Doors of Opportunity

Nineteenth-Century America

Heritage Studies 4

for Christian Schools®

HOME TEACHER'S EDITION

Second Edition

 Bob Jones University Press, Greenville, SC 29614

Advisory Committee
from the administration, faculty, and staff of Bob Jones University
James W. Deuink, Ed.D., *Dean of the School of Education*
Linda K. Hayner, Ph.D., *Chairman, Department of History*
Philip D. Smith, Ed.D., *Provost*
James R. Davis, M.A., *Director of Product Development, Bob Jones University Press*
Melva M. Heintz, M.A., *Principal Emerita, Elementary School*

Note:
The fact that materials produced by other publishers may be referred to in this volume does not constitute an endorsement of the content or theological position of materials produced by such publishers. Any references and ancillary materials are listed as an aid to the student or the teacher and in an attempt to maintain the accepted academic standards of the publishing industry.

Home Teacher's Edition for
HERITAGE STUDIES 4 for Christian Schools® Second Edition

for Christian Schools is a registered trademark of Bob Jones University Press.

A careful effort has been made to trace the ownership of selections included in this teacher's edition in order to secure permission to reprint copyrighted material and to make full acknowledgment of their use. If any error of omission has occurred, it is purely inadvertent and will be corrected in subsequent editions, provided written notification is made to the publisher.

Greenville, South Carolina 29614

Printed in the United States of America

ISBN 1-57924-269-3

15 14 13 12 11 10 9 8 7 6 5 4 3

CONTENTS

Heritage Studies 4 for Christian Schools
written especially for a home setting

1 Encourages Christian growth.

What a child learns in Heritage Studies can affect his spiritual growth and ministry. The child should learn discipline in his approach to and his performance of responsibilities. He should be prepared to evaluate and reject false philosophies. He should have a better testimony among unbelievers.

2 Develops good citizenship through the use of history, geography, economics, culture, and government skills.

The Heritage Studies program emphasizes Christian philosophy, character, and attitudes. It gives the child opportunities to use many skills, such as making decisions, inferring relationships, and showing respect for his heritage. It also teaches him practical skills, such as reading maps and charts, sequencing events, and working with time lines. Thus, the program promotes a balanced approach to social studies instruction.

3 Promotes historic and geographic literacy.

The goal of historic literacy is to emphasize God's plan for the individual, the family, and the nation. Although history is the study of man's actions, it is essentially the record of God's dealing with man. The Christian teacher must be able to distinguish God's leading in historical events and to impress upon the child the significance of the events. Learning history well helps the child more fully appreciate and comprehend his own times. This broad perspective, then, helps him make better decisions and become a responsible Christian citizen.

4 Presents events by incorporating a more traditional emphasis on skills.

The product of Heritage Studies is organized according to a scope and sequence. The scope is *what* knowledge will be covered in the program. There is disagreement among educators about the scope of knowledge that should be presented on the elementary level. Some still hold to the post-1920s experiment in "socializing" the study of history, organizing the material around the child and his environment. Recent research recommends, however, that true historic and geographic understanding rests on the more traditional emphasis on skills, such as working with maps and sequencing events.

5 Organizes knowledge in a spiral pattern and chronological order.

There are many ways to present Heritage Studies knowledge. For example, it can be organized around a unifying framework of themes. Another approach is a spiral pattern in which the same general topics are taken up periodically—every year, or two or three times in a program. Another option, supported by research and experience, is to study history chronologically, exploring eras in order, thereby helping the child see connections between events. This program combines the spiral pattern and the chronological approach.

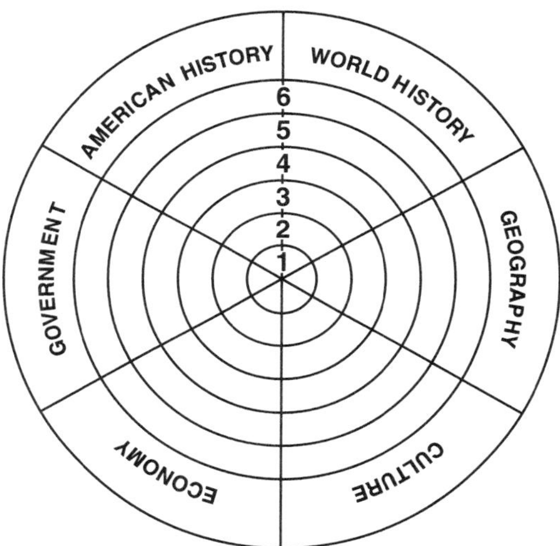

6 Promotes an understanding of and an ability to discern connections among events.

By viewing history in a chronological manner incorporating a time line, the child gains an understanding of and an ability to discern connections among events. He learns how events and people from other countries influenced his own American heritage and how they relate to each other in history.

7 Strengthens a knowledge of God.

Creation tells us about God (Ps. 19:1; Rom. 1:20). By studying the history of the world and the features of the earth, we can see illustrations of God's wisdom, omnipotence, sovereignty, and benevolence.

TEACHING HERITAGE STUDIES 4

How do I schedule the lessons?

You, the teacher, have a choice in scheduling the teaching of Heritage Studies. Some suggested methods follow.

- You may teach an entire lesson each day, completing the Heritage Studies program in a semester. Science could then be taught the other semester.
- You may teach an entire lesson of Heritage Studies two days a week for the whole year. Science would also be taught two days a week for the whole year.

Day 1

- You may use the scheduling plan provided by the Day symbols in each lesson. By following the numbered days throughout the lesson, you have logical starting and stopping points for discussions and activities. This plan will provide approximately 140 to 150 teaching days.

You will want to arrange the lessons to accommodate your schedule. Many lessons offer several procedures and activities. You may choose to use all of each lesson or only parts of a lesson. You may choose to adapt the material to your own methods. It is recommended that Heritage Studies be taught in thirty- to forty-minute sessions. The Supplemental lessons are optional.

Where will the needed materials be listed?

You can find lists of the materials you need in order to teach the Heritage Studies program in the following sections of the manual:

Instructional Materials, a section in the introduction to this manual, lists all the essential curriculum items that need to be purchased to teach Heritage Studies 4.

Chapter Overview, at the beginning of each chapter, contains a list of materials that need to be prepared or purchased ahead of time.

Materials, in the Preview of each lesson, lists the materials needed to present that particular lesson.

Materials List, found in the Supplement of the manual, lists all materials needed to teach the entire program.

What pages do I need to copy?

All the pages that you will need to copy for teaching the lessons can be found in the Appendix. The pages in the Supplement may also be copied, though copying is not essential. These pages may be viewed by your child directly from the teacher's manual. **Please note:** Although you are permitted to copy pages for your own use, copyright law prohibits the making of copies for any other purpose. Making copies and distributing them in whole or in part to other institutions or individuals is unlawful.

What is in the student text?

The student book presents for the child a summary of the more detailed study that the lessons will offer. It reinforces with grade-level text the concepts developed in the teaching time. Although it contains much information, it is only part of the complete package of learning provided by the combination of teacher's edition, TimeLine, student text, and Notebook.

The student book has twelve chapters, each emphasizing one of six categories: American history, world history, geography, government, culture, and economics. To determine the focus of the chapter, look at the color that highlights the chapter number. It corresponds to the color of one of the main category symbols.

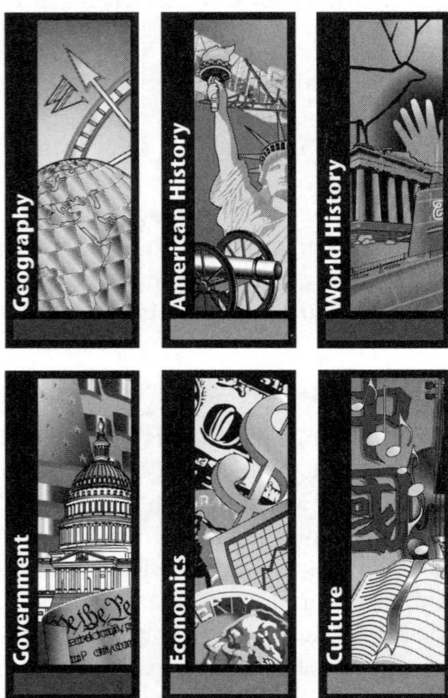

In addition, some chapters have special sections. One such section is *Famous People,* which highlights influential people of nineteenth-century America. *Things People Do* focuses on common trades, skills, or hobbies of the past and present. *How It Was* takes a detailed look at single moments in American history. *Echoes in History* connects past events with the present. *Learning How* sections provide hands-on activities that enliven the lesson and allow your child to experience some flavor of the times as well as learn map skills and develop thinking skills.

What is historic and geographic knowledge?

History and geography can be defined as a body of knowledge. History can also be defined as a way of thinking. The study of these topics, therefore, is a product (body of knowledge) and a process (way of investigating and thinking). The Bob Jones University Press Heritage Studies series continually interweaves the product and process of history and geography.

The products of history and geography are stated in several forms. For example, knowledge can be expressed as a fact. A *fact* is an event that has been observed and recorded by more than one person, the records showing no disagreement among the observers. (This does not mean that a fact cannot be in error.) Knowledge can also be expressed as a *concept,* a set of ideas derived from objects or events. Finally, knowledge can be expressed as a *principle,* a statement predicting interrelationships among concepts. The Bob Jones University Press Heritage Studies program uses the words *main idea* to include all three forms of knowledge. Note the following examples of each form of knowledge:

- *Fact:* The Separatists founded Plymouth Plantation.
- *Concept:* Religious freedom (The words *religious freedom* encompass the commitment to and struggles for worshiping as one believes proper.) To make a set of examples that accompany the label, think of people who have sacrificed for their beliefs.
  - William Tyndale—martyred for translating the Bible into English
  - John Bunyan—imprisoned for preaching
  - The Huguenots—persecuted in France for their beliefs, some fleeing to America
- *Principle:* The Constitution of the United States guarantees religious freedom. (Notice the interrelationship between the concepts *Constitution* and *religious freedom.*)

How should I teach history and geography skills?

The child should be deriving knowledge through practical experiences that involve action—"hands-on" or "learning-by-doing" activities. Christians can use the inductive method in good conscience, provided they remember that historical recording is fallible and changeable and often disregards many biblical truths. It would be helpful to all Christian teachers to study the principles discussed in *The Christian Teaching of History,* available from Bob Jones University Press.

It is not necessary to follow a certain set of steps, but there are *process skills* employed in this method of teaching. A list of the process skills in the program follows.

- Sequencing events
- Summarizing data
- Making predictions
- Inferring relationships
- Making decisions
- Formulating opinions
- Working with time lines
- Identifying sources of information
- Working with maps and globes
- Using cardinal directions
- Working with tables, graphs, charts, and diagrams
- Identifying key documents
- Valuing the rights of citizenship
- Showing respect for heritage

What attitudes are being developed as I teach?

The dictionary defines *attitude* as "a state of mind or feeling with regard to some matter." Some of the attitudes that you will see develop as your child learns through the Bob Jones University Press Heritage Studies program fall into the following broad categories.

- *Attitudes Toward Schoolwork*
  - Cooperatively share responsibilities and tasks.
  - Demonstrate proper care and handling of maps, globes, and other equipment.
  - Stay with the task in search of comprehension and evaluation of ideas.
- *Attitudes Toward Interests and Careers*
  - Pursue history- or geography-related leisure-time activities.
  - Voluntarily seek additional information about history and related studies.
  - Seek information about careers in research, history, and geography.
- *Attitudes Toward Personal Application of Heritage Studies Principles*
  - Use an objective approach in problem solving.
  - Display a willingness to consider other points of view.
  - Demonstrate divergent thinking in problem solving.
  - Demonstrate curiosity about history, geography, and related subjects.
  - Show an appreciation for his heritage.
  - Uphold foundational principles of his government.
  - Counteract influences detrimental to the perpetuation of his heritage.
  - Reflect a knowledge of history in everyday decision making.
- *Attitudes Toward Oneself*
  - Display confidence in his ability to use geographic skills successfully.
  - Demonstrate a scriptural view of himself through the study of history.
- *Attitudes Toward History and Society*
  - Select cause-and-effect relationships to explain contemporary problems.
  - Identify historical precedent as a way of solving some current problems.
  - Describe historians as persons sensitive to normal human concerns.
  - Demonstrate an awareness of the need for conservation, preservation, and the wise use of natural resources.
  - Demonstrate patriotism.
  - Explain how the study of history and geography can have positive (or, if unbalanced, negative) effects on one's personal life.

INSTRUCTIONAL MATERIALS

Student Materials

Text

HERITAGE STUDIES 4 for Christian Schools is a four-color text containing a variety of developmental subtopics built around six major topics: American history, world history, geography, culture, economics, and government.

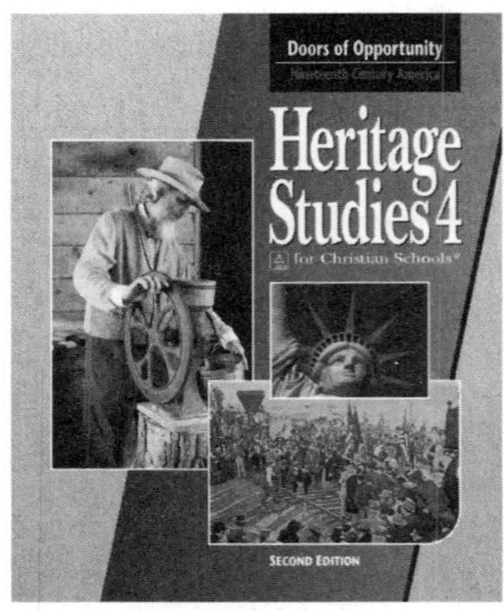

Notebook

The *HERITAGE STUDIES 4 Student Notebook* is a consumable companion tool for the text. It is used primarily for evaluating your child's understanding of the material. The Notebook will also save the teacher time. The pages are designed to be used in a notebook binder.

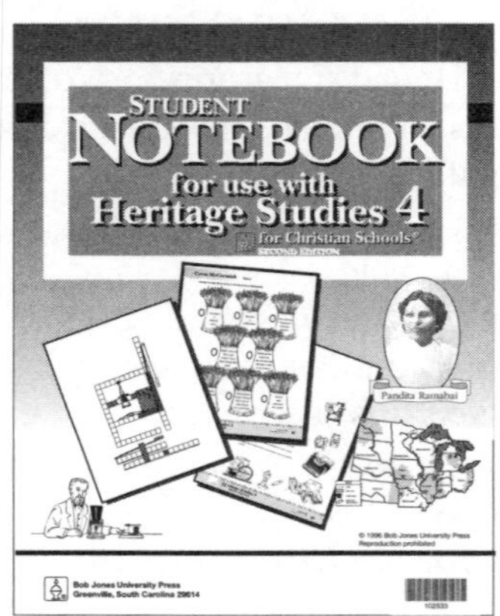

Miscellaneous school supplies

The child will need standard school supplies: crayons or felt-tip pens, pencils, scissors, glue, and so on.

Library trade books

No history program can provide enough information for enthusiastic young readers. A collection of trade books (library books) must be available to your child. Be careful of books that slant the history of certain events. For example, library books about Puritans are generally written by people who do not believe in the God of the Puritans. In these instances, try to find books that present a truthful and objective account of these people.

Teacher Materials

Teacher's edition

The home teacher's edition for *HERITAGE STUDIES 4 for Christian Schools* (this volume) is the foundation of the program from which all the activities originate. This volume contains the parts labeled below. Maps and More is a section of colored maps and visuals.

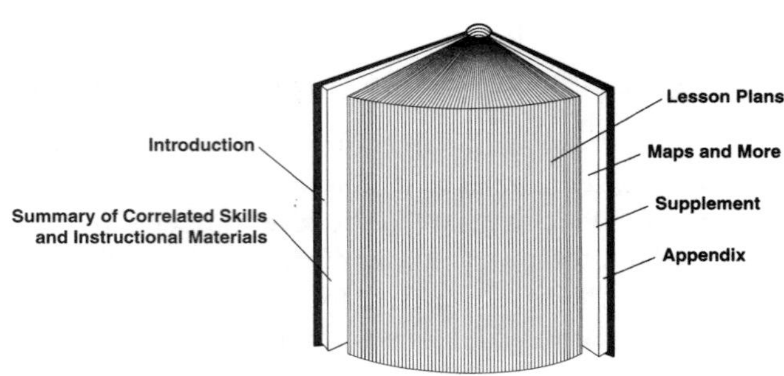

Optional Materials

TimeLine Snapshots

The *TimeLine Snapshots* is a visual working chart of the seventeenth through the twentieth centuries. It contains figures representing important events or people studied in grades 2-5, including pictures of all the presidents. It enhances the child's chronology skills. See Lesson 3 for additional details.

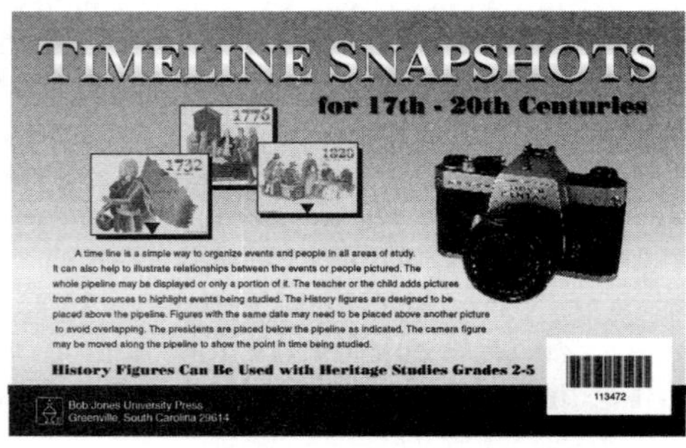

Heritage Studies Listening Cassette

The cassette tape contains songs and readings that will enhance the child's enjoyment of, understanding of, and participation in the study of history. Cassette B contains selections used in grades 4-6.

Heritage Studies supplies

Refer to the Materials List in the Supplement of this book.

Tests

The test packet includes a test for each chapter. A separate answer key is also available.

LESSON PLAN FORMAT

Preview

Main Ideas are short statements of historic or geographic knowledge.

Objectives are statements describing the outcome of instruction in terms of the child's behavior.

Materials is a list of items to be obtained or prepared.

Notes is a section of helpful hints.

Lesson

Introducing the Lesson suggests a way to start the lesson.

LESSON 9
Leaving the Old Country

Text, pages 32-35
Notebook, page 9

Preview

Main Ideas

- An interview is an important tool in the search for one's ancestors.
- Immigrants faced many hardships in their struggles to improve their lives.
- Many different people and groups have contributed to American culture.
- People have needs, feelings, interests, and preferences.

Objectives

- Write about an important personal possession
- Record information from an interview

Materials

- A Bible
- A cassette player/recorder
- A blank cassette*
- A family Bible (optional)*
- 15-20 play dollar bills or coins

Notes

In this lesson you will be conducting the model interview referred to in the Notes for Lesson 6. Before the interview, you will want to prepare a list of questions. Use Notebook page 9 as a guide.

The interviews in this lesson are designed to prepare your child to conduct an interview on his own. This will be done in Lesson 16.

Day 1

Lesson

Introducing the Lesson

Model Interview

Set up a special place with two chairs for the interview. Welcome the visitor warmly and direct him to sit down. Start the interview by thanking your visitor for taking the time to come and answer a few questions. Ask the visitor for permission to record the interview. After the cassette recorder is on, say the date and

◆ LEARNING HOW ◆

To Study Your Family History

1. Get a notebook and a pencil, or a cassette tape and a tape recorder.
2. Find out something new and interesting about your family history from one of the following sources:
   a. An older family member, such as a grandparent, aunt, or uncle.
   b. An old family Bible.
   c. Newspaper clippings.
   d. A bundle of old letters.
   e. Old photographs.
   f. Special family books, such as diaries, baby books, or autograph books.

3. In your notebook, record the things you find out. If you talk to an older family member, try to use a tape recorder. Then write a page telling the family story you learned. Be sure to include details like the year, the place, and the names and ages of the family members in the story.
4. Share your family information with your classmates. Then put your written work in a folder or scrapbook. If you like, find out about more family stories and add them to the folder or scrapbook too.

33

the name of the person you are interviewing and proceed with your list of questions.

Conduct the interview in a relaxed manner, giving the interviewee plenty of time to answer each question. Make sure that you are a good example by listening intently and responsively. When the interview is over, express how much you have enjoyed learning more about him and thank him again for coming.

Day 2

Teaching the Lesson

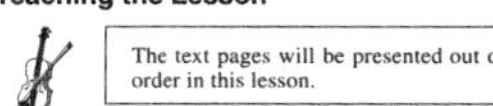

The text pages will be presented out of order in this lesson.

***Learning How* Activity, page 33**

- ➤ **Read page 33 to find ways of learning more about your family history.**
- ➤ **Read aloud the list of sources for gathering family history information.**

In the 1700s a traditional wedding present was a family Bible. Often between the Old and the New Testaments, there were pages provided for the recording of births, deaths, and marriages. Sometimes special events were written down and dated in the blank pages at the beginning or end of the Bible.

18 — Heritage Studies 4 Home TE

Teaching the Lesson suggests a procedure for instruction.

Evaluating the Lesson gives ideas to evaluate the child's grasp of the material presented.

Down steep, dark stairs the emigrants found rows of bunk beds. The first emigrants to board the ship chose the best bunks—near the stairs or on top. But even in the best spots, only the very smallest child could sit up in his bed without bumping his head.
Have you ever been on a ship before? Most emigrants had not. The unfamiliar rocking of the ship on the water made many sick. In the crowded space, colds and disease might spread quickly. Those who were not too sick to leave their beds spent time on the main deck, in the fresh air.
The sailing ships took two or three months to cross the ocean. Later, steamships cut the crossing time to about two weeks. How would you like to spend that long on a ship as a steerage passenger?
Steerage passengers, 1893

- ➤ **What kind of ticket would the poorer emigrant buy and how much would it cost?** *(A steerage ticket cost ten to fifteen dollars.)*

Text Discussion, page 35

- ➤ **Read page 35 to find out what it was like down in the lowest level of the ship.** *(dark, crowded, much sickness, very uncomfortable)*
- ➤ **How do you think the steerage passengers could stand the horrible conditions on the trip to America?**

The people knew that if they could endure the trip, they eventually would be in the land of their hopes and dreams.

Evaluating the Lesson

Review Activity

Pretend that you are an emigrant setting out for the New World. You will have the opportunity to earn money for a ticket to America. I will ask you some questions about the information we have been learning. For each correct answer you will receive one dollar. See if you can buy a steerage ticket with the money you earn. *(NOTE: You may choose to assign a greater value to a few questions so that your child can earn enough money for a first-class ticket.)*

1. **What was the first thing a family needed when they decided to emigrate?** *(money)*
2. **What was one thing money was used for?** *(a ticket or food)*
3. **If a family did not have enough money for the entire family to emigrate, what would they do?** *(send one person)*
4. **Name one thing the emigrants took with them to America.** *(clothes, pots, or tools)*
5. **What two things must a Christian do when God gives him a task?** *(trust and obey)*
6. **Name two ways that emigrants traveled to the port cities in their country.** *(by foot, horse and wagon, or train)*
7. **Name one thing emigrants saw when they reached the port cities.** *(posters or ships)*
8. **What did the emigrants have to wait for once they arrived at the port city?** *(the next ship)*
9. **What kind of ticket did poorer emigrants buy?** *(steerage ticket)*
10. **How much did a steerage ticket cost?** *($10 to $15)*
11. **On what level was the steerage portion of the ship?** *(lowest)*
12. **What happened to many of the emigrants as they traveled to America?** *(They got sick.)*
13. **About how many months did it take for the emigrants in sailing ships to get to America?** *(two to three)*
14. **About how many weeks did it take for steamships to cross the ocean?** *(two)*
15. **Besides the interview, what is another source of information about a family's past?** *(family Bible, newspaper clippings, old letters, old photographs, or special family books such as diaries, baby books, or autograph books)*

Going Beyond

Enrichment

Give your child a copy of the two-page Pedigree Chart, Appendix, pages A20-A21. *(NOTE:* A family tree and a pedigree chart differ in that a family tree includes aunts, uncles, cousins, and so on. A pedigree chart traces only an individual's direct ancestors.) Tape the pages together side by side to make one large chart. Encourage your child to become an "Ancestor Hunter" and to find out as much about his heritage as possible. Challenge him to check out library books to guide him in the search.

Additional Teacher Information

When the United States celebrated its two hundredth birthday in 1976, many people became interested in finding out their family histories and took up ancestor hunting as a hobby. Stories about family histories, such as Alex Haley's

Chapter 2: Lesson 9 — 21

Going Beyond

Enrichment includes activities and games. Some of these activities may be done independently.

Additional Teacher Information provides the teacher with extra information to help him expand his knowledge of related topics. It is not necessary to understand or even to read the information in this section to teach the lesson.

BIBLE ACTION TRUTHS

The quality and consistency of a man's decisions reflect his character. Christian character begins with justification, but it grows throughout the lifelong process of sanctification. God's grace is sufficient for the task, and a major part of God's gracious provision is His Word. The Bible provides the very "words of life" that instruct us in salvation and Christian living. By obeying God's commands and making godly decisions based on His Word, Christians can strengthen their character.

Too often Christians live by only vague guidance—for instance, that we should "do good" to all men. While doing good is desirable, more specific guidance will lead to more consistent decisions.

Consistent decisions are made when man acts on Bible principles—or Bible Action Truths. The thirty-seven Bible Action Truths (listed under eight general principles) provide Christians with specific goals for their actions and attitudes. Study the Scriptures indicated for a fuller understanding of the principles in Bible Action Truths.

Thousands have found this format helpful in identifying and applying principles of behavior. Yet there is no "magic" in this formula. As you study the Word, you likely will find other truths that speak to you. The key is for you to study the Scriptures, look for Bible Action Truths, and be sensitive to the leading of the Holy Spirit.

1. **Salvation—Separation Principle**
   Salvation results from God's direct action. Although man is unable to work for this "gift of God," the Christian's reaction to salvation should be to separate himself from the world unto God.
   a. **Understanding Jesus Christ** (Matthew 3:17; 16:16; I Corinthians 15:3-4; Philippians 2:9-11) Jesus is the Son of God. He was sent to earth to die on the cross for our sins. He was buried but rose from the dead after three days.
   b. **Repentance and faith** (Isaiah 55:7; Luke 13:3; Acts 5:30-31; 16:31; Hebrews 11:6) If we believe that Jesus died for our sins, we can accept Him as our Savior. We must be sorry for our sins, turn from them, confess them to God, and believe that He will forgive us.
   c. **Separation from the world** (John 17:6, 11, 14, 18; Romans 16:17-18; II Corinthians 6:14-18; James 4:4; I John 2:15-16; II John 10-11) After we are saved, we should live a different life. We should try to be like Christ and not live like those who are unsaved.
2. **Sonship—Servant Principle**
   Only by an act of God the Father could sinful man become a son of God. As a son of God, however, the Christian must realize that he has been "bought with a price"; he is now Christ's servant.
   a. **Authority** (Matthew 22:21; Romans 13:1-7; I Thessalonians 5:12-13; I Timothy 6:1-5; Hebrews 13:17; I Peter 2:13-19) We should respect, honor, and obey those in authority over us.
   b. **Servanthood** (Ephesians 6:5-8; Philippians 2:7-8) Just as Christ was a humble servant while He was on earth, we should also be humble and obedient.
   c. **Faithfulness** (Matthew 25:23; Luke 9:62; I Corinthians 4:2) We should do our work so that God and others can depend on us.
   d. **Goal setting** (Proverbs 13:12, 19; I Corinthians 9:24; Philippians 3:13; Colossians 3:2) To be faithful servants, we must set goals for our work. We should look forward to finishing a job and going on to something more.
   e. **Work** (Ephesians 4:28; II Thessalonians 3:10-12) God never honors a lazy servant. He wants us to be busy and dependable workers.
   f. **Enthusiasm** (Romans 12:11; Colossians 3:23) We should do *all* tasks with energy and with a happy, willing spirit.
3. **Uniqueness—Unity Principle**
   No one is a mere person; God has created each individual a unique being. But because God has an overall plan for His creation, each unique member must contribute to the unity of the entire body.
   a. **Self-concept** (Psalm 8:3-8; 139; II Corinthians 5:17; Ephesians 2:10; 4:1-3, 11-13; II Peter 1:10) We are special creatures in God's plan. He has given each of us special abilities to use in our lives for Him.
   b. **Mind** (Proverbs 4:23; 23:7; Daniel 1:8; Luke 6:45; Romans 7:23, 25; II Corinthians 10:5; Philippians 2:5; 4:8; James 1:8) We should give our hearts and minds to God. What we do and say really begins in our minds. We should try to think of ourselves humbly, as Christ did when He lived on earth.
   c. **Emotional control** (Proverbs 16:32; 25:28; Acts 20:24; Galatians 5:24; II Timothy 1:7) With the help of God and the power of the Holy Spirit, we should have control over our feelings. We must be careful not to act out of anger.
   d. **Body as a temple** (I Corinthians 3:16-17; 6:19-20) We should remember that our bodies are the dwelling place of God's Holy Spirit. We should keep ourselves pure, honest, and dedicated to God's will.
   e. **Unity of Christ and the Church** (John 17:21; Ephesians 2:19-22; 5:23-32; II Thessalonians 3:6, 14-15) Since we are saved, we are now part of God's family and should unite ourselves with others to worship and grow as Christians. Christ

is the head of His Church, which includes all believers. He wants us to work together as His Church in carrying out His plans, but He forbids us to work in fellowship with disobedient brethren.

4. **Holiness—Habit Principle**
Believers are declared holy as a result of Christ's finished action on the cross. Daily holiness of life, however, comes from forming godly habits. A Christian must consciously establish godly patterns of action; he must develop habits of holiness.
   a. **Sowing and reaping** (Hosea 8:7; Matthew 6:1-8; Galatians 6:7-8) We must remember that we will be rewarded according to the kind of work we have done. If we are faithful, we will be rewarded. If we are unfaithful, we will not be rewarded. We cannot fool God.
   b. **Purity** (I Thessalonians 4:1-7; I Peter 1:22) We should try to live lives that are free from sin. We should keep our minds, words, and deeds clean and pure.
   c. **Honesty** (Proverbs 16:8; Romans 12:17; II Corinthians 8:21; Ephesians 4:25) We should not lie. We should be honest in every way. Even if we could gain more by being dishonest, we should still be honest. God sees all things.
   d. **Victory** (John 16:33; Romans 8:37; I Corinthians 10:13; 15:57-58; I John 5:4) If we constantly try to be pure, honest, and Christlike, with God's help we will be able to overcome temptations.

5. **Love—Life Principle**
We love God because He first loved us. God's action of manifesting His love to us through His Son demonstrates the truth that love must be exercised. Since God acted in love toward us, believers must act likewise by showing godly love to others.
   a. **Love** (John 15:17; I Corinthians 13; Ephesians 5:2; I John 3:11, 16-18; 4:7-21) God's love to us was the greatest love possible. We should, in turn, show our love for others by our words and actions.
   b. **Giving** (Proverbs 3:9-10; Luke 6:38; II Corinthians 9:6-8) We should give cheerfully to God the first part of all we earn. We should also give to others unselfishly.
   c. **Evangelism and missions** (Psalm 126:5-6; Matthew 28:18-20; Romans 1:16-17; II Corinthians 5:11-21) We should be busy telling others about the love of God and His plan of salvation. We should share in the work of foreign missionaries by our giving and prayers.
   d. **Communication** (Isaiah 50:4; Ephesians 4:22-29; Colossians 4:6; James 3:2-13) We should have control of our tongues so that we will not say things displeasing to God. We should encourage others and be kind and helpful in what we say.
   e. **Friendliness** (Psalm 119:63; Proverbs 17:17; 18:24) We should be friendly to others, and we should be loyal to those who love and serve God.

6. **Communion—Consecration Principle**
Because sin separates man from God, any communion between man and God must be achieved by God's direct action of removing sin. Once communion is established, the believer's reaction should be to maintain a consciousness of this fellowship by living a consecrated life.
   a. **Bible study** (Psalm 119; II Timothy 2:15; I Peter 2:2-3) To grow as Christians, we must spend time with God daily by reading His Word.
   b. **Prayer** (I Chronicles 16:11; Psalm 145:18; John 15:7, 16; 16:24; Romans 8:26-27; I Thessalonians 5:17) We should bring all our requests to God, trusting Him to answer them in His own way.
   c. **Spirit-filled** (Romans 8:13-14; Galatians 5:16, 22-23; Ephesians 5:18-19; I John 1:7-9) We should let the Holy Spirit rule in our hearts and show us what to say and do. We should not say and do just what we want to do, for those things are often wrong and harmful to others.
   d. **Clear conscience** (Acts 24:16; I Timothy 1:19) To be good Christians, we cannot have wrong acts or thoughts or words bothering our consciences. We must confess them to God and to those people against whom we have sinned. We cannot live lives close to God if we have guilty consciences.
   e. **Forgiveness** (Matthew 18:15-17; Mark 11:25-26; Luke 17:3-4; Ephesians 4:30-32; Colossians 3:13) We must ask forgiveness of God when we have done wrong. Just as God forgives our sins freely, we should forgive others when they do wrong things to us.

7. **Grace—Gratitude Principle**
Grace is unmerited favor. Man does not deserve God's grace. However, after God bestows His grace, believers should react with an overflow of gratitude.
   a. **Grace** (I Corinthians 15:10; Ephesians 2:8-9) Without God's grace we would be sinners on our way to hell. He loved us when we did not deserve His love and provided for us a way to escape sin's punishment by the death of His Son on the cross.
   b. **Exaltation of Christ** (John 1:1-4, 14; 5:23; Galatians 6:14; Ephesians 1:17-23; Philippians 2:9-11; Colossians 1:12-21; Hebrews 1:2-3) We should realize and remember at all times the power, holiness, majesty, and perfection of Christ, and we should give Him the praise and glory for everything that is accomplished through us.

c. **Praise** (I Chronicles 16:23-36; 29:11-13; Psalm 107:8; Ephesians 1:6; Hebrews 13:15; I Peter 2:9) Remembering God's great love and goodness toward us, we should continually praise His name.

d. **Contentment** (Psalm 77:3; Proverbs 15:16; Philippians 4:11; I Timothy 6:6-8; Hebrews 13:5) Money, houses, cars, and all things on earth will last only for a little while. God has given us just what He meant for us to have. We should be happy and content with what we have, knowing that God will provide for us all that we need. We should also be happy wherever God places us.

e. **Humility** (Philippians 2:3-4; I Peter 5:5-6) We should not be proud and boastful but should be willing to be quiet and in the background. Our reward will come from God on Judgment Day, and men's praise to us here on earth will not matter at all. Christ was humble when He lived on earth, and we should be like Him.

8. **Power—Prevailing Principle**
Believers can prevail only as God gives the power. "I can do all things through Christ." God is the source of our power used in fighting the good fight of faith.

a. **Faith in God's promises** (Romans 4:16-21; 8:28; Philippians 4:6; I Thessalonians 5:18; Hebrews 3:18–4:11; I Peter 5:7; II Peter 1:4) God always remains true to His promises. Believing that He will keep all the promises in His Word, we should be determined fighters for Him.

b. **Faith in the power of the Word of God** (Jeremiah 23:29; Psalm 119; Hebrews 4:12; I Peter 1:23-25) God's Word is powerful and endures forever. All other things will pass away, but God's Word shall never pass away because it is written to us from God, and God is eternal.

c. **Fight** (Ephesians 6:11-17; I Timothy 6:12; II Timothy 4:7-8; I Peter 5:8-9) God does not have any use for lazy or cowardly fighters. We must work and fight against sin, using the Word of God as our weapon against the Devil. What we do for God now will determine how much He will reward us in heaven.

d. **Courage** (Joshua 1:9; I Chronicles 28:20; Acts 4:13, 31; Ephesians 3:11-12; Hebrews 13:6) God has promised us that He will not forsake us; therefore, we should not be afraid to speak out against sin. We should remember that we are armed with God's strength.

BIBLE PROMISES

A. **Liberty from Sin—**Born into God's spiritual kingdom, a Christian is enabled to live right and gain victory over sin through faith in Christ. (Romans 8:3-4—"For what the law could not do, in that it was weak through the flesh, God sending his own Son in the likeness of sinful flesh, and for sin, condemned sin in the flesh: that the righteousness of the law might be fulfilled in us, who walk not after the flesh, but after the Spirit.")

B. **Guiltless by the Blood—**Cleansed by the blood of Christ, the Christian is pardoned from the guilt of his sins. He does not have to brood or fret over his past because the Lord has declared him righteous. (Romans 8:33—"Who shall lay any thing to the charge of God's elect? It is God that justifieth." Isaiah 45:24—"Surely, shall one say, in the Lord have I righteousness and strength: even to him shall men come; and all that are incensed against him shall be ashamed.")

C. **Basis for Prayer—**Knowing that his righteousness comes entirely from Christ and not from himself, the Christian is free to plead the blood of Christ and to come before God in prayer at any time. (Romans 5:1-2—"Therefore being justified by faith, we have peace with God through our Lord Jesus Christ: by whom also we have access by faith into this grace wherein we stand, and rejoice in hope of the glory of God.")

D. **Identified in Christ—**The Christian has the assurance that God sees him as a son of God, perfectly united with Christ. He also knows that he has access to the strength and the grace of Christ in his daily living. (Galatians 2:20—"I am crucified with Christ: nevertheless, I live; yet not I, but Christ liveth in me: and the life which I now live in the flesh I live by the faith of the Son of God, who loved me, and gave himself for me." Ephesians 1:3—"Blessed be the God and Father of our Lord Jesus Christ, who hath blessed us with all spiritual blessings in heavenly places in Christ.")

E. **Christ as Sacrifice—**Christ was a willing sacrifice for the sins of the world. His blood covers every sin of the believer and pardons the Christian for eternity. The purpose of His death and resurrection was to redeem a people to Himself. (Isaiah 53:4-5—"Surely he hath borne our griefs, and carried our sorrows: yet we did esteem him stricken, smitten of God, and afflicted. But he was wounded for our transgressions, he was bruised for our iniquities: the chastisement of our peace was upon him; and with his stripes we are healed." John 10:27-28—"My sheep hear my voice, and I know them, and they follow me: and I give unto them eternal life; and they shall never perish, neither shall any man pluck them out of my hand.")

F. **Christ as Intercessor—**Having pardoned them through His blood, Christ performs the office of High Priest in praying for His people. (Hebrews 7:25—"Wherefore he is able also to save them to the uttermost that come unto God by him, seeing he ever liveth to make intercession for them." John 17:20—"Neither pray I for these alone, but for them also which shall believe on me through their word.")

G. **Christ as Friend—**In giving salvation to the believer, Christ enters a personal, loving relationship with the Christian that cannot be ended. This relationship is understood and enjoyed on the believer's part through fellowship with the Lord through Bible reading and prayer. (Isaiah 54:5—"For thy Maker is thine husband; the Lord of hosts is his name; and thy Redeemer the Holy One of Israel; the God of the whole earth shall he be called." Romans 8:38-39—"For I am persuaded, that neither death, nor life, nor angels, nor principalities, nor powers, nor things present, nor things to come, nor height, nor depth, nor any other creature, shall be able to separate us from the love of God, which is in Christ Jesus our Lord.")

H. **God as Father—**God has appointed Himself to be responsible for the well-being of the Christian. He both protects and nourishes the believer, and it was from Him that salvation originated. (Isaiah 54:17—"No weapon that is formed against thee shall prosper; and every tongue that shall rise against thee in judgment thou shalt condemn. This is the heritage of the servants of the Lord, and their righteousness is of me, saith the Lord." Psalm 103:13—"Like as a father pitieth his children, so the Lord pitieth them that fear him.")

I. **God as Master—**God is sovereign over all creation. He orders the lives of His people for His glory and their good. (Romans 8:28—"And we know that all things work together for good to them that love God, to them who are the called according to his purpose.")

SUMMARY OF CORRELATED SKILLS AND INSTRUCTIONAL MATERIALS

	Chapters and Lessons	Suggested teaching days	Lesson pages	Text pages	Notebook pages
1	**THE CONTINENTS**				
	1 Land and Water	2	2-6	2-5, 316-17	1
	2 Earth Locations	3	6-11	6-8	2
	3 Climates and Currents	2	11-15	9-12, 316-17	3
	4 Rain and Resources	2	16-20	12-17	
	5 Earth Exploration	2	20-24	18-20	4
2	**THROUGH THE GOLDEN DOOR**				
	6 A Nation of Immigrants	4	26-31	22-25, 306, 322-23	5-6
	The Presidents of the United States (Supplemental)		32-33	268-79	
	7 Reasons for Coming to America	2	34-37	26-28	7
	8 The New Immigrants	2	38-41	28-31	8
	9 Leaving the Old Country	3	42-46	32-35	9
	10 America at Last	3	46-51	36-41, 311	10-11
	11 A Fresh Start	3	51-55	42-45	12
	12 Becoming a Citizen	3	55-58	46-48, 307	13

Bible Action Truths; Bible Promises	Heritage Studies skills
Bible Promise: I. God as Master	inferring relationships, formulating opinions, working with maps and globes, using cardinal directions
Bible Promise: I. God as Master	summarizing data, inferring relationships, working with maps and globes, using cardinal directions, working with graphs
BAT: 8b Faith in the power of the Word of God; Bible Promise: I. God as Master	summarizing data, inferring relationships, formulating opinions, identifying sources of information, working with maps and globes, using cardinal directions, working with charts and diagrams
BAT: 8b Faith in the power of the Word of God; Bible Promise: H. God as Father	summarizing data, inferring relationships, making decisions, formulating opinions, working with maps and globes, using cardinal directions, working with charts and diagrams
BATs: 2e Work, 2f Enthusiasm, 8d Courage; Bible Promise: I. God as Master	summarizing data, inferring relationships, formulating opinions, working with time lines, working with maps, using cardinal directions
Bible Promise: H. God as Father	formulating opinions, working with maps, working with charts and graphs, showing respect for heritage
	inferring relationships, making decisions, formulating opinions, working with time lines, identifying key documents, valuing the rights of citizenship, showing respect for heritage
BATs: 2d Goal setting, 2e Work, 2f Enthusiasm, 7d Contentment, 8a Faith in God's promises, 8d Courage; Bible Promise: I. God as Master	sequencing events, summarizing data, inferring relationships, making decisions, working with maps, working with graphs, identifying key documents, valuing the rights of citizenship, showing respect for heritage
BATs: 5a Love, 5e Friendliness; Bible Promise: I. God as Master	sequencing events, summarizing data, inferring relationships, formulating opinions, working with maps, using cardinal directions, working with graphs and charts, showing respect for heritage
BAT: 4a Sowing and reaping; Bible Promises: G. Christ as Friend, H. God as Father, I. God as Master	sequencing events, summarizing data, inferring relationships, making decisions, showing respect for heritage
Bible Promise: H. God as Father	summarizing data, inferring relationships, formulating opinions, working with maps, valuing the rights of citizenship
BATs: 5a Love, 8b Faith in the power of the Word of God; Bible Promises: H. God as Father, I. God as Master	inferring relationships, formulating opinions, working with maps, valuing the rights of citizenship, showing respect for heritage
Bible Promise: I. God as Master	formulating opinions, identifying sources of information, valuing the rights of citizenship, showing respect for heritage

	Chapters and Lessons	Suggested teaching days	Lesson pages	Text pages	Notebook pages
	AMERICAN VOICES				
	13 Living the Dream	2	60-62	50-51, 316-17	14
	14 Helping One Another	2	63-66	52-53	15
3	**15 New Experiences**	3	66-70	54-57, 316-17	16-17
	16 Blending Cultures	3	71-75	58-61, 314-15	18
	17 "A Nation of Nations"	2	75-78	62-63, 316-19	19
	18 America's Language	3	79-82	64-66, 310, 318-19	20
	PREACHING THE WORD				
	19 Chaplains and Circuit Riders	2	84-87	68-69	21-22
	20 D. L. Moody: From Soles to Souls	3	87-92	70-77, 312	23-24
4	**21 Mary Slessor: White Ma of Calabar**	1	93-95	78-79	25
	22 Hudson Taylor—To China with Love	2	96-99	80-82	
	23 To Do the Work of Christ	2	99-104	83-84	26-35
	24 "Go . . . and Teach All Nations"	2	105-8	85-88	36-37

Bible Action Truths; Bible Promises	Heritage Studies skills
BATs: 5a Love, 5e Friendliness	summarizing data, inferring relationships, making decisions, formulating opinions, working with maps, showing respect for heritage
BATs: 2b Servanthood, 5a Love, 5b Giving	summarizing data, formulating opinions, working with time lines, showing respect for heritage
BATs: 2e Work, 3a Self-concept	making predictions, making decisions, formulating opinions, identifying sources of information, working with maps, showing respect for heritage
BATs: 3a Self-concept, 5a Love	inferring relationships, formulating opinions, identifying sources of information, working with maps, using cardinal directions, showing respect for heritage
BAT: 5d Communication	making predictions, formulating opinions, working with maps, showing respect for heritage, valuing the rights of citizenship
BATs: 5a Love, 5d Communication, 5e Friendliness, 7c Praise	working with maps, working with graphs, valuing the rights of citizenship, showing respect for heritage
BATs: 1a Understanding Jesus Christ, 1b Repentance and faith, 2c Faithfulness, 5c Evangelism and missions, 6a Bible study, 7a Grace, 8a Faith in God's promises	making predictions, inferring relationships, formulating opinions
BATs: 1a Understanding Jesus Christ, 1b Repentance and faith, 1c Separation from the world, 2c Faithfulness, 2d Goal setting, 2e Work, 2f Enthusiasm, 3b Mind, 4c Honesty, 4d Victory, 5c Evangelism and missions	sequencing events, summarizing data, making predictions, inferring relationships, making decisions, formulating opinions, working with time lines
BATs: 2b Servanthood, 2e Work, 4a Sowing and reaping, 5c Evangelism and missions, 7d Contentment, 8d Courage	making predictions, inferring relationships, making decisions, formulating opinions, working with maps, using cardinal directions
BATs: 2d Goal setting, 4b Purity, 5c Evangelism and missions, 5a Love, 5d Communication, 6b Prayer	sequencing events, summarizing data, making predictions, inferring relationships, making decisions, formulating opinions, working with maps, showing respect for heritage
BATs: 5c Evangelism and missions, 6b Prayer	summarizing data, making decisions, formulating opinions, working with maps
BATs: 3a Self-concept, 5c Evangelism and missions, 6a Bible study, 6b Prayer, 8a Faith in God's promises, 8b Faith in the power of the Word of God; Bible Promises: H. God as Father, I. God as Master	sequencing events, summarizing data, making predictions, inferring relationships, making decisions, formulating opinions, working with maps and globes

	Chapters and Lessons	Suggested teaching days	Lesson pages	Text pages	Notebook pages
	THE FIFTY STATES				
	25 The Northeast: Sweet Land of Liberty	3	110-18	90-96, 280-305, 320-21	38-40
	26 The Southeast: Let Freedom Ring	4	118-25	96-102, 280-305, 308-9, 320-21	41-42
	27 The Middle West: For Amber Waves of Grain	3	126-31	103-8, 280-305, 320-21	43-44
5	**28 The Southwest: My Native Country, Thee**	3	132-36	109-11, 280-305, 320-21	45-46
	29 The Rocky Mountains: For Purple Mountain Majesties	3	137-41	112-14, 280-305, 320-21	47-49
	30 The Pacific: From Sea to Shining Sea	3	141-47	115-18, 280-305, 320-21	50-52
	More About Our State(s) (Supplemental)		147-48	280-305, 326	
	NEWFANGLED IDEAS				
	31 From Alarm Clocks to Zippers	2	150-53	120-23	53
	32 Engines and More	2	153-57	123-26	54-55
	33 Sheaves of Success	2	158-61	127-30	56
6	**34 A Stitch in Time**	1	162-65	131-33	57
	35 For Home and Office	2	165-69	134-37	58
	36 What Inventors Are Made Of	2	169-73	138-42	59

Bible Action Truths; Bible Promises	Heritage Studies skills
BATs: 1b Repentance and faith, 2a Authority, 5c Evangelism and missions, 6b Prayer; Bible Promises: A. Liberty from Sin, B. Guiltless by the Blood	formulating opinions, working with maps, identifying key documents, showing respect for heritage
BATs: 1c Separation from the world, 2b Servanthood, 2e Work, 3d Body as a temple, 5a Love, 5d Communication, 6a Bible study, 6c Spirit-filled, 7a Grace, 7b Exaltation of Christ	summarizing data, making decisions, formulating opinions, working with time lines, working with maps, showing respect for heritage
BATs: 1c Separation from the world, 3c Emotional control, 4a Sowing and reaping, 5c Evangelism and missions, 5d Communication	summarizing data, inferring relationships, making decisions, formulating opinions, working with maps, showing respect for heritage
BATs: 2c Faithfulness, 7c Praise, 7d Contentment, 8a Faith in God's promises	making predictions, inferring relationships, making decisions, formulating opinions, identifying sources of information, working with maps, using cardinal directions, showing respect for heritage
BATs: 1a Understanding Jesus Christ, 1b Repentance and faith, 1c Separation from the world, 2c Faithfulness, 2e Work, 3d Body as a temple, 4a Sowing and reaping, 5c Evangelism and missions, 7c Praise, 8b Faith in the power of the Word of God; Bible Promise: I. God as Master	summarizing data, making predictions, formulating opinions, using cardinal directions, working with maps, showing respect for heritage
BATs: 5c Evangelism and missions, 7c Praise, 7d Contentment, 8a Faith in God's promises; Bible Promise: I. God as Master	making predictions, making decisions, formulating opinions, working with maps and globes, showing respect for heritage
	summarizing data, making decisions, formulating opinions, working with time lines, identifying sources of information, working with maps and globes, showing respect for heritage
BATs: 2c Faithfulness, 5a Love	summarizing data, making predictions, making decisions, formulating opinions
BATs: 2e Work, 5a Love, 5e Friendliness	summarizing data, inferring relationships, making decisions, formulating opinions
BATs: 2d Goal setting, 5b Giving	sequencing events, summarizing data, making predictions, inferring relationships, making decisions, formulating opinions
BATs: 2d Goal setting, 5a Love, 5b Giving, 5d Communication, 5e Friendliness	summarizing data, making predictions, making decisions, formulating opinions
BATs: 2a Authority, 2b Servanthood, 2d Goal setting, 2e Work, 3c Emotional control, 5a Love	summarizing data, making decisions, formulating opinions
BATs: 2c Faithfulness, 2d Goal setting, 2e Work, 3a Self-concept, 4a Sowing and reaping, 5d Communication, 7e Humility	summarizing data, making predictions, making decisions, formulating opinions, working with time lines, working with diagrams

Chapter	Chapters and Lessons	Suggested teaching days	Lesson pages	Text pages	Notebook pages
	In the Market				
	37 Buying and Selling	2	176-78	144-45	60
	38 The Landlord's Game	2	179-81	146-47	61
	39 What's It Worth?	1	182-85	148-51	62-63
7	**40 Supply and Demand**	2	185-88	152-55	64
	41 Capitalism	2	189-92	156-59	65-66
	42 Needs and Wants	1	193-94	160	
	Steam Engines and Smokestacks				
	43 By Hand	2	196-99	162-65	67
	44 By Machine	1	200-203	166-69	68
	45 More Machines	1	204-6	170-72	69
8	**46 The Industrial Revolution**	2	207-11	173-76, 271, 313	70-71
	47 The Workers	2	212-16	177-81	72-73
	48 Big Business	2	216-20	182-84	

Bible Action Truths; Bible Promises	Heritage Studies skills
BATs: 2c Faithfulness, 2d Goal setting, 2e Work, 4c Honesty	summarizing data, inferring relationships, making decisions, formulating opinions, working with tables, valuing the rights of citizenship
BATs: 5a Love, 5b Giving, 7d Contentment	summarizing data, making decisions, formulating opinions, identifying sources of information, working with maps
BATs: 1b Repentance and faith, 3a Self-concept, 3c Emotional control, 3d Body as a temple, 6d Clear conscience, 7c Praise, 7d Contentment	summarizing data, making predictions, inferring relationships, making decisions, formulating opinions
BAT: 7d Contentment	sequencing events, summarizing data, making predictions, inferring relationships, making decisions, formulating opinions, identifying sources of information, working with graphs and charts
Bible Promises: H. God as Father, I. God as Master	summarizing data, making predictions, inferring relationships, making decisions, formulating opinions, valuing the rights of citizenship, showing respect for heritage
BATs: 1b Repentance and faith, 7d Contentment, 8a Faith in God's promises	summarizing data, making predictions, inferring relationships, making decisions, formulating opinions
BATs: 2c Faithfulness, 2d Goal setting, 2e Work	sequencing events, summarizing data, working with charts
BATs: 2d Goal setting, 2e Work, 3c Emotional control; Bible Promise: I. God as Master	sequencing events, summarizing data, making predictions, inferring relationships, making decisions, formulating opinions, working with maps, working with graphs
BATs: 2c Faithfulness, 2e Work	sequencing events, summarizing data, inferring relationships, formulating opinions
BATs: 2c Faithfulness, 2d Goal setting, 2e Work, 2f Enthusiasm	sequencing events, summarizing data, making predictions, inferring relationships, making decisions, formulating opinions, working with time lines, working with maps, working with graphs and charts
BATs: 2a Authority, 2c Faithfulness, 2e Work, 3c Emotional control, 5a Love, 5b Giving	sequencing events, summarizing data, making predictions, inferring relationships, making decisions, formulating opinions, valuing the rights of citizenship
BATs: 2c Faithfulness, 2e Work, 3a Self-concept, 4a Sowing and reaping, 5b Giving, 7b Exaltation of Christ, 7d Contentment	sequencing events, summarizing data, making predictions, inferring relationships, making decisions, formulating opinions, working with time lines, working with maps, showing respect for heritage

Chapters and Lessons		Suggested teaching days	Lesson pages	Text pages	Notebook pages
	STOKING THE FIRES				
	49 The Railroad: Workmen and Weather	2	222-26	186-92, 320-21	
	50 Deliberations: The Chiefs and Government	2	227-31	193-97, 273, 322-23	74
9	51 Conflicts: The Laws and the Land	1	231-33	198-99	
	52 Towns: Changes Through Time	1	234-37	200-203	75-76
	53 War: The Beginning	2	237-41	204-6	77
	54 The Fighting: Important People and Events	2	241-45	207-10, 275	78
	GETTING THE MESSAGE				
	55 Hoofbeats A-Coming	1	248-50	212-13	79
	56 Read All About It!	2	251-52	213-14	80
	57 Morse and His Telegraph Machine	1	253-56	215-17	81-83
10	58 Dots and Dashes	2	257-60	218-20, 271	84
	59 Words over a Wire	2	260-63	221-24	85
	60 Better and Faster	1	264-67	225-28	

Bible Action Truths; Bible Promises	Heritage Studies skills
BATs: 2b Servanthood, 2c Faithfulness, 2d Goal setting, 2e Work, 2f Enthusiasm, 3a Self-concept, 3c Emotional control, 4a Sowing and reaping, 4b Purity, 5a Love, 5b Giving, 5d Communication, 5e Friendliness, 6b Prayer, 8d Courage; Bible Promises: H. God as Father, I. God as Master	sequencing events, summarizing data, inferring relationships, formulating opinions, showing respect for heritage
BATs: 3a Self-concept, 4c Honesty, 4d Victory, 5a Love, 5d Communication, 6c Spirit-filled, 6d Clear conscience, 7d Contentment	sequencing events, summarizing data, making predictions, inferring relationships, formulating opinions, valuing the rights of citizenship, showing respect for heritage
BATs: 2a Authority, 2b Servanthood, 2f Enthusiasm, 3a Self-concept, 3c Emotional control, 4c Honesty	sequencing events, summarizing data, making predictions, inferring relationships, making decisions, formulating opinions
	sequencing events, summarizing data, making decisions, working with maps, working with charts
BATs: 4b Purity, 4c Honesty, 4d Victory	sequencing events, summarizing data, making predictions, inferring relationships, making decisions, formulating opinions, working with maps, using cardinal directions, working with graphs, valuing the rights of citizenship, showing respect for heritage
BATs: 4a Sowing and reaping, 5a Love, 5b Giving, 6a Bible study, 6b Prayer, 8b Faith in the power of the Word of God	sequencing events, summarizing data, making predictions, inferring relationships, making decisions, formulating opinions, working with time lines, valuing the rights of citizenship, showing respect for heritage
BATs: 2c Faithfulness, 2d Goal setting, 2e Work, 2f Enthusiasm, 4a Sowing and reaping	sequencing events, making predictions, inferring relationships, formulating opinions, working with maps
BAT: 5d Communication	sequencing events, summarizing data, working with maps, showing respect for heritage
BATs: 2d Goal setting, 2e Work, 3a Self-concept	sequencing events, summarizing data, making predictions, making decisions, formulating opinions, working with time lines
BATs: 2d Goal setting, 2e Work, 7b Exaltation of Christ, 7c Praise	sequencing events, summarizing data, making predictions, inferring relationships, making decisions, formulating opinions, working with maps
BATs: 2c Faithfulness, 2d Goal setting, 2e Work	sequencing events, making predictions, inferring relationships, formulating opinions, working with time lines
BATs: 2c Faithfulness, 2d Goal setting, 2e Work, 2f Enthusiasm, 3a Self-concept	sequencing events, summarizing data, making predictions, inferring relationships, formulating opinions, working with time lines, working with graphs, valuing the rights of citizenship, showing respect for heritage

	Chapters and Lessons	Suggested teaching days	Lesson pages	Text pages	Notebook pages
11	**STRUGGLES FAR AWAY**				
	61 Diamonds and Gold	2	270-74	230-33, 316-17	86
	62 The Boer War	2	275-78	234-37	
	63 China in Conflict	2	278-82	238-41, 316-17	87-88
	64 Christians in the Boxer Uprising	2	283-86	242-44	89-90
	65 The Industrial Revolution and Imperialism	1	287-90	245-48	91-92
12	**BY THE PEOPLE**				
	66 By the People	1	292-95	250-53, 269-70	93
	67 Democracy Comes to America	3	296-99	254-57, 316-17	94
	68 Checks and Balances	2	299-303	257-61	95-96
	69 Citizenship	2	303-5	262-63	97
	70 We the People	2	306-8	264-66	98

Bible Action Truths; Bible Promises	Heritage Studies skills
BAT: 8d Courage	making predictions, inferring relationships, formulating opinions, working with maps, using cardinal directions, valuing the rights of citizenship
BATs: 8a Faith in God's promises, 8d Courage	sequencing events, making predictions, formulating opinions, working with maps and globes, valuing the rights of citizenship, showing respect for heritage
BATs: 1a Understanding Jesus Christ, 4c Honesty, 5c Evangelism and missions, 6d Clear conscience	sequencing events, summarizing data, inferring relationships, making decisions, formulating opinions, working with maps, showing respect for heritage
BATs: 1b Repentance and faith, 8a Faith in God's promises	sequencing events, summarizing data, making predictions, inferring relationships, making decisions, formulating opinions, working with maps, working with graphs
BAT: 5c Evangelism and missions	inferring relationships, making decisions, formulating opinions, working with maps, valuing the rights of citizenship, showing respect for heritage
BATs: 2a Authority, 3a Self-concept, 5a Love, 5d Communication, 7c Praise	making predictions, making decisions, formulating opinions, valuing the rights of citizenship, showing respect for heritage
BAT: 5a Love; Bible Promises: A. Liberty from Sin, B. Guiltless by the Blood, H. God as Father, I. God as Master	making decisions, working with time lines, working with maps, identifying key documents, valuing the rights of citizenship
BAT: 2a Authority	inferring relationships, working with maps, working with charts, identifying key documents
BATs: 2a Authority, 4a Sowing and reaping, 5b Giving	working with time lines, identifying key documents, valuing the rights of citizenship, showing respect for heritage
BATs: 2c Faithfulness, 2e Work, 2f Enthusiasm, 7c Praise	formulating opinions, working with time lines, identifying key documents, valuing the rights of citizenship, showing respect for heritage

LESSON PLANS

1 | LESSONS 1-5

The Continents

This chapter deals with the physical geography of the earth. Your child will locate and use the parallels of latitude and the meridians of longitude on maps and the globe. Additional map work highlights the discussion and location of the prime meridian, international date line, tropics of Cancer and Capricorn, and the Arctic and Antarctic Circles. Lessons 4 and 5 discuss factors affecting climate, as well as the relationship of climate and natural resources to the choices people make about where they live.

Exploration of the earth is also discussed, giving special attention to the accomplishments and character qualities of Matthew Maury, the "Pathfinder of the Seas," and Roald Amundsen, the first man to reach the South Pole.

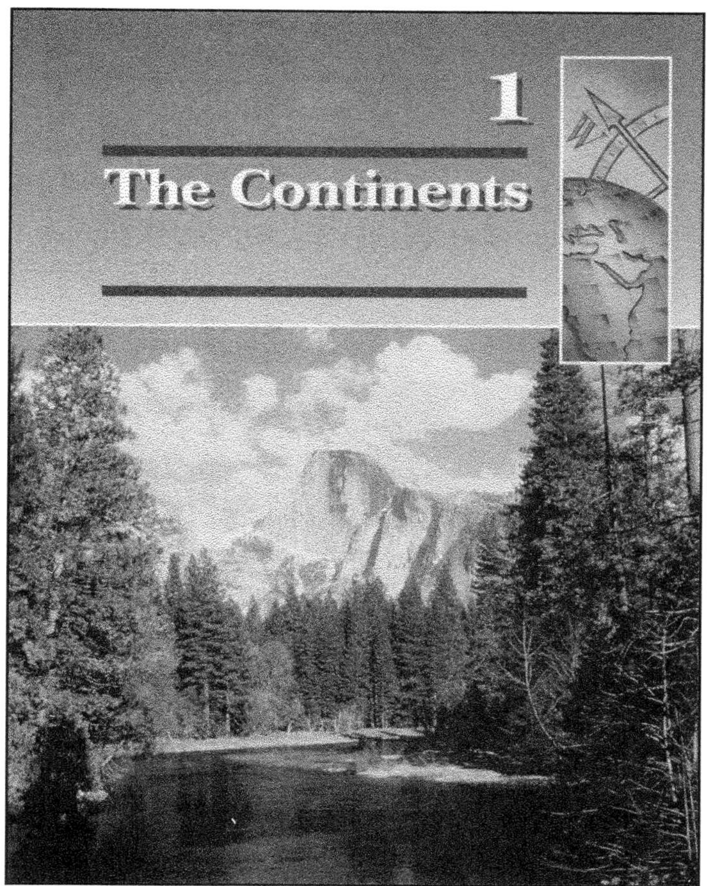

Materials

The following materials must be obtained or prepared before the presentation of the lesson. These items are labeled with an asterisk (*) in each lesson and in the Materials List in the Supplement. For further information see the individual lessons.

- A *Heritage Studies 4 Student Textbook*
- A *Heritage Studies 4 Student Notebook*
- A globe (Lesson 1) (*NOTE:* A globe will be used in many lessons throughout the curriculum.)
- Appendix, pages A2-A4 (Lesson 1)
- 2 oranges (Lesson 2)
- An atlas (Lessons 2, 4, and 5)

If you have not already purchased an easy-to-read atlas for your child to use, we recommend that you do so. The *Rand McNally Classroom Atlas,* available through the BJU Press, is appropriate for elementary usage.

- Appendix, page A5 (Lesson 2)
- The TimeLine Snapshots (Lesson 3) (*NOTE:* The TimeLine Snapshots will be used in many lessons throughout the curriculum.)
- 2 small toy boats (Lesson 3)
- Appendix, page A6 (Lesson 3)
- A packet of instant cocoa or a tea bag (Lesson 4)
- Appendix, pages A7-A8 (Lesson 4)
- Appendix, page A10 (Lesson 5)
- A labeled index card (Lesson 5)

Maps, charts, games, and other black-and-white visuals can be found in two places in your teacher's manual—the Supplement and the Appendix. All the pages that need to be copied for use in the lessons can be found in the Appendix. Those found in the Supplement can be used directly from your manual and do not need to be copied, though they may be copied if you so desire.

LESSON 1

Land and Water

Text, pages 2-5, 316-17
Notebook, page 1

Preview

Main Ideas

- Maps and globes represent real places.
- The earth's land is divided into seven continents.
- Most of the earth's water is contained in four oceans.
- The equator divides the earth into Northern and Southern Hemispheres.
- The prime meridian and the international date line divide the earth into Eastern and Western Hemispheres.

Objectives

- Identify the seven continents and four oceans on a map
- Locate the equator on a map
- Locate the prime meridian and the international date line on a map

Materials

School supplies, such as crayons, glue, scissors, pencils, and paper that you would have in your teaching area, are not listed in the Materials list of each lesson.

- A globe*
- A *Heritage Studies 4 Student Textbook**
- A *Heritage Studies 4 Student Notebook**
- Appendix, page A2: World Map 1*
- Appendix, page A3: World Map 2*
- Appendix, page A4: information cards*

You may choose to teach this lesson or other lessons in one day. If you would like to spread the lesson over more than one day, the suggested teaching days are marked for you.

Day 1

Lesson

As you read the lesson, you will notice that there is a variety of types or styles of print. **Questions to be given directly to your child are in the regular bold print.** Information to be given directly to your child is in the regular print. *(The answers to questions are shown in italics within parentheses.) Instructions and information directed to you as the teacher are given in a different italicized print.* (*NOTE*s give information to the teacher also.) ***Terms*** that you will want your child to become familiar with are in bold/italic print.

Introducing the Lesson

Role-Playing Activity

➤ **What are the features or characteristics of a person's face?** *(eyes, nose, mouth)*

When your child is asked to give his opinion (a "what-do-you-think" question), an answer may not be listed. Accept any answer and, if needed, guide your child by asking further questions to reach a better answer.

➤ **What do you think some of the features or characteristics of the earth are?**

In this chapter you will be learning about ***geography***, the study of the features of the earth.

➤ *Turn off the lights in the schoolroom.*

Imagine that you are strapped into a space shuttle, waiting to be launched into earth orbit. *Count down from ten to one; then say, "Launch."*

Imagine you are hurtling through the atmosphere up to earth orbit. The earth would be about two hundred miles below you.

➤ **What might you see out the window?** *(Answers will vary but should include a discussion of the earth falling away below.)*

➤ *Turn on the lights to continue the lesson.*

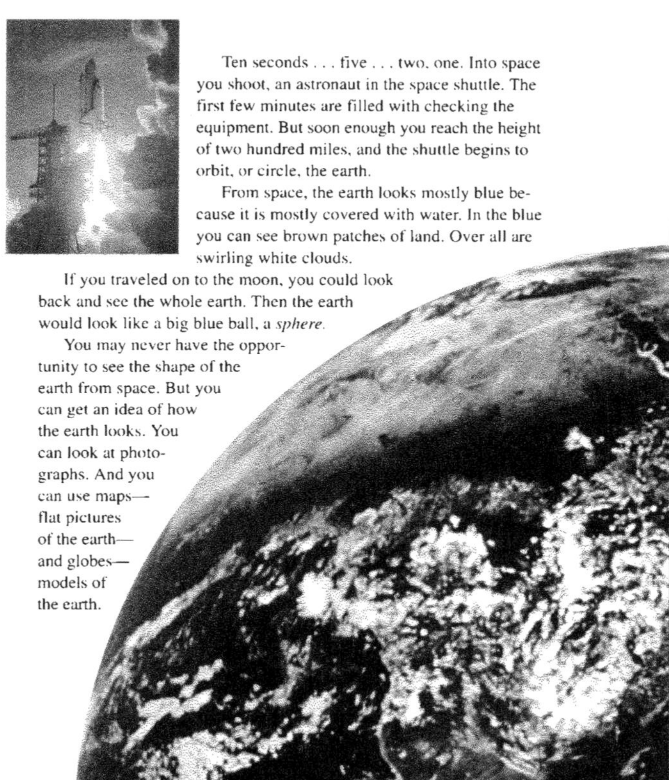

Ten seconds . . . five . . . two, one. Into space you shoot, an astronaut in the space shuttle. The first few minutes are filled with checking the equipment. But soon enough you reach the height of two hundred miles, and the shuttle begins to orbit, or circle, the earth.

From space, the earth looks mostly blue because it is mostly covered with water. In the blue you can see brown patches of land. Over all are swirling white clouds.

If you traveled on to the moon, you could look back and see the whole earth. Then the earth would look like a big blue ball, a *sphere*.

You may never have the opportunity to see the shape of the earth from space. But you can get an idea of how the earth looks. You can look at photographs. And you can use maps—flat pictures of the earth—and globes—models of the earth.

Like the earth, a globe is a sphere. It shows how the earth's water and land look. We divide the water into four oceans and the land into seven continents. Find all the oceans and continents on the globe.

Asia is the largest continent. It is connected to one of the smallest continents, Europe. Some *geographers*, people who study the earth, think these two continents should be just one. They call the one large continent *Eurasia*. Do you think that is an appropriate name?

The Arctic Ocean is the smallest ocean. Which ocean do you think is the biggest? The Pacific Ocean is the largest and the deepest. In some places, it is almost seven miles deep. All seven continents could fit into the space the Pacific takes up.

Teaching the Lesson

The Text Discussion is a guide to help as you read and discuss the text pages. When instructions say to read the text, your child should read silently for comprehension. He will be asked occasionally to read aloud for interpretation. You know your child best. Adjust the reading to meet his needs. Take time to help your child answer the questions found in the text.

Text Discussion, page 2

➤ **Read page 2 to learn what the earth looks like from earth orbit.** *(mostly blue water)*

➤ **What other colors does an astronaut see when he looks at the earth?** *(brown and white)*

➤ **What is the brown?** *(land)*

➤ **What are the white areas?** *(clouds)*

➤ Land and water are the main features of the earth. **How would the earth be different if there were no water?** *(Life could not exist.)*

Remind your child that God created the earth for His own glory. (Bible Promise: I. God as Master)

➤ **Would it be easy for us to hire a shuttle to take a field trip up to earth orbit?** *(no)*

➤ **How can we know the shape of the land and bodies of water if we cannot go up to earth orbit to look at them?** *(We can look at maps and globes.)*

Text Discussion, page 3

➤ **Read page 3 to find out how many continents and how many oceans there are.** *(seven continents, four oceans)*

➤ **What are people who study the earth called?** *(**geographers**)*

You will want to reinforce each concept in the following map activity with a globe. You may also use pages 316-17 in the student text if you so desire.

Globe Activity

➤ Look at the globe.

➤ Give characteristics of the globe. *(It is round like a ball, slightly tilted; it is a sphere.)*

➤ **What two major features cover the surface of the earth?** *(land and water)*

➤ **What are the large landmasses of the earth called?** *(continents)*

➤ Use the globe to name the seven continents. *(Africa, Antarctica, Asia, Australia, Europe, North America, and South America)*

- ➤ *As your child names the continents, label them on World Map 1.*
- ➤ *Point to Greenland on World Map 1.* **Does Greenland look large enough to be a continent?** *(yes)*

Although Greenland looks quite large on the map, it is actually only about one-third the size of the continental United States. Because it is difficult to portray the round earth as flat, map layouts—called ***projections***—make Greenland seem much larger than it is.

- ➤ Point to the landmass that contains both Europe and Asia.

This is the largest landmass on the earth. It is usually divided into two continents.

- ➤ Find on page 3 the name some geographers use for both continents combined. *(Eurasia)*
- ➤ **Why would some people think that these two continents might be considered one continent?** *(They are connected; no ocean separates them.)*
- ➤ Look at the blue areas on the globe. Name the four oceans. *(Pacific, Atlantic, Arctic, Indian)*
- ➤ *As your child names the oceans, label them on World Map 1.*
- ➤ **Which ocean is the largest?** *(the Pacific)*
- ➤ **How much of the world's land could fit in the Pacific Ocean?** *(all of it)*
- ➤ **Which ocean is the smallest?** *(Arctic)*

The surface of the Arctic Ocean is frozen on top, but the ocean beneath the icecap is not frozen. In 1958 the nuclear submarine *Nautilus* was the first submarine to sail under the North Pole in the Arctic Ocean.

Day 2

Text Discussion, page 4

- ➤ **Read page 4 to find out differences between the North Pole and the South Pole.**
- ➤ **Where is the actual geographical North Pole located?** *(in the Arctic Ocean)*

Explorers have been able to reach the North Pole by walking on the ocean.

- ➤ **How is such a walk as this possible?** *(Much of the surface of the Arctic Ocean is frozen.)*
- ➤ **Would you enjoy walking on a frozen ocean?**

The frozen part of the Arctic Ocean is called the ***icecap*** and is frozen seawater.

- ➤ **Where is the actual geographical South Pole located?** *(Antarctica)*
- ➤ **Is Antarctica also a frozen ocean?** *(No, it is a continent.)*

North Pole

Equator

South Pole

The North Pole is the northernmost point on the earth. It is in the Arctic Ocean. The southernmost point on the earth is called the *South Pole.* You can find it on the continent of Antarctica.

Halfway between the North and South Poles, an imaginary line circles the earth, the *equator.* The equator divides the earth into two half spheres, or *hemispheres:* the Northern Hemisphere and the Southern Hemisphere. Find the continent on which you live on the maps below. Which hemisphere do you live in?

Most of the land on earth is in the Northern Hemisphere. All of North America, Asia, and Europe are in the Northern Hemisphere. Parts of Africa and South America are also north of the equator. Which continents are found completely within the Southern Hemisphere?

Northern Hemisphere

Southern Hemisphere

4

Antarctica is actually a continent covered with ice and snow. There are approximately seven million cubic miles of ice in Antarctica. This amount of ice would cover the United States—including Alaska and Hawaii—with a sheet of ice two miles thick.

- ➤ **What is the imaginary line around the middle of the earth called?** *(the equator)*
- ➤ The equator divides the earth into two sections. **What is the part of the earth north of the equator called?** *(the Northern Hemisphere)*
- ➤ **What is the part of the earth south of the equator called?** *(the Southern Hemisphere)*

When it is summer in the Northern Hemisphere, it is winter in the Southern Hemisphere.

- ➤ **What season would it be in the Southern Hemisphere when it is winter in the Northern Hemisphere?** *(summer)*

Map Activity, page 4

- ➤ Find North America on the globe. **Which hemisphere is it in?** *(the Northern Hemisphere)*
- ➤ *Point to Brazil on the globe.* **What season is it in Brazil when it is summer in North America?** *(winter)*
- ➤ Locate several different countries on the globe, telling in which hemisphere they lie.

You cannot see the whole globe at one time. When you look at a globe, you can see about one half—a hemisphere. To see the other hemisphere, you must turn the globe. We divide the earth into hemispheres to make it easier to study.

There is a second way to divide the earth into hemispheres. Geographers draw a line from the North Pole to the South Pole and another line back to the North Pole again. These lines divide the Eastern Hemisphere from the Western Hemisphere.

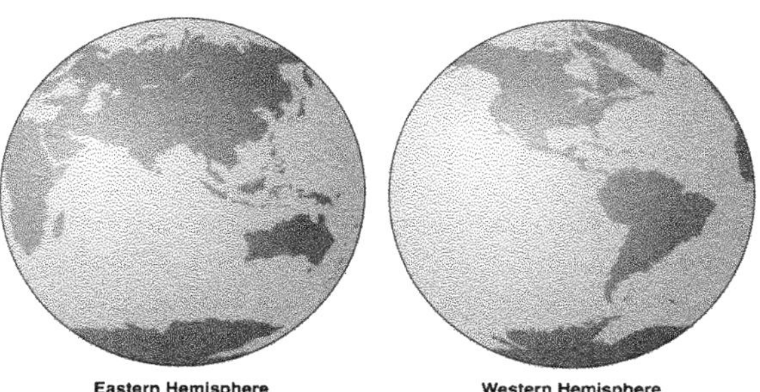

Eastern Hemisphere — Western Hemisphere

These lines have names too. One line runs from the North Pole to the South Pole through the Atlantic Ocean. It passes through England. This line is called the *prime meridian*. On the other side of the globe, the second line runs through the Pacific Ocean. It is called the *international date line*. Together these lines circle the globe from north to south, just as the equator circles the globe from east to west. When the earth is divided in this way, in which hemisphere is your country located?

5

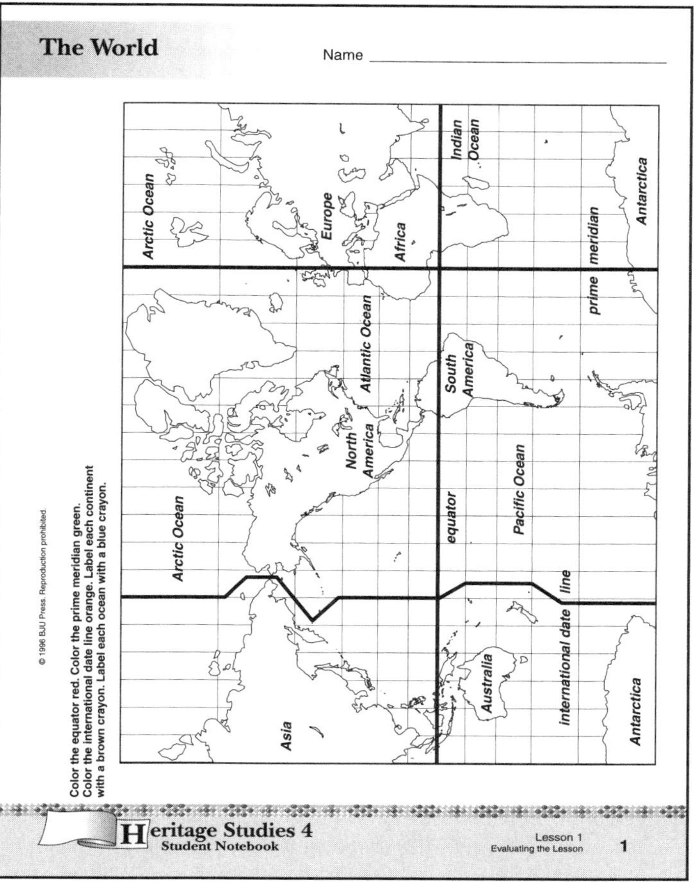

The World Name ______________________

Color the equator red. Color the prime meridian green. Color the international date line orange. Label each continent with a brown crayon. Label each ocean with a blue crayon.

Heritage Studies 4 Student Notebook — Lesson 1 Evaluating the Lesson 1

- ➤ Look at the maps on the bottom of page 4. **Which continents are contained entirely in the Northern Hemisphere?** *(North America, Asia, and Europe)*
- ➤ **Which continents are partly in the Northern Hemisphere and partly in the Southern Hemisphere?** *(Africa and South America)*
- ➤ **Which continents are contained entirely in the Southern Hemisphere?** *(Australia and Antarctica)*
- ➤ **In which hemisphere are you located?**

Text Discussion, page 5

- ➤ **Read page 5 to find out the names of the two imaginary lines that divide the earth from top to bottom.** *(the prime meridian and the international date line)*
- ➤ **Can you find these lines on World Map 2?**

> The prime meridian and international date line will be discussed in more detail in Lesson 2.

Information Activity

- ➤ *Give your child the information cards.*
- ➤ Find the continent card.
- ➤ **Which continent is your state or country in?** Write the name of the continent on the card.
- ➤ Repeat the activity for the state, country, and hemisphere cards. If your state borders an ocean, fill out the ocean card.

Evaluating the Lesson

Notebook Activity, page 1

- ➤ Read the directions on Notebook page 1.
- ➤ Complete the page.

> You may want to have your child label in pencil the names of the continents and oceans before he uses his blue and brown crayons.

Going Beyond

Enrichment

The following activity will help your child learn the hemispheres. It is designed for more than one player. Since the answers are on the back of the index cards, your child can practice by himself.

Have available a world map for your child to play Hemisphere Hunt. Prepare a set of twenty index cards with the name of a country on the front of each card and the name of the corresponding hemispheres in which the country is located on the back of the card. Make a set of four cards labeled *Northern Hemisphere, Southern Hemisphere, Eastern Hemisphere,* and *Western Hemisphere.* Place the Northern Hemisphere card at the top of the map, the Southern Hemisphere card at the bottom of the map, the Eastern Hemisphere card to the right of the map, and the Western Hemisphere card to the left of the map. The first player will choose a country card and tell all the hemispheres in which this country is located. *(For example, Canada is located in the Northern Hemisphere and the Western Hemisphere. France is located in the Northern Hemisphere, and since the prime meridian passes through France, it is also located in both the Eastern and Western Hemispheres.)* If he is correct, he will keep the card. If he is incorrect, he should place the card on the bottom of the deck of country cards. Players alternate until all the country cards are taken. The player with the most cards is the winner.

Additional Teacher Information

The earth's surface area covers approximately 196,800,000 square miles. Approximately 139,500,000 square miles (about 71 percent) is ocean. Only 29 percent of the earth's surface is land. It is interesting to note that the ratio of water to land on the earth is approximately equal to the ratio of water to other elements in the human body.

Recently, geographers have begun referring to Australia and the surrounding islands as the continent *Oceania.* Also, some oceanographers identify five oceans, rather than four, by counting the South Sea, the area around Antarctica.

LESSON 2
Earth Locations

Text, pages 6-8
Notebook, page 2

Preview

Main Ideas

- Parallels of latitude mark distance north or south of the equator.
- Meridians of longitude mark distance east or west of the prime meridian.

Objectives

- Identify parallels of latitude on a world map and globe
- Identify meridians of longitude on a world map and globe
- Identify the longitude of a given place
- Identify the latitude of a given place
- Locate a point on a map or globe given the latitude and longitude

Materials

- A globe
- 2 oranges*
- A permanent marker
- A knife
- Appendix, page A5: World Map 3*
- An atlas*

Day 1

Lesson

Introducing the Lesson

Location Activity

➤ Tell the location of your desk in the room. *(by the back door, next to parent's desk, below the window, etc.)*

➤ *Give the location of your own desk and another piece of furniture.*

Each time the location is given, we have mentioned its relationship to another object in the room.

➤ Tell the location of several items in the schoolroom in relation to your desk. *(The wastebasket is next to my desk; the clock is above my desk, etc.)*

Point to the equator and the prime meridian on the globe. Places on the earth are located by their relationship to the equator and the prime meridian.

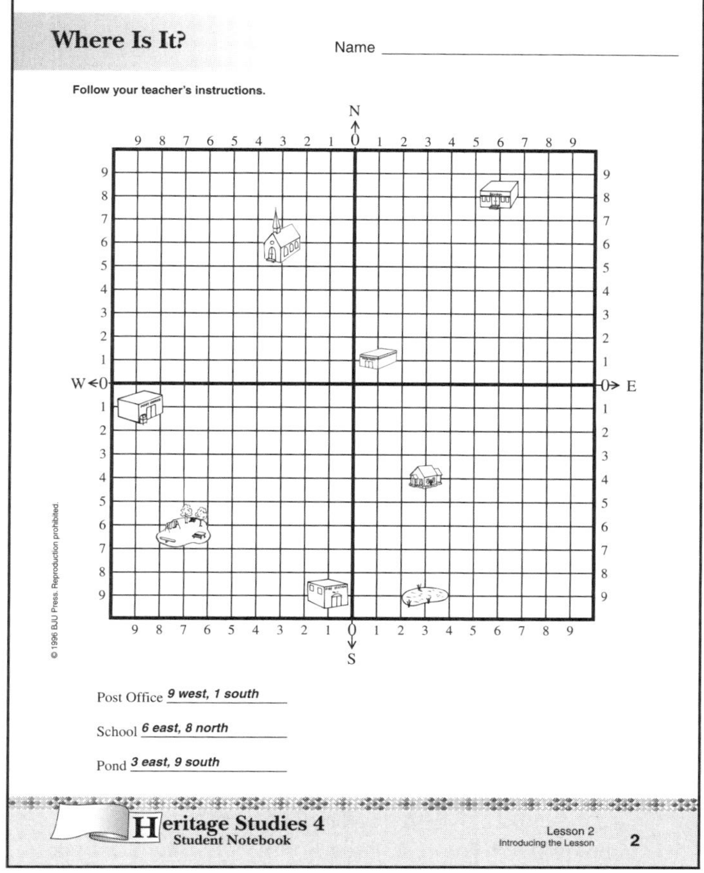
Where Is It? Name ____________________

Follow your teacher's instructions.

Post Office *9 west, 1 south*

School *6 east, 8 north*

Pond *3 east, 9 south*

Heritage Studies 4
Student Notebook

Lesson 2
Introducing the Lesson
2

Notebook Activity, page 2

➤ Look at Notebook page 2. Name the buildings and other features of the town. *(school, church, store, park, etc.)*

➤ **What is drawn over the map?** *(lines)*

The thick line going across the page from left to right will be called the *equator.*

➤ Trace with your finger the equator on your Notebook page. *Write the word* equator *beside the line for your child.*

➤ Find a line numbered *1* on each side of the equator.

Each of these lines is one line away from the equator. The numbers on the lines north and south of the equator indicate how far from the equator each line is.

➤ Find the thick line that runs north and south down the center of the town.

This line will be called the *prime meridian. Write the words* prime meridian *above the line on the Notebook page for your child.*

➤ Find the lines numbered *1* on each side of the prime meridian.

Each of these lines is one line away from the prime meridian. Each vertical line is numbered according to its distance from the prime meridian.

➤ Find the picture of the church. **How many lines from the prime meridian is the church?** *(three lines)*

➤ **Is the church east or west of the prime meridian?** *(west)*

In the white space below the map, write church—3 west *for your child.*

➤ **How many lines away from the equator is the church?** *(six lines)*

➤ **Is the church north or south of the equator?** *(north)*

Write 6 north *on the page.* The "address" of the church on the map is 3 west, 6 north.

Some children may remember coordinate graphs from math. They may refer to the "address" as coordinate points.

➤ *Repeat the above step-by-step procedure, allowing your child to tell the "address" of the fire station. (1 west, 9 south)*

➤ **What is located at the address 7 west, 6 south?** *(the park)*

➤ Draw your house at the address 5 east, 4 north.

➤ Complete the Notebook page by filling in the "addresses" of the post office, school, and pond.

In the back of the student text is a glossary. Encourage your child to look up any words that he is unfamiliar with.

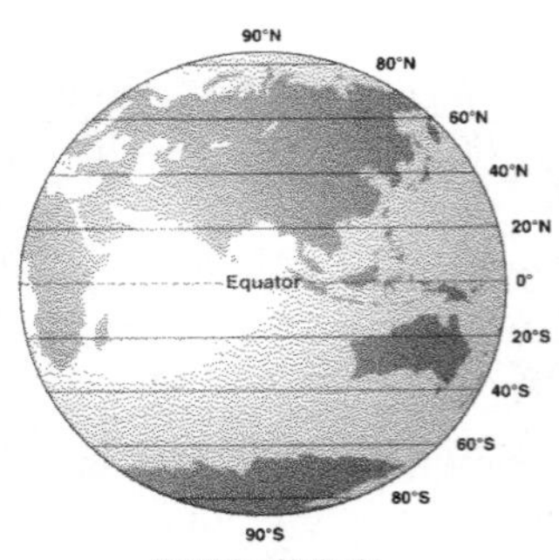

Parallels of latitude

Parallels and Meridians

The equator, prime meridian, and international date line are just three of the lines that geographers draw on globes and maps. Most globes and maps have many more lines on them, running north/south and east/west. Together the lines form a grid on the earth. The grid helps to locate places.

One set of the lines circles the globe from east to west. Each line is *parallel* to the equator. That means that each line is always an equal distance from the equator and every other line in this set. They are *parallels of latitude*.

The second set of lines runs along the globe from north to south. These lines are called *meridians of longitude*. Meridians are different from parallels in two ways. First, each meridian is drawn only half way around the globe. It takes two meridians to complete a circle. And meridians are not always an equal distance apart. All the meridians meet at both the North and the South Poles. Where are the meridians most far apart from each other?

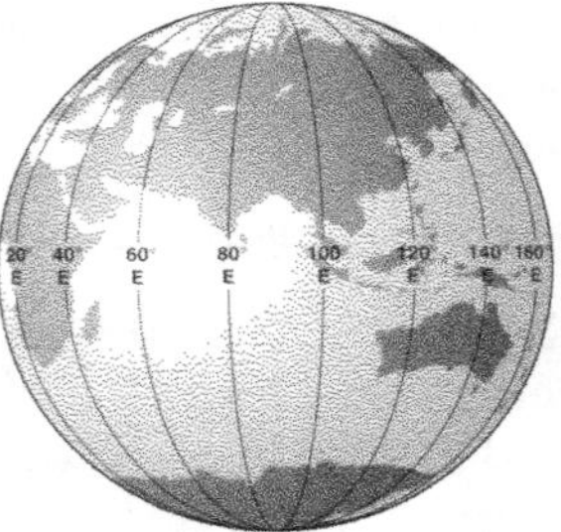

Meridians of longitude

6

Teaching the Lesson

Text Discussion, page 6

➤ Look at World Map 3. **What is the same about this map and the grid map on the Notebook page?** *(Both have lines going across and down, or both have a prime meridian and an equator.)*

➤ **Read the first two paragraphs on page 6 to find what the lines which circle the globe from east to west are called.** ***(parallels of latitude)***

Map Demonstration, page 6

➤ *Show your child an orange.*

➤ We will let this orange represent the globe.

I will write an *N* at the top of the orange to represent the North Pole. I will write an *S* at the bottom of the orange to represent the South Pole. I will draw a line around the center of the orange to represent the equator.

➤ Parallels of latitude tell the distance from the equator. **What does the word *parallel* mean?** *(Every point on a line is the same distance from another line.)*

➤ *Begin to cut the orange into parallel sections, making sure that each slice has approximately the same thickness.*

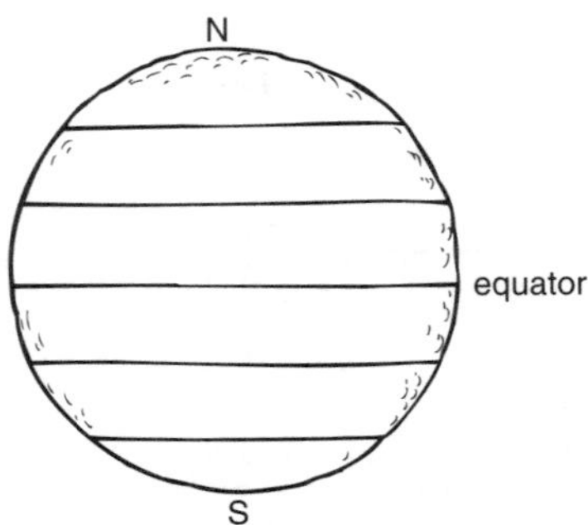

As you cut the sections north of the equator, tell your child with each cut that this is a north parallel of latitude. While cutting the slices south of the equator, tell your child this is a south parallel of latitude.

Notice that each section of the orange is of the same thickness and goes all the way around. These sections represent the parallels of latitude.

➤ **Read the last paragraph on page 6 to find out what the lines from the north to south are called.** ***(meridians of longitude)***

➤ We will let the second orange also represent the globe.

I will again write an *N* at the top of the orange to represent the North Pole and an *S* at the bottom of the orange to represent the South Pole. I will draw a line from the North Pole to the South Pole to represent the prime meridian.

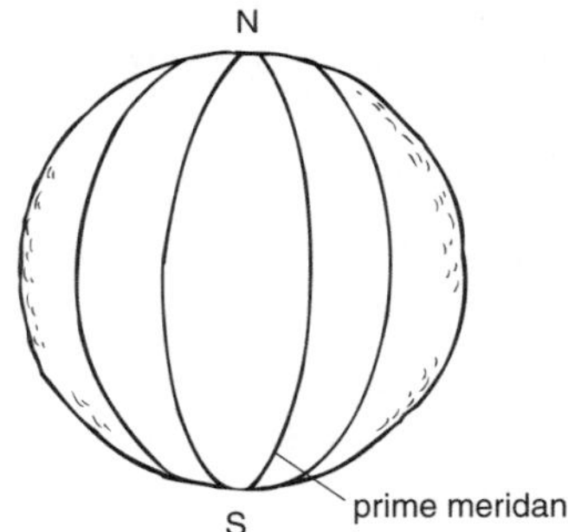

➤ **What are the lines going down the map from north to south called?** *(meridians of longitude)*

Begin to cut the orange to show meridians. Be sure to cut only partway into the orange as you slice from north to south, stopping at the South Pole. As you make a cut east of the prime meridian, tell your child this is an east meridian of longitude. Make a cut west of the prime meridian, saying this is a west meridian of longitude.

➤ All the sections meet at the top and bottom of the orange. **Are the sections the same width or distance apart at the ends as they are in the middle?** *(no)*

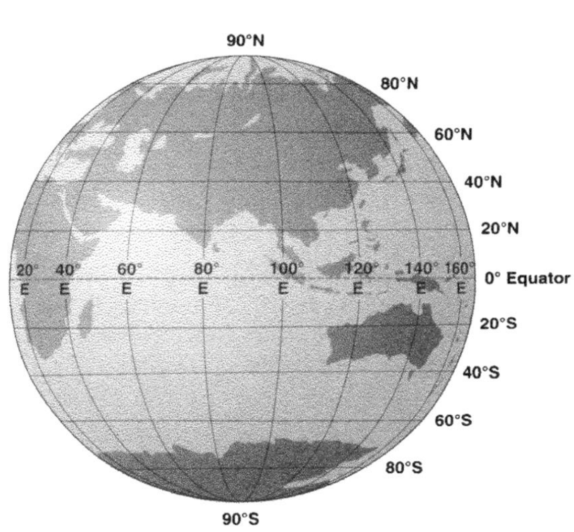

The number given to each parallel of latitude tells how far it is north or south of the equator. On the map above, the first parallel south of the equator is 20°S. We say it is 20 degrees south latitude. What label is given to the first parallel north of the equator? It is 20°N. The North Pole is 90°N. Can you guess the latitude of the South Pole?

Except for the prime meridian and the international date line, meridians of longitude are labeled with numbers and directions too. Each meridian east of the prime meridian is labeled in degrees east longitude. The meridians west of the prime meridian are labeled in degrees west longitude. East and west longitude meet at 180°, the international date line.

7

➤ **Are the meridians of longitude on the orange making a complete circle of the orange?** *(no)*

Meridians go only halfway around the globe. It takes two meridians to make a complete circle around the globe. *Demonstrate this as you continue to cut slices in the orange, completing the meridians.*

➤ Compare the "parallel" orange sections and the "meridian" orange sections.

➤ **In what two ways do meridians differ from parallels?** *(A meridian goes only halfway around the globe; the meridians are not always the same distance apart.)*

➤ **Where do the meridians meet?** *(at the North and South Poles)*

➤ **Where do parallels of latitude meet?** *(They don't.)*

Day 2

Text Discussion, page 7

Parallels of latitude and meridians of longitude can be used to locate places in the world just as you located places on the grid map on your Notebook page.

➤ **Read page 7 to find out how points on the globe are labeled.** *(by degrees of longitude and latitude)*

➤ Look at the map on page 7. **What degree of latitude marks the equator?** *(0°)*

Parallels of latitude north of the equator are called north latitudes.

➤ **What are the parallels of latitude south of the equator called?** *(south latitudes)*

➤ **What degree of latitude marks the North Pole?** *(90°N)*

➤ **What degree of latitude marks the South Pole?** *(90°S)*

Map Activity

Your child may ask why the spacing for 15° appears larger at the bottom and top of World Map 3 than in the center. Making the map flat but keeping an accurate representation seems to distort the parallels. In reality the markings are equidistant.

➤ Look at World Map 3.

Parallels of latitude tell how far away from the equator a place is located. Only a few of the 180 parallels of latitude are shown on World Map 3. The lines of latitude on the map are 15° apart, going north and south.

➤ Name the continents that are along the 30°N line of latitude. *(North America, Africa, Asia)*

➤ Point to the prime meridian on the map.

Meridians of longitude tell how far east or west a place is from the prime meridian.

➤ **How are meridians west of the prime meridian labeled?** *(degrees west longitude)*

➤ **Where do the degrees west longitude meet the degrees east longitude?** *(at the international date line)*

When it is Tuesday in Hawaii (east of the international date line), it is Monday on the island of Fiji (west of the international date line). *Point out these two places on a world map in an atlas or on a globe.*

➤ **What degree of longitude marks the international date line?** *(180°)*

This longitude is 180° east and 180° west of the prime meridian. *Show on a globe that the international date line is halfway around the world from the prime meridian.*

➤ Look at World Map 3. Name the continents that lie along 60°W longitude. *(North America, South America, Antarctica)*

➤ *Repeat this procedure for other degrees of longitude as desired.*

◆ **LEARNING HOW** ◆

To Find Places Using Latitude and Longitude

1. Get a globe, a flat map of the world, a pencil, and a piece of paper.
2. Find the equator and the prime meridian on the globe. Put one finger on each line. Follow the lines to the spot where they meet, 0° latitude, 0° longitude. Is it found on a continent or in an ocean? Do the same thing on the world map. Do the lines meet in the same spot?
3. You can find any place on the earth using latitude and longitude. Follow the lines to where 20°S meets 40°W. What continent are you on?
4. Think of a latitude and a longitude. Let your Heritage Studies partner find the place where the two lines meet on the globe or map. Make a list of latitude and longitude pairs, always writing the latitude first. Can your partner find these places? Can you find the latitude and longitude of your hometown?

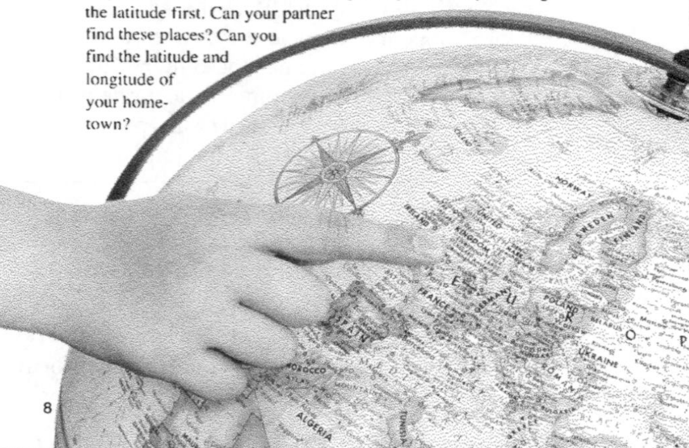

8

Day 3

State Map Activity

➤ Find your state on a map in the atlas.

➤ Determine the latitude and longitude of your state.

You will direct attention to a *Learning How* activity for the first time this year. One of your purposes in teaching these sections will be to teach your child to follow the directions for gathering materials, doing the activity, and considering the results of the activity.

Evaluating the Lesson

Learning How Activity, page 8

This activity calls for the use of a globe and a world map. It is not necessary to find each "address" on both maps. Alternate the "addresses" to give your child experience using both the flat world map and the globe.

➤ **Read the steps on page 8.**

God created a beautiful and orderly world. Scientists are able to find places easily using latitude and longitude because of the care God took in forming the earth. (Bible Promise: I. God as Master)

➤ **Read Step 2 again.** Answer the questions. *(in the ocean; the Atlantic Ocean; yes)*

If your child has difficulty following the latitude and the longitude at the same time, allow him to be the latitude finder. You take the job of longitude finder. Each of you will follow your own line with your fingers meeting at the point of location.

➤ **Read and do Step 3.** *(South America)*

➤ Point to 60°N latitude. Find 90°E longitude. **What is the continent that lies at the intersection of these lines?** *(Asia)*

➤ *Repeat the activity, directing your child to find what continents lie at the following locations:* 60°N latitude, 120°W longitude; 15°N latitude, 30°E longitude; 30°S latitude, 60°W longitude. *(North America, Africa, South America)*

➤ **Read and do Step 4.** *You will need to be your child's partner.*

Going Beyond

Enrichment

Set up an activity for your child to gain more experience using latitude and longitude. Cover a 3"×5" card file box with paper, adding designs to resemble the windows and doors of a house. Prepare several index cards to be placed in the box. On one side of each card write clues such as the following:

> My name is José. I live in an apartment building. My location on the earth is 15°S latitude, 45°W longitude. On what continent do I live?

Write the answer *(in this case, South America)* on the back of each card. Place the cards in the house box with the clue sides up. Instruct your child to read the clues and use the map to find the location. Direct him to look at the back of the card to check his answer. Encourage him to make a new card with clues on one side and the answer on the back to add to the card house.

Additional Teacher Information

The earth is divided into twenty-four time zones, each encompassing approximately 15° of longitude. Each time zone east of the prime meridian is one hour ahead of the previous zone up to the international date line, and each time zone west of the prime meridian is one hour behind the previous zone. Because of this time difference, when it is 1:00 P.M. on Sunday at the prime meridian (in Greenwich, England), it is twelve hours later (1:00 A.M. Monday morning) in Wellington, New Zealand. At the same time, it is twelve hours earlier than Greenwich (London) time on Midway Island (1:00 A.M. Sunday morning). Thus, though Wellington and Midway are in adjacent time zones, they are one whole day apart.

The international date line does not strictly follow the 180th meridian of longitude. In order to keep political entities in the same time zone, the line has been staggered. For example, the 180th meridian passes through the Aleutian Islands. Since these are all a part of western Alaska, however, the line is altered at that place so that all of Alaska will be on the same day.

Each degree of latitude indicates sixty nautical miles (sixty-six statute miles). When a more accurate positioning is required, degrees are divided into minutes ($\frac{1}{60}$ of a degree) and seconds ($\frac{1}{60}$ of a minute). At the equator, a degree of longitude is sixty-nine miles. Degrees of longitude become smaller closer to the poles. Degrees of longitude can also be divided into minutes and seconds.

LESSON 3
Climates and Currents

Text, pages 9-12, 316-17
Notebook, page 3

Preview

Main Ideas

- Climate is the typical weather of a given place.
- Climate is affected by latitude, altitude, distance from the ocean, and temperature of the air.
- Matthew F. Maury was the first to chart ocean currents.

Objectives

- Locate the Tropics on a map
- Locate the Arctic Circle and the Antarctic Circle on a map
- Answer questions about the climates of the Tropics and the circles
- Name benefits of Matthew Maury's ocean current charts

Materials

- World Map 3 used in Lesson 2
- A globe (optional)
- 2 small toy boats*
- The TimeLine Snapshots*
- The figure of Matthew Maury (1850) from the TimeLine Snapshots*
- Appendix, page A6: the temperature cards*

Notes

If you have purchased the TimeLine Snapshots, you will refer to it for the first time in this lesson. A time line is a simple way to organize the important events in history. It can easily be used to establish a sequence of events and illustrate relationships between the events pictured.

You will want to post the TimeLine before beginning this lesson. If you are teaching only fourth grade, post the TimeLine sections from 1725 to 1925. If you are teaching other grade levels also, be sure to include the years studied on those levels. If there is not enough space to hang the TimeLine along your schoolroom wall, consider hanging it in the hallway or garage. You may want to hang it in levels, leaving room between the layers for the pictures. The figures will be added throughout the year. You may also choose to add pictures of your own to the TimeLine as the opportunities arise.

Day 1

Lesson

Introducing the Lesson

Pretending Game

- ➤ Imagine that you are wrapped in a quilt while drinking hot chocolate in front of a cozy fire.
- ➤ **What might the weather be like outside on a day like that?** *(a cold winter day, perhaps a snowstorm)*
- ➤ **What outside activities can be done in snowy weather?** *(sledding, skiing, building snowmen or snow forts, etc.)*
- ➤ **What type of clothing is appropriate for very cold weather?** *(heavy coats, thick socks, etc.)*
- ➤ Now imagine that you are playing at the beach and that some of the adults are sitting under umbrellas to keep shaded.
- ➤ **What might the weather be like in this situation?** *(hot and sunny)*
- ➤ **What clothing might you wear?** *(short sleeves, light play clothes, sandals, etc.)*
- ➤ Different places have different types of weather. **What is the weather like in our town during the summer and winter?**

Teaching the Lesson

Text Discussion, page 9

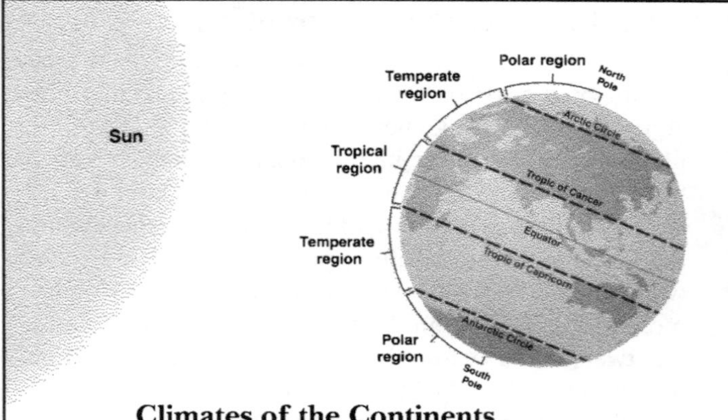

Climates of the Continents

What is the weather like where you live? Is it always the same? We can know much about a place when we know the kind of climate it has. *Climate* is the normal condition of the atmosphere near the earth's surface in a particular place.

You can find many different climates on each continent. In South America, you can find a hot, wet climate in the rain forest. You can find a desert in which rain has fallen just once in four hundred years. And high in the Andes Mountains, you can find the ground covered with snow all year. What causes these differences in climate?

How far a place is from the equator will affect its climate. Near the equator, the sun's light shines directly, or straight, on the land. The direct sunshine makes the land near the equator hot year-round. Would you like to live in a place that is always hot? We use two parallels of latitude to mark the boundaries of this hot-weather land. The lines are $23\frac{1}{2}$°N and $23\frac{1}{2}$°S. In the Northern Hemisphere the line is called the tropic of Cancer. Can you find the name of the line in the Southern Hemisphere? The area between these two lines is known as the *Tropics*.

9

- ➤ **Read the first paragraph on page 9 to find the definition of *climate*.** *(the normal condition of the atmosphere near the earth's surface in a particular place)*
- ➤ **What are some characteristics of a cold climate?** *(snow, rain, cold winds)*
- ➤ **What are some characteristics of a warm climate?** *(sunny days, warm breezes, no snow)*
- ➤ **Is the climate of most places exactly the same all year?** *(no)*
- ➤ **Read the rest of page 9 to find out what will affect the climate.** *(how far a place is from the equator)*
- ➤ Find the equator on World Map 3 or on the globe.
- ➤ **Why is the land on and near the equator hot throughout the year?** *(The sun shines directly on this area.)*
- ➤ **What parallels of latitude mark the boundaries of the hot-weather land?** *(23½°N latitude and 23½°S latitude)*
- ➤ **What is the 23½°N latitude called?** *(the tropic of Cancer)*
- ➤ **What is the 23½°S latitude called?** *(the tropic of Capricorn)*
- ➤ **What is the land between the tropic of Cancer and the tropic of Capricorn called?** *(the Tropics)*

Map Activity, pages 316-17

- ➤ Find the equator on the map on pages 316-17.
- ➤ Now find the tropic of Cancer and the tropic of Capricorn. The parallels are dotted lines on your map.
- ➤ Point out the Tropics. The land of the Tropics is consistently hot throughout the year.
- ➤ Name the continents that lie partly within the Tropics. *(North America, South America, Africa, Asia, Australia)*

If it is hottest near the equator, what do you think the climate is like at the poles? The poles are the coldest places on the earth. We use two more parallels of latitude to mark these cold areas. Both parallels are 66½° from the equator. North of the equator, the parallel is called the Arctic Circle. To the south, it is the Antarctic Circle.

The parallels at 23½° from the equator are called the Tropics. Most of the land on the earth falls between the Tropics and the Arctic or Antarctic Circles. Here the climate changes with the seasons. Places near the Tropics are warmer, but no place is always hot or cold.

How far a place is from an ocean or a large sea will also affect its climate. The hot summer sun warms the land quickly, but water warms up more slowly. The water stays cooler longer. Land near the cool water stays cooler too. During the winter, the opposite happens. The land loses heat quickly and becomes cool. But water loses heat slowly, so land near the water stays warmer as long as the water is warm. Which region would you like to visit?

10

Text Discussion, page 10

➤ **Read the first paragraph on page 10 to find which two areas of the earth are the coldest.** *(the poles)*

➤ **What do we call the parallels to mark these cold areas?** *(the Arctic Circle and the Antarctic Circle)*

➤ **How far from the equator are these parallels?** *(66½°)*

Map Activity, pages 316-17

➤ Find the Arctic Circle on the map on pages 316-17.

➤ **What lands are part of the Arctic Circle?** *(parts of Alaska, Canada, Greenland, Norway, Finland, Sweden, and Russia)*

➤ **Why do few people live within the Arctic Circle?** *(It is too cold.)*

➤ Find the Antarctic Circle on the map.

➤ **What land is part of the Antarctic Circle?** *(Antarctica)*

A temperature of ⁻128.6°F has been recorded at Vostok, Antarctica. There are no permanent settlements in Antarctica, but there are permanently manned scientific research stations.

Text Discussion, pages 10 (cont.), 9, 316-17

➤ **Read the second paragraph on page 10 to find where most of the land in the world is located.** *(between the Tropics and the circles)*

➤ Look at the map on page 9. Locate the areas between the Tropics and the circles.

➤ **What kind of climate can be found in the area between the Tropics and the circles?** *(temperate)*

Temperate means that the climate is not hot like the equator's climate or cold like the climate at the poles. It is a moderate temperature that changes with the seasons.

➤ Look at the map on pages 316-17. Name the continents or parts of continents that lie between the Tropics and the circles. *(North America, Europe, most of Asia, half of Africa and South America, and Australia)*

➤ **Read the last paragraph on page 10 to find how distance from the ocean affects the climate of a place.** *(Land near the ocean is warmed or cooled by the ocean water.)*

➤ **What type of climate is your favorite?**

Day 2

Demonstration

The ocean has currents. ***Currents*** are places where the water flows in a certain direction, like a path or a river. Ocean currents are created by wind pushing water along.

➤ Let's fill the kitchen sink full of water.

➤ **Is the water moving or calm?** *(calm)*

➤ *Place two small toy boats in the water, one in the center and the other along the side. Blow across the water behind the ship that is at the side of the sink.*

➤ **What happened to the boats?** *(The boat you are blowing behind is moving to the other end of the sink; the other boat is not moving.)*

➤ **Does the water stop moving when it gets to the other end of the sink?** *(No, it keeps moving along the outside of the sink.)*

Currents turn when they come close to continents, just as the current you have made follows the sides of the sink.

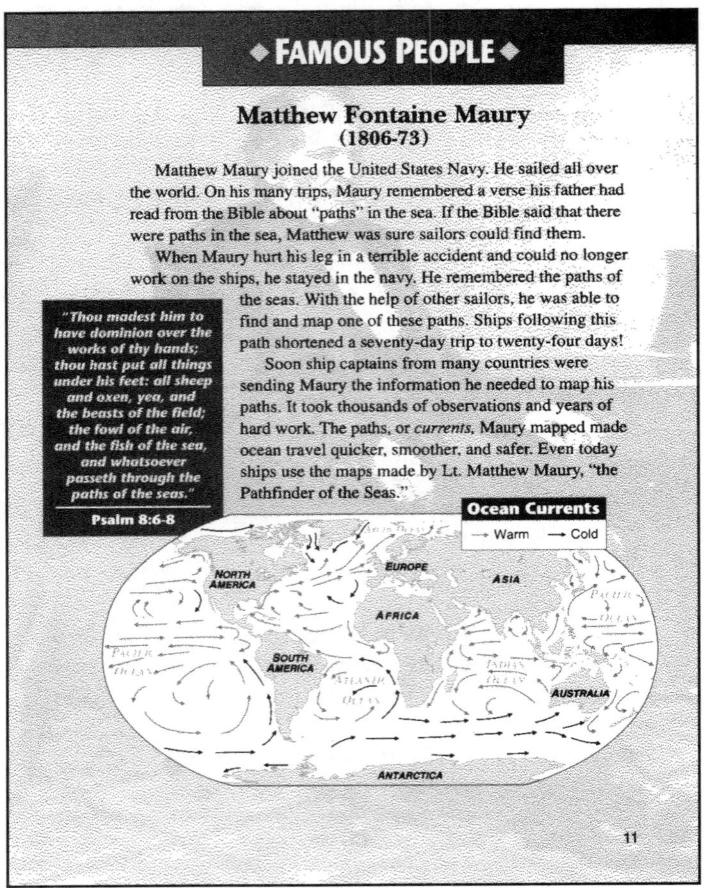

◆ FAMOUS PEOPLE ◆

Matthew Fontaine Maury
(1806-73)

Matthew Maury joined the United States Navy. He sailed all over the world. On his many trips, Maury remembered a verse his father had read from the Bible about "paths" in the sea. If the Bible said that there were paths in the sea, Matthew was sure sailors could find them.

When Maury hurt his leg in a terrible accident and could no longer work on the ships, he stayed in the navy. He remembered the paths of the seas. With the help of other sailors, he was able to find and map one of these paths. Ships following this path shortened a seventy-day trip to twenty-four days!

Soon ship captains from many countries were sending Maury the information he needed to map his paths. It took thousands of observations and years of hard work. The paths, or *currents,* Maury mapped made ocean travel quicker, smoother, and safer. Even today ships use the maps made by Lt. Matthew Maury, "the Pathfinder of the Seas."

"Thou madest him to have dominion over the works of thy hands; thou hast put all things under his feet: all sheep and oxen, yea, and the beasts of the field; the fowl of the air, and the fish of the sea, and whatsoever passeth through the paths of the seas."
Psalm 8:6-8

11

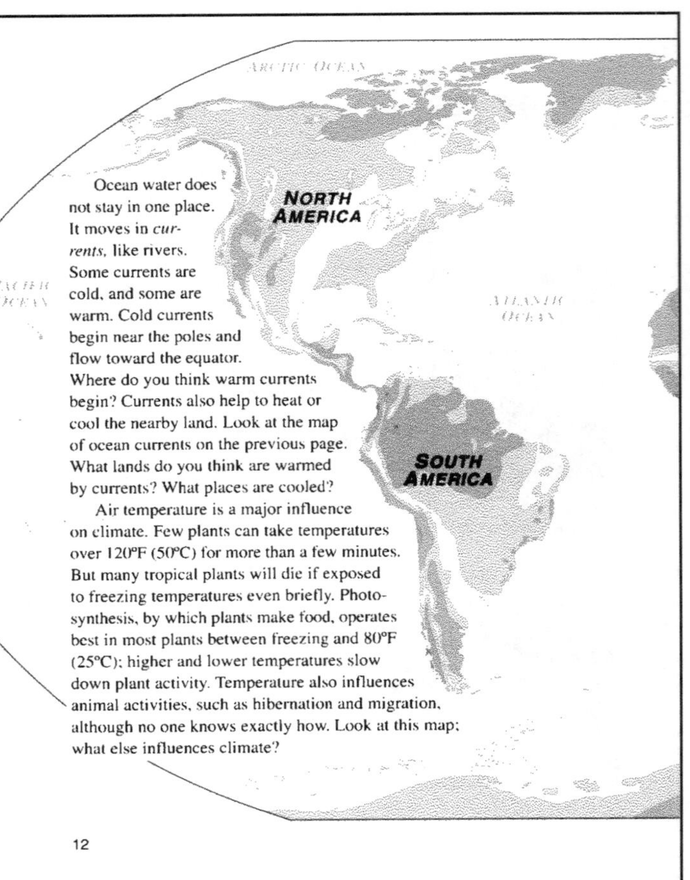

Ocean water does not stay in one place. It moves in *currents,* like rivers. Some currents are cold, and some are warm. Cold currents begin near the poles and flow toward the equator. Where do you think warm currents begin? Currents also help to heat or cool the nearby land. Look at the map of ocean currents on the previous page. What lands do you think are warmed by currents? What places are cooled?

Air temperature is a major influence on climate. Few plants can take temperatures over 120°F (50°C) for more than a few minutes. But many tropical plants will die if exposed to freezing temperatures even briefly. Photosynthesis, by which plants make food, operates best in most plants between freezing and 80°F (25°C); higher and lower temperatures slow down plant activity. Temperature also influences animal activities, such as hibernation and migration, although no one knows exactly how. Look at this map; what else influences climate?

12

Text Discussion, page 11

➤ **Read page 11 to find out who was the first person to map the ocean currents.** *(Matthew Maury)*

➤ **What job did Matthew Maury have?** *(He was in the U.S. Navy.)*

➤ **What happened to Maury that forced him off navy ships?** *(He had a terrible accident that injured his leg.)*

Since the leg did not heal properly, the doctors had to rebreak it to set it right. After the accident Matthew Maury was unable to return to duty on ship, but he devoted himself to gathering information about ocean currents.

➤ **How did knowing about ocean currents improve sea travel?** *(made it quicker, smoother, and safer)*

➤ Notice how the currents move on the ocean current map on page 11.

TimeLine Snapshots Activity

➤ Place the figure of Matthew Maury on the TimeLine at 1850.

After Maury's book, *Wind and Current Charts,* was published, ship captains were able to sail in the swift currents and arrive at their destinations in record time.

➤ Matthew Maury knew that the Bible was God's Word. Listen as I read a paragraph of a speech Maury gave in Tennessee in 1860.

> The Bible is authority for everything it touches. . . . When your men of science, with vain and hasty conceit, announce the discovery of disagreement between [the Bible and science], rely upon it, the fault is not with the witness of His records, but with the worm who essays to interpret evidence which he does not understand.

Read aloud Psalm 8:6-8 from text page 11, emphasizing the phrase "and whatsoever passeth through the paths of the sea." Matthew Maury understood that whatever the Bible says is true. (BAT: 8b Faith in the power of the Word of God; Bible Promise: I. God as Master)

Text Discussion, page 12

➤ **Read the first paragraph on page 12 to find out where cold currents begin.** *(near the poles)*

➤ **Where do warm currents begin?** *(near the equator)*

➤ Look at the ocean current map on page 11. **What lands are warmed by currents?** *(lands near currents that begin near the equator)*

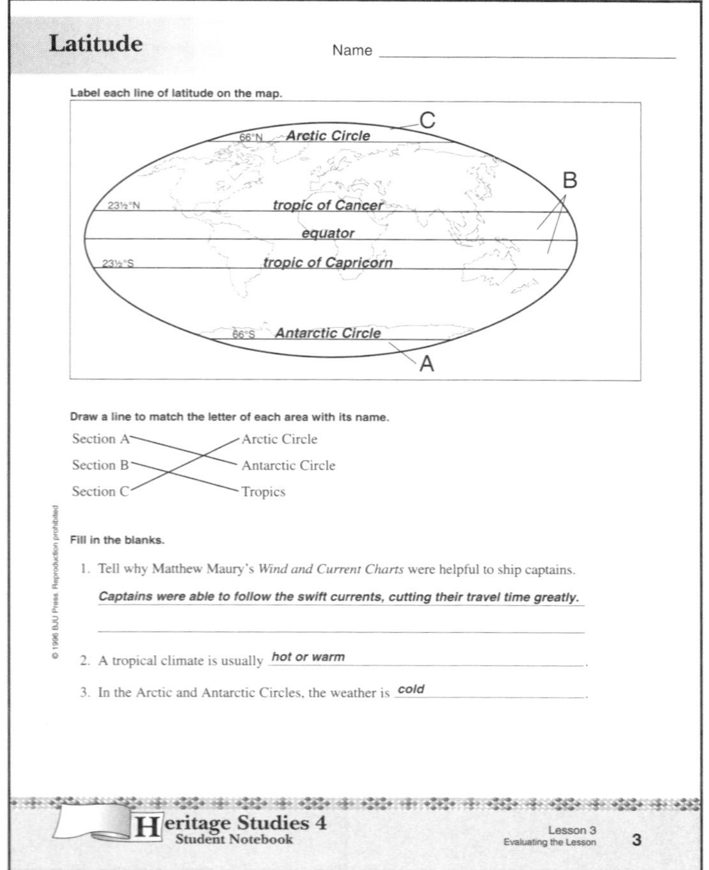

Latitude Name ______________________

Label each line of latitude on the map.

Draw a line to match the letter of each area with its name.

Section A — Arctic Circle
Section B — Antarctic Circle
Section C — Tropics

Fill in the blanks.

1. Tell why Matthew Maury's *Wind and Current Charts* were helpful to ship captains.
   Captains were able to follow the swift currents, cutting their travel time greatly.
2. A tropical climate is usually *hot or warm*.
3. In the Arctic and Antarctic Circles, the weather is *cold*.

Heritage Studies 4 Student Notebook — Lesson 3 Evaluating the Lesson 3

- ➤ **Read the last paragraph to find out what other factor affects the climate of a place.** *(air temperature)*
- ➤ **Can all plants live in all temperatures?** *(no)* God made some plants to live in warm climates and some to live in cool climates.
- ➤ **What is *photosynthesis?*** *(the way plants make food)*
- ➤ **What range of temperatures is best for photosynthesis?** *(between freezing and 80°F)*
- ➤ **How do the plants in our area reflect the climate in which we live?**

Temperature Cards Activity

- ➤ **What type of weather does our area have at different times of the year?**
- ➤ **What is today's weather?**
- ➤ *Give your child the temperature cards. Allow him to find the average January and July temperatures for your area by using reference material (newspapers, local weather station, etc.).*

Evaluating the Lesson

Notebook Activity, page 3

- ➤ Read the directions on Notebook page 3.
- ➤ Complete the page.

Going Beyond

Enrichment

Provide your child with a strip of paper one inch wide and five inches long, a black pen, clear Con-Tact paper, and a tall, narrow jar to make a rain gauge. Direct him to draw lines on the paper strip to mark each inch and to make ten equal divisions between each inch. Tell him to affix the marked piece of paper to the jar by placing clear Con-Tact paper over it so that all the paper is covered.

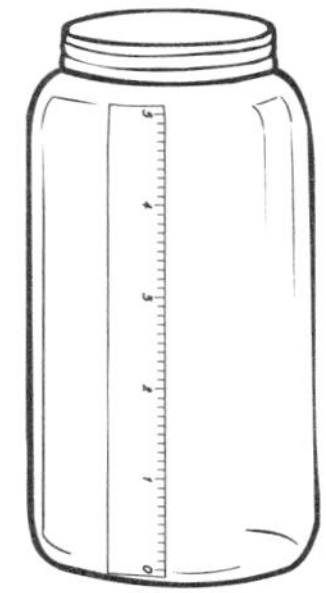

Tell your child to place his rain gauge outside the house, away from roofs or trees so that no runoff will fall into the jar. Explain that he should bring the jar into the house as soon as it stops raining so that no water will evaporate. The jar should then be placed on a flat table or counter to be read. Your child may wish to confirm his findings by listening to a radio or television weather report of how much rain fell.

Additional Teacher Information

Although seven nations have made claims in Antarctica, it has been agreed that no nation will settle the continent. Only scientific research can be carried on there. No military operations are allowed.

The Antarctic circumpolar current moves approximately 47,520,000,000 gallons of water each second. It is the largest ocean current in the world.

As Maury's *Wind and Current Charts* began to be used, it was estimated that millions of dollars were saved each year by American merchants because of the time saved. Maury was awarded five thousand dollars in gold by a group of New York merchants in 1855.

Maury noted that the Bible and nature have the same Author.

> Their records are equally true, and when they bear upon the same point . . . it is as impossible that they should contradict each other as it is that either should contradict itself. If the two cannot be reconciled, the fault is ours, and is because, in our blindness and weakness, we have not been able to interpret aright either the one or the other, or both.

Matthew Maury was interested in more than ocean currents. In 1860 he expressed a desire that someone explore Antarctica.

LESSON 4
Rain and Resources

Text, pages 12-17

Preview

Main Ideas

- Altitude affects climate.
- Climate affects where people live.
- Natural resources affect where people live.

Objectives

- Answer questions about the relationship between rainfall and climate
- Answer questions about the relationship between altitude and climate
- Explain how climate affects where and how people live
- Identify natural resources

Materials

- A pair of sunglasses
- A heavy coat
- A knit cap
- A straw hat
- A packet of instant cocoa or a tea bag*
- A glass of ice water
- An atlas with a map of the world
- A Bible
- Appendix, page A7: weather and rainfall cards*
- Appendix, page A8: thermometer*

Day 1

Lesson

Introducing the Lesson

Matching Game

➤ *Lay the sunglasses, knit cap, heavy coat, straw hat, packet of cocoa mix or tea bag, and glass of ice water in front of your child.*

➤ Pretend that you live in an extremely cold climate. Put on the items that you would wear in the winter. *(knit cap and heavy coat)*

➤ **Which of the drinks would be most appropriate?** *(hot cocoa or hot tea)*

➤ **What activities might you be involved in?** *(skiing, building a snowman, etc.)*

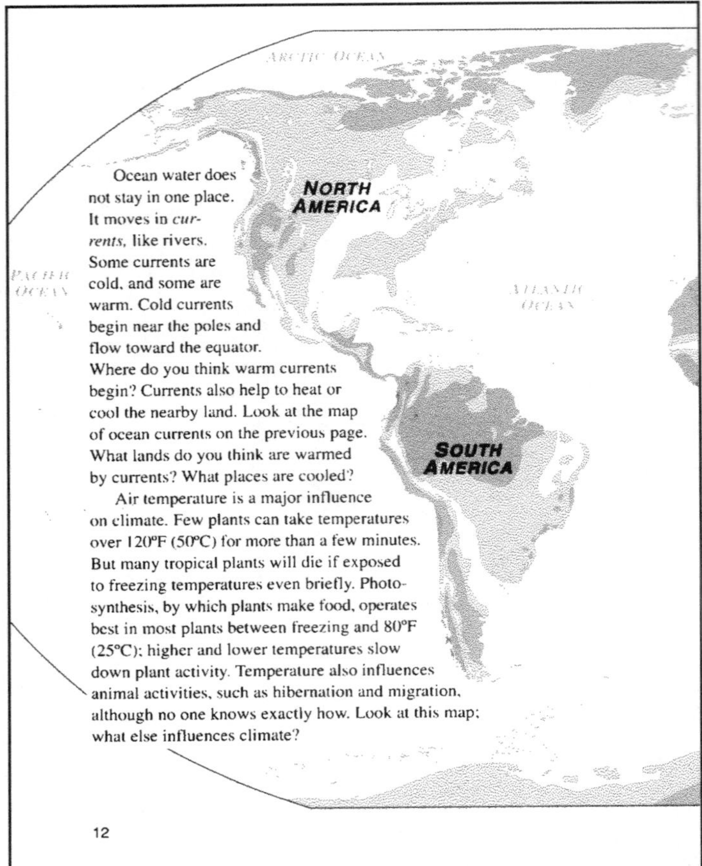

Ocean water does not stay in one place. It moves in *currents*, like rivers. Some currents are cold, and some are warm. Cold currents begin near the poles and flow toward the equator. Where do you think warm currents begin? Currents also help to heat or cool the nearby land. Look at the map of ocean currents on the previous page. What lands do you think are warmed by currents? What places are cooled?

Air temperature is a major influence on climate. Few plants can take temperatures over 120°F (50°C) for more than a few minutes. But many tropical plants will die if exposed to freezing temperatures even briefly. Photosynthesis, by which plants make food, operates best in most plants between freezing and 80°F (25°C); higher and lower temperatures slow down plant activity. Temperature also influences animal activities, such as hibernation and migration, although no one knows exactly how. Look at this map; what else influences climate?

12

➤ Now put on those things indicating a warm, tropical climate. *(sunglasses and straw hat)*

➤ **Which drink would be more appropriate in this climate?** *(ice water)*

➤ **What activities might you be involved in?** *(swimming, playing at the beach, picnicking, etc.)*

➤ **Which climate do you prefer?**

Teaching the Lesson

Map Activity, pages 12-13

➤ **What factors that we have studied affect climate?** *(latitude, distance from the ocean, and air temperature)*

➤ **What do the colors on the map on pages 12-13 represent?** *(the amount of rainfall per year)*

➤ *Discuss the meanings of the different colors.*

➤ **Would plants grow better in a place that receives no rain or in a place that receives plenty of rain?** *(in a place with plenty of rain)*

➤ **What kinds of animals might live in a place with very little rain?** *(lizards, snakes)*

➤ *Point out the Sahara Desert in northern Africa on the map.*

➤ **What color is the Sahara Desert?** *(brown, orange)*

➤ **How much rainfall do the brown areas receive?** *(0-2 inches)*

Some areas of the Sahara receive less than one inch of rain per year.

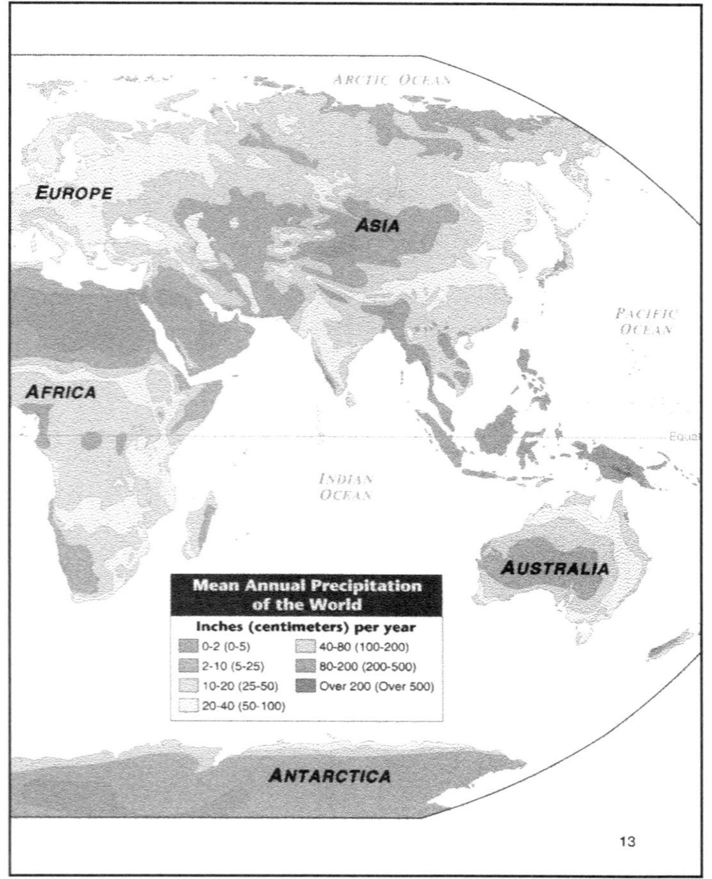

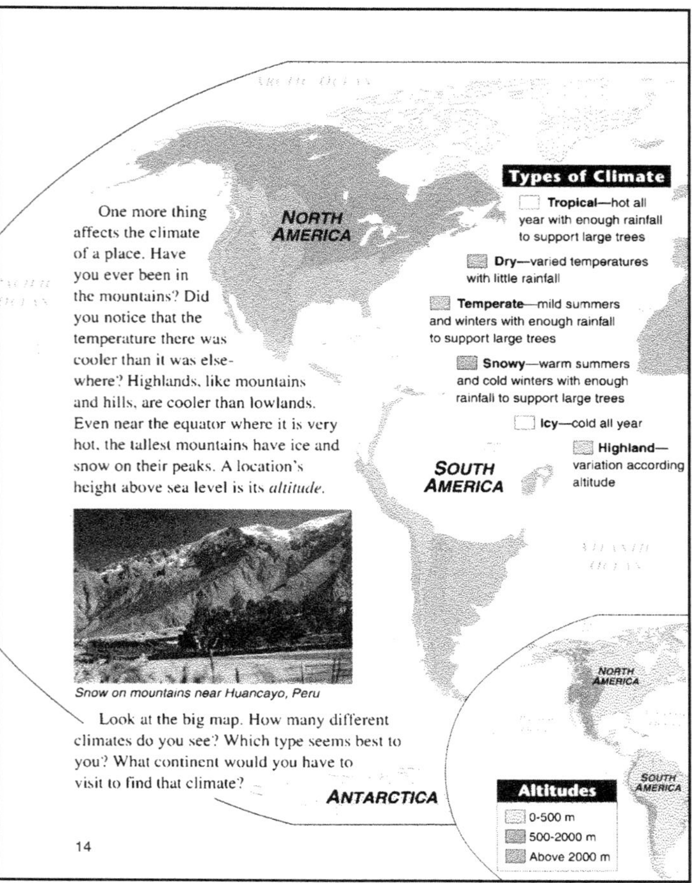
One more thing affects the climate of a place. Have you ever been in the mountains? Did you notice that the temperature there was cooler than it was elsewhere? Highlands, like mountains and hills, are cooler than lowlands. Even near the equator where it is very hot, the tallest mountains have ice and snow on their peaks. A location's height above sea level is its *altitude*.

Snow on mountains near Huancayo, Peru

Look at the big map. How many different climates do you see? Which type seems best to you? What continent would you have to visit to find that climate?

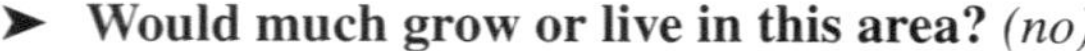

- ➤ **Would much grow or live in this area?** *(no)*
- ➤ Find your area on the map. **What is the amount of rainfall for your area?**

Text Discussion, pages 14-15

- ➤ **Read page 14 to find out what *altitude* is.** *(height above sea level)*
- ➤ **How is the climate at the top of a mountain different from the climate of lowlands?** *(It is cooler at the top of the mountains.)*
- ➤ Look at the altitude map at the bottom of pages 14-15. **What is the altitude of the area where you live?**

Map Activity

- ➤ *Point out the Himalayas (on the northern border of India) on the world map in an atlas.*

The Himalayan mountain range has the highest altitude on earth. Mount Everest, the highest mountain in the world, is in the Himalayan range. It is over twenty-nine thousand feet, or over six miles high. At the base of the Himalayan Mountains there is a tropical climate where palm trees and fruit trees grow.

- ➤ **Do you think the top of Mount Everest has a tropical climate?**
- ➤ **What would weather conditions be there?** *(snow, ice, cold)*
- ➤ **On what latitude are the Himalayas?** *(about 30°N latitude)*
- ➤ Find northern Africa on the world map.
- ➤ **Is this latitude approximately the same latitude as the Himalayan Mountains?** *(yes, approximately 30°N latitude)*
- ➤ **What natural formation is the main feature of northern Africa?** *(the Sahara Desert)*
- ➤ **Does the Sahara Desert have approximately the same climate as the Himalayan Mountains?** *(no)*
- ➤ **What might be one reason for the difference in climate?** *(The Himalayas have a higher altitude; they are higher above sea level.)*
- ➤ Discuss the altitude of your town in relation to its climate.

Text Discussion, pages 14-15 (cont.)

- ➤ **Read the last paragraph on page 14 again.**
- ➤ Answer the questions in the last paragraph.

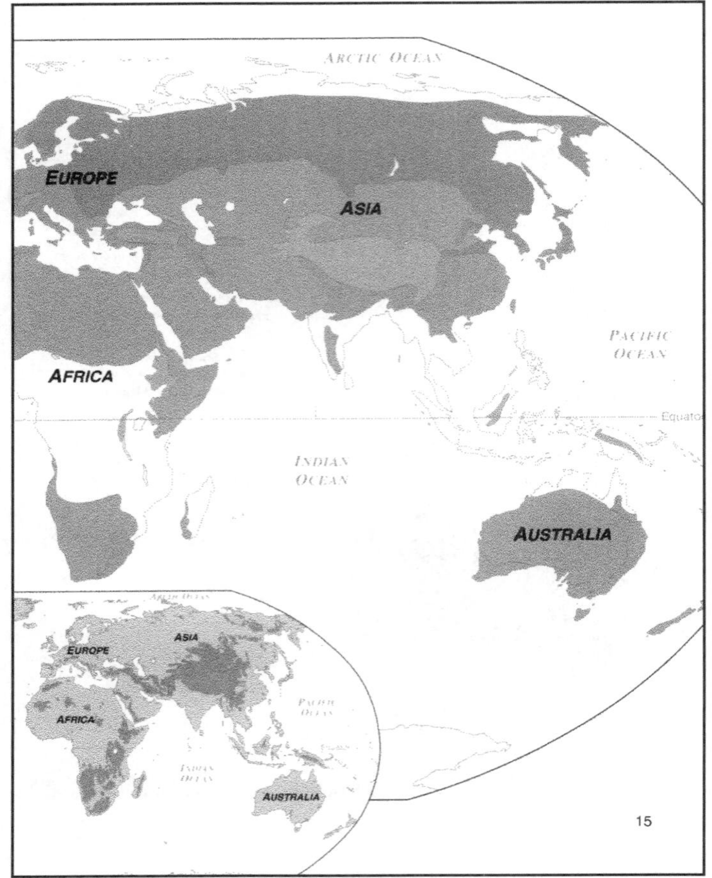

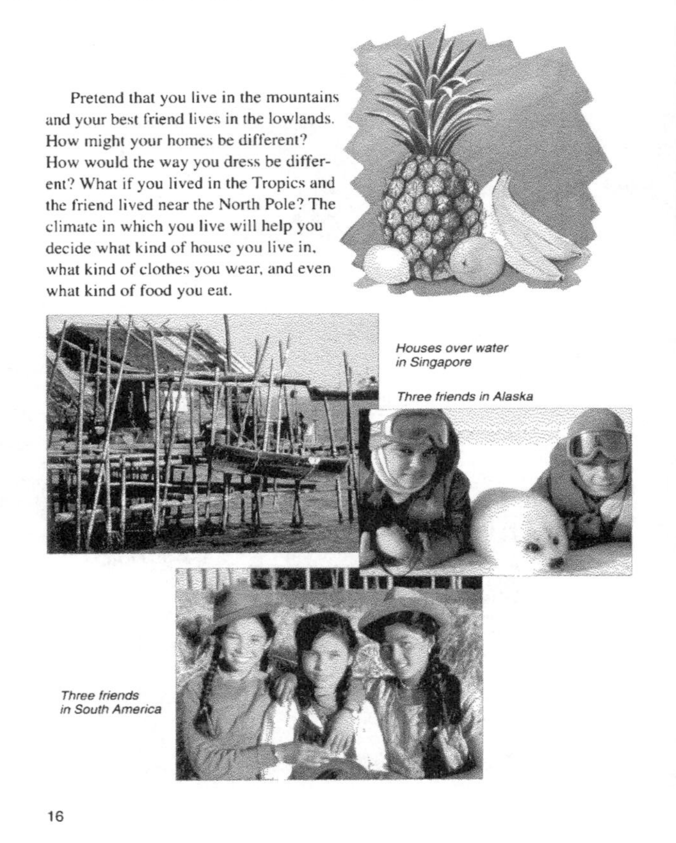

Pretend that you live in the mountains and your best friend lives in the lowlands. How might your homes be different? How would the way you dress be different? What if you lived in the Tropics and the friend lived near the North Pole? The climate in which you live will help you decide what kind of house you live in, what kind of clothes you wear, and even what kind of food you eat.

Houses over water in Singapore

Three friends in Alaska

Three friends in South America

16

Text Discussion, page 16

➤ **Read page 16 to find out how climate affects the way people live.** *(what kind of house they live in, what kind of clothes they wear, what kind of food they eat)*

➤ Listen as I read a paragraph to you.

For many years the Ballard family lived in Hawaii, where Mr. Ballard worked for the United States Navy. After he completed twenty years of service with the Navy, Mr. Ballard retired, and the family moved to Alaska.

➤ Think about the changes that the Ballard family would have to make when moving from Hawaii to Alaska.

➤ **What kind of clothes would they have owned in Hawaii?** *(lightweight clothes, because Hawaii's weather is tropical throughout the year)*

➤ **Would the Ballards need to buy different kinds of clothes to wear in Alaska?** *(Yes, they would need warm clothes.)*

➤ **What kind of heating system would the Ballards' house in Hawaii have?** *(probably none)*

➤ **Will they need a heating system in their house in Alaska?** *(yes)*

➤ **What other changes might the family experience?** *(changes in leisure activities, seasonal activities, periods of daylight and nighttime)*

➤ **What changes might be experienced by a missionary moving from the United States to Africa?** *(Answers will vary.)*

When Hudson Taylor moved from England to China as a missionary, he experienced great discomfort and illness because of the drastic change in climate. England has a cool climate, but parts of China become very hot.

➤ **Why did Hudson Taylor make these sacrifices?** *(so that people could hear about Jesus and be saved)*

Read aloud Philippians 4:19 and I Peter 5:7. Ask your child whether God gives Christians the grace to endure difficult climates when He calls them to serve Him in a faraway place. *(yes)* Explain that there will be difficulties of some type no matter where we live, but God is able to give us the grace we need to do His will. (BAT: 8a Faith in God's promises)

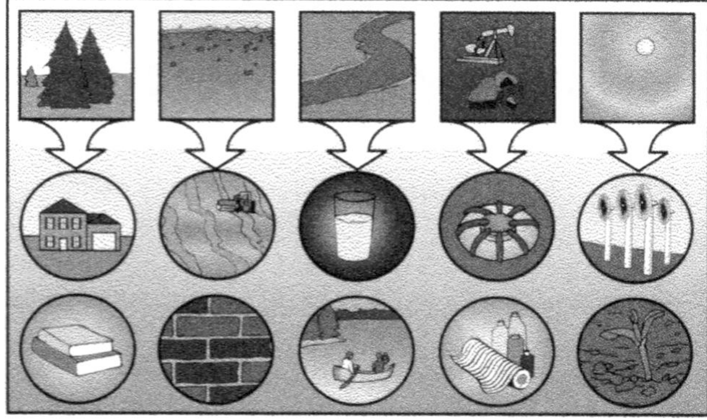

Natural Resources

Climate is not the only thing that determines how, or even whether, people live in a certain place. The natural resources of an area help people decide whether a place is good for living. *Natural resources* are the things God put on the earth for man to use and enjoy. How long do you think a list of natural resources would be?

This chart shows just a few of the natural resources God has given us. Could you find all of these resources in all places on the earth? Each *region*, or part of a continent, has its own natural resources. Which natural resources are found near your home? No natural resource, not even the sun, can be found in every region. Caves never get any sun. And in the Arctic and Antarctic Circles, the sun shines only during six months of the year. What other resources might you find in such places instead?

17

Day 2

Text Discussion, page 17

- **Read page 17 to find out what a *natural resource* is.** *(something God put on the earth for man to use and enjoy)*
- Name some natural resources. *(rivers, lakes, forests, etc.)*

Everything man makes—clothes, houses, cars, etc.— is made from natural resources that God placed on the earth.

> Lead your child to understand that even our lives depend on the nutrients in the soil that feed the plants and animals that we eat in order to survive. Explain that God carefully crafted the earth to be able to support life and allow us to enjoy our lives. (Bible Promise: H. God as Father)

- Look at the natural resource chart on page 17. Name the resources found in the square pictures at the top of the page. *(trees, soil, water, oil and coal [fuels], sun)*
- **What resources are found in your area?**
- **What ways can the natural resources in different areas be used?** *(Answers will vary. The pictures in the circles on page 17 show some ways: houses, paper or books, crops, bricks, drinking water, boating, gas cooking, oil byproducts, windmills for harvesting energy, and plants.)*

Weather Cards Activity

- Describe today's weather.
- **What is the weather like in your area at other times during the year?**
- *Give your child the weather and rainfall cards.*
- Choose the correct weather symbol card for today's weather. You may want to color it.
- Use reference material to find the average yearly rainfall in inches for your state. Fill out the rainfall card.

Evaluating the Lesson

Evaluating Activity

- *Place the thermometer page in front of your child.*

I will ask you some questions about what we have studied. For each correctly answered question, you may color in the thermometer 4°. See how hot you can make your thermometer.

> If you choose to ask fewer questions, you will want to adjust the number of degrees your child colors for each correct answer. If you are teaching more than one child, you may want to have two thermometers (labeled *Eskimos* and *Islanders*) and color 5° for each correct answer.

- **What altitude level is known for cold weather?** *(high altitude)*
- **What are natural resources?** *(things God put on the earth for man to use and enjoy)*
- **To what country did Hudson Taylor travel as a missionary?** *(China)*
- **Was China warmer or colder than England?** *(warmer)*
- **What might you need to buy when moving from a warm to a cold climate?** *(a heavy coat, boots, gloves)*
- **What type of climate do tropical countries have?** *(warm)*
- **What type of climate does the Antarctic Circle have?** *(cold)*
- **Do many people live above the Arctic Circle?** *(no)*
- **Is latitude the only factor that determines a country's climate?** *(no)*
- **What is altitude?** *(height above sea level)*
- **In what kind of place do plants grow best?** *(in a place that gets plenty of rain)*
- **On what continent is the Sahara Desert?** *(Africa)*

- ➤ **Why is there very little vegetation in the Sahara Desert?** *(because it gets so little rain)*
- ➤ **Name some natural resources.** *(rivers, lakes, forests)*
- ➤ **Where is the highest altitude on the earth?** *(Mount Everest in the Himalayas)*
- ➤ **What is the climate at the base of the Himalayan Mountains?** *(tropical)*
- ➤ **What is the climate at the top of the Himalayan Mountains?** *(snowy)*
- ➤ **At what latitude are the Himalayas located?** *(about 30°N latitude)*

Going Beyond

Enrichment

Allow your child to research the path of natural resources. Provide magazines or catalogs to be cut, scissors, and glue. Provide encyclopedias and other books for your child to research what products are made from these natural resources. Prepare an index card with a picture of a natural resource, such as cotton growing in a field or gold being mined. Instruct your child to cut out pictures from magazines or catalogs to show the natural resource in a finished, manufactured form—a cotton dress, a gold ring, and so on. Direct him to write a paragraph explaining how the natural resource was made into the finished product.

To reverse the procedure, provide your child with pictures of a manufactured product such as a car or a building. Challenge him to find pictures of the natural resources that make up the finished product.

Additional Teacher Information

Matthew Maury, the "Pathfinder of the Seas," said in an 1860 speech, "Physical geography confesses that 'the earth was made for man.' Upon no other theory can it be studied—upon no other theory can its phenomena be reconciled."

LESSON 5
Earth Exploration

Text, pages 18-20
Notebook, page 4

Preview

Main Ideas

- Commercial gain is a goal of earth exploration.
- Scientific research is a goal of earth exploration.
- Roald Amundsen was the first man to reach the South Pole.
- The ocean floor has mountains, trenches, and valleys.

Objectives

- Identify achievements and characteristics of Roald Amundsen
- Identify achievements and characteristics of David Livingstone
- Identify significant features of the earth's surface and the ocean floor

Materials

- An index card labeled with a "treasure," such as *an extra treat* or *stay up fifteen extra minutes**
- An atlas with a map of the world
- The figure of Roald Amundsen (1911) from the TimeLine Snapshots
- Appendix, page A9: exploration questions*

Cut apart the exploration questions and hide them around the schoolroom. Hide the index card in a different room of the house.

Notes

The game "Three in a Row" is introduced in the Enrichment section of this lesson. (*NOTE:* See the Appendix, pages A10-A13.)

Here are several suggestions for using prepared tests such as those in the *HERITAGE STUDIES Test Packet.* Teach the chapter as you normally would. Do not try to "teach to the test." Before giving your child the chapter test, preview the questions. If there is a question(s) covering material that you did not emphasize, you may mark through the question. You may also consider awarding bonus points for the question or replacing it with a question of your own.

Day 1

Lesson

Introducing the Lesson

An Investigation

- ➤ **What term is used for the things that God put on the earth for our use and enjoyment?** *(natural resources)*
- ➤ Men have always searched for valuable natural resources. Name some natural resources that the king of a country might desire enough to send an explorer somewhere to find. *(gold, silver, etc.)*
- ➤ I have hidden a treasure card somewhere in the house. It looks like an index card. The country that finds the treasure will be rich beyond its wildest dreams. The king of that country will become the most famous king in all the world.
- ➤ Try to find the treasure card.

Teaching the Lesson

Text Discussion, page 18

Exploration of the earth has been carried on mainly to find valuable natural resources or ways to get them. Columbus was hoping to find a quick water route to the rich islands of the East. If he could find a direct water route, Spain would gain immeasurable wealth.

- ➤ **Where did Columbus sail instead?** *(to the New World)*
- ➤ **Can you think of something other than wealth that makes people want to explore the earth?**
- ➤ Men have always been interested in discovering new lands and exploring the earth. **Read page 18 to find out when the continent of Antarctica was discovered.** *(1820)*

Scientists had predicted that a continent would be found at the bottom of the world. They had even named it—*Terra Australis Incognita,* which means "unknown southern land."

Victoria Falls, the world's highest

Exploring the Continents

We know that the tallest mountain in the world is Mount Everest. It is found between the countries of Nepal and China, on the continent of Asia. We know that the longest river is the Nile River on the African continent, and the largest island is Greenland. Today we know many things about the world in which we live. But men have not always known as much. How did they find out such things?

Do you remember how people in Europe learned about North and South America? Christopher Columbus sailed for Asia but instead found a land new to him. Later other explorers came. They learned about the land by looking around. They learned more from the people who had lived in the land for hundreds of years. When the explorers returned to their homes, they told about what they had learned.

Men have learned about the other continents in much the same way. Explorers have visited parts of Europe, Africa, Australia, and Asia. But for a very long time, no explorer had ever visited the seventh continent, Antarctica. In fact, until 1820 no one even knew that Antarctica was there. Would you like to explore unknown places?

Mount Everest in Nepal

18

- ➤ Look at the picture of Victoria Falls on page 18. In 1855 David Livingstone was the first European to see Victoria Falls.
- ➤ **Do you think he was the first man ever to see this waterfall?**

No, Africans had known it was there for many years. Livingstone named the waterfall for Queen Victoria. The African name for the falls is *Mosi oa Tunya,* which means "a smoke that thunders."

- ➤ Look at the picture of Mount Everest. **What is special about this mountain?** *(It is the highest mountain in the world.)*

Map Activity

- ➤ *Point out the Nile River (in northern Africa) on the world map in the atlas, tracing its length with your finger.*
- ➤ **What is special about the Nile River?** *(It is the longest river in the world.)* It is over four thousand miles long.
- ➤ *Point out Greenland on the world map.*

The Viking explorer Eric the Red founded a settlement in Greenland about one thousand years ago. This settlement lasted for over five hundred years.

Text Discussion, page 19

➤ **Read page 19 to find what location Roald Amundsen (ä´ mənd sən) was the first to reach.** *(the South Pole)*

Amundsen was a Norwegian explorer who had always wanted to be the first person to reach the North Pole. However, when he received word that Robert Peary had reached the North Pole in 1909, he decided to try to be the first to reach the South Pole.

➤ **When did Amundsen reach the South Pole?** *(1911)*

➤ **Did Roald Amundsen reach the South Pole alone?** *(no)*

Like most explorers, Amundsen was the leader of a team of experienced men who worked with him to achieve a shared goal. In 1906, Roald Amundsen was also responsible for finding the Northwest Passage, the route between the Atlantic and Pacific Oceans. This passage became important for ships traveling to the Alaskan oil fields, but the Panama Canal, which opened the same year, was used more.

➤ **Could Amundsen have made the expedition alone?** *(no)*

➤ *Share examples of other people who have gotten credit for big accomplishments but who in fact were significantly helped by others (for example, Columbus).*

> Helpers are just as important as leaders in almost any project. Encourage your child to work diligently and cheerfully whether he is the leader or the helper. Without the help and encouragement of others who are willing to follow, a leader cannot accomplish great things. (BAT: 2f Enthusiasm)

TimeLine Snapshots Activity

➤ Name the major accomplishments of Roald Amundsen's life. *(finding the Northwest Passage, finding the South Pole)*

➤ Amundsen devoted his life to earth exploration. Place the figure of Roald Amundsen on the TimeLine at 1911, the year he discovered the South Pole.

Text Discussion, page 19 (cont.)

➤ **Who arrived at the South Pole just a few weeks after Amundsen?** *(Robert Scott)*

Scott's team did not have warm enough clothing. They also had trouble because they had chosen to use ponies instead of dogs to pull their sledges. The ponies were unable to get through the ice and snow,

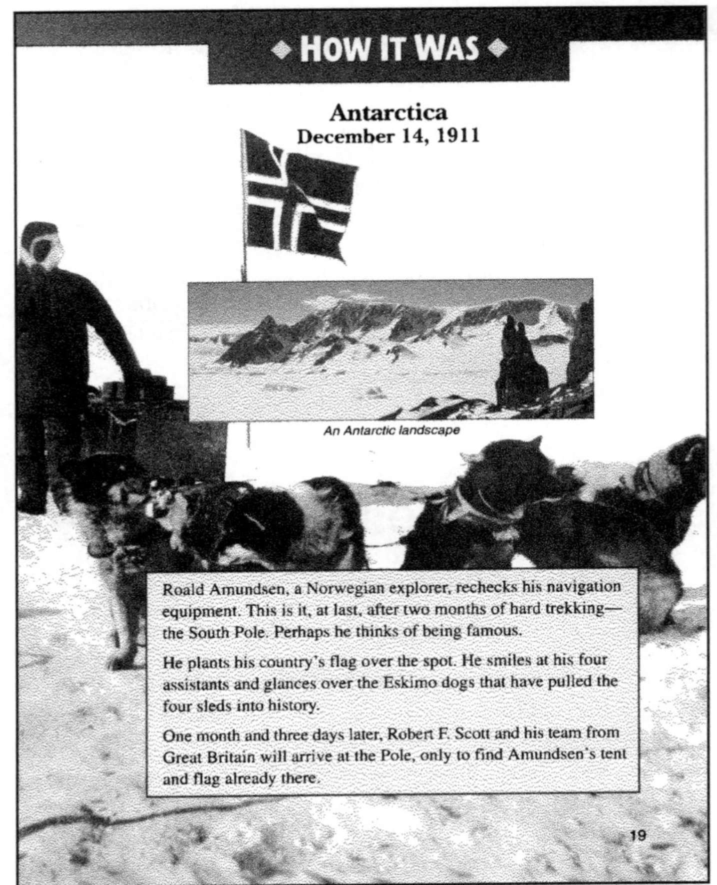

so the men had to pull the sledges and sleds themselves. Robert Scott's team reached the South Pole only to find Amundsen's flag already there. All the members of Scott's team died of cold and starvation on their way back from the South Pole.

◆ HOW IT WAS ◆
Antarctica
December 14, 1911
An Antarctic landscape
Roald Amundsen, a Norwegian explorer, rechecks his navigation equipment. This is it, at last, after two months of hard trekking—the South Pole. Perhaps he thinks of being famous.
He plants his country's flag over the spot. He smiles at his four assistants and glances over the Eskimo dogs that have pulled the four sleds into history.
One month and three days later, Robert F. Scott and his team from Great Britain will arrive at the Pole, only to find Amundsen's tent and flag already there.
19

➤ **Do you think that Robert Scott's team might have survived if they had used the right animals and worn the right clothing?**

It is important to make proper preparations for safety when setting out on an adventure.

Roald Amundsen continued to explore the Arctic regions. He was the first man to fly completely over the Arctic. During an Arctic trip in 1926, his ship was frozen in place for a whole year. During this time, Amundsen was attacked by a polar bear; however, he survived. After a year, the ice melted, but only for two weeks. Then the ship was frozen in place again for ten more months.

➤ **How would you feel being unable to move from a small area for an extended length of time?**

In 1928, while searching for a missing explorer, Roald Amundsen was lost. He was never found.

A landform map shows how the surface of an area looks. Look at this landform map of part of the earth. It shows the surface of the earth the way it would look if there were no water on it.

The Ocean Floor

GREENLAND
ICELAND
NORTH AMERICA
AFRICA
SOUTH AMERICA

"For the Lord is a great God, and a great King above all gods. In his hand are the deep places of the earth: the strength of the hills is his also. The sea is his, and he made it: and his hands formed the dry land. O come, let us worship and bow down: let us kneel before the Lord our maker."

Psalm 95:3-6

20

Explorations Name ____________________

Follow your teacher's instructions.

EXPLORATION 1	Clue Location: ____	Answer: *Mount Everest*
EXPLORATION 2	Clue Location: ____	Answer: *mountains, trenches, valleys*
EXPLORATION 3	Clue Location: ____	Answer: *false*
EXPLORATION 4	Clue Location: ____	Answer: *hard work, courage, determination, flexibility, strength*
EXPLORATION 5	Clue Location: ____	Answer: *Nile River*
EXPLORATION 6	Clue Location: ____	Answer: *David Livingstone*
EXPLORATION 7	Clue Location: ____	Answer: *to find riches; for knowledge*
EXPLORATION 8	Clue Location: ____	Answer: *false*

Heritage Studies 4 Student Notebook — Lesson 5 Evaluating the Lesson 4

Roald Amundsen's life showed the characteristics of hard work, courage, determination, flexibility, and strength. These are characteristics that Christians should try to develop in their lives as they serve the Lord. (BATs: 2e Work, 8d Courage)

Text Discussion, page 20

- ➤ **Read aloud the paragraph on page 20.**
- ➤ **What does the *landform map* show?** *(how the surface of the earth would look if there were no water)*
- ➤ **What do the gray areas represent?** *(the ocean floor)*
- ➤ **Is the ocean floor smooth?** *(no)*
- ➤ **What features are on the ocean floor?** *(mountains, trenches, canyons)*
- ➤ **How do you think scientists know what the bottom of the ocean looks like?**

Research ships carry equipment that measures the depth of the ocean by the use of sound waves. There are whole mountain ranges in the sea. Some of the mountains are as tall as thirteen thousand feet. When the tops of these mountains rise above the ocean surface, they form islands. The Hawaiian Islands are the tops of ocean mountains in the Pacific Ocean.

Read aloud the verses from page 20. Emphasize that God made and controls the earth and everything in it. (Bible Promise: I. God as Master)

Resource Activity (optional)

- ➤ Use reference materials to find what land formations are in your state.

Evaluating the Lesson

Investigation Game, Notebook page 4

- ➤ I have hidden exploration questions around the room.
- ➤ You may begin looking around the room for the questions.
- ➤ When you find a question, write where you found the question as well as the answer to the question on Notebook page 4.

Going Beyond

Enrichment

Prepare the game "Three in a Row." Have available nine buttons for each player, copies of the game cards, and a copy of the clue cards (Appendix, pages A10-A13). Cut apart the game cards and the clue cards. Give one game card (tic-tac-toe grid) to each player. Instruct the players to place the clue cards facedown in a stack. Instruct each player to place a game card in front of him with the stack of clue cards between the players. The first player will turn over the top clue card. Direct any player who has the corresponding words in any section of his game card to place a button in that section. Play continues with the next player's turning over a second card. The player who covers three sections in a row, vertically, horizontally, or diagonally, wins the round. Direct the players to exchange game cards before playing a second round.

Additional Teacher Information

The Greek explorer Pytheas is thought to be the first Arctic explorer. Around 325 B.C. he made a northern expedition. He called the land he reached *Ultima Thule,* which means "the outermost land." It is believed that this land was approximately where Trondheim, Norway, is today.

When David Livingstone died in 1873, his heart and other internal organs were removed from his body and buried in Africa. Faithful friends then guarded the body while it dried out in the hot African sun. Livingstone's friends feared that enemies of the great missionary explorer would not allow his remains to be returned home to England. So these friends folded and wrapped the mummified body so that it would fit into a parcel that could be carried inconspicuously through hostile territory. After a journey of many months, the body reached England. A doctor positively identified Livingstone's body on the basis of a wound the missionary had received when attacked by a lion years earlier. Livingstone's body was buried in Westminster Abbey in London.

2 LESSONS 6-12

Through the Golden Door

This chapter details the flow of immigration over two centuries. It emphasizes that, aside from the Native Americans, all Americans are either immigrants or descendants of immigrants. Your child will review the reasons for the first immigrants' coming to America and learn about later reasons, such as the potato famine in Ireland and the persecutions of Jews in Russia.

In the first lesson, your child makes a quilt square illustrating part of his unique heritage. In later lessons, he learns about conducting an interview to collect information for a family history. He also writes a citizenship pledge, memorizes part of Emma Lazarus's poem "The New Colossus," and re-enacts the testing of immigrants at Ellis Island. Throughout the chapter, your child will see the bravery of those who came through America's "golden door" and the privilege of citizenship in this great country. In the supplemental, or optional, lesson, he learns about the requirements and role of the president of the United States as presidential figures are added to the TimeLine.

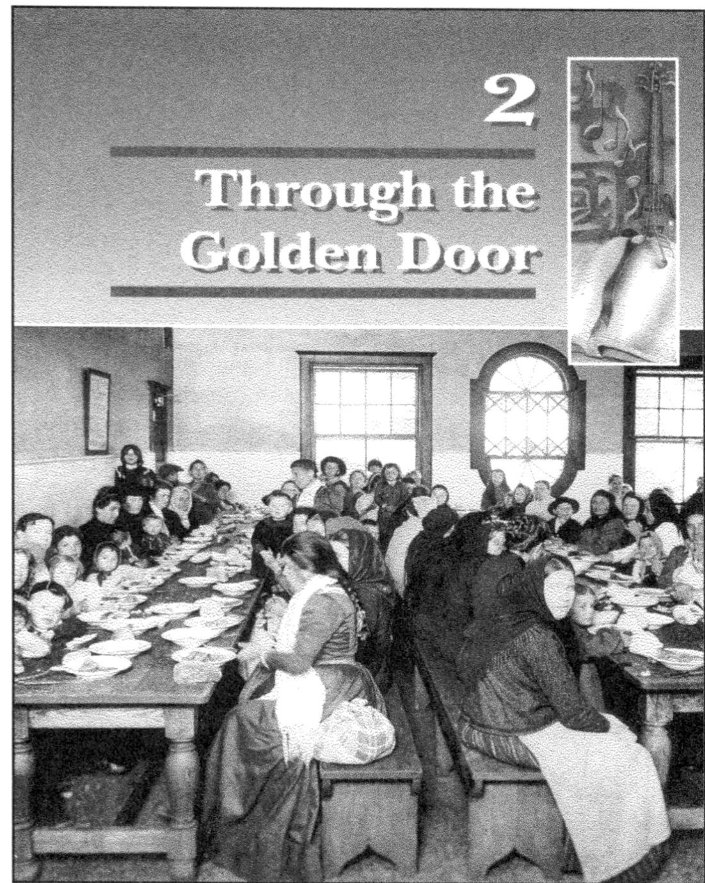

Materials

The following materials must be obtained or prepared before the presentation of the lesson. These items are labeled with an asterisk (*) in each lesson and in the Materials List in the Supplement. For further information see the individual lessons.

- *HERITAGE STUDIES Listening Cassette B* (Lesson 6)
- Family pictures (optional) (Lesson 6)
- Newspaper clippings (optional) (Lesson 6)
- Yellow construction paper (Lesson 6)
- A patchwork quilt or a piece of patchwork (Lesson 6)
- Appendix, pages A14-A15 (Lesson 6)
- Appendix, pages A17-A18 (Supplemental Lesson)
- Several potatoes (Lesson 7)
- A scarf and a shawl (Lesson 7)
- Appendix, page A19 (Lesson 8)
- A blank cassette (Lesson 9)
- A family Bible (optional) (Lesson 9)
- Appendix, page A22 (Lesson 10)
- Suitcases (optional) (Lesson 10)
- Appendix, pages A23-A24 (Lesson 11)

Lesson 6
A Nation of Immigrants

Text, pages 22-25, 306, 322-23
Notebook, pages 5-6

Preview

Main Ideas

- With the exception of Native Americans, all Americans immigrated from other countries.
- Many individuals and groups have shaped the heritage of the United States.
- The United States has provided freedom for people from many parts of the world.

Objectives

- Read a circle graph to answer questions
- Make a circle graph

Materials

- A patchwork quilt or a piece of patchwork*
- 9" square of colored construction paper
- Felt-tip pens and colored pencils of various colors
- Family pictures (optional)*
- Newspaper clippings (optional)*
- Supplement, page S2: symbols
- Supplement, page S3: New York Harbor
- Appendix, pages A15: flashcards*
- 8 pieces of yellow construction paper*
- A Bible
- A cassette player
- *Heritage Studies Listening Cassette B**
- Supplement, page S4: Terms
- Appendix, page A14: Native American map*
- Supplement, page S5: population chart

Prepare 8 "golden door" flashcards from the pieces of yellow construction paper by gluing the terms from Appendix page A15 on one side and the corresponding definitions on the other side.

Notes

Heritage Studies Listening Cassette B includes songs and readings for grades 4-6. This is the first use of the listening cassette for grade 4.

During this chapter you may want to create a corner for displaying memorabilia relating to your family's heritage. Lessons 6, 9, and 13 include opportunities for discussing these items.

You may want to invite a friend whose family members immigrated to America to share his stories with your child.

SPECIAL NOTE: Contact a relative, explaining that your child will be studying immigration and learning how to conduct an interview. Invite the relative to participate with you in a model interview. This interview will take place in Lesson 9. Inform him that you will ask questions about his background (his birthplace, brothers, sisters, salvation, schooling, and ancestors and where they immigrated from, and events that led him to what he is doing today). Encourage him to bring any pictures or memorabilia of his family history.

If you do not have any relatives who live nearby, you may ask a friend to participate so that you can model the interview process. You may wish to gather information from your relatives by phone or mail a questionnaire or a cassette on which to record the information.

Day 1

Lesson

Introducing the Lesson

Art Activity

➤ Examine the piece of patchwork.

➤ **Do you know how a patchwork quilt is made?**

Each square, or section, of patchwork is a separate piece of cloth. In some quilts, many types and colors of cloth are used. All the pieces are sewn together to make the large piece. *If you know the history of your quilt, tell about it.*

Some people think of the United States as a quilt. Each person represents a piece of the quilt—a special, small piece of "cloth" that is part of the bigger piece. In this chapter we will learn about some of the people that make up the American *quilt.*

If you are teaching several children, you may involve each of them in creating a quilt square. When the squares are complete, you can put them together to make a mini-quilt.

➤ You will be creating a quilt square about yourself. Use a felt-tip pen to write your name in the center of the construction-paper square, using your best handwriting.

An American Quilt Square

Name ____________________

Fill in the following information about yourself.

First name ____ Middle name ____ Last name ____

Date of birth ____ Place of birth (city, state) ____

Ask your family to help you answer these questions.

1. How were your first and middle names chosen? Do they have special meanings? Were you named after a relative? ____
2. From what country does your family name, or surname, come? What does it mean? Was it ever changed from another surname? ____
3. Did any of your relatives immigrate to America from another country? What country was that? Which family members came? When did they immigrate? ____

Heritage Studies 4 Student Notebook — Lesson 6 Introducing the Lesson 5

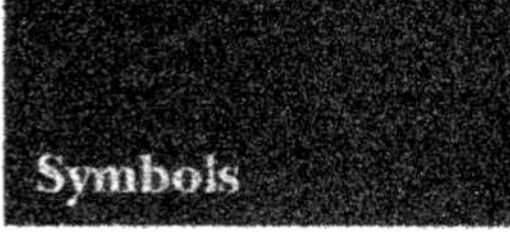

The Statue of Liberty

The Statue of Liberty raises her torch above New York Harbor.

The Statue of Liberty, or *Liberty Enlightening the World,* was a gift from France to the United States in 1884. Made of copper and standing on an enormous pedestal of steel and granite, Miss Liberty has become a symbol of the United States and a beacon of freedom for people all over the world.

The statue presents liberty as a proud lady, draped in a graceful, loose robe. In her right hand, she lifts on high a glowing torch. Her crown bears seven spikes, representing the seven seas and seven continents. In her left arm, she cradles a tablet that bears the date of the Declaration of Independence. At her feet lies a broken chain, symbolizing that unjust rule is gone. As millions of immigrants entered the United States seeking freedom and opportunity, their first image was of the Statue of Liberty. Seeming to speak for the "Lady with the Lamp," the poem "The New Colossus" by Emma Lazarus was inscribed on a bronze plaque on the pedestal of the monument.

". . . Give me your tired, your poor,
Your huddled masses yearning to breathe free,
The wretched refuse of your teeming shore.
Send these, the homeless, tempest-tost to me.
I lift my lamp beside the golden door!"

306

Notebook Activity, page 5

- ➤ Fill in the information that you know. We will complete the rest of the page together.
- ➤ Choose some of the information on this page to add to your quilt square. You may use colored pencils or felt-tip pens. You may also add family pictures or newspaper clippings.

Uncle Lee Cass
Immigrated July 4, 1939
John Lee Smith
Smithy—made horseshoes

Day 2

Teaching the Lesson

Text Discussion, page 306

- ➤ **Do you know what famous statue is shown in the photograph on page 306?** *(the Statue of Liberty)*
- ➤ **Have you ever visited the Statue of Liberty?** If you have, tell about your experience.
- ➤ *Show your child the page of symbols. Point to the first symbol.*
- ➤ **What do you think of when you see this sign?** *(handicapped people)*

Follow the same procedure for any of the other signs with which your child is familiar. *("Mr. Yuk" poison sign, divide, recycle, "no", stop, equals, multiply, camping)*

Each of these marks or figures is called a ***symbol*** because it represents or stands for something else.

- ➤ The Statue of Liberty is also a symbol. **Do you know what it symbolizes?** *(America, freedom, liberty)*
- ➤ **What is *liberty?*** *(Answers will vary but should include the freedom from control or rule of others.)*

> The most important liberty is found in Christ: liberty from sin. (BAT: lb Repentance and faith; Bible Promise: A. Liberty from Sin)

- **Read the inscription below the picture on page 306 to find out where the Statue of Liberty is located.** *(in New York Harbor)*

  Show the map of New York Harbor, tracing with your finger the dotted line illustrating the route that ships take entering the harbor. Point out where the statue stands.

- **What does Lady Liberty hold in her right hand?** *(a torch)*
- **Read page 306 to find a description of the Statue of Liberty.**
- **What is Lady Liberty wearing?** *(a graceful, loose robe)*
- **What is significant about the date located on the tablet she holds?** *(It is the date of the signing of the Declaration of Independence.)*
- **What other names are given for the Statue of Liberty?** *(Liberty Enlightening the World, Miss Liberty, the Lady with the Lamp)*

Only the last portion of the poem written by Emma Lazarus is quoted on this page. We will read the entire poem from our text after discussing some terms that we need to understand.

Discussion, page 22

- *Discuss the terms and their definitions that you have written on the "golden door" flashcards.*
- Follow in your text as I read aloud Emma Lazarus's poem "The New Colossus." (*NOTE:* You may use the flashcards for review.)
- **What names does the poet give to the statue?** *(New Colossus, Mother of Exiles)*
- **Why do you think Emma Lazarus calls the statue the Mother of Exiles?**

The Statue of Liberty, like a mother, welcomes people who have left their homes to come to America.

- **What words does the poet use for *light?*** (*torch, flame, lightning, beacon, lamp*)
- **What does the statue "say" to the lands from which people come to America?** *(the last six lines of the poem)*
- **How does the statue describe those people?** *(tired, poor, huddled masses, wretched refuse, homeless, tempest-tost)*

The New Colossus

by Emma Lazarus

Not like the brazen giant of Greek fame,
With conquering limbs astride from land to land;
Here at our sea-washed, sunset gates shall stand
A mighty woman with a torch, whose flame
Is the imprisoned lightning, and her name
Mother of Exiles. From her beacon-hand
Glows world-wide welcome; her mild eyes command
The air-bridged harbor that twin cities frame.
"Keep, ancient lands, your storied pomp!" cries she
With silent lips. "Give me your tired, your poor,
Your huddled masses yearning to breathe free,
The wretched refuse of your teeming shore.
Send these, the homeless, tempest-tost, to me,
I lift my lamp beside the golden door!"

22

- **What do you think the line "I lift my lamp beside the golden door" means?**

To many immigrants, America was a land of golden opportunity, a place with land, food, and jobs for everyone and where people could speak and pray as they wanted without being afraid. *Show the New York Harbor map again to further explain the image of Lady Liberty standing at the doorway to this "golden" land.*

> Although the sight of the Statue of Liberty has always been a comfort to people immigrating to America, God offers not only comfort but also protection, nourishment, and the gift of salvation. Read aloud Psalm 103:13, which compares God to a father who pities his children. (Bible Promise: H. God as Father)

- Listen to the recording of "Give Me Your Tired, Your Poor." The words of this song were taken from the last section of "The New Colossus" by Emma Lazarus.

After Columbus discovered America, people were inspired by the idea of a New World. They listened to the tales told by Columbus and other explorers. And they dreamed about a place full of forests and clear, blue lakes. There land and food were free for the taking. Why would such a place be so appealing?

Many people were interested in this new land because it seemed so different from where they were living. Some decided to become *emigrants*, people who move away from their old country to live in a new place. When they reached America, these brave pioneers became *immigrants*. Immigrants are those who go into a new country. They hoped to build a new home in the New World.

The United States is a nation of immigrants. Some Americans are immigrants themselves. Others are the children, grandchildren, or great-grandchildren of immigrants. Only one group of people has lived in America long enough to be thought of as native Americans. Can you tell which people? The American Indians are native Americans. Their people have lived in America for several thousand years.

Chiricahua Apache girl (a Native American)

23

Day 3

Text Discussion, page 23

➤ **Read page 23 to find the difference between *emigrants* and *immigrants.*** *(Emigrants move away from their old country; immigrants move into a new country.)* (*NOTE:* The word *migrate* means "to move from one country or region and settle in another" or "to move regularly to a different place at a certain time of year.")

➤ *Show your child the Terms page.* Look at the two terms on this page. This may help you to remember the meanings of *emigrants* and *immigrants.*

➤ **What word can we associate with the term *emigrant?*** *(exit)*

➤ **What word can we associate with the term *immigrant?*** *(into)*

Every emigrant is also an immigrant. When a person is referred to as an emigrant, we think about the country he left. When someone is called an immigrant, we think about the country to which he came.

At this time, you may also want to write on the page and discuss the words *export,* a product sent *from* a country, and *import,* a product brought *into* a country.

Map Activity, pages 322-23

➤ **Which groups of people are the only true native Americans?** *(American Indians)*

➤ **Why are they considered to be native Americans?** *(Their ancestors have lived in America longer than any other group of people.)*

➤ Turn to the map on pages 322-23. Find our state and identify which Native Americans once lived where we now live.

The Native American map page found in the Appendix will aid you in determining which tribes lived in a given territory. Keep this map for reference throughout the school year.

➤ Locate other areas on the map and identify which Native Americans once lived in those parts of the United States.

➤ **Do you know of any relatives who are immigrants?** *Discuss details about your relatives who immigrated to America.*

The Spanish built another fort, the Fort of Saint Mark, in St. Augustine in the 1600s.

The First Immigrants

Spanish immigrants built the first lasting settlement on the land that became the United States. They built a fort at St. Augustine, Florida, in 1565. Later, Spanish immigrants built towns in the Southwest. Today those settlements are part of Texas, New Mexico, Arizona, and California. Many of the Spanish immigrants planned to make their fortune and then go back to Spain.

Soon immigrants came from other countries; they were French, Dutch, and Swedish. They too planned to make as much money as they could and then return to their old homes. Many did. But a few decided to stay in their new homes. What might have made them change their minds?

Other immigrants came with the plan to stay in the New World. These immigrants settled in the East. They built towns up and down the Atlantic coast. These towns were part of thirteen colonies that belonged to England. Where do you think most of these immigrants came from?

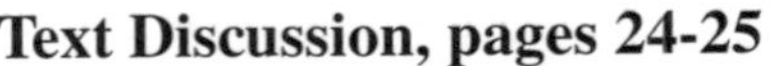

A Norwegian immigrant

24

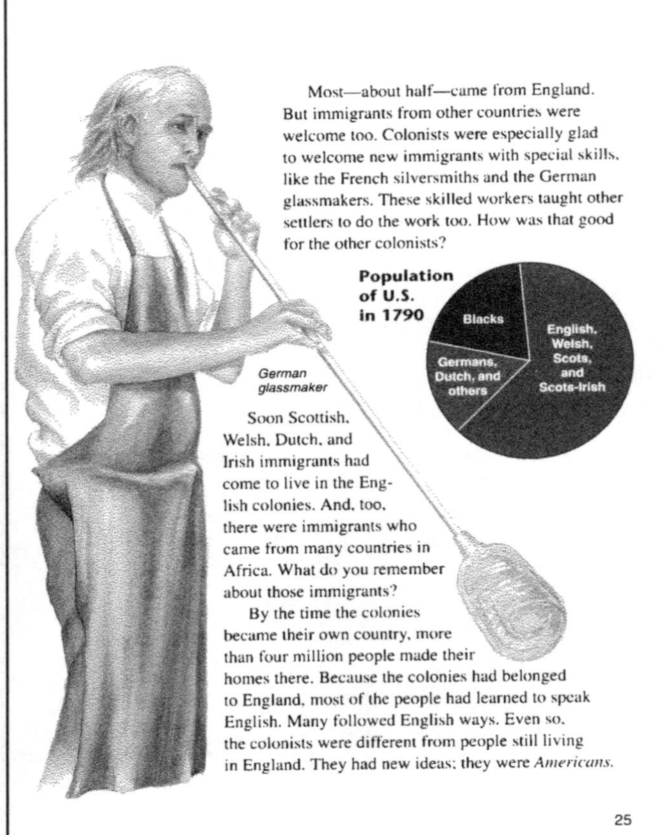

Most—about half—came from England. But immigrants from other countries were welcome too. Colonists were especially glad to welcome new immigrants with special skills, like the French silversmiths and the German glassmakers. These skilled workers taught other settlers to do the work too. How was that good for the other colonists?

German glassmaker

Soon Scottish, Welsh, Dutch, and Irish immigrants had come to live in the English colonies. And, too, there were immigrants who came from many countries in Africa. What do you remember about those immigrants?

By the time the colonies became their own country, more than four million people made their homes there. Because the colonies had belonged to England, most of the people had learned to speak English. Many followed English ways. Even so, the colonists were different from people still living in England. They had new ideas; they were *Americans.*

25

Text Discussion, pages 24-25

➤ **Read page 24 to find out what the first immigrants planned to do when they came to America.** *(Some planned to make money and then return to their homelands. Others planned to stay in the New World.)*

➤ **Why do you think some who had planned to return to their old homes might have decided to stay in America instead?**

➤ **Where did most of the immigrants who planned to stay in the New World settle?** *(in the East)*

➤ **Read the first sentence on page 25 to see where most of these immigrants came from.** *(England)*

➤ **Read the rest of the page to find out what other immigrants settled in the colonies.** *(German, Scots, Welsh, Dutch, French, Irish, and African)*

➤ **What did the immigrants do that helped the other colonists?** *(taught their skills to the settlers)*

As the colonists learned various skills, they could supply goods that were previously imported.

The African immigrants did not come of their own choice and were not given opportunity to display their skills. Most of them were brought to America and sold as slaves.

➤ **Reread the last paragraph to find the similarities and the differences between the colonists and the people still living in England.** *(Most non-English colonists had learned to speak English, and many followed English ways. On the other hand, the colonists developed new ideas and were American.)*

➤ **What new ideas do you think the colonists might have had?**

Some colonists thought they should be free to worship God as they believed, while others wanted freedom to say what they thought about their laws and their rulers.

Day 4

Graph-Reading Activity, page 25

➤ **What kind of graph is shown on page 25?** *(a circle graph, or pie graph)*

Some people call it a ***pie graph*** because it is shaped like a pie with different-sized pieces.

➤ **What information does the pie graph give?** *(the population of the United States in 1790)* The whole circle, or pie, stands for all the people in the United States in 1790.

➤ **Which section is the largest?** *(the one marked English, Welsh, Scots, and Scots-Irish)* (*NOTE:* In referring to the people who emigrated from Scotland and from Northern Ireland, we use the noun/adjective word, *Scots,* instead of *Scottish* or *Scotch.*)

➤ **Which group was the second largest?** *(Blacks)*

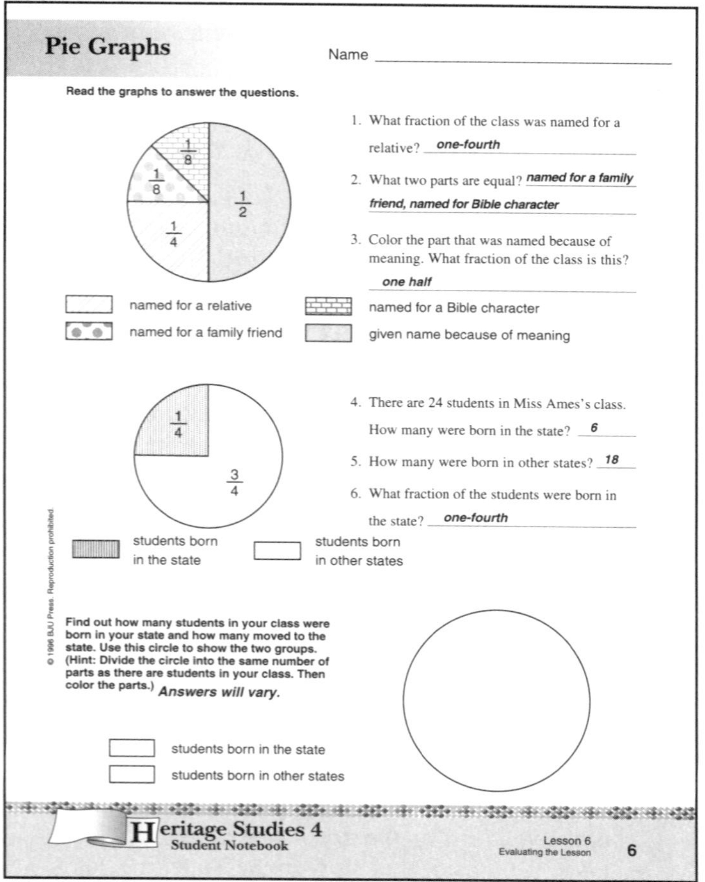

Pie Graphs Name ____________________

Read the graphs to answer the questions.

1/8, 1/8, 1/2, 1/4

1. What fraction of the class was named for a relative? *one-fourth*
2. What two parts are equal? *named for a family friend, named for Bible character*
3. Color the part that was named because of meaning. What fraction of the class is this? *one half*

named for a relative
named for a family friend
named for a Bible character
given name because of meaning

1/4, 3/4

4. There are 24 students in Miss Ames's class. How many were born in the state? *6*
5. How many were born in other states? *18*
6. What fraction of the students were born in the state? *one-fourth*

students born in the state
students born in other states

Find out how many students in your class were born in your state and how many moved to the state. Use this circle to show the two groups. (Hint: Divide the circle into the same number of parts as there are students in your class. Then color the parts.) *Answers will vary.*

students born in the state
students born in other states

Heritage Studies 4 Student Notebook — Lesson 6 Evaluating the Lesson 6

- ➤ **What groups make up the third largest section?** *(German, Dutch, and others)*
- ➤ **What nationalities are being referred to by the term *others*?** *(Spanish, French, Swedish—all named on pages 24 and 25)*
- ➤ **Why would all those groups be put together in the *others* category?** *(There were not enough of any of them to be put onto the graph alone.)*
- ➤ Look at the population chart on the Supplement page.

The pie graph was based on these numbers from the first census, which was taken in 1790.

- ➤ Tell the differences between the circle graph and the list of numbers. *(The circle graph gives a quick, overall picture of the general sizes of the three major groups in the population. The chart gives specific numbers, by nationality, of the population.)*
- ➤ **Do you prefer the chart or the graph and why?**

Evaluating the Lesson

Notebook Activity, page 6

- ➤ Read the pie graphs on Notebook page 6.
- ➤ Use the information from the graphs to complete the page. (*NOTE*: Your child may not have learned the math skills needed to solve questions 4 and 5. Give help as needed. You may choose to have him demonstrate the problem using twenty-four objects.)

To complete the pie graph at the bottom of the page, you will need to use your child's Sunday school class, create a pretend class, or use all the members of your family. It will be best to use an even number of people, such as 8 or 12.

Going Beyond

Enrichment

Direct your child to memorize the section of Emma Lazarus's poem that is inscribed on the pedestal of the monument. Encourage him to recite it to family members. If you are working with more than one child, allow them to recite the five lines together or alternately in a choral rendition.

Give your child a copy of the crossword puzzle and clues on Appendix page A16. Direct him to read the clues to complete the crossword puzzle. Refer him to the textbook if he needs help. *(Across: 4. France, 6. immigrants, 8. tablet, 10. copper, 11. seven, 12. robe; Down: 1. crown, 2. pedestal, 3. chain, 5. Lazarus, 7. golden, 9. torch)*

Additional Teacher Information

Family names, or surnames, originated in western countries in four basic ways. People often took the name of their village *(Somerset, Winthrop)* or a geographical feature *(Rivers, Hill, Fields, Meadows)*. The English occupational name *Baker* appears in French as *Boulanger* and in German as *Becker*. *Carpenter* is *Charpentier* in French, *Schreiner* in German, and *Martello* in Italian.

Patronymics is perhaps the most common way of forming surnames. The English name *Johnson* means "son of John," *O'Brian* is Irish for "descendant of Brian," and *Mendelssohn* is German for "son of Mendel."

Surnames are also derived from nicknames. A person named *Reid* may have had a red-haired ancestor centuries ago. The *Goodman* family probably had an ancestor who was known for his kindness. The names *Short, Little,* and *Long* probably indicate the stature of an ancestor.

The following comparisons offer a concrete idea of the Statue of Liberty's dimensions:

> If the statue and the pedestal were laid flat on a football field with the bottom of the pedestal on one goal line, the top of the torch would lie five and one-half feet beyond the other goal line—305' 6".
>
> The tablet Miss Liberty holds is about the size of a large room—13' 7"×23' 7".
>
> The statue's mouth is as wide as a yardstick is long—36".
>
> One of Miss Liberty's fingernails is larger than most textbooks—13"×10".
>
> One of her fingers would reach from the floor of an average room to its ceiling—8'.

SUPPLEMENTAL

LESSON

The Presidents of the United States

Text, pages 268-79

Preview

Main Ideas

- The president of the United States is to preserve, protect, and defend the Constitution of the United States.
- The Constitution assigns the president his duties.

Objectives

- Add presidential figures to the TimeLine in order
- Decide which people in a list qualify to be president according to the Constitution

Materials

- Supplement, page S6: excerpt from the Constitution
- Presidential figures 1-25 from the TimeLine Snapshots
- Appendix, page A17: research sheet*
- Appendix, page A18: presidential profile sheet*

Notes

This lesson discusses the presidency and provides the opportunity to put the presidential figures from George Washington to William McKinley on the TimeLine all at once. You would then be able to review the presidents as you put up associated TimeLine figures in the lessons to come. For example, when you use the Statue of Liberty figure in Lesson 10, you would point out that Grover Cleveland was president when France gave America the gift of Lady Liberty.

If you do not use this lesson, you may add presidential figures when you deem best.

Lesson

Introducing the Lesson

Inductive Activity

- ➤ *Place in front of your child the Supplement page showing the excerpt from the Constitution.*
- ➤ **Read this portion of the Constitution and find the qualifications listed for the presidency.** *(natural-born citizen, 35 years old or older, resident of the United States at least 14 years)*
- ➤ **Is your dad qualified to be president of the United States?** *Help your child to think inductively, asking questions about his dad's age and citizenship. Repeat the process using several other individuals.*

Teaching the Lesson

TimeLine Snapshots Activity, pages 268-79

- ➤ Select a strip of the presidents from Washington through McKinley. Choose one of the presidents on the strip.
- ➤ Turn to pages 268-79 to find the information about the president you selected. **Read the biographical information aloud.** *Repeat the procedure with the other presidents on the strip if time allows.*
- ➤ Place the presidential strip on the TimeLine below the appropriate dates.
- ➤ Continue the procedure until you have added all these strips to the TimeLine.
- ➤ Name the presidents in chronological order, using the TimeLine as a guide.

Research Activity, pages 268-79

- ➤ **Read the first question on the research sheet.** Find the answer by reading the appropriate information found on pages 268-79. *(vinegar-soaked cucumbers)*
- ➤ Follow the same procedure to complete the rest of the page.
  2. *July 4th, day that the Declaration of Independence was adopted*
  3. *George Herbert Walker Bush*
  4. *first to be communicated by telegraph*
  5. *swimming pool and movie theater*
  6. *John Quincy Adams, Andrew Jackson*
  7. *John Fitzgerald Kennedy*
  8. *Thomas Jefferson*
  9. *Abraham Lincoln*
  10. *false teeth carved from rhinoceros ivory*

Evaluating the Lesson

A "Qualified Candidate Search"

- ➤ Read the instructions on the presidential profile sheet.
- ➤ Complete the page, using the Constitutional excerpt page from the Supplement as an aid in determining whether the person described qualifies for the United States presidency. *(Numbers 1, 4, 6, and 8 should have an X over the number; numbers 2, 3, 5, and 7 should be circled.)*

Going Beyond

Additional Teacher Information

George Washington, the "Father of Our Country," embodied the ideals of America. As the first president, he defined many aspects of government, leaving a legacy to the American people.

George Washington's lineage traces back to seventeenth-century England. His great-grandfather, John Washington, survived a shipwreck during his journey to America and finally landed along the Potomac River. He married and established himself as a landowner and ironsmith. The Washington family began to "put its roots down" in America.

George grew up on a plantation that later became known as Mount Vernon. His education was informal, focusing more on history and geography than on literature and language. At an early age, he learned how to work a plantation. He lived an active life riding horses, working the land, and socializing.

As a teenager, George had a desire to explore the frontier—an interest he fulfilled by surveying uncharted land. Later, he was appointed county surveyor. In his early twenties, Washington wanted to help in the French and Indian War, so he volunteered to deliver a letter for the governor of Virginia. Later, Washington received the promotion of lieutenant colonel, leading his few troops into the first battle of the French and Indian War.

Washington married Martha Custis, a young mother of two who had been widowed. They were married in Martha's home, known as the White House. The Washingtons settled down to live a comfortable life in the countryside of Virginia. They had no children together, but George Washington reared Martha's children as his own.

Washington served in the colonial legislature, gaining popularity for his quiet integrity and valuable experience in leading a representative government. The Washingtons later moved to Mount Vernon, and George began his life as a landowner. He was a shrewd and capable businessman, supervising both his family estate and the one inherited by his wife. Mount Vernon produced first tobacco and then wheat. Its situation on the Potomac River yielded salted fish as an additional profit. Under Washington's careful hand, his property and wealth grew, culminating in the ownership of about forty thousand acres of land.

During this time, the atmosphere of the country was moving toward revolution. The colonists were growing angrier about the taxes imposed by the British government. Washington was one of the first to consider using force to protect the colonies. He was elected to go to the First Continental Congress. Here he met with other colonial leaders. He was re-elected to attend the Second Continental Congress. Washington wore his uniform from the French and Indian War to demonstrate his belief that the colonists should take forceful action. On June 14, 1775, George Washington was unanimously elected as commander in chief.

George Washington represented hope to the colonists. Though he sometimes expressed feelings of doubt, failure, and fear that the Americans could not win, he led them to victory over the British. He went on to serve as president of the United States. He was keenly aware of the magnitude of his duties, saying, "There is scarcely any part of my conduct that may not hereafter be drawn into precedent." Indeed, this planter, soldier, and gentleman set a precedent in his integrity, wisdom, and leadership—a precedent that future presidents would look back upon as a guide.

Not all of Washington's presidential career was smooth. At one point, one of the members of his cabinet, Edmund Randolph, was accused of selling secrets to the French. A scandal arose, and there was even talk of impeaching Washington. He regained popularity, however, after negotiating trade deals with Spain. In May 1796, Washington gave his farewell address and settled down to a retired life as a country gentleman. He maintained contact with many of his political friends and still kept current on governmental affairs. In December of 1799, Washington became ill with what seems to have been a cold or streptococcal infection. Doctors treated him by a process called *bleeding,* in which they drained blood from the patient in hopes of curing him. The president never recovered from this process, and on December 14, 1799, George Washington died at the age of sixty-seven. Even today, he remains a hero, a symbol of America and the American dream.

LESSON 7
Reasons for Coming to America

Text, pages 26-28
Notebook, page 7

Preview

Main Ideas

- People came to the New World for many reasons.
- Many people came to America in search of religious and political freedom.
- The desire for better jobs and greater opportunities influenced the settlement of the United States.
- Circumstances in America and in other countries affected the flow of immigration to the United States.
- Many individuals and groups have shaped the nation's heritage.

Objectives

- Answer questions about a bar graph
- Complete a bar graph

Materials

- A scarf*
- A shawl*
- A bowl with several unpeeled boiled potatoes*
- A small paring knife
- A table knife (optional)
- Some salt
- A globe

Day 1

Lesson

Introducing the Lesson

Monologue Activity

Adapt this monologue for your particular situation. You may want to attempt an Irish brogue or invite an Irish person to read with a genuine Irish accent. You or your Irish guest will act as an immigrant from Ireland who came to the United States as a child after the potato blight.

In preparation for the monologue, put on the scarf and the shawl, place the potatoes in a bowl, and then enter the room, carrying the bowl of potatoes and the small knife. Place the bowl on the table. Start to peel a potato with the knife and then thoughtfully put the knife down, look at your thumbnail, and try to peel the potato with it. As you are intently trying to peel the potato, act as if you suddenly realize that there are people watching you and begin reading the monologue.

"Oh, hello! I was just reliving some of the old days. My name is Maria O'Brien. Potatoes have played such a major part in my life. I can't look at a potato without praising God for the way He led my family, and thousands of other families, to the United States.

I was born in Ireland in 1840 to poor peasant farmers, Robert and Mary O'Reilly. I had three brothers and two sisters. Times certainly were hard. My father, as well as all the other peasant farmers, could rent only a small piece of land for farming. Since there was not enough land to grow several different crops, everyone's garden consisted of a field of potato plants.

So the potato was a very important food to an Irish family. For every meal my mother would boil up some potatoes. Each one of us would peel his own potato with his thumbnail. (We would let our thumbnails grow long just so we could peel potatoes with them.) We would sprinkle the potato with a dash of salt and then wash it down with a glass of water or sometimes milk. It was a luxury when we had a little butter on a potato.

Really, ours was a miserable lot there in Ireland. Often our stomachs ached for more food. My parents and all my brothers and sisters huddled together in our one-room house. Sometimes, even our pigs joined us for the night! Half of the people of Ireland lived this way. But even with all these miserable living conditions, we were a happy, lighthearted people—until death came to call on our country.

An Irish legend says that a king was being chased by Death. Now this king was very clever, and he convinced Death to step into a box. The king quickly closed the lid, threw the box into the sea, and went back home. According to the legend, the box floated in the ocean for weeks till it washed up on Ireland's shore. Men brought the box up on land and were curious about what was in it. Two big Irishmen finally broke the box open. Death flew out and started killing people all over Ireland. . . .

You will learn more about the terrible tragedy that happened in my homeland, but why don't you try peeling one of these potatoes with your thumbnail and let's have ourselves a taste of Ireland's past.

➤ *Give your child a knife.* Peel one of the boiled potatoes.

➤ You may salt and eat your potato.

➤ **How would you like having potatoes for every meal *every* day?**

ECHOES IN HISTORY

Reasons for Coming to America

Why would a person or a family or a whole community travel hundreds, even thousands, of miles to live in a strange place? Most immigrants to America have answered those questions in one of three ways.

Some came to find a better life. They had heard that America had plenty of land. Everyone could get a job there and no one had to be hungry. Everyone had the same chance—the poor as well as the rich.

Separatists came to Plymouth.

Others came to find freedom to worship God as they believed they should. The Separatists came for this reason in 1620. Later, Quakers and Roman Catholics and Huguenots and others came too.

Some came for a different freedom: *political* freedom. In most countries, people could not say whether they thought laws were good or bad. They might be put in jail or even killed for questioning them.

Thanks to the words of the Declaration of Independence, Americans believe that "all men are created equal." The Bill of Rights promises freedom to every person in America. The words of the Declaration of Independence and the Bill of Rights still "echo" around the world, drawing immigrants to America.

The Declaration of Independence

26

We *could* be happy even if boiled potatoes became our daily diet. Since God provides everything we need to be happy, we can learn, as Paul did, to be content in whatsoever state we are. (BAT: 7d Contentment)

Teaching the Lesson

Text Discussion, page 26

➤ **Read page 26 to find three reasons people left their homes to come to America.** *(to find a better way of life, to find religious freedom, to find political freedom)*

➤ **What character qualities would a person have to have to be willing to uproot his whole family and make the dangerous trip to a land he had never seen?** *(Answers will vary but should include courage, determination, faith, and a willingness to work.)* (BATs: 2d Goal setting, 2e Work, 2f Enthusiasm, 8a Faith in God's promises, 8d Courage)

➤ **Which groups of people came to America to find freedom to worship God as they believed they should?** *(Separatists, Quakers, Roman Catholics, and Huguenots)*

➤ **What facts can you remember about each of these four groups?**

The Separatists were from England and were separating from the Church of England. (The Puritans stayed in England to try to change the Church of England.)

The Quakers were shunned by many because they went neither to the Church of England nor to the Separatist or Puritan churches. The Quakers settled in Pennsylvania.

Catholics did not have any more freedom to worship in England than the Separatists or the Quakers did. They settled in Maryland.

The Huguenots were a group of Protestants who suffered much persecution and fled Catholic France after 1685, when the king revoked religious liberty. They settled in towns along the Atlantic coast, especially in Philadelphia, Boston, and Charleston.

➤ **Which American belief stated in the Declaration of Independence draws so many people to the United States?** *(the belief that "all men are created equal")*

➤ **What does the Bill of Rights promise for every person in America?** *(freedom)*

➤ **Read aloud the last paragraph on page 26.**

The Constitution was written shortly after the colonies gained freedom from England in 1776. As the American public became aware of what the Constitution said, some people worried because it did not mention the freedom to have ideas and to tell them to others. It was then that the Bill of Rights was added to the Constitution.

➤ Name some freedoms guaranteed by the Bill of Rights. *(freedom to have a fair trial, to worship, to speak, to gather in groups, and to print what one wants)* (*NOTE:* Further discussion of the Constitution and the Bill of Rights is provided in Chapter 12. You may want to refer to the pictorial version of the Bill of Rights from Maps and More 31.)

It is important that we do not take our freedoms for granted but thank the Lord for them. As Christian citizens we must become aware of new laws the government is passing and make sure that these laws continue to guard America's freedoms.

➤ **How can we stay informed about current issues?** *(read newspapers, listen to news programs with parents, and discuss politics with parents in light of the Bible)*

A crowded European city in the 1800s

Fewer immigrants came after the colonies became a country. At first, people in Europe did not believe that the American ideas of freedom could work. They thought that other countries would try to take over the new United States.

Soon, wars between France and England and between England and the United States kept people at home. It was not safe to travel across the ocean when countries were at war. Can you think why such travel would be dangerous?

After 1820, immigrants began coming to America again. Where do you think these immigrants came from? Many came from the same countries that sent the earliest immigrants. Some others came from Norway, and a few came from Canada. Which immigrants had the shortest trip?

Most immigrants who came during this time came to find a better life. In many countries of Europe, *landlords*, or landowners, forced the peasant farmers to move from their land. These poor farmers moved to the already crowded cities and towns. They hoped to find jobs there. But soon there were no jobs to find. Those who could scrape a bit of money together packed up their families and headed to America.

27

1,200,000
1,000,000
800,000
600,000
400,000
200,000
0
1836-45
1846-55
1856-65

Irish Immigration to America 1836-65

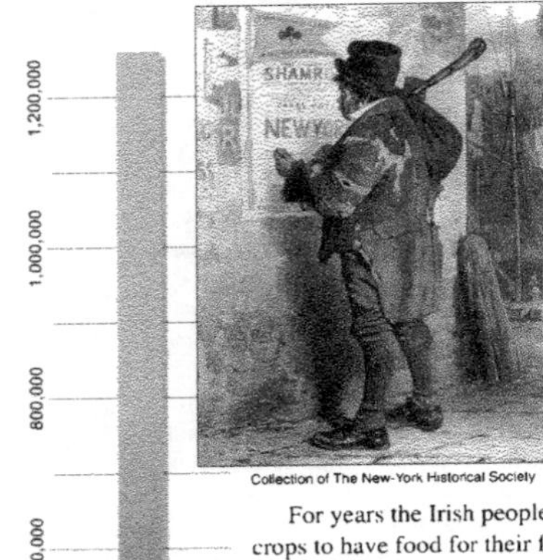

Collection of The New-York Historical Society

An Irish worker dreams of going to America.

The flow of immigrants into America was slow and steady for about thirty years. Then something terrible happened in Ireland that changed the flow into a flood.

For years the Irish people had planted potato crops to have food for their families. But during the years 1845-49, a potato blight struck the crops. The potatoes rotted in the ground. Suddenly the people in Ireland had no food to eat.

Many Irish people died from hunger. Those who did live made plans to leave their homeland. Between 1850 and 1860, as many immigrants came to America as had come in all the thirty years before. More than two million immigrants came; most were from Ireland.

The New Immigrants

Immigration slowed down almost to a stop in the years between 1860 and 1865. What do you think was the cause? During these years, Americans were at war with Americans. The horrible, bloody Civil War kept many would-be immigrants at home.

28

Text Discussion, page 27

- ➤ **Read page 27 to find out why fewer immigrants came to America after the colonies had become a country.** *(They did not think American ideas of freedom would work; it was not safe to travel after war broke out between France and England and between England and the United States.)*
- ➤ **Why did people begin coming to America again after 1820?** *(to find a better way of life)*
- ➤ **Where did the immigrants come from this time?** *(the same places as before, plus Norway and Canada)*
- ➤ Look at the globe or the world map on pages 316-17 to discover whether Norway or Canada is closer to America. *(Canada)*

Day 2

Text Discussion, page 28

The legend we heard at the beginning of the lesson indicated that there was trouble in Ireland.

- ➤ **Read the first three paragraphs on page 28 to find out what really happened to cause so many Irish to die.** *(The potato blight in Ireland left many of the Irish without food. Many were dying from hunger.)*

More than a million Irish came to America to escape starvation and disease. Because they were very poor, most stayed in the port cities where they landed—New York City and Boston—and worked in factories and on construction crews.

The rest of text page 28 will be read in Lesson 8.

Graphing Activity, page 28

- ➤ Look at the graph on page 28. **What kind of graph is this?** *(a bar graph)*
- ➤ **Why is a bar graph helpful?** *(It helps people to understand the information.)*
- ➤ **What information does the bar graph show?** *(Irish immigration to America between 1836 and 1865)*
- ➤ **From looking at the bars, can you tell what happened to the Irish immigration to America?** *(It jumped dramatically between 1846 and 1855.)*
- ➤ Point to the numbers along the left side of the graph. **How do these numbers help in reading the graph?** *(They assign an approximate number to the bars.)*
- ➤ **Does the graph show the exact number of immigrants that came in the three time periods?** *(No, it shows about how many.)*

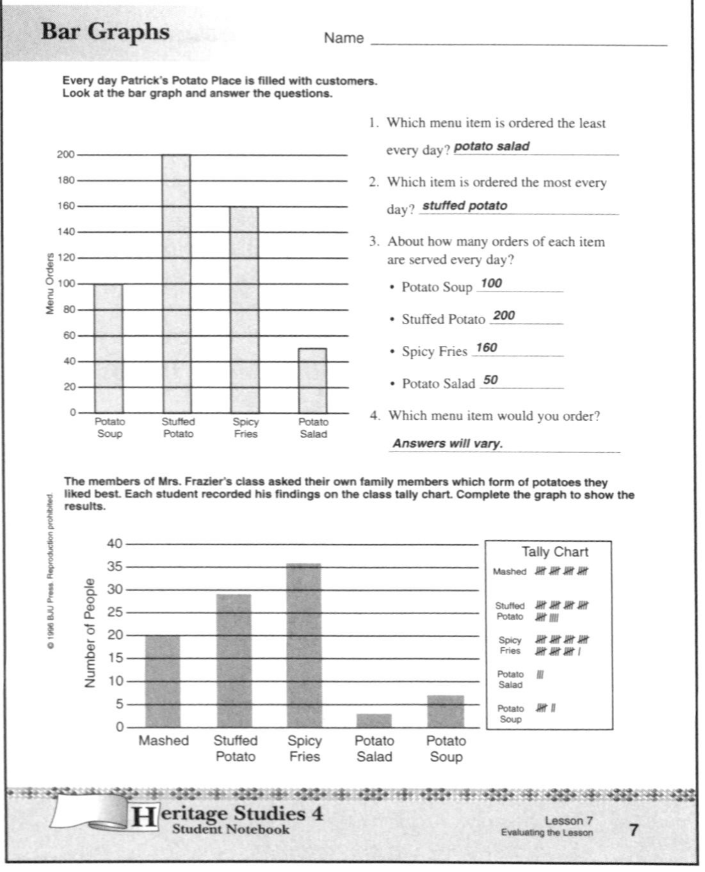

Bar Graphs Name ____________

Every day Patrick's Potato Place is filled with customers. Look at the bar graph and answer the questions.

1. Which menu item is ordered the least every day? *potato salad*
2. Which item is ordered the most every day? *stuffed potato*
3. About how many orders of each item are served every day?
   - Potato Soup *100*
   - Stuffed Potato *200*
   - Spicy Fries *160*
   - Potato Salad *50*
4. Which menu item would you order? *Answers will vary.*

The members of Mrs. Frazier's class asked their own family members which form of potatoes they liked best. Each student recorded his findings on the class tally chart. Complete the graph to show the results.

Heritage Studies 4 Student Notebook   Lesson 7 Evaluating the Lesson   7

➤ **About how many Irish immigrated to the United States between 1836 and 1845?** *(over 300,000)* **between 1846 and 1855?** *(over 1,250,000)* **between 1856 and 1865?** *(over 400,000)*

The graph makes it very clear that a major catastrophe was taking place between 1846 and 1855 and influencing the flow of immigration dramatically.

➤ **What was that catastrophe?** *(the potato blight)*

God has control over everything in a Christian's life, even in times of tragedy. A Christian does not always know why God allows difficulties in his life, but he does know that God works *all* things together for his good. (Bible Promise: I. God as Master)

Evaluating the Lesson

Notebook Activity, page 7

➤ Read the bar graph and answer the questions on the top half of Notebook page 7.

➤ Draw bars to complete the graph on the bottom half of the page, using the information given.

Going Beyond

Enrichment

Provide your child with graph paper, colored pencils, felt-tip pens, and rulers. Encourage him to make graphs to illustrate information about his family members, such as their favorite form of potatoes, favorite colors, favorite breakfast cereals, favorite sports teams, and so on.

Additional Teacher Information

During the height of immigration in the nineteenth century, American and British ships carried Irish immigrants to America. The fare for the American ships was much more expensive than the British fare. A family of six could sail on a British ship for about $30 as opposed to $105 on an American vessel. Although it was less expensive to sail on British ships, the inferior vessels cost many Irish their lives. The British ships were called "coffin ships" because often they were not strong enough to stand the trip. Sometimes these ships sank and many Irish immigrants drowned. Although the Irish knew of the danger of sailing on the British vessels, their desperation to flee Ireland forced them to take the risk.

It was not easy for the Irish to leave their homeland. As many of the Irish emigrated, they picked up a small bag full of their "ould sod," carried it across the ocean, and, upon setting foot in America, poured it out on the ground so they could still step on their beloved soil.

LESSON 8
The New Immigrants

Text, pages 28-31
Notebook, page 8

Preview

Main Ideas

- People have needs, feelings, interests, and preferences.
- Every individual is unique.
- Religious beliefs help shape cultures.
- Religious differences caused tension between old and new immigrants in America.
- America has provided freedom for people from many parts of the world.

Objective

- Unscramble letters to make words describing ways the "new immigrants" differed from most Americans

Materials

- A dictionary (optional)
- Appendix, page A19: Brainstorming*
- A Bible
- Maps and More 2, page M1

Maps and More is a collection of colored maps, visuals, charts, and graphs. Display the pages from your teacher's edition for use in the lessons. These visuals may not be copied.

Lesson

Introducing the Lesson

Problem-Solving Activity

This activity may best be accomplished if other members of the family are involved. You may prefer to do this the evening before you teach this lesson.

➤ **Read the paragraph at the top of the Brainstorming page.**

➤ **What does the word *brainstorming* mean?** *If your child is unsure, encourage him to use the dictionary. (the act of thinking of possible ideas, plans, and methods concerning a given situation)*

➤ Write each of your ideas on the worksheet.

➤ Act as a spokesperson and summarize the ideas for your family.
(Possible answers to the questions on the Brainstorming page are as follows:

1. *There will be a language barrier; he may not care for the food; the way of life will be different; he may be homesick for Brazil; and so on.*
2. *The family could prepare a room for him, make a banner that says "welcome" in Portuguese, research information about Brazil, and so on.*
3. *Smile and talk to him even though he cannot understand English; try to teach him English words; include him in your games and play; show him where everything is; and so on.)*

Read Galatians 6:2 aloud. A Christian is to be aware of problems and burdens that fellow Christians are bearing and do what he can to help. This demonstrates the love of God. (BATs: 5a Love, 5e Friendliness)

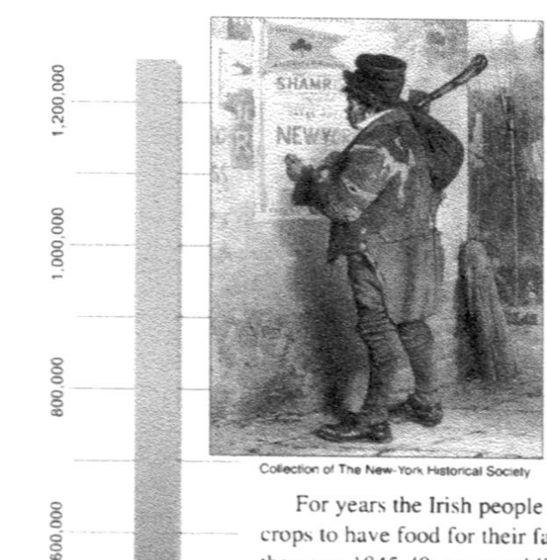

An Irish worker dreams of going to America.

Collection of The New-York Historical Society

Irish Immigration to America 1836-65

Years	
1836-45	
1846-55	
1856-65	

The flow of immigrants into America was slow and steady for about thirty years. Then something terrible happened in Ireland that changed the flow into a flood.

For years the Irish people had planted potato crops to have food for their families. But during the years 1845-49, a potato blight struck the crops. The potatoes rotted in the ground. Suddenly the people in Ireland had no food to eat.

Many Irish people died from hunger. Those who did live made plans to leave their homeland. Between 1850 and 1860, as many immigrants came to America as had come in all the thirty years before. More than two million immigrants came; most were from Ireland.

The New Immigrants

Immigration slowed down almost to a stop in the years between 1860 and 1865. What do you think was the cause? During these years, Americans were at war with Americans. The horrible, bloody Civil War kept many would-be immigrants at home.

28

As soon as peace was made between the North and the South, immigrants were again ready to come. For a while, most still came from the same countries of northern Europe. But more and more, immigrants began coming from different countries as well. What other countries do you think some immigrants came from?

These *new immigrants*, as they were called, came from countries in the south and east of Europe. They too had heard about the opportunities in America. When railroads were built through countries like Austria-Hungary, Russia, and Italy, the people finally had an easy way to travel. They rode the trains to cities on the coast. There they boarded ships bound for America.

29

Teaching the Lesson

Text Discussion, page 28

- ➤ **Read the last paragraph on page 28 to find out what caused immigration to America to stop almost completely.** *(the American Civil War)*
- ➤ **Why would the American Civil War hinder immigration to the United States?** *(People would not want to move to a place with so much fighting and turmoil.)*

Text Discussion, page 29

- ➤ **Read page 29 to find out where immigrants came from after the American Civil War.** *(They came from the same countries of northern Europe, and they started coming from countries of southern and eastern Europe.)*
- ➤ **Why were the immigrants from southern and eastern Europe called "new immigrants"?** *(They came from places different from those of earlier immigrants.)*

People were leaving countries such as Austria-Hungary, Russia, and Italy. People from these countries had wanted to emigrate much earlier, but traveling to the European coastal harbors was very difficult.

- ➤ **What invention made it easier for people from these countries to reach the coast so that they could emigrate from their homelands?** *(railroads)*
- ➤ **Why did so many people want to immigrate to America?** *(They had heard that America was full of opportunities for all.)*

Above: Austro-Hungarian immigrants

Left: Immigrants from Europe

Life in America was not as easy for these new immigrants as it had been for the first ones who came. Many of the early immigrants spoke the English language. They did things the same ways that the English settlers did. They looked and dressed the same. How would being like the people already in America help an immigrant who had just arrived?

The new immigrants were different in every way. They spoke languages that were much different from English. They ate different kinds of foods. They wore clothes that were strange and brightly colored. They were poorer too.

One more thing set many of these new immigrants apart: religion. The new immigrants were Roman Catholic or Jewish. But most Americans were *Protestant*. They went to churches that had separated from the Catholic Church. Why might this difference cause problems?

30

To be sure, many Jews and Roman Catholics had made their homes in America before the new immigrants came. But never before had so many come so quickly. Some Protestants feared that they would soon be outnumbered. Then the Catholics or the Jews might try to take away the freedom of all Americans to worship God as they thought they should. It had happened before in other countries. Do you think the Protestants were right to be afraid?

Many of the Jewish immigrants came from Russia. Like the Irish immigrants who had come thirty years before, the Russian Jews were forced to leave their homeland. But it was not hunger that made them leave. The Jewish people were blamed for everything that went wrong in Russia. The *czar,* Russia's king, encouraged his people to persecute the Jews.

The Isaak family, Russian immigrants

The Russian Jews gave a name to the persecutions—*pogroms*—and they lived in constant fear. They never knew when a pogrom might happen or what small thing might cause one. The czar's soldiers and the townspeople burned the homes and businesses owned by Jews. They stole and ruined all that the Jewish people had worked for. With nowhere else to go, the Russian Jews turned to America. Can you think of others who were persecuted for their beliefs and came to America?

31

Day 2

Text Discussion, page 30

- ➤ **Read page 30 to find out whether adjusting to life in America was easier for the immigrants who came first or for the new immigrants.** *(the first immigrants)* **Why?** *(They were very much like the English settlers. Many did not have to overcome a language barrier. Their ways and customs were similar, so it was easy for them to get along together.)*
- ➤ **What are five ways in which the new immigrants were different from immigrants who had come before them?** *(They spoke different languages, ate different foods, wore strange clothing, were poorer, and had different religions.)*
- ➤ **Why do you think these differences would make adjusting to America difficult?**

Not only did these people have to adjust to a new place, language, and manner of living, but they also had to deal with anti-immigration feelings from the people who were already in America. Because the immigrants would work for lower wages, employers often gave jobs to immigrants rather than Americans. This trend created ill feelings toward the new immigrants.

Text Discussion, page 31

- ➤ **Read page 31 to find out what the Protestants in America feared.** *(They feared that the masses of Jews and Catholics would try to take their religious freedom away.)*
- ➤ **What forced the Russian Jews to leave their homeland?** *(the czar's persecutions)*
- ➤ **What did the Russian Jews call the persecutions?** ***(pogroms)***
- ➤ **What happened to the Jews during a pogrom?** *(Jewish homes and businesses were burned. Their possessions were stolen.)*
- ➤ **What other groups had come to America earlier because they were being persecuted in their homelands?** *(Separatists, Quakers, Catholics, and Huguenots)*

Read Philippians 4:6-7 aloud. Remind your child that God's Word tells Christians not to worry about the future but to pray about everything. In whatever situation a Christian finds himself, he is to give thanks, trust the Lord, and remember that God is in control. (Bible Promise: I. God as Master)

Chart Activity

➤ Look at the chart on Maps and More 2.

This chart gives an overview of immigration into the United States from colonial days to 1920. It is divided into three time periods. Sometimes these periods of immigration are called **waves of immigration.** The first wave of immigration occurred between the years 1620 and 1820, the second wave between the years 1820 and 1870, and the third wave between the years 1870 and 1920.

➤ Study the chart to find the answers to the following questions:

1. **Why are there no bars shown in the section labeled 1620-1820?** *(because records of immigration were not kept until 1820)*
2. **Where did most of the immigrants come from in the first wave of immigration?** *(England)*
3. **What hindered the first wave of immigration?** *(the Revolutionary War of 1776 and the War of 1812)*
4. **How many immigrants came in the second wave?** *(7.5 million)*
5. **What happened in Ireland that caused the giant leap in the second wave of immigration?** *(the potato blight in Ireland)*
6. **How many immigrants came in the third wave?** *(26 million)*
7. **What were many of these immigrants called?** *(new immigrants)*
8. **Why were these immigrants called new?** *(because they came from new parts of Europe—southern and eastern)*
9. **During which years did immigration take a giant leap?** *(between 1900 and 1910)*

(*NOTE:* Events and overcrowding in industrial European cities caused the influx of immigration to America between 1900 and 1910.)

Evaluating the Lesson

Notebook Activity, page 8

➤ Read the instructions for Notebook page 8.
➤ Complete the page.

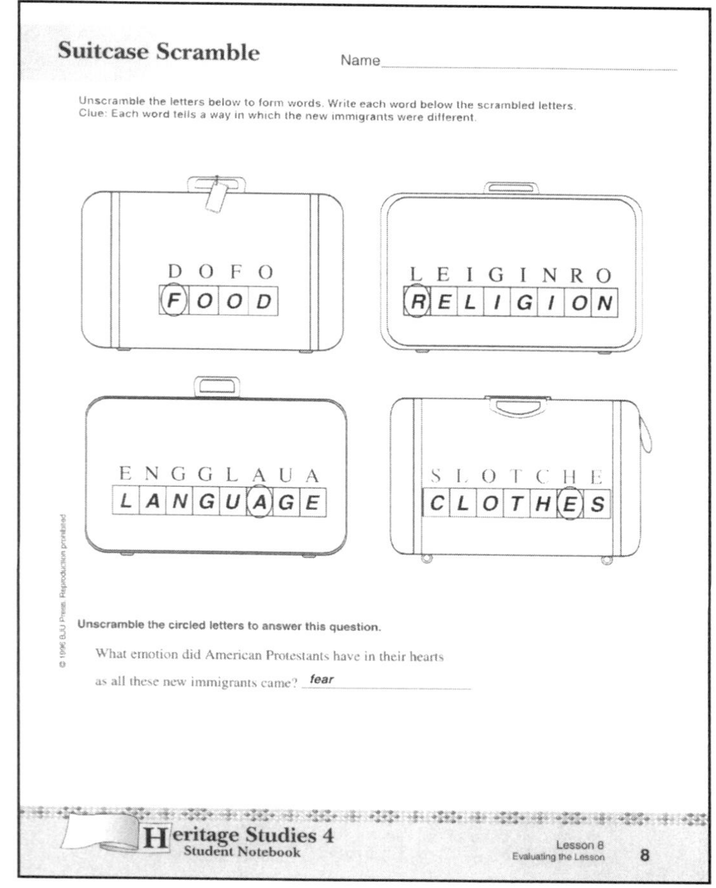
Suitcase Scramble Name ____________

Unscramble the letters below to form words. Write each word below the scrambled letters.
Clue: Each word tells a way in which the new immigrants were different.

D O F O — *FOOD*

L E I G I N R O — *RELIGION*

E N G G L A U A — *LANGUAGE*

S L O T C H E — *CLOTHES*

Unscramble the circled letters to answer this question.

What emotion did American Protestants have in their hearts as all these new immigrants came? *fear*

Heritage Studies 4 Student Notebook   Lesson 8 Evaluating the Lesson   8

Going Beyond

Enrichment

Take a field trip to make gravestone rubbings. Before going, call the cemetery to obtain permission for this type of activity. You will need masking tape, a whiskbroom, a large sheet of dressmaker's interfacing or thin white paper, and a large wax crayon.

To make the rubbing of the gravestone, gently clean the desired gravestone with the broom. Tape the interfacing or the paper over the inscription; then, using the side of the crayon, rub over the paper. The inscription will show up in white. Choose a place to display the rubbing.

Additional Teacher Information

After the American Civil War, immigration was stimulated by farming. States west of the Mississippi River placed advertisements in European papers, enticing Europeans to immigrate to America and settle in their regions. The railroads also advertised the land along the railways. The land was offered at low prices, and passenger fares were greatly reduced for immigrants. Entrepreneurs of America's growing industries also enticed immigrants to America since these newcomers would work for lower wages.

LESSON 9
Leaving the Old Country

Text, pages 32-35
Notebook, page 9

Preview

Main Ideas

- An interview is an important tool in the search for one's ancestors.
- Immigrants faced many hardships in their struggles to improve their lives.
- Many different people and groups have contributed to American culture.
- People have needs, feelings, interests, and preferences.

Objectives

- Write about an important personal possession
- Record information from an interview

Materials

- A cassette player/recorder
- A blank cassette*
- A family Bible (optional)*
- A Bible
- 15-20 play dollar bills or coins

Notes

In this lesson you will be conducting the model interview referred to in the Notes for Lesson 6. Before the interview, you will want to prepare a list of questions. Use Notebook page 9 as a guide.

The interviews in this lesson are designed to prepare your child to conduct an interview on his own. This will be done in Lesson 16.

Day 1

Lesson

Introducing the Lesson

Model Interview

Set up a special place with two chairs for the interview. Welcome the visitor warmly and direct him to sit down. Start the interview by thanking your visitor for taking the time to come and answer a few questions. Ask the visitor for permission to record the interview. After the cassette recorder is on, say the date and the name of the person you are interviewing and proceed with your list of questions.

Conduct the interview in a relaxed manner, giving the interviewee plenty of time to answer each question. Make sure that you are a good example by listening intently and responsively. When the interview is over, express how much you have enjoyed learning more about him and thank him again for coming.

◆ LEARNING HOW ◆

To Study Your Family History

1. Get a notebook and a pencil, or a cassette tape and a tape recorder.
2. Find out something new and interesting about your family history from one of the following sources:
   a. An older family member, such as a grandparent, aunt, or uncle.
   b. An old family Bible.
   c. Newspaper clippings.
   d. A bundle of old letters.
   e. Old photographs.
   f. Special family books, such as diaries, baby books, or autograph books.

3. In your notebook, record the things you find out. If you talk to an older family member, try to use a tape recorder. Then write a page telling the family story you learned. Be sure to include details like the year, the place, and the names and ages of the family members in the story.
4. Share your family information with your classmates. Then put your written work in a folder or scrapbook. If you like, find out more family stories and add them to the folder or scrapbook too.

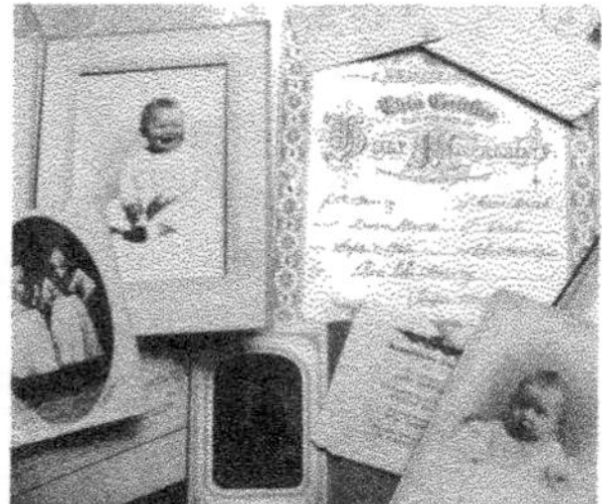

33

Day 2

Teaching the Lesson

The text pages will be presented out of order in this lesson.

***Learning How* Activity, page 33**

➤ **Read page 33 to find ways of learning more about your family history.**

➤ **Read aloud the list of sources for gathering family history information.**

In the 1700s a traditional wedding present was a family Bible. Often between the Old and the New Testaments, there were pages provided for the recording of births, deaths, and marriages. Sometimes special events were written down and dated in the blank pages at the beginning or end of the Bible.

Show a family Bible with information written on these special pages, if one is available.

If you have access to any of the items listed on page 33, help your child to collect these and create a nook of family memorabilia.

Interviewing Activity, Notebook page 9

The purpose of this activity is to provide your child with practice in the process of interviewing. You will want to give guidance as needed and to encourage formality in order to make the experience as valid as possible.

➤ It is your turn to conduct an interview. I will be the interviewee (the person being interviewed).

➤ Let's talk about some tips on interviewing a person to gain information. (*NOTE:* You may refer to the interview you conducted as you discuss the following points.)

1. Before any interview, tell the interviewee about your project and why he can be of help to you. This information will give him time to be more prepared and to make the interview more productive.
2. Prepare for the interview in advance. Find out all you can about the interviewee and prepare a list of questions that you would like him to answer. Since this is a practice session, you may use the same questions I used earlier.
3. Take a notebook and a pen to the interview. Take a cassette recorder or a camcorder if either one is available. If you want to record the interview, first ask the interviewee's permission.
4. During the interview, give the interviewee plenty of time to answer the questions. Do not be afraid of silence. Sometimes an interviewee will use the time to reflect and formulate an answer.
5. Be a good listener. Keep eye contact with the interviewee and be responsive and encouraging.
6. When the interview is over, be sure to thank the interviewee for his time and his help.

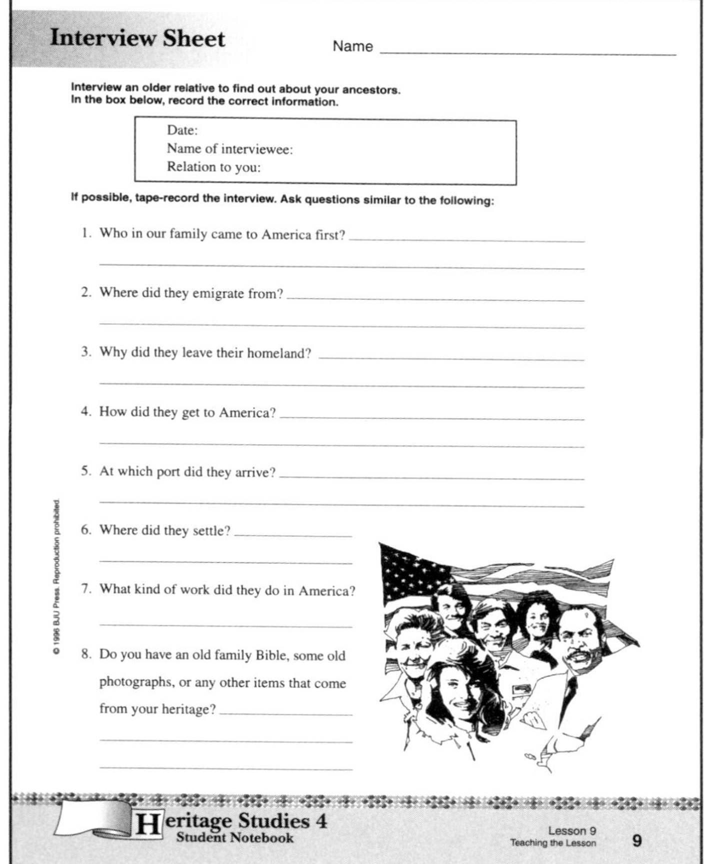

Interview Sheet Name ____________

Interview an older relative to find out about your ancestors. In the box below, record the correct information.

Date:
Name of interviewee:
Relation to you:

If possible, tape-record the interview. Ask questions similar to the following:

1. Who in our family came to America first? ____________
2. Where did they emigrate from? ____________
3. Why did they leave their homeland? ____________
4. How did they get to America? ____________
5. At which port did they arrive? ____________
6. Where did they settle? ____________
7. What kind of work did they do in America? ____________
8. Do you have an old family Bible, some old photographs, or any other items that come from your heritage? ____________

Heritage Studies 4 Student Notebook — Lesson 9 Teaching the Lesson 9

➤ When you have completed the interview, record the information onto Notebook page 9.

➤ **Reread Step 4 on text page 33.** Create a folder or scrapbook for your interview sheet.

You may want to allow some time for an oral presentation to friends or other family members. Your child might play parts of the recorded interview, show special pictures, or share something special he has collected representing his heritage.

Immigrants arriving with a few possessions from their old country

Leaving the Old Country

To many people in Europe, America seemed like a wonderful, golden place. And living in the old country was often horrible. But making the decision to leave the place that had been home for so many years was not easy. How would you have felt about making such a decision?

Once the decision was made, the emigrants began making plans. First, money had to be raised to pay for a ticket. Sometimes money was needed to pay for food on the ship as well. A whole family might have to put their money together. They would send one person to America, hoping that he would make a good living. Then he could send money back for the rest of the family to make the trip.

What things would you have taken to America? Nearly every emigrant took with him some clothing. If there was room left in the suitcase, trunk, or basket, some other things could go too. Perhaps a place could be found for a special doll or a favorite book. When Bessie Jane Priest came from England, she brought a bracelet her uncle had given her. Like many mothers, she probably brought pots and pans so that she could cook for her family in their new home.

32

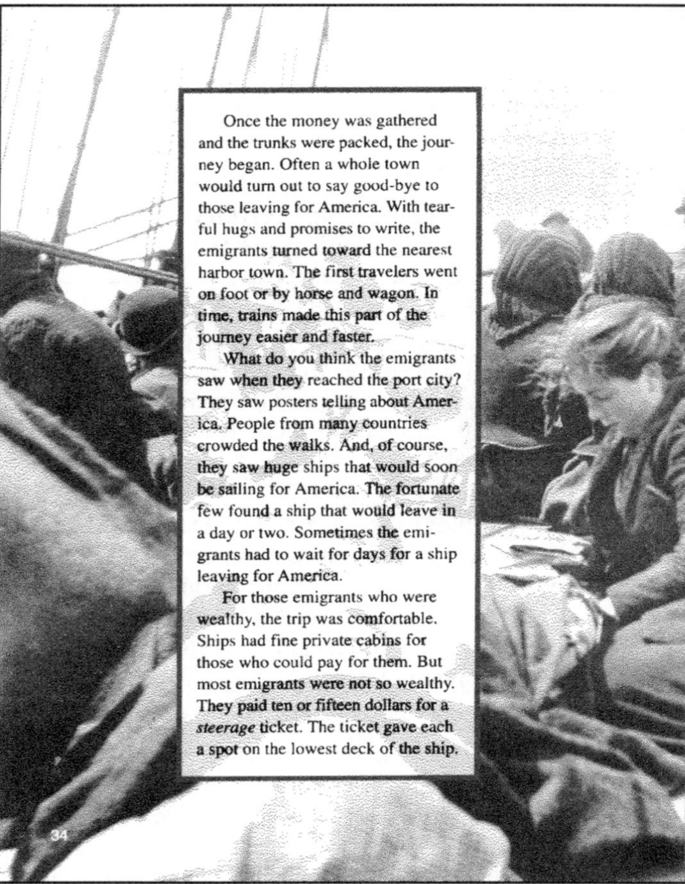

Once the money was gathered and the trunks were packed, the journey began. Often a whole town would turn out to say good-bye to those leaving for America. With tearful hugs and promises to write, the emigrants turned toward the nearest harbor town. The first travelers went on foot or by horse and wagon. In time, trains made this part of the journey easier and faster.

What do you think the emigrants saw when they reached the port city? They saw posters telling about America. People from many countries crowded the walks. And, of course, they saw huge ships that would soon be sailing for America. The fortunate few found a ship that would leave in a day or two. Sometimes the emigrants had to wait for days for a ship leaving for America.

For those emigrants who were wealthy, the trip was comfortable. Ships had fine private cabins for those who could pay for them. But most emigrants were not so wealthy. They paid ten or fifteen dollars for a *steerage* ticket. The ticket gave each a spot on the lowest deck of the ship.

34

Text Discussion, page 32

➤ **Read page 32 to find out what families had to do once they decided to immigrate to America.** *(raise money and decide what to take)*

➤ **What might have gone through the minds of the emigrants as they were deciding whether they should leave their homelands?** *(Possible answers include these: Will I survive the voyage across the sea? Will I ever see my family again? Can I leave my home and all my belongings behind? Will I be able to find work in the United States?)*

➤ **How would you feel if your father had to emigrate alone in hopes of sending for the rest of the family later?** *(Answers may include fearful, betrayed, lonely, or sad.)*

Emigrants had to leave almost all their possessions behind when they came to America. The men would often take tools with them that would help them make money in the New World; for example, a barrel maker would take a special knife with him.

No matter what God calls someone to do, He gives the grace and strength that is needed. Read I Thessalonians 5:24 aloud. God knows that a person does not have the strength to do what God wants him to do; that is why God promises to help him. It is the Christian's responsibility to obey and go through the doors God opens. The Lord may call us to leave our home country someday to be missionaries in another country. Questions and fears may arise, but the Christian must simply trust and obey God. (BAT: 4a Sowing and reaping; Bible Promises: G. Christ as Friend, H. God as Father, I. God as Master)

Day 3

Text Discussion, page 34

➤ **Read page 34 silently to find out how those leaving their countries got to the port cities.** *(by foot, by horse and wagon, and eventually by train)*

Often the people were so poor that they would not wear their shoes as they walked to the ports; they needed to save their shoes to wear in the new land.

➤ **What did the emigrants do once they reached the port cities?** *(They waited for the next ship leaving for America and bought their tickets.)*

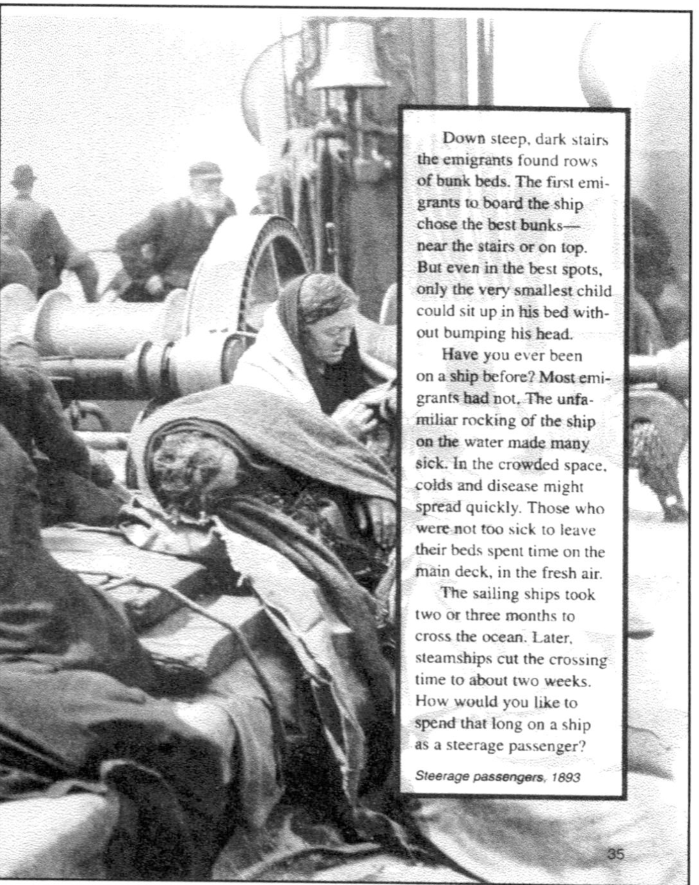

Down steep, dark stairs the emigrants found rows of bunk beds. The first emigrants to board the ship chose the best bunks—near the stairs or on top. But even in the best spots, only the very smallest child could sit up in his bed without bumping his head.

Have you ever been on a ship before? Most emigrants had not. The unfamiliar rocking of the ship on the water made many sick. In the crowded space, colds and disease might spread quickly. Those who were not too sick to leave their beds spent time on the main deck, in the fresh air.

The sailing ships took two or three months to cross the ocean. Later, steamships cut the crossing time to about two weeks. How would you like to spend that long on a ship as a steerage passenger?

Steerage passengers, 1893

35

➤ **What kind of ticket would the poorer emigrant buy and how much would it cost?** *(A steerage ticket cost ten to fifteen dollars.)*

Text Discussion, page 35

➤ **Read page 35 to find out what it was like down in the lowest level of the ship.** *(dark, crowded, much sickness, very uncomfortable)*

➤ **How do you think the steerage passengers could stand the horrible conditions on the trip to America?**

The people knew that if they could endure the trip, they eventually would be in the land of their hopes and dreams.

Evaluating the Lesson

Review Activity

Pretend that you are an emigrant setting out for the New World. You will have the opportunity to earn money for a ticket to America. I will ask you some questions about the information we have been learning. For each correct answer you will receive one dollar. See if you can buy a steerage ticket with the money you earn. *(NOTE: You may choose to assign a greater value to a few questions so that your child can earn enough money for a first-class ticket.)*

1. **What was the first thing a family needed when they decided to emigrate?** *(money)*
2. **What was one thing money was used for?** *(a ticket or food)*
3. **If a family did not have enough money for the entire family to emigrate, what would they do?** *(send one person)*
4. **Name one thing the emigrants took with them to America.** *(clothes, pots, or tools)*
5. **What two things must a Christian do when God gives him a task?** *(trust and obey)*
6. **Name two ways that emigrants traveled to the port cities in their country.** *(by foot, horse and wagon, or train)*
7. **Name one thing emigrants saw when they reached the port cities.** *(posters or ships)*
8. **What did the emigrants have to wait for once they arrived at the port city?** *(the next ship)*
9. **What kind of ticket did poorer emigrants buy?** *(steerage ticket)*
10. **How much did a steerage ticket cost?** *($10 to $15)*
11. **On what level was the steerage portion of the ship?** *(lowest)*
12. **What happened to many of the emigrants as they traveled to America?** *(They got sick.)*
13. **About how many months did it take for the emigrants in sailing ships to reach America?** *(two to three)*
14. **About how many weeks did it take for steamships to cross the ocean?** *(two)*
15. **Besides the interview, what is another source of information about a family's past?** *(family Bible, newspaper clippings, old letters, old photographs, or special family books such as diaries, baby books, or autograph books)*

Going Beyond

Enrichment

Give your child a copy of the two-page Pedigree Chart from the Appendix, pages A20-A21. (*NOTE:* A family tree and a pedigree chart differ in that a family tree includes aunts, uncles, cousins, and so on. A pedigree chart traces only an individual's direct ancestors.) Tape the pages together side by side to make one large chart. Encourage your child to become an "Ancestor Hunter" and to find out as much about his heritage as possible. Challenge him to check out library books to guide him in the search.

Additional Teacher Information

When the United States celebrated its two hundredth birthday in 1976, many people became interested in finding out their family histories and took up ancestor hunting as a hobby. Stories about family histories, such as Alex Haley's *Roots,* motivated many Americans to explore their heritage. Two major genealogical libraries exist to help in the search. One is in Doraville, Georgia, near Atlanta. The largest genealogical library, which contains one million rolls of microfilm, is in Salt Lake City, Utah. Many branches of this library have been started in other parts of the world. The Mormons' interest in genealogy stems from their belief that they can save the souls of their ancestors and reunite with them for eternity.

LESSON 10
America at Last

Text, pages 36-41, 311
Notebook, pages 10-11

Preview

Main Ideas

- People came to the New World for many reasons.
- The desire for better jobs and greater opportunities led to the settlement of the United States.
- Many immigrants came to the United States to escape dangers in their homelands.

Objectives

- Act out the part of a person at Ellis Island
- Write a journal entry about a young immigrant

Materials

- 3 pieces of colored paper or index cards
- New York Harbor map from Lesson 6
- The figure of the Statue of Liberty (1886) from the TimeLine Snapshots
- Scarves to be used as head coverings and shawls (optional)
- Suitcases (optional)*
- Paper bags (optional)
- Appendix, page A22: Immigrant Questionnaire (optional)*

Notes

Before the lesson begins, you will need to prepare three cards using the pieces of paper or index cards. Write one of the following letters on the front of each card in large black print: ***B, H, L***. On the back of the cards write the corresponding meaning. (**B** *means back trouble,* **H** *stands for heart problems, and* **L** *means the immigrant was lame or had trouble walking.)*

The materials labeled as optional in the Materials list are props. They may be used to act out the inspection of an immigrant, as explained in the Notebook Activity in the Teaching the Lesson section.

If you have not put up the presidential figures from the TimeLine Snapshots, you will want to do so at this time.

What excitement filled the crowded ship when land was finally sighted. America, at last! But where exactly would the immigrants be when they stepped off the ship? Look at the map. How many different cities does it show? Immigrants came into America in all these places. But most came to New York City.

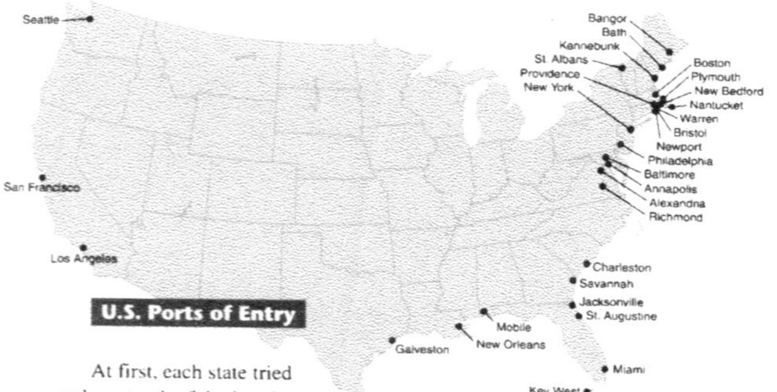

At first, each state tried to keep track of the immigrants that came to their part of America. Ship captains gave a list of their passengers to state officers. But not much was done to help or welcome the immigrants to their new country. Instead, some immigrants got an unfriendly welcome from thieves. They were robbed, and a few were even killed. With more and more immigrants coming all the time, the United States needed a better way of welcoming them.

In 1855, the first official station for receiving immigrants into the United States was opened. At Castle Garden in New York City, immigrants could exchange their money for American money. They could buy railroad tickets to take them to other parts of the country. And if they were sick after their long trip, they could see a doctor.

36

◆ THINGS PEOPLE DO ◆

Sculpting Statues

Most statues are carefully carved from a stone called *marble*. It is smooth and strong. The person who carves the statue is called a *sculptor.* He uses special tools to sculpt, or carve, the stone. What other things can statues be made from?

Frédéric Auguste Bartholdi was well known in his country of France. He liked to sculpt big statues. His first statue was twelve feet tall! He tried to make each statue he carved bigger and better than the one before.

A friend told Bartholdi about his idea for a gift from the people of France to the people of America. Such a statue would make a wonderful gift for the hundredth birthday of the United States.

Building the left hand of the Statue of Liberty

Bartholdi began to work. He drew many sketches of his ideas. Finally he had a drawing that he liked. He called his statue "Liberty Enlightening the World."

It took many years to sculpt the statue to liberty. Because Bartholdi wanted to make it huge, he did not make the statue from stone. He shaped each part from wood, then carefully hammered copper sheets over the wood until it was shaped just right. A skeleton of iron and steel held the copper parts in place.

Americans put the statue on an island in New York Harbor. For millions of immigrants, it was the first thing "American" they saw. The Statue of Liberty stood for American freedom and liberty.

37

Day 1

Lesson

Introducing the Lesson

Dramatization Activity

Place the letter cards face up on the table. The letters on the front of these cards represent a physical problem that an immigrant may have had. This problem might keep him from being able to stay in the United States.

> If you are teaching more than one child, choose a child to pick a card and act out the infirmity. The other children should try to guess what the infirmity is.

- Choose one of the cards and read silently the problem, or infirmity, on the back.
- Pretend you are an immigrant who has just arrived in America. Act out your infirmity. Follow the same procedure for the rest of the cards.

In this lesson we will learn more about these letters and the fear they brought to immigrants.

Teaching the Lesson

Text Discussion, page 36

- **Read page 36 to find out where most immigrants entered America.** *(New York City)*
- Look at the map on the page. **How many cities other than New York are marked as places where immigrants came?** *(twenty-nine, besides New York City)*
- **What unfriendly welcome met many of the immigrants?** *(Some were robbed and others killed.)*
- **What was done in 1855 to help immigrants?** *(The first official station to welcome them was opened.)*
- **What was the name of the station, and where was it located?** *(Castle Garden in New York City)*
- **What services were available to the immigrants?** *(They could exchange their money for American money, buy railroad tickets, and see a doctor there.)*
- Point to Castle Garden on the New York Harbor map. It is located on the tip of Manhattan Island.

Immigrants could not yet view the Statue of Liberty, since it was not unveiled until 1886.

Text Discussion, page 37

- **Read page 37 silently to find out how Frédéric Auguste Bartholdi made his huge statue.** *(Paragraph 5 tells about the process.)* **Read the fifth paragraph aloud.**

Inside the Great Hall

Castle Garden served for thirty-five years as an immigration station. During those years more than eight million immigrants passed through its doors. In time the number of immigrants grew too great for the small building. A bigger immigration station had to be built.

Ellis Island

The United States built a new place for receiving immigrants on Ellis Island. It opened in 1892. Its many buildings covered the whole island. A hospital gave the sick immigrants a place to stay while they received care. Many immigrants got their first taste of American food in the Ellis Island dining room.

Not every immigrant who came to Ellis Island visited the hospital or ate in the dining room. But everyone had to pass through the main building. The huge building looked like a castle to the immigrants. The workers in their uniforms reminded them of soldiers in the old country. The workers shouted orders at the immigrants in English. Do you think the immigrants understood the words?

38

Ellis Island

Ellis Island is located in New York Harbor, less than half a mile north of Liberty Island, where the Statue of Liberty stands. Ellis Island is named for the merchant and farmer Samuel Ellis, who owned the island in the late 1700s. The United States government bought the island in 1808 and, after the construction of thirty-five buildings, began using it as an immigration station in 1892.

Can you imagine how these immigrants felt upon their arrival on Ellis Island?

For more than twelve million immigrants, Ellis Island was their first glimpse of America with her promise of freedom and opportunity. Newcomers were questioned by government officials and examined by doctors before being allowed to enter the United States. Most of the immigration station at Ellis Island closed down in 1924, and the station was completely closed in 1954. In 1965, Ellis Island became a national historic site, part of the Statue of Liberty National Monument.

311

- **How are most statues made?** *(They are carved or **sculpted** from marble.)*
- **Why did Bartholdi not carve his famous statue from stone?** *(He wanted to make it very, very big.)*
- **What do we call people who sculpt?** *(**sculptors**)*
- **What did the sculptor do before beginning to shape the statue?** *(He drew many sketches until he had a drawing he liked.)*
- **What are some of the different names that have been given to Bartholdi's statue?** *(The New Colossus; Mother of Exiles [in Emma Lazarus's poem]; Statue of Liberty; Liberty Enlightening the World; Lady Liberty; the Lady with the Lamp; Miss Liberty)*
- Look again at the New York Harbor map and point to the location of the Statue of Liberty on Bedloe's Island. The island was renamed Liberty Island in 1956.

TimeLine Snapshots Activity

- **Do you remember when the Statue of Liberty was given to the United States?**

Although the presentation was made in Paris on July 4, 1884, the statue did not arrive in New York Harbor until July 1885. It was not completely ready and dedicated until October 28, 1886.

- Place the figure of the Statue of Liberty on the TimeLine at the year 1886.
- **Who was President of the United States in 1886?** *(Grover Cleveland)*

Day 2

Text Discussion, pages 38 and 311

- **Read page 38 to find out what happened when Castle Garden became too small for all the immigrants who were coming to the United States.** *(The United States built a new immigration station on Ellis Island.)*
- Point to Ellis Island on the New York Harbor map.

The new station offered improved care for the immigrants. However, many of them were frightened and confused.

- **What would have caused the immigrants to feel fearful at a place that was built especially to welcome and to help them?** *(The huge main building looked like a castle; the uniformed workers reminded them of soldiers in their home countries; the immigrants could not understand the orders that the workers shouted at them.)*
- **Read page 311 to find out what Ellis Island is today.** *(a national historical site; part of the Statue of Liberty National Monument)*

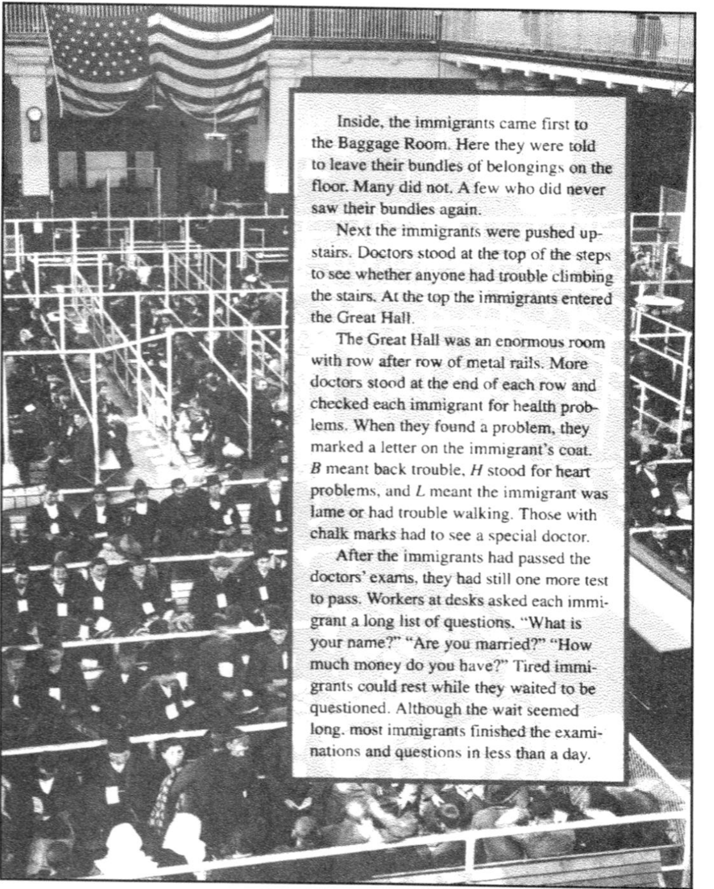
Inside, the immigrants came first to the Baggage Room. Here they were told to leave their bundles of belongings on the floor. Many did not. A few who did never saw their bundles again.

Next the immigrants were pushed upstairs. Doctors stood at the top of the steps to see whether anyone had trouble climbing the stairs. At the top the immigrants entered the Great Hall.

The Great Hall was an enormous room with row after row of metal rails. More doctors stood at the end of each row and checked each immigrant for health problems. When they found a problem, they marked a letter on the immigrant's coat. *B* meant back trouble, *H* stood for heart problems, and *L* meant the immigrant was lame or had trouble walking. Those with chalk marks had to see a special doctor.

After the immigrants had passed the doctors' exams, they had still one more test to pass. Workers at desks asked each immigrant a long list of questions. "What is your name?" "Are you married?" "How much money do you have?" Tired immigrants could rest while they waited to be questioned. Although the wait seemed long, most immigrants finished the examinations and questions in less than a day.

The Konshak family (Tillie is in the second row.)

Otillige Konshak often told the story of her arrival at Ellis Island. She had traveled from Poland with her mother and eight brothers and sisters. They could not wait to see Mr. Konshak; he had come to America to find a home and a job before sending for his family.

Otillige stood in line with her family, waiting for the first doctor to examine her. The doctor saw the deep, ugly scars on Otillige's neck. When she was very young, Otillige had many painful sores. The doctors in Poland did not know what to do for the sores, so when they healed, they left the bad scars. "I think your daughter is healthy," the doctor told Otillige's mother. "But I am afraid the next doctor will send her back because of these scars."

Otillige's mother made a quick plan. "Tillie, pull your shawl high around your neck. And don't look at the next doctor if he speaks. Maybe he won't look closely at you."

Otillige shuffled slowly behind her brothers and sisters. Her heart pounded. But she did everything her mother had told her. It worked! The doctor glanced at her, but he did not stop her. Soon the whole Konshak family was together again.

Text Discussion, page 39

➤ **As I read aloud page 39, listen for what the immigrants first experienced.**

➤ **In what ways were the immigrants "tested" on Ellis Island?** *(They were to leave their belongings in the Baggage Room, to climb some stairs while doctors watched them, to be checked for health problems and marked if problems were noticed, and to answer a long list of questions.)*

➤ **What happened to some of the immigrants' belongings that were left in the Baggage Room?** *(Some were stolen.)*

➤ **What would have frightened the immigrants about having to climb the stairs?** *(They were shouted at and pushed; doctors were watching them as they climbed.)*

The officials provided benches on which the immigrants could rest as they waited to be questioned at the end of the Great Hall.

➤ **Why do you think the letters might have scared the immigrants?**

An immigrant might not have understood what the letter was or why he had to see a special doctor. He also might have been afraid of the unknown.

➤ **Do new or unknown situations ever frighten you?**

Remember that God protects His children and knows their needs and fears. He will allow nothing to happen to Christians that is not for their good and His glory. (Bible Promise: H. God as Father)

Text Discussion, page 40

➤ **Read page 40 to find out about Mrs. Konshak's plan to get her daughter Tillie through the doctors' examinations.**

➤ Explain the plan in your own words. *(paraphrase of paragraph 3)*

➤ **Did Mrs. Konshak's plan work?** *(yes)*

➤ Point to Tillie in the picture of the Konshak family.

➤ **How do you think the younger brothers must have felt as they went through the examinations and questions on Ellis Island?**

Immigrant Questionnaire Name ______________________

Read these questions. Prepare to answer them as an immigrant coming to the United States.

OFFICIAL DOCUMENT

UNITED STATES OF AMERICA

1. What is your name? ______________________
2. How old are you? __________ Are you married or single? __________
3. What is your occupation? ______________________
4. Are you able to read and write? _____ What is your nationality? __________
5. Where was your last residence? ______________________
6. At which United States seaport did you land? ______________________
7. What is your final destination in the United States? ______________________
8. Do you have a ticket to your destination? ______________________
9. Did you pay for your passage to the United States? If not, who did? __________
10. Do you have money with you? How much? ______________________
11. Are you going to join a relative? What relative? Name and address? __________
12. Have you ever been to the United States before? Where and when? __________
13. Have you ever been in prison, in a poorhouse, or supported by charity? __________
14. Are you under contract to perform labor in the United States? __________
15. What is the condition of your health, mental and physical? __________

◆ HOW IT WAS ◆

Ellis Island
April 17, 1907

On this day 11,000 people are waiting on Ellis Island, or on ships nearby, to find out whether they can enter the United States.

This young Jewish girl has left Russia with her family. They wanted to escape the pogroms, cruel persecutions encouraged by the czar.

She is twelve—old enough to be sent back to Russia alone if she does not pass the examinations.

So far, she has passed every examination without receiving a chalk mark on her coat. She has seen others with many different marks given them by the doctors. Even though she does not know what they mean, she knows the marks are not good.

This is the most dreaded examination. The inspector will turn back her eyelids with a metal hook so that he can look beneath them.

41

Day 3

Notebook Activity, page 10

➤ Read the list of questions on Notebook page 10.

Think about someone you would like to represent as an immigrant. You may use props to portray the character. I will conduct a pretend "inspection." You are to respond in the manner that your chosen character would have responded.

➤ Reread the questions on page 10 as you think through what answers will be fitting for your character.

➤ *Conduct the inspection, completing the immigrant questionnaire. Then if you wish to switch roles, you may give your child the copy of the questionnaire from the Appendix to use.*

If you are teaching more than one child, they may take turns being the inspector and the immigrant.

Evaluating the Lesson

Creative Writing Activity, page 41 and Notebook page 11

A *How It Was* section in the student text takes a detailed look at a single moment in American history.

➤ **Read *How It Was* on page 41.**

➤ **What do you think might have happened to this young immigrant?**

➤ Pretend you are the Jewish immigrant or someone in line with her. Write a journal entry on Notebook page 11, telling something memorable about this day. *Offer assistance and encouragement as needed with this writing assignment.*

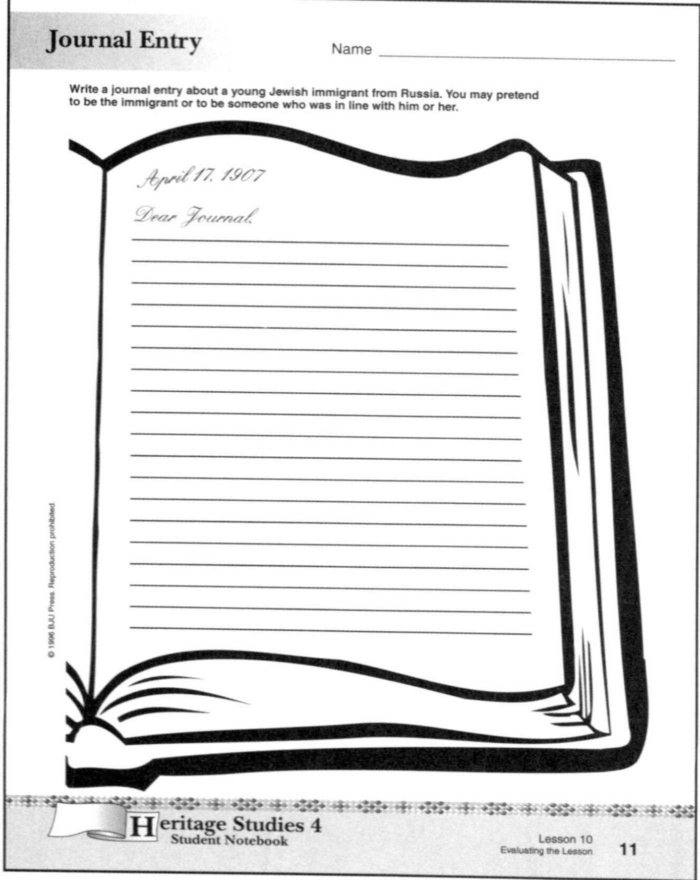
Journal Entry Name ____________________

Write a journal entry about a young Jewish immigrant from Russia. You may pretend to be the immigrant or to be someone who was in line with him or her.

April 17, 1907

Dear Journal,

Heritage Studies 4 Student Notebook

Lesson 10 Evaluating the Lesson 11

Going Beyond

Additional Teacher Information

Ellis Island was officially closed in 1954. In 1965, the National Park Service took over the property. Then, in 1976, Congress appropriated money to clean up the island. Some who visited wanted to construct a museum in the main building. The exhibits would keep alive the memory of the place and would tell the stories of the millions of immigrants whose first step through the "golden door" was taken on Ellis Island.

In 1990 the dream of an immigration museum became reality. The first-floor exhibit includes some of the luggage that immigrants brought across the ocean. Other memorabilia—tickets, passports, ships' passenger lists—are also on display. Visitors can walk up the long stairs, into the Great Hall, and picture where their relatives stood in line, awaiting inspection and word of whether they could stay in America.

In memory of ancestors who immigrated to America, thousands of people donated money for the rebuilding of Ellis Island. The name of each person honored by a donation is listed on the Immigrant Wall of Honor, an impressive tribute to the courage of those who left their homelands for a new home, a new hope, and a new life.

LESSON 11
A Fresh Start

Text, pages 42-45
Notebook, page 12

Preview

Main Ideas

- Some immigrants settle in *ethnic* communities in their new land.
- Ethnic communities offer familiarity and comfort to people in a new land.

Objective

- Write about what makes him proud of America

Materials

- Appendix, pages A23-A24: I Am an American*
- A calculator (optional)

Day 1

Lesson

Introducing the Lesson

Poem Discussion

Some sections of the poem "I Am an American" will not be grasped by your child. Spend as much time in discussion about it as he shows interest. The overriding theme of national pride will be understandable and should be the major emphasis as you present the poem.

➤ I will read aloud part of the poem "I Am an American" by Elias Lieberman. Follow along with me as I read. *Read aloud the first three lines.*

The groups to which the speaker's father and mother belong are clues to the family's history. The *Sons of the Revolution* is a patriotic organization whose members are descendants of men who served in the Revolutionary War or who contributed to establishing American independence. Each member of the *Colonial Dames* is descended from a person who came to an American colony before 1750 and who contributed to the founding of the nation.

➤ As I read the rest of this stanza, listen for the things that the ancestors of this American did. *(took part in the Boston Tea Party; fought with Joseph Warren at the Battle of Bunker Hill; served with George*

A Fresh Start

The examinations passed and the questions answered, the golden door to America swung wide open. Now the hard work of making a new life in a strange land began for each immigrant. Where would he go? Would he find work? Would he be accepted by his new neighbors?

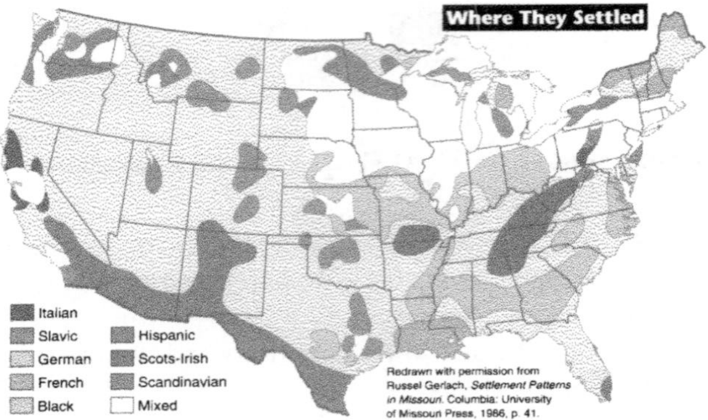

Most of the immigrants who came before 1870 went west. During those years the United States grew to cover the land from ocean to ocean. The country needed people to live on that land. As long as land could be found for a good price, immigrants followed their dreams and bought their own farms. Sometimes whole villages in the old country packed up and moved to the American West.

Look at the map. It shows where different groups of immigrants settled. What groups settled west of the Mississippi River? Why do you think so many Scandinavian and Slavic people settled in the West?

42

The Kvsvick family emigrated from Norway in 1918.

Not every immigrant who went west bought a farm. Nineteen-year-old John Kvsvick worked on a large farm owned by another man. John's brother, who had come from Norway earlier, helped him to find the job. Many immigrants got help finding work from family and friends. John worked hard and saved all his money. After four years John headed home to Norway. Do you think he stayed?

Back in Norway, John married Jennie Thomsen. They had three children, but John was not happy in Norway. It was hard to earn enough money to care for his growing family. And he did not agree with the way God's Word was preached in the church there. John remembered how things had been for him in America. He told his little family, "I must go back to America. I will send money for you as soon as I can."

The house that John Kvsvick built in America

John went again to Minnesota. But he did not work on a farm this time. Other kinds of work were easier to find now. New western cities needed factory workers. Other immigrants found work on the railroads. This time John worked in a lumber camp. It took a few years, but he finally saved enough money to send for his family.

43

Washington at Valley Forge; took part in the forming of America by speaking in councils, serving as soldiers, and working the land; thrilled at the promise of the growth of the United States)

➤ **What did this American say he is proud of?** *(his past)*

➤ **Does he have good reasons to be proud?** *(yes)*

Part of being a good American is looking back on the past with gratefulness, thanking God for His blessings on America, and then praying that He will continue to be gracious to this country. (Bible Promises: H. God as Father, I. God as Master)

Teaching the Lesson

Text Discussion, page 42

➤ **Read page 42 to find out where most of the immigrants who came before 1870 went after they arrived in America.** *(Most went west.)*

➤ **Why did so many immigrants settle in the West?** *(The land was open to settlement; people were needed to live on the land; land could be bought for a good price.)*

➤ **Why do you think whole villages would leave another country and move to the American West?**

The three concerns mentioned in the first paragraph—destination, work, and acceptance—would be more easily overcome when large groups of people relocated together.

➤ Look at the map to determine which groups settled in the West.

Many Scandinavian and Slavic immigrants were farmers; the West offered opportunities for them to own their own farmland. (*NOTE:* The Scandinavian immigrants include the Icelandic, Norwegian, Swedish, Finnish, and Danish peoples. Among the Slavic are the Wendish, Ukrainian, Serbo-Croatian, Slovene, Slovak, Russian, Polish, Macedonian, Czech, Bulgarian, and Belorussian peoples.)

Text Discussion, page 43

➤ *Point to and pronounce the name Kvsvick (kĭsvick or kūsvick) on page 43.*

➤ **Read this page to find out what kind of work John Kvsvick did in America.** *(At first he worked on a large farm, and later he worked in a lumber camp.)*

➤ **Why do you think John worked so hard and saved all his money during his first four years in America?**

Perhaps John came to America to earn money and never intended to settle here. All of his family were still in Norway, so he returned to be with them.

➤ **What kinds of work other than farming were available when John returned from Norway?** *(work in factories, on railroads, and in lumber camps)*

➤ **Why did John return to America?** *(It was hard to earn money in Norway, and he did not agree with the way God's Word was preached there.)*

➤ **What troubled John about the church in Norway?** *(God's Word was not preached the way he thought it should be.)*

A Christian realizes that preaching must be true to God's Word in order for it to minister to hearts. (BAT: 8b Faith in the power of the Word of God)

➤ **Has anyone in your family ever worked hard for a long time to save money for something?**

➤ **What did John work hard to save money for after he returned to Minnesota?** *(to bring his family to Minnesota to be with him)*

John worked very hard at his job in the lumber camp. He worked eleven hours a day and earned thirteen cents an hour.

➤ Calculate how much money John made daily. *($1.43) Give help as needed or allow your child to use a calculator.*

➤ **How do you think John's family felt during the years that John was away from them?**

➤ **Have you been away from someone you love? How did you feel when you finally got to see that person again?** (BAT: 5a Love)

Day 2

Listening Activity

Complete the story of John Kvsvick and his family by reading the following account aloud.

The Kvsvicks borrowed money to build a one-room house. After a while they bought a cow. When other children were born, the Kvsvicks added more rooms to their home.

John and his brother Henry decided to change their last name so that it would sound American. Their father's name was Jacob, so they chose to be called Jacobsen (Jacob's son). John was still not satisfied. "Jack is a nickname for Jacob," he thought. "I will change Jacobsen to Jackson. That is a real American name."

The Jacksons always worked hard. Jennie taught her girls how to sew, knit, and do beautiful embroidery. The family enjoyed good music and good books. They loved the beauty of the outdoors and tried to make their home simple and tranquil, yet beautiful. The parents encouraged their children to go to college.

Little Italy, about 1899

A butcher in his shop in Chinatown

After 1870, many immigrants went no further than the city where their ship had landed. In New York City, three of every four people were immigrants or the children of immigrants. Most were poor people who did not have money to travel any farther. They had spent all they had to get to America.

Others stayed in the cities because they did not want to be farmers. Remember the Irish immigrants? After their experience with the potato blight, many Irishmen did not want to be farmers ever again. Instead they worked in factories in the cities. Some Irish immigrants did go west but not to farm. They helped to build the railroads and canals.

Often immigrants formed their own communities. German farmers bought land near other farmers from Germany. Italian immigrants found places to live in neighborhoods settled by other Italians. Why would the immigrants want to live near others from their old countries?

44

John and Jennie Jackson visited Norway two times, but they never wanted to stay there. They did not forget their old ways, but they had become real Americans.

Text Discussion, page 44

➤ **Read page 44 to find out why many immigrants who came to America after 1870 stayed in the city where their ship landed.** *(Some had no money to travel farther; some did not want to be farmers; some stayed to live in neighborhoods settled by others from their old country.)*

➤ **What kinds of work did many of the Irish immigrants do in America?** *(They worked in factories and built railroads and canals.)*

➤ **Why do you think immigrants would want to live near others from their old countries?**

Things such as a common language, familiar customs and food, similar clothing styles, and shared religious beliefs were of great comfort to people in a new land.

➤ Look at the photographs on page 44 and read the captions to find out what neighborhoods are shown. *(Chinatown and Little Italy)*

tunnpannkakor med lingonsylt:
Swedish thin pancakes with lingonberry sauce

At first, most immigrants felt like strangers in a strange new land. It was comforting to live near people who spoke their language and understood their customs. These *ethnic* communities were small copies of the old country. There the immigrants could buy the foods they had eaten all their lives. They could find newspapers written in their language. Parties and celebrations were just like the ones in the old country. And sermons at the community church were preached in the immigrants' language.

Enoch Malmfeldt and Hattie Hallberg lived in an ethnic community in Kansas City. Both young people had emigrated from Sweden. They met at the Old Swedish Baptist Church in Kansas City and were married there. What language do you think the preacher at the church spoke? In the small Swedish community, many of the people spoke only Swedish.

Enoch and Hattie Malmfeldt

Enoch worked as a tailor, and Hattie worked as a maid in the home of a wealthy family. They could speak a little English, but at home they spoke Swedish. But that changed when their oldest son went to school. "Papa, the other children make fun of the way I talk. I do not want to go back to school anymore," the young boy told his father. Enoch decided that, for the sake of the children, the family would speak only English from then on. Do you think that was a good idea?

45

I Am an American Name ____________________

Write a paragraph using the following sentence starter.

I am an American. I am proud of my country because ____________________

Heritage Studies 4 Student Notebook — Lesson 11 Evaluating the Lesson 12

Text Discussion, page 45

➤ **Read the first paragraph on page 45 to find the term used to describe communities such as those in the pictures on page 44.** *(an* ***ethnic*** *community)* Ethnic communities exist in most major cities.

➤ **Read the rest of page 45 to find out why the Malmfeldt family decided to speak only English.** *(Children at school were making fun of the way their son talked.)*

Day 3

Poem Discussion

➤ I will read the second stanza of Elias Lieberman's poem "I Am an American." Follow along as I read. *Read aloud the first four lines.*

➤ **Why do you think the poet would use the words *an atom of dust* and *a straw in the wind* to describe the speaker's father and mother?**

A piece of dust and a straw blowing in the wind are two small, unimportant things, especially in the mind of a great king, *His Serene Majesty.*

➤ As I read the rest of the stanza aloud, listen for the things that the ancestors of this American did. *(died in Siberian mines; became crippled in a beating with a leather whip [Russian knout]; were killed in a massacre; came to America; became American citizens)*

Place the two stanzas of the poem side by side. Discuss the differences between the American in the first stanza and the American in the second stanza.

➤ **What is the American in the second stanza proud of?** *(his future)*

➤ **Why do you think he feels that way?**

This American looks back to all that his ancestors suffered in the past, then forward to all that America, the "promised land," offers to him in the future; he is proud of being a citizen of such a land.

Evaluating the Lesson

Notebook Activity, page 12

➤ Write on Notebook page 12 the reasons that you are proud to be an American. (*NOTE:* If you are citizens of another country, you may want your child to write why he is proud to be a citizen of his country.)

➤ Read aloud what you have written.

Going Beyond

Enrichment

Take your child to the local library. Help him to select several juvenile fiction and nonfiction books about immigrants and immigration.

Additional Teacher Information

Among the immigrants from eastern Europe were great numbers of Jews. Many people hated the Jews because of their religion. Russia was the home of more Jews than any other European country, and often the government encouraged attacks upon the Jews. Stories of freedom and riches in America caused many Jews—sometimes even whole villages—to come to this country. Many called America the promised land, as did Elias Lieberman in his poem.

The Jews have been persecuted for thousands of years. But they have been treated more kindly in the United States than in most other countries. Many believe that God has blessed America greatly because of its kindness to His people.

LESSON 12

Becoming a Citizen

Text, pages 46-48, 307
Notebook, page 13

Preview

Main Ideas

- Despite different heritages, people in the United States share the common quest for freedom and opportunity.
- To become a citizen of the United States, an immigrant must make certain promises.

Objectives

- Write part of the immigrant's citizenship pledge in his own words
- Write his own citizenship pledge

Materials

- Supplement, page S7: pledge
- An American flag
- A dictionary
- *HERITAGE STUDIES Listening Cassette B*

Day 1

Lesson

Introducing the Lesson

Text Activity, page 307

➤ *Place the pledge in the Supplement in front of your child.*

➤ **Read the Pledge of Allegiance.**

➤ **What is the proper way to stand when pledging to the American flag?** *(face the flag with your right hand over your heart)*

➤ **Stand. Let's pledge to the flag.**

➤ **What do you think the pledge means?**

➤ Use your dictionary to help you give the meaning of the following words:

> ***pledge***—*to make a formal promise or vow*
> ***allegiance***—*loyal and faithful devotion to someone or something*
> ***republic***—*a form of government in which the power rests with the voters, who elect representatives to govern the country; usually headed by a president*

The Pledge of Allegiance

The Pledge of Allegiance is a promise of loyalty to the United States. Bostonians James B. Upham and Francis Bellamy wrote the original pledge. School children first recited the Pledge of Allegiance in 1892 as they commemorated the 400th anniversary of the discovery of America. In 1923 and 1924, the National Flag Conference expanded the wording of the pledge. In 1942 Congress sanctioned the use of the Pledge of Allegiance with the display of the flag. Then in 1954 Congress added the words "under God" to the pledge.

The Pledge of Allegiance reads:

I pledge allegiance to the flag of the United States of America and to the Republic for which it stands, one Nation under God, indivisible, with liberty and justice for all.

307

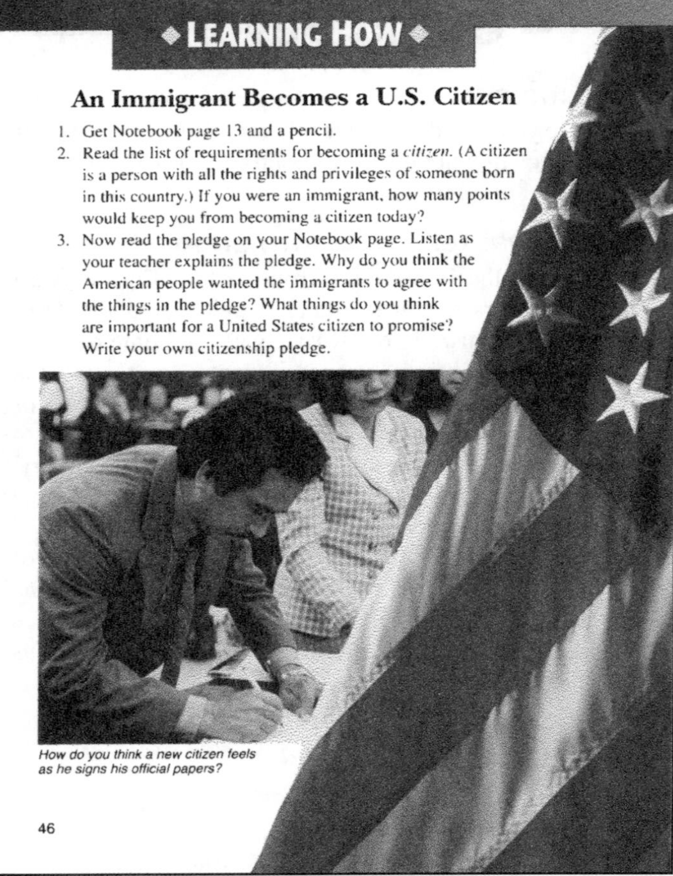

◆ LEARNING HOW ◆

An Immigrant Becomes a U.S. Citizen

1. Get Notebook page 13 and a pencil.
2. Read the list of requirements for becoming a *citizen.* (A citizen is a person with all the rights and privileges of someone born in this country.) If you were an immigrant, how many points would keep you from becoming a citizen today?
3. Now read the pledge on your Notebook page. Listen as your teacher explains the pledge. Why do you think the American people wanted the immigrants to agree with the things in the pledge? What things do you think are important for a United States citizen to promise? Write your own citizenship pledge.

How do you think a new citizen feels as he signs his official papers?

46

indivisible—not able to be divided
liberty—freedom
justice—fair treatment according to law or honor

- ➤ **To what two things does a person pledge his allegiance?** *(to the United States flag and to the country, or republic, itself)*
- ➤ **Read page 307 to learn more about the Pledge of Allegiance.**
- ➤ **When was the pledge recited for the first time by schoolchildren?** *(in 1892)*
- ➤ **What special occasion was being celebrated?** *(the 400th anniversary of the discovery of America)*
- ➤ **What phrase was not a part of the pledge until 1954?** *(under God)* (Bible Promise: I. God as Master)
- ➤ Calculate how many years the Pledge of Allegiance was recited without the words *under God. (62 years)*

In this lesson we will learn about another important pledge.

Day 2

Teaching the Lesson

Learning How Activity, page 46 and Notebook page 13

If you are teaching more than one child, they may work together to rewrite their version of the pledge. Give help and guidance as needed.

- ➤ **Read the steps in the *Learning How* section on page 46.**
- ➤ Complete Steps 1 and 2 as stated on page 46.

The pledge, or oath, that an immigrant must make before becoming a United States citizen is written on the Notebook page. An ***oath*** is a promise to act in a certain way.

- ➤ **Read the entire pledge, underlining the word *that* every time it appears in the pledge.** (*NOTE:* It appears seven times.) After every *that* is a promise.
- ➤ *Reread each promise one at a time, discussing what each one means.*
- ➤ Now rewrite the pledge in your own words on a separate sheet of paper. Use your dictionary to help you. When you have finished, we will proofread and revise your version. (*NOTE:* The following is a sample rewriting of the pledge.)

A Citizen's Pledge

Name ______________________

Pretend you are an immigrant. Could you become a citizen? Read the following list of requirements. Which thing(s) would keep you from becoming a citizen today?

To become a citizen of the United States of America, an immigrant must

1. Be eighteen years old.
2. Have lived in the United States for at least five years.
3. Show that he understands the English language.
4. Obey all the laws of the United States.
5. Know something about the history of the United States.

When an immigrant can pass all those tests, he must make these promises:

I hereby declare, on oath, that I absolutely and entirely renounce and abjure all allegiance and fidelity to any foreign prince, potentate, state or sovereignty, to whom or which I have heretofore been a subject or citizen; that I will support and defend the Constitution and laws of the United States of America against all enemies, foreign and domestic; that I will bear true faith and allegiance to the same; that I will bear arms on behalf of the United States when required by the law; that I will perform noncombatant service in the armed forces of the United States when required by the law; that I will perform work of national importance under civilian direction when required by the law; and that I take this obligation freely without any mental reservations or purpose of evasion; so help me God.

Rewrite the promises in your own words.

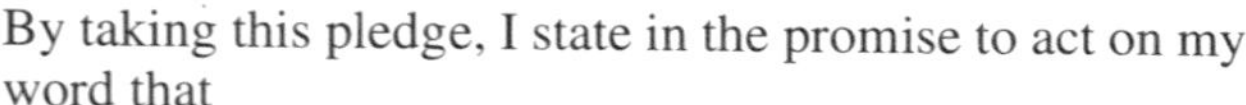
Heritage Studies 4
Student Notebook

Lesson 12
Teaching the Lesson
13

Learning the customs of a new country

After a time, immigrants became more comfortable in their new country. They began to think of home as the United States rather than the old country. No matter where they went, the children of immigrants became "American" more quickly than their parents. In schools and in the streets and playgrounds, children learned the language and ways of their new home.

Life was often not as easy as an immigrant had dreamed it would be. Even when an immigrant's life in America was not all he hoped for, it was better than it might have been in the old country. Few ever went back to their old homes, except to visit. All in all, they were glad they had made the decision to come to the land of liberty.

Ending the Flood

As more and more immigrants poured into the United States, Americans began to get worried. Land for farming was getting hard to find. Cities were crowded. And what if the new immigrants did not become "American"? Shouldn't America be for Americans? Perhaps, some thought, it is time to close the golden door.

47

By taking this pledge, I state in the promise to act on my word that

1. I completely give up all loyalty and faithfulness to any leader of another country where I have been a citizen.
2. I will stand behind the Constitution and the laws of the United States and will protect them against any enemies from other lands or here in this country.
3. I will show true faithfulness and loyal devotion to the Constitution and the laws of the United States.
4. I will be ready to fight with weapons for the United States when the law demands it.
5. I will do nonfighting work in an army of the United States when the law demands it.
6. I will do work important to the United States under orders from a citizen when the law demands it.
7. I accept the responsibilities of these promises without any doubts or thoughts of avoiding them.

➤ **Read aloud the wording of your pledge.**

➤ **Why do you think the American people wanted immigrants to agree with the things in the pledge?**

The last part of Step 3 on page 46—the child's writing of his own citizenship pledge—is an optional activity. He may choose to do this instead of copying his pledge explanation on the Notebook page for the Evaluating the Lesson section.

Day 3

Text Discussion, page 47

➤ **Read the first two paragraphs to find out who became "American" more quickly, children or parents.** *(children)*

➤ **Why do you think children might learn a new language and customs more quickly than their parents?**

In school, children read, hear, and speak English throughout the day. They are taught to understand what they hear and read. As they play, children become aware of and practice certain American expressions and customs. Children do not have the many years of language and custom "accumulation" that parents have.

➤ **As I read aloud the last paragraph on page 47, listen for the reasons Americans began to worry about immigration.** *(They worried about farmland being lost, cities becoming crowded, and immigrants not becoming "American.")*

People from all over still come to America.

Some Americans wanted to make laws that would keep more immigrants from coming. In 1882, laws were made that said criminals, people with mental handicaps, and anyone who could not take care of himself could not come in. Then people in California complained about the ways of the Chinese immigrants there. Soon a law said that no one could come to America from China. Every few years, a new law kept more people from coming. By 1924, almost no new immigrants were coming to America.

Today immigrants are again coming to America. They come from different places—South America, Mexico, and Asia. But they come for the same reasons that brought the very first immigrants. During the past two hundred years, about fifty million people have come to America. They left 140 different homelands searching for freedom or better opportunity in the New World.

Today's immigrants do not often come by boat. Most come by car or bus or plane. And they do not have to go through immigrant stations like Ellis Island. Instead, Ellis Island is a national monument. Hundreds of people visit Ellis Island each day. They remember their brave family members who came to a new home, a new hope, and a new life.

"Now the Lord had said unto Abram,
Get thee out of thy country,
and from thy kindred,
and from thy father's house,
unto a land that I will shew thee."
Genesis 12:1

48

➤ **What did some people think they should do about these concerns?** *(close the door to further immigration)*
➤ **Why does the author use the expression "golden door?"** *(Answers will vary. Remind your child of the last line in Emma Lazarus's poem on page 22.)*

Text Discussion, page 48

➤ **Read page 48 to find out why, by 1924, almost no new immigrants were coming to America.** *(Laws were made every few years, from 1882, to limit the number of immigrants.)*
➤ **From what places are immigrants coming to America today?** *(from South America, Mexico, and Asia)*
➤ **Why are the immigrants coming now?** *(for the same reasons that brought the first immigrants: to have a better life, to worship God as they believe they should, and to gain political freedom)*
➤ **How do immigrants come to America now?** *(mostly by car, bus, or airplane, though some still come by boat)*
➤ **What has happened to Ellis Island?** *(It is a national monument, not an immigrant station.) (NOTE:* For more of the history of Ellis Island, see the Additional Teacher Information section in Lesson 10 and student text page 311.)

Although some people visit Ellis Island because it is a tourist attraction, many people visit the island each day to remember their family members who came to America.

➤ **Why do you think those family members are referred to as "brave?"** It must have been very difficult for families to leave everything that they had known and to come to a new country.

Read aloud Genesis 12:1 from text page 48. God told Abram to leave his country. Abram was willing to do a hard thing because he wanted to obey God. In Canaan, the place where God led Abram, God built a great nation. (Bible Promise: I. God as Master)

Evaluating the Lesson

Notebook Activity, page 13

➤ On Notebook page 13, write a clean copy of the citizenship pledge which you wrote in your own words.
➤ Sing along with the recording as I play "America" from the listening cassette.

Going Beyond

Enrichment

Provide for your child red, white, and blue construction paper, scissors, self-adhesive stars, glue, felt-tip pens, and poster board. Encourage him to make a small copy of the American flag. Remind him to be careful to include the correct number and arrangement of stars and stripes.

Additional Teacher Information

Naturalization, the process by which a person becomes a citizen of an adopted country, involves three steps. A person must first apply to the Immigration and Naturalization Service. Along with an application, he must submit a fingerprint card and biographical information.

The second step involves the applicant's proving his qualifications for citizenship. The person must be eighteen years old and must have lived in the United States for the previous five years. He must prove that he has lived by certain moral standards during those years and has been loyal to American principles of government during the previous ten years. Except for certain elderly applicants, every person applying for citizenship must read, write, and speak English and show that he has a basic knowledge of American history and government.

The last step is the final hearing, held after a judge has decided to grant citizenship to the applicant. The person takes the loyalty oath, receives certificates of naturalization, and is declared a citizen.

3 LESSONS 13-18

American Voices

This chapter focuses on the immigrants' journey from their homeland to America. One of the major adjustments they encountered was learning a new language. Ridicule and prejudice made the immigrants' lives in America even more difficult. They were often disliked merely because they wore different clothes, ate different foods, and spoke another language. These differences have made America the country it is today—a pluralistic one. By studying how the early immigrants contributed to and influenced America and its culture, your child should gain a greater appreciation for his heritage, which sprang from the desire for the freedom and new life offered by the Land of Opportunity.

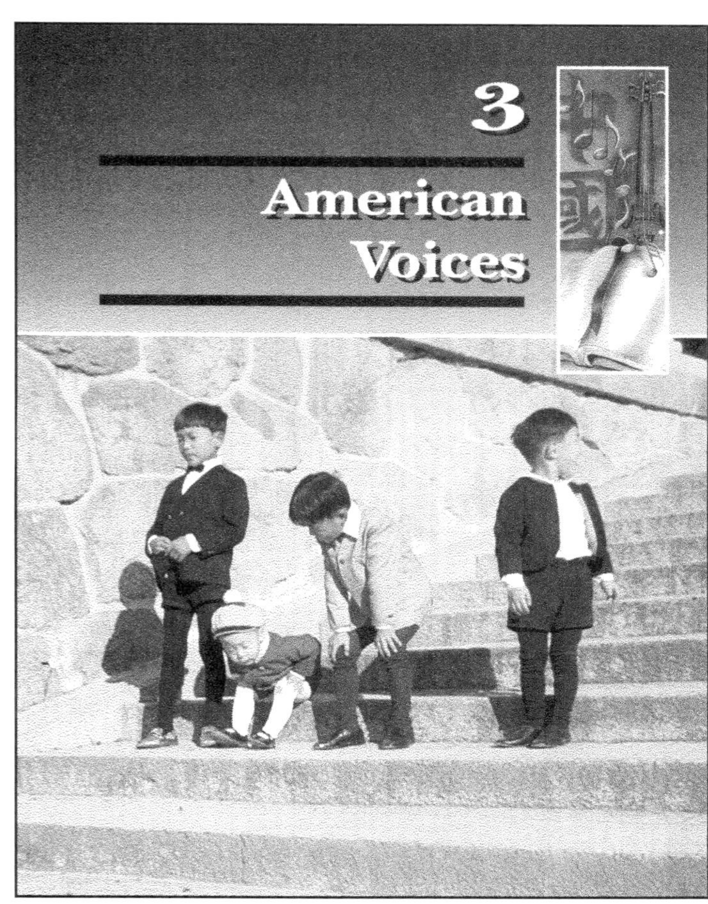

Materials

The following materials must be obtained or prepared before the presentation of the lesson. These items are labeled with an asterisk (*) in each lesson and in the Materials List in the Supplement. For further information see the individual lessons.

Lesson 16 offers the opportunity for your child to interview an immigrant. You may need extra time to make arrangements for this activity.

- Construction paper (Lesson 13)
- Appendix, pages A27-A28 (Lesson 14)
- Safety pins and hairpins (Lesson 14)
- A set of encyclopedias (Lesson 15)
- Appendix, page A29 (Lesson 17)
- Yarn or ribbon (Lesson 18)

Lesson 13
Living the Dream

Text, pages 50-51, 316-17
Notebook, page 14

Preview

Main Ideas

- Despite their different heritages, people in the United States share a common quest for freedom and opportunity.
- Upon coming to America, immigrants faced many changes.

Objectives

- Give reasons that America was appealing to many people from other lands
- Pantomime how language differences affected immigrants who came to the United States

Materials

- *Heritage Studies Listening Cassette B*
- An atlas with a world map
- 2 pieces of construction paper*
- A hole punch

Prepare the pieces of construction paper by punching three holes to align with holes punched in Notebook pages. The construction paper will be used to make a cover for a booklet.

Day 1

Lesson

Introducing the Lesson

Listening Activity

➤ *Play the German reading from the listening cassette, without explaining what is being read.*

➤ **Could you understand the recording?**

➤ **Do you know what language was being spoken?**

➤ **What do you think was being said?**

➤ **How did you feel listening to this speaker but not being able to understand the language?** *(Answers will vary; probably frustrated or confused)*

The reading was text page 50 being read in German. In this chapter we will discuss the adjustments immigrants faced, particularly the adjustments to a different language and customs.

People from All Over

Imagine for a moment that you live in a small village in Hungary about one hundred years ago. There are only a dozen houses there, forty cows, a few pigs, and some chickens. The land you live on was your grandfather's; the house you live in has only two rooms.

Then imagine what you think when someone returns to your village from America and tells you that there the trees have grown for a thousand years by the big ocean and have gotten to be one hundred feet around. Think how your heart pounds when he tells about gold mines where men get rich as kings in a single day and how your mind races when he says that Americans in a place called Texas own ranches fifty times bigger than your whole village.

And then imagine your surprise when you hear that in that far-off America one can go up to the president and shake his hand. Incredible! But suddenly you begin to think that perhaps you could go to America too. And once you were there, you could become more than you had ever hoped. The idea gets bigger and bigger in your heart, until one day, you decide you have to go; you have to become an American.

50

Teaching the Lesson

Text Discussion, pages 50 and 316-17

➤ **Follow along as I read page 50 aloud.**

➤ *Point out Hungary on the map on pages 316-17 or a world map in the atlas.*

➤ Point to America on the map. **How far do you think it is from Hungary to America?**

Part of the hardship involved in emigrating was traveling such great distances to an unknown part of the world.

➤ Give at least two reasons that America appealed to people from other countries. *(rumors of wealth, vast amount of land available to anyone, more freedom)*

➤ Compare the old way of life in Hungary to the new life in America. *(In Hungary the villages were smaller, families had been there for generations, and the way of living was modest-to-poor. Rumors held that America was full of gold, land, and opportunity.)*

➤ **Why do you think it was hard for people to leave their homeland?**

➤ **Have you ever heard someone tell stories of a distant place that made you want to visit there?** Many people heard about America this way and decided to move there.

Immigrants arriving at Ellis Island, hoping to start a new life

In many villages, cities, and farms all over the world, men and women, boys and girls had much the same idea. They saved their money, sold their houses, and said good-bye to all that was familiar—customs, family, friends, language, and even food. And they set off for America from Turkey, from China, from Poland, from Russia, from Scotland, from Greece, from France, from Norway, from Mexico, from everywhere. Once they passed through customs at Ellis Island in New York or a few other places, these newcomers found that being in America was not all grandeur and gold.

The first problem was always the language. Few of the immigrants could speak much English. Those who could speak it usually did so with an accent. The way immigrants spoke often made them targets for ridicule and the subjects of jokes. Many times it kept them from getting jobs. What do you think the immigrants did about this serious problem?

Learning English

A boy from Turkey arrived at Ellis Island when he was eleven. His father and mother did not speak English; neither did he. He had not been able to go to school in his homeland because there was a war going on there. Once in America and in school, he began to learn some English words. That is not to say that he had an easy time—older boys teased him, and boys his own age picked fights with him because he dressed differently and because his accent was thick. How do you think you would have treated him?

51

Day 2

Map Activity, pages 316-17

- Look at the world map on pages 316-17 or in the atlas.
- Find these countries on the map: Turkey, China, Poland, Russia, Greece, France, Norway, and Mexico.

Long ago people started to immigrate to America from these countries and others as well.

Text Discussion, page 51

- **Read page 51 to find out one of the first problems immigrants faced when coming to the new land.** *(the language)*
- Name other changes the immigrants had to get used to. *(different customs, food, clothing)*
- A ***barrier*** is something that holds back or stops movement or passage. **What do you think a *language barrier* is?** It is the differences in language that hinder communication.
- **How did immigrants from all of these countries contribute to the language barrier in America?** *(The more languages brought into the United States, the harder the communication process became.)*
- Name some of the specific problems that resulted from the language barrier. *(The immigrants were teased and found it hard to find jobs.)*
- Define the word ***ridicule.*** *(to make fun of, to laugh at, to mock)*
- **How were some immigrant children treated by the other students in school?** *(They were teased because of their different clothes and accents; they did not fit in.)*

Ask your child how he treats others who are different from himself. Remind him that Christians should show love to everyone, regardless of who the person is or what he looks like. Encourage your child to be friendly to others and to make newcomers feel welcome. (BATs: 5a Love, 5e Friendliness)

Evaluating the Lesson

Booklet Cover Activity

You will be making a booklet about the early immigrants, examining the experiences the immigrants had when they sought to fulfill their American dream. Throughout this chapter, you will be adding Notebook pages to your booklet.

- *Give your child two pieces of construction paper for the front and back of his booklet.* Write the title "Living the Dream" on the front of your booklet.
- Draw and decorate the front cover with any kind of travel theme such as a boat, a map or a globe, or the Statue of Liberty.

Keep your child's completed Notebook pages in between the construction-paper cover until Lesson 18, during which he will bind together all the Notebook pages to complete his booklet.

Homelands Name ______________________

Choose a country to be your "homeland." Fill in the blanks and then draw in the boxes things you like about your homeland and things in America that attract you.

My country is ______________ on the continent of ______________.

HOMELAND AMERICA

On the lines provided, write a brief paragraph explaining your drawings.

Heritage Studies 4 Student Notebook Lesson 13 Evaluating the Lesson 14

Notebook Activity, page 14

➤ Read the instructions on Notebook page 14.

➤ Complete the page. You may refer to the world map on pages 316-17 to help in choosing your country.

Going Beyond

Enrichment

Give your child the figures of people in ethnic costumes representing different countries (Appendix, pages A25-A26). Allow him to color the figures and add them to his "Living the Dream" booklet.

Additional Teacher Information

Schools have not always tried to accommodate immigrant children as they do today. Because of the language barrier, immigrant children were at first placed in the regular classes, but with the younger children. It was not uncommon to see a twelve year old in the midst of second graders. If the immigrant child progressed in his learning, particularly in learning English, he was promoted. Eventually, special classes were created to help these immigrant children adjust and learn.

It was not unusual for immigrant children to drop out of school to work full-time. Finishing grammar school was considered a great accomplishment. It is the school system, however, that introduced these immigrant children to the American way of life. In school, the new students learned about the heroes, folklore, manners, and customs of the United States. These children became a bridge between the old country with its customs and the new, very different America.

LESSON 14
Helping One Another

Text, pages 52-53
Notebook, page 15

Preview

Main Ideas

- Individuals have unique attributes and skills.
- People have needs, feelings, interests, and preferences.
- Prejudice is unfair and harmful.
- Jane Addams reached out in kindness to immigrants.

Objectives

- Recognize situations that show prejudice
- Write a paragraph on why Jane Addams is admirable
- Find hidden words in a puzzle

Materials

- 2 crib-sized bed sheets, towels, pieces of cloth, or women's long rectangular scarves
- Some safety pins and some hairpins*
- Appendix, page A27: a man in ethnic costume*
- Appendix, page A28: a woman in ethnic costume*
- The figure of Jane Addams (1889) from the Time-Line Snapshots

Day 1

Lesson

The Coloring Activity and the Dress-Up Activity found in the Introducing the Lesson section discuss ethnic costumes for a man and a woman. You may choose to do both coloring pages and dress-up activities, or you may choose to do the one that corresponds to your child's gender.

Introducing the Lesson

Dress-Up Activity

➤ *Help your child "dress-up" with the turban or the veil, or try on both.*

To make a turban, fold the sheet or towel in half lengthwise and wrap it loosely around the head and then over the head again. Tuck the ends in. You may use a procedure similar to wrapping your head with a towel after shampooing your hair. Pin the ends to the top if necessary to hold the turban in place.

To make the veil, simply drape the scarf over the head and loosely place one end over the face and then the shoulder. Use hairpins if necessary to keep the scarf on the head.

You may want to allow your child to wear one of the unusual head coverings during the lesson.

➤ **Would people wearing clothing such as this look normal in your community?** *(probably not)* **Why?** *(They would stand out in a crowd and look different from everyone else.)*

When the first immigrants came to America, differences such as these in clothing and language made some people dislike the immigrants.

➤ **Do these seem like good reasons not to like someone?**

Remind your child that we are to love all people, regardless of their clothing, their language, or their nationality. Jesus set the example when He showed love to the poor, the tax collectors, and the sick. (BAT: 5a Love)

Coloring Activity

➤ *Give your child the page of the man in ethnic costume, the page of the woman in ethnic costume, or both pages.*

➤ Color the picture(s).

➤ **Read the paragraph(s) and fill in the blanks.**

➤ Place the page(s) between the covers of your booklet.

Immigrant children (and some adults) learned English in schools like this one.

To dislike someone without knowing anything about him is to be *prejudiced.* Many Americans have felt such unjust dislike directed at them. And even some who have felt prejudice from others have been prejudiced themselves. Why do you think some people dislike those whom they do not know?

Some of the other students helped the new boy. At recess, they pointed out objects and repeated the English words for them over and over: *chair, window, shoes, collar, cat.* Soon, because he was bright and because he really tried hard, the Turkish boy learned the language of his new home. His father was learning a little English too at his job as a dishwasher in a big restaurant. But his mother stayed inside the room they rented and did not learn the new speech.

Some schools had special classes for students who knew little English. And there were classes at night for adults who needed help with the new language. But mostly people picked up the American way of talking by being with others in the neighborhood.

52

◆ FAMOUS PEOPLE ◆

Jane Addams and Lillian Wald
(1860-1935) (1867-1940)

Jane Addams

Although many Americans were unkind to new immigrants (forgetting that all but Native Americans were immigrants or descendants of immigrants), others tried hard to help.

Jane Addams, a woman with a kind heart and a good mind, decided that it was not only wrong but harmful to everyone for immigrants to be treated badly. She thought that helping them become "Americanized" would make the whole country stronger. How do you think that might be true?

Addams started a center for helping immigrants, Hull House, in Chicago in 1889. Hull House ran nurseries for small children whose mothers worked, offered English classes as well as other classes, provided instruction in cleanliness and housekeeping skills, and even gave music and art lessons. Why do you think Hull House had so many services?

Hull House

Other cities also started *settlement houses,* such as the Henry Street settlement in New York, run by Lillian Wald. All the settlements were staffed by volunteers. But as hard as they worked, they could not do all that was needed. So Jane Addams and others pushed for the government to help. Before long, New Jersey, New York, Massachusetts, and California were providing classes in English, hygiene, and American history.

53

Day 2

Teaching the Lesson

Text Discussion, page 52

➤ **Read the last paragraph on page 51 again to refresh your memory about the boy from Turkey.**

➤ **Read page 52 to find out how most immigrants learned to speak English.** *(by being with others in the neighborhood)*

➤ **What do you think the word *prejudice* means?**

Some ***prejudice*** is disliking a person without really knowing anything about him or her. Some people show prejudice against others because they do not like others who are different from themselves.

➤ I am going to read several situations. Tell me whether the situation demonstrates prejudice or kindness.

- Sue Chang brought chopsticks in her lunch box. Other children on the field trip laughed and said, "This is America. We use forks here. You need to use them too if you want to be a real American." *(prejudice)*
- Romero had just come to America from Mexico. He did not know much English. When the coach instructed the team to put on their gloves, Romero looked at a boy nearby and shrugged his shoulders. The boy, John, smiled and pointed to his glove. "Glove," he said, still smiling. *(kindness)*
- Camille recently came to America from Holland. At a birthday party, the other children would not let her play tag because she had on funny wooden shoes. They said she needed "real" shoes if she wanted to play. *(prejudice)* (BAT: 5a Love)

Text Discussion, page 53

➤ **Read the first paragraph on page 53 to find out which group of people has been in America the longest.** *(Native Americans)*

➤ **What do we call all other people who came to America?** *(immigrants)*

It is unfair for Americans to be unkind to new immigrants because everyone other than the Native Americans either immigrated to America or descended from immigrants.

➤ Although many Americans mistreated immigrants, there were some who befriended them. **Read the rest of page 53 to find out the name of one lady who helped immigrants.** *(Jane Addams)*

➤ **What does the text mean when it says that Jane Addams wanted to help the immigrants to become "Americanized"?** *(adapted or adjusted to* *the American way of living—becoming a part of the American culture)*

➤ **What seemed to motivate Jane Addams to help the people around her?** *(She thought that by helping others she could improve the entire country.)*

➤ **How do you think a person can make a country stronger by helping others?**

Being kind to one another helps to build unity and joins communities together. When people work toward a common goal and show that they care, everyone's attitude improves.

> Remind your child that Christians are to serve others as Jesus Christ served. Allow him to give ways in which we can serve people in our church, in our neighborhood, and even at home. (BAT: 2b Servanthood)

➤ **What do you think a *settlement house* was?**

It was a home, often located in the midst of slums or tenements, where immigrants could get help.

➤ **Why was the government needed to help with these settlement houses?** *(The population of the poor and needy far exceeded the number of settlement houses.)*

➤ **When and where was Hull House established?** *(1889 in Chicago)*

➤ **What did the workers at Hull House do to help people?** *(ran nurseries for working mothers, taught English classes, taught valuable housekeeping and cleanliness skills, gave lessons in music and art)*

➤ **Why did Hull House offer so many different services?** *(People have different needs, and Jane Addams wanted to help as many people as possible.)*

> Remind your child that Christians should be kind and giving because they are to reflect Christ in all that they do. Invite him to name ways in which he can be giving to others. (BATs: 5a Love, 5b Giving)

TimeLine Snapshots Activity

➤ Place the figure of Jane Addams on the TimeLine at 1889.

➤ **What did Jane Addams do in 1889?** *(established Hull House in Chicago)*

Jane Addams Name ____________________

In a few sentences, tell what you admire about Jane Addams.

Find and circle the listed words in the puzzle.

Jane Addams	Hull House	prejudice
Chicago	immigrant	settlement houses
helping	learning	Lillian Wald
Henry Street		

```
I X O L I L L I A N W A L D E J
J M T E R O P R E J U D I C E A
H S M Z A C Q P G I X V R U L N
U H U I N U H O Y F L B U W O E
L A Y B G I B I X G I A K O F A
L M I O Q R Y N C O N Z O R Y D
H J L P O F A L P A Q I R G I D
O P O L E A R N I N G J P A M A
U Q L A F J O R T I S O R L D M
S E T T L E M E N T H O U S E S
E T A B O D L I K F E Z Y I X H
A H E N R Y S T R E E T E R O S
```


Heritage Studies 4 Student Notebook — Lesson 14 Evaluating the Lesson — 15

Evaluating the Lesson

Notebook Activity, page 15

➤ Read the instructions on Notebook page 15.

➤ Complete the page.

➤ Add the page to your booklet.

Going Beyond

Enrichment

Give your child one sheet of white poster board, crayons, scissors, yarn, a stapler, and a hole punch. Tell him to draw or trace a circle in pencil on his poster board. (*NOTE:* The circle needs to have a 15" diameter.) Tell him to color the circle, using brown colors to make his coloring look like a basket weave. When he has finished coloring, allow him to cut out the circle. Cut a slit to the center of the circle, overlapping the sides and stapling the two edges so that the hat has a cone shape. Punch holes on opposite sides of the cone to loop a piece of yarn through. Tie each end of the yarn in a knot to keep it from slipping through the hole. The string should hang loosely yet fit around the chin to hold the hat on. Explain that many people from Asian countries and the Pacific Islands wear this type of hat to protect their heads from the hot sun.

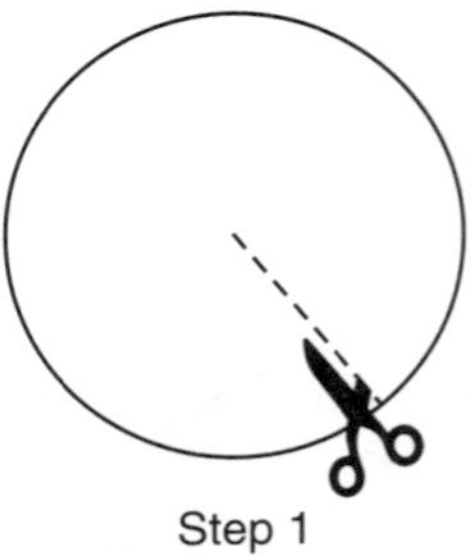

Step 1

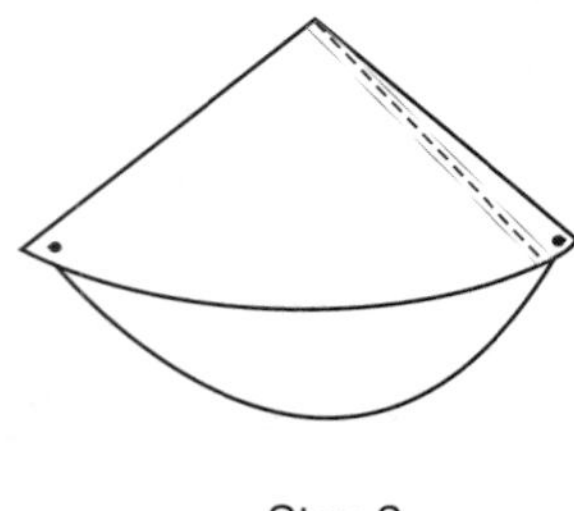

Step 2

Additional Teacher Information

At an early age, Jane Addams learned the values of integrity and kindness from her father, a prestigious statesman in Illinois. Jane dedicated her life to helping people who lived in the Chicago slums surrounding Hull House as well as people around the world.

Jane became inspired when she saw an English settlement house, Toynbee Hall, where young Englishmen were educating poor people around them. She was greatly impressed that the men actually lived in the midst of the people with whom they worked. Using her substantial inheritance, Jane and a friend, Dr. Ellen Starr, bought Hull House in 1889. They moved in with the idea of starting a settlement house in the Chicago slum. That was merely the beginning of what became a lifelong work. Jane and her friends helped many of Chicago's poor, particularly needy immigrants. Her work was not limited to the slums of Chicago. In Washington, D.C., she lobbied for governmental aid and even attended conferences in Europe, where she championed world peace.

In 1931, Jane Addams won the Nobel Peace Prize and donated the money to charity. One newspaper columnist, Walter Lippman, wrote this tribute to Jane Addams: "She had compassion without condescension, and a pity without a retreat into vulgarity. She had infinite sympathy for common things without forgetfulness of those that are uncommon. That, I think, is why those who have known her say that she was not only good, but great."

LESSON 15
New Experiences

Text, pages 54-57, 316-17
Notebook, pages 16-17

Preview

Main Ideas

- Many different people and groups have contributed to American culture.
- Many of the immigrants had to make difficult adjustments in America.
- The language barrier affected the immigrants' social interactions.
- Many of the foods Americans enjoy today were introduced by the immigrants.

Objectives

- Use encyclopedias to compare a state in the U.S. to a foreign country
- Solve riddles about food from other countries
- Identify and locate on a map the continent from which a favorite food originated

Materials

- A cookbook
- A world map in an atlas (optional)
- A set of encyclopedias*

Day 1

Lesson

Introducing the Lesson

Cookbook Activity

➤ Let's look through the cookbook and find recipes for ethnic foods that have been associated with or passed on from other countries.

➤ **Were you able to find more than one recipe?** We get many of our foods from other places.

You may want to have your child try out one of the simpler recipes with you.

A young man named Leon Surmelian, from Armenia, arrived in New York with little money but much hope. He had been given a train ticket to Kansas, where he was wanting to go to college. On the train he bought a bag of peanuts and a Coca-Cola. He thought the drink had a "peculiar taste," but drinking it made him "feel more American."

Two days later, Surmelian arrived in Kansas and took a taxi to the college campus. He set out to find the vice president. He showed a student the vice president's name on the letter he carried, and the student took him to the right office. Surmelian pretended to know English, but soon had to admit he did not. The man asked Surmelian whether he could speak German. Surmelian said no. But he could speak French. The vice president sent for the French teacher. Now Surmelian could communicate, but the news was not good.

He was too late to get a job to pay for his schooling. He had to live in a basement and sweep floors. He worked hard all that winter, living at first on only bread and cheese and water. The next summer, he went to work on a farm. In a book he wrote much later, after graduating from the University of Kansas, he tells how his desire to be an American came alive again that summer.

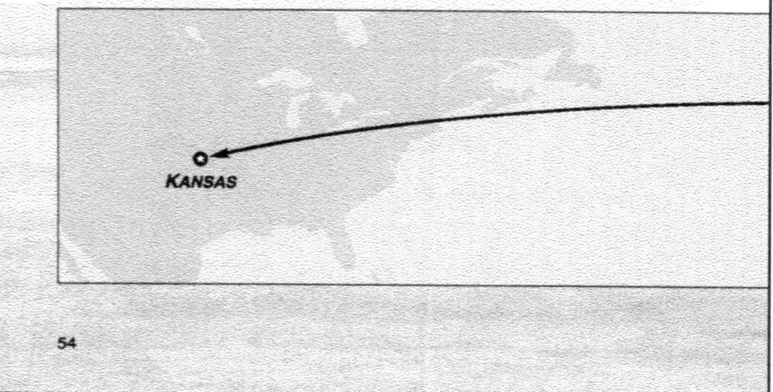

54

Early the next morning I began my apprenticeship on an American farm, wearing overalls. In them I felt like an American. Harry and I went to the pasture to bring in the cows. It was a golden June morning. The young corn crackled in the breeze, and the orchard was ablaze with ripe sour cherries. I was in secret rapture over those cherry trees.

"Do you know," I said to Harry, who majored in horticulture, "cherries come from a place near my hometown, from Cerasus, or Kerasund, on the Black Sea. That's why they're called cherries."

He was surprised.

"And do you know the scientific name of the apricot?"

"No," he said.

"*Prunus armeniaca.* Armenian prune. Oh, a lot of other fruits from my country! Chestnuts, for example. The English word chestnut is derived from the Armenian word *kaskeni,* which means chestnut tree."

A little brook ran through the pasture, where I saw blackberry and gooseberry bushes. To complete this miraculous picture, a spring flowed from under a rock through a narrow wooden trough, with a leaf dangling from its end! I wondered if I was dreaming. . . .

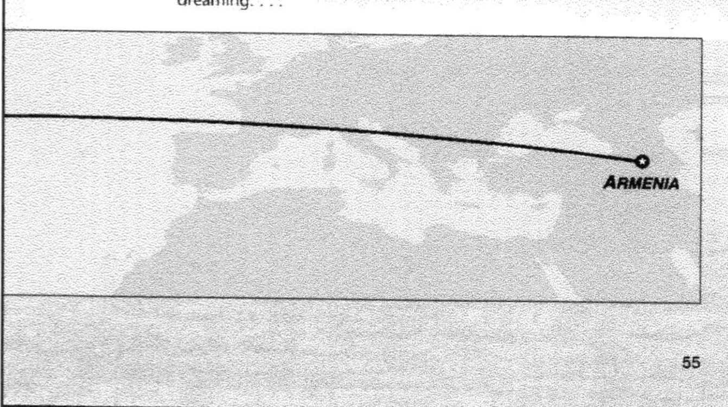

55

Teaching the Lesson

Text Discussion, pages 54-55

- ➤ **Read the first paragraph on page 54 to find out where Leon Surmelian wanted to go.** *(Kansas)*
- ➤ Look at the map on pages 54-55. Estimate the distance from Armenia to Kansas from this map or the world map in the atlas.
- ➤ **How do you think Leon might have felt about traveling all that way from his homeland to America?** *(scared, excited)*
- ➤ **Why do you think that the Coca-Cola had a "peculiar taste"?** *(This was the first time Leon had ever tasted the drink, and it probably tasted different from anything else he had ever had.)*
- ➤ **How could drinking Coca-Cola make Leon "feel more American"?** *(By drinking an American beverage, he probably felt as though he were doing what everyone else was doing, and so he felt more like the other Americans around him.)*

State/Country Data Sheet

Name ______________________

Research with a partner the state and country assigned to you by your teacher. Fill in the information below. Draw and color the flag of each place.

State ______________________

Capital ______________________

Agriculture ______________________

Manufacturing ______________________

Mining ______________________

Climate: summer ______________________

winter ______________________

First people to live in the area ______________________

Country ______________________

Capital ______________________

Agriculture ______________________

Manufacturing ______________________

Mining ______________________

Climate: summer ______________________

winter ______________________

First people to live in the area ______________________

Heritage Studies 4 Student Notebook — Lesson 15 Teaching the Lesson — 16

Encyclopedia Activity, Notebook page 16

The following activity will give your child experience using resources such as the encyclopedia. If your child has not had experience using an encyclopedia, give him help by asking questions to lead him in finding the information that he needs. (Which encyclopedia will have the information you need? Look at the main topics. Look at the charts. What do the maps tell you?)

- ➤ Choose a foreign country and a state, such as Armenia and Kansas.
- ➤ Use a set of encyclopedias to fill in the information about the country and the state on Notebook page 16. You may find some of the information about the state you chose on text pages 280-305.
- ➤ Draw and color the flags for each area researched.
- ➤ When the page has been completed, add it to your booklet.

Day 2

Text Discussion, page 54 (cont.)

- ➤ **Read the last two paragraphs on page 54 to find out what language Leon could speak.** *(French)*
- ➤ **What hopes did Leon probably have about coming to America?** *(a different way of life, better education)*
- ➤ **Why did Leon pretend that he could speak English when he went to the college?** *(He wanted to be accepted to study there.)*
- ➤ **What did Leon do that proved he really wanted to go to college?** *(He lived in a basement, swept floors, and ate only bread, cheese, and water in order to save money to pay for schooling.)*

Leon worked hard to reach his goal of going to college. He was willing to do what was necessary to pay his bills. Remind your child that God expects us to work hard and to fulfill our responsibilities. A Christian's main goal in working hard, however, should be to please the Lord. (BATs: 2e Work, 3a Self-concept)

Text Discussion, pages 55 and 316-17

An ***apprenticeship*** is the process by which a person learns a trade by working for a skilled craftsman. He usually works for a very small salary because he is learning a skill from a professional.

- ➤ **What type of apprenticeship would you like to try?**

Two pronunciations to help you as read the story on page 55 are Cerasus (sĕr´ ə səs) and Kerasund (kĕr ə sün´).

- ➤ On page 55 Leon begins to tell us of his first summer day as an apprentice on the farm. **Follow along as I read page 55 aloud.**
- ➤ **How did wearing overalls make Leon feel like an American?** *(Overalls were associated with the American farmer, so they made him feel like an American.)*

Harry studied ***horticulture,*** the "study or art of growing vegetables, fruits, or other plants."

- ➤ **Why did Leon become excited about the cherry trees?** *(because his homeland, Armenia, produces many cherries)*
- ➤ Leon said the "cherries come from a place near my hometown, from Cerasus or Kerasund, on the Black Sea." Find the Black Sea on the world map on pages 316-17 or in the atlas.
- ➤ Name the three food items that Leon said came from Armenia. *(cherries, apricots, and chestnuts)*
- ➤ **How do you know that Leon was proud of his Armenian heritage?** *(because he was excited to tell Harry about all the foods Americans get from his country)*

It was an excellent breakfast they served when we finished milking—grapefruit, bran flakes and cream, home-cured ham and eggs, fresh country butter, homemade bread, good hot coffee. Mr. Schultz said grace, thanking God for His many blessings—the God of America. Yes, America seemed to have a different God, a more generous one. . . .

A field had to be plowed, and I begged Harry to let me do it. What a thing of beauty and precision the modern steel plow was! Harry showed me how to cut furrows of uniform depth and width, turning the surface completely under.

A no less heroic task was pitching hay in the afternoon. This was sheer poetry. True, my hands became blistered, my face, neck, and shoulders sunburned and the blue shirt on my back wringing wet with perspiration. . . . But I exulted in the powerful heat of the earth, in the dust and odor of alfalfa hay.

By nightfall I was dead tired, with a fine fatigue.

Something important had happened to me, but I did not know how to word it, not even to myself. Somehow I felt as if the earth and sun of Kansas flowed through my veins, that I had suddenly become an American. . . .

What is it makes nations? Language, history, traditions, political organizations? These are contributing factors, yes; but fundamentally it is the land . . . with dandelions and moonlight and crickets and the crackling of young corn.

56

Like Surmelian, many new Americans found that not knowing English gave them a bad start. A French girl was invited to a tea party. She knew only one English word—*yes*. A lady at the party asked her whether her clothes were like what the girls were wearing in France. "Yes," she said. Then the lady asked her what kind of hats they were wearing. "Yes," she said. The lady, puzzled, asked again about the hats, what sort of trims they had on them. "Yes," said the girl. The lady, thinking the girl was being rude, asked her, "Do you think I'm stupid?" The girl, still smiling brightly, said, "Yes." Another woman rescued the girl and told her she must start learning English right away!

Keeping Customs

Like Surmelian, many Americans also wanted familiar things in the new country to comfort them and to make them feel at home. Most people liked to have some of the food they were used to. Italian settlers brought lasagna and a round, hard bread. The Greeks made pita bread; the Austrians made croissants. Today Americans eat these foods often; but before 1900, the foods from other countries were looked on with as much suspicion as the people.

Breads from many countries are popular in America.

57

Day 3

Text Discussion, page 56

➤ **Read page 56 to find out what Leon said truly makes a nation.** *(the land)*

➤ **What do you think Leon meant when he said, "Yes, America seemed to have a different God, a more generous one"?**

The land in America was so rich and fertile, compared to his home country, that it seemed as if God had been more generous to the United States than to Armenia.

➤ **What kind of person did Mr. Schultz seem to be?** *(He seemed to be a man who respected and honored the Lord and was thankful for God's blessings.)*

➤ **Why did Leon want Harry to let him do the plowing?** *(Leon wanted to use the modern steel plow because it was a new tool to him.)*

➤ **What do you think the word *furrows* means?**

It is the long, narrow cuts or grooves made in the ground by a plow or other tool.

➤ Explain why Leon described his hard work as a "heroic task," "sheer poetry," and "fine fatigue." *(Working hard in this American soil made Leon feel like a true American, and he really enjoyed the work and the feeling of being part of America.)*

➤ **How do you think the land makes a place a nation?**

The land determines the jobs of the people, the types of lifestyles, the wealth, and even the health of a nation. All of these factors are influenced by the resources a nation's land offers.

Text Discussion, page 57

➤ **Read page 57 to find out some common foods Americans eat that come from other countries.** *(lasagna, pita bread, and croissants)*

➤ **How did not being able to speak English cause the French girl to say the wrong thing?** *(Because she did not know how to speak or understand English, people thought she was being rude and insulting.)*

➤ **Why did Americans not immediately accept the different foods the immigrants brought with them?** *(They were suspicious of both the people and their foods because they were different from what most Americans were used to.)*

Remind your child that even though people are different and make different choices than we would, they are not necessarily bad or wrong. Remind him that God made each person to be a unique individual. (BAT: 3a Self-concept)

Foreign Foods Name ______________________

Solve the riddles and write the name of the food on the line provided.

hot dog wonton pizza sandwich hamburger

wonton 1. I am the Chinese version of a dumpling. I am meat in a noodle-dough wrapper. Some people like me fried, but others like me served in soup.

hot dog 2. I am named after Frankfurt, Germany. I was first made during the Middle Ages. About 1900 an American food seller called me a "hot dachshund sausage" because I looked like the long body of those small dogs.

sandwich 3. I was named after a certain earl from England during the 1700s. He was playing cards when he wanted something to eat. He ordered a servant to bring him a piece of roast meat between two slices of bread. Today, many children take me to school in their lunches.

pizza 4. I was born in Italy. My name is the Italian word for pie. Some like me with pepperoni and some with extra cheese.

hamburger 5. I came from Germany too. I was originally called a Hamburg steak. Many people today consider me to be an American food because so many fast-food restaurants serve me.

In the box, draw a picture of your favorite food and then write the name of the country in which that food originated. You may need to use an encyclopedia or another research source to find out where your food came from.

Evaluating the Lesson

Notebook Activity, page 17

➤ Read the instructions on Notebook page 17.

➤ Complete the page.

Your child may not know what a wonton, the answer to the first riddle, is. Encourage him to work the other riddles and come back to the first question. He should be able to find the answer by process of elimination.

➤ Place the completed page in your "Living the Dream" booklet.

Going Beyond

Enrichment

Provide a wooden skewer or long party toothpick, plus four large marshmallows, six small, colored marshmallows, and one red or black licorice stick cut into small pieces for your child. Explain that we get shish kebabs from the country of Turkey, where they are made with cooked meat and vegetables. Tell your child that he may make "candy kebabs." He may want to alternate the marshmallows and licorice on the skewer to make the kebabs more decorative.

Additional Teacher Information

Much of American culture, custom, and food is borrowed from other countries. Pretzels were first made in southern Europe as a reward for good students who learned their prayers. The crossed pieces represent praying hands. Shish kebabs originated in Turkey and consist of grilled, skewered pieces of lamb, tomatoes, peppers, and onions.

In an interesting reversal, many of the Native Americans introduced new foods to those first Europeans who immigrated to the New World. These new foods included avocados, chocolate, corn, peanuts, peppers, pineapples, sweet and white potatoes, squash, and tomatoes. Eventually they were introduced into Europe from the New World.

LESSON 16
Blending Cultures

Text, pages 58-61, 314-15
Notebook, page 18

Preview

Main Ideas

- People in neighborhoods may share languages, traditions, and customs.
- Individuals have unique attributes and skills.
- Immigrants bring different traditions with them, creating a pluralistic America.

Objectives

- Use a dictionary to find the etymologies of words
- Create questions for an interview with an immigrant
- Conduct an interview

Materials

- A dictionary

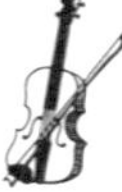

The text pages are taught out of order in this lesson.

Day 1

Lesson

Introducing the Lesson

Learning How Activity, page 61

The *Learning How* Activity in this lesson is similar to the one in Lesson 9. In that lesson your child practiced interviewing after watching you model an interview. In this lesson he will write the questions and conduct an interview on his own. You will want to review the tips for interviewing from Lesson 9.

➤ **Read page 61 to find out what you will be doing in the *Learning How* Activity.**

➤ **Reread Step 1.**

➤ **What does it mean to become *Americanized*?** *(It means to become adapted or adjusted to the American way of living—to become a part of the American culture.)*

◆ LEARNING HOW ◆

Immigrants Came to the United States

1. Prepare a list of questions that you would like to ask an immigrant. Perhaps you would like to ask when the person learned to speak English or when he began to feel "Americanized." You may want to ask what customs from his old home he still keeps. Let your teacher read over your questions.

The Zoltán Gaal family immigrated to America from Hungary.

2. Ask an immigrant to let you interview him. If you do not know an immigrant, ask your teacher or your parents to help you. You may need to write a letter to the person if he lives far away.
3. After you get your answers, remember to write a thank-you note to the person. Then write about the person you met. When you report to the class, be prepared to show on a globe or map the country that was once home to the person you interviewed.

61

➤ Write a list of questions that you would like to ask an immigrant.

Be sure to include in your list questions about learning how to speak English, adjusting to different customs, and becoming Americanized.

➤ Let me read over your questions to help with any corrections.

The *Learning How* Activity will be completed in the Evaluating the Lesson section.

Many American immigrants like to dress as they did in their homelands.

Another thing people liked to bring with them from their old homes was *tradition*. A tradition is a practice or a belief that is handed down from generation to generation. Another word for *tradition* is *custom*. Italian people liked to eat fish on Christmas Eve. Germans liked to put up Christmas trees. The Chinese liked to shoot off fireworks to bring in their new year. Japanese people bowed to each other in greeting. In places like New York City, many different kinds of people lived close together, observing each other. Some traditions began to spread to other people. Can you think of any?

Most immigrants came from places where all the people dressed alike, spoke the same language, and had the same traditions. But in America, immigrants had to learn to get along with others who had different ideas and customs. Sometimes the clash led to new problems; sometimes it helped form a new *culture*. A culture is the way of life of the people who live in a certain place.

58

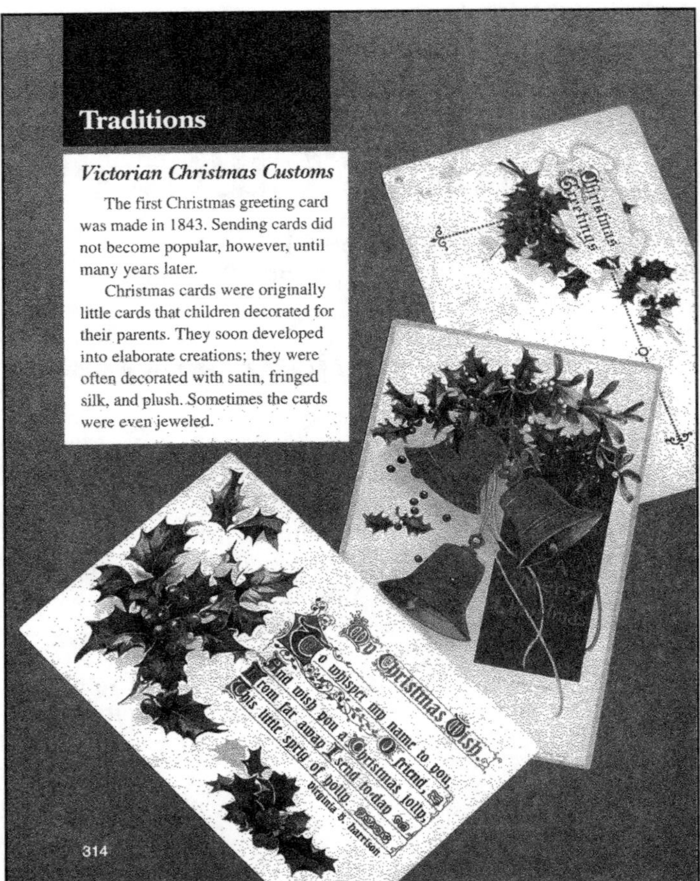

Traditions

Victorian Christmas Customs

The first Christmas greeting card was made in 1843. Sending cards did not become popular, however, until many years later.

Christmas cards were originally little cards that children decorated for their parents. They soon developed into elaborate creations; they were often decorated with satin, fringed silk, and plush. Sometimes the cards were even jeweled.

314

Teaching the Lesson

Day 2

Text Discussion, pages 58 and 314-15

➤ **Read the first paragraph on page 58 to find out the definition of *tradition*.** *("a practice or a belief that is handed down from generation to generation")*

America is a mixture of traditions that vary from one area of the country to the next or from one family to another.

➤ **Can you name one of our own family traditions?** *If your child cannot think of a tradition, help him by asking about Thanksgiving or Christmas traditions or other things that are unique to your family.*

➤ **Read pages 314-15 to learn the origin of some Christmas traditions.**

Discuss any traditions in your family that you have learned from other families or that have been passed down for many generations.

➤ **Read the second paragraph on page 58 to find the definition of *culture*.** *("the way of life of the people who live in a certain place")*

➤ **What do you think the word *neighborhood* means?** A neighborhood is made up of people who live in the same area or district.

➤ Tell about our neighborhood.

As immigrants moved to the United States, those from the same country, speaking the same language, often settled near one another. These immigrants formed a neighborhood in which the people shared similar backgrounds and traditions. In other neighborhoods, however, the immigrants were different from those around them. They had their own language and customs.

➤ **What do you think some of the problems might have been when two different types of people lived near one another?** Some disagreements probably occurred because the groups did not speak the same language.

➤ **How can new cultures be formed?** *(Sometimes the people in a neighborhood create a new custom or language by combining their own ways with the ways of others.)*

➤ **Do you think these same types of neighborhood problems occur today?**

Remind your child that God made all people. Each person is unique and special to Him. Although each person is different, all people, particularly Christians, should get along with others. (BATs: 3a Self-concept, 5a Love)

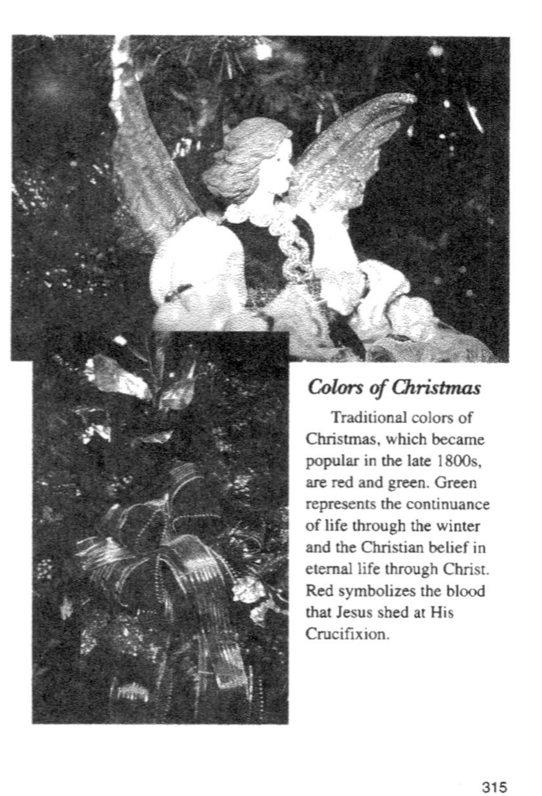

Colors of Christmas

Traditional colors of Christmas, which became popular in the late 1800s, are red and green. Green represents the continuance of life through the winter and the Christian belief in eternal life through Christ. Red symbolizes the blood that Jesus shed at His Crucifixion.

315

America has a *pluralistic culture*. What does that mean? *Plural* means "more than one." So a pluralistic culture is a way of life that has more than one way within it. If Japanese, German, Korean, Bulgarian, Welsh, Australian, and English people all live near each other in, say, California but keep many of their native customs, they form a pluralistic culture. They are all Americans, but they are all different from each other in many ways. How can this arrangement be good for a country? How can it be bad?

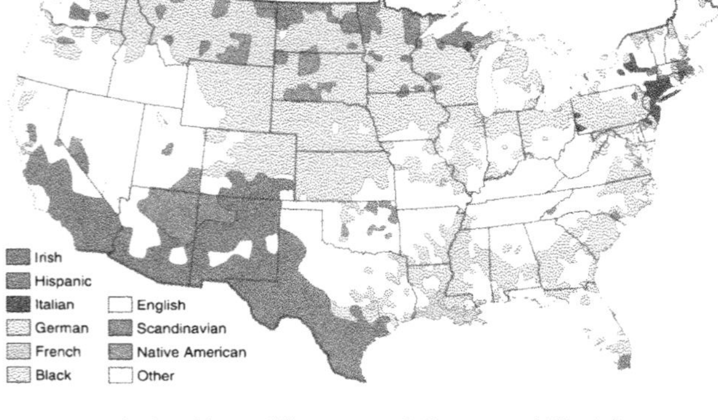

Look at this map. What groups settled in your area? What influences do you see from these people? Look in a telephone book for names that represent the group or groups of settlers who came to your area. What street and city names, foods, games, sayings, and traditions may the settlers have contributed?

59

Text Discussion, page 59

- ➤ **Read the first paragraph on page 59 to find what type of culture America has.** *(pluralistic)*
- ➤ **What do the words *singular* and *plural* mean?** (Singular *means "one" and* plural *means "more than one.")*
- ➤ **Read aloud from the text a definition of the term *pluralistic culture.*** *("a way of life that has more than one way within it")* It is one culture consisting of many different cultures.
- ➤ **How do you think a pluralistic culture could be good for a country?**

A pluralistic culture can allow for many different traditions and customs that offer a variety of rich experiences.

- ➤ **How do you think a pluralistic culture could be bad?**

A pluralistic culture could keep a country from being united and in harmony because there are too many differences. It can also be bad if the particular groups cling too closely to their own ways and do not care about the country as a whole.

Map Activity, page 59

- ➤ Look at the map on page 59.
- ➤ **Which groups settled in the Midwest?** *(mainly German and Scandinavian, but some Native Americans, Italian, and English)*
- ➤ **Which groups settled in the Southwest?** *(mainly Hispanics, Native Americans, and English)*
- ➤ **Which groups settled in the Southeast?** *(mainly Blacks or African Americans and English, but some French and Hispanics)*
- ➤ **Read aloud the last paragraph on page 59, answering the questions.**
- ➤ Name your favorite food or favorite subject.

Tell your child your favorite food or favorite subject. Everyone has different likes and dislikes even though we are part of the same family.

ECHOES IN HISTORY

Borrowing Words

An Old World food, now an American standard

Many words we use every day come from other languages. *Kindergarten*, for example, is German for "child garden." And when you eat a hamburger, you pay tribute to the German city the food came from—Hamburg.

Many of our cities, lakes, and rivers have names that are Native American: Tioga, Omaha, Susquehanna, and Huron, to name only a few. Other places and bodies of water have Spanish names: Colorado, Los Angeles, and Rio Grande.

When you say you want a cookie, you are using a word from Holland. When you point out New Orleans on the map, you find a city name from the French. When you talk about putting horses in a corral, you are using an African-derived word. Having goulash for supper? That is a Hungarian dish.

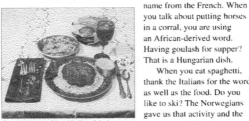

Spaghetti, a traditional Italian dish, is now a favorite in America.

When you eat spaghetti, thank the Italians for the word as well as the food. Do you like to ski? The Norwegians gave us that activity and the name we call it by. Browse through a dictionary and you will hear "echoes" of people who came before. Even the very name of our country, *America*, is an "echo" of the Italian name *Amerigo*.

60

Foreign Names

Name ______________________

Find Omaha and New Orleans and circle them in green. Find at least five other non-English names and circle them in red.

Answers in Teacher's Edition

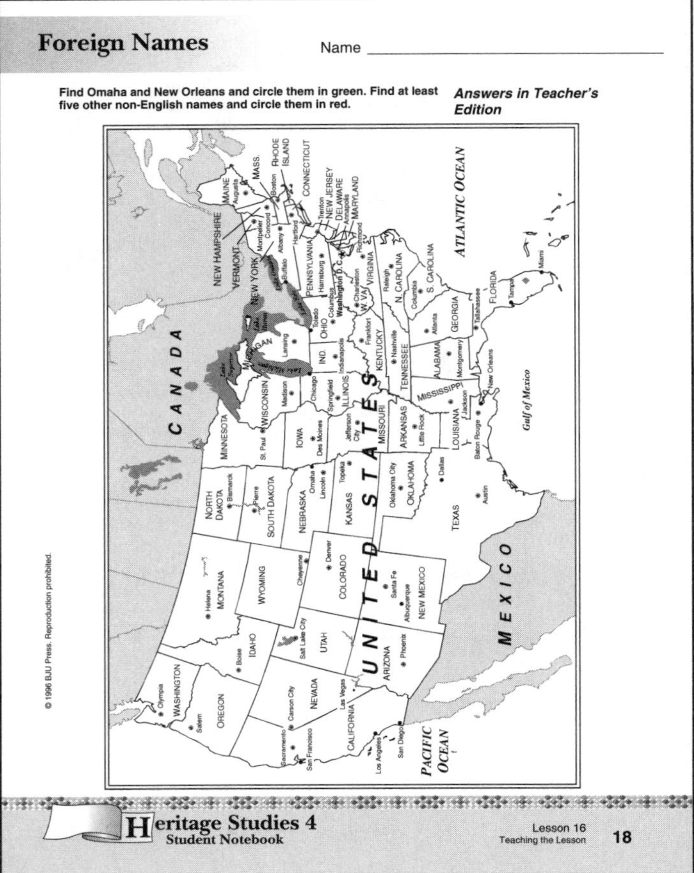

Heritage Studies 4 Student Notebook — Lesson 16 Teaching the Lesson 18

Text Activity, page 60 and Notebook page 18

- ➤ **Read page 60 to find out where the word *corral* comes from.** *(from Africa)*
- ➤ Study the map on the Notebook page 18 to find a few of the names mentioned in your text, such as Omaha and New Orleans.
- ➤ Circle these names in green.
- ➤ Find at least five foreign names other than those mentioned in the textbook, circling them in red. *(Los Angeles, Albuquerque, Toledo, Mississippi, San Diego, etc.)*
- ➤ Place Notebook page 18 in your booklet.

Dictionary Activity

> The etymology of a word is usually in brackets at the end of the dictionary entry.

- ➤ Write the word ***etymology.*** An etymology is the history of a word, including where it came from and how it got its present form and meaning.
- ➤ *Show your child the word* science *in the dictionary, demonstrating how to read the etymology of the word.*
- ➤ Find and read the etymology of these words: *dynamite, fix, parent,* and *work.*

Day 3

Evaluating the Lesson

Learning How Activity, page 61 (cont.)

- ➤ Conduct your interview.
- ➤ **After you have conducted your interview, read and follow Step 3 on page 61.**

Going Beyond

Enrichment

Explain to your child that a collage contains many pictures that may overlap somewhat. Give him magazines to be cut, newspapers, colored construction paper, scissors, and glue. Remind him that we get many different foods, names, and traditions from immigrants. Instruct your child to find pictures that represent some of the influences the immigrants brought to America. You may need to give him ideas such as different ethnic foods like tacos, chop suey, and pizza, or some foreign names like Garcia, Chung, and Pierre. Tell your child to cut out the pictures and/or words and glue them onto the construction paper, creating a collage.

Additional Teacher Information

The American culture has been influenced by countries around the world. Language, food, and tradition have all been influenced by the immigrants who moved to America over the years. One of the greatest traditions passed on through the ages is the celebration of Christmas. According to Dane legend, the holly branches were used to symbolize the crown of thorns placed on the Savior's head before His death. The red berries symbolize the drops of blood on His brow.

Some say that the tradition of sending Christmas cards began in England in 1846. Sir Henry Cole hired a printer to make copies of cards with a drawing of a sprig of holly or mistletoe and a few words to send to his friends. The printer thought he would experiment and made many copies to sell.

The tradition of the Christmas tree supposedly comes from Martin Luther in Germany. The story holds that while traveling home on December 24, he noticed the beauty of the stars and trees. When he arrived at home, he tried to describe to his family what he had seen. In an endeavor to portray the beautiful sights, he brought in a tree from outside and placed candles on it to show the light of the stars.

Lesson 17

"A Nation of Nations"

Text, pages 62-63, 316-19
Notebook, page 19

Preview

Main Ideas

- Although America is a country of diverse cultures, it is strong and unified as one nation.
- Throughout history, cultures have borrowed from each other.
- The language barrier often creates difficulties among groups.

Objectives

- Create a new word by blending two words
- Answer questions about a poem written by Walt Whitman

Materials

- Appendix, page A29: signs in Spanish and German to be cut out*

> If your child knows how to read Spanish or German, you will want to make the "Wet Paint" signs in a language that your child does not read.

- Supplement, page S8: Definitions for Notebook Page 19

Day 1

Lesson

Introducing the Lesson

Word Activity

➤ Create a word of your own by combining two words you already know. For example, *yark* is a combination of *yard* and *work. Write the word* yark.
➤ Write your new word and its definition.
➤ Now write a sentence using the word.

People actually did create new words by combining two or more words from different languages. In this lesson, you will read about the Pennsylvania Dutch and the Gullah people who created their own unique languages.

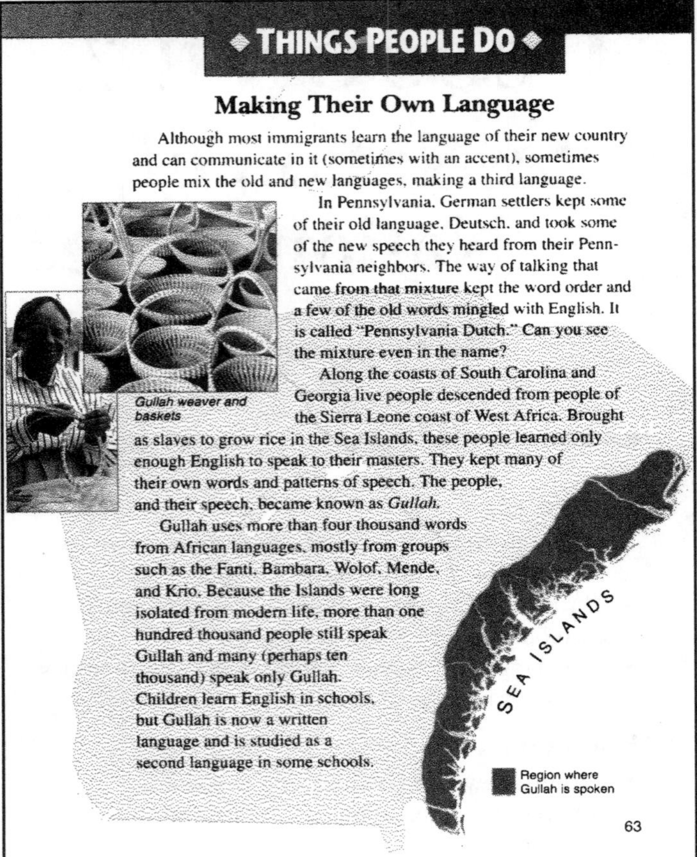

◆ THINGS PEOPLE DO ◆

Making Their Own Language

Although most immigrants learn the language of their new country and can communicate in it (sometimes with an accent), sometimes people mix the old and new languages, making a third language.

In Pennsylvania, German settlers kept some of their old language, Deutsch, and took some of the new speech they heard from their Pennsylvania neighbors. The way of talking that came from that mixture kept the word order and a few of the old words mingled with English. It is called "Pennsylvania Dutch." Can you see the mixture even in the name?

Along the coasts of South Carolina and Georgia live people descended from people of the Sierra Leone coast of West Africa. Brought as slaves to grow rice in the Sea Islands, these people learned only enough English to speak to their masters. They kept many of their own words and patterns of speech. The people, and their speech, became known as *Gullah.*

Gullah uses more than four thousand words from African languages, mostly from groups such as the Fanti, Bambara, Wolof, Mende, and Krio. Because the Islands were long isolated from modern life, more than one hundred thousand people still speak Gullah and many (perhaps ten thousand) speak only Gullah. Children learn English in schools, but Gullah is now a written language and is studied as a second language in some schools.

Gullah weaver and baskets

63

Teaching the Lesson

In order to preserve the flow of the lesson, page 63 is used ahead of page 62.

Text Discussion, pages 63 and 316-19

➤ **Do you know someone who speaks with an accent?**

➤ **Read the first two paragraphs on page 63 to find out what languages are mixed to make what is called "Pennsylvania Dutch."** *(German and English)*

➤ **How can we see a mixture even in the name "Pennsylvania Dutch"?** *(The word* Pennsylvania *is American while the word* Dutch *is from the German word* Deutsch.*)*

➤ **Why do some people have accents?** *(They carry the sound of their old language over into the English language.)*

Some accents also are regional within one country like the Southern or New England accent.

➤ Find Pennsylvania on the map on pages 318-19.

The German immigrants' influence affects us even today, particularly in people's accents but also in their customs and art.

➤ **Read the rest of page 63 to find out who the Gullah people are.** *(people living along the coasts of South Carolina and Georgia who descended from people from Sierra Leone)*

➤ Find South Carolina and Georgia on the map on pages 318-19. They are located on the southeast coast of the United States.

➤ Find Sierra Leone on the map on pages 316-17. Remember that it is on the west coast of Africa.

➤ Use your finger to trace a path from Sierra Leone to the southern part of the United States.

➤ **What differences might there be between these two places?** *(different climates, languages, customs)*

Many of these people still carry on some of the traditions that they have had for many years.

➤ **Do you think the Gullah children should learn the Gullah language or the English language?**

It is important for people to learn their native language and to retain their heritage. It is also important for people to learn English because so many parts of our society depend upon English.

➤ **What does the prefix *bi-* mean in words such as *bicycle* and *bifocals?*** *(two)*

Someone who is said to be ***bilingual*** is able to use two languages fluently.

➤ **How can being bilingual help a person?** *(He can communicate with more people.)*

Encourage your child to take advantage of any opportunities he may have to learn to speak another language. Remind him that regardless of what language he speaks or how many languages he speaks, he should always be in control of his speech. What Christians say and how they say it should always be pleasing to God. (BAT: 5d Communication)

A writer named Walt Whitman once said that our country is "a nation of nations." What do you think he meant? Do you agree? Try to name as many proofs as you can that America is the result of many cultures coming together in one place.

Some products have labels in two languages.

It may also be said, however, that America is entirely one nation. How is that so? It has one Constitution, one central government, and one president. How else are Americans one people? Do most Americans speak English? Do you think they should?

What reasons might some people give for not learning the language of their new home? People who were forced to immigrate—slaves—would resent the language that their captors used. Native Americans often felt that it was wrong to forget the speech that their people had used for centuries, to take up the language used by those who had invaded their lands. Some immigrants perhaps felt they were too old or too slow to learn another tongue. Still others could not learn until someone would teach them. If there were no others kind enough to teach them, they would sometimes give up trying to learn.

Today there is much debate over whether every American should learn to speak English. Some schools offer classes taught in two or more different languages. Many street signs have two or three languages giving the same message. Do you see this as a good or bad method of dealing with the language problem?

62

Day 2

Text Discussion, page 62

- **Read page 62 to find the sentences that tell why some people did not want to learn English in the new country.** *(Answers may be found in sentences two through five of the third paragraph.)*

Walt Whitman was an American poet who lived during the American Civil War. His experiences led him to write several poems about America.

- **What did Walt Whitman say about our country?** *(It is "a nation of nations.")*
- **What do you think the phrase "a nation of nations" means?**

America is one nation, yet it consists of many different people and cultures. When people immigrated to America, they brought with them the traditions, lifestyles, and cultures of their homelands. Many of them kept their old ways but also adopted some of the new traditions and customs of America, making it "a nation of nations."

- Name some things in American society today that are a result of the immigrants' coming to America. *(Possible answers include ethnic foods, many words that are traced to different languages, various traditions and festivals, and different types of clothing.) (NOTE:* Review Lessons 13-16 for specific answers.)
- To illustrate that America is one nation, name ways in which America operates as one country. *(one Constitution, one central government, one president, and one monetary system)*
- **What is the one major thing that most Americans have in common?** *(the English language)*

Language-Issue Discussion, page 62

- *Place the copies of the signs in German and Spanish on a chair in the room.*
- **Do you know what the signs say?**
- Please sit in the chair.
- The signs read "Wet Paint." **Why did you not read the signs before sitting in wet paint?**

It is not possible to read signs when they are written in a language we do not understand.

- **Read aloud the last paragraph on page 62.**

Many people want to have more than one language in America for things like street signs, menus, and even in schools.

- **What do you think a major problem may be with using several languages within one country?**

A major problem would be in choosing the languages to be used. Although the signs on the chair were in two languages, neither language was one you understood. It is impossible to provide all languages for everyone.

- Explain the advantage of having one language within a country. *(One language helps increase communication between groups and is much easier to place on signs and in schools.)*

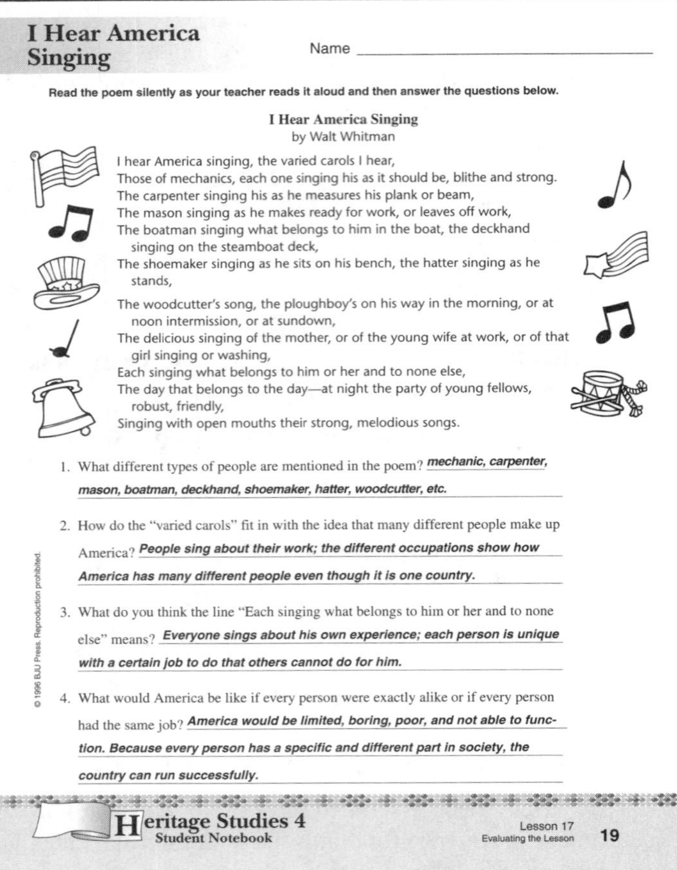

I Hear America Singing Name ______________________

Read the poem silently as your teacher reads it aloud and then answer the questions below.

I Hear America Singing
by Walt Whitman

I hear America singing, the varied carols I hear,
Those of mechanics, each one singing his as it should be, blithe and strong.
The carpenter singing his as he measures his plank or beam,
The mason singing as he makes ready for work, or leaves off work,
The boatman singing what belongs to him in the boat, the deckhand
singing on the steamboat deck,
The shoemaker singing as he sits on his bench, the hatter singing as he
stands,
The woodcutter's song, the ploughboy's on his way in the morning, or at
noon intermission, or at sundown,
The delicious singing of the mother, or of the young wife at work, or of that
girl singing or washing,
Each singing what belongs to him or her and to none else,
The day that belongs to the day—at night the party of young fellows,
robust, friendly,
Singing with open mouths their strong, melodious songs.

1. What different types of people are mentioned in the poem? ***mechanic, carpenter, mason, boatman, deckhand, shoemaker, hatter, woodcutter, etc.***
2. How do the "varied carols" fit in with the idea that many different people make up America? ***People sing about their work; the different occupations show how America has many different people even though it is one country.***
3. What do you think the line "Each singing what belongs to him or her and to none else" means? ***Everyone sings about his own experience; each person is unique with a certain job to do that others cannot do for him.***
4. What would America be like if every person were exactly alike or if every person had the same job? ***America would be limited, boring, poor, and not able to function. Because every person has a specific and different part in society, the country can run successfully.***

Heritage Studies 4 Student Notebook — Lesson 17 Evaluating the Lesson — 19

Evaluating the Lesson

Notebook Activity, page 19

➤ Read the page with the Definitions for Notebook Page 19.

➤ Follow along on Notebook page 19 while I read the poem aloud.

The poem shows that America has many different types of people, yet each person has a significant or major part in society. America would not be America without the many different "voices" that exist.

The poem on Notebook page 19 is presented to give your child exposure to historical poetry. It will begin to help him enhance his critical thinking skills. Please give him as much help and guidance as needed in answering the questions on the Notebook page.

➤ Answer the questions on the Notebook page.

➤ When you have completed the Notebook page, put it in your booklet.

Going Beyond

Additional Teacher Information

The African people now known as the Gullahs were originally brought to the coastal area of the South to help the English settlers work the rice crops. These early settlers were unfamiliar with rice planting and had a low resistance to the malaria bred in the swampy land. The slaves were, for the most part, left alone to work the crops, and they kept much to themselves—a fact that has helped their culture to remain intact even until today. In the Low Country areas such as Charleston, South Carolina, and along the Georgia coast, the Gullah people retain traces of their African heritage. Gullah women line the marketplace, selling their handwoven baskets made from the sweet grass that grows in the marshes.

Walt Whitman, one of America's most influential poets, was born in New York in 1819. He worked as a teacher, printer, and journalist, writing articles about government and politics. He wrote several poems praising the freedom and democracy of America. He portrayed a deep respect for Abraham Lincoln in his poem "When Lilacs Last in the Dooryard Bloom'd" and in the famous "O Captain! My Captain!" Whitman is best known, however, for his *Leaves of Grass,* a collection of humanistic poems presenting his philosophical views. He believed that Americans were capable of reaching perfection. He stated this belief when he wrote, "The chief reason for the being of the United States of America is to bring about the common good will of all mankind, the solidarity of the world."

LESSON 18
America's Language

Text, pages 64-66, 310, 318-19
Notebook, page 20

Preview

Main Ideas

- Throughout history, cultures have borrowed from each other.
- The early English settlers influenced all other immigrants.

Objective

- Answer questions about pie graphs

Materials

- A dictionary (optional)
- Three 4" lengths of yarn or ribbon*
- The figure of the immigrants (1820) from the TimeLine Snapshots
- Supplement, page S9: Major Points of Entry, 1985

Day 1

Lesson

Introducing the Lesson

Text Discussion, page 310

➤ **Read page 310 to find out how the figure of Uncle Sam came to represent the United States.**

➤ **Whose packing plant supplied meat in boxes for America's soldiers?** *(Sam Wilson)*

➤ Describe the figure that has come to symbolize the United States of America. *(It is an old man with a white beard, red and white striped trousers, and a tall top hat covered with stars and stripes.)*

Teaching the Lesson

Text Discussion, page 64

➤ **Read page 64 to find out who had the most influence on the American language and culture.** *(the English)*

➤ **Why is English the primary language spoken in the United States?** *(Many early settlers came from England, speaking English and bringing English books and traditions from their country.)*

Uncle Sam

During the War of 1812 Sam Wilson's packing plant supplied meat in boxes that were stamped "U.S.," for America's soldiers. Though it was the abbreviation for United States, U.S. also came to mean "Uncle Sam," sometimes referring to Sam Wilson and sometimes a nickname for the United States government.

James Montgomery Flagg's famous painting of Uncle Sam inspired young men to enlist in the U.S. Army during World War I.

The figure of Uncle Sam with his white beard, red and white striped trousers, and tall top hat covered with stars and stripes has come to symbolize the United States of America. Probably the most famous picture of Uncle Sam is the one on a World War I recruitment poster. Uncle Sam is pointing his finger and saying "I want you!"

310

➤ **What does the word *communication* mean?** *(the exchange of thoughts, information, or messages) Encourage your child to use his dictionary if he needs help in explaining the definition.*

When people live near each other and work with one another, they must communicate all the time.

➤ **How is communication hindered when people do not know the same language?** *(They cannot understand one another easily.)*

➤ **How did the early English settlers influence the people who moved into their community?** *(They shared their English books and traditions from their homeland.)*

Every time they communicated with other settlers, the newcomers had to learn a little more English because the majority of the community spoke English. More and more people learned English, and eventually, most people living in America could speak English.

Becoming "American"

Why do you think English is the main language of America? Why do you think that one of the Native American languages or French or Chinese or Spanish is not? There are many people from many places here in the United States. Why are there not many languages?

For people to live in one place together, they have to be able to communicate with each other. Early settlers sometimes used sign language to talk with their Native American neighbors. But eventually, both parties had to learn some of the other's words. There were many languages spoken by the Native Americans, too many to find one that all should learn.

The first newcomers who had the most influence were English—they built permanent towns much like the ones in England, set up English laws, and brought English books and traditions. Some English settlers learned Sioux, some Cree, some Algonquian. But all Native Americans who met Englishmen had to know a little English. When other immigrants came to America, they usually came into towns where English was already being spoken and English laws were being obeyed. To fit in, the later immigrants had to adapt to English talk and English ways. Thus English became the language of America.

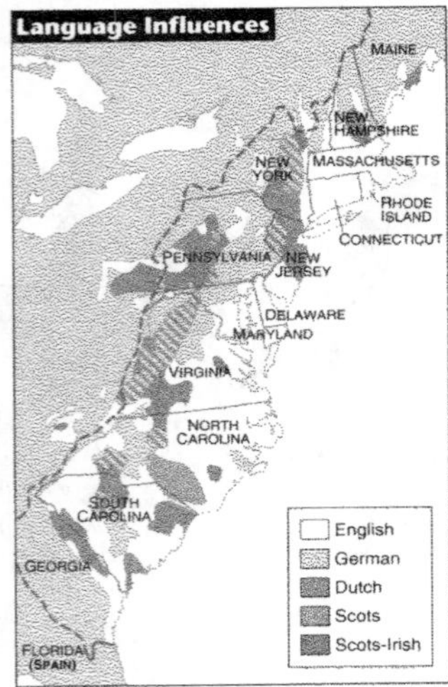

64

One Swedish woman who came into an English settlement and could not understand the neighbors said, "It is like standing outside looking in, with the door locked on both the inside and the outside. You cannot go in and they cannot let you in, but I have decided that I shall be one of the neighbors. I am going to learn the American language!"

And she did, trading English lessons for spinning wool for someone. The next spring, she taught English to Danish immigrants. Then later she taught English to some people she would never have believed she would.

One day, Anna saw that a group of Chippewa had camped nearby. She took some bread and yarn that she had made and went to visit. At first, she did not know how to talk to the Chippewa. She wrote in her diary, "There is a strong conviction inside myself: that all human beings . . . have certain rights that no other human beings have the right to violate."

Anna and Mia, a daughter of one of the Chippewa chiefs, became good friends. Soon Anna was welcome in the camp, and Anna looked forward to the time every year when her friends would come back.

After many years, other settlers wanted to run the Chippewa off, to "put them in their place." Anna asked, "What is 'their place' in their own country?"

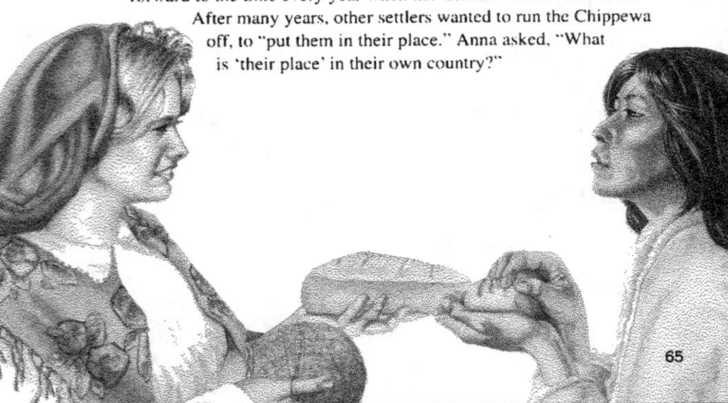

65

Map Activity, page 64

- ➤ Look at the map on page 64.
- ➤ **Which group was the main group to settle in the Northeast?** *(the English)*
- ➤ **Which groups settled in South Carolina?** *(the English, German, and Scots-Irish)*
- ➤ **Which groups settled mainly in New York and New Jersey?** *(the Dutch)*
- ➤ **In which state did the Scots mainly settle?** *(North Carolina)*

Day 2

Text Discussion, pages 65 and 318-19

- ➤ **As I read page 65, follow along to find out who Anna's friend was.** *(Mia, the daughter of a Chippewa chief)*
- ➤ **What did the Swedish woman mean when she said, "It is like standing outside looking in, with the door locked on both the inside and the outside. You cannot go in, and they cannot let you in"?** *(The language difference keeps people from communicating.)*

The door seems "locked" because they do not speak the same language. The only way to be "let in" is to learn the language that the other person speaks.

- ➤ Find the sentences in the first paragraph that tell what decision the immigrant woman made. *("I have decided that I shall be one of the neighbors. I am going to learn the American language!")*
- ➤ **What things did the Swedish lady do that proved she really wanted to learn to speak English?** *(She spun wool as payment for her English lessons. She taught others English once she learned how to speak it.)*
- ➤ Find Minnesota on the map on pages 318-19. This is where Anna settled.
- ➤ **Why did Anna take bread and yarn when she went to visit the Chippewa camp?** *(She wanted them to know she was friendly and wanted peace.)*

Remind your child that Christians should be kind to others, including people who are different. (BAT: 5e Friendliness)

- ➤ **Read aloud what Anna wrote in her diary.**
- ➤ **What do you think Anna meant by these words?**

She meant that we are all humans, regardless of our race or country, and we all have certain rights. Anna was probably thinking about how the Chippewa were mistreated and disliked by the settlers.

> "And Ruth said, Intreat me not to leave thee, or to return from following after thee: for whither thou goest, I will go; and where thou lodgest, I will lodge: thy people shall be my people, and thy God my God."
>
> **Ruth 1:16**

Anna did not see her friends for a long time. Then she got a letter from a preacher rather far away. It said that he had met some Chippewa people who could spin and weave and who talked "the American language with a Swedish accent." Anna smiled. There might be much wrong in the new country; but when people wanted to, they could work together to overcome it.

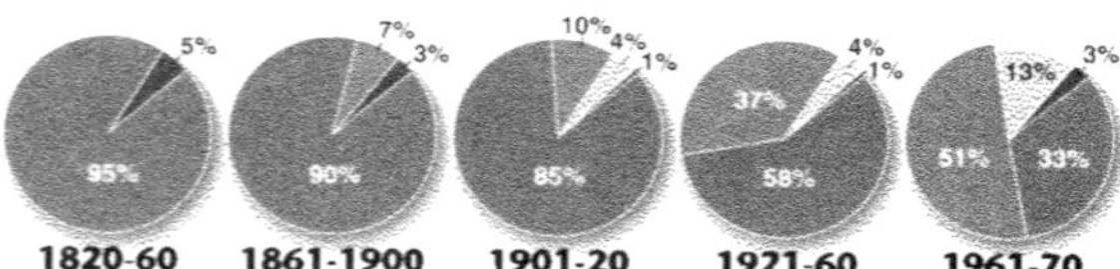

Immigration Today

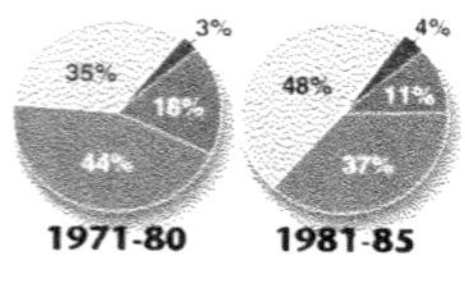

Europe
Canada/Mexico/Latin America
Asia
Other

Compare the graphs above. Were the same groups of people coming in 1960 that came in 1860? Can you say what group of immigrants increased most between 1961 and 1985? Is the heritage of your family represented on the charts?

People are still coming to America. Sometimes they come illegally, crossing the borders without proper admittance. Some come on small, risky boats from Haiti and Cuba; some come on foot from Mexico; some brave the Pacific to come from the Asian coasts. Many come legally, from Haiti, Cuba, Mexico, and all over the world. Wherever they come from, immigrants bring their ways of cooking and talking, thinking and celebrating. And they all enter a culture that has certain expectations of them—and for them.

66

- **What was admirable about Anna and her dealings with the Chippewa?** *(Answers will vary. She was kind and friendly toward them. She did not have prejudice against them. Instead, she made it a point to help them learn English.)* (BATs: 5a Love, 5d Communication)
- **Why do you think the settlers wanted to put the Chippewa "in their place"?**

Some settlers felt that they, not the Chippewa, owned the land. They wanted to make sure the Chippewa did not interfere with this owning of the land.

- **What was Anna's response to these settlers?** *(She told them that the land was already the Chippewa's.)*

The Chippewa belonged there because they were there before the settlers came. The land was their own country. It did not totally belong to the settlers.

Day 3

Text Discussion, page 66

- **Read the first paragraph on page 66 to find out the effects of Anna's contact with the Chippewa.** *(She taught them English, which helped them communicate with white settlers.)*
- **Read the rest of the page to find out if people are still coming to America.** *(yes)*
- Look at the graphs on page 66. **What was the main group of people who came to the United States between 1820 and 1860?** *(people from Europe)*
- **What group was the largest during the American Civil War (1861-65)?** *(immigrants from Europe)*
- **What continent was represented by the countries in green?** *(North America)*
- Compare the groups of people that came in 1960 to those that came in 1860. *(In 1960 fewer people came from Europe; many came from North America and a few came from Asia. The group of "Others" was smaller.)*
- **What group of immigrants increased the most between 1961 and 1985?** *(Immigrants from Asia increased from 13 to 48 percent.)*
- **Which groups remained almost the same between the years 1921 and 1985?** *(Those immigrants falling into the "Other" category and the North America group changed the least among all the groups represented on the pie graphs.)*
- **Which groups came to the United States during the time in which you were born?**
- Tell where your ancestors came from.
- **Is your heritage represented on the graphs?**

TimeLine Snapshots Activity

- Place the figure of the immigrants coming to America on the TimeLine at 1820.
- The year 1820 marks the beginning of the flow of immigration.

Map Activity

- *Show your child the Major Points of Entry, 1985 page.*
- **Which city received the most immigrants in 1985?** *(New York City)*
- Name other cities that received large numbers of immigrants in 1985. *(Possible answers include Chicago, Illinois; El Paso, Texas; Seattle, Washington; Honolulu, Hawaii; and San Francisco and Los Angeles, California.)*
- Name ways in which people try to get to America. *(some on small, risky boats; some on foot; some across the Pacific Ocean by plane)*
- **What do these different ways of getting here tell about the people and their motivations?** *(They are willing to make a great sacrifice, even risk their lives, to come to America.)*

They believe that America is a land worth all the risk. It is this land of opportunity that motivates them to come.

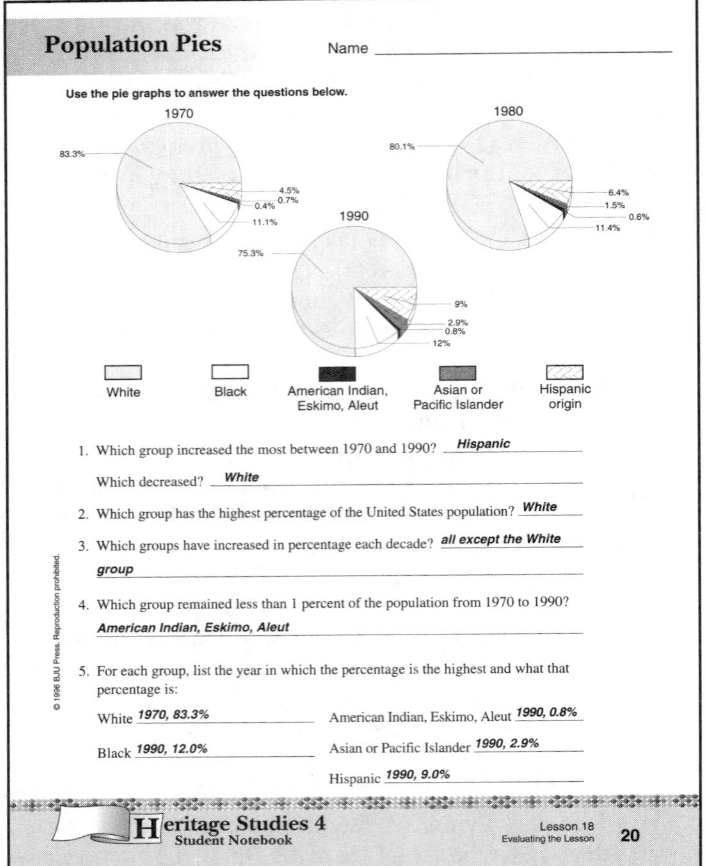

Population Pies Name ____________

Use the pie graphs to answer the questions below.

1. Which group increased the most between 1970 and 1990? *Hispanic*

   Which decreased? *White*
2. Which group has the highest percentage of the United States population? *White*
3. Which groups have increased in percentage each decade? *all except the White group*
4. Which group remained less than 1 percent of the population from 1970 to 1990? *American Indian, Eskimo, Aleut*
5. For each group, list the year in which the percentage is the highest and what that percentage is:

   White *1970, 83.3%* American Indian, Eskimo, Aleut *1990, 0.8%*

   Black *1990, 12.0%* Asian or Pacific Islander *1990, 2.9%*

   Hispanic *1990, 9.0%*

Americans today do not have to endure the hardships or struggles that the immigrants of long ago had to endure. Encourage your child to make a list of the different ways Americans have been blessed. Remind him to give thanks to the Lord for His blessings. (BAT: 7c Praise)

Evaluating the Lesson

Notebook Activity, page 20

- ➤ Read the instructions on Notebook page 20.
- ➤ Study the pie graphs and complete the page.
- ➤ Place the completed page in your booklet.

Living the Dream Booklet Activity

- ➤ Place your Notebook pages in order between your construction-paper covers, making sure the holes line up.
- ➤ Loop one piece of yarn through each hole, tying the ends in a bow to bind your booklet.

Going Beyond

Enrichment

Give your child one 3"×8" sheet of paper, one 8" piece of yarn, colored pencils or crayons, and glue. Tell him to write on one side of the paper a list of things that he is thankful for. Then allow him to decorate and illustrate his list on the other side of his bookmark. You may wish to laminate the bookmark or use clear Con-Tact paper to make it durable. Punch a hole at the top of the bookmark. Loop the piece of yarn through the hole and tie as a tassel.

Additional Teacher Information

The Chippewa, also known as the Ojibwa, lived primarily in northern Minnesota, Wisconsin, North Dakota, Michigan, and Canada. Even today, some Chippewa still live in these regions. The Chippewa are well known for their harvesting of the wild rice that grows in the lake country. For these Native Americans, rice harvesting is more than a livelihood. It is an important part of their heritage and custom. If the harvesters choose to keep the rice instead of selling it, then the gathering is merely the first step. This gathering takes place in a canoe that the Chippewa harvesters navigate through shallow, grassy waters. They use long poles called knockers to "knock" the rice into the boat. Once they have collected a load, the rice must be parched, removed from the husks, and separated from the chaff.

4 LESSONS 19-24

Preaching the Word

Spanning the time period from 1861 to the mid-1900s, this chapter highlights men and women who caused others to reflect on their spiritual conditions. These men and women of faith—D. L. Moody, Hudson Taylor, Pandita Ramabai, Andrew Murray, chaplains, and missionaries—illustrated their love and obedience to God by willingly taking the gospel of Christ "to all the world." By learning about these champions of the Faith, your child will be challenged to commune with the Lord daily, to support missionaries, and perhaps even to become a missionary himself.

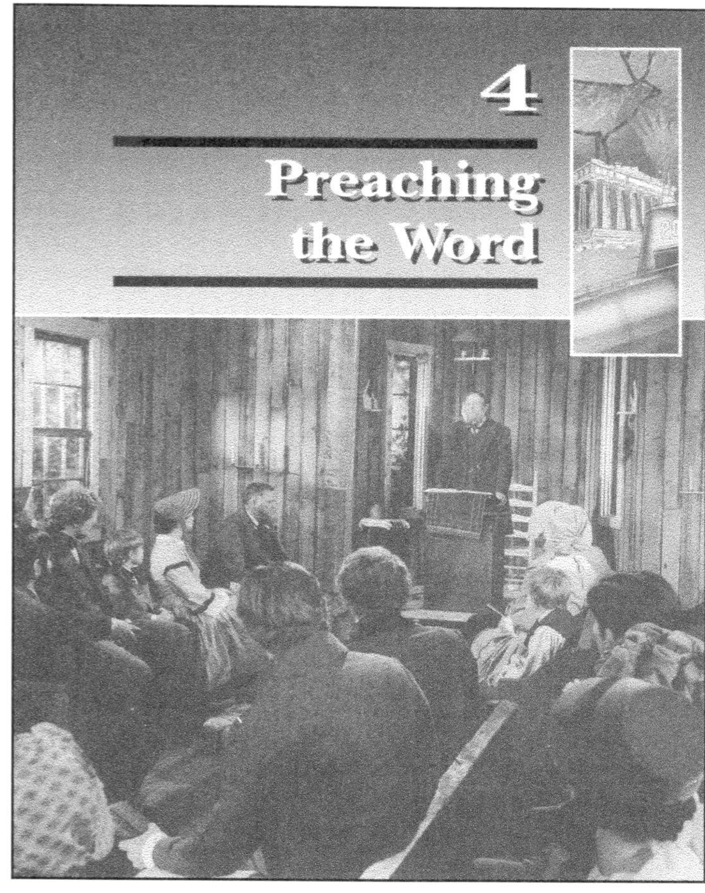

Materials

The following materials must be obtained or prepared before the presentation of the lesson. These items are labeled with an asterisk (*) in each lesson and in the Materials List in the Supplement. For further information see the individual lessons.

- Appendix, page A30 (Lesson 20)
- Men's shoes in a shoe box (Lesson 20)
- Appendix, page A31 (Lesson 22)
- Cookie ingredients (Lesson 22)
- Construction paper (Lessons 22 and 23)
- Two missionary prayer cards or letters (Lesson 23)
- Metal brads or yarn (Lesson 23)

LESSON 19
Chaplains and Circuit Riders

Text, pages 68-69
Notebook, pages 21-22

Preview

Main Ideas

- God has ordained evangelism.
- War and imminent death often make people mindful of their need for Christ.
- Chaplains and circuit-riding preachers took the gospel of Christ to the needy.

Objectives

- Sing along with the recording of the "Battle Hymn of the Republic"
- Relate items either to the Civil War and chaplains or to the circuit riders

Materials

- *HERITAGE STUDIES Listening Cassette B*
- Maps and More 5, page M2

Day 1

Lesson

Introducing the Lesson

Listening Activity, Notebook page 21

➤ **Read the words on Notebook page 21 as you listen to this recording.** *Play the "Battle Hymn of the Republic." Do not reveal the title of the song until you have played the recording.*

➤ **What kind of song does this sound like—a playful song, a sad song, a church song, or a marching song?** *(Answers will vary.)*

➤ Quietly tap your pencil on the desk or pat your feet as the song plays again, noting the rhythm.

➤ **Is the rhythm mostly even or mostly uneven?** *(mostly uneven)*

➤ **Do you know the title of the song?** *("Battle Hymn of the Republic")*

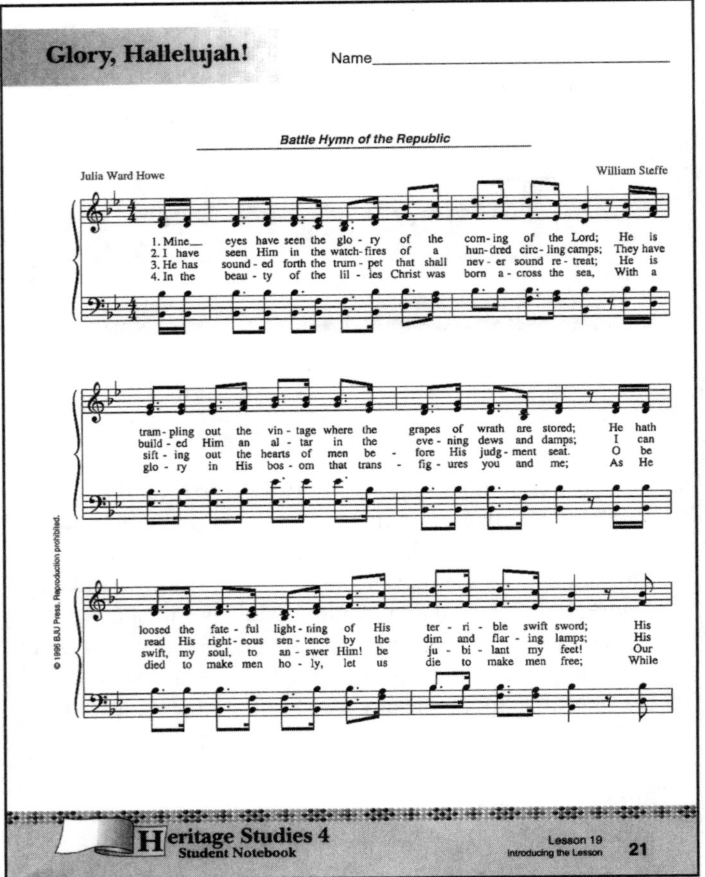

➤ Write this title on the blank at the top of Notebook page 21. *Guide your child with the spelling.*

The "Battle Hymn of the Republic" is a marching song, a war song, written during the American Civil War. The words of this hymn remind Christians that the Lord is coming again and that God's truth will always remain. We will learn about the songwriter in this lesson. (BAT: 8a Faith in God's promises)

➤ Sing along with the recording as I replay the "Battle Hymn of the Republic."

Julia Ward Howe looked out upon the fires that night, dozens and dozens warming the Union soldiers near Washington, D.C. She heard the soldiers singing; she felt the coming of war in her heart, weighing her with sadness and determination. She turned to God for comfort and strength. And the next morning she wrote a poem that told in grand and somber words how many Americans were feeling. The poem became one of America's most famous patriotic songs, "The Battle Hymn of the Republic." This is the second verse:

I have seen Him in the watchfires of a hundred circling camps;
They have builded Him an altar in the evening dews and damps;
I can read His righteous sentence by the dim and flaring lamps;
His day is marching on.

Men who sat around campfires awaiting the morning, and battle, had much to think about. Death was near for many, and many did not feel ready. Some tried not to think about death too much—they played cards and joked with each other. Others wrote letters, telling their wives not to worry and their children to keep watching for them to come home. But others, many others, started to think about their souls and what would happen if they were killed.

An actor at a reenactment plays a flute as soldiers in the Civil War did.

68

A scene from the film Sheffey, showing how a camp meeting would have looked

There were, among the men in most camps, preachers who knew how to talk to men facing death. Called *chaplains*, these preachers told the soldiers how Christ had already suffered death for them so that when they died—whether tomorrow on the battlefield or at home as old men—they need not fear. They told the men that they had only to believe in Christ. Many soldiers accepted Christ during the war.

After the war, many American soldiers were different. The terrible battles they had seen and the destruction they still saw everywhere kept them thinking about how short life was. Those who had lived through battles and cannon fire often came back determined to live better lives. It had been many years since there was so much interest in godly things.

The revival did not stop on the battlefields and in the camps. It swept across the country, touching almost every city, every village. Songwriters wrote many more hymns and gospel songs. Circuit-riding preachers went out by the hundreds. They traveled on horseback and held camp meetings. Church attendance grew. And in the hearts of Christians in America and other countries was a growing desire to take the gospel to the ends of the earth.

69

Teaching the Lesson

Text Discussion, page 68 and Maps and More 5

- ➤ **Read page 68 to find the name of the writer of the song "Battle Hymn of the Republic."** *(Julia Ward Howe) Show the picture of Mrs. Howe on Maps and More 5.*
- ➤ **Read the stanza on text page 68, noting especially the words *Him* and *His*.**
- ➤ **Why are these words capitalized?** *(They refer to God.)*
- ➤ **What did many of the soldiers think about as they sat around the campfires?** *(death and what would happen to them after death)*

People in desperate situations are sometimes easier to witness to than those who seem content and at peace. Death is closer and more real during war or in other life-threatening situations, so people often are more concerned about their souls. (BATs: 1a Understanding Jesus Christ, 1b Repentance and faith, 7a Grace)

Text Discussion, page 69

- ➤ **Read the first two paragraphs on page 69 to find out the name given to those who preached among the soldiers.** *(chaplains)*

There are still men who serve as chaplains in the armed services in modern times. Many, but not all, chaplains preach the true gospel of Christ. They are concerned about winning soldiers to Jesus Christ. (*NOTE:* If you are acquainted with any chaplains or missionary endeavors directed toward servicemen, bring these to your child's attention and take time today to pray for these individuals.) (BATs: 1a Understanding Jesus Christ, 1b Repentance and faith, 5c Evangelism and missions)

Day 2

- ➤ **Do you remember what name was given to the preachers in the 1700s and 1800s who rode on horseback from church to church or community to community preaching the gospel of Christ?** ***(circuit-riding preachers)***

A ***circuit*** is a path. The preachers on horseback would ride the trail, taking the same path month after month to several towns and churches.

- ➤ **Read the caption below the picture on page 69.**

Robert Sheffey was a circuit-riding preacher during the 1800s. He rode through the hills of Virginia and neighboring states spreading the gospel. On many occasions he participated in camp meetings.

➤ **What are *camp meetings?*** *(Answers will vary.)*

Sometimes a number of circuit riders would decide to join efforts to hold a series of large meetings in one location. The circuit riders would arrange the place, usually one with a large barnlike meeting place, and would spread the news to the folks on their circuit. Then at the appointed time, the campground would fill up with wagonloads of families from neighboring states and territories, coming together to worship the Lord.

Many new friends would be made and old friendships rekindled. The services were held several times during the day and night, with the families camping right there for about a week. Many souls were saved, and Christians were encouraged and taught the Scriptures during these camp meetings. (BATs: 5c Evangelism and missions, 6a Bible study)

People in the 1800s were very much interested in hearing about the Lord. This interest brought about a great revival in America.

➤ **What does the word *revival* mean?** *(Answers will vary.)*

Revival is a reawakening (bringing back interest and excitement) of spiritual things in the heart of a Christian, causing that person to want to serve the Lord wholeheartedly. The singing and preaching of the gospel that an unsaved person hears during a revival will often result in his salvation. Revival begins in the heart; it is a personal decision between an individual and the Lord.

➤ **Read the last paragraph on page 69 to learn about the results of this revival.** *(It spread all across America; people wrote hymns and gospel songs; churches grew; people desired to share the gospel.)*

➤ **Read aloud the last sentence on page 69.**

➤ **What name is given to a person who takes the gospel to the ends of the earth?** *(a **missionary**)*

What we know today as foreign missions began as a result of this desire to take the gospel to other nations. In this chapter we will learn more about some of the early missionaries. (BATs: 1b Repentance and faith, 2c Faithfulness, 5c Evangelism and missions)

Chaplains and Circuit Riders

Name ____________________

Read the following list of people and events.
Put an *X* in the column to which each item refers.
(*NOTE:* One item applies to *both* columns.)

The War and Chaplains		Circuit Riders
x	soldiers worry about death	
x	Julia Ward Howe	
	preacher on horseback	x
	Robert Sheffey	x
x	campfires	
x	"Battle Hymn of the Republic"	
	after the war	x
x	revival	x
	camp meetings	x
	foreign missions established	x

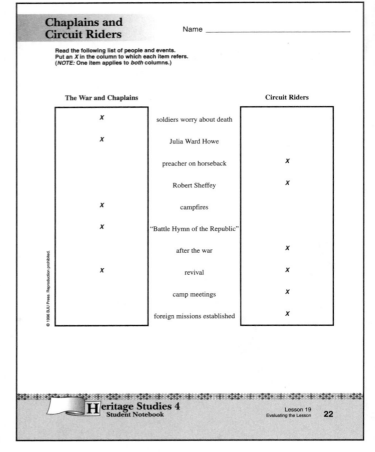

Heritage Studies 4 Student Notebook — Lesson 19 Evaluating the Lesson 22

Evaluating the Lesson

Notebook Activity, page 22

➤ Read the instructions for Notebook page 22.

➤ Complete the page.

Your child's choices may differ from what is shown here. For instance, it would be correct to say that both categories had campfires and camp meetings. You may suggest he look for more than one item that applies in both columns, or you may accept whichever column he chooses.

Going Beyond

Enrichment

Arrange to show the video *Sheffey* about the circuit-riding preacher Robert Sheffey. (*NOTE:* This video is available from Bob Jones University Press.) After viewing the story of Sheffey, give your child the song "Brethren, We Have Met to Worship," found in the Supplement, page S10. Encourage him to listen to the recording of the song on the listening cassette as he follows along with the words. Encourage him to try to learn the song.

Additional Teacher Information

One night as soldiers marched past her window, Julia Ward Howe was greatly stirred and wrote out the words for a marching song. The next day, she copied her song to submit to the *Atlantic Monthly.* The magazine gave Mrs. Howe ten dollars for her song, which the magazine entitled "Battle Hymn of the Republic." Often called one of the greatest songs of the American Civil War, "Battle Hymn of the Republic" gives glory to God and offers courage and hope to those who trust in Him.

Circuit-riding preachers, often called *backwoods preachers,* began riding their regular routes in the United States in the 1760s. The circuit rider covered great distances, usually on horseback, to conduct preaching services and revivals.

One famous circuit-riding preacher of pioneer America was Peter Cartwright (1785-1872). Saved at the age of sixteen, Peter preached his first sermon at age eighteen, taking as his text Isaiah 26:4—"Trust ye in the Lord for ever: for in the Lord Jehovah is everlasting strength." Having been in the Methodist denomination since 1801, Mr. Cartwright rode circuits and preached in camp meetings in Kentucky, Tennessee, Ohio, and Illinois for over sixty years. While in Illinois, Peter Cartwright was twice elected to the Illinois state legislature. He ran for Congress to represent the state of Illinois but was defeated by Abraham Lincoln.

Another noted circuit rider was the Methodist preacher Robert Sayers Sheffey (1820-1902). In the saddle for almost twelve months of the year, Robert Sheffey carried the message of Christ throughout the Virginia countryside and surrounding states for sixty-three years after his own conversion. Devoted to doing good and giving people the gospel of Christ, this "saint in the wilderness" helped to shape the character of the American frontier.

LESSON 20
D. L. Moody: From Soles to Souls

Text, pages 70-77, 312
Notebook, pages 23-24

Preview

Main Ideas

- Man's view of God determines his philosophy and history.
- God has ordained evangelism.
- The Lord greatly used D. L. Moody in evangelism in nineteenth-century America.
- Religious beliefs help shape cultures.

Objective

- Complete statements about Dwight L. Moody

Materials

- Appendix, page A30: shoes*
- A felt-tip pen (optional)
- A shoebox containing a pair of men's shoes*
- The figure of D. L. Moody (1861) from the TimeLine Snapshots

Day 1

Lesson

Introducing the Lesson

Description Activity

- ➤ Collect the materials to design paper shoes. You will need scissors, crayons, a felt-tip pen, and the paper shoes.
- ➤ Print your first initial on the back of one shoe and your middle initial on the back of the other shoe. (*NOTE:* If your child does not have a middle initial, allow the initial of his last name to be used.)
- ➤ Color or design the paper shoes and then cut them out.
- ➤ On the back of each shoe, write an adjective that describes yourself. Choose a word that begins with the initial you have written there.

This lesson is about a man who was often known by his initials, D. L.

Missions Begins at Home: Dwight L. Moody (1837-99)

Dwight was tired. Cutting broomcorn was a hard job, and he had been working since morning. But he had almost finished the field, and the eight-year-old knew his mother would be pleased with the money he had earned.

The Moody family lived in Massachusetts. All the Moody children learned to work when they were young. Their father had died when Dwight was only four. Mrs. Moody taught her nine children to trust the Lord for the things they needed, but she also expected them to work.

When Dwight was older, he agreed to work for a neighboring farmer. He received his meals for his pay. But Dwight did not like the way things turned out. "Mother," Dwight said, "I am not going to work for that man any longer."

"Why not, Son? The work isn't too hard for you, is it?" Mrs. Moody was puzzled. Dwight had been pleased to get the job. "Are you getting enough to eat?" she asked.

70

Dwight answered, "I guess I get enough, Mother. But do you know what I've had for the last nineteen meals? Cornmeal mush and milk. That's all! Meal after meal! I'm tired of it. I'm not going back!"

Mrs. Moody sighed. She knew how he felt. "Dwight, you promised to work all winter. You must keep your promise. You must keep every promise you make, even when it is hard or unpleasant. God expects us to keep our word." Dwight went back to work, but he never learned to like farming.

One day when Dwight was seventeen, an older brother gave him five dollars. Dwight believed that this was his chance. He told his family good-bye and took a train for Boston. Dwight's uncle, Sam Holton, had a shoe store in Boston, but Dwight did not ask him for a job. He wanted to get a job on his own.

71

➤ *Display the shoebox, revealing the men's shoes inside. Point out the upper, the heel, and the sole of the shoe.*

All the sections of the upper part of the shoe are stitched together and then fastened to the sole of the shoe. The ***sole,*** or underside, of a shoe must be well made and durable to make the shoe last and to make the fit comfortable for the wearer.

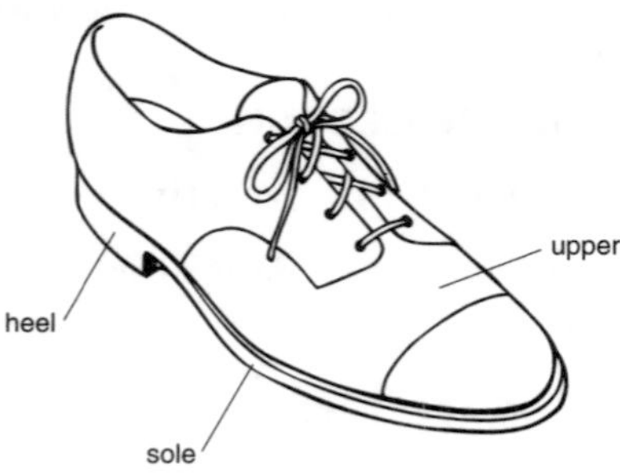

➤ Write the word *sole*. **Do you know a homonym for this word?** *(soul)*

Every human has a soul, the part of his being that accepts or rejects spiritual things. The person in this lesson went from selling shoes with durable soles to telling people about Christ, the most important message for their souls. (BATs: 1a Understanding Jesus Christ, 1b Repentance and faith, 5c Evangelism and missions)

Teaching the Lesson

Text Discussion, pages 70-71

➤ **Read the title on page 70 to find out the name of the man in this lesson.** *(Dwight L. Moody)*

➤ **Read pages 70-71 to find out what D. L. Moody did with the first money he received.** *(took a train to Boston to get a job)*

➤ **Why did Dwight and his brothers and sisters have to work so hard at home even when they were young?** *(Their father had died; they needed to help their mother with the jobs around the house and yard; they worked to earn money for food.)*

Mrs. Moody was a Christian who trusted God to provide for her family and to give them the strength to fulfill their responsibilities. (BATs: 2c Faithfulness, 2e Work, 2f Enthusiasm)

➤ **Read aloud the second paragraph on page 71, telling what Mrs. Moody said about promises.**

➤ **What is meant by the words *Dwight believed that this was his chance* when he headed to Boston?** *(This was his chance for a change in his life.)*

➤ **Why did Dwight not ask his uncle for a job in the shoe store?** *(He wanted to find a job on his own, maybe to prove he was a man or was more grown up.)* (BATs: 2c Faithfulness, 2d Goal setting, 4c Honesty)

For a week the country boy hunted for work, but no one would hire him. He ran out of money, and he was hungry. Finally, he went to his uncle and asked for a job in his shoe store.

Mr. Holton thought it over. He did not like his nephew much because the boy was bold and liked to have things his own way. At last he told Dwight he could have a job if he would make three promises. First, he must do his best. Second, he must ask about things he did not understand. Third, he must go to Sunday school and church every Sunday. Dwight agreed.

Dwight had gone to church almost every Sunday of his life, but he was not a Christian. One day his Sunday school teacher in Boston decided to tell Dwight that he needed to be saved. He went to the shoe store and found the young man in the back, wrapping up shoes. The man reminded Dwight that Christ loved him and that the Lord wanted Dwight to love Him too. He asked Dwight whether he wanted to be saved. And there in the back room of a shoe store, Dwight L. Moody gave his life to Christ.

72

In those days, the talk was always about going west. Moody listened and thought about it. At last he made up his mind and told his uncle he was leaving. He went to the train station, bought a ticket to Chicago, and got on the train.

One of Moody's Sunday school classes; Moody is in the back row on the left.

Two days after Moody reached Chicago, he found a job in another shoe store. On the first Wednesday night in Chicago, he went to a prayer meeting. He quickly made many friends there.

Moody did not forget that he had given his life to the Lord. He worked as hard for the Lord on Sunday as he did for himself during the week. His special job was bringing children to a mission Sunday school that was held on Sunday afternoons.

Three years passed. By then almost a thousand children were coming to his Sunday school, most of them poor. They all loved Mr. Moody. He understood them because he had been poor too.

One Sunday afternoon Abraham Lincoln visited Moody's class. He heard the songs and prayers. He told the children, "I was once as poor as any boy in this school, but I am now president of the United States. If you will attend to what is taught you here, some of you may yet be president of the United States."

73

Day 2

Text Discussion, page 72

- ➤ **Read page 72 to find out whom D. L. Moody went to work for and why.** *(his uncle, because he was hungry and could not find any other work)*
- ➤ **What promises did his uncle tell him he must make in order to have a job at the shoe store?** *(First, he must do his best. Second, he must ask about things he did not understand. Third, he must go to Sunday school and church every Sunday.)*
- ➤ **What wonderful happening occurred in the back room of that store?** *(His Sunday school teacher led him to Jesus.)*
- ➤ **How old was D. L. Moody when he received Christ as his Savior?** *(seventeen)* (BATs: 1a Understanding Jesus Christ, 1b Repentance and faith)

Text Discussion, pages 73-74

- ➤ **Read page 73 to find out what Dwight L. Moody did after he was saved.** *(moved to Chicago to work in another shoe store)*
- ➤ **What was Moody's special job every Sunday?** *(to bring children to learn about the Lord at a mission Sunday school)*
- ➤ **What important man visited the Sunday school one afternoon?** *(President Abraham Lincoln)*
- ➤ **Read what President Lincoln told the class.**

Lincoln encouraged the children to listen to and obey what they were taught at Sunday school, for it would benefit them all their lives.

Mr. Hibbert, a fellow teacher, became too sick to teach his Sunday school class any more. He asked Moody to visit each of his pupils with him before he died. He wanted to ask each one to become a Christian. Moody wanted to work that day, but he thought he should help his friend. In house after house, Moody watched Mr. Hibbert plead with his students, sincerely grieving over their souls. Almost all the students were saved that day.

Now young Mr. Moody knew what he was going to do. He knew that he would rather see people saved than be the richest man in the world. The next day he quit his job. He chose to work only for God.

74

In April 1861, Fort Sumter fell. Now Moody had another choice to make. Should he join the army? He agreed with President Lincoln that the Southern states should not be allowed to leave the Union. He thought slavery was wrong. But he did not think he could kill a person. Besides, he had promised God that he would work for Him.

Some friends made a suggestion. Why not take the Word of God to the soldiers? Who needed to hear the gospel more than men who were going into battle or men who were wounded and perhaps dying? His friends promised to raise the money he would need if he would go.

So Moody went to the soldiers. He preached in army camps, in prison camps, in hospitals, on trains, and on boats. He took a trip on a boat down the Tennessee River. Four hundred fifty men were on the boat, many of them badly wounded. Moody made up his mind that he would not let any man on the boat die without hearing of Christ and heaven. And he did not; he went to each one with a drink of water and told him about the Lord.

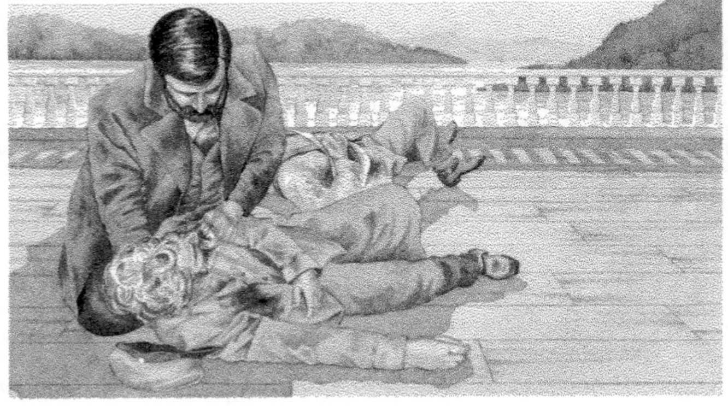

75

➤ **Read page 74 to find out what Moody's new mission in life became.** *(to tell people about the Lord)* (BAT: 5c Evangelism and missions)

Text Discussion, pages 75-76

➤ Locate the presidential figure of Abraham Lincoln on the TimeLine at 1861.

➤ **What was going on in the United States during the time that Lincoln was president?** *(The American Civil War, or the War Between the States, was being fought between the North and the South.)*

➤ **Read pages 75-76 to find out what D. L. Moody did to serve his country *and* God during this war.** *(He told the soldiers about Christ.)*

➤ **What do we call a man who preaches to soldiers?** *(a chaplain)*

➤ **Did Moody ever preach to soldiers from the Southern army?** *(Yes, he preached to prisoners from the Southern army in a camp near Chicago.)*

Many soldiers, Union and Confederate, heard the gospel from D. L. Moody during the American Civil War.

Nine times Moody went to the battlefields. Hundreds, even thousands of times, he knelt beside wounded and weary men and told them of Christ.

"Chaplain, help me die." The soldier wounded in a battle in Tennessee could only whisper. "I've been fighting Christ all my life."

Moody gave him many verses from the Bible, but the man did not understand. Then Moody read the story of Nicodemus in the third chapter of John. He came to verse fifteen: "That whosoever believeth in him should not perish, but have eternal life."

The soldier lifted his hand. "What's that? Is it true? Read it again. That's good! Won't you read it again?"

Moody read the verse three times. The man smiled with understanding now and died a forgiven man.

Moody also went to a camp near Chicago where prisoners from the Southern army were held. Hundreds of these men were saved as they listened to God's Word.

76

Days

Memorial Day

Memorial Day, also called Decoration Day, is a holiday in the United States to honor those who died in war while serving the United States. In 1971 a federal law declared that Memorial Day would be celebrated on the last Monday in May.

On Memorial Day, many communities have parades and special ceremonies to honor the nation's war dead. People often place flowers and small American flags on the graves of military personnel.

312

One night Moody heard a preacher say, "The world has yet to see what God can do with one man who is wholly committed to Him." Moody could not get the words out of his mind. Before he went to sleep that night, he told God that he would be that man.

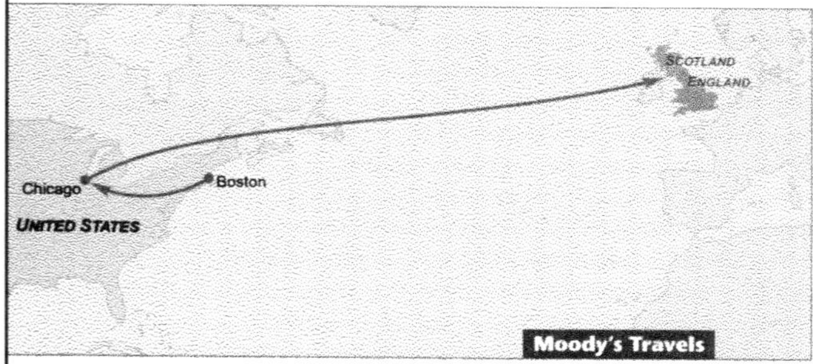

Moody met a singer named Ira Sankey and asked him to work with him. Moody, Sankey, and their wives went to England and Scotland to hold gospel meetings. Their American ways were strange to the people there. Dwight spoke as he had back home in the country, and Ira sang solos in the meetings. No one else did that in English churches. Crowds of people—about two million in the London services alone—came to hear the "crazy Americans." Thousands accepted the Lord Jesus as their Savior.

Mr. Moody started a school for girls and then a school for boys in his hometown of Northfield, Massachusetts. In Chicago he started a Bible school to train young men and women to serve God. When he died at age sixty-two, Dwight L. Moody had lived a life that showed the world what God could do through a man who was wholly committed to Him.

77

Text Discussion, page 312

The United States honors all soldiers who have served in wars. We have a special day set aside for this purpose.

➤ **Read page 312 to find out what this special day is called.** *(Memorial Day)*

➤ **When is this day celebrated?** *(the last Monday in May)*

Day 3

Text Discussion, page 77

➤ **Read page 77 to find out what else Moody did for God.** *(preached in England and Scotland; started a school for girls and a school for boys in Massachusetts; started a Bible school in Chicago)*

➤ **Read aloud the statement that D. L. Moody heard.** *("The world has yet to see what God can do with one man who is wholly committed to Him.")*

➤ **What does it mean to be wholly committed to God?** *(Everything a person does or thinks or says is based on doing the Lord's will.)*

➤ **Whom did Moody ask to help him with the music in his gospel campaigns?** *(Ira Sankey)*

Moody and Sankey conducted many meetings all over the world, telling people about the Lord. Thousands of people accepted Christ as their Savior.

➤ Look at the map of Moody's travels on page 77. Trace the path as we review the life of D. L. Moody. *Review the key events in Moody's life as a Christian.*

Remember that the term *Christian* means "one who follows Christ." (BATs: 1c Separation from the world, 3b Mind, 4d Victory)

Shoe Clues Name ____________________

Read each statement. Then color the shoe on page 24 with the corresponding answer for each statement. Finally, color the correct ending for Moody's life pathway.

1. Dwight's father ________ when Dwight was only four years old.
2. Dwight's mother ________ God.
3. Uncle Sam Holton gave Dwight a job if he promised to do his best, ask questions when he didn't understand, and go to ________ every Sunday.
4. Dwight worked in a ________ store.
5. Dwight L. Moody got saved ________ .
6. One Sunday afternoon ________ came to visit at the mission.
7. A singer, ________, joined Moody in his gospel meetings.
8. In Chicago, Dwight L. Moody started a ________ to train men and women to serve God.

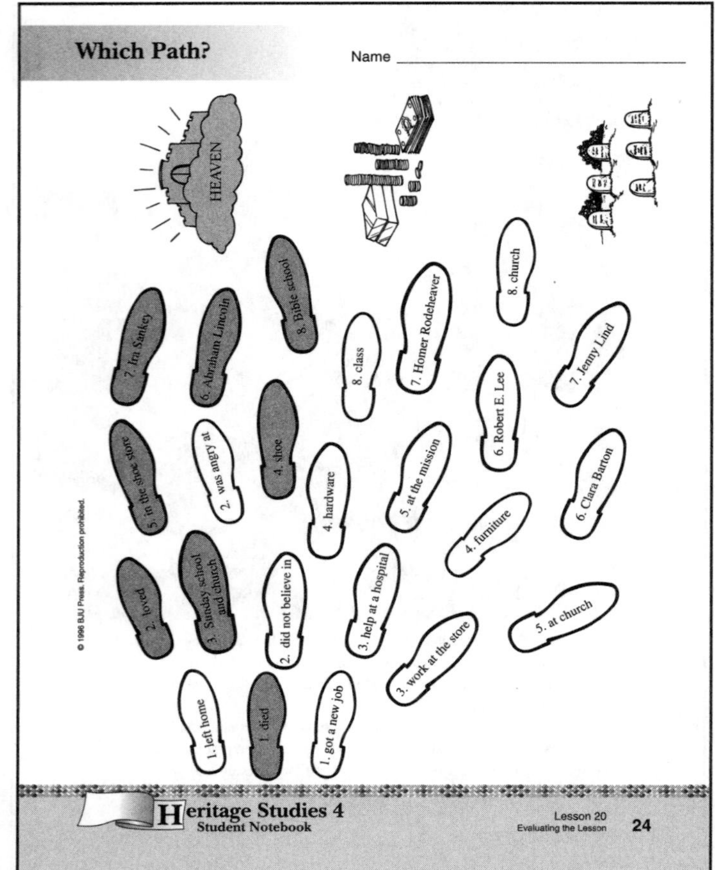

TimeLine Snapshots Activity

➤ Add the figure of Dwight L. Moody to the TimeLine at 1861.

➤ **Do you remember what Moody did in 1861?**

Fort Sumter fell in 1861, marking the beginning of the American Civil War. In that same year Moody quit his shoe business and began his ministry to soldiers. It was only the beginning of a long life devoted to winning lost souls for Christ.

Evaluating the Lesson

Notebook Activity, pages 23-24

➤ Read the instructions and statements on Notebook page 23.

➤ Complete Notebook page 24.

Going Beyond

Enrichment

Provide books for your child to read about Dwight L. Moody. Books available from Bob Jones University Press include *D. L. Moody* by David Bennett and *D. L. Moody* by Faith Coxe Bailey.

Additional Teacher Information

Dwight Lyman Ryther Moody (1837-99) was led to the Lord in his uncle's shoe store by his Sunday school teacher, Ed Kimball. For years after that, every Sunday Moody brought children to the mission on North Wells Street, in a slum district in Chicago. In 1861 Moody quit the shoe business to work full-time in the Sunday school, in the YMCA (Young Men's Christian Association), and with the soldiers engaged in the American Civil War. In August 1862 he married Emma Revell, who joined him in his ministry for the Lord. In 1864 Moody's Sunday school became a church, the Illinois Street Church.

Moody's meeting with George Mueller in 1867 influenced his prayer life and his ultimate trust in the Lord for all things. It is said that Mueller rebuked Moody, saying, "It is not what Dwight Moody can do for God; it is what God can do for Dwight Moody." Later, while attending a prayer meeting in a private home, Moody listened intently to the words of the minister, Henry Varley. "We try. We fail. We are sure we can succeed if we try harder tomorrow. We fail again. And if we succeed, it is only half success, half of what it would have been with God. We are all guilty. All. For I tell you tonight—*the world has yet to see what God can do with one man wholly committed to Him.*" Moody referred to this experience as the turning point of his ministry. That statement gripped his thinking and changed his life. From that day he determined to be wholly given over to the service of the Lord.

LESSON 21

Mary Slessor: White Ma of Calabar

Text, pages 78-79
Notebook, page 25

Preview

Main Ideas

- God has ordained evangelism.
- Religious beliefs help shape culture.
- Mary Slessor took the gospel to the heathen of Africa, influencing and changing many customs and beliefs.

Objectives

- Identify statements about Mary Slessor as either true or false
- Correct statements about Mary Slessor by changing words

Materials

- Maps and More 6 and 7, pages M2-M3

Lesson

Introducing the Lesson

**Discussion,
Maps and More 7**

➤ **Do you know any children who are twins?**
➤ **Do you think that the parents knew they were having twins before the babies were born?**
➤ **What do you think people's reactions were to the twins' birth?** *Discuss any twins that you know about and how their family reacted to their birth.*

Twins are not always welcomed with excitement. Twins who were born in Nigeria, Africa, anytime before the 1870s probably were killed. The Africans in those tropical jungles believed that twins were evil and would bring destruction upon the whole village. But hope came to these African people and especially to twins and their parents when "Ma" came.

➤ *Show Maps and More 7.*

SCOTLAND

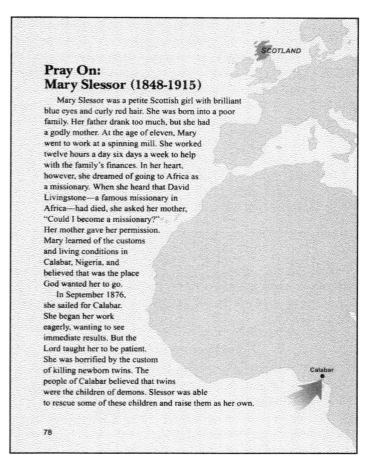

**Pray On:
Mary Slessor (1848-1915)**

Mary Slessor was a petite Scottish girl with brilliant blue eyes and curly red hair. She was born into a poor family. Her father drank too much, but she had a godly mother. At the age of eleven, Mary went to work at a spinning mill. She worked twelve hours a day six days a week to help with the family's finances. In her heart, however, she dreamed of going to Africa as a missionary. When she heard that David Livingstone—a famous missionary in Africa—had died, she asked her mother, "Could I become a missionary?" Her mother gave her permission. Mary learned of the customs and living conditions in Calabar, Nigeria, and believed that was the place God wanted her to go.

In September 1876, she sailed for Calabar. She began her work eagerly, wanting to see immediate results. But the Lord taught her to be patient. She was horrified by the custom of killing newborn twins. The people of Calabar believed that twins were the children of demons. Slessor was able to rescue some of these children and raise them as her own.

Calabar

78

This is "Ma," or Mary Slessor. She rescued as many twin babies as she could and raised many of them in her own home. In this lesson we will learn more about this amazing woman who changed the way of life for many Africans by bringing them the message of God's love.

Teaching the Lesson

**Text Discussion, page 78
and Maps and More 6**

➤ **Read page 78 to find out where Mary Slessor was born and what she dreamed of doing.** *(Scotland; becoming a missionary in Africa)*
➤ **Who was David Livingstone?** *(a famous missionary to Africa)*
➤ **What area did Mary Slessor study about after she learned of the death of David Livingstone?** *(Calabar, Nigeria)*
➤ *Show Maps and More 6.*
➤ Point to Scotland on this map and tell the name of the continent on which it lies. *(Europe)*
➤ Point to Calabar and name the continent on which it lies. *(Africa)*

Scotland is about four thousand miles away from Calabar.

- ➤ **Which direction did Mary Slessor have to travel to get from Scotland to Calabar?** *(south)*
- ➤ **How would she have made the journey?** *(by ship)*
- ➤ **How old was Mary Slessor when she first went to Calabar?** *(1876–1848=28 years old)*

The long, hard work that Mary Slessor endured as a child prepared her for the work in Calabar. The customs and beliefs of the people of Calabar were very different from what Mary Slessor was used to. The Europeans thought that the African people were uncivilized and cruel, but Mary knew that that was where God wanted her, so she was content.

God wants us to exhibit a contented spirit wherever He places us and in whatever situations we find ourselves. God knows what is best for each of us. We must trust His plans for our lives. (BATs: 2b Servanthood, 2e Work, 5c Evangelism and missions)

Text Discussion, page 79

- ➤ Write the word ***cannibal.***
- ➤ **What does this word mean?** *(a person who kills and eats other people)*
- ➤ **Read page 79 to find out what Mary Slessor did for the cannibals in Africa.** *(She took care of them, loved them, and told them about Jesus.)*
- ➤ **Why do you think Mary Slessor was burdened to take the gospel of Christ to these people?**
- ➤ **What was Mary chosen to do when the British government took over Calabar in 1889?** *(to be the vice consul for the interior of the Niger Coast Protectorate; to establish law and order)*

Even while she worked for the government in Calabar, Mary never ceased to share the gospel of Jesus Christ with the African people.

- ➤ **How many years did Mary Slessor serve the Lord in Africa?** *(thirty-nine years)*

After spending a few years at the mission station on the coast, Slessor felt God wanted her to go up the river to witness to several cannibal tribes. At first the mission was opposed to the idea, but finally she was allowed to go. Taking her children with her, she settled in one of the cannibal villages. Her love for the people was clear: she tended the sick and cared for the unwanted. The people returned her love by giving her the honored title of Ma ("mother").

Mary Slessor

When Calabar was taken over by the British government in 1889, Mary Slessor was made vice consul for the interior of the Niger Coast Protectorate. She was responsible for establishing law and order there. But she remained true to her primary task of winning people to the Lord: she faithfully gave out God's Word. When she moved fifteen years later, she left behind many Christians.

After thirty-nine years of loving service, her frail body could take no more; she went to be with the Lord on January 13, 1915. What was the secret to her successful work for the Lord? Mary Slessor said, "I have no idea how and why God has carried me over so many hard places, and made these hordes submit to me . . . except in answer to prayer at home for me. It is all beyond my comprehension. The only way I can explain it is on the ground that I have been prayed for more than most. Pray on power lies that way."

79

The cannibal tribes had never seen a white woman, nor had they ever heard of Christ before Mary Slessor came. They valued only three things: guns to have power, chains to keep slaves, and liquor. Often, whenever there was any trouble, the cry would come: "Run, Ma, run!" And Mary Slessor would hurry to the scene, bringing medicine or wisdom to settle the disputes. God gave her protection and provided for her during all those years. (BATs: 4a Sowing and reaping, 5c Evangelism and missions, 7d Contentment, 8d Courage)

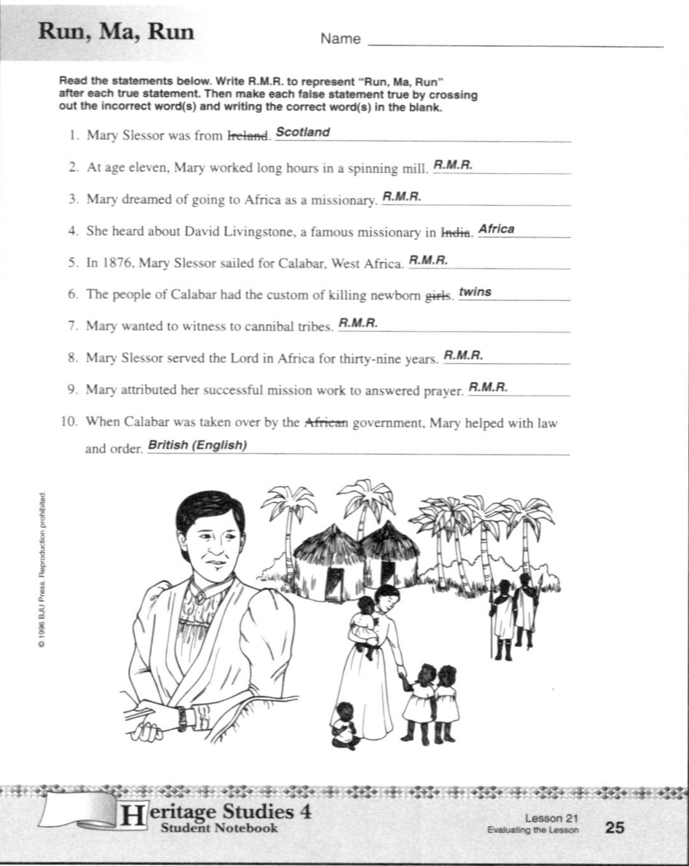

Run, Ma, Run Name ____________

Read the statements below. Write R.M.R. to represent "Run, Ma, Run" after each true statement. Then make each false statement true by crossing out the incorrect word(s) and writing the correct word(s) in the blank.

1. Mary Slessor was from ~~Ireland~~. *Scotland*
2. At age eleven, Mary worked long hours in a spinning mill. *R.M.R.*
3. Mary dreamed of going to Africa as a missionary. *R.M.R.*
4. She heard about David Livingstone, a famous missionary in ~~India~~. *Africa*
5. In 1876, Mary Slessor sailed for Calabar, West Africa. *R.M.R.*
6. The people of Calabar had the custom of killing newborn ~~girls~~. *twins*
7. Mary wanted to witness to cannibal tribes. *R.M.R.*
8. Mary Slessor served the Lord in Africa for thirty-nine years. *R.M.R.*
9. Mary attributed her successful mission work to answered prayer. *R.M.R.*
10. When Calabar was taken over by the ~~African~~ government, Mary helped with law and order. *British (English)*

Heritage Studies 4 Student Notebook — Lesson 21 Evaluating the Lesson 25

Evaluating the Lesson

Notebook Activity, page 25

➤ Read the instructions on Notebook page 25 and complete the page.

➤ *After your child has completed the page, read the statements aloud, instructing him to provide the word he wrote to correct the false statements and to say "Run, Ma, Run" for each true statement.*

Going Beyond

Enrichment

Borrow or purchase the audio cassettes "Run, Ma, Run" for your child to listen to during his free time. (*NOTE:* The audio cassettes and story visuals by the same name, "Run, Ma, Run," are available from Bob Jones University Press.)

Additional Teacher Information

Even as a child Mary Mitchell Slessor (1848-1915) longed to be a missionary in the jungles of Africa. She was twenty-eight years old when she first arrived in Calabar, with its hot, tropical jungles and its cannibal tribes and cruel, superstitious beliefs. Desiring to teach the love and forgiveness of Christ, she quickly came to realize that the truth of God's love must be lived before it can be taught. Slessor adopted the motto "Learn of me," representing Christ in her actions as well as in her words. Among the Christians who assisted Mary Slessor in her mission work was King Eyo Honesty VII, the chief at Creek Town.

To recognize Slessor's years of work for the Lord, the Mission Committee in Scotland established a medical base in Itu and named the hospital the Mary Slessor Mission Hospital. At age sixty-five, she was elected to membership in the Order of the Hospital of St. John of Jerusalem in England and received its Silver Cross. Though these recognitions were kindly received, Mary Slessor's only desire was to do the work that God had sent her to do. Of her sixty-six years, she spent thirty-nine teaching—and living—the gospel in the jungles of Calabar, Nigeria, on the continent of Africa. Mary Slessor was buried on a hillside by the mission station at which she first served in Duke Town.

Lesson 22
Hudson Taylor—To China with Love

Text, pages 80-82

Preview

Main Ideas

- God has ordained evangelism.
- Throughout history, cultures have borrowed from each other.
- Religious beliefs help shape cultures.
- Hudson Taylor's adaptation to the Chinese culture and his love for the Chinese people and for the Lord helped his ministry to flourish.

Objective

- Participate in a matching game about Hudson Taylor

Materials

- Ingredients and utensils for baking fortune cookies (see below) *OR* construction-paper circles (about 3" diameter)*
- Maps and More 8, page M3
- A globe or atlas with a world map
- 2 rice bowls or baskets
- A metal saucepan
- A rubber hammer or a large metal cooking spoon
- 24 fortune cookies, either baked or made of paper, with a strip containing one of the sentence parts inside each. (*NOTE:* If you are baking the fortune cookies, bake them a few days ahead to allow the cookies to harden. Refer to the following recipe.)
- Appendix, page A31: sentence beginnings and endings

Cut apart the strips, including the two parts of the sentences. Keep the cookies (real or paper) containing the beginning strips separate from those with the endings.

Fortune Cookies

3 egg whites	$\frac{1}{2}$ cup margarine, melted
$\frac{3}{4}$ cup granulated sugar	$\frac{1}{2}$ cup all-purpose flour
$\frac{1}{8}$ teaspoon salt	2 teaspoons almond extract

Preheat oven to 350°F. Beat egg whites until frothy. Beat in sugar and salt. Stir in butter, flour, and almond extract. Making no more than six cookies at a time, drop batter by rounded teaspoons onto an ungreased baking sheet about three inches apart. Bake eight to ten minutes or until edges are light golden brown.

While cookies are warm and pliable, hold each cookie in your palm and place a half-sentence strip on one-half of the cookie. Fold the cookie in half over the slip of paper. Drape the center of the folded cookie over the handle of a wooden spoon or over the edge of the batter bowl. Fold the edges of the cookie around the spoon until the sides touch; slide off the spoon. Repeat with the remaining cookies. If cookies become brittle, return them to the oven for one minute to soften.

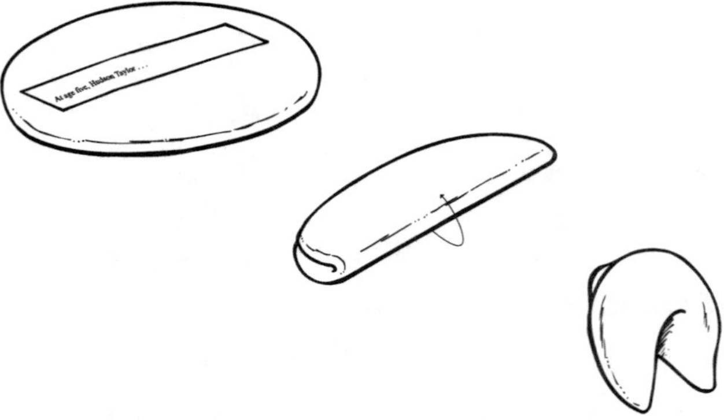

Notes

If you prefer to make paper fortune cookies, fold the construction-paper circles in half, placing a half-sentence strip inside each one. Staple the rounded edges of the "cookie" in two or three places to hold the paper inside. Bend the paper cookie slightly to resemble a fortune cookie.

Day 1

Lesson

Introducing the Lesson

Listening Activity, Maps and More 8

➤ *Show your child Maps and More 8.* This is a picture of a man named Hudson Taylor.

➤ Listen as I read aloud a narrative poem about Hudson Taylor.

In long-ago England was born a dear lad.
Hudson learned of the Lord every day.
With the family he prayed and the Bible obeyed,
To know God's will and His way.

South of the Clouds,
North of the Lake,
West of the Mountains,
Clear Sea—
The great Master of life laid the plans.

Sweet tea and some crumpets, manners, and style—
The evangelist's son was well bred.
Hudson Taylor soon learned the value of prayer
And was willing to go where God led.

South of the Clouds,
North of the Lake,
West of the Mountains,
Clear Sea—
Merely faraway names on the map.

To do God's work was his only desire,
So to China he willingly sailed.
The Chinese were different, their language was strange.
Hudson tried to preach—but he failed.

South of the Clouds,
North of the Lake,
West of the Mountains,
Clear Sea—
He must reach them for Christ—but how?

He shaved his head, wove a braid in the back,
Wore a robe with fullness of sleeve.
Whatever it took to serve his great God
And to help the Chinese believe.

South of the Clouds,
North of the Lake,
West of the Mountains,
Clear Sea—
He wanted to be more like them.

He moved among them, fitting in with the crowd,
And taught of his dear Lord above.
With prayer and much work through all the long years
The Chinese learned of God's love.

South of the Clouds,
North of the Lake,
West of the Mountains,
Clear Sea—
China's faraway names were now home.

We will learn more about this missionary to China in this lesson.

To the Uttermost:
J. Hudson Taylor (1832-1905)

J. Hudson Taylor was a man who set himself to do God's will. At the age of five, after hearing his father talk about the need for taking the gospel to China, he declared, "One day I will go to that country." In 1849, at seventeen, he dedicated himself to the Lord's service. In 1853, after receiving a medical degree, he set sail for China.

A Chinese city such as Taylor might have seen

After nearly six months, the twenty-two-year-old Hudson Taylor arrived in Shanghai. In the city streets were men with long pigtails and women with tiny bound feet. Everywhere he heard the Chinese language. Later, he wrote in his journal: "Mingled with thankfulness for deliverance from many dangers and joy at finding myself at last on Chinese soil came a vivid realization of the great distance between me and those I loved, and that I was a stranger in a strange land."

Taylor spent many hours learning to speak and read Chinese. He came to believe that the best way to reach the Chinese was to become as nearly Chinese as possible. After much prayer, Taylor decided to follow Paul in being made all things to all men (I Cor. 9:22). He knew the other missionaries would think he was wrong, even crazy. But Taylor was sure it was God's leading:

80

Teaching the Lesson

Text Discussion, page 80

- **Read page 80 to find out what Hudson Taylor believed to be the best way to reach the Chinese for Christ.** *(become as nearly Chinese as possible)*
- **How old was Hudson Taylor when he said he wanted to take the gospel to China?** *(five years old)*

The Lord kept this desire within Hudson Taylor's heart, and he sailed for China in 1853.

- Point to England and China on the globe or world map.
- **How long was Hudson Taylor onboard ship, sailing from England to China?** *(six months)*
- **Read aloud what Hudson Taylor wrote in his journal after arriving in China.** *("Mingled with thankfulness. . . I was a stranger in a strange land.")*
- **Why do you think Hudson Taylor felt that he was "a stranger in a strange land" and that there was a "great distance" between him and the Chinese people?** *(Answers will probably include that he was a long way from home and that he did not look, talk, or act like the Chinese.)*

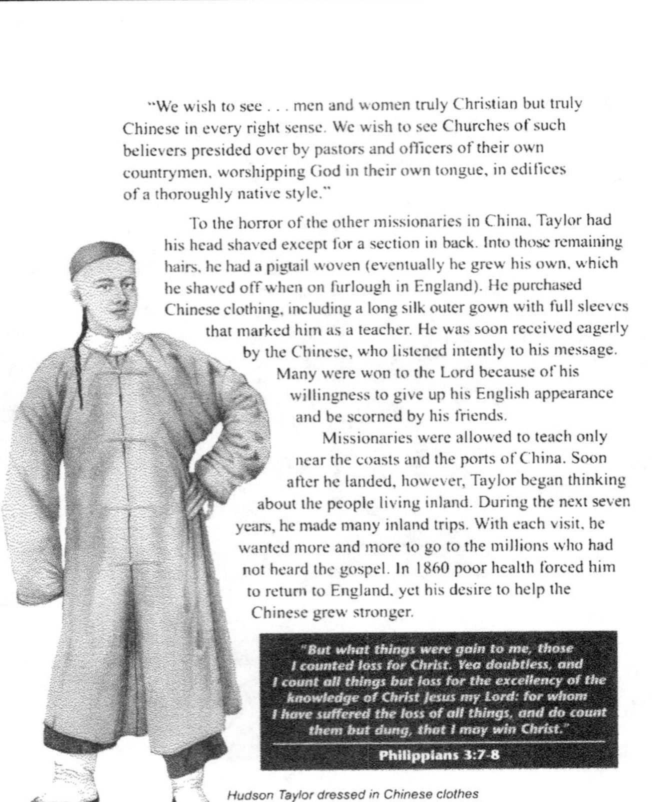

"We wish to see . . . men and women truly Christian but truly Chinese in every right sense. We wish to see Churches of such believers presided over by pastors and officers of their own countrymen, worshipping God in their own tongue, in edifices of a thoroughly native style."

To the horror of the other missionaries in China, Taylor had his head shaved except for a section in back. Into those remaining hairs, he had a pigtail woven (eventually he grew his own, which he shaved off when on furlough in England). He purchased Chinese clothing, including a long silk outer gown with full sleeves that marked him as a teacher. He was soon received eagerly by the Chinese, who listened intently to his message. Many were won to the Lord because of his willingness to give up his English appearance and be scorned by his friends.

Missionaries were allowed to teach only near the coasts and the ports of China. Soon after he landed, however, Taylor began thinking about the people living inland. During the next seven years, he made many inland trips. With each visit, he wanted more and more to go to the millions who had not heard the gospel. In 1860 poor health forced him to return to England, yet his desire to help the Chinese grew stronger.

"But what things were gain to me, those I counted loss for Christ. Yea doubtless, and I count all things but loss for the excellency of the knowledge of Christ Jesus my Lord: for whom I have suffered the loss of all things, and do count them but dung, that I may win Christ."

Philippians 3:7-8

Hudson Taylor dressed in Chinese clothes

81

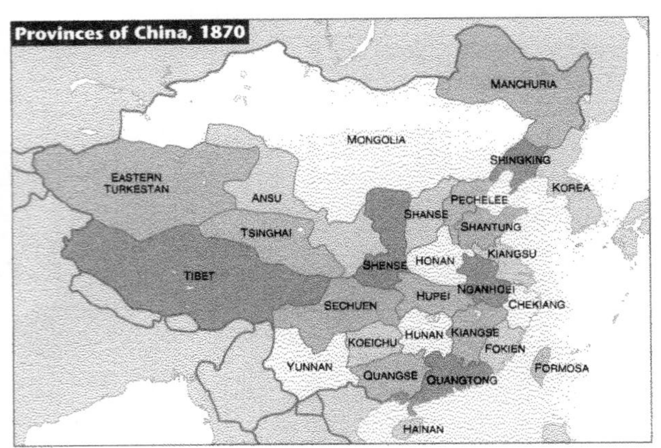

Five years went by. Taylor revised the Chinese New Testament, waiting to go where there were "a million a month dying without God." But in the summer of 1865, he prayed that God would send twenty-four workers to inland China. Immediately he felt a peace in his heart and strength in his body. He opened a bank account in the name of the China Inland Mission, an organization dedicated to missionary work in China. He was acting on faith: the account held only ten pounds. God honored his faith. On May 26, 1866, Taylor, his family, and twenty-four dedicated men and women set sail for China.

Hudson Taylor and the other missionaries were often called "foreign devil" or "Western dog." Some Chinese people hated foreigners so much that they spread terrible stories. The worst was that the missionaries kidnapped children to use their eyes and hearts for medicine. Returning good for evil, the missionaries won respect among the people. By the time he died in 1905, Hudson Taylor had seen mission stations set up in every province.

82

Text Discussion, page 81

- Notice the picture of Hudson Taylor on page 81.
- **Read this page to find out what Hudson Taylor did to make himself "as nearly Chinese as possible."** *(He learned the Chinese language. He shaved his head except for a section in the back that he had woven into a pigtail. He wore Chinese clothing, including a long silk gown with full sleeves.)*

The Chinese called the pigtail a ***queue***. Chinese women were forced to bind their feet. Among the Chinese customs of long ago, the queue of the men and the tiny feet of the women were favored.

- **What did the Chinese people think about Hudson Taylor after he changed?** *(They received him eagerly and listened to him.)*
- **What did Hudson Taylor's English friends think about his change in appearance?** *(They thought he was crazy. They scorned him.)*
- **In what areas of China were missionaries allowed to preach in those early days?** *(near the coast and the ports)*
- **Where else did Hudson Taylor desire to take the gospel?** *(to the Chinese who lived inland)*

This desire became an earnest prayer of Hudson Taylor. Taylor's illness only temporarily slowed his progress with the Chinese people. God greatly used him even during his illness. (BATs: 2d Goal setting, 5c Evangelism and missions, 6b Prayer)

Day 2

Text Discussion, page 82

- **Read page 82 to find out how God used Hudson Taylor while he was ill.** *(He revised the Chinese New Testament and prayed for more workers.)*
- **How did God answer the prayer of Hudson Taylor for more missionaries for China?** *(God supplied twenty-four missionaries for inland China. This group began the China Inland Mission.)*
- Look at the map of early China on page 82.

The twenty-four people that God supplied were sent throughout the land of China. There were two missionaries for each province that did not yet have any mission work, as well as two missionaries for Mongolia.

Though the missionaries were not always welcomed by the Chinese, God protected them and enabled them to preach the gospel of peace. No matter what happened, the missionaries tried to have a good testimony and to show God's love to the Chinese. (BATs: 4b Purity, 5a Love, 5d Communication)

Evaluating the Lesson

Matching Game

Place the fortune cookies in two rice bowls or baskets, keeping the cookies with the beginning statements separate from the cookies with the conclusions.

➤ Choose one fortune cookie containing the first part of a statement and then choose one cookie containing the completion of a statement.

Demonstrate the sound of the "Chinese gong" by striking the metal saucepan with the rubber hammer or large metal cooking spoon.

➤ If your two parts of sentences form a correct sentence, sound the gong. If they do not, choose another ending cookie until you find matching parts. Continue until all the sentences have been matched.

You may want your child to tape together the matching portions of the statements.

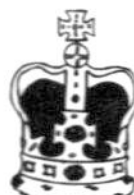

If you are teaching a group of children, you may make this more interesting by passing out beginning strips to half the children and ending strips to the other half. The children will then try to find their partners by matching the beginnings and endings of the sentences.

Going Beyond

Enrichment

Encourage your child to look around your home to find items that are stamped *Made in China.*

Additional Teacher Information

Hudson Taylor (1832-1905) was born in Barnsley, Yorkshire, England, to a godly family. Hudson Taylor tells in his autobiography, *To China . . . with Love,* that seven years after sailing to China he learned of his father's prayer before Hudson was born for a son who might be called of the Lord to minister in the needy empire of China. God answered that prayer in the life and service of Hudson Taylor. At age twenty-two, he sailed to Shanghai, China.

Hudson Taylor was not only a missionary and preacher but also a medical doctor and writer. He served with the China Inland Mission for fifty years, many times asking the Lord for more missionaries and seeing the Lord faithfully supply the need. Hudson Taylor believed that nothing was too small to pray about. In his autobiography, he relates: "There is nothing small, and there is nothing great. Only God is great. We should trust Him fully." And he did.

Lesson 23
To Do the Work of Christ

Text, pages 83-84
Notebook, pages 26-35

Preview

Main Ideas

- God has ordained evangelism.
- Religious beliefs help shape cultures.
- People everywhere have needs and wants.
- Missionaries take the gospel to people of many lands.
- Missionaries are supported by the prayers and financial aid of other Christians.

Objectives

- Read and summarize a prayer letter from a missionary
- Locate a mission field on a world map
- Make a missionary booklet

Materials

- Two missionary prayer cards or letters* (*NOTE:* Letters should represent different missionaries and different countries of the world.)
- A globe or atlas with a world map
- Two sheets of construction paper or tagboard*
- 3 metal brads or 3 four-inch lengths of yarn*
- A hole puncher

Prepare the construction paper or tagboard to be used as the front and back of the missionary booklet by punching holes on the left to line up with the holes on Notebook pages 26-35.

Notes

If you are not able to acquire two different prayer cards or letters, adjust the management of the *Learning How* activity to fit your situation.

◆ THINGS PEOPLE DO ◆

Getting Missionary Support

Most missionaries are supported by money from churches and people in their home country. The missionaries use this money to pay for the things they need: food, clothing, and housing. The money often pays the costs of their ministry too. Because other Christians give money to their work, the missionaries can spend their time spreading the gospel and training Christians.

Missionaries receive money for their work in different ways. Sometimes one church will support just a few missionaries. Sometimes many churches give money to a *mission board.* The mission board uses the money to support missionaries. Most often, missionaries visit many churches and ask each one to give a part of the money they need.

When missionaries go to a field, they usually go with the promise of a certain amount of money to support them each month. If, after they arrive on the field, prices rise faster than expected, the missionaries may have to move to cheaper housing and cut food and clothing expenses. It is important that God's people make themselves aware of missionaries' needs and strive to meet them.

The Randall Studdard family, missionaries in northern Cameroon

83

◆ LEARNING HOW ◆

To Help Missionaries

1. Get your Notebook, a pen or pencil, and the letter or card your teacher gives you.

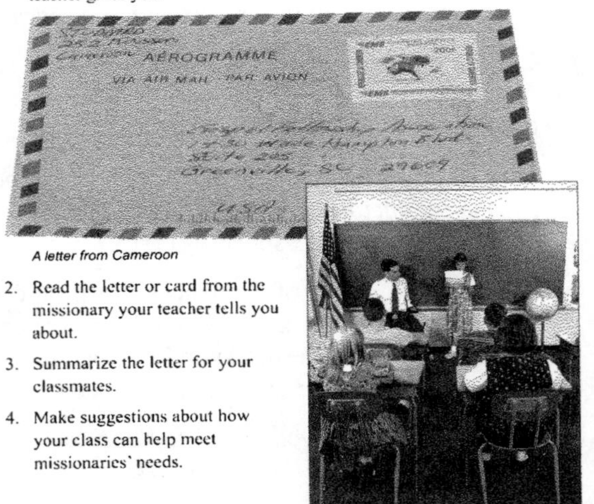

A letter from Cameroon

2. Read the letter or card from the missionary your teacher tells you about.
3. Summarize the letter for your classmates.
4. Make suggestions about how your class can help meet missionaries' needs.

Talking about how to be a help to missionaries

84

Day 1

Lesson

Introducing the Lesson

Map Activity

➤ Look at the two missionary cards or letters. Select the one that you would like to learn more about.

➤ Scan the card or letter to find the country in which your missionary is ministering. Locate that country on the map or the globe.

➤ Keep the missionary prayer letter to use later in the lesson. We will be learning more about the missionary's ministry.

➤ Make it your goal to pray for this particular missionary every day for at least a month. (BATs: 5c Evangelism and missions, 6b Prayer)

You will be using the other missionary card or letter as a teaching model. Locate this missionary's country on the map or the globe as well.

Teaching the Lesson

Text Discussion, page 83

➤ **Read page 83 to find out why missionaries need to raise money for their support on the mission field.** *(to help pay for their food, clothing, and housing, and to help with the ministry too)*

Missionary families need the same things that our family needs. Whatever will help the missionary family stay on the mission field to accomplish God's work is important. Whatever helps them reach people for the Lord is important also.

➤ **How can God's people keep up with the current needs of missionaries?** *(Write letters to missionaries. Read missionary letters. Talk with the missionaries at church. Visit them on the mission field.)*

Missionary Report: Part I

Name ______________________

Use your missionary prayer letter to complete the following information.

Prepared by ______________________

1. Missionary's name: ______________________
2. Date of letter: ______________________
3. Address of missionary:

____

____

____

4. Name of mission board or sponsoring church:

____

Heritage Studies 4 Student Notebook — Lesson 23 Teaching the Lesson 26

Missionary Report: Part II

Complete the following information about your missionary.

1. What details does the writer give about his home or about his family?

____

____

____

____

2. What seems to be the main theme of the letter? ______________________

____

____

____

3. What prayer requests does the writer give?

- ______________________
- ______________________
- ______________________
- ______________________

Heritage Studies 4 Student Notebook — Lesson 23 Teaching the Lesson 27

Learning How Activity, page 84 and Notebook pages 26-28

The purpose of the first part of this lesson is to model the steps in researching and summarizing material. Guide your child through the steps of reading the letter, summarizing, and writing the information asked for on Notebook pages 26-28. Notebook pages 29-35 will be completed independently, using the chosen letter. If you are teaching more than one child, you may all work together on the first missionary letter.

- ➤ **Read the steps in the *Learning How* activity on page 84.**
- ➤ **Read your prayer letter.**
- ➤ We will be working together to fill out the information on Notebook pages 26-28.

Missionary Report: Part III

Name ______________________

Complete the following information.

1. The two most important needs that ____________ (name of missionary) has are ____________

____

____

______________________.

2. What I can do for ____________ (name of missionary) is ____________

____

____

______________________.

3. Our class might also help by ______________________

____

____

______________________.

Heritage Studies 4 Student Notebook — Lesson 23 Teaching the Lesson 28

Checklist

Name ______________________

Use the following checklist as a guide in completing a missionary booklet for Lesson 23. Check off when each item is complete.

	I Have Done This	Points Earned
Cover (Design and color. Include missionary's name and/or field plus your name and the date.)	________	________
page 1—family information	________	________
page 2—map study	________	________
page 3—flag and capital	________	________
page 4—culture	________	________
page 5—the gospel	________	________
page 6—items of interest	________	________
Include any pictures, drawings, foreign stamps, or foreign currency	________	________

Missionary Booklet: 1

Name ______________________

The missionary's family includes

______________________ (father) ______________________ (mother)

____

____

____

____

____

______________________ (children)

(Staple missionary letter here.)

Day 2

Evaluating the Lesson

Missionary Booklet Activity, Notebook pages 29-35

➤ Today you will begin making a missionary booklet to represent your missionary, his field, his ministry, and his needs.

The two pieces of construction paper or tagboard will serve as the cover and backing for the booklet.

➤ Design a cover to represent the missionary or his place of service.

➤ Use Notebook page 29 as a checklist of items to include in your booklet.

➤ Collect the resource materials you will need to help you find the information for completing Notebook pages 30-35.

➤ Complete all the Notebook pages.

Assign a date for final completion of the booklet. Guide your child in setting daily goals for work to be accomplished in order to meet the due date. Encourage him to work independently to achieve his goals.

Missionary Booklet: 2

______________________ (missionary's name) serves the Lord in ______________________ (city),

______________________ (country or state), on the continent of ______________________ (continent).

Draw or trace a map to show that mission field.

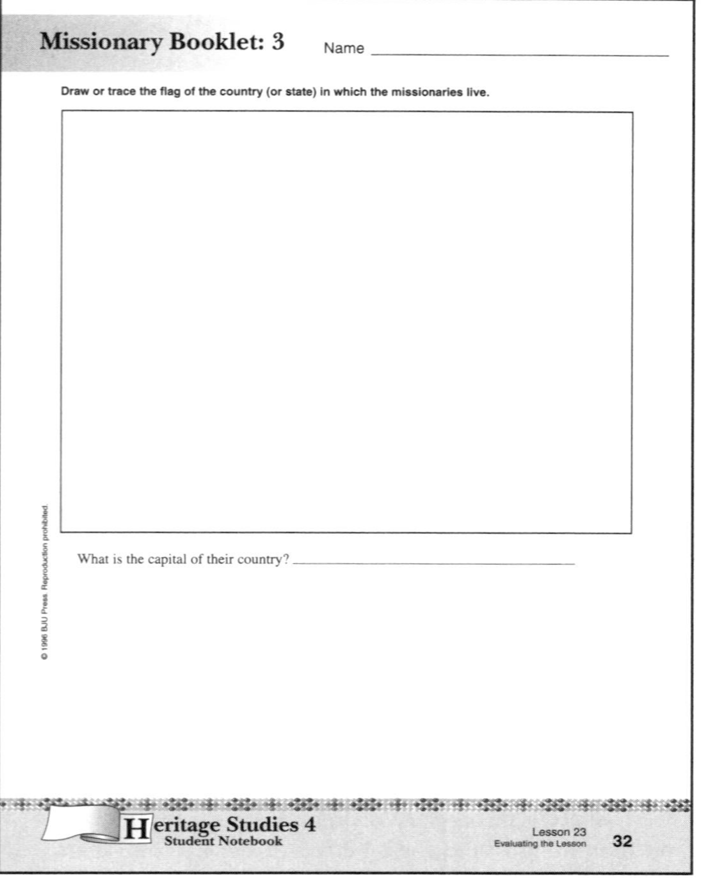

Missionary Booklet: 3

Name ______________________

Draw or trace the flag of the country (or state) in which the missionaries live.

What is the capital of their country? ______________________

Missionary Booklet: 4

Name ______________________

One interesting food of the country is ______________________.

The main language in the country is ______________________.

The weather is usually ______________________.

The temperature sometimes goes as high as ______ and sometimes as low as ______.

The average rainfall is about ______________________.

The main religion of the country is ______________________.

The currency is called ______________________.

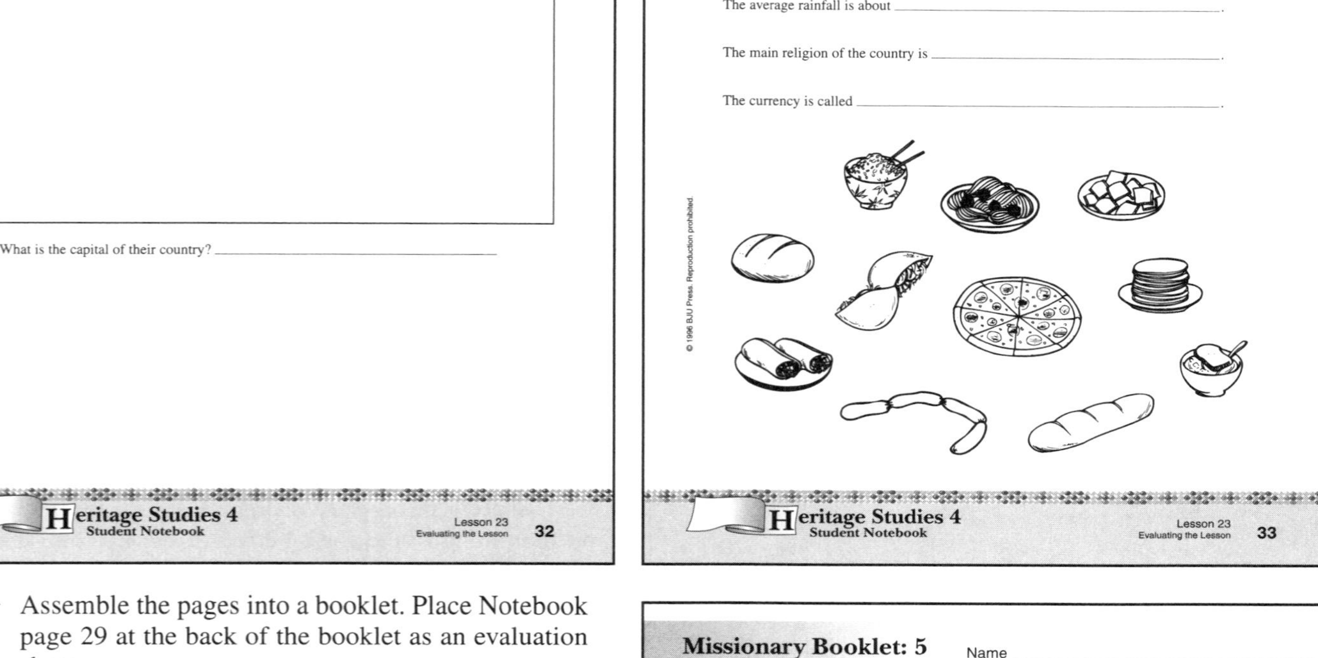

- ➤ Assemble the pages into a booklet. Place Notebook page 29 at the back of the booklet as an evaluation sheet.
- ➤ Staple the center portion of the missionary letter or card to the first report page.
- ➤ Use the yarn or brads to fasten the pages together.

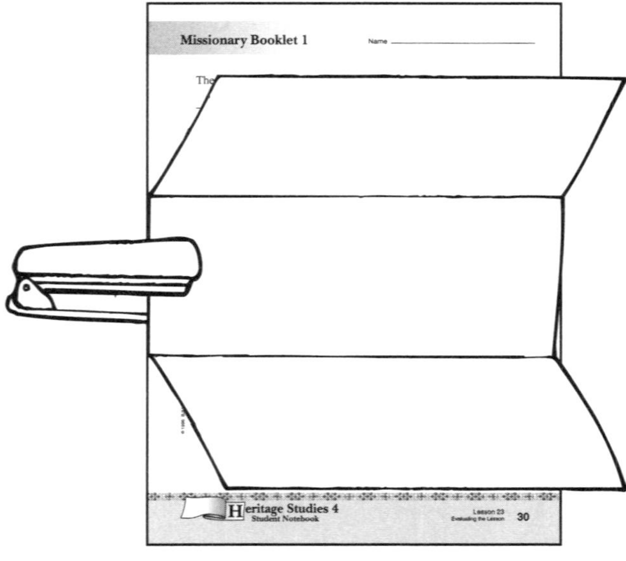

Missionary Booklet: 5

Name ______________________

The missionaries teach the gospel to people who are ______________________ (describe)

____

______________________.

Here is a verse they might use. ______________________

____

____

____

Here is a prayer request from the missionary. ______________________

____

____

____

I want to help the missionaries by ______________________

____

____

______________________.

Missionary Booklet: 6 Name ____________

Here are some interesting things I've learned about the missionaries. ____________

Here is a picture of an interesting place to visit on the mission field.

Heritage Studies 4 Student Notebook — Lesson 23 Evaluating the Lesson — 35

Oral Report

- ➤ Review the information you have learned about your missionary. Organize a summary.
- ➤ Present an oral report about your missionary.

It is very beneficial for your child to learn to present oral reports. It is often easier to begin this process while the child is young. You may help him choose a setting, such as Sunday school, children's church, family devotions, or other appropriate gatherings.

Going Beyond

Enrichment

Set up a small area in your schoolroom where your child may display pictures, post cards, artifacts, and so on that represent the mission field that he has learned about. This may become a part of his oral presentation about the missionary and his field of service.

Additional Teacher Information

Before going to the mission field, many missionary candidates join a mission board that offers advice and often assists them with prayer letters and distribution of funds. The missionary candidates usually enter a period of about two to three years called *deputation,* during which they travel to various churches around the country, presenting their mission field and their goals for service. Often the host church presents a *love offering* to the missionary to help with travel expenses as he journeys to another church. Churches and individuals are encouraged to pledge to support the missionary financially for a certain amount each month while he is on the mission field. When the missionary raises 100 percent of the amount needed to live on and to serve the Lord, he journeys to the mission field to start his work.

Usually a missionary or missionary family remains on the mission field for a period of two to four years, building churches, witnessing to the unsaved, giving out tracts, and helping in any way possible to win the people to Christ. At the completion of two to four years, the missionary family usually returns home for a period of *furlough.* The family gets a much needed time of refreshment with family and friends during the furlough. Often the missionary travels to the churches that support him, showing slides of the mission work and reporting on what has been accomplished for the Lord in the area. It is then that the churches decide to continue with support, discontinue support, or increase the support. Usually the missionary returns to his mission field at the end of the furlough.

LESSON 24
"Go . . . and Teach All Nations"

Text, pages 85-88
Notebook, pages 36-37

Preview

Main Ideas

- Man's view of God determines his philosophy and history.
- God has ordained evangelism.
- Religious beliefs help shape cultures.
- Missionaries teach the gospel to people in many countries around the world.

Objectives

- Locate continents on a globe/map
- Complete the answers for a crossword puzzle

Materials

- A globe or world map
- A Bible

Day 1

Lesson

Introducing the Lesson

Review Activity

➤ **What evangelist have we studied in this chapter?** *(Dwight L. Moody)*

➤ Find on the globe or world map the continents on which Moody served. *(North America and Europe)*

➤ **What two missionaries have we studied, and where did they serve?** *(Mary Slessor—Africa; Hudson Taylor—Asia)* Point to these places on the globe.

Evangelists and missionaries serve the Lord around the world, sharing the gospel of Christ. In this lesson we will learn about four more missionaries. They served on the continents of South America, Asia, Australia, and Africa. (BATs: 5c Evangelism and missions)

➤ Find these continents on the globe.

Other Missionaries

Francisco Penzotti

In 1864, thirteen-year-old Francisco Penzotti received an amazing offer. One of his relatives was moving from Italy to South America, and he asked Francisco to go with him. The young Italian eagerly agreed, and soon he was living in Montevideo, Uruguay. One day when he was about twenty-five years old, Penzotti attended a church service, and he was converted.

Penzotti began passing out Bibles in Bolivia, Chile, and Peru. While in Peru, Penzotti realized the people needed more than just Bibles. He moved his family to the city of Callao and began a church. Laws about non-Catholic churches were very strict in Peru. Penzotti carefully obeyed the rules, but in 1890 the authorities arrested him for breaking the religious laws. Protestants and other lovers of freedom all over Latin America rallied to support Penzotti. Newspapers, ministers, and politicians in the United States urged Peru's government to release the preacher. For two years his case dragged through the courts while Penzotti lived in a filthy jail known as "the house that kills." At last the government released Penzotti. He had won not only his own freedom but also the freedom to preach the gospel even more widely throughout Peru.

Modern seller of Bibles in area where Penzotti worked

85

Teaching the Lesson

Text Discussion, page 85

➤ **Read page 85 to find out what nationality Penzotti was.** *(Italian)*

➤ Locate Italy on a map or globe. **What continent is Italy on?** *(Europe)*

➤ **To which continent did Francisco Penzotti move?** *(South America)*

➤ Locate on the map the country in South America where Penzotti first lived. *(Uruguay)*

➤ Find on the map the South American countries in which Penzotti passed out Bibles. *(Uruguay, Bolivia, Chile, and Peru)*

➤ Describe how Penzotti ended up in "the house that kills" and what he did after he was released. *(He preached and started a church in Peru and was thrown in prison. When he was released from jail, he preached God's Word again.)*

Penzotti had been very diligent in obeying all the laws. He was falsely accused of breaking the religious laws. God preserved him for an even greater ministry.

Pandita Ramabai

Pandita with the people that she helped

Pandita Ramabai was born in India in 1858. Her father, a high-caste Hindu teacher, unlike other Hindu leaders of that time, believed that women should receive the same education as men. He taught Pandita to read and memorize the religious literature of India.

After her parents died in a famine, Pandita married an Indian lawyer. Within two years, her husband died, leaving her with a small child. A widow in Hinduism had to shave her head, was forced to wear special garments, and could associate with very few people. Pandita began studying English and the Scriptures with a Christian schoolteacher from Great Britain. Pandita became convinced that Christianity was the true religion. She believed the Bible, but she did not personally accept Christ as Savior.

Pandita Ramabai

Pandita began a home for young widows. And she kept reading the Bible. Soon she realized that she needed the Savior. She led her students to Christ as well. Many Hindus who had been giving her money and other help pulled away. With the help of God, however, Pandita continued her home. And the work flourished; as many as nineteen hundred girls lived at the home at one time. By the time of her death in 1922, Pandita Ramabai had taken in and helped over three thousand people.

86

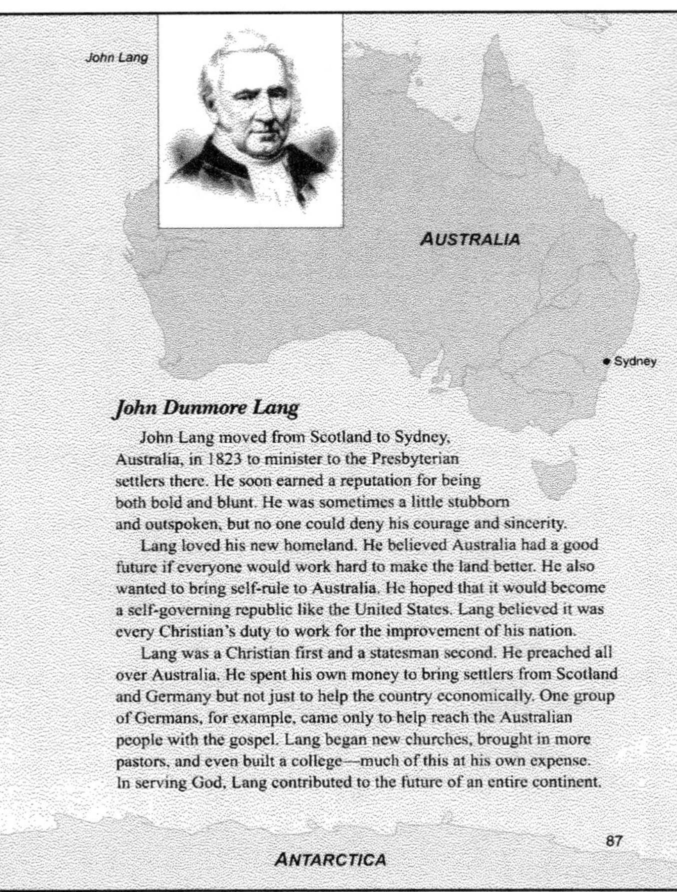

John Dunmore Lang

John Lang moved from Scotland to Sydney, Australia, in 1823 to minister to the Presbyterian settlers there. He soon earned a reputation for being both bold and blunt. He was sometimes a little stubborn and outspoken, but no one could deny his courage and sincerity.

Lang loved his new homeland. He believed Australia had a good future if everyone would work hard to make the land better. He also wanted to bring self-rule to Australia. He hoped that it would become a self-governing republic like the United States. Lang believed it was every Christian's duty to work for the improvement of his nation.

Lang was a Christian first and a statesman second. He preached all over Australia. He spent his own money to bring settlers from Scotland and Germany but not just to help the country economically. One group of Germans, for example, came only to help reach the Australian people with the gospel. Lang began new churches, brought in more pastors, and even built a college—much of this at his own expense. In serving God, Lang contributed to the future of an entire continent.

87

Text Discussion, page 86

Another missionary ministered on the continent of Asia, specifically in the country of India.

- ➤ Find India on the globe. **On what continent is India located?** *(Asia)*
- ➤ **Read page 86 to find out how Pandita Ramabai from India became interested in the Bible.** *(She studied English with a Christian schoolteacher who used the Bible in the lessons.)*
- ➤ **What is the main religion in India?** *(Hinduism)*
- ➤ **What did Pandita Ramabai's father do that was against the Hindu religion?** *(He taught his daughter to read and memorize the religious literature of India.)*
- ➤ **Was this the true gospel?** *(no)*

Because of her knowledge of the Hindu religion, Ramabai was able to compare its beliefs and doctrines with those that she learned from the Bible. This comparison and study convinced her that Christianity is the true religion.

- ➤ **How did Pandita Ramabai come to realize her need of the Savior?** *(When she read the Bible, the Holy Spirit convicted her and showed her her need for Christ.)*
- ➤ **What kind of home did Ramabai start?** *(a home for young widows)*

In India, young girls of eleven or twelve often were married to old men. When the old men died, the young wives were dismissed from the family and were thrust out on their own. In Pandita Ramabai's home these child widows were given a place to live and were taught about Christ. God used this educated, compassionate woman to meet the physical and spiritual needs of many people in India.

Day 2

Text Discussion, page 87

- ➤ **Read page 87 to find out what John Lang believed to be every Christian's duty.** *(to work for the improvement of his nation)*
- ➤ Show on the world map where John Lang was born. *(in Scotland)*
- ➤ Point to the city that he claimed as his new homeland. *(Sydney, Australia)*
- ➤ **Why did Lang use his own money to bring in more settlers to Australia from other countries?** *(to help Australia become a self-governing republic like the United States and to reach the Australian people with the gospel)*
- ➤ **What term have we learned that would describe these settlers that came to live in Australia?** *(immigrants)*

SCOTLAND

Andrew Murray

Andrew Murray was born in South Africa, where his parents had moved from Scotland to minister to the Dutch settlers. When Andrew was only ten, his father sent him to Scotland to study. There Murray decided to follow in his father's footsteps and enter the ministry. After graduating from Aberdeen University, Murray went to Holland. Although he had studied the Bible and theology for years, he did not feel sure that he was saved. But while in Holland, young Murray trusted the Lord completely. He began to practice his Dutch intensely so that he could teach both British and Dutch settlers in South Africa.

Andrew Murray, who spent his long life in God's service

In 1848 Murray returned to his homeland. He pastored several churches and became a leader in the Dutch Reformed Church. Some Dutch Reformed pastors began to teach that Christ was not the Son of God and that His blood could not save people from their sins. Murray and the other Bible-believing pastors did everything they could to stop such preaching in South Africa. Murray followed the Bible's command to "earnestly contend for the faith which was once delivered unto the saints" (Jude 3).

Andrew Murray was both a preacher and a writer. He toured South Africa, preaching in churches all over the country. He also helped start a school for training preachers and another for missionaries. He wrote more than 250 books, in both Dutch and English. He organized missions in other parts of Africa. He, like many other missionaries, found that having compassion for others' souls did indeed make a difference (Jude 22).

SOUTH AFRICA

88

Text Discussion, page 88

➤ **Read page 88 to find out where Andrew Murray was born and where God led him.** *(He was born in South Africa, moved to Scotland and Holland, and then back to South Africa again.)*

➤ Trace on the map the path that Andrew Murray's life followed. *(South Africa, Scotland, Holland, and then back to South Africa)*

➤ **What did Andrew's father do for a living?** *(He was a preacher.)*

➤ **Why was Andrew Murray sent to Scotland as a young boy?** *(to study)*

➤ **When did Murray gain full assurance that he was saved?** *(as an adult, after he moved to Holland)*

Murray was studying to be a minister when he finally came to know Christ as personal Savior. After his salvation he was strongly concerned for the people in South Africa. He determined to go back to minister as his father had done in South Africa.

➤ **Do we have family members involved in the same types of jobs or professions as other family members?**

The Lord directs the lives of Christians but often uses the influences of people close to them as instruments in His leading.

The Lord expects Christians to be faithful in daily Bible reading and prayer to develop a close relationship with Him. (BATs: 3a Self-concept, 6a Bible study, 6b Prayer; Bible Promises: H. God as Father, I. God as Master)

Andrew Murray practiced what he preached. He tried to stop false Bible teaching in South Africa.

➤ **Read aloud Jude 21-22.** Andrew Murray showed his love and compassion for both the saved and the unsaved.

➤ **Read aloud the last paragraph on page 88 to summarize Andrew Murray's work for the Lord.**

Murray's work for the Lord was based on a fervent prayer life. Listen as I read aloud the following statements from Andrew Murray's book *The Kingdom of God in South Africa.*

> Prayer is the life of missions. Continual and believing prayer is the secret of life-giving power and fruitfulness of mission work. The God of missions is the God of prayer.

Many of the books Andrew Murray wrote deal with prayer. God wants us to pray daily for missionaries. (BATs: 5c Evangelism and missions, 6b Prayer, 8a Faith in God's promises, 8b Faith in the power of the Word of God)

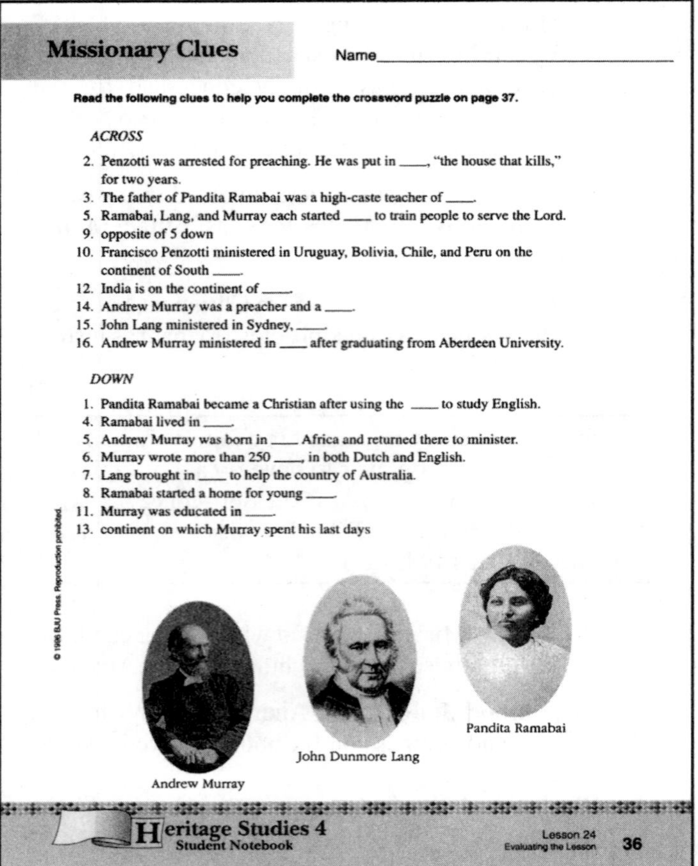

Missionary Clues Name________________

Read the following clues to help you complete the crossword puzzle on page 37.

ACROSS

2. Penzotti was arrested for preaching. He was put in ____, "the house that kills," for two years.
3. The father of Pandita Ramabai was a high-caste teacher of ____.
5. Ramabai, Lang, and Murray each started ____ to train people to serve the Lord.
9. opposite of 5 down
10. Francisco Penzotti ministered in Uruguay, Bolivia, Chile, and Peru on the continent of South ____.
12. India is on the continent of ____.
14. Andrew Murray was a preacher and a ____.
15. John Lang ministered in Sydney, ____.
16. Andrew Murray ministered in ____ after graduating from Aberdeen University.

DOWN

1. Pandita Ramabai became a Christian after using the ____ to study English.
4. Ramabai lived in ____.
5. Andrew Murray was born in ____ Africa and returned there to minister.
6. Murray wrote more than 250 ____, in both Dutch and English.
7. Lang brought in ____ to help the country of Australia.
8. Ramabai started a home for young ____.
11. Murray was educated in ____.
13. continent on which Murray spent his last days

Andrew Murray

John Dunmore Lang

Pandita Ramabai

Heritage Studies 4 Student Notebook — Lesson 24 Evaluating the Lesson 36

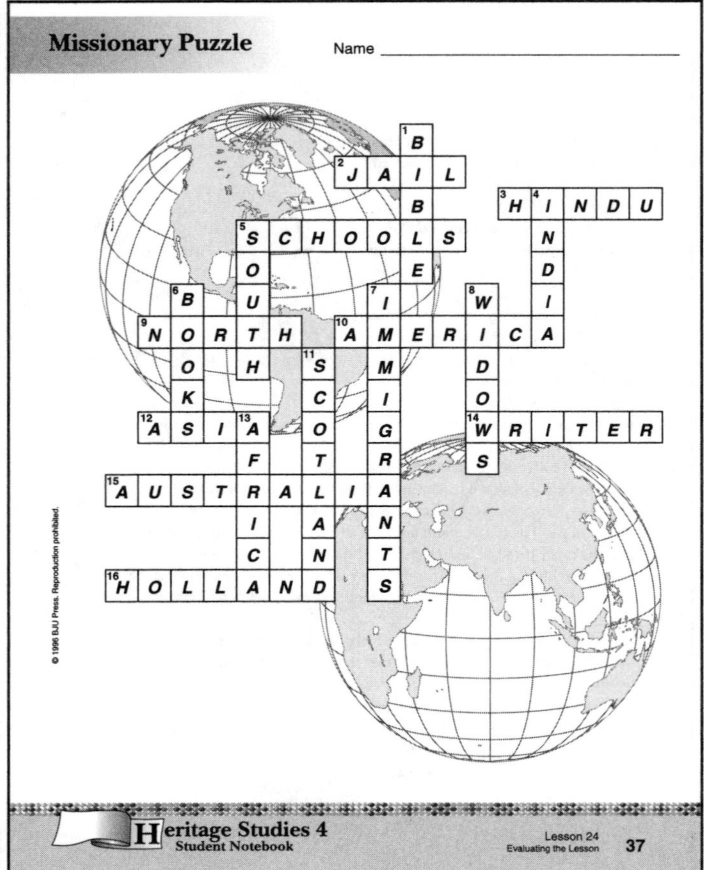

Missionary Puzzle Name________________

Heritage Studies 4 Student Notebook — Lesson 24 Evaluating the Lesson 37

Evaluating the Lesson

Notebook Activity, pages 36-37

- ➤ Read the instructions on page 36.
- ➤ Complete the crossword puzzle on page 37.

Going Beyond

Enrichment

Encourage your child to prepare an illustrated booklet of a missionary song. Have available several missionary songs, drawing paper, crayons or felt-tip pens, and a stapler. Direct him to select one verse of a missionary song to illustrate. Tell him to fold and staple together the papers to form a little booklet. Allow him to display his booklet as your family sings the missionary song.

Additional Teacher Information

Rama was born in India in 1858 in a high-caste family. Her father was a Hindu teacher. (In India the term *bai,* meaning "lady," refers to the mistress of the house and is part of the title attached to the end of a woman's name.) The fame of Ramabai spread across India. She was not only knowledgeable about the sacred books of India but also able to speak seven languages fluently. A college of learned men, or "pandits," gave her the name *Pandita,* recognizing her learning to be the equivalent to theirs. Though Pandita Ramabai believed Christianity to be the true religion and accepted its doctrines, it was not until 1883 that she received Christ as her personal Savior.

Pandita Ramabai's mission work included the establishment of the Mukti Mission (*Mukti* means "salvation"); Sharada Sadan ("House of Wisdom"), a widows' home; Sadananda Sadan ("House of Unending Gladness"), a school for orphaned boys; and Priti Sadan ("House of Love"), a school for orphaned girls. Ramabai was also involved in translating God's Word and gospel tracts into the common language of the people of India. (*NOTE:* The common people speak over one hundred thirty distinct languages and dialects.) The Mukti press issued more than one hundred thousand Scripture portions, particularly the Gospels and the Psalms, in addition to printing more than fifty thousand Bibles. On the morning of April 5, 1922, at age sixty-four, Pandita Ramabai "fell asleep in Jesus" while translating another portion of the Bible.

Andrew Murray (1828-1917) served the Lord as a writer, preacher, evangelist, and founder of a seminary and missionary school. He wrote approximately two hundred forty books and tracts, published in fifteen languages. His first two books were for children: *Jesus, the Children's Friend* and *What Manner of Child Shall This Be?* One of his most famous works is the devotional book *Abide in Christ.* Andrew Murray did indeed abide in Christ, serving and loving the Lord to the end of his life. He died while praying.

5 | LESSONS 25-30

The Fifty States

This chapter discusses the entire United States as well as its territories and commonwealths. The states are grouped into six regions; however, the focus is on individual states. State capitals, nicknames, famous people, important crops, geography, and interesting places to visit are topics included. Your child will gain a greater knowledge of the vastness and variety of the United States as well as a greater appreciation for God's blessings as he "journeys" across America.

This chapter contains a wealth of information about each of the states. Focus on helping your child enjoy his "journey" through America rather than memorizing all the details. It is enough for your child to memorize the states, their capitals, and the regions.

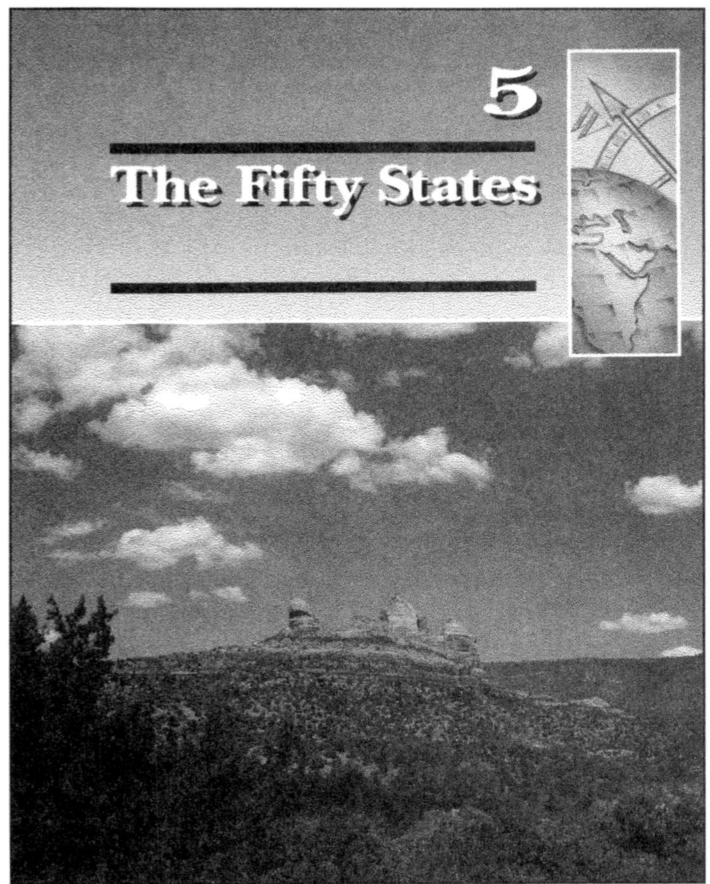

Materials

The following materials must be obtained or prepared before the presentation of the lesson. These items are labeled with an asterisk (*) in each lesson and in the Materials List in the Supplement. For further information see the individual lessons.

- A pine cone (Lesson 25)
- A piece of granite (Lesson 25)
- A maple cookie (optional) (Lesson 25)
- Appendix, page A32 (Lesson 25)
- Several items derived from peanuts (Lesson 26)
- Several roasted peanuts in the shell (Lesson 26)
- A piece of coal (Lesson 26)
- A model of a horse (Lesson 26)
- A picture of the Smoky Mountains (Lesson 26)
- Appendix, page A35 (Lesson 26)
- Several kernels of corn or a can of corn (Lesson 27)
- A cereal box (Lesson 27)
- A model or picture of a cow (Lesson 27)
- Appendix, pages A36-A38 (Lesson 27)
- A picture of the Grand Canyon (Lesson 28)
- A road atlas (Lesson 28)
- Several road maps for adjoining states (Lesson 28)
- Appendix, pages A39-A40 (Lesson 28)
- A large cardboard box with "Rocky Mountain Treasures" (optional) (Lesson 29)
- Appendix, page A41 (Lesson 29)
- Approximately 25 buttons or dried beans (Lesson 30)
- Encyclopedias, travel brochures, and/or library books (Supplemental Lesson)
- Appendix, pages A42-A47 (Supplemental Lesson)

LESSON 25
The Northeast: Sweet Land of Liberty

Text, pages 90-96, 280-305, 320-21
Notebook, pages 38-40

Preview

Main Ideas

- Maps represent actual places.
- The United States can be divided into six regions: Northeast, Southeast, Middle West, Southwest, Rocky Mountain, and Pacific.
- Each of the eleven states of the Northeast region is unique.
- Names have their origins in words with special meanings.
- Every state has a nickname, state tree, state flower, state bird, as well as other symbols to represent the state.

Objectives

- Label the Northeast states and capitals on a map
- Complete a crossword puzzle about the Northeast states

Materials

- A maple cookie (optional) (See Notes section for a recipe.)*
- Maps and More 10 and 11, pages M4-M5
- Appendix, page A32: Regions map*
- A pine cone*
- A piece of granite*
- Supplement, page S11: fishermen with lobster pots
- A Bible
- An atlas (optional)
- The figure of the Declaration of Independence (1776) from the TimeLine Snapshots
- The figure of the signing of the Constitution (1787) from the TimeLine Snapshots
- The figure of Francis Scott Key (1812) from the TimeLine Snapshots
- *Heritage Studies Listening Cassette B*

Notes

Maple Krinkle Cookies

$\frac{3}{4}$ cup shortening	1 teaspoon baking soda
1 cup sugar	1 teaspoon maple extract
1 egg	$\frac{1}{2}$ cup sugar
$\frac{1}{4}$ cup pure maple syrup	$\frac{1}{2}$ teaspoon maple extract
2 cups all-purpose flour	

In a mixing bowl, cream together shortening, sugar, egg, and maple syrup until well mixed. Combine flour and baking soda; add to creamed mixture. Add 1 teaspoon maple extract and mix well.

In a small dish, combine $\frac{1}{2}$ cup sugar and $\frac{1}{2}$ teaspoon maple extract. Stir until well blended. Roll dough into one-inch balls and then roll in the sugar mixture. Place on an ungreased baking sheet two inches apart. Put a drop of water on top of each ball. Bake at 350 degrees for eight to ten minutes. Yield: 5-6 dozen

If you live in the Northeast region, you may wish to devote additional time for the study of your state. If you do not live in the United States, you will need to adjust some of the questions in this chapter.

Day 1

Lesson

Introducing the Lesson

Instead of serving your child a maple cookie, you may want to serve him pancakes or waffles with maple syrup for breakfast to introduce this lesson.

Tasting Activity

➤ *Give your child one maple cookie without telling him what kind of cookie it is.*

➤ Eat your cookie and try to guess the special ingredient that is produced in the Northeast region of the United States. *If he does not guess correctly, tell him that the special ingredient is maple syrup, produced in the state of Vermont.*

➤ *Show Maps and More 10 of the Northeast region, pointing out Vermont.*

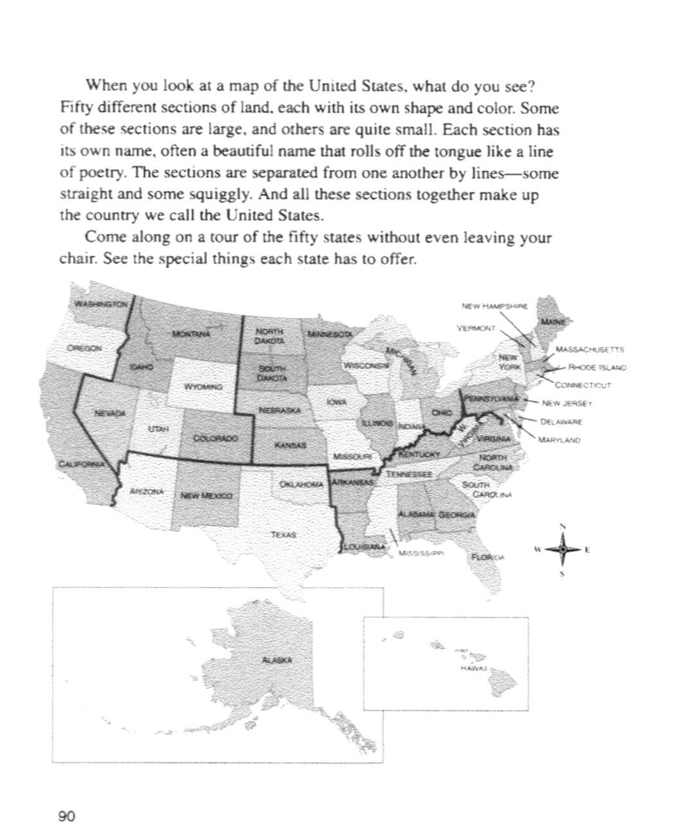

When you look at a map of the United States, what do you see? Fifty different sections of land, each with its own shape and color. Some of these sections are large, and others are quite small. Each section has its own name, often a beautiful name that rolls off the tongue like a line of poetry. The sections are separated from one another by lines—some straight and some squiggly. And all these sections together make up the country we call the United States.

Come along on a tour of the fifty states without even leaving your chair. See the special things each state has to offer.

90

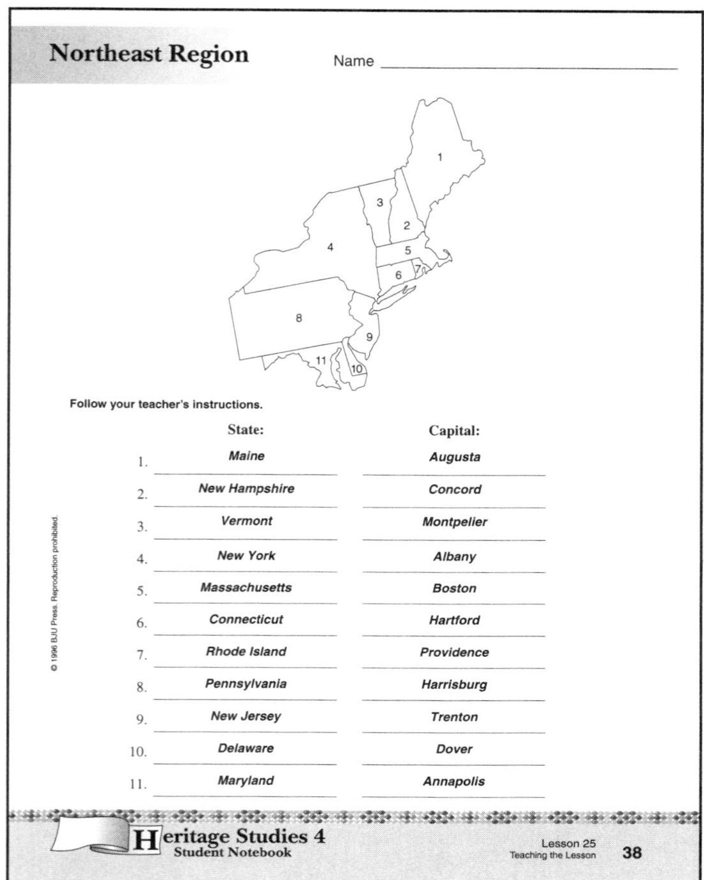

Northeast Region Name ______________________

Follow your teacher's instructions.

	State:	Capital:
1.	*Maine*	*Augusta*
2.	*New Hampshire*	*Concord*
3.	*Vermont*	*Montpelier*
4.	*New York*	*Albany*
5.	*Massachusetts*	*Boston*
6.	*Connecticut*	*Hartford*
7.	*Rhode Island*	*Providence*
8.	*Pennsylvania*	*Harrisburg*
9.	*New Jersey*	*Trenton*
10.	*Delaware*	*Dover*
11.	*Maryland*	*Annapolis*

Heritage Studies 4 Student Notebook — Lesson 25 Teaching the Lesson 38

Teaching the Lesson

Text Activity, page 90

- ➤ **Read page 90 to find out how many states make up the United States.** *(fifty)*
- ➤ *Point out the six regions of the United States on the Regions map, instructing your child to locate these regions on his map in the text. (Northeast, Southeast, Middle West, Southwest, Rocky Mountain, and Pacific)*
- ➤ Locate your state on the Regions map. **In what region is your state located?**
- ➤ Look at the Northeast region again. Count how many states it includes. *(eleven)*

The chapter makes extensive use of several of the Maps and More. You will find it helpful to mark the page with a bookmark or paper clip.

Map Activity, page 90, Notebook page 38, and Maps and More 10

- ➤ Look at the numbered states at the top of Notebook page 38.
- ➤ Write the name of each state next to the corresponding number. You may look at the map on text page 90 and Maps and More 10 to help with labeling the states.
- ➤ Read the names of the eleven states aloud as you point to each state.
- ➤ Keep Notebook page 38 on your desk during this lesson to fill in the information about the capitals.

Northeast

Portland Head Light

Maine

In the Northeast, the nation's easternmost state is Maine. Because of Maine's cool climate, pine trees grow well in its forests. Maine's nickname is "the Pine Tree State," and the white pine is its official state tree.

Maine is well known for its long, rocky coastline. A famous lighthouse called the Portland Head Light stands on Maine's southeast coast. This 101-foot lighthouse has steered ships away from the rocky shore since 1791. Because of their nearness to the sea, many people in Maine like to fish. Lobsters are most often the catch of the day.

New Hampshire

New Hampshire still boasts many buildings and churches built during the Colonial period.

Southwest of Maine is New Hampshire. "The Granite State" gets its nickname from the large granite quarries found there. New Hampshire was the only colony that British soldiers never invaded during the War for Independence. New Hampshire took as its motto "Live Free or Die."

People often visit New Hampshire to see its mountains dressed in their fall colors. One peak in the White Mountains has an interesting rock formation that people call "Old Man of the Mountain." What do you think it looks like? It looks like the head of an old man frozen in stone, looking out across the valley.

91

Text Discussion, page 91 and Maps and More 10 and 11

- ➤ *Point out Maine and New Hampshire on the Regions map, discussing their locations in relation to the whole United States.*
- ➤ Point to Maine on Maps and More 10.
- ➤ **What is the capital of Maine?** *(Augusta)*
- ➤ Write *Augusta* next to *Maine* on Notebook page 38.
- ➤ Point to New Hampshire on Maps and More 10.
- ➤ **What is the capital of New Hampshire?** *(Concord)*
- ➤ Write *Concord* next to *New Hampshire* on the Notebook page.
- ➤ *Show your child the pine cone and the granite, telling him that these items represent the nicknames for Maine and New Hampshire.*
- ➤ **Read page 91 to find out which item goes with which state's nickname.** *(The pine cone represents Maine, "the Pine Tree State." The granite represents New Hampshire, "the Granite State.")*

Every state has a nickname, state tree, state flower, state bird, as well as other symbols to represent the state.

- ➤ **What do you think the name *Maine* means?**

It means mainland. This name was given by explorers long ago to tell the main part of Maine from the thousands of offshore islands that would one day be part of the state of Maine.

- ➤ Look at Maps and More 11. Point to and name several of the offshore islands shown on the map.

Most of Maine's islands are too small to include on this particular map.

- ➤ **If you were driving along Maine's coast, what things would you be able to see?** *(fishing or lobstering and lighthouses)*
- ➤ *Show the picture of the fishermen with their lobster pots, explaining that pots like these are used to catch lobster.*
- ➤ **Why are lighthouses needed along Maine's coast?** *(to warn sailors of dangerous rocks and to guide ships safely into the harbors)*

> Christians are to be like lighthouses, giving the light of salvation through Christ to people in a dark world of sin. Read Matthew 5:14-16 to your child to illustrate the importance God places on witnessing for Him. (BAT: 5c Evangelism and missions)

- ➤ Find the state of New Hampshire again on Maps and More 10.
- ➤ Run your finger along the coastline. Its short coastline of eighteen miles is the shortest coastline of any state.
- ➤ Name an interesting rock formation in the Granite State. *(Old Man of the Mountain)*

This natural rock formation is shaped by five stone ledges reaching a height of forty feet (twelve meters) on Profile Mountain. "Great Stone Face," as Old Man of the Mountain is sometimes called, is New Hampshire's official trademark.

> Your child will find information about each state on pages 280-305 in his text. The next activity is an example of how you may use these pages after discussing each state. This activity will not be repeated after each state.

Northeast

Vermont

Autumn on a Vermont farm

New Hampshire's neighbor to the west is Vermont, "the Green Mountain State." Can you guess how it got its nickname? If you stand at any given spot in Vermont, you can see mountains in at least one direction. Vermont got its name from the French phrase *vert mont* meaning "green mountain."

Do you like to eat maple syrup on pancakes? Vermont is the state to thank for most of the maple syrup produced in this country. In autumn its thousands of maple trees turn to bright oranges and golds. The Bennington Battle Monument, a 306-foot granite tower, was built to honor the men who won a famous battle against the British in 1777.

New York

West of Vermont lies the largest northeastern state, New York. George Washington took his oath of office as our first president in New York. He once said that New York might become the seat of a new empire. New York is nicknamed "the Empire State."

New York City

When you think of New York, do you think first of New York City? With its busy streets and tall skyscrapers, the city is a major center of New York life. Have you ever heard of a building so large that it took up more than one zip code? The World Trade Center has a separate zip code for each of its two towers. Another attraction is the magnificent Niagara Falls near Buffalo. And what famous lady raises her torch above New York Harbor?

92

Information Activity, pages 289 and 294

- ➤ **Turn to page 294 and read aloud the information given about New Hampshire.**
- ➤ Look at the date next to the state's name. This is when this area became a state.
- ➤ Look at the number in the bold box under the state's name. This number represents the order in which this state joined the United States of America.
- ➤ *Follow a similar procedure using page 289 to read about Maine.*

Day 2

Text Discussion, page 92 and Maps and More 10

- ➤ Find Vermont on Maps and More 10.
- ➤ **What is the capital of Vermont?** *(Montpelier)*
- ➤ Write *Montpelier* next to *Vermont* on Notebook page 38.
- ➤ **Read the first two paragraphs of page 92 to find the nickname of Vermont.** *("the Green Mountain State")*

You may want to use different maps in your atlas in place of the map on pages 320-21 throughout this chapter.

Map Activity, pages 320-21

- ➤ Find Vermont on the map on pages 320-21.
- ➤ Find the Green Mountains of Vermont and run your finger down the mountains.

These mountains are part of a larger chain of mountains called the Appalachian Mountains. Because the Green Mountains run down the center of the state, some people call these mountains the "backbone of Vermont." Men from Vermont who fought in the Revolutionary War were known as the "Green Mountain Boys."

- ➤ Name the monument that was built to honor these men. *(Bennington Battle Monument)*

(*NOTE:* The fighting for this battle actually took place across the border in the state of New York; however, since it was planned in Vermont and fought by Vermonters, the Battle of Bennington is a major part of Vermont's history.)

Text Activity, page 92 and Maps and More 10 (cont.)

- ➤ **Read the rest of page 92 to find out how large the state of New York is.** *(the largest northeastern state)*
- ➤ Find New York on Maps and More 10.
- ➤ **What is the capital of New York?** *(Albany)*
- ➤ Write *Albany* next to *New York* on Notebook page 38.
- ➤ Name some special sights in New York. *(skyscrapers, the World Trade Center, Niagara Falls, the Statue of Liberty)*
- ➤ Point to New York City on Maps and More 10.

Although New York City is not the capital of New York, it is the largest U.S. city with over seven million people.

Remember that the Statue of Liberty symbolizes freedom to people all over the world. Just as the torch held in her right hand represents the spread of freedom as a light across the world, the freedom from sin that Christians have through salvation in Christ is a beacon of hope to the unsaved. (BATs: 1b Repentance and faith, 5c Evangelism and missions; Bible Promises: A. Liberty from Sin, B. Guiltless by the Blood)

This minuteman statue stands at Lexington Battle Green.

Northeast

Massachusetts

Massachusetts, New York's neighbor to the east, is one of four states that are known as *commonwealths*. Massachusetts is named for the people who first lived there. Its nickname is "the Bay State" because it used to be the Massachusetts Bay Colony.

Can you remember any important historical events that happened in Massachusetts? At Plymouth Plantation, visitors can see what Pilgrim villages might have looked like in the 1620s. In Boston they can walk the Freedom Trail, visiting sixteen Colonial sites. At Lexington Battle Green they can learn about the first battle of the War for Independence. Cape Cod, the state's southeastern peninsula, offers sandy beaches, quaint houses, and boat rides.

Mark Twain's Victorian home in Rocky Hill

Connecticut

Connecticut is south of Massachusetts. In the Algonquian language, *Connecticut* means "on the long tidal river." The Connecticut River divides the state in two. Do you remember the Great Compromise at the Constitutional Convention of 1787? A man from Connecticut thought of that. Connecticut also had the first written state constitution. Those are two reasons that Connecticut is nicknamed "the Constitution State."

Connecticut has the nation's largest ship museum, called Mystic Seaport. With its tall-masted boats and old buildings, it looks like a whaling village from the 1800s. Since 1701, Connecticut has been the home of Yale University. Many aircraft engines and parts are produced in Connecticut.

93

Northeast

Rhode Island

Slater Mill

East of Connecticut is Rhode Island, our country's smallest state. Its official nickname is "the Ocean State," but it is often called "Little Rhody." Rhode Island was begun by people who disagreed with the Puritan religion. They named its capital Providence because they wanted to thank God for His care and protection.

Rhode Island is actually not an island. It is a mainland and thirty-six small islands in Narragansett Bay. Would you like to live in a mansion? The city of Newport has mansions and other historic buildings. Trinity Church in Newport has a specially marked pew where George Washington once sat and prayed. In Pawtucket is Slater Mill, where the American textile industry began. Rhode Island is also a center for jewelry making.

Liberty Bell

Pennsylvania

South of New York is Pennsylvania. *Pennsylvania* means "Penn's Woods." William Penn started the colony for Quakers. Pennsylvania is nicknamed "the Keystone State" because it was at the center of the arch formed by the first thirteen states.

Do you like chocolate? You would probably enjoy a trip to the world's largest chocolate factory in Hershey, Pennsylvania. Even the streetlamps in Hershey are shaped like chocolate kisses. Pennsylvania Dutch people live in southeast Pennsylvania. They are skilled in cooking, arts, and crafts. Philadelphia, which means "city of brotherly love," displays the Liberty Bell, a famous symbol of American freedom. Two of our nation's most important documents were drawn up in Philadelphia. Can you name them?

94

Text Discussion, page 93 and Maps and More 10

➤ **Read the first two paragraphs on page 93 to find out what Massachusetts' nickname is.** *("the Bay State")*

➤ Find Massachusetts on Maps and More 10.

➤ **What is the capital of Massachusetts?** *(Boston)*

➤ Write *Boston* next to *Massachusetts* on Notebook page 38.

➤ **What special name is given to Massachusetts and three other states?** *(commonwealth)*

The other three commonwealths are Kentucky, Pennsylvania, and Virginia. ***Commonwealth*** is another name for *state*. Each of these states has chosen to refer to itself as a commonwealth.

➤ Find Cape Cod on Maps and More 10. It is near Massachusetts.

A ***cape*** is a section of land extending into a body of water. Cape Cod is a famous vacation spot.

➤ **Read the rest of page 93 to find out what Connecticut means.** *("on the long tidal river")*

➤ Find Connecticut on Maps and More 10.

➤ **What is the capital of Connecticut?** *(Hartford)*

➤ Write *Hartford* next to *Connecticut* on Notebook page 38.

➤ **What divides Connecticut in two?** *(the Connecticut River)*

➤ Tell about the Great Compromise of 1787.

If your child needs help, explain that Connecticut helped states come to an agreement in order to accept, or ratify, the Constitution. The Great Compromise, also called the Connecticut Compromise, called for equal representation in the Senate and representation based on population in the House of Representatives.

Day 3

Text Discussion, page 94 and Maps and More 10

➤ **Read page 94 to find out which states have the nicknames "Little Rhody" and "the Keystone State."** *(Rhode Island is "Little Rhody," and Pennsylvania is "the Keystone State.")*

➤ Find Rhode Island on Maps and More 10.

- **What is the capital of Rhode Island?** *(Providence)*
- Write *Providence* next to *Rhode Island* on Notebook page 38.
- **Why do you think Rhode Island was given the nickname "Little Rhody"?** Rhode Island is the smallest state in the United States.
- Find Pennsylvania on Maps and More 10.
- **What is the capital of Pennsylvania?** *(Harrisburg)*
- Write *Harrisburg* next to *Pennsylvania* on Notebook page 38.
- **What city has street lamps shaped like chocolate candy kisses?** *(Hershey, Pennsylvania)*
- **Where would we find the Liberty Bell?** *(Philadelphia)*
- Find Philadelphia on Maps and More 10.
- **What does *Philadelphia* mean?** *("city of brotherly love")*

The city was planned as a center for religious freedom and later became America's birthplace.

- **Can you name the two important documents that were signed in Philadelphia?** *(Declaration of Independence and the Constitution)*

> In this chapter about the states, you will have the opportunity to review some events that your child has studied in Grades 2 and 3. You will want to add these figures to the TimeLine Snapshots. If you have left the figures from these grades on the TimeLine, please refer to them as you discuss the events.

TimeLine Snapshots Activity

- **Do you remember what year the Declaration of Independence was signed?** *(1776)*
- Place the figure of the Declaration of Independence (1776) on the TimeLine.
- **Do you remember what year the Constitution was signed?** *(1787)*
- Place the figure of the signing of the Constitution (1787) on the TimeLine.

Northeast

Workers harvest cranberries from a bog.

New Jersey

New Jersey, "the Garden State," is east of Pennsylvania. Its nickname comes from its flower gardens, farms, and orchards. New Jersey is the most crowded state; it has more people per square mile than any other state.

Have you ever tasted juice or sauce made from cranberries? Cranberries are often grown in New Jersey's bogs, or swampy areas. At Batsto State Historic Site, visitors can stroll through a Colonial village and watch ironmakers and glassmakers at work. Would you like to know what a fort from the War for Independence looked like? Morristown National Historical Park includes Fort Nonsense, a restored fort that was first built in 1777.

Delaware

Fishing is a popular industry.

South of New Jersey is Delaware. Delaware is nicknamed "the First State" because it was the first of the thirteen colonies to accept the United States Constitution. Because of their brave fighting during the War for Independence, Delaware's troops came to be called the "Blue Hen's Chickens," after a famous breed of fighting gamecock. The blue hen chicken is now the state bird of Delaware.

People from many different European countries have lived in Delaware. At the Zwaanendael Museum in Lewes, visitors can learn about the Dutch colony founded in Delaware in 1631. Swedish and Finnish settlers built America's first log cabins in this state. The Old Swedes Church in Wilmington is our nation's oldest church still in use. In the southwest corner of Delaware live descendants of the Nanticoke people, who hold a special powwow in Millsboro every September.

95

Text Discussion, page 95 and Maps and More 10

- Find New Jersey and Delaware on Maps and More 10.
- **What is the capital of New Jersey?** *(Trenton)*
- **What is the capital of Delaware?** *(Dover)*
- Write *Trenton* next to *New Jersey* and *Dover* next to *Delaware* on Notebook page 38.
- **Read page 95 to find out which state—New Jersey or Delaware—is the most crowded of all fifty states.** *(New Jersey)*
- **Why is New Jersey called "the Garden State"?** *(because of all its flower gardens, farms, and orchards)*
- **What is Delaware's nickname?** *("the First State")*
- **How did it receive that title?** *(It was the first colony to become a state.)*
- **What was first built in Delaware?** *(The first log cabins in the United States were built by Swedish and Finnish settlers in Delaware.)*

Northeast

Chesapeake Bay is dotted with sailboats every summer.

Maryland

We complete our tour of the northeastern states with Maryland. Named for the wife of King Charles I of England, Maryland is nicknamed "the Old Line State." The soldiers in the Maryland line were famous for their courage in the War for Independence.

If you have ever wanted to be a knight, Maryland would be a good place to visit. Maryland's state sport is jousting, or fighting with lances on horseback. Jousting contests are held there each year. Maryland is also the home of Fort McHenry. The British attacked this fort in 1814, but its soldiers held their ground. Francis Scott Key wrote "The Star-Spangled Banner" as he watched the American flag flying over Fort McHenry the next morning.

Southeast

Virginia

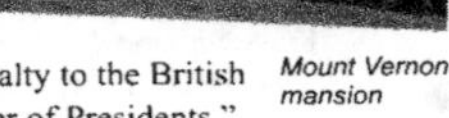

Virginia is our first stop in the Southeast region of the United States. Virginia, a commonwealth, was named after Elizabeth I of England, the "Virgin Queen." It is nicknamed "Old Dominion" because of its loyalty to the British crown in the 1600s. Virginia is often called "Mother of Presidents." Eight presidents were born there. Can you name any of them?

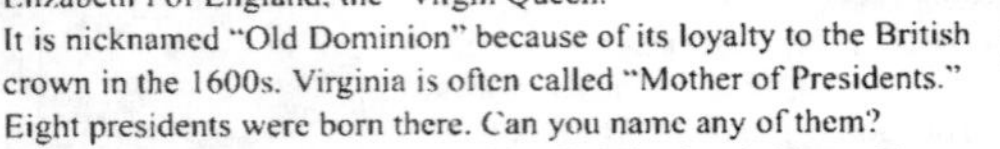

Mount Vernon mansion

Two famous homes are located in Virginia. One is Mount Vernon, George Washington's home. Another is Monticello, the mansion Thomas Jefferson designed for himself. Would you like to see what a Colonial wigmaker's or candlemaker's shop looked like? Williamsburg has these and many other shops. It also has The College of William and Mary, the second-oldest college in the United States. In Arlington National Cemetery, visitors can see memorials to Robert E. Lee and John F. Kennedy as well as the tombs of honored military heroes.

96

Text Discussion, page 96 and Maps and More 10

- Find Maryland on Maps and More 10.
- **What is the capital of Maryland?** *(Annapolis)*
- Write *Annapolis* next to *Maryland* on Notebook page 38.

The states and capitals listing for the Northeast region is now complete. You may use Notebook page 38 to study and memorize the states and capitals of this region.

It is important for your child to learn the states and capitals. Encourage him to study them after each region instead of waiting until all the regions have been studied.

- **Read the first two paragraphs of page 96 to find out for whom Maryland was named.** *(the wife of King Charles I of England)*

Queen Mary was the wife of King Charles I of England.

- Find the Chesapeake Bay on Maps and More 10. It divides Maryland almost in half.

TimeLine Snapshots Activity

- **What is the name of the famous fort that was attacked by the British in 1814?** *(Fort McHenry)*

Fort McHenry is located in the city of Baltimore, which is above Annapolis.

- **What famous song did Francis Scott Key write as he saw the American flag waving over the fort after the battle?** *("The Star-Spangled Banner")*
- Place the figure of Francis Scott Key (1812) on the TimeLine.

The battle at Fort McHenry took place in 1814. We are placing the figure on the TimeLine at the beginning of the war, which is called the War of 1812.

- Sing along with the recording of the "Star-Spangled Banner" as I play the listening cassette.
- Name some specific freedoms Americans have. *(Answers will vary but should include religious freedom.)*

Remind your child of the great responsibility Christians have to pray for their country and its leaders. (BATs: 2a Authority, 6b Prayer)

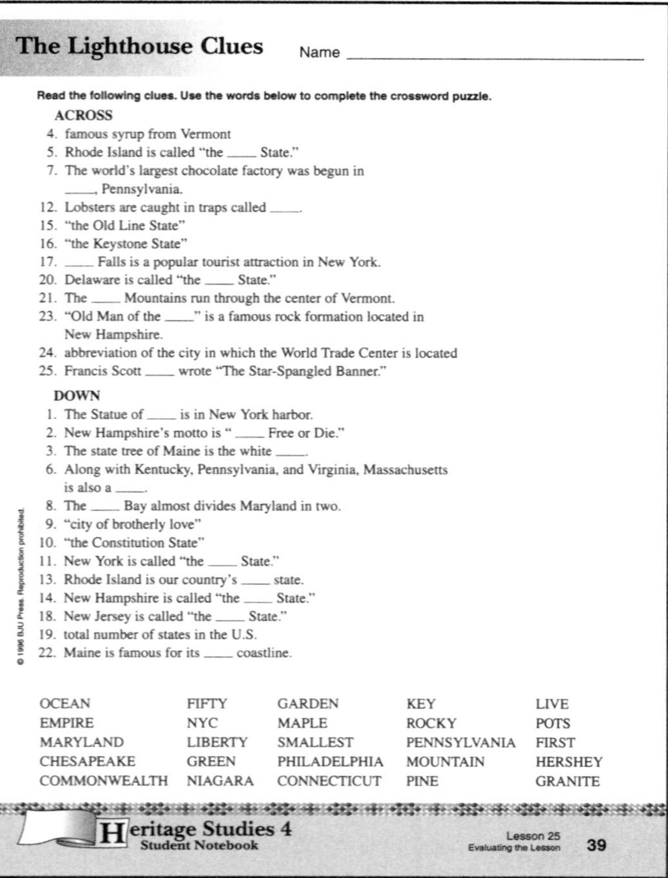

The Lighthouse Clues

Name ______________________

Read the following clues. Use the words below to complete the crossword puzzle.

ACROSS

4. famous syrup from Vermont
5. Rhode Island is called "the ____ State."
7. The world's largest chocolate factory was begun in ____, Pennsylvania.
12. Lobsters are caught in traps called ____.
15. "the Old Line State"
16. "the Keystone State"
17. ____ Falls is a popular tourist attraction in New York.
20. Delaware is called "the ____ State."
21. The ____ Mountains run through the center of Vermont.
23. "Old Man of the ____" is a famous rock formation located in New Hampshire.
24. abbreviation of the city in which the World Trade Center is located
25. Francis Scott ____ wrote "The Star-Spangled Banner."

DOWN

1. The Statue of ____ is in New York harbor.
2. New Hampshire's motto is "____ Free or Die."
3. The state tree of Maine is the white ____.
6. Along with Kentucky, Pennsylvania, and Virginia, Massachusetts is also a ____.
8. The ____ Bay almost divides Maryland in two.
9. "city of brotherly love"
10. "the Constitution State"
11. New York is called "the ____ State."
13. Rhode Island is our country's ____ state.
14. New Hampshire is called "the ____ State."
18. New Jersey is called "the ____ State."
19. total number of states in the U.S.
22. Maine is famous for its ____ coastline.

OCEAN	FIFTY	GARDEN	KEY	LIVE
EMPIRE	NYC	MAPLE	ROCKY	POTS
MARYLAND	LIBERTY	SMALLEST	PENNSYLVANIA	FIRST
CHESAPEAKE	GREEN	PHILADELPHIA	MOUNTAIN	HERSHEY
COMMONWEALTH	NIAGARA	CONNECTICUT	PINE	GRANITE

Evaluating the Lesson

> Since the emphasis of the chapter should be on memorizing the states and the capitals, you may want to allow your child to use his textbook as he completes the Notebook pages in the Evaluating the Lesson sections.

Notebook Activity, pages 39-40

- Read the instructions on Notebook page 39.
- Complete the crossword puzzle on Notebook page 40.

Going Beyond

Enrichment

To assist your child in learning the states and capitals of each region, you may wish to use the following activities.

1. Have available state flash cards to review and practice the identification, location, and basic information of the states.
2. Have available envelopes, each labeled with the name of a state. Prepare an enlargement of each state shape; cut it apart into puzzle pieces. Place the state puzzle inside a labeled envelope. Instruct your child to choose an envelope, remove the puzzle pieces, and assemble them to form the shape of that state. Direct him to find that state on the map (Appendix, page A34) and to name the capital.
3. Have available purchased puzzles of the United States.
4. Cover a blank map of the United States (Appendix, page A34) with clear Con-Tact paper. Give your child a nonpermanent pen to identify the states. The marks can be wiped off and the map used again. You may need to experiment with your pen on the back side of the map to be sure that it will work.

Additional Teacher Information

Many people have never tasted *real* maple syrup because it is much more expensive than the many other sweeteners used today. It takes approximately thirty-five to forty-five gallons of sap to produce one gallon of maple syrup since about 97 percent of the sap is boiled away during processing. After the maple processing is complete, many sugar makers celebrate with an old Native American tradition called "sugar on snow," "toffee snowballs," or "leather aprons." This treat is made by spooning the boiled maple syrup onto clean snow. The syrup immediately stiffens and can be twisted around a spoon or a Popsicle stick and eaten like caramel.

Samuel Slater learned the textile trade after working for six years in an English mill. In order to maintain its world leadership in textiles, England refused to allow anyone with knowledge of this trade to leave the country. Slater disguised himself in order to come to America. The English would not even allow copies of their machines to leave the country; however, Slater was able to construct America's first textile machines completely from memory at the Old Slater Mill in Pawtucket, Rhode Island.

LESSON 26

The Southeast: Let Freedom Ring

Text, pages 96-102, 280-305, 308-9, 320-21
Notebook, pages 41-42

Preview

Main Ideas

- Maps represent actual places.
- Each of the twelve states of the Southeast region is unique.
- Names have their origins in words with special meanings.
- Many people have contributed to the heritage of the Southeast region.

Objectives

- Identify the Southeast states and label their capitals on a map
- Match events or accomplishments with famous people
- Gather information about a famous person from the Southeast
- Present the information as an oral report

Materials

- Several roasted peanuts in the shell*
- Several of the following items derived from peanuts: shoe polish, ink, soap, face powder, shaving cream, shampoo, paint, cooking oil, milk, flour, and coffee*
- Maps and More 12 and 13, pages M5-M6
- Appendix, page A35: Carver Story*
- A piece of coal*
- A model of a horse*
- A picture of the Smoky Mountains*
- A Bible
- The figure of Wilbur and Orville Wright (1903) from the TimeLine Snapshots
- An atlas (optional)

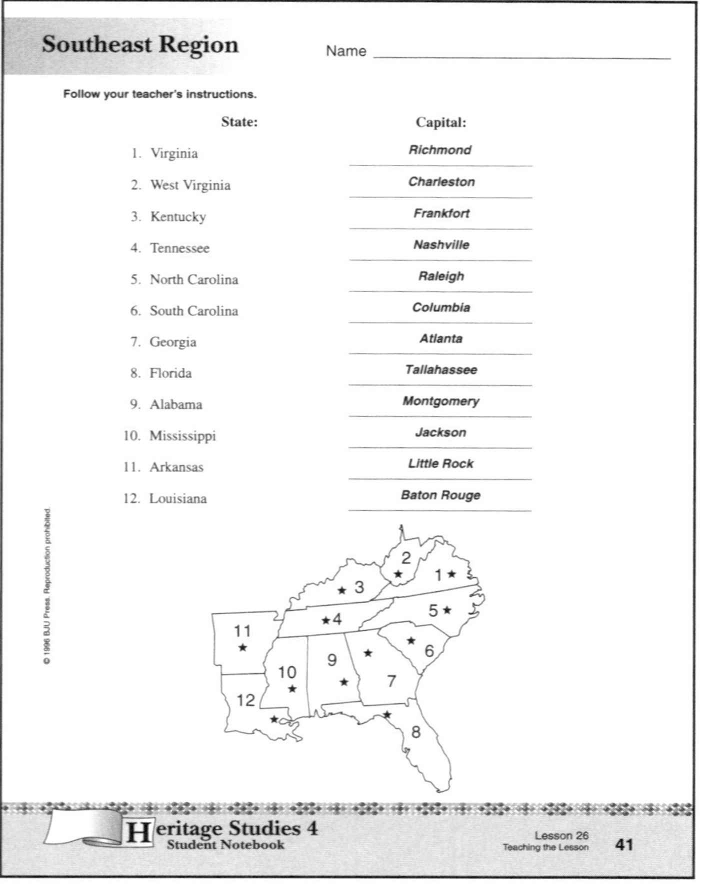

Southeast Region Name ____________________

Follow your teacher's instructions.

State:	Capital:
1. Virginia	*Richmond*
2. West Virginia	*Charleston*
3. Kentucky	*Frankfort*
4. Tennessee	*Nashville*
5. North Carolina	*Raleigh*
6. South Carolina	*Columbia*
7. Georgia	*Atlanta*
8. Florida	*Tallahassee*
9. Alabama	*Montgomery*
10. Mississippi	*Jackson*
11. Arkansas	*Little Rock*
12. Louisiana	*Baton Rouge*

Northeast

Maryland

Chesapeake Bay is dotted with sailboats every summer.

We complete our tour of the northeastern states with Maryland. Named for the wife of King Charles I of England, Maryland is nicknamed "the Old Line State." The soldiers in the Maryland line were famous for their courage in the War for Independence.

If you have ever wanted to be a knight, Maryland would be a good place to visit. Maryland's state sport is jousting, or fighting with lances on horseback. Jousting contests are held there each year. Maryland is also the home of Fort McHenry. The British attacked this fort in 1814, but its soldiers held their ground. Francis Scott Key wrote "The Star-Spangled Banner" as he watched the American flag flying over Fort McHenry the next morning.

Southeast

Virginia

Mount Vernon mansion

Virginia is our first stop in the Southeast region of the United States. Virginia, a commonwealth, was named after Elizabeth I of England, the "Virgin Queen." It is nicknamed "Old Dominion" because of its loyalty to the British crown in the 1600s. Virginia is often called "Mother of Presidents." Eight presidents were born there. Can you name any of them?

Two famous homes are located in Virginia. One is Mount Vernon, George Washington's home. Another is Monticello, the mansion Thomas Jefferson designed for himself. Would you like to see what a Colonial wigmaker's or candlemaker's shop looked like? Williamsburg has these and many other shops. It also has The College of William and Mary, the second-oldest college in the United States. In Arlington National Cemetery, visitors can see memorials to Robert E. Lee and John F. Kennedy as well as the tombs of honored military heroes.

96

If you live in one of the Southeast states, you may wish to devote additional time to the study of your state. Refer your child to pages 280-305 for additional information about each of the Southeastern states.

Day 1

Lesson

Introducing the Lesson

Story, Maps and More 12

- *Lay the peanuts and the items derived from the peanut in front of your child.*
- **What do you think all of the items on the table have in common?**
- *Show your child the pictures of George Washington Carver on Maps and More 12 as you read the Carver Story from the Appendix copy.*
- **Now that you have heard the story, what do the items in front of you have in common?** *(All come from peanuts.)*

Even though George Washington Carver worked with many other plants, developing various foods, cosmetics, and household items, he is most famous for his work with the peanut. In this lesson you will learn about other people of the Southeast who contributed greatly to America's heritage.

Teaching the Lesson

Map Activity, Notebook page 41 and Maps and More 13

- Read the names of the states in the Southeast region from Notebook page 41.
- Look at Maps and More 13. Write the number of each state in the correct place on your map using Maps and More 13.
- Keep Notebook page 41 on your desk during the lesson to fill in more information about these states.

Text Discussion, page 96 and Maps and More 13

- Find Virginia on Maps and More 13.
- **What is the capital of Virginia?** *(Richmond)*
- Write *Richmond* next to *Virginia* on Notebook page 41.
- **Read the last two paragraphs on page 96 to find Virginia's nickname.** *("Old Dominion")*
- **Can you name any of the eight presidents born in Virginia?** *(George Washington, Thomas Jefferson, James Madison, James Monroe, William Henry Harrison, John Tyler, Zachary Taylor, and Woodrow Wilson)*

Southeast

The Washington Monument and the Capitol Building

Washington, D.C.

Located between Virginia and Maryland is our nation's capital, Washington, D.C. *D.C.* stands for "District of Columbia." The city of Washington takes up the entire District of Columbia. Washington, D.C., is not a state. It is a section of land owned by the United States government.

West Virginia

West Virginia is northwest of Virginia. It is nicknamed "the Mountain State" because of its rugged land. The mountains and hills of the Appalachian Range nearly cover the state. West Virginia was once part of Virginia. When Virginia joined the Confederacy, the northwestern part of the state broke away and formed its own government, remaining loyal to the Union. West Virginia has as its motto "Mountaineers Are Always Free."

West Virginia is rich with an important resource. Over half of its land has coal buried beneath it. Coal mining is one of West Virginia's primary industries, along with pottery and glassmaking. Have you ever played with glass marbles? West Virginia makes most of the nation's glass marbles at factories in Parkersburg. The historic town of Harpers Ferry, on the northern boundary of the state, has been restored to the way it was when John Brown seized its armory just before the Civil War.

Perhaps you have played with West Virginia's famous product?

97

Washington, D.C.

Washington, D.C., is the capital of the United States, serving as the headquarters of the federal government and a symbol of the country's history. Washington, D.C., is the only American city or town that is not part of a state; it covers all of the District of Columbia, a section of land under the rule of the federal government.

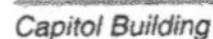
Capitol Building

Jefferson Monument (above) and Washington Monument (right)

Lincoln Memorial

308

White House

In 1791 President George Washington chose the site for the city, along the Potomac River, between Maryland and Virginia. He hired Pierre Charles L'Enfant, a French engineer, to draw up the plans for the city. L'Enfant's plan made the Capitol building the center of the city with streets leading out from it like spokes on a wheel. Every year, millions of visitors from all over the world visit Washington, D.C., learning of America's government and her history. Some of the most-visited points of interest include the Capitol, the White House, the Washington Monument, the Lincoln Memorial, and the Smithsonian Institution.

309

➤ **What are the names of the famous homes of George Washington and Thomas Jefferson?** *(Washington's home—Mount Vernon; Jefferson's home—Monticello)*

Text Discussion, pages 97, 308-9, and Maps and More 13

➤ Find Washington, D.C., on Maps and More 13.

Maryland and Virginia gave land for America's capital. This land was the center of the country at that time. It has been the capital of the United States since 1800.

➤ **Read the first paragraph on page 97 to find out what *D.C.* means.** *(District of Columbia)*

➤ **Read aloud more about Washington, D.C., on pages 308-9.**

Day 2

Text Discussion, page 97 (cont.) and Maps and More 13

➤ *Show the coal.* Coal mining is very important to West Virginia.

➤ **Read the rest of page 97 to find out how much of West Virginia has coal buried beneath it.** *(over half)*

Southeast

Kentucky

A horse farm in Kentucky's Bluegrass region

Kentucky borders West Virginia on the northeast and Virginia on the east. Kentucky, a commonwealth, is nicknamed "the Bluegrass State." Kentucky's bluegrass actually looks green, but during the spring it blossoms with tiny blue flowers.

Have you ever watched the Kentucky Derby? It is the oldest horse race still being run each year in the United States. The first running was in 1875. The Bluegrass region of Kentucky, around Lexington, is an ideal place for raising Thoroughbred racehorses. Does the thought of buried treasure excite you? Most of the gold owned by the United States—worth more than six billion dollars—is stored in Fort Knox's underground vaults.

Lookout Mountain

Tennessee

Tennessee is Kentucky's neighbor to the south. It got its name from a Cherokee village in that region called *Tanasie*. Tennessee is nicknamed "the Volunteer State" because its people were known for being willing to volunteer for military service.

The Great Smoky Mountains are located in eastern Tennessee. On a peak called Lookout Mountain, an important battle was fought in the War Between the States. Visitors to this battleground can see parts of five different states on a clear day. Another popular place to see is the Hermitage, Andrew Jackson's home near Nashville. Tennessee has another nickname: "the Big Bend State." The Tennessee River has a large bend in it, and it flows through the state twice.

98

- **Do you remember the name of the war that caused West Virginia to separate from Virginia?** *(the American Civil War)*
- Find West Virginia on Maps and More 13.
- **What is the capital of West Virginia?** *(Charleston)*
- Write *Charleston* next to *West Virginia* on Notebook page 41.
- **What is the nickname of West Virginia?** *("the Mountain State")*
- **Why is this a good nickname for West Virginia?** *(because of the ruggedness of the land)*

Text Discussion, page 98 and Maps and More 13

- *Show a model of a horse and a picture of the Smoky Mountains.*
- **Read page 98 to find out which state is famous for the Great Smoky Mountains and which state is known for horses.** *(Tennessee—the Great Smoky Mountains; Kentucky—horses)*
- Find Kentucky on Maps and More 13.
- **What is the capital of Kentucky?** *(Frankfort)*
- Write *Frankfort* next to *Kentucky* on Notebook page 41.
- Find Tennessee on Maps and More 13.
- **What is the capital of Tennessee?** *(Nashville)*
- Write *Nashville* next to *Tennessee* on Notebook page 41.
- **In which state is Fort Knox located?** *(Kentucky)*
- Name the valuable mineral stored in Fort Knox's underground vaults. *(gold)*

During World War II, the Constitution, the Declaration of Independence, a Gutenberg Bible, Lincoln's Gettysburg Address, and the Magna Carta were placed in a depository at Fort Knox for safekeeping.

- Name your most valuable possessions.

Even though possessions are enjoyable, people and relationships should be more important. Remember that the Word of God should be precious to Christians, who are instructed to hide it in their hearts. Read or recite Psalm 119:11. (BATs: 5a Love, 5d Communication, 6a Bible study)

Map Activity, pages 320-21

- The seven states that can be seen from Lookout Mountain are Georgia, Tennessee, North Carolina, South Carolina, Mississippi, Kentucky, and Alabama.
- Find the Great Smoky Mountains on the map on pages 320-21. Notice how these mountains form the boundary between Tennessee and North Carolina.
- **Can you guess where the mountains get their name?**

The Great Smoky Mountains contain thick forests that create a humid atmosphere, which at times forms a smoky mist or haze over the mountains.

- **What is so unusual about the Tennessee River?** *(It flows through the state twice.)*
- Trace the river with your finger on the map as I describe the path.

The Tennessee River begins in the Appalachian Mountains in Knoxville, Tennessee. This is about where the "r" is in "Great Smoky Mtns." on the map. It flows south through the state and then into Alabama where it turns north. The river then flows back through Tennessee and on into Kentucky before emptying into the Ohio River at Paducah, Kentucky.

Southeast

Wright Brothers National Memorial

North Carolina

East of Tennessee is North Carolina. North Carolina's nickname is "the Tar Heel State." Most people think this name goes back to the Civil War. Soldiers from North Carolina offered to "tar the heels" of some other Confederate soldiers who had fled from a battle and left them to fight on their own.

Cape Hatteras, at the tip of an island off North Carolina's coast, is known as "the Graveyard of the Atlantic." Many ships have been wrecked there, as well as on the other islands and reefs offshore. North Carolina contains parts of the Great Smoky Mountains and the Blue Ridge Mountains. Why do you think this state is often called "First in Flight"? In Kitty Hawk, the Wright brothers made the first successful flight in a powered aircraft.

South Carolina

The gardens of Middleton Plantation in Charleston

South Carolina is North Carolina's neighbor to the south. It is nicknamed "the Palmetto State" after its state tree.

South Carolina played a key role in the American Civil War. It was the first state to secede from the Union. The first shot of the war was fired at Fort Sumter, on an island off South Carolina's coast. Visitors can still view the remains of this fort in Charleston Harbor. Charleston also has many stately houses from before the war. Have you ever been inside a fabric store? There is a good chance that some of the fabrics you see were produced in South Carolina. Making textiles is its biggest industry.

99

Southeast

Stone Mountain

Georgia

Georgia is southwest of South Carolina. Georgia is famous for the large, sweet peaches it grows. It is nicknamed "the Peach State." Another nickname is "the Empire State of the South" because it is the largest southern state. It has more land than any other state east of the Mississippi River.

Near Atlanta is Stone Mountain, which displays a huge sculpture of three Confederate leaders on horses. Which three men do you think these are? They are Jefferson Davis, Robert E. Lee, and Stonewall Jackson. Underneath Georgia are large deposits of marble. Georgia marble was used to build the Lincoln Memorial. Do you like peanuts? Georgia produces more of them than any other state.

Florida

Orange groves

South of Georgia is Florida, one of the states people visit most often. Florida's nickname is "the Sunshine State" because of its warm, mild climate. The Spanish explorer Juan Ponce de León first claimed this land for Spain in 1513. He saw all of the flowers there and named it Florida, or *flowery* in Spanish.

Florida contains the oldest city in the United States. St. Augustine was founded in 1565, and in this city is the oldest house in the nation, built in the late 1500s. Florida offers many beautiful beaches and palm trees. It is also the home of Walt Disney World. The southern tip of Florida lies near the island of Cuba. Many Cuban people have come to live in Florida. Did you drink orange juice with your breakfast this morning? Florida produces almost all of the nation's orange juice.

100

Text Discussion, page 99 and Maps and More 13

➤ Find North Carolina and South Carolina on Maps and More 13.

These states were once part of one colony, the Carolina Colony.

➤ **What is the capital of North Carolina?** *(Raleigh)*
➤ Write *Raleigh* next to *North Carolina* on Notebook page 41.
➤ **What is the capital of South Carolina?** *(Columbia)*
➤ Write *Columbia* next to *South Carolina* on Notebook page 41.
➤ **Read page 99 to find out which state is known for a set of famous brothers.** *(North Carolina)*
➤ **Who are these famous brothers?** *(the Wright brothers)*
➤ **Where was the first shot fired in the American Civil War?** *(Fort Sumter in South Carolina)*
➤ Find Charleston and Fort Sumter on Maps and More 13.

Even though it took the Confederates thirty-four hours to defeat this Union fort, the only death in the first battle of America's bloodiest war was the death of a horse.

TimeLine Snapshots Activity

➤ **What is the famous accomplishment of Wilbur and Orville Wright?** *(first powered airplane flight)*

On December 17, 1903, the Wright brothers started the age of aviation with a flight that went for 120 feet and lasted twelve seconds.

➤ Add the figure of Wilbur and Orville Wright to the TimeLine at 1903.

Part of the Wright brothers' plane was placed on the moon in 1969 by Neil Armstrong and Buzz Aldrin.

Day 3

Text Discussion, page 100 and Maps and More 13

➤ Find Georgia on Maps and More 13.
➤ **What is the capital of Georgia?** *(Atlanta)*
➤ Write *Atlanta* next to *Georgia* on Notebook page 41.
➤ **Read the first two paragraphs on page 100 to find Georgia's popular fruit, which is also part of the state's nickname.** *(peaches; "the Peach State")*
➤ Look at the picture of the stone sculpture.
➤ **Who are the three Confederate leaders honored in the sculpture?** *(Jefferson Davis, Robert E. Lee, and Stonewall Jackson)*

Stone Mountain, a huge gray mass of granite, is the largest stone mountain in North America. This sculpture was carved as a memorial of the South's struggle during the American Civil War.

Remind your child that Christians should live to honor and glorify the Lord. Encourage him to share ways that Christians can honor the Lord with their lives. *(Answers will vary.)* (BATs: 2b Servanthood, 2e Work, 3d Body as a temple, 6c Spirit-filled, 7b Exaltation of Christ)

- ➤ Find Florida on Maps and More 13.
- ➤ **What is the capital of Florida?** *(Tallahassee)*
- ➤ Write *Tallahassee* next to *Florida* on Notebook page 41.
- ➤ **Read the rest of page 100 to find the name of the oldest U.S. city.** *(St. Augustine)*
- ➤ **What does the Spanish word *Florida* mean?** *(flowery)*
- ➤ **Who discovered Florida and where was he from?** *(Ponce de León [pŏns′ də lē′ ən]; Spain)*

Ponce de León was in search of the Fountain of Youth, a legendary spring that could restore youth to those who drank from or bathed in its waters.

- ➤ **Do you think he ever found the Fountain of Youth?** He never did.
- ➤ **Why would someone not want to grow old?** *(Answers will vary but should include a fear of dying.)*

Read I Peter 1:24-25. Explain that growing older and dying are part of life's process; however, Christians know that through Christ they can have assurance of eternal life in heaven. (BATs: 1c Separation from the world, 7a Grace)

Text Discussion, page 101 and Maps and More 13

- ➤ **Read page 101 to find the nicknames of Alabama and Mississippi.** *(Alabama—"the Yellowhammer State"; Mississippi—"the Magnolia State")*
- ➤ Find Alabama on Maps and More 13.
- ➤ **What is the capital of Alabama?** *(Montgomery)*
- ➤ Write *Montgomery* next to *Alabama* on Notebook page 41.
- ➤ Find Mississippi on Maps and More 13.
- ➤ **What is the capital of Mississippi?** *(Jackson)*
- ➤ Write *Jackson* next to *Mississippi* on your Notebook page.
- ➤ **Why is Huntsville, Alabama, known as "Rocket City, U.S.A."?** *(Redstone Arsenal and the George C. Marshall Space Flight Center, where rockets and space equipment are developed, are located there.)*

Rocket Park in Huntsville

Southeast

Alabama

Georgia's western neighbor is the state of Alabama. Alabama's nickname is "the Yellowhammer State," after the state bird, which has yellow spots beneath its wings. During the Civil War, some of the Alabama soldiers, also called *yellowhammers,* wore uniforms trimmed with bright yellow cloth.

The city of Huntsville has been called *Rocket City, U.S.A.* It is the home of Redstone Arsenal and the George C. Marshall Space Flight Center, where scientists develop rockets and other space flight equipment. In Mobile Bay, visitors can see the U.S.S. *Alabama,* a famous battleship preserved from World War II. Do you remember the man who discovered over three hundred uses for the peanut? George Washington Carver taught at Tuskegee Institute in Alabama, a college for African Americans. Today the college houses a museum in his honor.

Mississippi

West of Alabama is Mississippi. Mississippi takes its name from the river that borders it on the west. The name means "Great Water." Mississippi is nicknamed "the Magnolia State."

Natchez, the oldest town along the Mississippi River, is a good place to find old plantation homes and colorful flowers. Do you remember which battle was a turning point in the American Civil War? Vicksburg National Military Park is a memorial of the battle of Vicksburg, which ended in victory for the Union. Biloxi, on the southern coast of Mississippi, is often called "the Shrimp Capital" of the United States because its bay is well supplied with shrimp. Mississippi is also known for its wooded, swampy areas like Cypress Swamp near Jackson.

Shrimp is the catch of the day for these boats.

101

Scientists at the Marshall Space Center developed the spacecraft that took U.S. astronauts to the moon. The world's largest space museum, the U.S. Space and Rocket Center, is also located in Huntsville. Visitors to Space Camp can experience how it feels to travel and walk in outer space.

Map Activity, pages 320-21

- ➤ **What is the meaning of *Mississippi?*** *(Great Water)*
- ➤ Find St. Paul, Minnesota, on the map on pages 320-21.

The river you see here is the Mississippi. The source, or beginning, of the Mississippi River is actually in northwestern Minnesota.

- ➤ Trace the entire river south to its mouth, or end, in Louisiana at the Gulf of Mexico.
- ➤ **What makes the Mississippi River so "great"?** *(It is very long.)*

The Mississippi River, flowing 2,350 miles, is the longest river in the United States. (*NOTE:* Some sources list the Missouri River and others the Mississippi as the longest river in the United States. It depends on how the river is measured. We have chosen to recognize the Mississippi as the longest.)

Southeast

Waterfalls on a river in the Ozarks

Arkansas

Arkansas is northwest of Mississippi. Arkansas was once nicknamed "the Land of Opportunity." What opportunities does Arkansas offer? It has beautiful mountains and valleys, good farmland, rich mines, and busy factories. Arkansas means "land of downstream people."

Now Arkansas is "the Natural State." Hot Springs, Arkansas, is the only city in the United States that has almost an entire national park within it. People believe the park's natural hot springs relieve pain from arthritis and other diseases. How would you like to search for diamonds? Arkansas also has a public diamond mine near Murfreesboro. Visitors who find diamonds there are allowed to keep them. The people of Arkansas, especially those in the Ozark region, are skilled in music and crafts such as woodcarving.

Egrets are a common sight on Avery Island.

Louisiana

South of Arkansas is Louisiana. Louisiana was named in 1682 by the explorer La Salle in honor of the king of France, Louis XIV. Louisiana is nicknamed "the Pelican State." Brown pelicans live along its coast. It is also often called "Sportsman's Paradise."

Louisiana is well known for its bayous. A bayou is a marshy, slow-moving body of water that flows into a lake or river. Many of Louisiana's people are descendants of its French and Spanish settlers. They are called Creoles. Others, known as *Cajuns*, descended from French settlers in Canada. Both groups have their own special types of spicy food. Visitors often stop in New Orleans to see the French and Spanish parts of the city. In the French Quarter are old buildings with fancy iron balconies and a large open marketplace called the French Market.

102

Faces of the South

Name ____________________

Draw a line to match each statement with the correct person(s).

included in famous carving on Stone Mountain	explorer who searched for the "fountain of youth"	performed the first airplane flight on December 17, 1903	discovered over 300 uses for the peanut

Gather information about one person from the Southeast region. Use this information to give an oral report.

Name of Person: ____________________

Place of Birth: ____________________

Date of Birth: ____________________

Date and Cause of Death: ____________________

Early Childhood: ____________________

Accomplishments: ____________________

Heritage Studies 4 Student Notebook — Lesson 26 Evaluating the Lesson 42

➤ **What is the oldest town along the Mississippi?** *(Natchez)*

In Natchez visitors can enjoy seeing *Rosalie,* a beautiful mansion once used as headquarters for Union troops during the Civil War.

Day 4

Text Discussion, page 102 and Maps and More 13

- ➤ Find Arkansas on Maps and More 13.
- ➤ **What is the capital of Arkansas?** *(Little Rock)*
- ➤ Write *Little Rock* next to *Arkansas* on Notebook page 41.
- ➤ Find Louisiana on Maps and More 13.
- ➤ **What is the capital of Louisiana?** *(Baton Rouge)*
- ➤ Write *Baton Rouge* next to *Louisiana* on your Notebook page.

The states and capitals listing for the Southeast region is now complete. You may use Notebook page 41 to study and memorize the states and capitals of the Southeast.

➤ **Read page 102 to find out which state is known for its diamond mine.** *(Arkansas)*

This mine is located in the Crater of Diamonds State Park. Visitors learn how to identify and hunt for diamonds.

- ➤ **What would you do if you found a diamond?**
- ➤ **What are the French and Spanish descendants in Louisiana called?** *(Creoles and Cajuns)*
- ➤ **What is typical of the foods these people like to eat?** *(spicy)*

Special Creole dishes include gumbo, an okra soup or stew, and jambalaya, spicy rice cooked with shrimp, oysters, ham, or chicken.

➤ **Why would seafood be popular in Louisiana?** *(It has a coastline suitable for fishing.)*

Evaluating the Lesson

Notebook Activity, page 42

- ➤ Look at the men at the top of Notebook page 42. They are George Washington Carver; Jefferson Davis, Robert E. Lee, and Stonewall Jackson; Ponce de León; and Orville and Wilbur Wright.
- ➤ Complete the matching section at the top of Notebook page 42.
- ➤ Complete the research project on the Notebook page.
- ➤ You will use your notes to present an oral report.

This oral report will give your child another opportunity to express what he has learned orally. The report does not need to be more than several minutes long. Encourage him to dress as the person he researched to present his report. You may wish to use the following list of people associated with the South.

Hank Aaron	Dolley Madison
Belle Boyd	James Madison
John Brown	Margaret Mitchell
Pearl S. Buck	James Monroe
John C. Calhoun	Garrett A. Morgan
Jimmy Carter	Jesse Owens
Bill Clinton	William Sydney Porter
Davy Crockett	Leontyne Price
George Guess (Sequoya)	Edmund Kirby-Smith
Wade Hampton	Zachary Taylor
William H. Harrison	Strom Thurmond
Thomas Jefferson	John Tyler
Percy L. Julian	Booker T. Washington
Helen Keller	George Washington
Juliette Gordon Low	Woodrow Wilson
Douglas MacArthur	

Going Beyond

Enrichment

Help your child make peanut butter. You will need roasted peanuts in the shell, cooking oil, salt, a measuring cup, a food grinder (for crunchy style) or food blender (for smooth style), a tablespoon, and a jar.

Your child should be able to follow each step on his own.

1. Crack open the shells and remove the peanuts. Measure out about one cup of peanuts.
2. Remove the red skin from the peanuts.
3. If you want chunky peanut butter, put the peanuts into a food grinder and run the chopped mixture through three or more times until the peanuts are the size you like. For creamy style peanut butter, chop up the peanuts in a food blender.
4. Add one to two tablespoons of cooking oil in small amounts and regrind or blend the mixture until the peanut butter is the familiar paste consistency.
5. Add one-half teaspoon of salt for each cup of peanuts. Homemade peanut butter contains no preservatives or other additives, so keep any unused portion in a closed jar in the refrigerator.

Additional Teacher Information

George Washington Carver was born a slave around 1864 in Diamond, Missouri. Both he and his mother were kidnapped by raiders; however, Moses Carver, the owner, was able to recover George. George's mother was never seen again. Moses chose to raise both George and his brother, Jim. After the Civil War, the Carvers gave the boys their freedom. Because this was the only home they had ever known, both George and Jim chose to stay with the Carvers. George was curious about nature and loved walking through the woods and observing plants, insects, and rocks. At a young age George showed a talent with plants by growing his own garden. He always had a strong desire to know more than anyone could teach him, and in time he went on to receive an advanced college degree in agriculture from Iowa State College of Agricultural and Mechanical Arts before accepting a teaching position at Tuskegee Institute in Alabama.

The Capitol in Washington, D.C., displays two statues donated from each state. These statues portray famous people from each state.

Mammoth Cave National Park is located in central Kentucky. This park contains the longest cave system in the world. With more than three hundred miles of mapped trails, the caves offer visitors a variety of interesting sights.

LESSON 27

The Middle West: For Amber Waves of Grain

Text, pages 103-8, 280-305, 320-21
Notebook, pages 43-44

Preview

Main Ideas

- Maps represent actual places.
- Each of the twelve states of the Middle West region is unique.
- Names have their origins in words with special meanings.
- U.S. maps have changed over the years.
- People rely upon crops from farms and products from factories.
- Farms and factories help make the Middle West region unique and valuable.

Objectives

- Identify the Middle West states on a map
- Identify pictures representing the Middle West states

Materials

- Appendix, pages A36-A37: product cards (cut apart and shuffled)*
- Appendix, page A38: Products Chart*
- Maps and More 15, 16, 17, and 18, pages M6-M8
- Several kernels of corn or a can of corn*
- A cereal box* (*NOTE:* You may wish to display a cereal brand based in Michigan, such as Kellogg's, Post, or General Foods.)
- A Bible
- A model or picture of a cow*
- A loaf of bread
- An atlas (optional)

If you live in one of the Middle West states, you may wish to devote additional time to the study of your state. Refer your child to pages 280-305 for additional information about each of the Middle West states.

Lesson

Introducing the Lesson

Identifying Activity

➤ *Give your child the product cards.*

➤ **Read the name on each card.**

These items are very important to the Middle West region of the United States.

➤ *Place the Products Chart in front of your child.*

Some of the items on the product cards are agricultural products. They are raised or grown on farms. Other items are manufactured products or products made in factories.

➤ Think about where the products on the cards came from—either a farm or factory.

➤ Place each product card under the correct word. *(farm—hog, dairy cow, wheat, and corn; factory—bacon, butter, flour, and breakfast cereal)*

People on farms and factories work closely together. People depend on both for jobs and needed goods.

➤ Match each farm product with its related factory product by placing the cards next to each other. *(hog—bacon; dairy cow—butter; wheat—flour; and corn—breakfast cereal)*

Farms and factories help make the Middle West region unique and valuable.

Teaching the Lesson

Map Activity, Notebook page 43 and Maps and More 15

➤ Read the names of the twelve states and capitals on Notebook page 43.

➤ Use Maps and More 15 to help locate each state on the Notebook page.

➤ Color each state according to the color code.

You will probably need to help your child see both parts of Michigan.

➤ Use Notebook page 43 to study and memorize the states and capitals of the Middle West region.

This region of the country is also referred to as the Midwest. You may use these terms interchangeably so that your child is familiar with both.

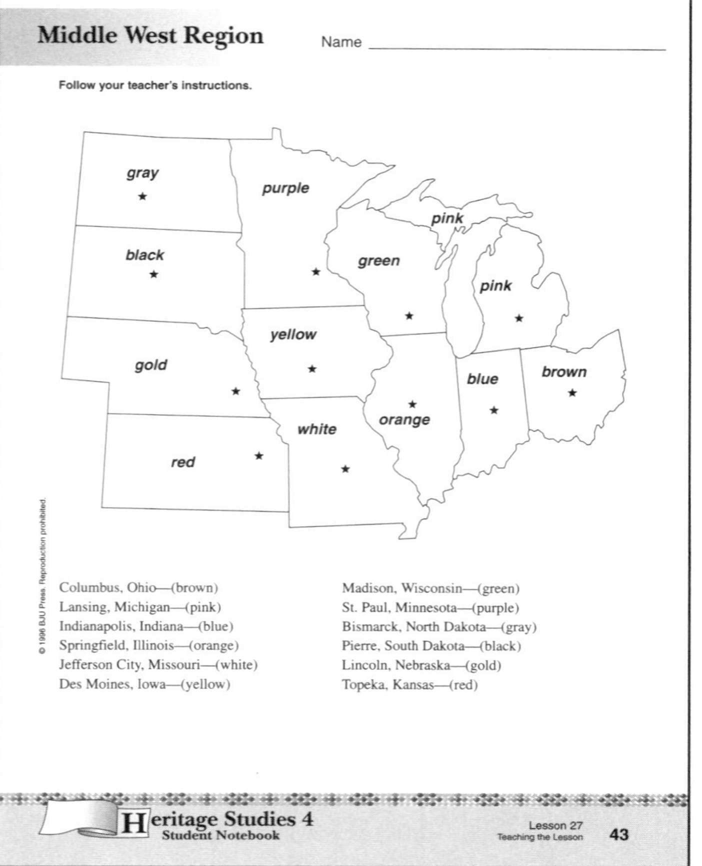
Middle West Region

Name ____________________

Follow your teacher's instructions.

Columbus, Ohio—(brown)
Lansing, Michigan—(pink)
Indianapolis, Indiana—(blue)
Springfield, Illinois—(orange)
Jefferson City, Missouri—(white)
Des Moines, Iowa—(yellow)

Madison, Wisconsin—(green)
St. Paul, Minnesota—(purple)
Bismarck, North Dakota—(gray)
Pierre, South Dakota—(black)
Lincoln, Nebraska—(gold)
Topeka, Kansas—(red)

Heritage Studies 4 Student Notebook — Lesson 27 Teaching the Lesson 43

Middle West

Ohio

In the Middle West region of the United States, our first stop is Ohio, "the Buckeye State." A buckeye is a type of tree that once grew in the state, but most are gone now because settlers used them to build their cabins. *Ohio* means "something great" in the Iroquois language.

Ohio was the first part of the Northwest Territory to become a state. In 1833, Oberlin College opened for both men and women to attend. Before that time, only men could go to college. Much of Ohio is farmland. Its two major crops are corn and soybeans. In Hillsboro is the Great Serpent Mound, a hill in the shape of a snake built by Native Americans. The Pro Football Hall of Fame is in Canton. In its museum, visitors can see uniforms and equipment worn by famous players.

The Great Serpent Mound contains seven deep curves and extends for more than a quarter of a mile.

Michigan

North of Ohio is Michigan, which consists of two separate land areas, the Upper Peninsula and the Lower Peninsula. Can you find these two sections on a map? Michigan's nickname is "the Wolverine State" because its wolverine pelts were once valuable items for trade.

Michigan's two peninsulas are connected by the five-mile-long Mackinac Bridge. The shoreline of Michigan touches four of the five great lakes, so water sports and fishing are popular there. Michigan produces more automobiles than any other state. Two men who built some of the first automobiles came from Detroit: Henry Ford and Ransom Olds. Battle Creek, Michigan, is known as the "Cereal Bowl of America." It is the world's leading cereal producer.

Mackinac Bridge

103

Text Discussion, page 103 and Maps and More 15 and 16

➤ *Display the kernels of corn and the cereal box.*

➤ **Read page 103 to find which product goes with Ohio and which product goes with Michigan.** *(corn—Ohio; cereal—Michigan)*

➤ Find Ohio on Maps and More 15.

➤ **What is the capital of Ohio?** *(Columbus)*

Your child already has the states and capitals on his Notebook page for this lesson. It is important for him to become familiar with the shape of each state and the location of its capital by referring to the map.

➤ **What famous territory was Ohio once a part of?** *(the Northwest Territory)*

➤ Look at Maps and More 16.

This map shows the Northwest Territory. It was land north of the Ohio River, west of Pennsylvania, and east of the Mississippi River.

➤ Name the Middle West states that were carved out of the Northwest Territory. *(Wisconsin, Michigan, Illinois, Indiana, Ohio)*

➤ **What is most of the land in Ohio used for?** *(farming)*

➤ **What crop other than corn grows in abundance in Ohio?** *(soybeans)*

Since farmland covers much of the Middle West, most people live in the big cities.

➤ Find Michigan on Maps and More 15.

➤ **What is the capital of Michigan?** *(Lansing)*

➤ Find Michigan's two peninsulas.

➤ **What are the names of Michigan's two sections of land?** *(Upper Peninsula and Lower Peninsula)*

A ***peninsula*** is an area of land surrounded on three sides by water. Michigan's Lower Peninsula is shaped like a giant mitten. Most people live in the large cities on this peninsula. The Upper Peninsula is more rugged, with a countryside boasting thick forests, swamps, and many rivers and waterfalls.

➤ **Which peninsula would you prefer to live on?**

➤ **What is the bridge connecting the two peninsulas called?** *(Mackinac [Măk′ə·nô′] Bridge)*

➤ **What two products rank the highest in Michigan?** *(the automobile and cereal)*

Detroit, also called "the Automobile Capital of the World" or "Motor City," is America's number one producer of automobiles.

➤ **Which city is the "Cereal Bowl of America"?** *(Battle Creek)*

Middle West

Quick teamwork during pit stops helped Gordon Johncock win this Indianapolis 500 by only 0.160 seconds.

Indiana

Indiana, west of Ohio, is called "the Hoosier State." Most people think *Hoosier* was once a slang word used as a greeting, meaning "Who's here?" Indiana is smaller than all the states west of it, except Hawaii.

Indiana is part of a wide section of the Middle West states called the Corn Belt. Its broad, flat plains make good farmland for corn, its main crop. Do you like car races? The nation's most famous automobile race, the Indianapolis 500, has taken place in Indiana each year since 1911. In the 1820s, people in New Harmony, Indiana, tried an experiment. They began teaching boys and girls together in their school. Most other American schools soon adopted their idea. Would you like to have attended the first professional baseball game? It was played in Fort Wayne, Indiana, in 1871.

The Sears Tower dominates the Chicago skyline.

Illinois

Illinois is west of Indiana. The rolling plains that produce one-sixth of all our nation's corn gave Illinois its nickname, "the Prairie State." Another nickname for the state is "the Land of Lincoln" because it was Abraham Lincoln's home for most of his life.

Illinois's most famous city is Chicago, on the coast of Lake Michigan. Almost half of the people in Illinois live in or near Chicago. The city is the home of the Sears Tower, one of the tallest buildings in the world. It is also famous for its industries, museums, and works of art. The first Ferris wheel was put into use at the World's Fair in Chicago in 1883. In Springfield, visitors can see where Lincoln lived before he went to Washington, D.C., as president. His gravesite is there also.

104

St. Louis arch

Missouri

Missouri, southwest of Illinois, has been given the nickname "the Show Me State." In a speech, a Missouri congressman said that he must be shown something, not just told it, to believe it. The name *Missouri* comes from an Indian word that means "town of the large canoes."

The Mississippi River borders Missouri on the east, and the Missouri River flows across the state. These two waterways, once a major center for transportation, make the land fertile for farming soybeans and corn, especially in the southern Boot Heel region. Can you see from the map how this region got its name? The two largest cities are Kansas City and St. Louis. People often call the tall arch in St. Louis the "Gateway to the West."

Iowa

North of Missouri is Iowa. Iowa is nicknamed "the Hawkeye State" in honor of Chief Black Hawk, whose people once owned some of Iowa's land. Sometimes Iowa is called "the Corn State" or "the land where the tall corn grows." It produces more corn than any other state.

Many of Iowa's farms also produce hogs and dairy cattle. Over 90 percent of Iowa is farmland. But only about 10 percent of Iowa's people are farmers. Most live in cities and small towns. Do you like popcorn? The largest popcorn factory is in Sioux City. In Elk Horn, Iowa, is a Danish windmill that was brought from Denmark piece by piece and rebuilt. In the Amana Colonies, founded by Germans, visitors can see how a woolen mill weaves sweaters and blankets.

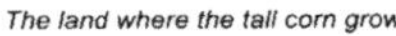

The land where the tall corn grows

105

Map Activity, Maps and More 15

- ➤ Look at the map on Maps and More 15.
- ➤ Name the Great Lakes that touch the state of Michigan. *(Lake Superior, Lake Michigan, Lake Huron, and Lake Erie)*
- ➤ **What is the name of the fifth Great Lake that does not touch Michigan?** *(Lake Ontario)*

Day 2

Text Discussion, page 104 and Maps and More 15 and 17

- ➤ Find Indiana and Illinois on Maps and More 15 and give the capital of each. *(Indiana—Indianapolis; Illinois—Springfield)*
- ➤ **Read page 104 to find the common crop of Indiana and Illinois.** *(corn)*
- ➤ Look at Maps and More 17.
- ➤ **What are the states in the Middle West that produce corn called?** *(the Corn Belt)*

The Corn Belt is an area stretching from Minnesota to Missouri and from Nebraska to Ohio.

- ➤ **What does the darker shaded portion of the map represent?** *(major corn-producing areas; the Corn Belt)*
- ➤ **Which states are the chief corn producers?** *(Iowa, Illinois, Nebraska, Minnesota, Indiana, Ohio, Wisconsin, Missouri, Michigan, and South Dakota)*
- ➤ **Why do you think this land would be suitable for growing corn?**

It is broad and flat and has fertile soil, abundant rainfall, and a long growing season.

- ➤ **What does the lighter shaded portion represent?** *(other corn-producing areas)*
- ➤ **What Illinois city is located on Lake Michigan?** *(Chicago)*
- ➤ Name the tallest building in Chicago. *(the Sears Tower)* This skyscraper has 110 stories, which include stores and an observation deck.

Text Discussion, page 105

- ➤ **Read page 105 to discover more about other states that produce corn.** *(Missouri and Iowa)*
- ➤ **Which state produces the most corn?** *(Iowa)*
- ➤ **What is Missouri's nickname?** *("the Show Me State")*

Remember that all Christians should be "Show Others" Christians. Read James 2:17-20. Christians should not just say they follow Christ; they should prove their faith through their actions. Ask your child to name ways that Christians can demonstrate their faith in Christ. (BATs: 1c Separation from the world, 3c Emotional control, 5c Evangelism and missions, 5d Communication)

Map Activity, pages 320-21

- Find the two major rivers in Missouri on the map on pages 320-21. *(the Mississippi and Missouri Rivers)*
- Trace with your finger these rivers through Missouri and along its border.
- **Why are these rivers important?** *(They make the land fertile and provide transportation.)*

Map Activity, Maps and More 15

- Find Missouri and Iowa on Maps and More 15, naming the capital of each. *(Missouri—Jefferson City; Iowa—Des Moines)*
- **Where is Missouri's most fertile region?** *(the Boot Heel region)*
- Locate this region on Maps and More 15. It is the area that looks like the high heel of a boot.
- Find St. Louis on Maps and More 15.
- **What do people often call the Gateway Arch?** *(the "Gateway to the West")* This monument stands in silent tribute to the opening of the West for the early pioneers.

Map Activity, Maps and More 17

- Look at Maps and More 17. Notice how much of Iowa is shaded dark green.
- **What percentage of land in Iowa did your text say is devoted to farming?** *(more than 90 percent)*
- **Why do you think only 10 percent of Iowa's people work on farms?**

Modern farming requires less manpower. More jobs are available in cities and small towns.

Text Discussion, page 106

- *Show your child the picture/model of the cow and the loaf of bread.*
- **Read page 106 to find out which state is known as "America's Dairyland" and which state is known as "the Bread and Butter State."** *(Wisconsin—"America's Dairyland"; Minnesota—"the Bread and Butter State")*
- **How did Wisconsin get this nickname?** *(Wisconsin produces more milk than any other state.)*
- Name some milk products. *(cheese, butter, ice cream, yogurt)*

Middle West

Some Holsteins in the Dells

Wisconsin

Wisconsin is east of Iowa and north of Illinois. In the 1820s, lead miners worked in Wisconsin and lived in caves they dug in the hillsides. They were called *badgers*. Wisconsin is nicknamed "the Badger State."

Black-and-white Holstein dairy cows dot Wisconsin's green pastures. It is often called "America's Dairyland" because it produces more milk than any other state. It also produces one-third of America's cheese and one-fourth of its butter. Two of the Great Lakes—Michigan and Superior—touch Wisconsin. Wisconsin Dells has interesting rock formations carved out of its sandstone cliffs and offers boat rides and water sports. Every year in Oshkosh, Wisconsin, airplanes fly in from around the world for a large experimental aircraft convention.

Minnesota

Minnehaha Falls in Minneapolis

Wisconsin's neighbor to the west is Minnesota. *Minnesota* means "sky-tinted waters" in the Sioux language. Its nickname is "the Gopher State," but it is also known as "the Bread-and-Butter State," "the North Star State," "Land of Sky-Blue Waters," and "Land of 10,000 Lakes."

Have you eaten any bread or butter today? Minnesota produces more butter than any other state and is also well-known for its flour mills. Two of the state's largest cities, Minneapolis and St. Paul, are so close together that they are called the Twin Cities. Minnesota has very long, cold winters. At the St. Paul Winter Carnival, people make beautiful ice sculptures and compete in sports like ice-skating and ski-jumping. Duluth, on Minnesota's northeastern coast, is the busiest freshwater port in the nation.

106

- **What kind of winters does Minnesota have?** *(long and cold)*
- **Where is the Winter Carnival held?** *(St. Paul)*

St. Paul's Winter Carnival is a two-week celebration of parades, entertainment, ice fishing, sled-dog racing, and snowmobile racing.

Map Activity, Maps and More 15

- Find Wisconsin and Minnesota on Maps and More 15. Name the capital of each. *(Wisconsin—Madison; Minnesota—St. Paul)*
- Locate Minnesota's two largest cities. *(Minneapolis and St. Paul)*
- **What are these two cities called?** *(Twin Cities)* **Why?** *(because they are located close together)*

Minneapolis and St. Paul lie on opposite sides of the Mississippi River. Half of the people in Minnesota live in the Twin Cities.

Day 3

Map Activity, Maps and More 15

- Find North Dakota and South Dakota on Maps and More 15.
- Name the capital of each. *(North Dakota—Bismarck; South Dakota—Pierre)*

A farm on North Dakota's Red River

North Dakota

West of Minnesota is North Dakota. North Dakota is nicknamed "the Flickertail State" because so many flickertail ground squirrels live there. *Dakota* is a Sioux word meaning "allies" or "friends."

Nearly all of North Dakota is covered with farms and ranches. Grains like winter wheat and durum wheat are its chief crops. Visitors to North Dakota may see oil wells at work on the prairies. Some of the state's soft-coal beds burn constantly with a soft glow that can be seen for miles at night. The Badlands in the southwest part of the state are a beautiful stretch of natural sandstone rock formations. At the Canadian border is the International Peace Garden, a park built in honor of the long-time friendship between the United States and Canada.

Mount Rushmore

South Dakota

South Dakota is North Dakota's southern neighbor. How do you think the two states are alike? Both contain the Badlands, grow wheat as their main crop, and have many ranches. South Dakota's nickname is "the Coyote State." Why do you think that is?

South Dakota is also different from North Dakota in several ways. Southwestern South Dakota contains the Black Hills region. These low, rocky mountains are covered with pine trees that look black when seen from the plains. South Dakota also has the Mount Rushmore National Memorial. Four presidents' heads are carved into the top of a 6,000-foot cliff. Can you name these presidents? The Corn Palace in Mitchell, South Dakota, has wall murals made of different colors of corn and other grains.

107

Chimney Rock was an important landmark to pioneers heading west.

Nebraska

Nebraska is south of South Dakota. "The Cornhusker State" is one of America's chief farming states. The nickname comes from the cornhusking contests once held there. *Nebraska* comes from an Oto word meaning "flat water."

About 95 percent of Nebraska is farmland. Wheat, corn, and cattle are its main products. Pioneers drove their wagons westward through Nebraska on the Oregon Trail. Some of their wagon ruts can still be seen now, more than a century later. Chimney Rock, shaped like a tall spire, is one site that marked the Oregon Trail. Nebraska's government is unique. Its legislature is unicameral, having one house instead of two.

Kansas

Windmill on a Kansas plain

Kansas, south of Nebraska, is nicknamed "the Sunflower State," after its state flower. The fighting between proslavery and antislavery groups centered in Kansas before the American Civil War. Kansas settlers took as their motto "To the Stars Through Difficulties." What do you think this means?

If you drove across Kansas in late summer, you would see fields and fields of golden, waving wheat. Kansas, often called the "Breadbasket of America," produces more wheat than any other state. Another of its nicknames is "Midway, U.S.A." The exact center of North America is in Osborne County, Kansas. In Dodge City, called "the Cowboy Capital of the World," visitors can see Front Street as it was in the days of the Wild West.

108

Text Discussion, page 107

- ➤ **Read page 107 to find four main things that North and South Dakota have in common.** *(Both mean "allies" or "friends," contain the Badlands, grow wheat as their main crop, and have many ranches.)*
- ➤ **What two types of wheat are grown in North Dakota?** *(winter wheat and durum wheat)*

Winter wheat is used for breads, cakes, cookies, and crackers. Durum wheat is used for spaghetti and other pasta.

Map Activity, pages 320-21

- ➤ Find the Badlands of North and South Dakota on the map on pages 320-21.

Wind and water carved out this area, making unusual formations of sandstone, shale, and clay.

- ➤ **What are the low, rocky mountains in South Dakota called?** *(the Black Hills)*
- ➤ **Why were these mountains given this name?** *(The pine trees look black from a distance.)*
- ➤ Locate the Black Hills on the map.

TimeLine Snapshots Activity, page 107

- ➤ **What famous memorial is found in the Black Hills?** *(Mount Rushmore National Memorial)*
- ➤ Look at the picture of the Mount Rushmore National Memorial on page 107.
- ➤ **Can you identify any of the four presidents honored there?** They are George Washington, Thomas Jefferson, Theodore Roosevelt, and Abraham Lincoln.
- ➤ Find these presidents on the TimeLine.

Text Discussion, page 108 and Maps and More 18

- ➤ **Read the first two paragraphs on page 108 to find the name of Nebraska's unique state government.** ***(unicameral)***
- ➤ **What is the meaning of this type of government?** *(one-house legislature)*

The state senate is Nebraska's only lawmaking group.

- ➤ Look at the picture of Nebraska's capitol on Maps and More 18.

Products and Places Name ____________________

Label each picture representing each Middle West state.

OHIO BUCKEYE tree	MICHIGAN CEREAL	INDIANA automobile RACING
ILLINOIS SEARS Tower	MISSOURI GATEWAY to the WEST	IOWA CORN
WISCONSIN DAIRY products	MINNESOTA the BREAD and BUTTER State	NORTH DAKOTA OIL and coal
SOUTH DAKOTA MOUNT RUSHMORE	NEBRASKA 95% FARMLAND	KANSAS WHEAT

Unscramble the circled letters from the words above to answer the following question.

What term describes products raised or grown on farms?

A G R I C U L T U R A L

Nebraska's capitol is different from the capitols of other states. This "Tower of the Plains" rises four hundred feet into the air and is topped with a bronze statue of a "sower" sowing seeds of goodwill for the state.

➤ **Read the last two paragraphs on page 108 to find Kansas' motto.** *("To the Stars Through Difficulties")*

➤ **Why is Kansas called the "Breadbasket of America"?** *(It produces more wheat than any other state.)*

This abundant harvest reminds us of another harvest—a spiritual harvest. Read Matthew 9:37-38. Explain that many people are lost in sin. Like a crop that needs to be harvested, these people need to be led to Christ. The Lord is calling Christians to go out into this world to win lost souls for His kingdom. (BATs: 4a Sowing and reaping, 5c Evangelism and missions)

Map Activity, Maps and More 15

➤ Find Nebraska on Maps and More 15 and name its capital. *(Lincoln)*

➤ Locate Kansas and name its capital. *(Topeka)*

Evaluating the Lesson

Notebook Activity, page 44

➤ Read the instructions for Notebook page 44.

➤ Complete the page.

Going Beyond

Additional Teacher Information

Gutzon Borglum came to South Dakota in 1924 to study the idea of carving a national memorial. Mount Rushmore, a sixty-two-hundred-foot mountain, was chosen as the site of the carving, and the work began in 1927. Four presidents, each representing a unique quality of America, were chosen for the memorial. Thomas Jefferson represents self-government; George Washington represents independence; Abraham Lincoln represents equality of citizens; and Theodore Roosevelt represents conservation. Towering five hundred feet above its surroundings, the granite face of the mountain is approximately one thousand feet long and four hundred feet high. Each head was carved to a scale of a man 465 feet tall. From the top of the head to the chin is sixty feet; the nose is twenty feet long; the mouth is eighteen feet wide; and one eye is eleven feet across. The carving faces southeast, allowing the sun to light the surface most of the day. Gutzon Borglum died March 6, 1941, after complications arose from surgery; however, his son, Lincoln, continued the project and completed drilling on October 31, 1941, fourteen years after the project began.

LESSON 28
The Southwest: My Native Country, Thee

Text, pages 109-11, 280-305, 320-21
Notebook, pages 45-46

Preview

Main Ideas

- Maps represent actual places.
- Each of the four states of the Southwest region is unique.
- Names have their origins in words with special meanings.
- Native Americans have contributed to the unique culture of the Southwest.

Objectives

- Label the Southwest states and capitals on a map
- Locate places on a road atlas
- Answer questions using a road atlas
- Answer oral questions about the Southwest region

Materials

- Appendix, page A39: United States map*
- Maps and More 19 and 21, pages M8-M9
- The figure of the Alamo (1836) from the TimeLine Snapshots
- A picture of the Grand Canyon*
- A Bible
- Several road maps for adjoining states*
- A road atlas*
- Appendix, page A40: the four Southwest state cards*
- An atlas (optional)

> If you live in one of the Southwest states, you may wish to devote additional time to the study of your state. Refer your child to pages 280-305 for additional information about each of the Southwest states.

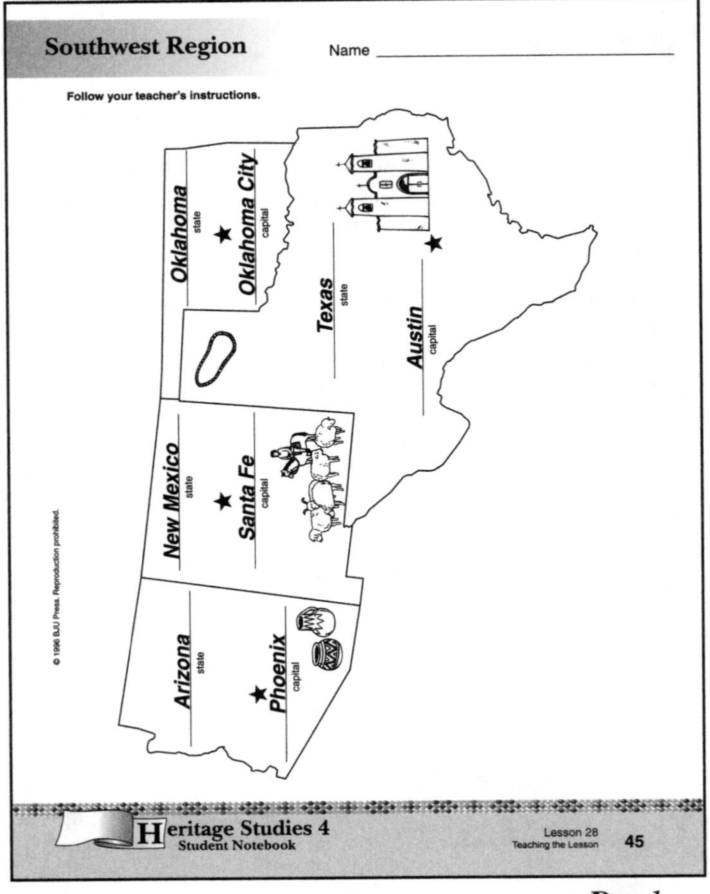

Day 1

Lesson

Introducing the Lesson

State and Capital Review

➤ *Give your child the United States map.*
➤ I will name a state that you have studied.
➤ Point to the state on the map.
➤ Name the capital and the region of the United States that the state is located in.

Teaching the Lesson

Map Activity, Notebook page 45

➤ Look at Notebook page 45, showing the states of the Southwest region.
➤ Fill in the names of the four Southwest states and capitals on Notebook page 45, using Maps and More 19.
➤ Use Notebook page 45 to study and memorize the states and capitals of the Southwest region.

Southwest

Native Americans in traditional dress

Oklahoma

Oklahoma, south of Kansas, is our first stop in the Southwest region of the United States. *Oklahoma* comes from two Choctaw words that mean "red people." Oklahoma's nickname is "the Sooner State" because some of its settlers arrived in the land before it officially opened.

What do you think the state of Oklahoma is shaped like? Many people think it looks like a long-handled pan. The long thin section is called the Panhandle. Wheat fields and oil wells are common sights on Oklahoma's plains. It is also a leading producer of natural gas. People from more than sixty different Native American tribes live in Oklahoma. Indian City, U.S.A., and the Cherokee Heritage Center are two places in which visitors can experience Plains Indian and Cherokee culture.

Texas

At a rodeo, people can demonstrate their skills in riding and roping.

South of Oklahoma is Texas, nicknamed "the Lone Star State" after the single white star on its flag. Texas is the only state allowed to fly its flag as high as the American flag because it was once an independent republic.

Texas is the second largest state. It contains more farmland and produces more cattle and sheep than any other state. As you might expect, rodeos are popular events in Texas. Do you remember any of the history behind the statehood of Texas? The Alamo chapel in San Antonio is all that is left of the fort where the Texas soldiers defended themselves against the Mexican army in 1836. Near Houston is the San Jacinto Monument, a tribute to theTexans who fought in the battle that won Texas independence.

110

The text pages are taught out of order in this lesson.

Text Discussion, page 110 and Maps and More 19

- ➤ Find Oklahoma on Maps and More 19, naming the capital. *(Oklahoma City)*
- ➤ **What does the shape of Oklahoma look like to you?**
- ➤ **Read the first two paragraphs on page 110 to discover a special name for the long thin section of the state.** *(the Panhandle)*
- ➤ **What are two common sights in Oklahoma?** *(wheat fields and oil wells)*

The capitol in Oklahoma City is located on a major oil field that was productive until the 1980s.

- ➤ **What does *Oklahoma* mean? *("red people")***

Today about one-third of all Native Americans live in Oklahoma.

- ➤ **Which two Native American nations are mentioned in the text?** *(Plains Indians and Cherokee)*
- ➤ Look at the Texas flag on page 301. The nickname of Texas is represented on the state flag.
- ➤ **Read the last two paragraphs on page 110 to find the nickname of Texas.** *("the Lone Star State")*

For ten years Texas was a separate country with its own president, its own paper money, and its own flag. Every state has a flag, and each color and symbol on the flag has significant meaning. The blue stands for loyalty, the red for bravery, and the white for purity. The single star reminds us of a time in history when Texas was a separate country.

- ➤ **How does Texas rank in size compared to the other states?** *(second largest)*

The state of Texas is larger than Wisconsin, Iowa, Illinois, Indiana, and Michigan combined.

- ➤ Find the state of Texas on Maps and More 19.
- ➤ **What is the capital of Texas?** *(Austin)*
- ➤ Find the city of San Antonio.

TimeLine Snapshots Activity

- ➤ **What is the name of the famous fort in San Antonio where Texas soldiers defended themselves against the Mexican army?** *(the Alamo)*
- ➤ Add the figure of the Alamo (1836) to the TimeLine.

Map Activity, pages 320-21

- ➤ Find Texas on the map on pages 320-21.
- ➤ Trace the southern border of the state of Texas with your finger.

The Rio Grande runs the entire length of Texas' border with Mexico. The Rio Grande is the longest river in Texas.

Day 2

Map Activity, Maps and More 19

- ➤ Find the state of New Mexico on Maps and More 19.
- ➤ **What is the capital of New Mexico?** *(Santa Fe)*
- ➤ Find Arizona on the map.
- ➤ **What is the capital of Arizona?** *(Phoenix)*

Southwest

New Mexico

West of Texas is New Mexico. Its beautiful scenery has earned it the nickname "the Land of Enchantment." It has rugged mountains, deserts with colorful rocks, and a beautiful river, the Rio Grande.

Would you like to ride on a four-hundred-year-old highway? *El Camino Real,* meaning "the Royal Highway," is the oldest road used by Europeans in America. New Mexico's capital, Santa Fe, is the oldest place of government in the United States. The Palace of Governors houses a museum about the Spanish government that ruled there in the early 1600s.

White Sands, a rugged New Mexico scene

Have you ever seen a bat? At Carlsbad Caverns, a group of caves in southeastern New Mexico, you will see hundreds of thousands of bats. Every evening at dusk, the sky is filled with flapping wings as the bats fly out of the caves.

Arizona

Arizona, the last of the Southwestern states, is west of New Mexico. Its nickname, "the Grand Canyon State," comes from its most well-known feature. The Grand Canyon, located in northern Arizona along the Colorado River, is the largest canyon in the world.

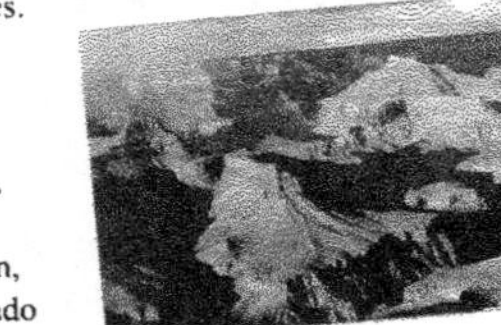

The Grand Canyon

When Arizona was first given to the United States after the Mexican War, many people called it a worthless stretch of desert. But it contains some of our country's most beautiful scenery. The Painted Desert is made up of sand of many different colors. The Petrified Forest and Monument Valley are filled with unusual rock formations. The cactus grows well in Arizona's climate. Would you like to stand in four states at one time? At Four Corners, the borders of Arizona, Colorado, New Mexico, and Utah meet.

111

Text Discussion, page 111

➤ New Mexico and Arizona, along with two other states, come together at one point. **Read page 111 to find the name of this special place where four states touch.** *(Four Corners)*

➤ **What are the two other states at Four Corners?** *(Colorado and Utah)*

➤ **What is the nickname of New Mexico?** *("the Land of Enchantment")*

➤ **What is the reason for this nickname?** *(beautiful scenery—rugged mountains, deserts with colorful rocks, and the Rio Grande)*

➤ Name two old sights found in New Mexico. *(El Camino Real and Santa Fe)*

Map Activity, pages 320-21 and Maps and More 21

➤ Find the area known as Four Corners on the map on pages 320-21.

Visitors to this barren site enjoy placing their hands and feet in the four states for a picture or visiting the craft booths set up around the monument.

➤ *Show the picture of the Grand Canyon.*

➤ **What is the nickname of Arizona?** *("the Grand Canyon State")*

➤ Locate the Grand Canyon on the map.

You may want to explain to your child that this canyon is not an evolutionary evidence as many believe and teach. Instead, it is another record of the Great Flood of Genesis.

➤ Locate the important river that flows through the Grand Canyon. *(the Colorado River)*

➤ **Why do you think this river would be important to the people of the Southwest?**

It supplies water and power to a dry, hot region.

➤ Look at Maps and More 21, the pictures of the Painted Desert and the Petrified Forest.

Colorful sand, petrified wood, and unusual rock formations make these places beautiful.

Text Discussion, page 281

➤ Look on page 281 to find the name of the state flower of Arizona. *(the saguaro cactus flower)*

➤ **Why would this flowering cactus grow well in the state?** *(because of Arizona's climate)*

The saguaro (sə gwär´ ō) cactus grows to sixty feet, making it the largest cactus in the United States. This particular plant can grow only in this region where there is little rainfall. It produces a flower and food.

Remember that Christians can experience a time of discouragement in which there seem to be little or no spiritual showers of blessing. Just like the saguaro cactus, a Christian can still produce fruit for the Lord and be a magnificent testimony of God's grace. Read aloud Isaiah 35:1. (BATs: 2c Faithfulness, 7c Praise, 7d Contentment, 8a Faith in God's promises)

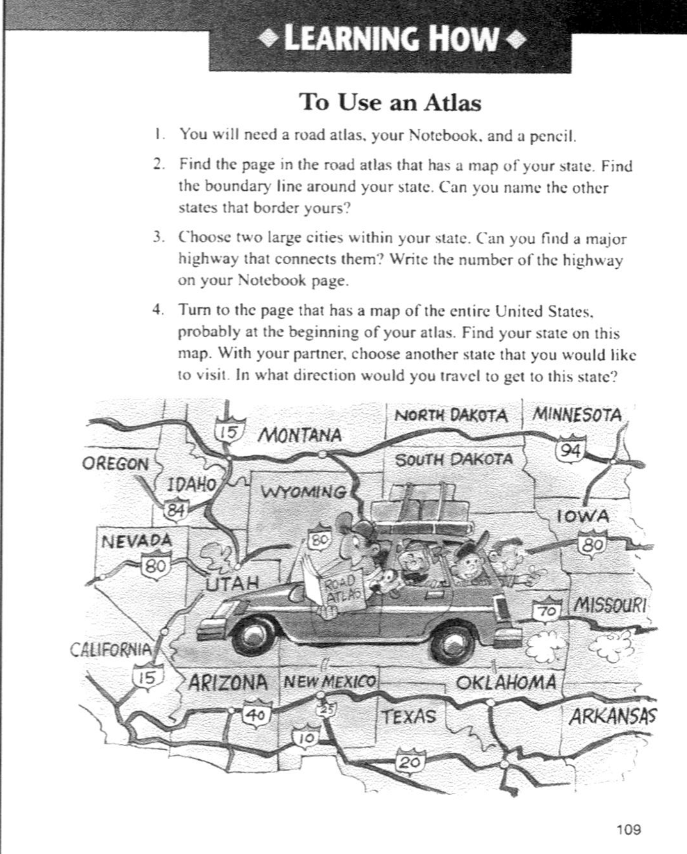

◆ LEARNING HOW ◆

To Use an Atlas

1. You will need a road atlas, your Notebook, and a pencil.
2. Find the page in the road atlas that has a map of your state. Find the boundary line around your state. Can you name the other states that border yours?
3. Choose two large cities within your state. Can you find a major highway that connects them? Write the number of the highway on your Notebook page.
4. Turn to the page that has a map of the entire United States, probably at the beginning of your atlas. Find your state on this map. With your partner, choose another state that you would like to visit. In what direction would you travel to get to this state?

109

Using a Road Atlas

Name ______________________

Follow your teacher's instructions to answer the following questions. ***Answers will vary.***

1. Your state is __________; its capital is __________.
   Find the capital on the map.
2. Name the other states that border yours. __________
   Does your state border an ocean, bay, or gulf? If so, which one? __________
3. Two large cities in your state are __________.
   What major highway connects these two cities? __________
4. Place your finger in the center of the state. If you were to travel directly west and cross the border, where would you be? __________
5. Write the name of a lake or reservoir in your state. __________
   In what part of the state is it located? __________
   Name a city that is near this body of water. __________
6. Two major rivers in your state are __________.
7. List two cities or towns with unusual names. __________
8. What is the name of your town? __________ Find it on the map.
   What major city is it closest to? __________
9. What is a point of interest in your state? __________ To go from your town to this point, in which direction would you travel? __________
10. Turn to the United States map in your atlas and find your state on the map.
11. Choose another state that you would like to visit. __________
    Which direction would you travel to get to this state? __________
    What is the capital of this state? __________ Find it on the map.
    Why would you like to visit this state? __________

Heritage Studies 4 Student Notebook — Lesson 28 Teaching the Lesson 46

Day 3

Learning How Activity, page 109 and Notebook page 46

- The most important part of taking a trip is getting accurate directions. *Show the road maps needed to make a trip through several states in the United States.*
- **What might be some problems with using several different maps?** *(The maps may get out of order, get lost, or be difficult to handle.)*
- **Read Step 1 on page 109 and gather the materials needed.** *Give your child a road atlas.* This book is called an atlas.
- Flip through the book to see what is in it. *(This is a book of maps.)*
- **How could using an atlas, rather than several maps, make a trip easier?** *(Answers will vary.)*
- **Read Step 2.**
- Complete numbers 1-2 on Notebook page 46.
- **Read Step 3.**
- Complete numbers 3-9 on the Notebook page.
- **Read Step 4.**
- Complete number 11 on the Notebook page.

Evaluating the Lesson

Oral Evaluation

➤ *Give your child the four Southwest state cards.*

➤ I will be asking questions about the Southwest.

➤ Hold up the card of the state that answers each question. *You may wish to use the following questions, varying the order of the questions by alternately asking one from each section.*

For OKLAHOMA:

1. Which state name comes from two Choctaw words that mean "red people"?
2. Which state has a thin section of land called the Panhandle?
3. Which state is nicknamed "the Sooner State"?
4. Which state has an abundance of wheat fields, oil wells, and natural gas?
5. Which state's capital is Oklahoma City?
6. What is this state? *Point to Oklahoma on the United States map.*

For TEXAS:

1. Which state has San Antonio and Houston as major cities?
2. Which state is the second largest state in the United States?
3. Which state is nicknamed "the Lone Star State"?
4. Where is the Alamo located?
5. Which state's capital is Austin?
6. What is this state? *Point to Texas on the United States map.*

For NEW MEXICO:

1. Which state has America's oldest road, known as *El Camino Real*, or "the Royal Highway"?
2. Where are the Carlsbad Caverns located?
3. Which state is nicknamed "the Land of Enchantment"?
4. Where is the Palace of Governors?
5. Which state's capital is Santa Fe?
6. What is this state? *Point to New Mexico on the United States map.*

For ARIZONA:

1. Which state has the cactus as its state flower?
2. Where is the Petrified Forest located?
3. Which state is nicknamed "the Grand Canyon State"?
4. Where is the Painted Desert located?
5. Which state's capital is Phoenix?
6. What is this state? *Point to Arizona on the United States map.*

Going Beyond

Enrichment

To make a sand painting, have available drawing paper, pencils, glue, and colored sand. Colored sand can be made by placing sand in a container and stirring in food coloring to tint the sand. Ask your child to draw a southwest scene based on his studies in this lesson. Suggestions might include the Painted Desert or the Grand Canyon. Instruct him to outline the picture with very thin streams of glue. Carefully sprinkle one color of sand in the areas where that particular color is needed. Hold the picture over the container of that color and bend to allow excess sand to pour back into the container. Continue this process with each color chosen until the picture is completely filled in with colored sand. Allow time for the picture to dry.

Additional Teacher Information

The Gila monster is a poisonous lizard found in the deserts of the Southwest. This reptile's coloring is a mixture of brown or black and orange or salmon. With a wide head, heavy body, and thick tail, the Gila monster can grow to a length of sixteen inches. It feeds on the eggs of birds and other reptiles but can live for months without eating because of the fat stored in its tail. The Gila monster has a powerful venom secreted from the teeth of its lower jaw. This venom is mainly for defense and is painful, but not fatal, to humans.

The Grand Canyon, one of the most remarkable canyons in the world, stretches for 277 miles in the northwest section of Arizona. With a depth of approximately one mile and a width ranging from one to eighteen miles, the Grand Canyon is truly grand. Visitors to the Grand Canyon National Park can drive along the roads, stopping at the overlooks; walk along the canyon rim; or hike any one of the thirty-eight trails in the park. Other visitors may choose to ride a helicopter into the canyon for a breathtaking aerial view. Still others may take a mule trip into the canyon or enjoy a boat ride down the Colorado River. Phantom Ranch, with its cabins, campground, and dining hall, is located at the bottom of the canyon as a resting place for tourists.

LESSON 29

The Rocky Mountains: For Purple Mountain Majesties

Text, pages 112-14, 280-305, 320-21
Notebook, pages 47-49

Preview

Main Ideas

- Maps represent actual places.
- Each of the six states of the Rocky Mountain region is unique.
- Names have their origins in words with special meanings.

Objectives

- Identify the Rocky Mountain states on a map
- Match characteristics, places, and other facts with each appropriate Rocky Mountain state

Materials

- Maps and More 22 and 23, pages M9-M10
- A large cardboard box with "Rocky Mountain treasures" (optional) (See Introducing the Lesson for suggestions.)*
- Appendix, page A41: "America the Beautiful"*
- *HERITAGE STUDIES Listening Cassette B*
- An atlas (optional)

If you live in one of the Rocky Mountain states, you may wish to devote additional time to the study of your state. Refer your child to pages 280-305 for additional information about each of the Rocky Mountain states.

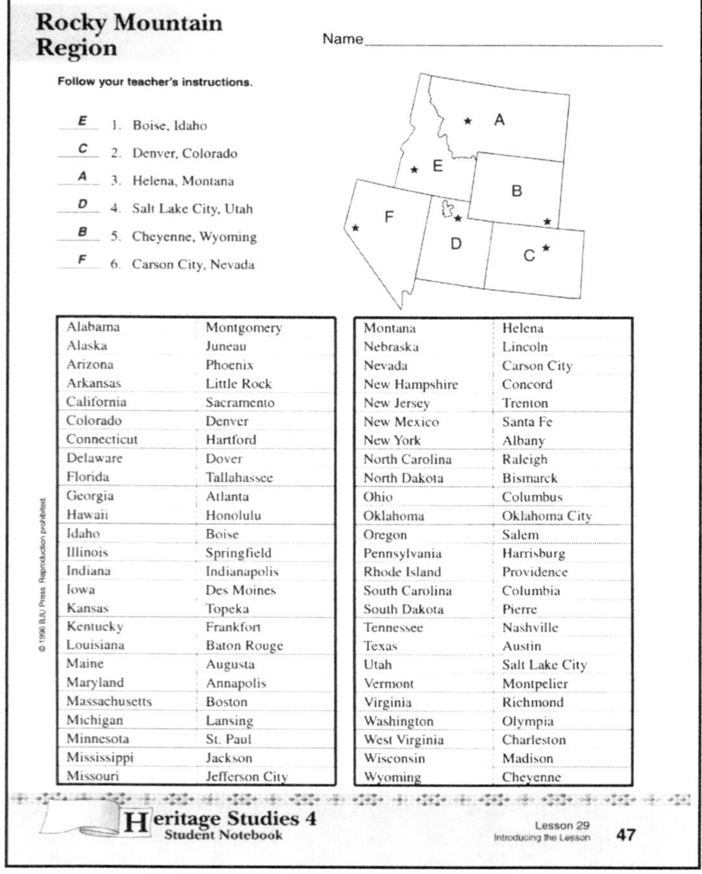

Rocky Mountain Region

Name__________

Follow your teacher's instructions.

E 1. Boise, Idaho
C 2. Denver, Colorado
A 3. Helena, Montana
D 4. Salt Lake City, Utah
B 5. Cheyenne, Wyoming
F 6. Carson City, Nevada

Alabama	Montgomery
Alaska	Juneau
Arizona	Phoenix
Arkansas	Little Rock
California	Sacramento
Colorado	Denver
Connecticut	Hartford
Delaware	Dover
Florida	Tallahassee
Georgia	Atlanta
Hawaii	Honolulu
Idaho	Boise
Illinois	Springfield
Indiana	Indianapolis
Iowa	Des Moines
Kansas	Topeka
Kentucky	Frankfort
Louisiana	Baton Rouge
Maine	Augusta
Maryland	Annapolis
Massachusetts	Boston
Michigan	Lansing
Minnesota	St. Paul
Mississippi	Jackson
Missouri	Jefferson City

Montana	Helena
Nebraska	Lincoln
Nevada	Carson City
New Hampshire	Concord
New Jersey	Trenton
New Mexico	Santa Fe
New York	Albany
North Carolina	Raleigh
North Dakota	Bismarck
Ohio	Columbus
Oklahoma	Oklahoma City
Oregon	Salem
Pennsylvania	Harrisburg
Rhode Island	Providence
South Carolina	Columbia
South Dakota	Pierre
Tennessee	Nashville
Texas	Austin
Utah	Salt Lake City
Vermont	Montpelier
Virginia	Richmond
Washington	Olympia
West Virginia	Charleston
Wisconsin	Madison
Wyoming	Cheyenne

Heritage Studies 4 Student Notebook — Lesson 29 Introducing the Lesson 47

Day 1

Lesson

Introducing the Lesson

Map Activity, Notebook page 47 and Maps and More 22

➤ *Show your child Maps and More 22.*

➤ Use the map to fill in the blanks on Notebook page 47 with the correct letter from the outlined states.

The Rocky Mountain region is like a treasure box, filled with wonder and beauty. We will be talking about these treasures in this lesson.

You may want to take a cardboard box and fill it with the gold and silver jewelry, pictures of Yellowstone National Park, pictures of the Rocky Mountains, a rock or a desert picture representing the state of Utah, a potato, and a light bulb. Each one of these "treasures" can be revealed from the treasure box as you discuss the corresponding state.

➤ Cut out the two large rectangles listing all the states and capitals at the bottom of the Notebook page.

- ➤ Fold each rectangle along the dotted line to show the states on one side and the corresponding capitals on the other side.
- ➤ Use these lists to practice the states and capitals.

Teaching the Lesson

Text Discussion, page 112 and Maps and More 22

- ➤ Find the state of Montana on Maps and More 22.
- ➤ **What is the capital of Montana?** *(Helena)*
- ➤ **Read the first two paragraphs on page 112 to find the nicknames of Montana.** *("the Treasure State" and "Big Sky Country")*
- ➤ **What two treasures were discovered in the mountains of Montana?** *(gold and silver)*
- ➤ **What changes do you think the discovery of gold and silver brought to the West?**

Thousands of settlers went to the Rocky Mountain region in search of these riches. Permanent cities, states, and transportation systems were established. Many of these gold rush sites have become popular tourist attractions.

- ➤ Name one of Montana's restored gold-mining camps. *(Virginia City)*
- ➤ **Where can you go in the state of Montana to see glaciers?** *(Glacier National Park)*
- ➤ Find the state of Wyoming on Maps and More 22.
- ➤ Name the capital of Wyoming. *(Cheyenne)*
- ➤ **Read the last two paragraphs on page 112 to find the name of America's first and largest national park.** *(Yellowstone National Park)*
- ➤ Locate Yellowstone National Park on Maps and More 22.

This park covers 3,472 square miles in the northwest corner of Wyoming and also spreads over the border into Idaho and Montana.

- ➤ Name some sights that visitors enjoy at Yellowstone. *(geysers, canyons, waterfalls)*
- ➤ **Do you know what a *geyser* is?**

A ***geyser*** is a bursting fountain of hot water, caused by pressure from heated water under the ground.

- ➤ Name another national park in Wyoming. *(Grand Teton National Park)*

Rocky Mountain

A view of the Rockies in Glacier National Park

Montana

Montana comes from the Spanish word for "mountainous." Does Montana's nickname, "the Treasure State," give you a clue as to what might be there?

When gold and silver were discovered in Montana's mountains, settlers rushed to the territory to set up mining camps. Many of the gold-mining camps, like Virginia City, near Dillon, have been restored. Another state nickname is "Big Sky Country" because of the wide, flat plains in eastern Montana. One landmark on the plains is Pompey's Pillar, a two-hundred-foot rock on the bank of the Yellowstone River. In the Rocky Mountains of northwestern Montana is Glacier National Park.

Wyoming

South of Montana is Wyoming. *Wyoming* in the Delaware language means "upon the great plain." Wyoming's nickname is "the Equality State" because women in Wyoming were the first in our nation to vote, serve on juries, and hold public office.

Although Wyoming has the lowest population of all the states, it attracts many visitors. Our country's first and largest national park is in Wyoming. Millions of people come to Yellowstone National Park each year to hike, camp, and view its geysers, canyons, and waterfalls. Grand Teton National Park, with its beautiful rocky mountain peaks, is nearby. Do you know what a *butte* is? Wyoming's low areas have many of these tall, rocky towers. Devils Tower, a volcanic tower in northeastern Wyoming, has become a national monument.

Grand Teton National Park

112

Discussion, Maps and More 23

- ➤ **Do you know the meaning of *butte (byo͞ot)*?**
- ➤ Look at Maps and More 23. It shows a butte and other landforms.

A ***butte*** is a hill with sloping sides and a flat top, usually found in an area of level land. Many states in the Rocky Mountain region have these distinctive land formations.

- ➤ Examine the picture and name other landforms found in the Rocky Mountain region.

Day 2

Text Discussion, page 113 and Maps and More 22

- ➤ Find Colorado on Maps and More 22.
- ➤ Name the capital of Colorado. *(Denver)*
- ➤ **Read the first two paragraphs on page 113 to find the famous mountain range running through Colorado and the other states in this region.** *(the Rocky Mountains)*

Rocky Mountain

Pikes Peak

Colorado

South of Wyoming is Colorado. *Colorado* is a Spanish word meaning "colored red." Spaniards first gave this name to the river that flowed through canyons of red-tinted stone. Colorado's nickname is "the Centennial State" because it joined the Union one hundred years after the United States declared its independence.

The beautiful Rocky Mountains draw skiers, hikers, and nature lovers to Colorado every year. Pikes Peak is the most well known peak in the Rockies. Katherine Lee Bates wrote the words to "America the Beautiful" after she enjoyed a view from the top of Pikes Peak. The world's highest suspension bridge crosses the Royal Gorge, a huge chasm between two mountains near Canon City.

Sandstone rocks in Bryce Canyon National Park

Utah

Colorado's neighbor to the west is Utah, "the Beehive State." Utah's nickname comes from the days when Mormons settled that region. They called their state *Deseret*, meaning "honey bee." The bee symbolized hard work and industry.

Deserts, canyons, and natural rock formations cover much of Utah. Bryce Canyon National Park is filled with red sandstone rocks that have towering spires like those on a church. Utah's Great Salt Lake is saltier than ocean water. Even people who do not swim can easily float in the lake. About 70 percent of Utah's people are Mormons. America's first continental railroad was completed in Utah at Promontory. The Golden Spike National Historic Site now marks the spot where the Union Pacific and Central Pacific railroads were joined.

113

Map Activity, pages 320-21

➤ Find the Rocky Mountains on the map on pages 320-21.

This is the largest mountain system in North America, stretching for three thousand miles from the Mexican border, through the Rocky Mountain states, and on into Canada.

➤ Run your finger over the Rocky Mountains on the map.

➤ Locate and name Colorado's most famous peak. *(Pikes Peak)*

Pikes Peak, with an elevation of 14,110 feet (4,301 meters), is the first peak travelers see as they journey west.

Song Activity

➤ **What famous patriotic song was written after the author had stood at the top of Pikes Peak?** *("America the Beautiful")*

➤ **Who wrote this song?** *(Katherine Lee Bates)*

➤ *Give your child the copy of "America the Beautiful."*

➤ Sing the first stanza along with the recording from the listening cassette.

Remember how thankful Americans should be to God to live in a country filled with breathtaking beauty. (BAT: 7c Praise; Bible Promise: I. God as Master)

Map Activity, Maps and More 22

➤ Find the state of Utah on Maps and More 22.

➤ **What is the capital of Utah?** *(Salt Lake City)*

➤ **What is the lake in Utah that is labeled on your map?** *(Great Salt Lake)*

The capital is located fifteen miles (twenty-four kilometers) from Great Salt Lake.

➤ **What direction would you travel from the Great Salt Lake to Salt Lake City?** *(southeast)*

Text Discussion, page 113 (cont.)

➤ **Read the last two paragraphs on page 113 to find three landscapes that cover much of Utah.** *(deserts, canyons, and natural rock formations)*

➤ Name Utah's lake that is saltier than ocean water. *(Great Salt Lake)*

The water in Great Salt Lake is more than four times as salty as ocean water.

➤ Name the religious group that founded and named Salt Lake City. *(the Mormons)*

➤ **What percentage of Utah's population follows the Mormon faith?** *(about 70 percent)*

Mormonism began in 1830 under the leadership of Joseph Smith. Mormons view *The Book of Mormon* and other books from their religion as more reliable than the Bible. They teach that God was once a man and that people can become equal with God by a combination of grace and good works.

➤ **Does salvation mean that men become God?** *(no)*

➤ **Do men get to heaven by good works?** *(no)*

There is only one God, and men can fellowship with Him only through faith in His Son, Jesus Christ. The Bible alone is the final source of authority and truth. (BATs: 1a Understanding Jesus Christ, 1b Repentance and faith, 8b Faith in the power of the Word of God)

➤ **Which insect represents the people of Utah?** *(the honeybee)*

➤ **Why is the honeybee appropriate?** *(The nickname of Utah is "the Beehive State," and early settlers of Utah were hard working and industrious, like busy bees.)*

Rocky Mountain

Shoshone Falls plunges into the Snake River.

Idaho

Northwest of Utah is Idaho. Some people say the word *Idaho* was the name of a Native American people meaning "gem of the mountains." Others say *Idaho* is a made-up word. In any case, Idaho took "the Gem State" as its nickname.

Have you eaten mashed potatoes, French fries, or potato chips lately? Idaho is the leading producer of potatoes in the United States. Idaho also has fascinating scenery. National forests, including canyons, waterfalls, lakes, and mountains, cover much of its land. Hells Canyon, the deepest canyon in North America, is near Lewiston, Idaho. Cut out by the Snake River, it is about a mile and a half deep at one point.What do you think a frozen waterfall might look like? Idaho has one in its Crystal Ice Cave.

Nevada

Hoover Dam

Nevada, the last Rocky Mountain state, is southwest of Idaho. *Nevada* comes from the Spanish word for "snow-clad." Nevada has not only snowcapped mountains but also barren deserts. Nevada is nicknamed "the Silver State" because large amounts of silver were once found in its mines.

Nevada receives the least amount of rainfall of any state. Its farmers must use special forms of irrigation to grow their crops. Nevada's Hoover Dam is one of the largest concrete dams in the world. It has a power plant that provides electricity for Arizona, California, and Nevada. Would you like to see a rock shaped like an elephant? This and other red rock formations can be found in Nevada's Valley of Fire State Park.

114

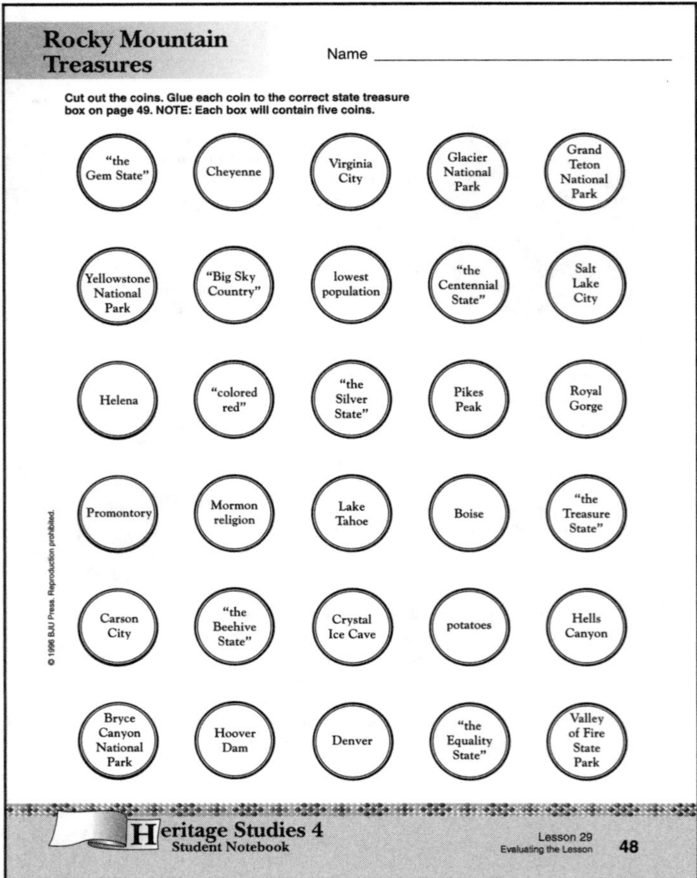

Rocky Mountain Treasures Name ____________

Cut out the coins. Glue each coin to the correct state treasure box on page 49. NOTE: Each box will contain five coins.

"the Gem State"	Cheyenne	Virginia City	Glacier National Park	Grand Teton National Park
Yellowstone National Park	"Big Sky Country"	lowest population	"the Centennial State"	Salt Lake City
Helena	"colored red"	"the Silver State"	Pikes Peak	Royal Gorge
Promontory	Mormon religion	Lake Tahoe	Boise	"the Treasure State"
Carson City	"the Beehive State"	Crystal Ice Cave	potatoes	Hells Canyon
Bryce Canyon National Park	Hoover Dam	Denver	"the Equality State"	Valley of Fire State Park

Heritage Studies 4 Student Notebook — Lesson 29 Evaluating the Lesson 48

> Remember that Christians have a special responsibility to be busy about the work of the Lord. (BATs: 2c Faithfulness, 2e Work, 5c Evangelism and missions)

Text Discussion, page 114 and Maps and More 22

- ➤ Find the state of Idaho on Maps and More 22 and name the capital. *(Boise)*
- ➤ **Read the first two paragraphs on page 114 to find Idaho's nickname.** *("the Gem State")*
- ➤ **What is a *gem?*** *(a precious stone or something of great value)*
- ➤ Name Idaho's most valuable crop. *(potatoes)* Idaho produces approximately twenty-five percent of the U.S. potato crop every year.

Day 3

Text Discussion, page 114 (cont.)

- ➤ **Read the last two paragraphs on page 114 to discover several treasures found in the state of Nevada.** *(Answers will vary but should include silver, Hoover Dam, and Valley of Fire State Park.)*
- ➤ **Which one of Nevada's "treasures" produces electricity?** *(Hoover Dam)*

Map Activity, Maps and More 22

- ➤ Find the state of Nevada on Maps and More 22 and name the capital. *(Carson City)*
- ➤ Find the Hoover Dam.
- ➤ Name three states that benefit from the electricity generated by Hoover Dam. *(Arizona, California, and Nevada)*

The Hoover Dam has a concrete base that is 660 feet (201 meters) thick—enough concrete to pave a two-lane road from New York to San Francisco. Hoover Dam is one of the largest dams in the world. Elevators can go down forty-four stories into the dam and still not reach the bottom.

- ➤ **Why does Nevada need an irrigation system?** *(It receives the least amount of rainfall of any state.)*

Evaluating the Lesson

Notebook Activity, pages 48-49

> Instead of cutting out the coins on Notebook page 48, direct your child to color each treasure box on Notebook page 49 a different color. He would then color each coin to correspond with the appropriate treasure box.

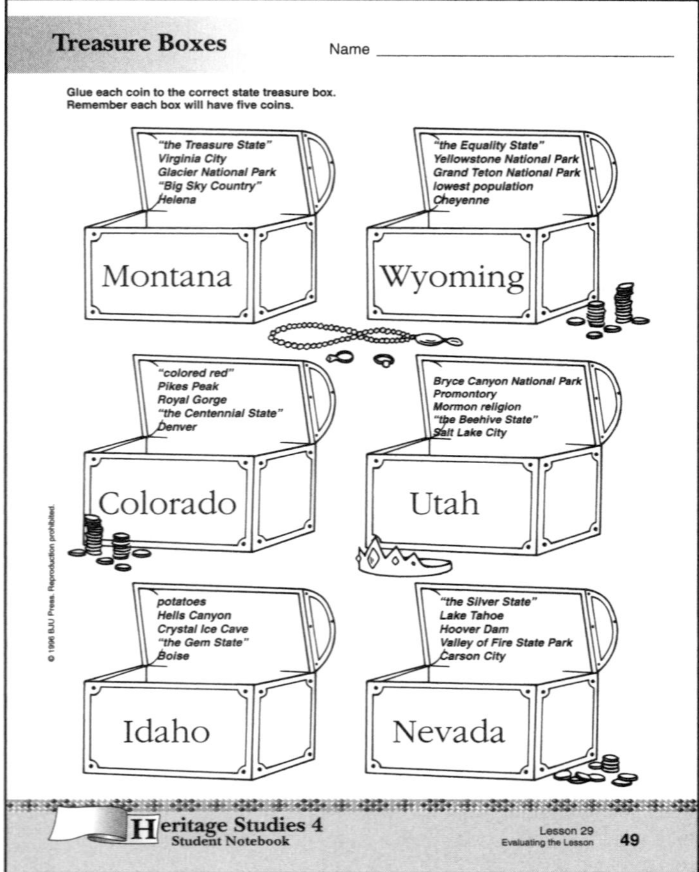

Treasure Boxes Name ____________________

Glue each coin to the correct state treasure box.
Remember each box will have five coins.

Montana
"the Treasure State"
Virginia City
Glacier National Park
"Big Sky Country"
Helena

Wyoming
"the Equality State"
Yellowstone National Park
Grand Teton National Park
lowest population
Cheyenne

Colorado
"colored red"
Pikes Peak
Royal Gorge
"the Centennial State"
Denver

Utah
Bryce Canyon National Park
Promontory
Mormon religion
"the Beehive State"
Salt Lake City

Idaho
potatoes
Hells Canyon
Crystal Ice Cave
"the Gem State"
Boise

Nevada
"the Silver State"
Lake Tahoe
Hoover Dam
Valley of Fire State Park
Carson City

Heritage Studies 4 Student Notebook — Lesson 29 Evaluating the Lesson — 49

➤ Read the instructions on Notebook pages 48-49.
➤ Complete the pages.

Going Beyond

Additional Teacher Information

Yellowstone National Park is the oldest national park in the world. Explorers of the Yellowstone National Park area during the 1800s told of mysterious, steaming fountains, bubbling springs, and sparkling pools. However, it was not until 1870 that photographs and drawings of these phenomena were shown to the U.S. Congress. In 1872 the U.S. government established Yellowstone National Park.

With more than two hundred active geysers and thousands of hot spring, Yellowstone contains more thermal (heated water) attractions than any other place in the world. "Old Faithful," Yellowstone's most famous geyser, sprays fifteen thousand gallons of hot water about 180 feet into the air on the average of once every hour and fifteen minutes. Other geysers may blow harder or higher; however, "Old Faithful" was rightly named because it blows more predictably day and night.

LESSON 30
The Pacific: From Sea to Shining Sea

Text, pages 115-18, 280-305, 320-21
Notebook, pages 50-52

Preview

Main Ideas

- Maps and globes represent actual places.
- Each of the five states of the Pacific region is unique.
- The United States has many territories and two commonwealths.
- Names have their origins in words with special meanings.

Objectives

- Label the Pacific states and capitals on a map
- Identify the United States territories and commonwealths on a map
- Complete information about the Pacific region

Materials

- Maps and More 23, 24, and 25, pages M10-M12
- A Bible
- A globe
- Approximately 25 buttons or dried beans*
- An atlas (optional)

If you live in one of the Pacific states, you may wish to devote additional time to the study of your state. Refer your child to pages 280-305 for additional information about each of the Pacific states.

Day 1

Lesson

Introducing the Lesson

Map Activity, Maps and More 23

➤ *Show your child Maps and More 23.*
➤ In today's lesson about the Pacific states, we will talk about several geographic terms. Let's find the terms and the definitions on this chart.

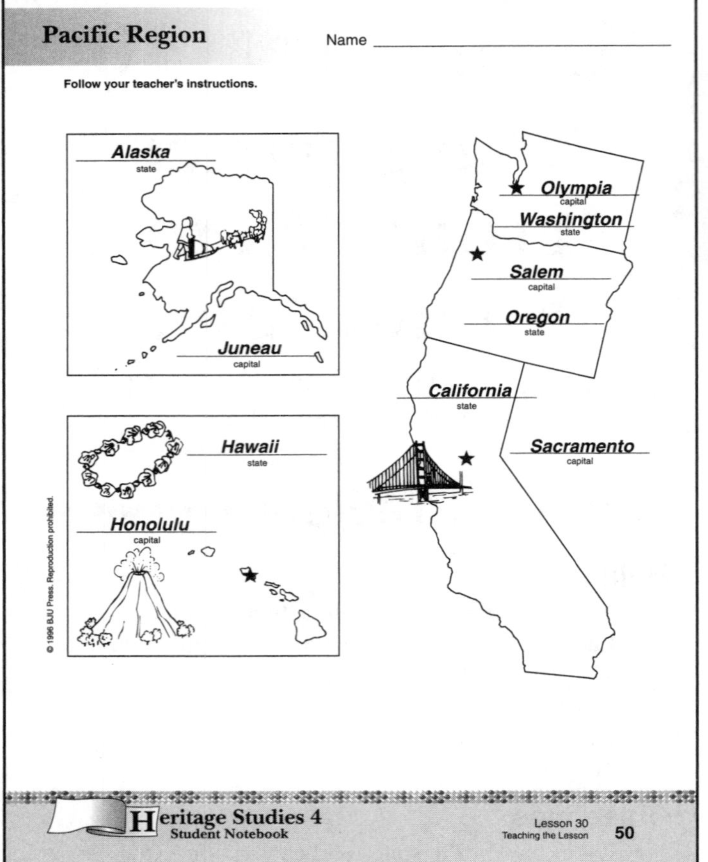
Pacific Region Name ____________________

Follow your teacher's instructions.

Heritage Studies 4 Student Notebook — Lesson 30 Teaching the Lesson — 50

Pacific

Mount Rainier

Washington

Finally we come to the Pacific region of the United States, where Washington is our first stop. Washington's nickname is "the Evergreen State" because of all its evergreen trees. Do you know for whom the state of Washington was named? It is the only state named after a president.

What would you expect to find in a city named George? The city of George, Washington, has different types of cherries, such as Bing and Maraschino, for its street names. With its snowcapped mountains, Washington is a popular state for skiers. Rainier Paradise Ranger Station on Mount Rainier holds the North American record for the most snow in one season. Mount Saint Helens is famous for its volcanic eruption in 1980. More apples come from Washington than from any other state.

Oregon

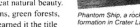

Phantom Ship, a rock formation in Crater Lake

South of Washington is Oregon. Its nickname is "the Beaver State." Beaver skins were the most common item of trade there in its early days. The name *Oregon* probably comes from the French word for the Columbia River. It means "hurricane."

Oregon is a state of great natural beauty. Its snow-covered mountains, green forests, and rocky coastline have earned it the title of "Pacific Wonderland." Oregon has the deepest lake in the United States. Crater Lake, which fills an extinct volcano in the Cascade Mountains, is 1,932 feet deep—more than a third of a mile! In the 1840s and 1850s, many people braved a rugged journey across America to settle in Oregon. The area where they settled, Willamette Valley, is now the center of industrial life in Oregon.

115

- ➤ *Guide your child as he finds and reads the definitions for the following words:* ***mountain, volcano, valley,*** *and* ***island.***

Teaching the Lesson

Notebook Activity, page 50 and Maps and More 24

- ➤ *Show your child Maps and More 24.*
- ➤ Write the five Pacific states and their capitals on Notebook page 50, using Maps and More 24.
- ➤ Use the page to study and memorize the states and capitals of the Pacific region.
- ➤ Find the state of Washington on Maps and More 24 and name the capital. *(Olympia)*

Text Discussion, page 115

- ➤ **Can you guess for whom the state of Washington was named?** *(George Washington)*
- ➤ **Read the first two paragraphs on page 115 to find the names of two famous mountains in Washington State.** *(Mount Rainier [rə nîr′] and Mount St. Helens)*

Map Activity, pages 320-21

- ➤ Find Mount Rainier and Mount St. Helens on the map on pages 320-21.

- ➤ **Which of these two mountains holds the North American record for the most snow in one season?** *(Mount Rainier)*

Mount Rainier, the highest mountain in the state of Washington, recorded 1,122 inches of snow from July 1971 through June 1972.

- ➤ **What is Mount St. Helens most famous for?** *(a volcanic eruption in 1980)*

Map Activity, Maps and More 24

- ➤ Find Oregon on Maps and More 24.
- ➤ Name the capital. *(Salem)*

Text Discussion, page 115 (cont.)

- ➤ **Read the last two paragraphs on page 115 to find the title Oregon has been given based upon the state's natural beauty.** *("Pacific Wonderland")*
- ➤ Name three natural features of the state that helped Oregon earn this title. *(snow-covered mountains, green forests, and rocky coastline)*
- ➤ **What is the deepest lake in the United States?** *(Crater Lake)*
- ➤ **How was this lake formed?** *(The crater of an extinct volcano filled with water.)*

➤ Name the area in the state where settlers during the 1840s and 1850s built their homes. *(Willamette [wə lăm′ it] Valley)*

Today most of the people of Oregon live in Willamette Valley.

➤ **What is this area known for today?** *(It is the center of industrial life in Oregon.)*

Willamette Valley is a fertile land with a mild, cool climate. This area is known for its fruit, including pears, plums, peaches, apples, and cherries.

Day 2

Map Activity, Maps and More 24

➤ Find California on Maps and More 24.
➤ Name the capital. *(Sacramento)*
➤ The four largest cities in California are Los Angeles, San Diego, San Jose, and San Francisco. **Can you find them on the map?**
➤ Find Death Valley. You will learn about this area as you read about California.

Text Discussion, page 116

➤ **Read the first two paragraphs on page 116 to find California's nickname.** *("the Golden State")*
➤ Name two things that contribute to the state's nickname. *(gold rush of 1849 and golden sunshine)*
➤ **What is the famous bridge in the state that reminds you of California's nickname?** *(the Golden Gate Bridge)*
➤ California is a record setter in many ways. **Read aloud the sentence that tells about California's rank in population.** *("More people live in California than in any other state.")*

California's population was recorded in the 1990 census as 29,839,250.

➤ Name the lowest point in the Western Hemisphere. *(Death Valley)*

Most of Death Valley is located in east-central California with a small portion in Nevada. Death Valley reaches a depth of 282 feet below sea level.

➤ **What was unusual about the temperature in Death Valley in 1913?** *(It was the hottest temperature ever recorded in the United States.)*

On July 10, 1913, the temperature in Death Valley reached a scorching 134°F.

➤ **Why do you think *Death Valley* is an appropriate name for this place?**

Rainfall averages three inches a year, limiting life in this desert region to certain plants and animals. Visitors enjoy the warm climate in this area during the winter.

Pacific

California

The Golden Gate Bridge spans San Francisco Bay.

California is south of Oregon. Its nickname is "the Golden State." California was the site of a famous gold rush in 1849. It is also known for its golden sunshine and fair weather nearly all the year around.

Do you know anyone who lives in California? Chances are that you do, because more people live in California than in any other state. Four of the nation's largest cities are in California. How many of them can you name? Death Valley, on California's eastern border, is the lowest point in the Western Hemisphere. In 1913, this area had the hottest temperature ever recorded in the United States—134°F. California's long Pacific coastline is a popular place for water sports. California's redwood trees are the tallest and oldest trees in the world.

Alaska

In summer, fireweed adds color to Alaska's mountain scenery.

Alaska, the northernmost state, is nicknamed "the Last Frontier" because much of its land has not yet been settled. William Seward, the secretary of state under President Andrew Johnson, bought Alaska from Russia in 1867. At the time, Americans called it things such as "Seward's Folly," "Icebergia," and "Johnson's Polar Bear Garden."

Do you think buying Alaska was a foolish decision? Alaska is rich in natural resources like fish, minerals, timber, and oil. Mount McKinley, the tallest peak in the United States, is located there. Alaska is the largest state. Its coastline is longer than those of all the other states put together. Although it is very big, it has the second fewest people in the nation.

116

➤ **What is the name of the world's tallest and oldest trees found in California?** *(redwood trees)*

The Bible refers to Christians as trees. Read aloud Psalm 1:3. Ask how a Christian is like a tree. *(Answers should include producing spiritual fruit.)* (BAT: 5c Evangelism and missions)

Map Activity, Maps and More 24

➤ Find the state of Alaska on Maps and More 24.
➤ Name the capital. *(Juneau [jo͞o′ nō])*

Text Discussion, page 116 (cont.)

➤ **Read the last two paragraphs on page 116 to find several names that have been given to Alaska.** *("the Last Frontier," "Seward's Folly," "Icebergia," and "Johnson's Polar Bear Garden")*
➤ **Why has Alaska been nicknamed "the Last Frontier"?** *(Much of its land has not yet been settled.)*
➤ Name the man responsible for the purchase of Alaska. *(William Seward)*
➤ **Did most Americans like the idea of buying Alaska?** *(no)*

Pacific

Hawaii

Hawaii, a state made up of islands in the Pacific, is our nation's youngest state. It joined the Union in 1959. Hawaii is nicknamed "the Aloha State" because of its friendliness toward visitors. *Aloha* is the Hawaiian word for "love," "greetings," "welcome," or "farewell."

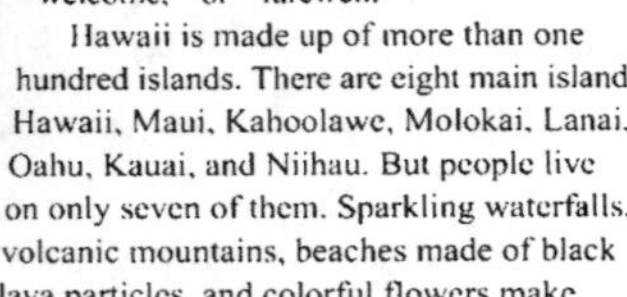

One of Hawaii's dramatic tropical landscapes

Hawaii is made up of more than one hundred islands. There are eight main islands: Hawaii, Maui, Kahoolawe, Molokai, Lanai, Oahu, Kauai, and Niihau. But people live on only seven of them. Sparkling waterfalls, volcanic mountains, beaches made of black lava particles, and colorful flowers make Hawaii beautiful. If you were to visit the islands, you would probably be greeted with the word *aloha*, and someone would place a *lei*, a wreath of flowers, around your neck. Do you like pineapple? That is one of Hawaii's most famous products.

Territories

Other U.S. Lands

Charlotte Amalie, on the island of St. Thomas, is the capital city of the Virgin Islands.

In addition to the fifty states, the United States owns other lands, called *territories*. The U.S. Virgin Islands are located in the Caribbean Sea, about a thousand miles east of the tip of Florida. The United States bought them from Denmark. Guam, an island in the Pacific Ocean, is nearly four thousand miles west of Hawaii. An important American naval base during the Spanish-American War, Guam was later ceded to the United States by Spain. American Samoa, in the south-central Pacific Ocean, is another island territory that our navy once used as a coaling station. Other small Pacific islands like Wake Island, the Midway Islands, and most of Micronesia are United States territories also.

117

➤ **Why do you think most Americans did not approve of the purchase?**

They considered it foolish. It was looked upon as a giant iceberg. It was thought to be fit only for polar bears.

➤ **Which country sold Alaska to the United States?** *(Russia)*

Russia sold Alaska to the United States for just over seven million dollars (two cents per acre).

➤ Name the tallest peak in the United States. *(Mount McKinley)*

At 20,320 feet, Mount McKinley is actually the tallest peak in all of North America and is appropriately referred to as the "top of the continent."

➤ Name four valuable natural resources that are abundant in the state. *(fish, minerals, timber, and oil)*

The resources of Alaska have paid back the price of purchase hundreds of times.

Globe Activity

➤ Find Alaska on the globe.

➤ **What is Alaska's rank in size compared to the other states?** *(the largest state)* Alaska is twice as large as Texas.

➤ **What is Alaska's rank in population compared to the other states?** *(second fewest)*

➤ **Why would the largest state have so few people?** *(Answers will vary but should include that a great amount of the land is unsuitable for living.)*

➤ Find the Arctic Circle on the globe. One-third of Alaska lies north of the Arctic Circle.

➤ **What would the weather be like in this part of the state?** *(cold most of the year)*

Day 3

Text Discussion, page 117

➤ **Read the first two paragraphs on page 117 to find out how many islands make up the state of Hawaii.** *(more than one hundred)*

➤ **How many main islands make up Hawaii?** *(eight)*

Map Activity, Maps and More 24

➤ Find the state of Hawaii on Maps and More 24.

➤ Name the capital. *(Honolulu)*

➤ *Point to and name each main island on the map, instructing your child to repeat each name after you pronounce it.*

Hawaii *(hə wä′ ē)*	Lanai *(lə nī′)*
Maui *(mou′ ē)*	Oahu *(ō ä′ hōō)*
Kahoolawe *(kä hō′ ō lä′ wē)*	Kauai *(kou′ ī)*
Molokai *(mŏl′ ə kī′)*	Niihau *(nē′ ē hou′)*

➤ **How many main islands do people actually live on?** *(seven)*

➤ Point to the island of Kahoolawe, the smallest of the islands.

Kahoolawe is the driest of all the main islands, and only U.S. Army, Air Force, and Navy bases are found there.

➤ **What is the Hawaiian name for a wreath of flowers? (lei [lā])**

➤ **What is a famous product in Hawaii?** *(pineapple)*

Use a globe to show the location of Hawaii in relation to the continental U.S.

Text Discussion, page 117 (cont.)

➤ **Read the last paragraph on page 117 to find out about other lands owned by the United States.**

➤ **What is the name given to these other lands?** *(territories)*

Territories are lands and waters under the authority of the United States. All but nineteen states, the original thirteen and six others, were once territories.

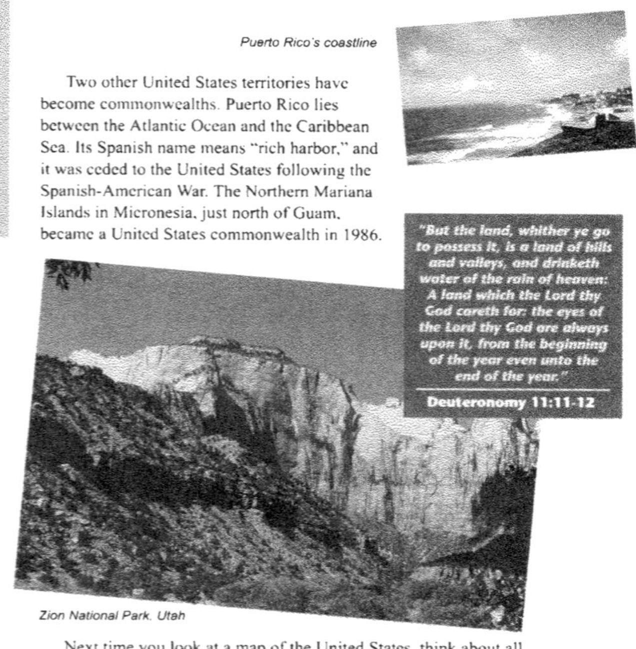

Commonwealths

Puerto Rico's coastline

Two other United States territories have become commonwealths. Puerto Rico lies between the Atlantic Ocean and the Caribbean Sea. Its Spanish name means "rich harbor," and it was ceded to the United States following the Spanish-American War. The Northern Mariana Islands in Micronesia, just north of Guam, became a United States commonwealth in 1986.

"But the land, whither ye go to possess it, is a land of hills and valleys, and drinketh water of the rain of heaven: A land which the Lord thy God careth for: the eyes of the Lord thy God are always upon it, from the beginning of the year even unto the end of the year."
Deuteronomy 11:11-12

Zion National Park, Utah

Next time you look at a map of the United States, think about all the different places and people that make up this country. If you could visit any of the fifty states, which one would you choose?

118

Map Activity, Maps and More 25

- ➤ Find some of the United States territories on Maps and More 25: U.S. Virgin Islands, Guam, American Samoa, and several Pacific islands, including Wake Island and Midway Islands.
- ➤ **Which country sold the Virgin Islands to the United States?** *(Denmark)*

The Virgin Islands are divided into two main groups—those owned by Great Britain and those owned by the United States.

- ➤ **In which ocean are the Virgin Islands located?** *(Atlantic)*
- ➤ Name the ocean in which the other territories are located. *(Pacific Ocean)*
- ➤ **Do you know the definition of the prefix *micro?*** *(small or tiny)*

Micronesia means "tiny islands." More than two thousand islands make up the territory of Micronesia. The Pacific islands total from twenty thousand to more than thirty thousand islands. No one knows exactly how many islands there are. Some of these islands are quite large, covering thousands of square miles, while others barely rise out of the water.

- ➤ Find the Northern Mariana Islands on Maps and More 25. Micronesia is located just south of these islands.

Text Discussion, page 118

- ➤ **Read page 118 to find out the special name given to Puerto Rico and the Northern Mariana Islands.** *(commonwealth)*

Commonwealth can also mean land that is voluntarily associated with the United States government. The government of the commonwealth controls its own internal affairs, but the United States is responsible for the commonwealth's foreign affairs and defense.

- ➤ **Read aloud the verses on page 118.**

Deuteronomy 11:11-12 reminds Christians of God's continuous, watchful care. (BATs: 7c Praise, 7d Contentment, 8a Faith in God's promises; Bible Promise: I. God as Master)

Map Activity, Maps and More 25

- ➤ Locate the United States commonwealths on Maps and More 25.
- ➤ **Which commonwealth has a Spanish heritage?** *(Puerto Rico)*
- ➤ Give the Spanish meaning of *Puerto Rico. ("rich harbor")*

Some people would like Puerto Rico to become the fifty-first state; however, many in Puerto Rico do not agree.

Evaluating the Lesson

Game, Notebook pages 51-52

- ➤ Cut out the twenty-five boxes on Notebook page 51.
- ➤ Glue each box in any order to the grid on page 52.
- ➤ I will call out questions about the Pacific states.
- ➤ Find and cover the answers on your grid with the game markers (buttons or beans).
- ➤ When you have covered five boxes in a row (across, down, or diagonally), call out "Five Alive!"

If you are teaching more than one child, you may choose to allow them to exchange grids between rounds.

Following are examples of questions you can use. Vary the order of the questions and make up new questions if desired.

1. **What bridge is similar to California's nickname?** *(Golden Gate Bridge)*
2. **Which state is the largest in the United States?** *(Alaska)*

Places Name ____________________

Cut out the twenty-five boxes to use in playing Five Alive on page 52.

	Alaska	Oregon	Washington	Hawaii
Puerto Rico	Northern Mariana Islands	lei		Mount McKinley
Death Valley	Crater Lake	Mount St. Helens	Mount Ranier	Willamette Valley
"Aloha!"	Denmark	Russia	Guam	Juneau
Sacramento	Honolulu	Salem	Olympia	U.S. Commonwealths

Places Name ____________________

Follow your teacher's instructions.

FIVE ALIVE

3. **Which state comes from a French word meaning "hurricane"?** *(Oregon)*
4. **Which state is known for its apples?** *(Washington)*
5. **Which state is made up of more than one hundred islands?** *(Hawaii)*
6. **Which U.S. commonwealth comes from a Spanish name meaning "rich harbor"?** *(Puerto Rico)*
7. **Which United States commonwealth lies north of Guam?** *(the Northern Mariana Islands)*
8. **What is a Hawaiian wreath of flowers called?** *(lei)*
9. **What term is given to the U.S. Virgin Islands, Guam, American Samoa, and other lands owned by the United States?** *(territories)*
10. **What is the highest peak in the United States?** *(Mount McKinley)*
11. **What is the lowest point in the Western Hemisphere?** *(Death Valley)*
12. **What is the deepest lake in the United States?** *(Crater Lake)*
13. **Which volcano in Washington erupted in 1980?** *(Mount St. Helens)*
14. **Which mountain in Washington holds the North American record for the most snow in one season?** *(Mount Rainier)*
15. **Where is the center of industrial life in Oregon?** *(Willamette Valley)*
16. **What is the Hawaiian word for love, greetings, welcome, or farewell?** *(Aloha)*
17. **Which country sold the Virgin Islands to the United States?** *(Denmark)*
18. **Which country sold Alaska to the United States?** *(Russia)*
19. **Which United States territory was an important U.S. naval base during the Spanish-American War?** *(Guam)*
20. **What is the capital of Alaska?** *(Juneau)*
21. **What is the capital of California?** *(Sacramento)*
22. **What is the capital of Hawaii?** *(Honolulu)*
23. **What is the capital of Oregon?** *(Salem)*
24. **What is the capital of Washington?** *(Olympia)*
25. **What term applies to lands that are voluntarily associated with the U.S. government?** *(U.S. commonwealths)*

Going Beyond

Enrichment

To make leis, have available a ruler, scissors, stapler, needle, thread, and colored tissue paper. Your child may be able to independently follow the directions from your teacher's edition.

1. Cut each sheet of tissue paper into twelve 6"×6" squares.
2. Place four squares in a neat stack.
3. Begin folding the edges like a fan in approximately one inch folds.
4. Staple the center of the fan; bend the two sides up.
5. Firmly holding the stapled section with one hand, carefully separate the layers of tissue, turning up and in to form the flower petals.
6. Measure and cut three feet of thread.
7. Thread a needle and string the flower onto the thread. Repeat with more flowers (approximately twelve), spacing them apart so that the petals can fan out.
8. Tie the ends of the thread together and place the lei around your neck.

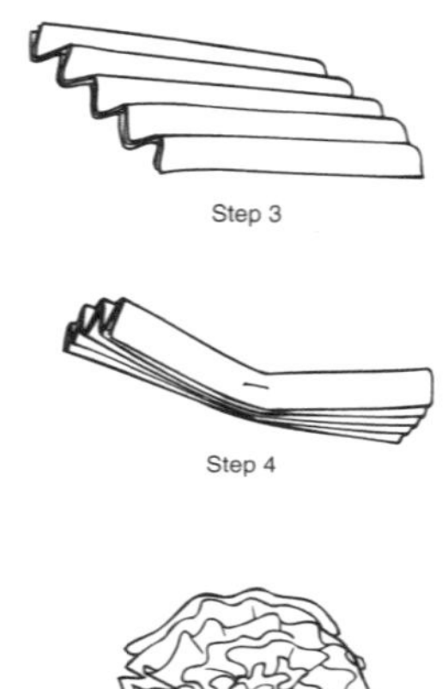
Step 3

Step 4

Step 5

Additional Teacher Information

On May 18, 1980, Mount St. Helens erupted for the first time in 123 years, leaving a huge crater where a mountain had once been. The eruption blew volcanic ash miles into the air and showered towns with as much as seven inches of ash. The hot ash and rock in turn created massive forest fires, and melting snow caused floods and mudslides. Crops and wildlife were destroyed, and millions of trees were leveled by the explosion.

There are two main types of redwoods growing in the state of California. The California redwood tree, the tallest tree in the world, may grow as high as a thirty-story building, with trunks that are eight to twelve feet in diameter. The bark is twelve inches thick, providing a special protection against fire; the wood is soft, giving a unique resistance to decay, insect enemies, and disease. The giant sequoia, the oldest tree in the world, is also found in California on the western slopes of the Sierra Nevada. These trees have been dated as old as thirty-five hundred years. Though not so tall as the California redwood, the giant sequoias can reach a diameter of one hundred feet at the base of the trunk.

Supplemental Lesson

More About Our State(s)

Text, pages 280-305, 326

Preview

Main Idea

- Each of the fifty states is unique, contributing to the vastness and great variety found within the United States.

Objectives

- Complete a state booklet
- Make a miniature state float

Materials

- Encyclopedias, travel brochures, and/or library books about the state that your child has chosen*
- Appendix, pages A42-A47: the state booklet pages*
- Materials to build a float: small box and art supplies

Notes

You may choose to devote this lesson to the study of your state. The writing and art activities are designed to be adapted for such purposes. You may allow your child to choose a state that he would like to learn more about.

To assemble the booklet, place the pages in order, one on top of another as shown below, neatly stacking the three pages. Fold the stack in half with the cover entitled "My State" on top. Bind each booklet by stapling the edge of the cover twice.

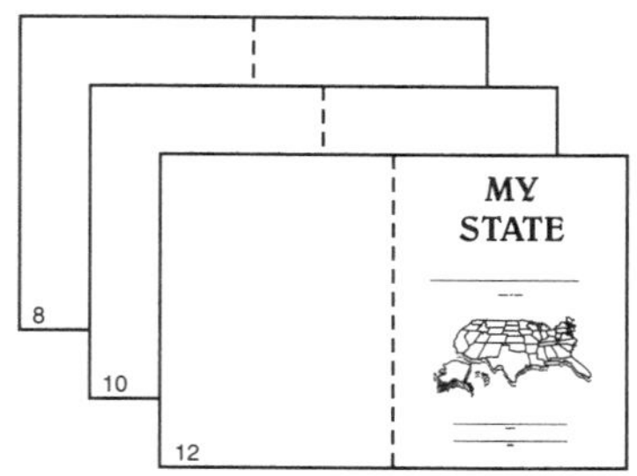

Lesson

States-and-Capitals Review Game

- We are going to review states and capitals by playing Rhythm.
- *Demonstrate the rhythm pattern "clap, clap, snap, snap; clap, clap, snap, snap" to your child. Invite him to join in clapping and snapping this pattern. As the rhythm continues, say a state or capital on the snaps, and help your child respond with the corresponding capital or state on the next snaps.*

Example 1
Teacher: Clap, clap, Augusta.
Child: Clap, clap, Maine.
Example 2
Teacher: Clap, clap, Maine.
Child: Clap, clap, Augusta.

Teaching the Lesson

Resources Activity, pages 280-305 and 326

- Locate your state on pages 280-305.

This section will serve as a valuable tool when gathering information about your state. You may also find information about your state in Chapter 5. Some of the maps in the text may also give you information.

- **In what part of the book can you quickly locate specific pages in the text on which a particular topic is discussed?** *(the index)*
- Turn to the index on page 326.
- **How are the topics listed?** *(alphabetically)*
- **What other sources can you use in gathering information?** *(encyclopedias, travel brochures, and library books)*

Research Activity

- *Give your child the state booklet.*
- Use the resources you have gathered to fill in the information about your state.

Evaluating the Lesson

Miniature Float Art Activity

- *Give your child scissors, a ruler, glue, and a shoe box, tissue box, or other small box.*
- Turn the box upside down.

The decorative, moving displays in a parade are called *floats.* Floats often advertise a certain product or carry famous people. You will build a float to represent your state.

- The edge of the box should be covered with a "float skirt" made of tissue paper or construction paper.
- The top of the float should display interesting objects representative of your state. Information from the state booklet may be used to give ideas of what to include on the float.

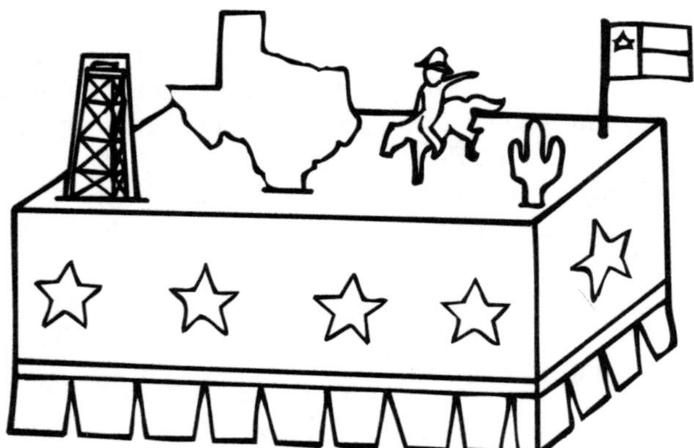

Going Beyond

Additional Teacher Information

The Hawaiian written language was developed by missionaries during the early 1800s. Twelve letters (five vowels: *a, e, i, o, u* and seven consonants: *h, k, l, m, n, p, w*) were chosen to match the sounds spoken in the Hawaiian language.

Certain regions of the United States are known for their unique foods. Pennsylvania Dutch refers to the seventeenth- and eighteenth-century German settlers of Pennsylvania and their descendants. They are known for such dishes as dried apples and dumplings, cottage cheese, and a sauerkraut and pork specialty known as *sauerkraut un schpeck.*

Southern Louisiana cooking has a flavor all its own. The two main styles of cooking found in this part of the state are *Cajun* and *Creole.* Famous dishes include *blackened redfish* (redfish with a mixture of black spices), *jambalaya* (a spicy rice dish cooked with shrimp, oysters, ham, or chicken), and *gumbo* (an okra soup or stew).

In Hawaii, some people enjoy eating *poi.* This starchy food is actually a paste made from the root of the taro plant. Another specialty of the islands includes *laulau* (a combination of chopped taro leaves, pork, chicken, and fish wrapped in the leaves of the ti plant). A popular feast called a *luau* features a whole roasted young pig, called *kalua pig,* wrapped in leaves and cooked in a pit, or *imu.*

6 | LESSONS 31-36

Newfangled Ideas

From James Watt's steam engine to George Washington Carver's peanut butter, this chapter highlights important inventions and the men who developed them. As your child studies the lives of these inventive people, he will learn that inventors possess such qualities as curiosity, confidence, imagination, and persistence. He will also have an opportunity to develop an invention of his own and present it to family members. The board game Patent Path provides a helpful enrichment tool.

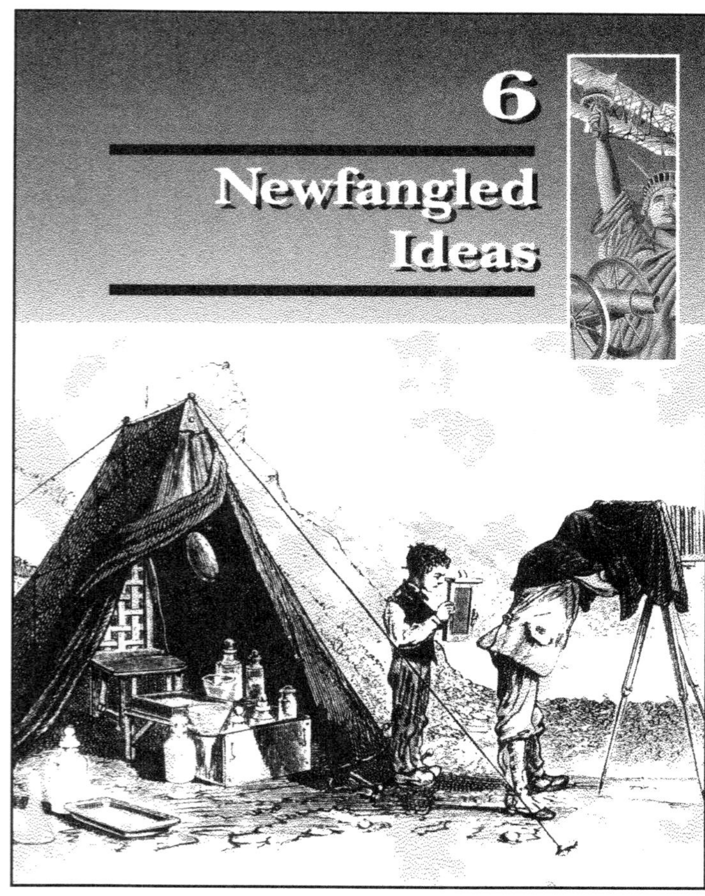

Materials

The following materials must be obtained or prepared before the presentation of the lesson. These items are labeled with an asterisk (*) in each lesson and in the Materials List in the Supplement. For further information see the individual lessons.

- A large plate or tray with 10 items (Lesson 31)
- Wheat flour (Lesson 33)
- Packaged items containing wheat (Lesson 33)
- A stalk of wheat or a picture of a stalk of wheat (Lesson 33)
- A sewing machine (Lesson 34)
- Pieces of fabric (Lesson 34)
- Needles and thread (Lesson 34)
- Books about inventions (Lesson 36)

LESSON 31
From Alarm Clocks to Zippers

Text, pages 120-23
Notebook, page 53

Preview

Main Ideas
- An invention is a new object, idea, or way of doing something.
- Inventions make life easier for us.

Objective
- Write a journal entry about the thoughts of a person using a new invention for the first time

Materials
- A large plate or tray
- 10 items to go on the tray (See box below.)*
- A large towel
- A blank sheet of paper
- A clock with a second hand or a stopwatch
- A button-up sweater with many buttons
- A zip-up jacket

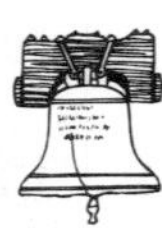

Before the lesson begins, place ten items on a tray or a large plate and cover them with a towel. Use items that have been invented, for example, a safety pin, a fork, a toothbrush, a stick of chewing gum, a ballpoint pen, a paper clip, a tissue, a pair of scissors, a pair of eyeglasses, and a small alarm clock.

Day 1

Lesson

Introducing the Lesson

Memory Activity

- ➤ *Remove the towel from the tray.*
- ➤ Observe the items on the tray, trying to remember as many as you can. *Allow a few moments for your child to view the items. Cover the items again with the towel.*
- ➤ On a sheet of paper write down the names of as many of the ten items as you can remember.

When your child has finished writing, uncover the tray and let him check how many items he remembered correctly.

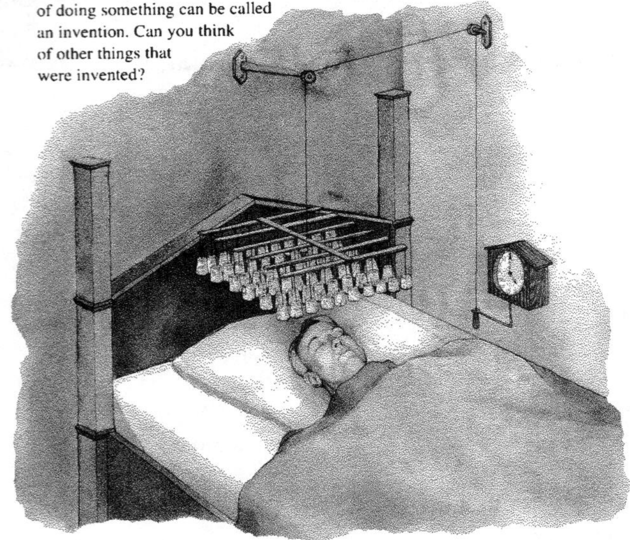

Have you ever seen anything quite like this device before? In 1882, a man named Samuel Applegate had an idea for getting people up on time each day. Can you figure out how his contraption works?

We call Samuel Applegate's idea an *invention*. Do you know what an invention is? An invention might be a new object, or it might be an old object made better. An invention might make a difficult job easier. It could help make a long process quicker. In some way, an invention helps to make life better for the people who use it. Any new idea or way of doing something can be called an invention. Can you think of other things that were invented?

120

All of the items on the tray have one important thing in common: they are all inventions. Each one was thought up by someone at some time in history and was tried out to see whether people would like it and want to use it. Each one has now become a commonplace object. In this lesson, we will learn about the beginnings of three common items.

Teaching the Lesson

Text Discussion, page 120

- ➤ Look at the picture on page 120. **What do you think an invention like this might do?**
- ➤ **Read page 120 to find out what this object was really designed to do.** *(to get people up on time)*
- ➤ **How do you think this contraption might work?**

Later in the lesson we will find out exactly how Samuel Applegate's invention helped people to get to school or work on time.

Demonstration

- ➤ **How do inventions help us?** *(They make difficult jobs easier; they make long processes shorter; they make life better in some way.)*
- ➤ When I say "Go," put on the sweater and fasten it up the front as fast as you can. I will time you.

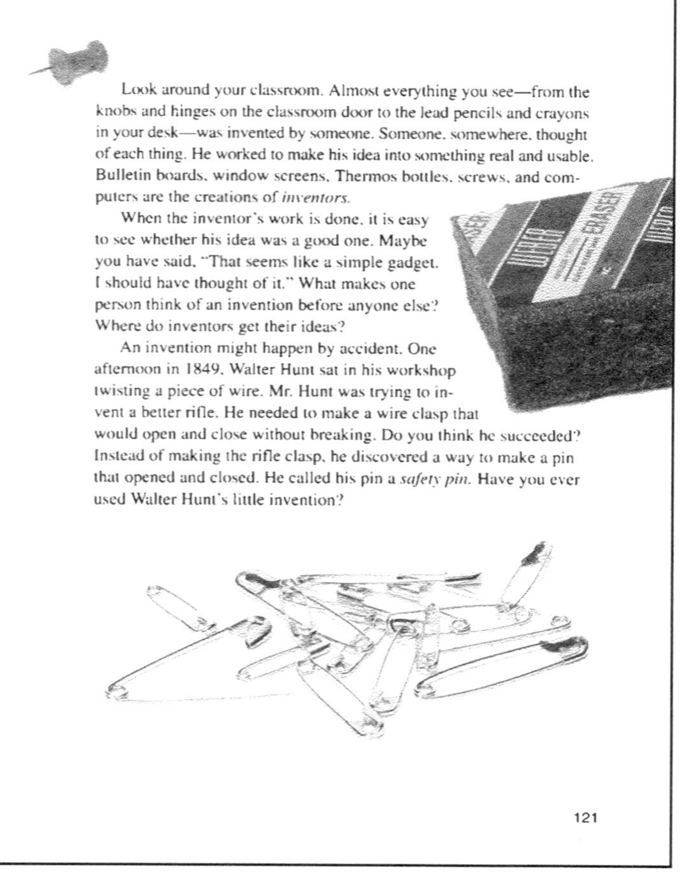

Look around your classroom. Almost everything you see—from the knobs and hinges on the classroom door to the lead pencils and crayons in your desk—was invented by someone. Someone, somewhere, thought of each thing. He worked to make his idea into something real and usable. Bulletin boards, window screens, Thermos bottles, screws, and computers are the creations of *inventors*.

When the inventor's work is done, it is easy to see whether his idea was a good one. Maybe you have said, "That seems like a simple gadget. I should have thought of it." What makes one person think of an invention before anyone else? Where do inventors get their ideas?

An invention might happen by accident. One afternoon in 1849, Walter Hunt sat in his workshop twisting a piece of wire. Mr. Hunt was trying to invent a better rifle. He needed to make a wire clasp that would open and close without breaking. Do you think he succeeded? Instead of making the rifle clasp, he discovered a way to make a pin that opened and closed. He called his pin a *safety pin*. Have you ever used Walter Hunt's little invention?

121

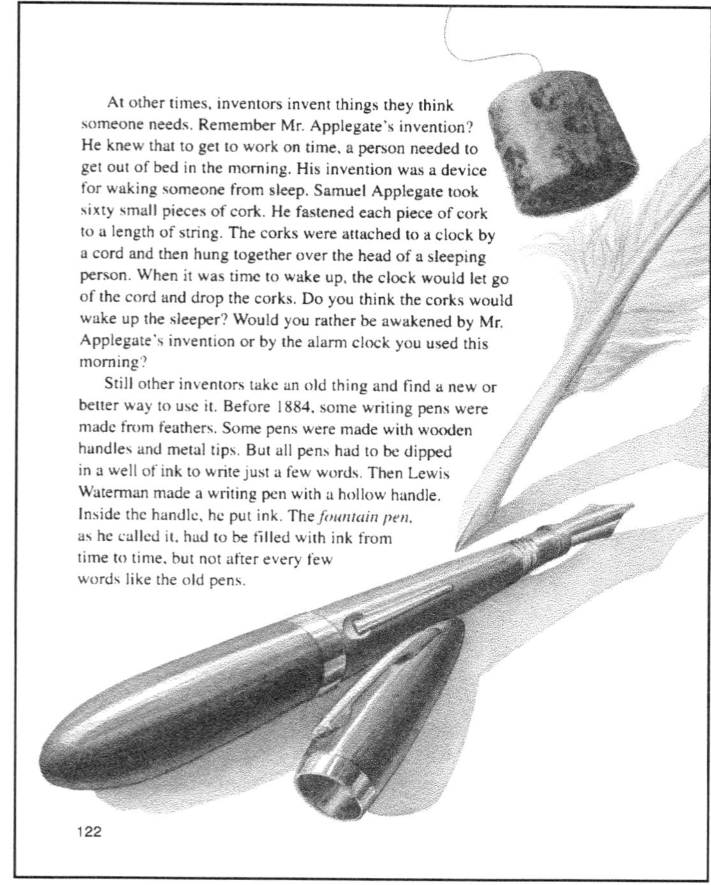

At other times, inventors invent things they think someone needs. Remember Mr. Applegate's invention? He knew that to get to work on time, a person needed to get out of bed in the morning. His invention was a device for waking someone from sleep. Samuel Applegate took sixty small pieces of cork. He fastened each piece of cork to a length of string. The corks were attached to a clock by a cord and then hung together over the head of a sleeping person. When it was time to wake up, the clock would let go of the cord and drop the corks. Do you think the corks would wake up the sleeper? Would you rather be awakened by Mr. Applegate's invention or by the alarm clock you used this morning?

Still other inventors take an old thing and find a new or better way to use it. Before 1884, some writing pens were made from feathers. Some pens were made with wooden handles and metal tips. But all pens had to be dipped in a well of ink to write just a few words. Then Lewis Waterman made a writing pen with a hollow handle. Inside the handle, he put ink. The *fountain pen*, as he called it, had to be filled with ink from time to time, but not after every few words like the old pens.

122

➤ Remove the sweater. Repeat the procedure, putting on the jacket and fastening it as fast as possible.

It will be obvious that the zipper fastens quicker than the buttons do. Before the zipper was invented by Whitcomb Judson in 1891, most clothing used buttons as fasteners. The zipper provided a way to fasten coats and other clothing more quickly.

Text Discussion, page 121

➤ **Read the first paragraph on page 121 to discover some more inventions that may be found in the schoolroom.** *(doorknobs and hinges, lead pencils, crayons, bulletin boards, window screens, Thermos bottles, screws, and computers)*

➤ Name some inventions we have around our house.

➤ **What do we call people who think up inventions?** *(inventors)*

➤ **Read the next two paragraphs on page 121 to find out how one inventor got his idea for a very popular invention.**

➤ **What was Walter Hunt's invention?** *(the safety pin)*

➤ **Have you ever used this invention? What for?**

➤ **How has Walter Hunt's accidental invention made our lives easier or better?** *(Answers will vary but should include that the safety pin prevents pricks and is sturdier than a straight pin.)*

Day 2

Text Discussion, page 122

➤ Look again at the picture of Samuel Applegate's invention on page 120.

➤ **Read the first paragraph on page 122 to find out exactly what it was.** *(an alarm clock)*

➤ **Do you think Samuel Applegate's invention would wake people up?**

➤ **Would you like to be awakened in this way? Why or why not?**

➤ **Why is it so important to be on time for church or work?**

> Being punctual is part of being faithful to the work God calls Christians to do, and it is also a courteous way to let others know Christians have respect for them and their time schedules. (BATs: 2c Faithfulness, 5a Love)

➤ **Read the second paragraph on page 122 to find out what Lewis Waterman's invention was.** *(the fountain pen)*

Pens up until this time had no ink inside them. The tips of the pens had to be dipped in ink again and again while a person wrote.

➤ **How did Lewis Waterman's invention make people's lives better?** *(They could write faster and save time with fountain pens.)*

In 1820, a visitor to the United States said, "The moment an American hears the word invention, he pricks up his ears." Why did Americans want to know about new inventions? Almost every invention made life easier for a few people. And some made a difference to almost everyone. If you were asked to make a list of the most important inventions, which ones would you choose?

A New Engine

One invention that changed life for many people in America was built in England in 1712. There an inventor heated water until it became steam and then cooled it quickly to make the engine run. At first the steam engine could only pump water from the bottom of deep mines.

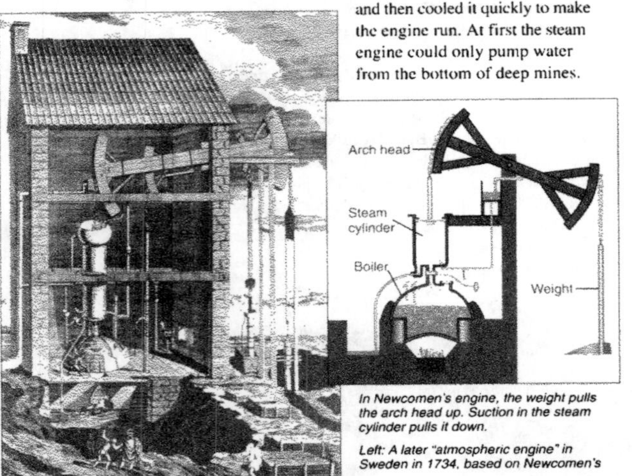

In Newcomen's engine, the weight pulls the arch head up. Suction in the steam cylinder pulls it down.

Left: A later "atmospheric engine" in Sweden in 1734, based on Newcomen's

123

My Journal Name ______________________

Write a journal entry as though you were someone who has just used for the first time one of the inventions studied in this lesson.

My Journal

Date ______________

Invention I used ______________

Before I used this invention ______________

I used this invention to ______________

Now that I have used it, ______________

Heritage Studies 4 Student Notebook — Lesson 31 Evaluating the Lesson 53

Text Discussion, page 123

- ➤ **Read the first paragraph on page 123.**
- ➤ **Why do you think early Americans were so interested in new inventions?**

Early Americans had to do a lot of hard things, such as build their own homes, make their own clothing, and farm their own land. They were eager to try new things to make life easier.

- ➤ **Do you think that early Americans would have liked to have had tractors and chain saws and microwave ovens to help them do their work faster?**
- ➤ **Name the inventions you consider to be most important to us.**

The rest of page 123 will be read and discussed in the next lesson.

Evaluating the Lesson

Notebook Activity, page 53

- ➤ Read the instructions on the page. Think about how that person might have thought about the invention before he used it, what he might have used it for, and what he thought of it after he used it.
- ➤ Write your entry as if you had just finished using the invention for the first time.

Going Beyond

Enrichment

Allow your child to "invent" safety pin jewelry. Provide yarn, safety pins, and small beads in a variety of colors. Direct your child to unclasp the safety pins, to slip beads onto them in colorful patterns, and then to clasp them again. Girls may want to make necklaces and bracelets by stringing several decorated pins on a piece of yarn and tying a knot to fasten them. Boys may want to use the safety pins as ornaments on their shoelaces or as gifts for their mothers or grandmothers.

Additional Teacher Information

People have been wearing pins since ancient times. The Greeks and Romans fastened their clothing with fibulae, a type of pin similar in design to the safety pin. In the 1800s the brooch gained popularity as a decorative ornament on clothing. The stickpin was used around the turn of that century as a fastener for men's ties and cravats. The public welcomed Walter Hunt's invention because it would not fall out of fabric and because it prevented injuries caused by other types of pins.

Samuel Applegate's device for waking people from sleep actually received a patent. Applegate claimed that this invention could also be used as a burglar alarm or as a device for turning on a gas heater at a certain time.

Before the invention of the fountain pen, people wrote with quill pens or steel-nib pens. Lewis Waterman's fountain pen had a steel nib. The ballpoint pen was invented by John Loud four years after the fountain pen. The ballpoint pen gained its popularity during World War II because pilots could use it at high altitudes and it would not leak.

LESSON 32
Engines and More

Text, pages 123-26
Notebook, pages 54-55

Preview

Main Ideas

- James Watt improved the steam engine.
- Eli Whitney invented the cotton gin and a machine that made interchangeable parts for muskets.

Objectives

- Associate key words with either James Watt or Eli Whitney
- Locate these key words in a word search puzzle

Materials

- The figure of James Watt (1769) from the TimeLine Snapshots

Day 1

Lesson

Introducing the Lesson

Listening Activity

➤ Listen to find out the first names of two importan men in this lesson.

A man named James and his friend Matthew were walking around the grounds of Matthew's handsome stone mansion in Birmingham, England. "A fine day, isn't it, James?" asked Matthew.

James glanced up at the sunny sky and frowned. "It will be raining again tomorrow," he said with a sigh.

Matthew let out a booming laugh and slapped James on the back. "When will you ever learn to look on the bright side, James? Just enjoy the sunshine while it's here today instead of worrying about tomorrow." He squinted at his companion's gloomy face. "What's on your mind, my friend? You seem troubled over something—even more so than usual."

"It's my invention. Matthew, of all things in life, there is nothing more foolish than inventing."

"Why do you say that?"

"I'm not accomplishing anything on this engine. I don't know why I'm even trying. I don't have enough talent to be a good inventor. And if I spend much more time fooling around with this thing that will probably never work, I will lose money. My wife and children will go hungry. I would never be able to forgive myself if something happened to one of them because of my failure to provide for them. I think I'm going to quit work on the engine."

Matthew threw back his head and laughed so hard that his hat fell backwards off his head. He stooped to pick it up. "James, my fine fellow," he said, "you have just given me the best laugh I've had in a long time."

James stopped walking. He stared at Matthew. "What on earth was funny about what I just said?"

"It's funny because there's not an ounce of truth in it!" Suddenly Matthew's face became serious, and he leaned toward James. "Your invention, my friend, is going to make you a very wealthy man someday. But first you just need someone to believe in you and to get you going. James, I'm your man. I'd like you to go into business with me as your partner."

James's mouth dropped open. "But—but my invention isn't even finished yet. And I live in Scotland, and you live here in England. How would it ever work?"

"That is not a problem at all. Look." They stopped at the crest of a little hill, and Matthew pointed down to a large brick building in the valley. "There's my little enterprise—Soho Manufactory. It's doing very well, James. I expect a large increase in my income over the next two years. I have the money right now to back you and your family while you work on the invention. I'll pay you to work on it. I'll pay for your tools, the workers you need to help you, your supplies—anything you need. You and your wife and children can move here to England, and you may set up an office in my factory. Then, when your invention begins to sell, you will earn more than enough money to pay me back every penny."

"You are very kind, Matthew," said James. "I appreciate your offer. But as I said before, I don't think I will ever finish my invention. And I know it will never be useful to very many people even if I do finish it."

"That's where you're wrong, James." Matthew clapped his hand down on James's shoulder and looked at him with earnest eyes. "When are you going to realize how much talent you have? You are a very clever inventor! Your engine is going to change the world—I say, it will change the whole way we live! All you need is someone like me to help you introduce it to the world. What do you say, James? Will you let me help you?"

➤ **Who were the two men discussing the new engine?** *(James and Matthew)*

➤ **Where did James live?** *(Scotland)*

➤ **What did Matthew want to do for James?** *(go into business with him)*

➤ **Why did James not want to accept Matthew's help?** *(Matthew lived in England, not Scotland; James would probably never finish his invention.)*

In 1820, a visitor to the United States said, "The moment an American hears the word invention, he pricks up his ears." Why did Americans want to know about new inventions? Almost every invention made life easier for a few people. And some made a difference to almost everyone. If you were asked to make a list of the most important inventions, which ones would you choose?

A New Engine

One invention that changed life for many people in America was built in England in 1712. There an inventor heated water until it became steam and then cooled it quickly to make the engine run. At first the steam engine could only pump water from the bottom of deep mines.

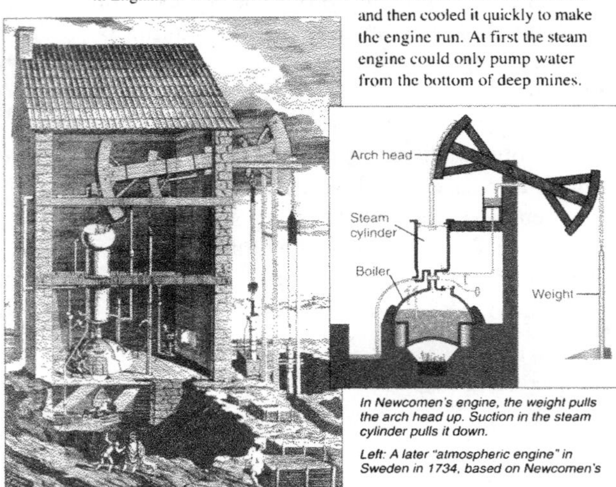

In Newcomen's engine, the weight pulls the arch head up. Suction in the steam cylinder pulls it down.

Left: A later "atmospheric engine" in Sweden in 1734, based on Newcomen's

123

Several years passed before James accepted Matthew's offer of help. We will learn more about James's invention and his friendship with Matthew in this lesson.

Teaching the Lesson

Text Discussion, pages 123-24

➤ **Read the last paragraph on page 123 and all of page 124 to find out how the new type of engine was powered.** *(by steam)*

The inventor who designed this first steam engine was not James but an earlier inventor.

➤ **Why was the first steam engine not very important to the world?** *(It did not work very well.)*

The engine James was trying to invent was an improved version of the earlier steam engine.

➤ **What was James's full name?** *(James Watt)*

James Watt was sickly as a child and did not go to school regularly until he was ten or eleven years old. But his mother had taught him so well at home that he immediately rose to the head of his class and eventually learned the trade of instrument making.

Instrument making involves making things such as craftsmen's tools, musical instruments, and other mechanical gadgets. It requires good mathematical

A steamboat in use around 1860

More than fifty years after the steam engine was first used, twenty-seven-year-old James Watt was busy in his shop. A steam engine had broken down, and Watt had been asked to fix it. The engine broke often. When it did work, it lost steam quickly. And it took huge amounts of coal to keep the engine hot. "There must be a way to make this engine work better," Watt thought.

Encouraged by his family and friends, Watt began work on a better steam engine. He found a way to save steam and coal by cooling the steam in a separate tube, or *cylinder.* After ten years of hard work, James Watt's better steam engine was ready to use. In five more years, Watt built almost three hundred new steam engines.

Throughout the rest of his life, James Watt thought of new ways to make his steam engine better. When he died in 1819, the steam engine was an important tool for many businesses in England. Before this invention, men had used their own muscle power or the power of animals, wind, or water to get work done. Now one steam engine could do the work of one hundred horses.

Soon people in other countries heard about the steam engine and the things it could do. Do you think they wanted to use the new steam engine?

124

skills. This was James Watt's trade when the broken steam engine was brought to him for repair.

- ➤ **What idea did Watt have to make the steam engine better?** *(He cooled the steam in a separate cylinder so that the engine could stay hot.)*
- ➤ **How long did it take James Watt to turn his idea into a real, usable engine?** *(ten years)*
- ➤ **Do you think you would have given up on the idea before ten years had passed?**
- ➤ Think about the story of James Watt I read earlier. **Did he seem to be a happy person?** *(No, he seemed sad.)*
- ➤ **Did James act as though he had a lot of confidence in his abilities?** *(No, he seemed to lack confidence or to be a worrier.)*
- ➤ *Write the word* ***pessimist.*** This word refers to a person who always sees the bad rather than the good in life.
- ➤ **Did James Watt seem to be a pessimist?** *(yes)*
- ➤ *Write the word* ***optimist.*** This is the opposite of *pessimist.*
- ➤ **What do you think *optimist* means?**

An optimist is a person who always sees the good in life and always looks on the bright side of things.

- ➤ **Do you think that Matthew was an optimist or a pessimist?** Matthew was more of an optimist.
- ➤ **What was Matthew like in the story?** *(Answers will vary but should include that Matthew was cheerful, kind, and encouraging.)*

Matthew's full name was Matthew Boulton. He was the one who gave James Watt the most encouragement to keep trying to make his invention work.

Matthew Boulton was the wealthy owner of a factory in which all the workers were treated with care and given pleasant, comfortable surroundings in which to work. Boulton was also an excellent businessman. After he and Watt went into business together, the steam engine brought them both a great deal of wealth.

- ➤ **Why was Matthew Boulton's encouragement such an important thing for James Watt?** *(Without encouragement from a friend who believed in him, he might never have finished his steam engine.)*
- ➤ Think of someone you know who tends to be pessimistic. **What kinds of things can you say or do to encourage that person?** *(Answers will vary.)* (BATs: 5a Love, 5e Friendliness)
- ➤ **Was James Watt satisfied with his engine after the ten years he spent inventing it?** *(No, he kept trying to improve it for the rest of his life.)* (BAT: 2e Work)
- ➤ *Write the term* ***horsepower.***

This is a unit of measurement introduced by James Watt. His steam engine eventually replaced horses in driving machinery in mills.

- ➤ **How many horses would it have taken to do the work his steam engine could do?** *(one hundred)*

Since his steam engine could do the same amount of work as one hundred horses, he said it had a horsepower of one hundred. The term *horsepower* is still used as a unit of measurement today.

TimeLine Snapshots Activity

James Watt's improved steam engine revolutionized (greatly changed) the way everyone lived and worked. The steam engine allowed for work to be done faster in factories, and it also became a source of power for many types of transportation.

- ➤ Add the figure of James Watt to the TimeLine at the year 1769.
- ➤ **Who was president of the United States at this time?** *(America did not yet have its first president.)*
- ➤ Name several events shown on the Time Line that occurred before or after James Watt made his invention. *This activity will help your child gain historical perspective.*

The Cotton Gin and Interchangeable Parts

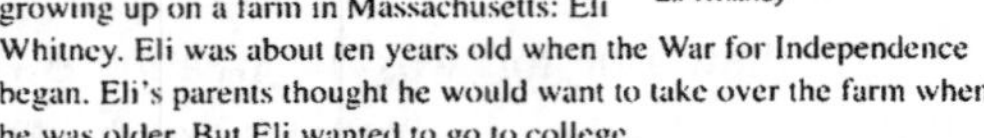

Eli Whitney

While James Watt worked on his steam engine in England, another inventor was growing up on a farm in Massachusetts: Eli Whitney. Eli was about ten years old when the War for Independence began. Eli's parents thought he would want to take over the farm when he was older. But Eli wanted to go to college.

After college, Whitney planned to teach the children of a rich Georgia planter. But he never made it to the plantation. On the way, Whitney saw the cotton plant for the first time. He heard how hard it was to remove the seeds from the sticky cotton. And he learned that the people of the South could become rich from selling cotton if only someone could find an easy way to remove the seeds.

Slaves worked this cotton gin by turning the crank.

Whitney decided to build a machine that would remove the seeds from cotton. It took six months of constant work. But by early 1793, he had a machine that could clean as much cotton as one thousand slaves could. The machine could be worked by a man, a team of oxen, or a water wheel. Later, the *cotton gin* would be run by another machine. Can you guess which one?

125

The Eli Whitney Gun Factory by William Giles Munson, painted 1826-28

We remember Eli Whitney most for his cotton gin. But the cotton gin was not his only invention. His next invention was not an object but a new way of doing things. This idea was even more important than his cotton gin.

In Whitney's day, all the parts for machines and tools were made by hand. No two parts were quite the same. And no two finished tools were exactly alike. Replacing parts and fixing broken equipment was very difficult.

Whitney began making muskets for the new United States army in 1798. In his factory, Whitney built machines for making each part of the musket. The machines made each part exactly alike. Now each trigger was just like all the other triggers. And each trigger would fit any one of Whitney's muskets. Suddenly, making the muskets was quicker. Fixing broken muskets was easier too because the parts were *interchangeable*. How do you think Whitney's idea helped other inventors?

126

Day 2

Text Discussion, page 125

➤ **Read the first paragraph on page 125 to find the name of another inventor who was growing up in the United States at the same time that James Watt was building his steam engine.** *(Eli Whitney)*

Eli Whitney showed promise as an inventor even when he was very young. During the War for Independence, he and his father found that the nails they needed for their work in their repair shop had skyrocketed in price. Eli thought of installing a forge to make their own nails in the workshop. Eventually, people were buying so many nails from them that they had to hire an extra person to help.

➤ **What qualities can we see in Eli Whitney from this incident?** *(Answers will vary but might include that he was creative, smart, and determined.)*

➤ **Read the next paragraph on page 125 to find out what Whitney planned to do after college.** *(teach the children of a planter)*

➤ **What other challenge did Eli Whitney encounter on his way to the plantation?** *(trying to find a way to remove seeds from cotton)*

➤ **Read the final paragraph on page 125 to find out whether Eli Whitney was successful.** *(yes)*

➤ **What was his machine called?** *(the cotton gin)*

The word *gin* comes from the word *engine,* but at the time of Eli Whitney, the power used for operating machinery came only from water, animals, and men.

➤ **What engine being invented across the ocean at that time would eventually power the cotton gin?** *(Watt's steam engine)*

Text Discussion, page 126

➤ **Read page 126 to find out what other important idea came from Eli Whitney?** *(interchangeable parts)*

➤ **How did Whitney's idea help the United States army?** *(He built machines for making the parts of muskets exactly alike so that it was quicker to make muskets and to fix broken ones.)*

➤ **How did Eli Whitney's idea help other inventors?** *(They could produce their inventions faster and in greater quantities than ever before. Broken parts could be easily replaced.)*

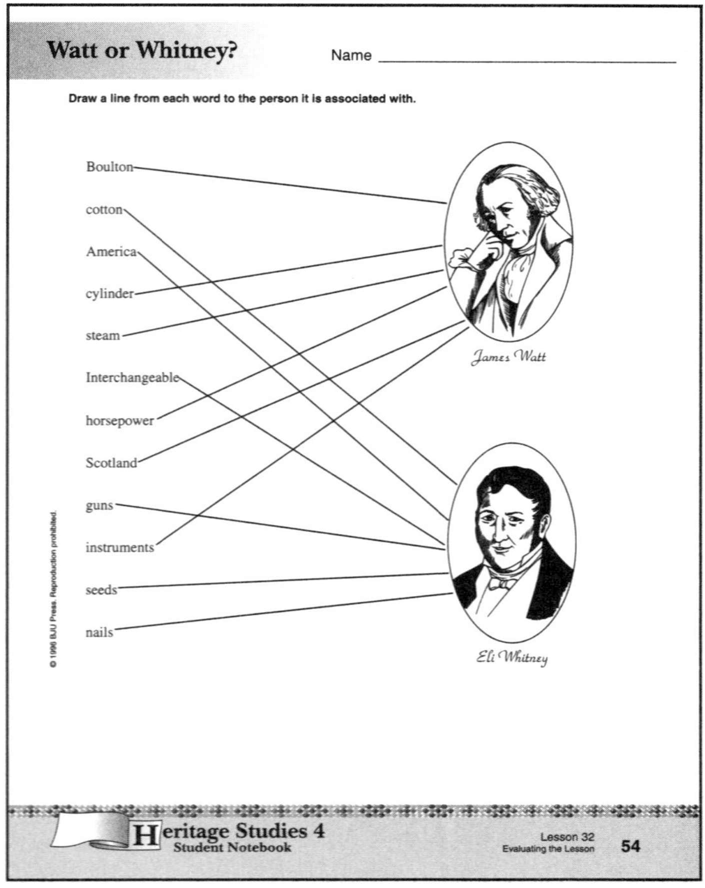

Watt or Whitney? Name ______________________

Draw a line from each word to the person it is associated with.

Boulton
cotton
America
cylinder
steam
Interchangeable
horsepower
Scotland
guns
instruments
seeds
nails

James Watt

Eli Whitney

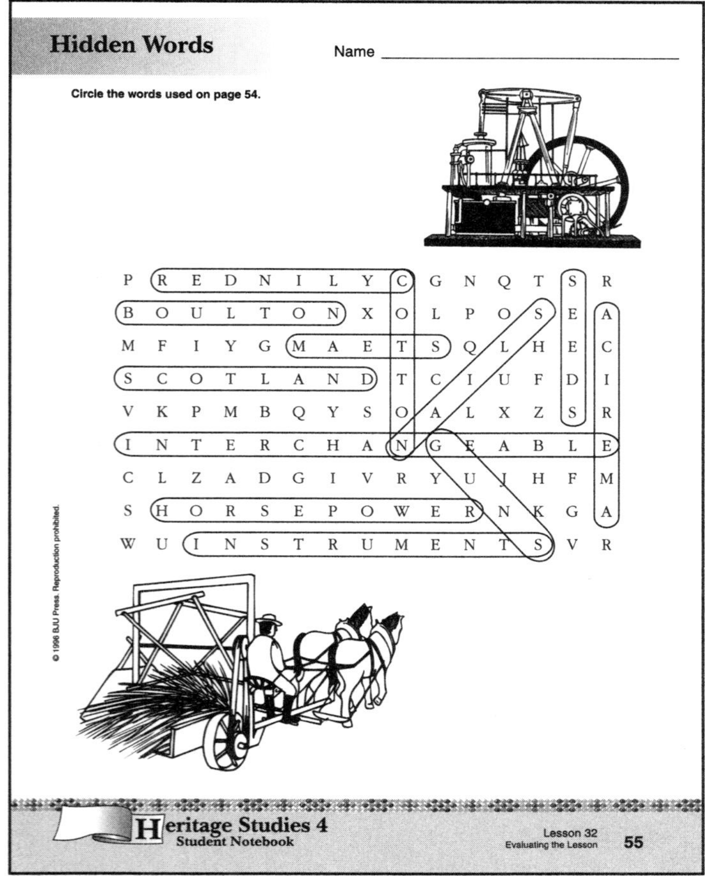

Hidden Words Name ______________________

Circle the words used on page 54.

P R E D N I L Y C G N Q T S R
B O U L T O N X O L P O S E A
M F I Y G M A E T S Q L H E C
S C O T L A N D T C I U F D I
V K P M B Q Y S O A L X Z S R
I N T E R C H A N G E A B L E
C L Z A D G I V R Y U J H F M
S H O R S E P O W E R N K G A
W U I N S T R U M E N T S V R

Evaluating the Lesson

Notebook Activity, pages 54-55

- ➤ Read the instructions on Notebook page 54 and complete the page.
- ➤ Complete the word search on Notebook page 55.

Going Beyond

Enrichment

Provide your child with magazines or catalogs, glue, scissors, and construction paper. Encourage him to make picture collages of things made of cotton or things that might once have been powered by steam (such as boats, trains, cars, machines, and so on).

Additional Teacher Information

James Watt needed the constant encouragement of his friend Matthew Boulton to keep him working on improving the steam engine. Watt had a tendency to give up every time he encountered a small problem. But Boulton's persistent faith in him kept James Watt going. Watt's steam engine went on to become the source of power for automobiles, steamboats, trains, and entire factories.

Like James Watt, Eli Whitney was also motivated to invent through the encouragement of a good friend. He was a guest on the plantation of Catherine Greene, who was the widow of Nathaniel Greene, an important general in the War for Independence. Mrs. Greene had noticed Whitney's skill with his hands, and she urged him to try to invent a seed-removing machine for the South. Financed by Mrs. Greene's manager, Phineas Miller, Whitney built and patented the cotton gin. Miller and Whitney went into business together, claiming exclusive rights to make and sell the cotton gin. Because they could not produce enough machines for all the southern planters, other inventors began producing their own cotton gins. Whitney and Miller fought so many court battles to protect their invention rights that they lost more money than they earned on their cotton gin. Though not as well known as the cotton gin, Whitney's machine that made interchangeable musket parts was a much more profitable venture for him.

LESSON 33
Sheaves of Success

Text, pages 127-30
Notebook, page 56

Preview

Main Ideas

- Cyrus McCormick invented the reaper.
- Cyrus McCormick's marketing skills and giving spirit helped him to be successful.
- A patent is an agreement between an inventor and the government to protect the inventor's rights.

Objectives

- Make an invention that will solve a specific problem
- Sequence the events of Cyrus McCormick's life

Materials

- Packaged items containing wheat (bread, crackers, cereal, pasta, cookies)*
- A stalk of wheat or a picture of a stalk of wheat*
- A bowl of wheat flour*

Notes

Places where wheat might be found include craft stores, florist shops, or farms.

The packaged food items should have the word *wheat* somewhere in the ingredients on the labels.

Day 1

Lesson

Introducing the Lesson

Label-Reading Activity

➤ *Place the packaged food items on the table.*

Even though we might not think of or talk about wheat very often, it is one of the most important crops grown in America. Each of the items on the table is made from wheat. See if you can find wheat listed in the ingredients on the label of each item.

➤ *Show your child the stalk of wheat or a picture of a stalk of wheat.*

◆ LEARNING HOW ◆

An Inventor Works

1. You will need a pencil, some paper, and materials to build your invention.
2. Think about things you use that could work better or problems you would like to solve. Make a list of as many things as you can think of. Then reread each idea. Is it really new? Would other people think it was a good idea? How easy would the thing be to make?
3. Choose one of your ideas and try to draw a picture that shows how it would work. Do you need more information to make your invention? Where can you find the information?
4. Try to put your invention together. Does it work? Do you need more information? Can you do something another way? Show your working invention to your classmates. Is your invention something they can use?

127

This is what the head of a wheat stalk looks like. The stalks of wheat are harvested when the grain is ripe. Notice the individual kernels in the head. After the wheat has been harvested, millers grind the kernels into a fine powder to make flour.

➤ Look closely at the wheat flour in the bowl and feel its texture.

For many years wheat was harvested by hand with a scythe. It was a tedious task. In this lesson we will learn about a man who had an important idea to help farmers harvest their wheat faster.

Teaching the Lesson

Learning How Activity, page 127

➤ **Read all the steps on page 127.**

Inventors often begin with a problem that they would like to solve. Then they begin to experiment and take practical steps to solve that problem.

➤ To begin this activity, you will need only the paper and pencil listed in Step 1.

➤ **Reread Step 2.** Begin brainstorming about problems that you would like to solve. Write your list as you think of ideas.

Cyrus McCormick's Reaper

Ripe wheat must be gathered quickly. But harvesting the grain with a scythe was slow and difficult work. A good worker would spend a whole day cutting just two acres of wheat. For years people tried to make a machine that would reap, or harvest, wheat. How would such a machine help farmers?

Robert McCormick was one of many who tried to build a reaping machine. When he gave up, his oldest son, Cyrus, decided to try. Cyrus McCormick and his helper, a slave named Jo Anderson, were ready to test their invention.

McCormick tests his reaper in Virginia

McCormick set up his reaper in one of his father's fields. People came from across the Virginia countryside to watch. A horse pulled the reaper slowly across the field, and the cut wheat stalks fell neatly behind the machine. It worked! How do you think the crowd of farmers felt as they watched the machine?

128

You may give some ideas such as having shoes that come off too easily or often come untied, snagging clothing on wooden chairs, losing important items like school papers or gloves, spilling beverages at meals, keeping food hot or cold in a picnic basket, or not being able to stop biting fingernails.

If you are teaching more than one child, allow them to work together in pairs.

- ➤ Choose one problem to work on independently.
- ➤ Think about what kind of invention would solve that problem.
- ➤ **Reread Step 3 and follow the instructions given.**

During the next few days, you will be working on your invention. You may ask other family members for ideas about building or improving your invention. *Assign a date for completion and presentation to the family.*

Text Discussion, page 128

- ➤ **Read page 128 to find out what Cyrus McCormick's reaper was and what it did.** *(a machine that cut down wheat stalks quickly and neatly)*
- ➤ **What is a *scythe?*** *(a tool with a wide blade and a bent handle)*
- ➤ **Who else in Cyrus McCormick's family had tried to invent a machine to harvest wheat?** *(Cyrus's father, Robert McCormick)*

Robert McCormick had already invented a few pieces of farm machinery—a thresher and a hemp binder. Young Cyrus often watched his father tinkering in his workshop and developed an interest in inventing mechanical things.

Before the reaper, Cyrus McCormick invented a lighter version of an existing farm tool, a set of surveying instruments, and a hillside plow. McCormick was twenty-two years old when he finished his first reaper.

- ➤ **Who helped him with the machine?** *(a slave named Jo Anderson)*
- ➤ **How many acres of grain could hand-held tools cut in an eight-hour day?** *(two acres)*

McCormick's reaper could harvest at least fourteen acres in the same amount of time. McCormick's reaper also piled the cut stalks on a platform on which they could easily be tied into sheaves.

- ➤ **How do you think Robert McCormick felt as he watched his son that day?** *(proud, happy)*

Text Discussion, page 129

- ➤ **Read the first paragraph on page 129 to find out whether Cyrus McCormick's reaper was an instant success.** *(no)*
- ➤ **Why did the farmers in Virginia, where McCormick lived, not want to buy the reaper?** *(Their farms were small and hilly, so they did not think they needed it.)*

The farmers also wanted to keep using tools that they were used to rather than try something new. They thought the mechanical reaper cost too much money or was too hard to operate.

- ➤ **Did this discourage Cyrus McCormick?** *(no)* (BAT: 2d Goal setting)

Cyrus McCormick did several important things to make people interested in his invention.

- ➤ **Read the second paragraph on page 129 to find out the first things Cyrus did to help his reaper sell better.** *(He went to the Midwest and found farmers who liked his reaper. Then he moved to Chicago and built a factory for making reapers.)*

Cyrus McCormick

McCormick spent more time making his machine work even better. But when he was ready to sell his reaper, the farmers in the East were not ready to buy it. Most thought they did not need such a contraption on their small, hilly farms. But McCormick would not give up.

On a visit to the Midwest, McCormick saw stretches of flat land ready for planting with wheat. When some farmers in the Midwest bought his reaper, McCormick made a decision. He moved to Chicago, Illinois. There he built a factory for making his reapers. How might moving nearer to his customers help McCormick to sell more of his reapers?

In his factory, Cyrus McCormick made his reapers from interchangeable parts. If a part broke on a reaper, the farmer simply sent for a new part to replace it. When the part came in the mail, the farmer could fix the reaper himself. What other inventor had thought of the idea of interchangeable parts?

Soon McCormick was a very rich man. He had earned more than a million dollars by selling his reapers. He gave money to build schools and churches. He gave money to the evangelist D. L. Moody. And he printed two Christian magazines. As long as Cyrus McCormick lived, he used his money to help in the Lord's work.

"Honour the Lord with thy substance, and with the firstfruits of all thine increase: So shall thy barns be filled with plenty, and thy presses shall burst out with new wine."

Proverbs 3:9-10

129

◆ THINGS PEOPLE DO ◆

Obtaining a Patent

All the inventors you will read about in this chapter have one thing in common: each applied for and received a *patent* from the United States government. Obtaining a patent is an important way to make an invention known to other people. But what is a patent?

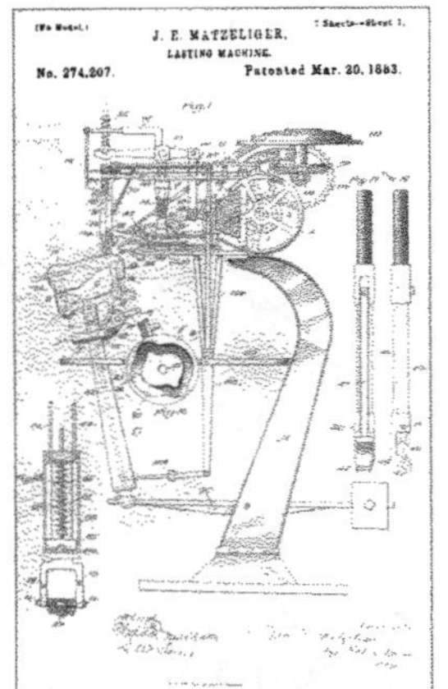

Jan Matzeliger's patent application for a machine that would last shoes

A patent is an agreement. The inventor agrees to explain all the details of his invention to anyone who wants to know. Then the U.S. government agrees to protect the rights of the inventor. A patent says that only the inventor may make or sell his invention for seventeen years. Why would an inventor want to make this agreement?

It is not easy to qualify for a patent. An invention must be a new idea, and it must work. The inventor needs to write a description of his invention. If he can, he should include a drawing of the invention, inside and out. The drawing helps the people at the Patent and Trademark Office understand how the invention works.

A worker at the Patent and Trademark Office looks over the description and drawings. If there is no other invention like his, the inventor is granted a patent. The Massachusetts Colony granted the first American patent to Joseph Jenks. He had made a better *scythe*, a tool for cutting wheat. Today more than one hundred thousand patents are given to inventors each year.

130

➤ **Why might farmers in the Midwest have been more interested in buying a reaper than farmers in the East?** *(It was easier to operate reapers on midwestern farms because the land was flatter; midwestern farms were usually larger and more spread out than eastern farms.)*

Another thing McCormick did to promote his reaper was to make posters with pictures of men using the machine. On the posters he described the different parts of the reaper and how each part worked. He posted these flyers on fence posts and gave them to shopkeepers to use as wrapping paper. He also advertised in many country newspapers. The McCormick reaper became well known all across the Midwest. Cyrus was good at marketing his invention.

➤ **What kinds of things could you do to advertise the invention you are going to make?** *(Answers will vary.)*

Cyrus McCormick also made his reapers easy for farmers to afford. He charged $125 for a reaper, but he allowed farmers to pay only $35 as a down payment if they bought their reapers in July. Then in December, after their crop had been harvested, they had to pay him the rest of the money. Buying on credit was a totally new concept then. Today it is a common practice.

➤ **How much money do you think you would charge for your invention if you were going to sell it?**

➤ **Read the third paragraph on page 129 to learn about another important idea that Cyrus McCormick used with his reaper.** *(He made his reapers with interchangeable parts.)*

➤ **What other inventor had begun the idea of using interchangeable parts in machines?** *(Eli Whitney)*

➤ **Read the last paragraph on page 129 to find out how much money McCormick earned from selling his reapers.** *(more than a million dollars)*

➤ **What would you do with that much money if you had it?**

➤ **How did Cyrus McCormick use his money?** *(He gave it to build schools and churches; he gave some to evangelist D. L. Moody; and he printed two Christian magazines.)*

Read aloud the verse on page 129. As Christians, we should follow Cyrus McCormick's example of giving to the Lord's work even if we do not have as much money to give as he did. (BAT: 5b Giving)

Text Discussion, page 130

➤ **Read page 130 to find out what all the inventions in this chapter have in common.** *(a patent)*

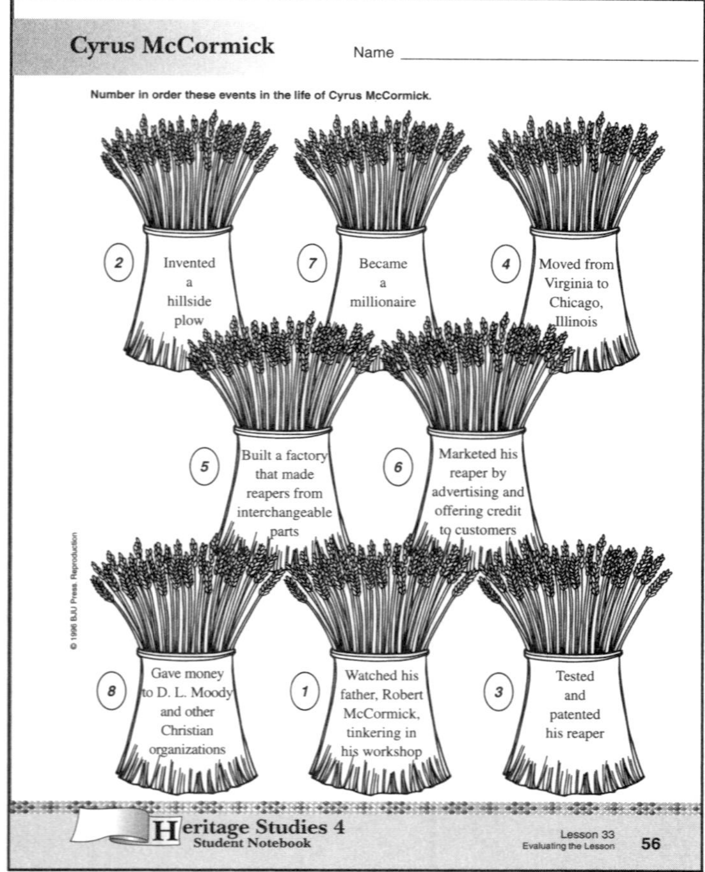

Cyrus McCormick Name ______________________

Number in order these events in the life of Cyrus McCormick.

2 Invented a hillside plow

7 Became a millionaire

4 Moved from Virginia to Chicago, Illinois

5 Built a factory that made reapers from interchangeable parts

6 Marketed his reaper by advertising and offering credit to customers

8 Gave money to D. L. Moody and other Christian organizations

1 Watched his father, Robert McCormick, tinkering in his workshop

3 Tested and patented his reaper

Heritage Studies 4 Student Notebook — Lesson 33 Evaluating the Lesson 56

- ➤ **What is a *patent*?** *(an agreement that the U.S. government will protect the inventor's rights to make and sell his invention for seventeen years)*
- ➤ **How would an agreement like this benefit an inventor?** *(No one else could copy his ideas and take business away from him.)*
- ➤ **What things must an inventor do to qualify for a patent?** *(He must have a new and working invention; he must write a description of his invention; and he must draw a picture of his invention, inside and out, that shows how it works; he must send all this information to the Patent and Trademark Office.)*
- ➤ **Who was the first American to receive a patent, and what did he invent?** *(Joseph Jenks invented a better scythe.)*

Evaluating the Lesson

Notebook Activity, page 56

- ➤ Read the instructions given on Notebook page 56.
- ➤ Read all the statements before you begin completing the page.

Going Beyond

Enrichment

Provide paper, crayons, felt-tip pens, scissors, and old magazines from which pictures may be cut. Encourage your child to design an advertisement for any of the inventions studied so far in this chapter or for the one he is making himself. The advertisement may be illustrated by a hand-drawn or a cut-out picture. It should include the name of the invention. Remind your child that the purpose of an advertisement is to get people to buy a product; therefore, the advertisement should focus only on the advantages of the invention, not on its problems.

If you live in a region where wheat is produced, arrange a field trip to a wheat farm to watch farmers working.

Additional Teacher Information

Cyrus McCormick grew up in a strict Presbyterian home in which family prayer, Bible memorization, and drilling in the Shorter Catechism played an important part. He remained loyal to the Presbyterian Church throughout his life. He did not marry until the age of forty-eight, when he met twenty-four-year-old Nancy Fowler. "Nettie," as Cyrus called her, shared his Presbyterian convictions, and they had a very strong marriage. Although McCormick had trouble keeping secretaries because of his fiery temper and harsh personality, he respected his wife's good sense and often followed her advice in his business affairs. Seven children were born to them.

Cyrus McCormick's pioneer spirit shone not only in the field of inventing but also in marketing. He became the first American manufacturer to promise a money-back guarantee on his product. In 1853, when the gears on his reapers failed, he remained true to his word and replaced every one of them at no charge to the customers. McCormick's marketing genius was a major factor in his success at selling his reapers.

Lesson 34
A Stitch in Time

Text, pages 131-33
Notebook, page 57

Preview

Main Ideas

- Elias Howe invented the sewing machine.
- Jan Matzeliger invented a shoe-lasting machine.

Objective

- Identify true and false statements about Elias Howe and Jan Matzeliger

Materials

- Two 4"×4" pieces of fabric for your child and four pieces for you*
- A needle and thread for each of you*
- A watch or clock with a second hand
- A sewing machine*

Each length of thread should be about 24" long. You may find it helpful to thread the needles and tie the knots to make a double strand before the lesson.

Day 1

Lesson

Introducing the Lesson

Sewing Demonstration

➤ *Give your child two pieces of fabric and a threaded needle.* We will each stitch two pieces of fabric together on one side by hand.

➤ Check the clock and record the starting time. When we finish, check the clock again and record the ending time.

➤ I will stitch two more pieces of fabric together, using the sewing machine this time. You will keep track of the time for me by watching the second hand while I sew.

➤ Compare the hand sewing with the machine sewing by amount of time taken and the quality of the stitching. *(Machine stitching took seconds rather than minutes, and the stitches are tighter and more even.)*

In this lesson we will learn about two inventors that developed machines to help people sew faster.

Elias Howe and His Sewing Machine

Elias Howe could not help overhearing his boss talking to a friend. "Someone needs to invent a machine that can take the place of sewing by hand," he said. "That person would make a fortune." What would you have done if you had heard that?

In 1841 Howe worked in a shop making different kinds of machines. The more he thought about what he had heard, the more he felt sure that he could build a machine for sewing. So Howe quit his job at the machine shop. And he spent all his time working on his idea.

For five years Howe worked on his sewing machine. For five years his family made do with only a little bit of money. But things would be better when Howe finished his machine. When he finally made a sewing machine that worked, he received a patent and made plans to sell his wonderful invention.

Howe patented his sewing machine in 1846.

Elias Howe

131

Teaching the Lesson

Text Discussion, page 131

From his childhood on, Elias Howe had a talent for working with mechanical things. He often helped his father in the sawmill on their farm, and when he was older, he worked in a number of machine shops in the Boston area.

➤ **Read page 131 to learn how Elias Howe got the idea for a sewing machine.** *(He overheard his boss telling a friend that if someone would invent a sewing machine, he would make a fortune.)*

➤ **What did Howe decide to do about his idea?** *(He quit his job to start working on the machine.)*

➤ **How many years did his family do without things so that he could work on this invention?** *(five years)*

➤ **Have you ever had to wait a long time for something you wanted?**

➤ **How do you think Howe and his family felt when he finished his sewing machine?**

➤ **What important thing did Elias Howe do to protect his rights to the sewing machine?** *(He got a patent on it.)*

➤ **How do you think other people felt about Howe's machine when he showed it to them?**

The sewing machine saved hours of work on every garment made.

What do you think happened then? It was not what Howe had expected. The tailors and seamstresses did not like his machine! They thought that the sewing machine could not do the fine work as well as they could. And they feared that it would take away their jobs. Besides, the machine cost too much to make. Even if someone wanted to buy a sewing machine, no one had enough money to spend on such nonsense.

Howe tried to sell his machine in the United States. He left his home and sailed for England to try selling the sewing machine there. Finally he gave up. No one seemed to be interested in Howe's invention. Had his old boss been wrong?

Discouraged, Elias Howe came home to the United States. And what do you think he found? People everywhere were using his sewing machine! But they had not bought the machines from Howe. Other men had used Howe's ideas to make and sell sewing machines.

Howe had done a smart thing. Do you remember what he had done? He had gotten a patent on his invention. Now all the people who were selling his sewing machine had to pay money to Howe. Soon Elias Howe was a millionaire. But he never forgot how hard it had been to be poor. He used his money to help other people get the things they needed.

132

◆ HOW IT WAS ◆

A shoe-making factory
Lynn, Massachusetts
May 29, 1885

After it was invented in 1846, Elias Howe's sewing machine was used to sew parts of a shoe together. But one part of the work could not be done with a sewing machine—the *lasting*.

Preparing to sew a shoe upper to a sole by hand

Lasting meant sewing the upper of a shoe to the sole. Lasting had to be done by hand. The lasters believed that a machine could never do such difficult work.

Jan Matzeliger was an immigrant who worked in a shoe factory. He studied the way the lasters did their work.

Jan Matzeliger

Matzeliger began building a machine in a room over the old West Lynn Mission. His machine copied the way a laster's hands worked. On this day, Matzeliger's machine lasted seventy-five pairs of ladies' shoes perfectly.

133

Text Discussion, page 132

➤ **Read the first two paragraphs on page 132 to find out what other people thought.** *(People did not like it; they thought it did not do fine work well; they thought it cost too much; they thought it would take away people's jobs.)*

➤ **What did Elias Howe do when he realized people in America were not interested in his machine?** *(He took it to England to try to sell it there.)*

Howe finally managed to interest one English shop owner in his machine and was offered a job in the shop. But the job lasted only eight months, and Howe was forced to return to America.

➤ **Read the last two paragraphs on page 132 to find out what Elias Howe found when he came home.** *(Other people had used his ideas to make and sell sewing machines.)*

➤ **What smart thing had Howe done earlier?** *(gotten a patent)*

Elias Howe had to go to court and pay lawyers a lot of money to help him get everything sorted out. But in the end he got all the money back with the profits from his sewing machine. Howe received five dollars from every sale of a sewing machine in the United States.

➤ **How did he use his money when he became rich?** *(to help poor people)*

When the American Civil War began, Howe enlisted in the Seventeenth Connecticut Regiment. It is said that one day Howe heard a soldier grumbling because he had not been paid yet. Howe went to the paymaster, asked him how much money was needed to pay the whole regiment, and wrote him a check for $31,000!

➤ **Why was Elias Howe so generous?** *(He remembered how it felt to be poor; he did not want others to go through what he had been through.)* (BATs: 5a Love, 5b Giving)

Text Discussion, page 133

➤ Notice the picture of the young man on page 133.

His name is Jan Matzeliger *(măt′ zə lī′ gər)*. Matzeliger was an immigrant from a South American country called Suriname *(sü′ rē nä′ mə)*.

➤ **Read page 133 to learn about the machine he invented to do a special type of sewing.**

➤ **What was Matzeliger's special type of sewing called?** *(lasting)*

➤ **What does *lasting* mean?** *(sewing the upper portion of a shoe to the sole)*

The shoe factory where Matzeliger worked had many people who spent the whole day lasting shoes by hand. All of the other jobs in the factory were done by machines, so often the other factory workers would be slowed down by the lasters who could not finish their jobs as quickly.

Many people in the factory laughed at Jan Matzeliger when he said that he could make a lasting machine.

➤ **Do you think Jan Matzeliger was discouraged by their jokes about him?**

Matzeliger was determined to make a lasting machine, and nothing others said discouraged him. (BAT: 2d Goal setting) Matzeliger was also a Christian, and the love and support of his friends at church helped to keep him going in his work. (BATs: 5a Love, 5d Communication, 5e Friendliness)

Matzeliger rented the room over the West Lynn Mission so that he could work in secret.

➤ **Why would he want to keep his ideas for the invention a secret?** *(because others might want to steal his ideas and copy them)*

➤ **What was Jan Matzeliger's machine able to do on the day that it was tested?** *(It lasted seventy-five pairs of ladies' shoes perfectly.)*

In a typical ten-hour day, Matzeliger's lasting machine could last seven hundred pairs of shoes, while hand lasters could finish only about fifty pairs a day. Matzeliger's idea quickly spread to other countries, and soon shoemakers all over the world were using his lasting machine.

Jan Matzeliger used the money he earned from his machine to help the poor and to help the young people at his church. He even paid for one young man to attend college and seminary to become a preacher. (BAT: 5b Giving)

➤ **Do you think the Lord was pleased with the way Jan Matzeliger used his money?**

Evaluating the Lesson

Notebook Activity, page 57

➤ Read the instructions on Notebook page 57.
➤ Complete the page.

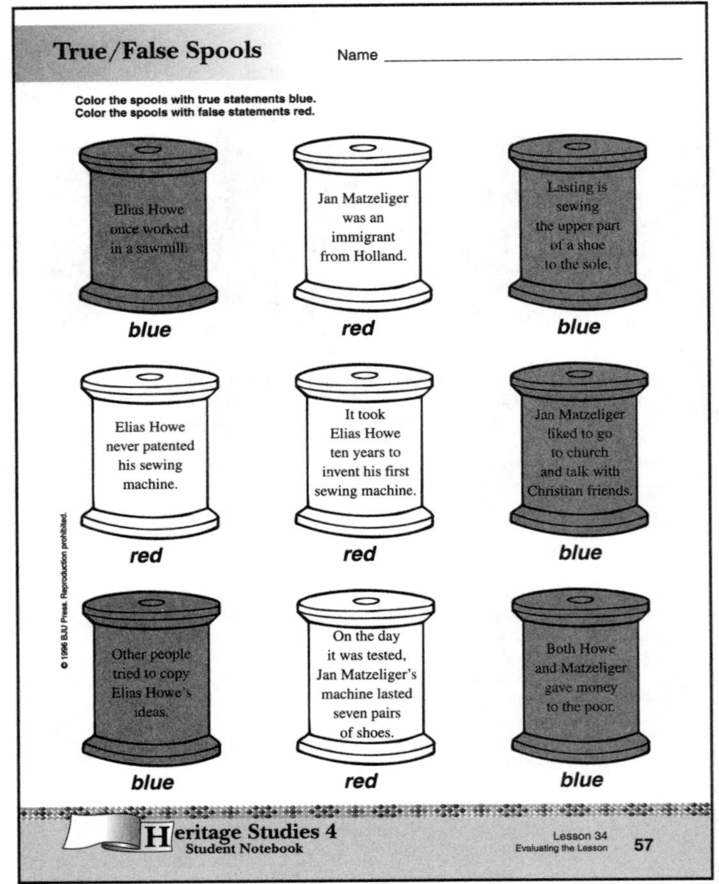

True/False Spools Name ______________________

Color the spools with true statements blue.
Color the spools with false statements red.

Elias Howe once worked in a sawmill. — *blue*

Jan Matzeliger was an immigrant from Holland. — *red*

Lasting is sewing the upper part of a shoe to the sole. — *blue*

Elias Howe never patented his sewing machine. — *red*

It took Elias Howe ten years to invent his first sewing machine. — *red*

Jan Matzeliger liked to go to church and talk with Christian friends. — *blue*

Other people tried to copy Elias Howe's ideas. — *blue*

On the day it was tested, Jan Matzeliger's machine lasted seven pairs of shoes. — *red*

Both Howe and Matzeliger gave money to the poor. — *blue*

Going Beyond

Enrichment

If there is a shoe factory or a shoe repair shop in your area, plan a visit for you and your child.

Additional Teacher Information

Although Elias Howe is greatly respected for his invention of the sewing machine, his work ethic and treatment of his family were less than admirable. Before he started work on the sewing machine, his employment was sporadic because he seemed to feel he should make suggestions to his employers rather than follow their orders. For many years after Howe quit formal work to experiment with the sewing machine, his wife had to take on sewing jobs for other people to support the family. Night after night Howe would sit and watch her hands as she worked, trying to discover a way he could copy her movements with a machine. When he finally finished his machine and secured a job in England, his family traveled across the sea with high hopes. But eight months later, when the job ended after Howe's quarrel with his employer, the family actually wandered the streets of England, homeless. Howe built another sewing machine and sold it to buy boat fare for his family to return to Boston. A few months later he pawned everything he owned and found passage on an emigrant ship as a cook. When he arrived in New York City, he learned that his wife was dying. He borrowed money to go to her bedside in Boston and arrived just before she passed away. His sympathy for the poor throughout the rest of his life was probably due to the suffering he and his own family had undergone in their days of poverty.

Jan Matzeliger was the son of a white Dutch father and a black West African mother. The color of his skin made it hard for him to be accepted in Philadelphia in the 1870s. The African American church was at first the only place that welcomed him. It is probable that Matzeliger accepted Christ while attending this church. When he moved to Lynn, Massachusetts, the capital of shoemaking, he had to knock on doors for many days before he could get work in a shoe factory. He was an active member of the North Congregational Church in Lynn, where he soon became a Sunday school teacher and leader of the young people's group. There the encouragement of the Bible studies and of his friends gave him courage to keep working on his machine in spite of ridicule and opposition. This brave man's lasting machine was adopted all over the world and revolutionized the shoe industry. When Matzeliger died of tuberculosis in 1889, he left North Church a third of his stock in the company that made his lasting machines.

LESSON 35
For Home and Office

Text, pages 134-37
Notebook, page 58

Preview

Main Ideas

- Christopher Sholes invented the typewriter.
- Thomas Alva Edison brought electricity into the home and invented such items as the phonograph and the light bulb.

Objective

- Use clues to fill in blanks with words about inventions

Materials

No additional materials needed.

The Enrichment section suggests a trip to an office to observe inventions used there. You may prefer to use that activity as an introduction to this lesson.

Day 1

Lesson

Introducing the Lesson

Discussion

➤ Get a pencil and a sheet of paper.
➤ Listen as I tell what I did this morning from the time I got up until we began school. (*NOTE*: Focus on details such as turning off the alarm clock, turning on the light, putting toothpaste on your toothbrush, and so on.)
➤ As I tell my story, write down names of any inventions that I mention.
➤ **Which of the inventions listed are most common in people's homes?**

If you are teaching more than one child, you may ask a child to tell about his morning while the others write down the inventions used.

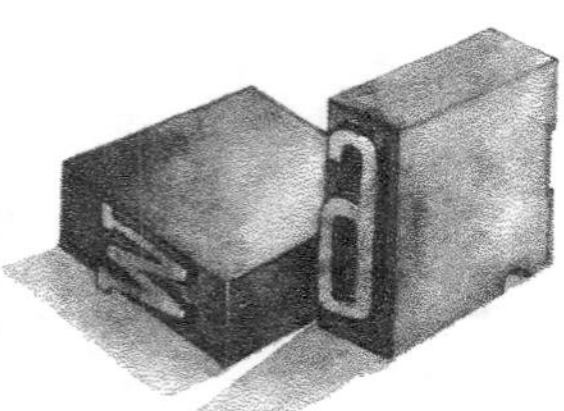

A Machine for the Office

Do you know someone who works in an office? He may use Christopher Sholes's invention. Since 1872, it has made the job of many office workers easier. Christopher called his machine a *Type-Writer.*

Christopher grew up around printing presses and cases of type. His older brother owned a printing shop. When Christopher was fourteen years old, he became a printer's apprentice. He learned his job quickly. When he was eighteen, he went to work for his brother's newspaper.

Before a machine could set type in 1886, a compositor picked each letter from a type case.

During the next twenty years, Sholes worked in many printing shops. In the last of these shops, Sholes printed a newspaper. He also made sure that blank books, tickets, and other small items were printed. Each thing the shop printed needed to be stamped with a number. It was slow work, and it was easy to make mistakes. Sholes and a friend decided to make a machine to print the numbers.

134

Samuel Clemens (Mark Twain) was the first author to type his manuscript. The book was Life on the Mississippi. He used a machine similar to the one shown below.

When Sholes finished his numbering machine, it worked just as he had planned. He showed his invention to a friend. "Chris," he said, "if you can make a machine to print numbers, why can't you make one to print letters and words too?" Sholes thought it was a good idea. So he set to work on a second invention.

Look at one of Sholes's typewriters. What do you think it looks like? The machine printed only capital letters. But people liked the clear, neat pages the typewriter printed. Sholes kept working.

He found a friend who was willing to try the typewriter in his office. Whenever he found a problem with the machine, he brought it back to Sholes. Each time, Sholes fixed the problem by making a new and better typewriter. He made more than fifty typewriters before he had a machine that worked perfectly.

Before Christopher Sholes built his typewriter, the office was a man's place. Letters and notes and forms were slowly written by hand. With the typewriter came big changes. Letters were written quickly and neatly. And ladies were hired to work the new machine. Today there are as many women as men who work in offices. Some still use a machine like Christopher Sholes's.

William Burt made an attempt at a typewriter in 1829. But Sholes and his friends Carlos Glidden and Samuel Soulé developed the model that is considered standard. The three sold out to the Remington Company, which manufactured guns and sewing machines before making the first commercial typewriter.

135

Teaching the Lesson

Text Discussion, page 134

- ➤ **Read page 134 to learn of an important invention for the office.**
- ➤ **What was the invention and who invented it?** *(the typewriter; Christopher Sholes)*
- ➤ **What trade did Christopher Sholes become interested in as a young boy?** *(printing)*
- ➤ **Where did Sholes go to work when he turned eighteen?** *(at his brother's newspaper)*

For the next twenty years of his life, Sholes worked as an editor for many different newspapers and was also the boss at several pressrooms.

- ➤ **What kind of machine did Christopher Sholes and his friend want to make?** *(a machine to print numbers on the shop's products)*
- ➤ **What problems would such a machine solve?** *(Stamping numbers by hand was slow, and it was easy to make mistakes.)*

Text Discussion, page 135

- ➤ **Read the first two paragraphs on page 135 to learn whether Sholes's machine worked.** *(yes)*
- ➤ **What idea did Christopher Sholes's friend have when he saw how well Sholes had done with his machine?** *(He told him he should design a machine that would print letters and words also.)*

This friend's name was Carlos Glidden. Eventually Glidden invented an important farming machine that would replace the plow. He helped Sholes and another man work on the typewriting machine.

- ➤ **Do you think it would be easier to work on an invention as a team or as an individual?**
- ➤ Name some good things about working as a team. *(Answers will vary but might include that work would go faster, that each person could share helpful ideas the others might not have thought about, and that they could all encourage each other to keep trying when things go wrong.)* (BATs: 2b Servanthood, 2e Work)
- ➤ Notice the picture of the finished typewriter on page 135. **What was the disadvantage of this typewriter?** *(It printed in only capital letters.)*

➤ **Read the last two paragraphs on page 135 to find out how Christopher Sholes's friend helped him.** *(He tried the typewriter out in his office and told Sholes about the problems he found while using it.)*

Sometimes Sholes felt a little angry that his friend hardly ever had anything good to say about the typewriter.

➤ **Did the criticisms make Sholes want to give up improving his typewriter?** *(no)*

➤ **What did Christopher Sholes do each time his friend pointed out a new problem?** *(He made a new and better typewriter.)*

Sholes listened to the criticism of his friend, even though it sometimes made him feel angry inside, and he used the criticism to help him improve his machine. (BAT: 3c Emotional control)

➤ **How did Sholes feel toward that friend when his typewriter was all finished?** *(grateful, happy)* (BAT: 5a Love)

➤ **What kinds of changes did Christopher Sholes's machine bring to offices?** *(Letters were written quickly and neatly; ladies came to work as typists in offices.)*

The letter arrangement that Christopher used on his typewriter is the one used today on typewriters and computer keyboards.

Day 2

Text Discussion, page 136

➤ **Read page 136 to learn how another famous inventor became interested in inventing.** *(He tried out experiments in his basement from a book his parents gave him.)*

➤ **What was this inventor's name?** *(Thomas Alva Edison)*

Edison patented 1,093 inventions, more than anyone else in history.

➤ **What did Thomas Edison promise to do?** *(to build a little invention every ten days and a big one every six months)*

➤ **Where did Edison go to school?** *(at home)*

From his earliest days, Thomas Alva Edison, or Al as he was called, was a curious boy. Listen as I read a story from his childhood.

> When Al was five years old, he came to his mother with a puzzled frown on his face. "Mother, why does the goose squat on her eggs?"
>
> "To keep them warm." Mother was busy taking bread from the oven.
>
> "Why does the goose want to keep her eggs warm?"

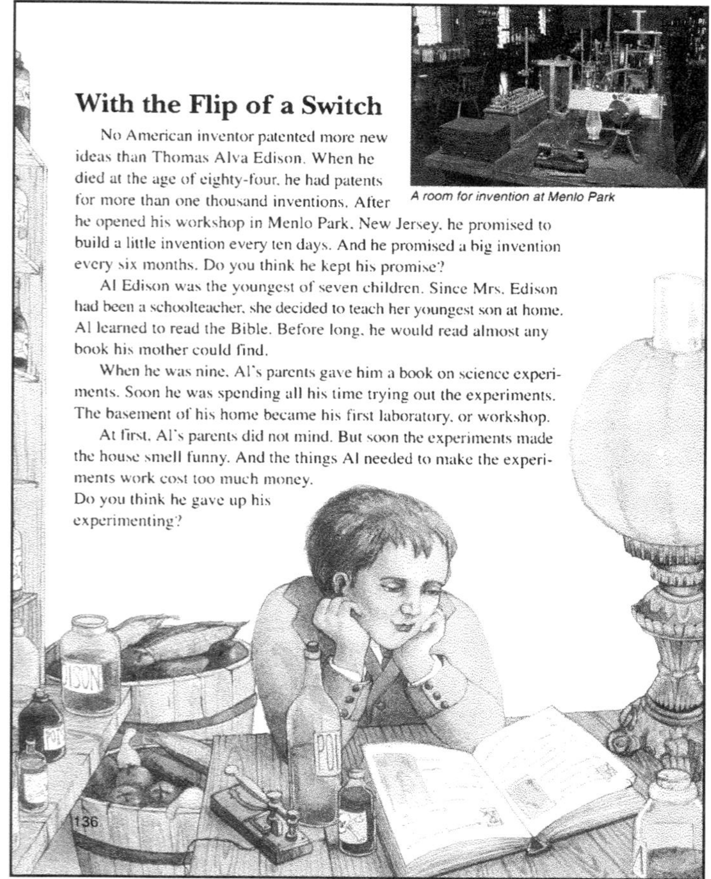

With the Flip of a Switch

No American inventor patented more new ideas than Thomas Alva Edison. When he died at the age of eighty-four, he had patents for more than one thousand inventions. After he opened his workshop in Menlo Park, New Jersey, he promised to build a little invention every ten days. And he promised a big invention every six months. Do you think he kept his promise?

Al Edison was the youngest of seven children. Since Mrs. Edison had been a schoolteacher, she decided to teach her youngest son at home. Al learned to read the Bible. Before long, he would read almost any book his mother could find.

When he was nine, Al's parents gave him a book on science experiments. Soon he was spending all his time trying out the experiments. The basement of his home became his first laboratory, or workshop.

At first, Al's parents did not mind. But soon the experiments made the house smell funny. And the things Al needed to make the experiments work cost too much money. Do you think he gave up his experimenting?

A room for invention at Menlo Park

136

> "So that they will hatch." Mother placed the last loaf pan on the cooling rack and began setting the table for supper.
>
> Al watched her quietly for a moment. "Mother, what does *hatch* mean?"
>
> "That's when the baby geese come out of their shells."
>
> "Oh." Al quickly turned and left the room.
>
> Mother began to grow worried when Al did not return for supper. She and Father searched the entire house and yard. "Where could he be?" she wondered.
>
> "I'll go to the neighbors and ask if they've seen him today," said Father. Over an hour later, Al's father found him. He was sitting on a pile of goose eggs and chicken eggs in the neighbor's barn!

➤ **What did Edison's parents think about having Al's laboratory in the house?** *(It made the whole house smell funny, and the things he used in his experiments cost too much money.)*

Edison and his phonograph

He did not. Al found a job selling newspapers and sandwiches on a train. He set up a new laboratory in one of the train cars.

Between the ages of twelve and twenty-two, Edison had many different jobs. Each new job gave him just a bit more money to spend on his experiments. And his experiments gave him ideas for new inventions. Soon he began building and trying out his ideas.

The *phonograph*, or record player, finished in 1877, was one of Edison's first inventions. Two years later he invented the electric light bulb, and later he found a way to bring electricity into people's homes. Soon other inventors were finding ways to use electricity too. How many things that need electricity have you used today?

Edison and his movie camera

Edison often worked more than one hundred hours a week on his inventions. About how many hours did he work each day? Edison did not work hard so that he would become rich. He wanted to be the best inventor and to make the most inventions. Did he reach his goal?

137

Invention Puzzle

Name ______________________

Fill in the acrostic below with the answers to the clues given. The letters in the boxes will spell out something that has become common in our homes.

1. the last name of the man who invented the typewriter
2. Thomas ______ Edison
3. Edison's factory was in ______ Park, New Jersey.
4. the kind of letters the first typewriter printed
5. the trade Christopher Sholes learned as a young boy
6. a scientific workshop
7. Typewriters brought these people into the office.
8. Sholes learned to accept his friend's ______ of his machine.
9. place where Edison worked and set up his second laboratory
10. Edison had more of these than anyone else.
11. number of typewriters Sholes built before making a perfect one

	Before box	Box	After box
1.	S H O L	E	S
2.	A	L	V A
3.	M	E	N L O
4.		C	A P I T A L
5.	P R I N	T	I N G
6.	L A B O	R	A T O R Y
7.	L A D	I	E S
8.	C R I T I	C	I S M
9.	T R A	I	N
10.	P A	T	E N T S
11.	F I F T	Y	

Heritage Studies 4 Student Notebook — Lesson 35 Evaluating the Lesson 58

Text Discussion, page 137

- ➤ **Read page 137 to find out whether Thomas Alva Edison gave up his experimenting.** *(no)*
- ➤ **How did Al honor his parents' wishes but still keep experimenting?** *(He set up a new laboratory in a train car.)* (BATs: 2a Authority, 2d Goal setting)

Edison then worked in a number of different places as a telegraph operator.

- ➤ **How did he spend the money he earned?** *(on experiments)*
- ➤ Name some things that Edison invented. *(the phonograph, the electric light bulb, a way to bring electricity into people's homes, etc.)*
- ➤ Name the things that you have used today that need electricity to work. *(Answers will vary but might include lamps, alarm clock, hair dryer, radio, television, refrigerator, and microwave oven.)*

Some other famous inventions of Thomas Alva Edison are the microphone and the motion-picture projector.

Most adults who work at full-time jobs work about forty hours a week, and the average time worked each day is eight hours.

- ➤ **How many hours a week did Edison work on his inventions?** *(one hundred)*
- ➤ Calculate how many hours a day this would be if Edison worked five days a week. *(twenty)*
- ➤ **Do you think Edison might have worked on Saturdays too?** *(yes)*
- ➤ **What was Edison's goal?** *(to be the best inventor and make the most inventions)*
- ➤ **Did Thomas Edison reach his goal?** *(Yes, he holds the record number of patents.)* (BAT: 2d Goal setting)

Evaluating the Lesson

Notebook Activity, page 58

- ➤ Read the instructions on Notebook page 58.
- ➤ Complete the page.

Going Beyond

Enrichment

Arrange a time for your child to visit an office. Instruct him to take along paper and pencil. As he observes the activity going on in the office, he should write down the names of inventions that he sees being used.

Additional Teacher Information

Christopher Sholes received financial aid from a businessman named James Densmore. Densmore became a friend to Sholes as well as a business advisor. He also had a share in Sholes's patent. When the Remington factory offered to buy the patent rights from Sholes and Densmore, Sholes eagerly sold his share for twelve thousand dollars. Densmore chose to keep his rights and be paid on a royalty basis. The sales of the typewriter brought him one and a half million dollars during the remainder of his life. Meanwhile Sholes finished his life quietly but comfortably, the father of ten children. He died of tuberculosis in 1890.

Thomas Alva Edison was given the nickname "Al" as a child. He was a difficult child to rear because of his stubbornness and his love of playing pranks. At the age of six he set fire to his father's barn out of curiosity "to see what would happen." For this his father gave him a thrashing in front of the townspeople, a punishment that Edison never forgot. During his later life, he became known as the Wizard of Menlo Park. Menlo Park in New Jersey was the first factory built for the sole purpose of making inventions. Edison had three children by his first wife, Mary Stilwell, and shortly after her death, he married eighteen-year-old Mina Miller, who also bore him three children. He was too engrossed in his inventions to spare much time for his family, yet one son inherited some of his skill and became a mathematical physicist. During World War I, Edison predicted that one day there would "spring from the brain of Science a machine so fearful in its potentiality . . . that even man . . . will be appalled." The atomic bombs of today seem to fulfill this great American scientist's prediction.

Lesson 36
What Inventors Are Made Of

Text, pages 138-42
Notebook, page 59

Preview

Main Ideas

- Inventors have curiosity, confidence, imagination, and persistence.
- George Washington Carver was an important inventor in the field of botany.

Objectives

- Construct a time line of important inventions since 1750
- Read a cross-sectional diagram comparing a home from 1800 to a home from 1900
- Read sentences about various inventors and determine what quality each illustrates

Materials

- A ruler
- A large piece of paper
- Scrap paper
- Some books about inventions (from the library or your personal collection)*

Notes

If your child has not already done so, he should be prepared to present his completed invention.

The board game Patent Path (Appendix, pages A48-A52) is introduced in the Enrichment section. If you choose to use the game, take the following steps to prepare the game pieces.

First, to assemble the **game board,** make one copy of each game board sheet and affix the copies side by side to the inside of a manila file folder. (*NOTE:* You will need to trim the inside edges of the pages to make the game board path line up.) You may want to add color with colored pencils or felt-tip pens before laminating the board or covering it with Con-Tact paper.

Next, make one copy of both sheets of **game cards** (the front sheet and the back sheet). You may copy them front and back or glue the two sheets together. Laminate or cover with Con-Tact paper. Cut the cards apart.

Finally, make one copy of the **spinner** sheet. Affix the copy to a stiff backing. After laminating, cut out the numbered square and the arrow. Place the straight end of

◆ LEARNING HOW ◆

To Construct a Time Line

1. You will need a ruler, a pencil, a large piece of paper, some scrap paper, crayons, and some books about inventions.
2. Draw a straight line across the middle of your large piece of paper. Use the ruler to divide the line into small sections. Will each section on your time line stand for one year, five years, or ten years? Beginning with 1750, mark the years on your time line.
3. Look through your textbook to find inventions. Write the name of the inventors and the names and years of the inventions on your scrap paper. Then add the inventions to your time line. If you like, draw a picture for each invention.
4. Find out about other important or unusual inventions. Add them to your time line. How many different things were invented during the years your time line shows? Why are time lines useful?

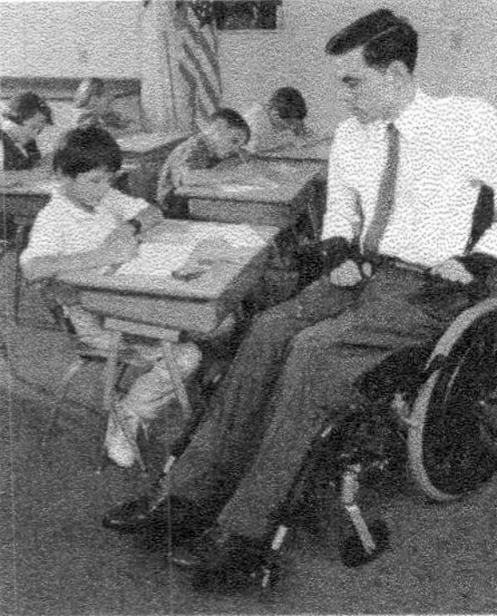

138

Few inventions work perfectly the first time. Do you think this one will?

What Makes a Good Inventor?

Many inventors are adults. But children can be inventors too. Thomas Alva Edison built his first invention when he was just sixteen years old. And George Washington Carver began working with plants before he was ten. People of all ages have received patents for their ideas. Young or old, a good inventor needs to have four things. Do any of the words describe you?

Inventors have *curiosity*. When they do not understand how or why something works, they ask questions. They study and experiment until they figure it out. Do you like to figure out how things work?

Good inventors should have *confidence*. A person who has confidence is sure of himself and his ideas. He does not give up when people tell him his invention will not work. He keeps looking for someone who likes his idea. Did any of the famous inventors you have read about need confidence?

139

the arrow over the center of the numbered square. Add an adhesive paper reinforcement to the arrow for extra durability around the hole. Then push the brad through to assemble the spinner. To let the arrow spin freely, bend the prongs of the brad approximately $\frac{1}{8}$" from the head. Tape the prongs to the back of the square to keep the brad from spinning with the arrow. For additional spinning ease, bend the square slightly away from the arrow. The square will curve slightly downward, and the arrow will spin freely.

Put the spinner, game cards, and game markers (buttons in eight different colors) in a resealable plastic bag or an envelope. Attach the bag or envelope to the back of the game board folder.

Day 1

Lesson

Introducing the Lesson

Learning How Activity, page 138

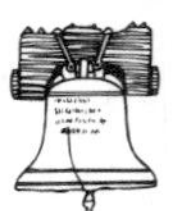

You may prefer to adapt the following activity by having your child put the information and pictures on separate cards and add them to the Snapshots TimeLine.

➤ **Read the directions given on page 138.**

The time line should begin in 1750 and should extend at least to 1880.

➤ Consider the size of your paper and the years covered. **How many years do you think each section should represent?**

Caution your child that since the time line must encompass more than one hundred years, it would be wise to make each section stand for more than one year. He should include all the inventions studied in this chapter and any others that he finds interesting.

➤ Display the finished time line somewhere in the schoolroom.

Day 2

Teaching the Lesson

Text Discussion, page 139

➤ **What character qualities do you think all the inventors in this chapter had in common?**

➤ **Read page 139 to find out two of the qualities of a good inventor.** *(curiosity and confidence)*

➤ **Which inventors that we studied had curiosity?** *(Answers will vary; accept all answers.)*

➤ **Which inventor demonstrated his curiosity in a funny way as a child?** *(Thomas Edison—when he sat on the eggs)*

Curiosity is a good quality to have. A good inventor needs to keep asking questions about things he does not understand. We too can learn new things by asking questions. It is important to be patient when younger brothers and sisters ask questions. (BAT: 5d Communication)

➤ **Which inventor that we have studied needed confidence?** *(James Watt)*

➤ Name the friend who helped build up Watt's confidence in himself. *(Matthew Boulton)*

Confidence is a good quality if we do not have too much of it.

➤ **What is a person with too much confidence like?** *(proud, boastful)*

> The Lord wants Christians to have a healthy confidence in the abilities He has given them, but He does not want Christians to be proud and think that they are better than others who do not have the same abilities. (BATs: 3a Self-concept, 7e Humility)

Text Discussion, page 140

➤ **Read page 140 to learn about a man people called the "plant doctor."**

➤ **How did George Washington Carver become interested in the study of plants?** *(He was often sick as a child and could not help with the hard jobs on the farm, but he loved to care for plants.)*

➤ Find the first sentence of the third paragraph: "George wanted to learn more." **Which quality of an inventor does this statement show about George?** *(He had curiosity.)*

➤ **How old was George when he left home to go to school?** *(twelve)*

There was a school near George's home, but African Americans were not allowed to go there. The nearest school he could go to was eight miles away. George lived with an older couple and did jobs for them to earn his room and board while he attended school.

Over the next fifteen years, George Carver moved from place to place, doing odd jobs to earn his living and trying to find schools where he could learn the things he wanted to know.

➤ **What do these incidents tell us about Carver?** *(Answers will vary; he was determined to get his education; he was not easily discouraged; he was a goal setter; he was diligent; he was thrifty with his money; etc.)* (BATs: 2c Faithfulness, 2d Goal setting, 2e Work, 4a Sowing and reaping)

◆ FAMOUS PEOPLE ◆

George Washington Carver
About 1864-1943

No one knows for sure exactly when George Washington Carver was born. His mother was a slave. When she was kidnapped near the end of the Civil War, her owners took the baby George and raised him as their son.

George Washington Carver

Young George was not a healthy child. He could not help with the hard jobs on the farm. But he loved to care for plants, and he learned to tell sick plants from strong ones. He also learned what things would make a plant stronger. Soon neighbors called George the "plant doctor."

George wanted to learn more. To learn, he needed to go to school. So when he was twelve, he left his home with the Carvers. He worked hard at his studies. And he worked hard to earn money to pay for the things he needed. It took many years for George to finish school. When he did, he knew he wanted to share the things he had learned.

George Carver began teaching at the Tuskegee Institute, a school for African Americans. While teaching the southern farmers about plants, Carver found out that the cotton plant was ruining the soil. He tried to get the farmers to grow other plants. But other plants would not bring as much money to the farmers as cotton could.

So Carver began experimenting. He invented 325 ways to use the peanut, from peanut butter to pickles to ink. He found 118 uses for the sweet potato. And he found many ways to use cowpeas as well. Soon farmers were planting peanuts, sweet potatoes, and cowpeas. And they were selling them and making money. Even today these crops are important to southern farmers.

140

➤ **What did George Carver do at Tuskegee Institute?** *(taught African Americans)*

Carver started a department of agriculture at the college and conducted many experiments with plants to help farmers grow better crops.

➤ **What important thing did Carver learn about cotton?** *(It was ruining the soil.)*

At the time, southern farmers did not know of any other plants they could grow in their type of soil.

➤ **What did George Carver do to help them solve this problem?** *(He experimented with different plants and found new ways to use the peanut, the sweet potato, and cowpeas. He encouraged some southern farmers to start growing these plants instead of cotton.)*

➤ **What kinds of things did Carver produce from the peanut?** *(peanut butter, pickles, and ink)*

➤ **What happened when the farmers took Carver's advice and planted these new crops?** *(They were able to sell the crops and make money from them.)*

➤ **Are farmers still growing these crops today?** *(yes)*

An inventor needs *imagination* too. It takes an imaginative inventor to think of new ways of doing things. Sometimes an inventor's imagination helps him to think of a new use for something old. Do you know anyone who uses his imagination?

The most important thing an inventor needs is *persistence*. Most times it takes more than one try to solve a problem. An inventor cannot give up if his first idea does not work. He must keep trying until he finds the best solution to his problem. Thomas Edison tried 9,990 different experiments before he made an electric light bulb that worked well. He said, "Genius is 99 percent perspiration and 1 percent inspiration." What do you think he meant?

Edison's largest experimental light bulb

Some of Edison's nearly 10,000 attempts at a good light bulb

141

Look at the two houses below. One shows how a house would have looked in colonial times. Can you tell which one? The other picture shows a house in 1900. How many new inventions can you see in the 1900 house? Can you think of anything in your house today that you do not see in either of these houses?

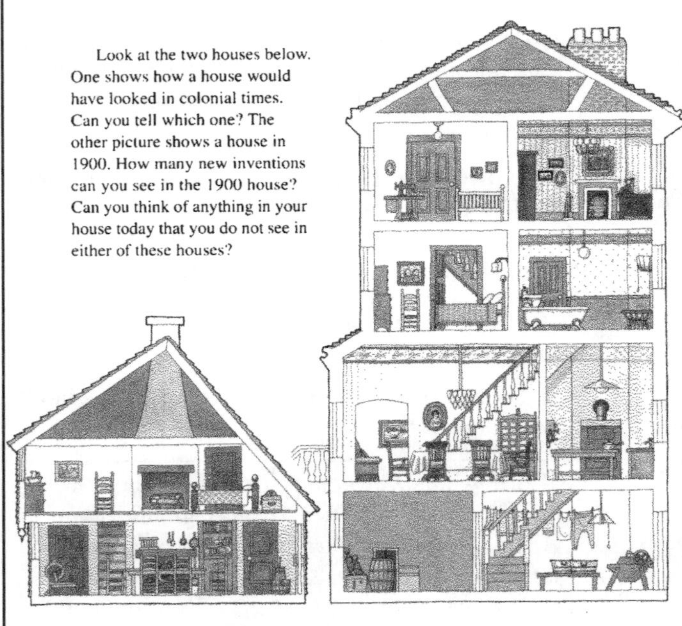

Many inventions have been built during the last two hundred years. Everyday, you use inventions that your great-grandparents could not have imagined. What inventions might your grandchildren and great-grandchildren be using seventy-five years from now? How many of those new things will have been invented by you?

142

Text Discussion, pages 141-42

- ➤ **Read page 141 to find out two more qualities of an inventor.** *(imagination and persistence)*
- ➤ **What does it mean to be *imaginative?*** *(Answers will vary but should include finding new ways of doing things or finding new uses for old things.)*
- ➤ **What does it mean to be *persistent?*** *(Answers will vary but should include not giving up easily or trying until the best solution to a problem is found.)*
- ➤ **Which inventor is described as being persistent?** *(Thomas Edison)*
- ➤ **Read aloud the quotation by Edison about genius.**
- ➤ **What do you think this quotation means?**

More great things are accomplished by people who work hard and refuse to give up than by people who have great talent or mental ability but do not work hard. (*NOTE*: If time allows, direct a discussion of how Edison's quotation might apply to schoolwork.)

- ➤ **Read page 142, following the directions given.**
- ➤ List the inventions you see in the 1800 house and the inventions in the 1900 house.

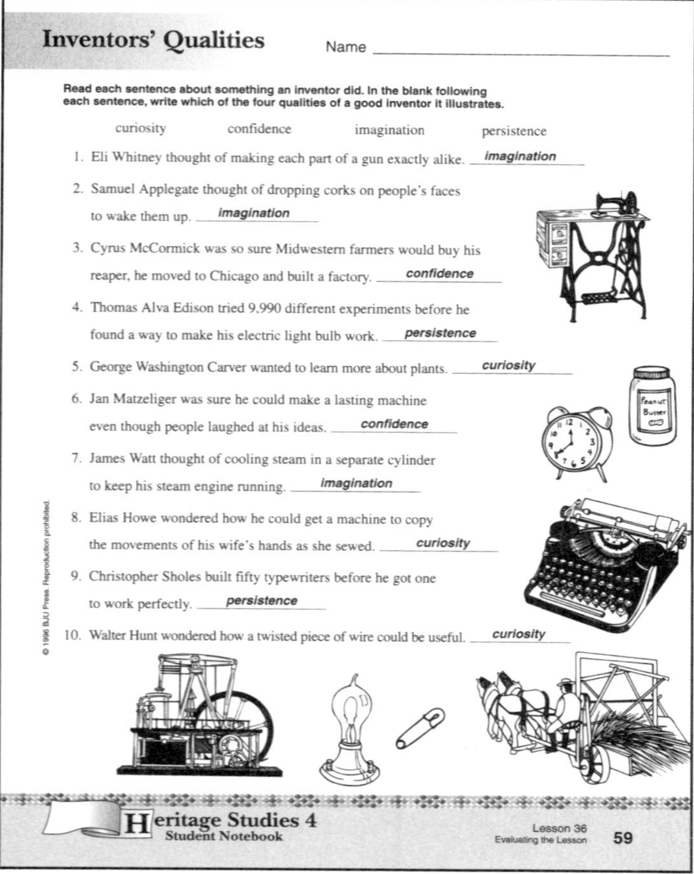

Inventors' Qualities Name ____________________

Read each sentence about something an inventor did. In the blank following each sentence, write which of the four qualities of a good inventor it illustrates.

curiosity confidence imagination persistence

1. Eli Whitney thought of making each part of a gun exactly alike. *imagination*
2. Samuel Applegate thought of dropping corks on people's faces to wake them up. *imagination*
3. Cyrus McCormick was so sure Midwestern farmers would buy his reaper, he moved to Chicago and built a factory. *confidence*
4. Thomas Alva Edison tried 9,990 different experiments before he found a way to make his electric light bulb work. *persistence*
5. George Washington Carver wanted to learn more about plants. *curiosity*
6. Jan Matzeliger was sure he could make a lasting machine even though people laughed at his ideas. *confidence*
7. James Watt thought of cooling steam in a separate cylinder to keep his steam engine running. *imagination*
8. Elias Howe wondered how he could get a machine to copy the movements of his wife's hands as she sewed. *curiosity*
9. Christopher Sholes built fifty typewriters before he got one to work perfectly. *persistence*
10. Walter Hunt wondered how a twisted piece of wire could be useful. *curiosity*

Heritage Studies 4 Student Notebook — Lesson 36 Evaluating the Lesson — 59

Evaluating the Lesson

Notebook Activity, page 59

- ➤ Read the instructions on Notebook page 59.
- ➤ Complete the page.

Going Beyond

Enrichment

Set up the board game Patent Path. Explain to your child that this game will help him to review the inventors he has studied as well as provide insight into an inventor's life. You may become one of the players, or he may test the knowledge of other members in his family.

Show the game board, calling attention to the words or pictures on each space. Point out that some spaces contain instructions to move forward or backward on the game board or to spin again. Some spaces give no instructions but have pictures. Call special attention to the six spaces throughout the board that contain pictures of inventors he has studied. Explain that these spaces are called Famous Inventor spaces. The object of the game is to see which player will reach the *Finish* space first.

Show the game cards. The sixteen Famous Inventor cards ask questions about the inventors. These cards are for use anytime a player lands on a Famous Inventor space on the game board.

Show the spinner and demonstrate how to spin it correctly. The numbers on the spinner will indicate the number of spaces a player may move on each turn.

Show the buttons to be used as game markers. Each player will have one button to move around the game board.

Give directions for playing the game. Play begins with all the buttons on *Start* and the cards placed face-down. Each player spins the spinner. The player spinning the highest number goes first. That player spins again and moves his button the number of spaces indicated. The player must follow any instructions on each space on which he lands. If a player lands on a Famous Inventor space, another player selects the top Famous Inventor card from the pile and asks him the question printed on it. If the player answers correctly, he may spin again. If he answers incorrectly, he must leave his marker there until his next turn. If a player lands on a space with a picture of an invention, he simply leaves his marker there until his next turn. The next player then spins and follows any instructions on the space on which he lands. Play continues until one player reaches the *Finish* space. (*NOTE:* The exact number is *not* needed to land on the *Finish* space.)

Additional Teacher Information

George Washington Carver grew up in southwest Missouri just after the American Civil War had ended. Racial prejudice against black people was strong throughout his younger life, and he found few schools that would accept him as a student. Through the influence of a college art teacher, he entered Iowa State University in 1891 and soon became a popular figure on campus. One of his professors called him "the ablest student" that the school had. In 1896 he finished his studies as a graduate assistant in the field of botany. When Booker T. Washington asked him to join the faculty of Tuskegee Institute, Carver found the decision a hard one to make. Although his career as a professor at Iowa State appeared promising, his desire to benefit those of his own race won out. He went to Tuskegee and remained there for the rest of his life. A fervent Christian, Carver believed that God has provided in nature all that man needs for food, and he sought to teach others how to utilize God's gifts to their fullest. Upon his death in 1943, he left his entire estate to a research foundation in which African American young people could do advanced studies in the subjects of chemistry, botany, and agronomy.

7 Lessons 37-42

In the Market

This chapter introduces your child to market economies, supply and demand, and needs versus wants. Throughout the lessons, he will see the connections among all the facets of the market, including human desires and expectations. The chapter ends with a comparison of temporal and eternal values.

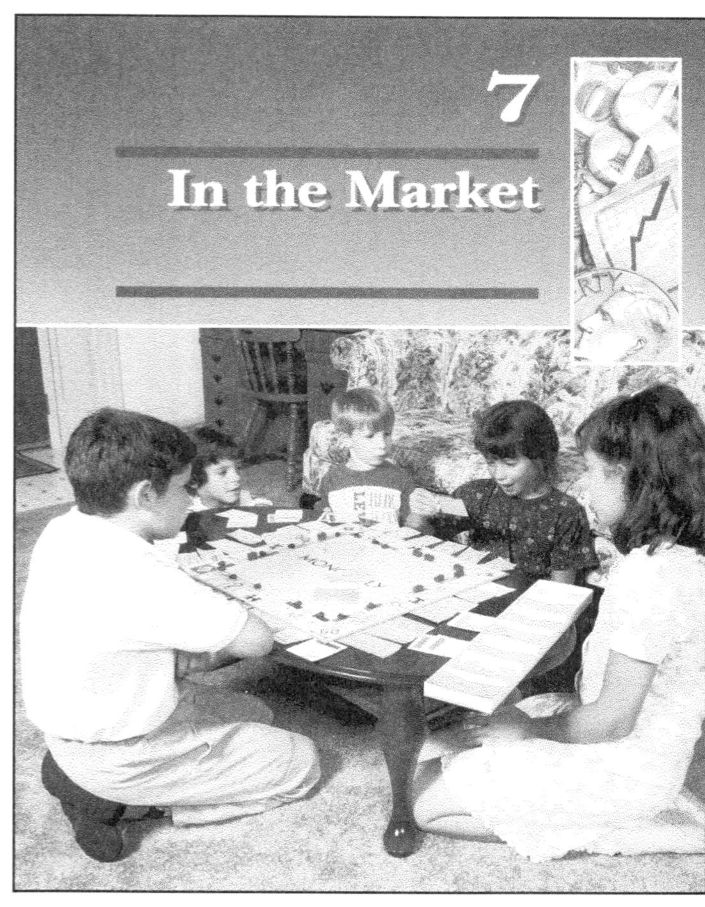

Materials

The following materials must be obtained or prepared before the presentation of the lesson. These items are labeled with an asterisk (*) in each lesson and in the Materials List in the Supplement. For further information see the individual lessons.

- 2 pieces of candy (Lesson 37)
- Several quarters (Lesson 37)
- Appendix, page A53 (Lesson 37)
- A Monopoly game (Lessons 37-38)
- An expensive-looking necklace (Lesson 39)
- Appendix, page A56 (Lesson 40)
- A candy bar (Lesson 40)
- Appendix, pages A58-A59 (Lesson 41)
- A magazine with advertisements (Lesson 42)
- Appendix, page A62 (Lesson 42)

LESSON 37
Buying and Selling

Text, pages 144-45
Notebook, page 60

Preview

Main Ideas

- Bartering and using a monetary system are two types of trade.
- An amount that is more than the original cost of something is a *profit*.
- The way a country handles its money and resources is called its *economy*.
- Every society has an economic system through which goods and services are produced and distributed.
- People work at different kinds of jobs.
- People are interdependent.
- A good economist uses time, money, and resources wisely.

Objectives

- Identify and evaluate types of trade
- Choose the best way to use resources and money
- Complete an evaluation of the Proverbs 31 woman as an economist

Materials

- 5 stones, beans, or buttons
- 2 pieces of candy*
- Several quarters*
- Several stickers
- A Monopoly game*
- Appendix, page A53: Bookmarks*
- A Bible

Day 1

Lesson

Introducing the Lesson

Demonstration

➤ *Give your child the stones, beans, or buttons. Display the candy.*

➤ You may "purchase" two pieces of candy by using your items to bargain with me.

Do not accept the first offer your child makes for the candy. You want your child to see that it takes longer and is not as easy to trade with items as it is with money. If you are teaching more than one child, you may allow trading between the children as well.

➤ *Give your child the quarters. Display the stickers.*

➤ You may purchase a sticker for a quarter. **How many stickers would you like to buy?**

Discussion

➤ What is the meaning of the word ***trade?*** *(exchange or swap)* The candy and stickers were both traded.

➤ **Which method of trade did you like best and why?**

Long ago people traded or exchanged goods or services directly without money. This method of trade is called ***bartering.*** It takes much time and limits the items to fewer people.

➤ **Which item did you get through bartering?** *(candy)*

➤ **How are goods and services today mainly traded?** *(with money)*

This method of trade is called a ***monetary system.*** Money is easy to handle and makes goods and services readily available to more people.

➤ **Which item was exchanged by the monetary system?** *(stickers)*

Teaching the Lesson

Text Discussion, page 144

➤ **Read page 144 to find the name of a game that is like the real business of buying and selling.** *(Monopoly)*

➤ *Show the Monopoly game board, money, and several of the game pieces.*

➤ **What are the players buying in this game?** *(property)*

➤ **What do you need to consider when making a purchase?** *(Answers will vary but should include the price of the item.)*

It can be very easy to overspend; however, with careful planning, we can make wise purchases.

Demonstration

➤ *Show your child the Bookmarks page. Cover the equations below the bookmarks with a sheet of paper. Uncover each one as you discuss it.*

I am selling four bookmarks for one dollar. I bought them for forty cents. Look at these two prices.

Some Monopoly player has a hotel on Boardwalk!

Do you know how to play the game Monopoly? Players buy property and try to improve it, collecting money from renters and paying taxes. The game teaches, among other things, that you have to pay more taxes when you own more land and that it is easy to be ruined by overspending.

The game of Monopoly is something like the real business of buying and selling. People buy property they think will be valuable. They sell property when they need money or when they can make a *profit*. A profit is an amount that is more than the original cost of something. For example, if you buy a used bicycle for ten dollars and spend five dollars to fix it up and then sell it for twenty dollars, you make a profit of five dollars.

144

Buying a bicycle

In the United States much buying and selling goes on every day. Citizens buy and sell within the country, and the United States government buys from and sells to other governments. The way a country handles its money and resources is called its *economy*. Perhaps you have heard adults talking about "the state of the economy." They are referring to the way the government uses money and goods.

Goods being loaded onto a ship for foreign export

145

➤ Compare the two prices, $0.40 and $1.00. *($0.40 < $1.00)*

I am charging more for the bookmarks than I paid for them.

➤ *Uncover the next equation.* Calculate the difference in cost between the original price and the price at which the bookmarks are being sold. *(sixty cents)*

➤ **What is the term used for this extra amount?** ***(profit)***

There is nothing wrong with making a profit; however, Christians should avoid being dishonest about the quality of the product being sold or charging an outrageous amount just to receive a large profit. (BAT: 4c Honesty)

Day 2

Text Discussion, page 145

➤ **Read page 145 to find out what *economy* means.** *(the way a country handles its money and resources)*

The word *economy* comes from Greek words meaning "management of a household." A country's economy is influenced first by the way each person handles his money. That economy then expands to include the family, community, state, country, and the world. Just as family members affect each other, the way a country handles resources and money affects everyone involved.

➤ **Read the words at the bottom of the Bookmarks page.** *(Goods, Services)*

The occupation you choose in life will fall mainly into one of two categories: jobs that produce goods (products) or jobs that offer services.

➤ Give examples of goods and services. I will write your ideas in the appropriate columns. *(Examples of jobs that produce goods: baker, house builder, factory worker, and farmer. Examples of jobs that offer services: mechanic, barber, teacher, telephone operator, secretary, and firefighter.)*

Long ago people produced almost everything for themselves and their own families. Today trade is necessary because people cannot produce everything they need themselves.

➤ *Write the word* economist.

Economy is a root of the word ***economist.*** A good economist is a person who uses his time, money, and resources wisely. Resources are the tools and supplies needed to make a product. If you are making tables, all the things you need to make the tables, such as wood, a hammer, saws, and nails, would be called resources.

The Proverbs 31 Woman

Name ______________________

An economist handles time, money, and resources. Read Proverbs 31:10-31. Look at the chart below. Read each phrase and determine which of the three areas each characteristic of the Proverbs 31 woman refers to. Check one. (The first one has been done for you.)

		Time	Money	Resources
1.	"no need of spoil" (verse 11)		✓	
2.	"wool and flax" (verse 13)			✓
3.	"bringeth her food from afar" (verse 14)			✓
4.	"riseth also while it is yet night" (verse 15)	✓		
5.	"considereth a field and buyeth it" (verse 16)		✓	
6.	"planteth a vineyard" (verse 16)			✓
7.	"strengtheneth her arms" (verse 17)			✓
8.	"candle goeth not out by night" (verse 18)	✓		
9.	"layeth her hands to the spindle" (verse 19)			✓
10.	"stretcheth out her hand to the poor" (verse 20)			✓
11.	"clothed with scarlet"; "clothing is silk and purple" (verses 21-22)			✓
12.	"maketh fine linen" (verse 24)		✓ or	✓
13.	"selleth it" (verse 24)		✓	
14.	"openeth her mouth with wisdom" (verse 26)			✓
15.	"eateth not the bread of idleness" (verse 27)	✓		

16. A good economist uses time, money, and resources wisely. Is the Proverbs 31 woman a good economist? *yes*

17. Read verse 28. Is her family proud of her accomplishments? *yes*

18. Give two words that indicate the feelings of her children and husband. **blessed, praiseth**

Heritage Studies 4 Student Notebook — Lesson 37 Evaluating the Lesson — 60

➤ **Read I Corinthians 4:2.**

➤ **Which word in the verse could be substituted for *economist?*** (*steward*) *Write the word* steward *next to the word* economist.

A ***steward*** manages another's property, finances, or other affairs. Remind your child that God has equipped Christians with unique talents or abilities. The Lord expects Christians to be good stewards, careful in the use of their time, money, and resources. (BATs: 2c Faithfulness, 2d Goal setting, 2e Work)

Evaluating the Lesson

Notebook Activity, page 60

➤ Read the instructions on Notebook page 60.

➤ Complete the page.

The Notebook page was designed to show your child that economy was part of life in Bible times. Accept any reasonable answers. Please do not grade the page.

Going Beyond

Enrichment

To develop a product, have available a chart with the following instructions.

IMAGINATION STATION

1. Think of a need for a product.
2. Research or learn about similar products that meet similar needs.
3. Develop your product.
4. Decide about distribution of your product.
5. Set a price for your product.
6. Advertise your product.

Encourage your child to use his imagination in developing a product and in following each step thoroughly in order to be successful in selling the product. Allow time for him to give commercials and advertise his product.

Additional Teacher Information

Numismatics, the collection or study of paper money or coins, is one of the most popular hobbies in the world. Some people collect money for enjoyment, while others collect as an investment. The most valuable coins and bills are those that are both unused (uncirculated) and scarce. "Mistakes" can also be valuable. Each three-legged buffalo nickel, for example, minted in 1937, is valued from $80 to $1,500.

Recycling is a process whereby useful products are created from what otherwise would be considered waste. The meat-packing industry is just one example of consuming natural resources with less waste, thereby helping a country's economy grow. Meat from beef cattle accounts for only half of the animals' use. In order to make a profit, ranchers must take advantage of byproducts. Leather items, such as shoes and furniture upholstery, come from the hides. Hair from cows' ears is used to make artists' brushes. Drugs and medical supplies are derived from glands. And candles, soap, and shaving cream are produced from the animals' fat. It has even been discovered that shoe polish and buttons can be made from cows' blood. Many other animal parts are used to make violin strings, glue, gelatin, and cosmetics.

LESSON 38
The Landlord's Game

Text, pages 146-47
Notebook, page 61

Preview

Main Ideas

- A *monopoly* is formed when products or services are controlled by one person or one group.
- Monopolies affect the economy in a negative way.
- The game of Monopoly has an interesting history.
- Economic principles are taught and practiced in the game Monopoly.

Objectives

- Play the game Monopoly
- Answer questions about Monopoly
- Write an economic principle used in playing Monopoly

Materials

- A Monopoly game*
- The Community Chest and Chance cards from a Monopoly game
- A Bible
- An atlas

Day 1

Lesson

Introducing the Lesson

Discussion

➤ *Give your child several of the Chance and Community Chest cards.*

➤ **Read one of the cards.**

➤ Decide whether what is stated on the card would help or hinder you economically if you wanted to own all the property on the Monopoly board.

Community Chest:
Get out of Jail Free *(help)*
Go to Jail *(hinder)*
Pay School Tax of $150 *(hinder)*
Pay Hospital $100 *(hinder)*
Grand Opera Opening—Collect $50 from Every Player *(help)*

◆ THINGS PEOPLE DO ◆

Inventing Games

The game that became Monopoly was probably invented by Elizabeth Magie Phillips, a woman who wanted to teach children that it was wrong to try to own everything. She called her game The Landlord's Game and had it patented in 1904.

But since The Landlord's Game was never packaged for sale, people in the area who played the game began to make up their own rules and to change some of the names of the places. And they called it Monopoly. Then others, especially college students going home on breaks, took the game to other states. Dan Layman took his new pastime to Indiana. There he made many changes and called the game Finance.

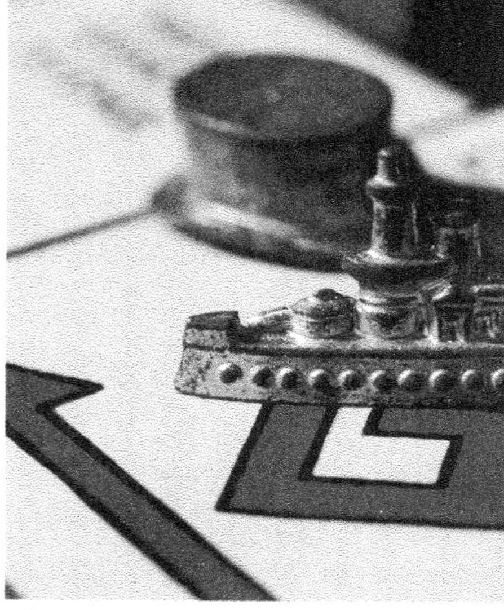

Many Monopoly games have markers that are miniatures of hats, cars, ships, and other objects.

146

You Have Won Second Prize in a Beauty Contest—Collect $10 *(help)*

Chance:
Bank Pays You Dividend of $50 *(help)*
Pay Poor Tax of $15 *(hinder)*
Your Building and Loan Matures—Collect $150 *(help)*
Advance to Go—Collect $200 *(help)*
You Have Been Elected Chairman of the Board—Pay Each Player $50 *(hinder)*

Teaching the Lesson

Text Discussion, page 146

➤ **Read page 146 to find the name of the woman who probably invented the game of Monopoly.** *(Elizabeth Magie Phillips)*

➤ **What did she call her game?** *(The Landlord's Game)*

➤ **What was she trying to teach?** *(It is wrong to try to own everything.)*

➤ Look at the word *monopoly* on your text page.

➤ **Do you know its definition?**

Mono- means "one" and *-poly* comes from the Greek word *polein,* which means "to sell."

An Indiana woman took the game of Finance to New Jersey, where she and her friends named places on the board after places in Atlantic City—places such as Boardwalk and Marvin Gardens. Then the game came into the hands of Philadelphian Charles Darrow, who made his own board and rules and sold the package to Parker Brothers, a large manufacturer of games and toys.

But the game was not Darrow's invention; it was a folk game that had grown out of Mrs. Phillips's idea. When Parker Brothers discovered Darrow's lie, the company was already making a lot of money on the game. So the owners decided to buy out all other claims to Monopoly, including the original one. Mrs. Phillips got five hundred dollars for her rights to the game that became the world's most popular board game.

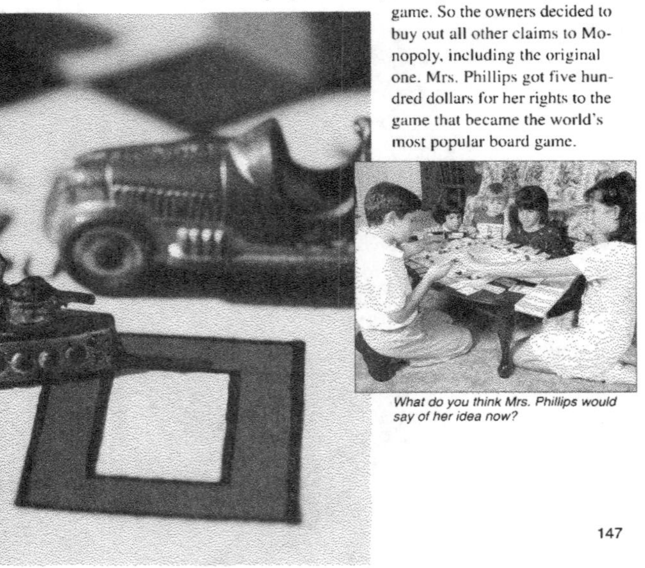

What do you think Mrs. Phillips would say of her idea now?

147

A ***monopoly*** is formed when products or services are controlled by one person or one group. In both The Landlord's Game and Monopoly, everyone starts out with the same amount of money. The game ends when one person has complete control of everything, and everyone else has little or no money or property.

Read I Corinthians 10:24 and Philippians 2:4. Ask your child what the Bible teaches about gaining wealth. *(Christians should not be overly concerned about money but should rather be thinking about the needs of other people.)* (BATs: 5a Love, 5b Giving, 7d Contentment)

The Bible gives Christians economic principles to help us to be successful with our money. It teaches us to be wise in the use of our money. For instance, we should not spend more money than we have. We should give to help others.

Text Discussion, page 147

➤ **What happened to the game of Monopoly as it was carried into other states?** *(The names and rules changed.)*

➤ **Read page 147 to find the name of the city whose street names were chosen for properties on the final playing board of Monopoly.** *(Atlantic City, New Jersey)*

➤ **Who sold Monopoly to Parker Brothers?** *(Charles Darrow)*

Parker Brothers published the game in 1935, thirty-one years after Elizabeth Magie Phillips patented her game. Charles Darrow retired at age forty-six, a millionaire.

➤ **How much money was Elizabeth Phillips paid by Parker Brothers?** *($500)*

➤ **Do you think she was paid enough for inventing the game?**

Map Activity

➤ Turn to a map of the United States in the atlas.

➤ Find Atlantic City, New Jersey, on the map. Atlantic City is a large seashore resort.

➤ Look at the Monopoly game board.

➤ The colored squares are the properties named for the streets in Atlantic City. **Read some of the names of the properties on the game board.**

Day 2

The rules for Monopoly given in the lesson have been simplified to save time and to encourage play for children who have never played the game. There are many variations of these rules. Keep the activity as simple as possible with the emphasis on exposure and experience.

Game of Monopoly

➤ *Explain the rules of Monopoly to your child.*

- Each player chooses a token to use throughout the game.
- Whoever has the highest throw on the dice goes first, and the person to the left goes next.
- One person is selected to serve as the banker. The banker is in charge of money, Title Deed cards, houses, and hotels.
- To begin the game, place the tokens on the space marked "Go." Players follow the direction of the arrow. More than one token may rest on each square.
- If a player rolls doubles, he gets another turn.
- Each time a player passes "Go," he receives $200 from the banker.
- The properties are grouped by colors, railroads, and utilities.
- A player may purchase a property separately when he lands on it during his turn. The prices are marked on the game board.

- The Title Deed card for a particular property is given out at the time of purchase.
- Once a property is purchased, any player who lands on that square must pay the owner rent as shown on the rent section of the Title Deed card.
- A property owner who has purchased all properties in one color group may purchase houses (green) and later a hotel (red) to place on the properties. Once a player owns a complete group of properties, explain how to "build" on the properties and increase rent. (*NOTE:* See Monopoly's official rules.)
- When a player lands on a "Chance" or "Community Chest" square, he will take a card from the top of the pile corresponding to the square. Instructions on the card must be followed and the card placed on the bottom of the pile. If the card can be useful later ("Get out of Jail Free"), it can be saved until needed or sold to another player at any time.
- When a player lands on the "Free Parking" square, this is a resting space.
- A player landing on the "Go to Jail" square must go to the space marked "In Jail." A player must also "Go to Jail" if he rolls doubles three times in a row. (*NOTE:* See Monopoly's official rules for getting out of jail.)
- Any player landing on the "Luxury Tax" or "Income Tax" square must pay the bank the amount indicated.
- The mortgage price of the property may be found on the back of the Title Deed card. If a player is in need of money, he may mortgage a property. (*NOTE:* See Monopoly's official rules for instructions on how to mortgage property.)
- When a player runs out of money and cannot pay his bills, he must withdraw from the game.

➤ *Play Monopoly with your child.*

It is not necessary to finish a game of Monopoly. Set a certain amount of time aside for the game or play until your child has had adequate experience with buying and selling.

Evaluating the Lesson

Notebook Activity, page 61

➤ Read the instructions on Notebook page 61.
➤ Complete the page.

Monopoly: The Landlord's Game Name ____________

Choose the correct answer to complete each statement.

wrong	Atlantic City
Parker Brothers	The Landlord's Game
Monopoly	Elizabeth Magie Phillips
Charles Darrow	

Elizabeth Magie Phillips probably invented the game of Monopoly. She called her game ***The Landlord's Game***. The main purpose of her game was to teach children that it is ***wrong*** to try to own everything. The game was never packaged for sale. Later the name of the game changed to ***Monopoly*** and the places on the board were named after places in ***Atlantic City***. ***Charles Darrow*** made his own version of the game and sold it to ***Parker Brothers***.

After playing the game of Monopoly, answer the following questions.

1. What did you enjoy most about the game? ***Answers will vary.***
2. What did you like least about the game? ***Answers will vary.***
3. Write one economic principle you used while playing Monopoly. ***Possible answers:*** ***To be successful, I need to use my money wisely. I should not overspend or get greedy in obtaining property and wealth.***

Heritage Studies 4 Student Notebook — Lesson 38 Evaluating the Lesson 61

Going Beyond

Enrichment

Give your child a copy of the map of Atlantic City (Appendix, page A54) and instruct him to circle all street names that correspond to property names on the Monopoly game board.

Additional Teacher Information

One of the most ancient board games has been dated to be forty-five hundred years old. The game was discovered in the city of Ur, located in present-day Iraq. Players used dice and playing pieces to race around a track on the game board.

Monopoly is a highly popular game known throughout the world. Since its publication by Parker Brothers in 1935, the game has sold more than eighty-five million copies worldwide and is available in over nineteen languages with street names and currency to match particular countries. Using a Braille version consisting of raised dots on a coating of plastic, blind people can also play Monopoly.

LESSON 39
What's It Worth?

Text, pages 148-51
Notebook, pages 62-63

Preview

Main Ideas

- *Value* is worth in money, usefulness, or importance.
- The value of items can change.
- An item of value satisfies a desire or need and/or is limited in quantity.

Objectives

- Identify items of value
- Distinguish changes in value

Materials

- A Bible
- An expensive-looking necklace*
- A book
- A wooden pencil
- A piece of paper
- A large rock

Day 1

Lesson

Introducing the Lesson

Discussion

➤ Imagine that you have two similar containers. One is full of gasoline and one is full of water.

➤ **Which item is more valuable?** *(Answers will vary; however, he may say the gasoline.)*

➤ Give a reason for your answer. *(Answers will vary but should include the idea that gasoline is more expensive.)*

➤ Imagine that you have spent all day without drinking and you are extremely thirsty.

➤ **Which item would then be more valuable?** *(water)*

➤ **Which item would be more valuable if your car were out of gas?** *(gasoline)*

➤ **Would gasoline be valuable to you if you did not have a car or if your car broke down?** *(no)*

➤ *Write the word* valuable.

Items that are valuable are not necessarily more expensive. An item that is ***valuable*** is worth something in money, usefulness, or importance.

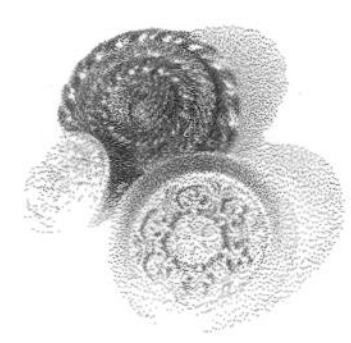

A diamond has many qualities that make it valuable.

What's It Worth?

Suppose you have a button and a diamond. Which do you think would bring more money? You probably said the diamond. And you might be right. Diamonds have great *value*, or worth in money. Why do you think they do? For one thing, they are beautiful, and many people want them for their beauty. A good rhinestone can look as lovely, yet rhinestones are not nearly as expensive as diamonds. Why is that?

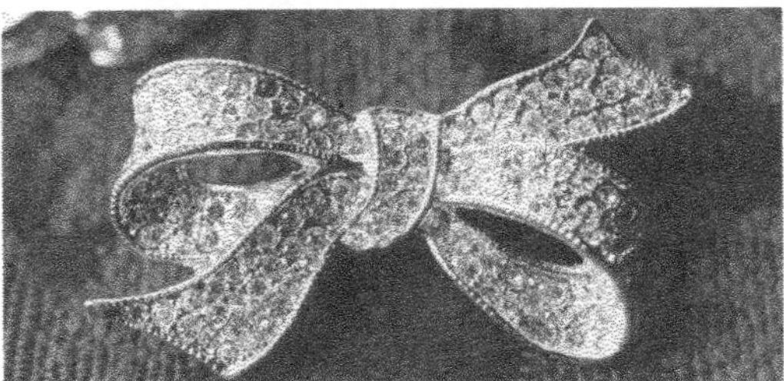

Rhinestones may look like diamonds, but they are worth far less.

148

➤ **What made the value of the water and gasoline change?** *(The value changed according to the immediate need.)*

Teaching the Lesson

Text Discussion, pages 148-49

➤ **Read pages 148-49 to discover a situation in which a button is more valuable than a diamond.** *(The button is an old button from George Washington's military uniform, and the diamond is small and has a flaw in it.)*

Many people decide value based on how something looks. Remind your child that he should value people without passing judgment on outward appearance. Read I Samuel 16:7. Ask what the Lord looks on to determine value. *(the heart)* (BATs: 1b Repentance and faith, 3c Emotional control, 3d Body as a temple, 6d Clear conscience)

➤ *Write the word* utility *under* valuable.

A ***utility*** is something that meets a need; therefore electricity is a utility.

➤ **What needs can electricity meet?** *(Answers will vary but might include the provision of light and heat.)*

➤ *Write the word* scarce *under the word* valuable.

Mining for diamonds

Diamonds are hard to get. They are not at all plentiful. Rhinestones, on the other hand, can be made easily, by the millions. Because real diamonds are scarce, they have more value. Can you think of other things that are valuable because they are rare?

Pretend again that you have a button and a diamond. The diamond, though real, is quite small and has a flaw in it. But the button is rather old. In fact, it is one of the buttons from George Washington's military uniform. Now which item do you think might bring more money? Why?

George Washington in military attire—how much for a collar button?

149

One man's junk is another man's treasure!

When people decide they want to buy or sell something, they think about the value of the item going up for sale. Some items have value because of what they are. Gold, for instance, is rare, useful, and hard to get. Therefore, it has value in itself. But there are other ways of deciding value too.

Suppose you were in a foreign country and could not get home. There is one airplane ticket to the United States left, but you do not have any money to pay for it. However, you have a gold necklace worth two thousand American dollars. The plane ticket costs only six hundred American dollars. The person who owns the ticket is willing to trade it for your necklace. At that time, the gold chain may not seem as valuable as the last ticket out of the country. How have the values changed?

150

➤ **What makes the diamond more valuable than the rhinestone?** *(The diamond is rare, scarce, or hard to get.)* Items that are valuable have utility (meet a need) and/or are scarce (few in number).

Text Discussion, pages 150-51

➤ Perhaps you had a blanket or a stuffed bear that you carried when you were younger. Name something that was very important to you when you were little.

➤ **Is that item as important to you now?**

The value of goods and services is always changing.

➤ **Read pages 150-51 to find out what changes the value of items.** *(Answers will vary but should include the availability of an item and the ability of an item to meet a particular need.)*

➤ **Why did the plane ticket become more valuable than the gold necklace?** *(There was only one plane ticket left, and there was a need to leave the country.)*

➤ **What changes when the value of an item changes?** *(the price)*

➤ Look at the Demand Curve on page 151.

➤ **What does the vertical set of numbers tell us?** *(the price of tickets)* This is the price of plane tickets.

➤ **What do the numbers across the bottom of the chart represent?** *(quantity or number of tickets sold)*

➤ **How high could the price of a plane ticket go?** *($1,000)*

➤ **According to the curve, how low could the price of a plane ticket be?** *($200)*

➤ **Were more tickets sold at the lower or higher price?** *(lower)*

The general goal of a business is to offer services or goods at a price that most people will be willing to pay. The business must be able to make money or a profit at that price. We will discuss the Demand Curve more in the next lesson.

Read aloud Matthew 10:29-31. Ask what animal the Scripture mentions in reference to God's watchful care. *(the sparrow)* Remind your child that God places a far greater value on people than on the sparrow. The Lord looks at each soul individually and sees potential and worth in His will. (BATs: 3a Self-concept, 7c Praise, 7d Contentment)

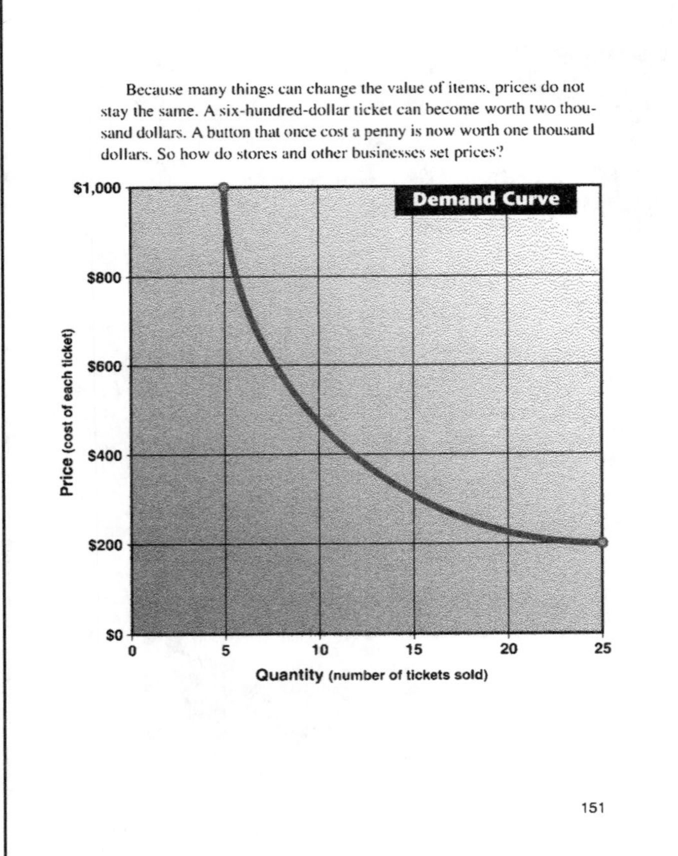

Because many things can change the value of items, prices do not stay the same. A six-hundred-dollar ticket can become worth two thousand dollars. A button that once cost a penny is now worth one thousand dollars. So how do stores and other businesses set prices?

151

Items and Their Values

Name ______________________

Follow your teacher's instructions.

Group I

Group II

Heritage Studies 4
Student Notebook

Lesson 39
Evaluating the Lesson 62

Evaluating the Lesson

Notebook Activity, pages 62-63

- *Place the necklace, book, wooden pencil, piece of paper, and large rock in front of your child. Do not make any comments about the objects.*
- Examine the items and consider their values.
- Cut out the Group I pictures on Notebook page 62.
- Glue them on Notebook page 63 in the order that you consider to be most valuable to least valuable.
- Look at the five items again. Let me tell you about them.

The necklace does not contain precious jewels—it is just fake costume jewelry. The book is signed by a famous author. The wooden pencil is covered with gold. The piece of paper is actually an old U.S. document thought to be lost. The large rock has a large diamond inside.

- Consider this new information about the five items as you reconsider their values.
- Cut out the Group II pictures on Notebook page 62.
- Glue them on Notebook page 63 in order from the most valuable to the least valuable.

The purpose of this evaluation is for your child to show recognition of changing values. The first set of pictures is based purely upon observation. After the description of the items, the second set of pictures should reflect changing values.

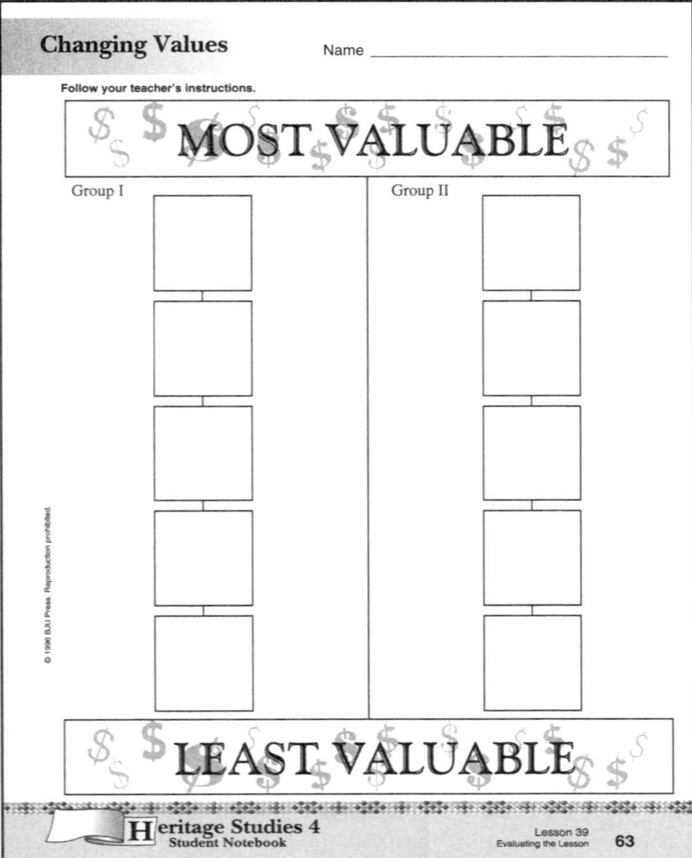

Changing Values Name ______________________

Follow your teacher's instructions.

MOST VALUABLE

Group I

Group II

LEAST VALUABLE

Going Beyond

Enrichment

Ask your child to evaluate an item that he considers valuable by completing the My Treasure page (Appendix, page A55).

Additional Teacher Information

Early money took many forms. If a particular item was considered useful, a group of people may have chosen to trade with it. Salt, animal hides, cloth, cattle, and tobacco were once used in the same way money is used today. Value might also be placed upon a common, everyday object. The people of the northwest coast of North America chose fishhooks as their money. Teeth, feathers, shells, and human skulls have also been traded for other goods. Giant round stones served as money for people of the South Pacific islands as recently as 1940. Larger stones, weighing as much as one hundred pounds, were worth more.

Because of the scarcity of certain items and because many people were able and willing to pay, prices during the California gold rush of 1849 were astronomical. For instance, one egg cost $3.00; a loaf of bread, $2.00; one pound of flour, $1.00; one potato, $1.00; one watermelon, $5.00; and one bottle of vinegar, $1.00.

LESSON 40
Supply and Demand

Text, pages 152-55
Notebook, page 64

Preview

Main Ideas

- Prices change.
- *Supply* is the quantity of a product that businesses are willing and able to offer.
- *Demand* is the quantity of a product that buyers are willing and able to purchase.
- Prices are affected by the laws of *supply and demand.*

Objectives

- Define *supply* and *demand*
- Interpret a demand curve

Materials

- A candy bar*
- Appendix, page A56: Demand Curve*

Day 1

Lesson

Introducing the Lesson

A Story Discussion

➤ Listen as I read a story.

The neighborhood children would meet under the big oak tree and trade baseball cards. On this hot summer day Jonathan brought a Mark McGwire trading card, picturing the neighborhood's favorite baseball player. Everyone knew this card was difficult to find.

Without hesitating Timothy said, "I'll trade you two of my John Smoltz cards for your Mark McGwire card."

"But I'll give you a John Smoltz card, a David Cone card, and my new green yo-yo," Chris interjected.

Benjamin was not going to be left out of this trade. He offered a John Smoltz card, a Greg Maddux card, and his yellow yo-yo. Now, all the boys knew that a Greg Maddux card was better than a David Cone card.

Jonathan sat cross-legged, waiting patiently for the next offer. After several minutes of calculating, Chris said, "I can give you my John Smoltz card, a

David Cone card, my green yo-yo, and I will throw in my rookie Greg Maddux card."

"I don't have anything else to offer. I guess I'm out of the trading." Benjamin laid back to watch a squirrel in the tree above.

Timothy had a wide grin on his face. He just knew he had a better offer than Chris. "I'll give you two John Smoltz cards, my Greg Maddux card, and I will take out the trash for two weeks." Since Jonathan was his younger brother, he was the only one who could offer to do his household chore.

Jonathan slowly looked at each of the boys. Benjamin had already made his final offer. Timothy's offer was much better than Chris's.

Jonathan reached out to shake Timothy's hand. "The Mark McGwire card is yours," he said.

➤ **What would you have traded for the Mark McGwire baseball card?**

➤ **What determined the price of the Mark McGwire baseball card?** *(the neighborhood boys' desire to obtain the card and their ability to raise the price)*

➤ *Write the word* supply.

Supply is the Mark McGwire baseball card or the items people want or need to buy.

➤ *Write the word* demand.

Demand is the number of offers made on the baseball card.

➤ **Why did the demand for the baseball card change?** *(Answers will vary but should include that the price of what was being offered was lower at the beginning of the trade. All the boys could offer something. As the price increased, some of the boys did not have enough to offer to trade.)*

Day 2

Teaching the Lesson

Text Discussion, pages 152-53

➤ **Read pages 152-53 to find the name of laws that affect prices.** *(laws of supply and demand)*

➤ *Hold up the candy bar.* **Would the candy bar be an example of supply or demand?** *(supply)*

➤ **Would you be willing to purchase a candy bar for five dollars?**

➤ **Why would you refuse to pay such a high price?** *(Answers will vary but should include being able to buy the same candy bar at a lower price elsewhere.)*

➤ **Would you be willing to purchase a candy bar for five cents?**

➤ Look at the Demand Curve chart. **Read the prices for the candy bars given on the chart.**

➤ Find the area on the chart that tells you the quantity, or number, of candy bars sold.

➤ **How many candy bars sold for twenty cents?** *(twenty-five)*

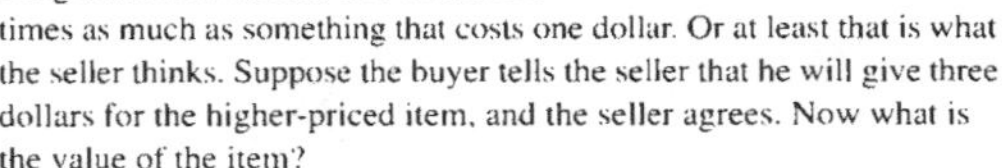

Supply and Demand

Prices are numerical ways of saying how much value an item has. If something costs five dollars, it is worth five times as much as something that costs one dollar. Or at least that is what the seller thinks. Suppose the buyer tells the seller that he will give three dollars for the higher-priced item, and the seller agrees. Now what is the value of the item?

Suppose now that the seller, who has many of the same item priced at five dollars, lowers the price to three dollars. What do you think will happen? People who were interested in the item but thought it was too highly priced may buy it. If you were the seller, what would you think was better: to sell a few items for five dollars or to sell more for three dollars? If you choose to sell more at a lower price, you are responding to the laws of *supply and demand.*

A price tag tells what the seller believes his item is worth. How does a buyer indicate what he thinks?

152

If your child is not familiar with reading graphs, you will want to give him step-by-step instructions. For example, put your finger on twenty cents. Slide your finger to the right until you reach the demand curve. Now look at the bottom of the chart to see how many candy bars sold for that amount.

➤ **At what price were the fewest candy bars sold?** *(one dollar)*

➤ **How many candy bars sold for that price?** *(five)*

➤ **About how many candy bars sold for seventy cents?** *(about eight)*

Your child may need your help as he figures prices or amounts when the exact line to follow is not on the graph.

➤ **What kind of prices allows more candy bars to sell—higher prices or lower prices?** *(lower prices)*

➤ **Which do you think will bring in more profit for the salesman—higher or lower prices?**

It depends on how many items he can sell at each price. If the candy bars are too cheap or too expensive, the salesman will not make any money. In fact, he will probably lose money.

For people to pay a high price, they must believe the product is especially good or scarce.

If there is a large supply of an item, the price usually must be lower. People think they can get the item anywhere and will try to get the best price. Sellers who keep the price high will not sell as many as those who lower the price. As long as the supply remains, the demand will keep the price low.

If many stores have the same product, the prices will usually stay lower.

153

Can you think of an item that would not be in great supply, that could not be made easily, and that people would want a great deal? Paintings are such items. An artist who is no longer living cannot make any more paintings. The supply of paintings is limited. What do you think will happen to the prices? They will probably go up. Why do you think sellers can raise the prices?

How does supply effect price in this case? What else may affect the price? If the artist is not a good artist, no one may want to buy his work no matter how scarce it is. What does that tell you about the laws of supply and demand?

Art museums are full of paintings upon which people have placed a high value.

If you are a seller, you want to find a price that will not only get people to buy but will also let you make a profit. Why do you think stores sometimes put things "on sale"?

154

➤ Find the *X* on the demand curve.

The "best price" for the candy bar is somewhere in the middle of the demand curve—high enough for the seller to make a profit but low enough for the buyer to purchase the item.

➤ **Which price on the chart would be the best price for both the seller and the buyer?** *(approximately forty-five cents)*

➤ Think of factors other than price that will affect the demand for a certain item. **Would you take a moldy candy bar for free?**

In addition to price, the *quality of the item* affects the demand.

➤ **How do you think the demand would change if the buyer were on a strict diet?**

Demand is also affected by *the item's ability to meet a need.*

➤ **Would you be willing to drive fifty miles in order to purchase the candy bar for five cents?**

The convenience of an item will also determine the demand for that item.

Text Discussion, page 154

➤ **Read page 154 to find out about the prices of fine paintings by deceased artists.**

➤ **Why do you think the price of famous paintings by a deceased artist would go up?**

The price is high because the supply is low and there is a demand for high-quality paintings.

➤ **Why is the demand for the paintings high?** *(Answers will vary but should include the idea that the paintings are scarce and valuable.)*

Some people buy paintings as an investment, hoping to make a profit. Others buy paintings because they like the paintings and have the money to buy them.

➤ Think of other items that are low in supply, high-priced, and high in demand. *(Answers will vary: gold, jewels, rare baseball cards, antiques.)*

➤ Many people collect expensive, rare things. **Have you ever heard the term *limited edition* used to describe a Christmas ornament?**

➤ **What do you think this phrase means?** There are a limited number of these ornaments for sale.

➤ **How will limits affect the price?** *(The price will increase over time.)*

◆ LEARNING HOW ◆

To Read a Demand Curve

1. Get Notebook page 64 and a colored pencil or pen.
2. Listen as your teacher explains the demand curve pictured on the graph.
3. Answer the questions on the page.

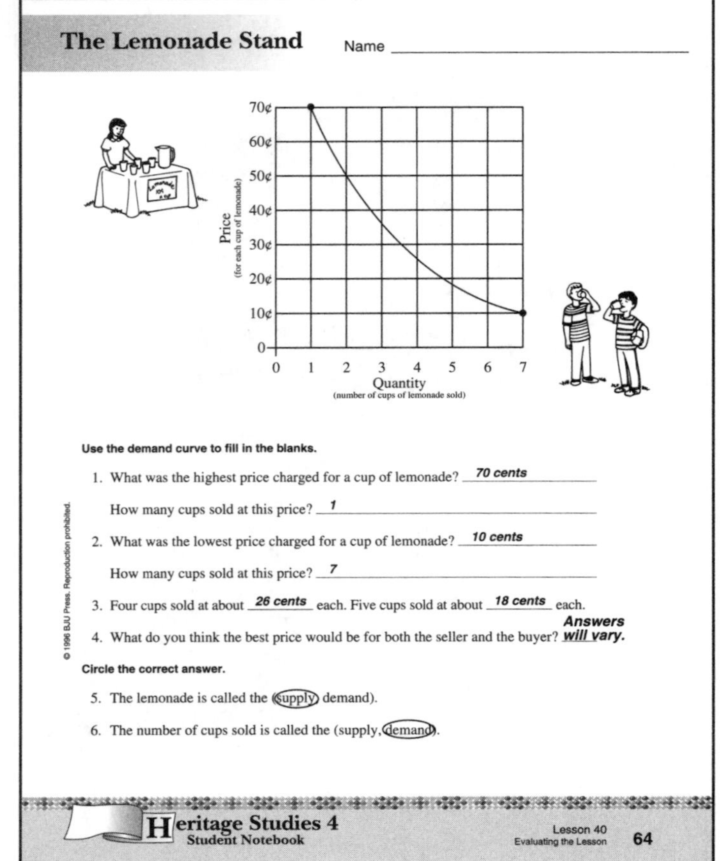

The Lemonade Stand Name ______________________

Use the demand curve to fill in the blanks.

1. What was the highest price charged for a cup of lemonade? ***70 cents***
   How many cups sold at this price? ***1***
2. What was the lowest price charged for a cup of lemonade? ***10 cents***
   How many cups sold at this price? ***7***
3. Four cups sold at about ***26 cents*** each. Five cups sold at about ***18 cents*** each.
4. What do you think the best price would be for both the seller and the buyer? ***Answers will vary.***

Circle the correct answer.

5. The lemonade is called the (supply, demand). [supply circled]
6. The number of cups sold is called the (supply, demand). [demand circled]

Remember that contentment comes not from expensive, rare things but from knowing that God will provide all that a person needs. (BAT: 7d Contentment)

Evaluating the Lesson

Learning How Activity, page 155 and Notebook page 64

- **Read and follow Step 1 on page 155.**
- **Read Step 2.**
- Locate on the chart the price per cup of lemonade. **Read aloud the prices given.**
- Locate the quantity of cups sold. **Read the number of cups given.**
- Place your pencil or pen on *fifty cents.*
- Slide your pencil over to the right until you reach the demand curve.
- **How many cups of lemonade sold for fifty cents?** *(two)*
- **Read and follow Step 3 on page 155.**

Going Beyond

Enrichment

Set up the activity Money Match (Appendix, page A57). Prepare the Money Match cards by cutting them apart and mounting each one on construction paper or tagboard. Mix up all cards and turn them facedown.

The game begins with the first player turning over two cards. If the two cards match (money amount with the correct portrait), then that player keeps the two cards and takes another turn. If the two cards do not match, then those cards are turned facedown again and play continues with the opponent taking a turn. The game ends when the last two cards are correctly matched. When only one player plays Money Match, he may wish to time himself to see how quickly he can match the cards.

Additional Teacher Information

The selection of pictures on paper money in the United States is the responsibility of the secretary of the Treasury. In 1929, when all bills were reduced to their present size, the secretary of the Treasury appointed a committee to choose pictures for the bills. It was decided that paper money should portray something of historical significance and not depict a living person. The committee thought that only presidents should appear on the bills; however, a few exceptions were made. The $100 bill portrays Benjamin Franklin—famous statesman and signer of the Declaration of Independence. Alexander Hamilton was chosen for the $10 bill because he was the first secretary of the Treasury.

LESSON 41
Capitalism

Text, pages 156-59
Notebook, pages 65-66

Preview

Main Ideas

- *Capital* is wealth that is owned and used by one person or a group of people working together.
- A *capitalist* country allows people to own businesses and exercise the freedom of choice.
- The United States has a *capitalist* economy.
- A *socialist* country insists that the government own businesses.
- A *socialist* country severely limits the freedom of individual choice.

Objective

- Distinguish between *capitalist* and *socialist* forms of government

Materials

- Appendix, page A58: occupation cards (Choose one.)*
- Maps and More 27, page M13
- Appendix, page A59: 3 price tags*
- Appendix, page A60: Socialist Prices cards (optional)*
- Appendix, page A61: Capitalist Prices cards (optional)*

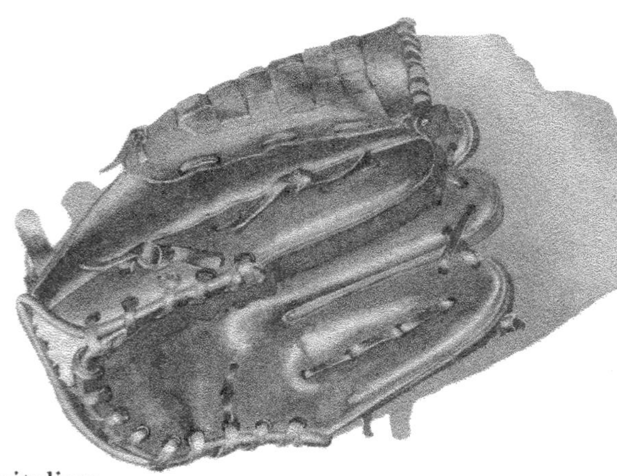

Capitalism

In the United States, businesses and individual sellers can choose to raise or lower prices for their goods and services. For example, if a toy store has many of a certain kind of toy, the manager could decide to lower the price so that more people would buy it. Why is having a choice important?

In the United States, the government does not own the businesses or the goods. Individual people and groups of people do. They choose what to make and sell and what to offer as services. They choose how they will market the goods or provide the services. A country that allows the people this ownership and the freedom to make choices is called *capitalistic*. *Capital* is wealth that is owned and used by one person or a group of people working together. Do you see where capitalism gets its name?

156

Day 1

Lesson

Introducing the Lesson

Listening Activity

➤ Listen as I read of two boys' situations.

Story 1

Kevin looked down at the items in the basket and carefully compared them to the list his mother had given to him. He slowly stepped up to the checkout line.

"Bread, milk, and cheese," he thought to himself. "Now, which candy bar should I get this time?"

Each week when Kevin rode his bike to pick up a few needed items, his mother would give him extra money to buy a treat for them to share. Suddenly, Kevin looked up from the candy rack to see that the line had moved rapidly, and it was almost his turn.

"I know—the chocolate almond bar." Kevin grinned to himself. That was his mother's favorite; he would surprise her.

Kevin proceeded toward the cashier. Soon the cashier was quickly ringing up each of his items.

Placing his money on the counter, he exclaimed, "Wow! I'll be home in record time!"

Story 2

Ivan shifted his weight from one foot to the other. The silent hour had passed by slowly. He strained his neck to peer down the seemingly endless line of people. It seemed that every person had had the same thought—arrive early to the bread line. Finally he felt a slight surge forward and heard a sigh from the crowd. The line was moving!

"I wonder whether there will be enough loaves for everyone here," Ivan thought.

Forty-five minutes later, Ivan stepped up to the counter. "One loaf, please," Ivan said. He placed his bread coupon on the counter.

Comparing Activity

➤ Compare the two stories, telling of similarities. *(Answers will vary but should include that the main characters are boys. They purchase bread. They stand in line.)*

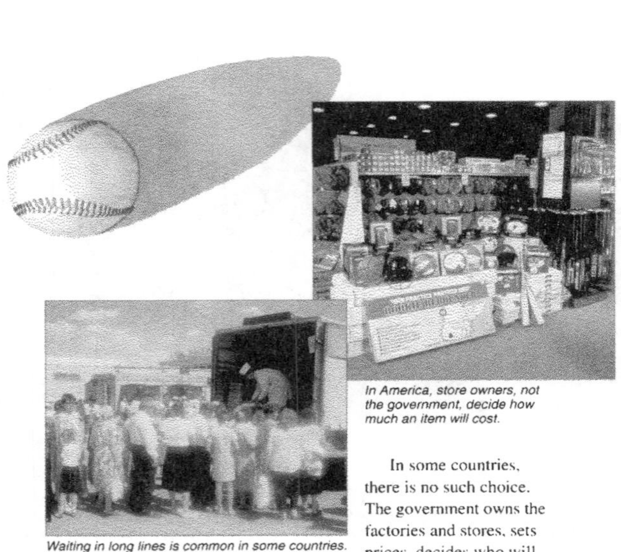

In America, store owners, not the government, decide how much an item will cost.

Waiting in long lines is common in some countries.

In some countries, there is no such choice. The government owns the factories and stores, sets prices, decides who will be allowed to work and where, and selects who gets the profits. Such countries are called *socialistic*. The word *social* comes from a Latin word that means "partner." Do you think socialism is a fitting name?

According to capitalism, the best way to run business is to let profits cause people to make decisions. For example, if a toy is popular, many companies will want to make it. The company that makes it best and sells it for the best price will be the one that makes the profits. How is such competition between the companies good for the people who buy toys?

157

How would things be different in a socialist country in which the price of the toy must be the same in every store? Why is this kind of pricing not good for the consumer? Can you think of any other reasons this system would not be good?

In socialist countries in which everyone has to have a job, businesses do not improve rapidly. If a machine could do the work of ten people more economically, the capitalist country would use it. But the socialist country would not, unless jobs could be found for the ten people who would be put out of work. Which country, then, would likely make more progress?

A shoe factory in a socialist country

A modern textile factory in Adana, Turkey

A car factory in the United States

158

- ➤ Name some differences between the two stories. *(Answers will vary but should include types of stores, certainty/uncertainty of purchasing items, choice of items, length of line, waiting time, and means of purchase.)*
- ➤ **Which line would you rather be in to make a purchase?**
- ➤ **Which story shows a typical American grocery store scene?** *(Story 1)*

Teaching the Lesson

Text Activity, pages 156-57

- ➤ **Read pages 156-57 to compare two different types of government, capitalist and socialist.**
- ➤ **Who owns the businesses in the United States?** *(individual people and groups of people)*
- ➤ **What kind of country allows its people to own businesses?** *(capitalistic)*
- ➤ **What is the base word of *capitalistic?*** *(capital)*
- ➤ Give synonyms for the word *capital. (wealth, money, goods, businesses)*
- ➤ **Who owns the businesses in a *socialist* country?** *(the government)*
- ➤ Give the Latin meaning of the word *social. (partner)*

A socialist government does not display partnership; instead it represents a master/slave relationship, with the government making all the decisions and controlling all the businesses.

- ➤ **Which kind of economy—socialist or capitalist—encourages competition?** *(capitalist)*

In a socialist economy the government sets all the prices. Businesses do not need to compete by setting different prices.

Text Activity, page 158

- ➤ **Read page 158 to find out which country, socialist or capitalist, would not improve rapidly.** *(socialist)*
- ➤ **What would be true about the price of a toy in all stores in a socialist economy?** *(Prices would be the same.)*
- ➤ **What would be true about the price of a toy in stores in a capitalist economy?** *(Prices would be different.)*
- ➤ **Why would the prices all being the same in a socialist economy not be good for the consumer or the buyer?** *(Answers will vary. The consumer would not be able to shop to get the best bargain or price. The government could set the price as high as it wanted.)*

A Demonstration

➤ *Give an occupation card to your child.*
➤ **Read the side of the card that already has information in the blanks.**

The government has issued this card and decided your future occupation, product/service, and salary.

➤ **Are you satisfied with the government's choices for you?**
➤ **What type of government controls businesses?** *(socialist)*
➤ Write the word *socialism* at the bottom of your card.
➤ Turn your card over and write your own choice of occupation, what good or service you would sell, and what price you would set.
➤ **What type of government allows individuals or groups to control businesses?** *(capitalist)*
➤ Write the word *capitalism* at the bottom of this side of your card.
➤ **What is the main difference between socialism and capitalism?** *(choice, decision, control, or ownership)*

Christians living in socialist countries suffer also from lack of religious freedom. Ask what promises those Christians can claim. *(God is in control and will protect His children wherever they are.)* (Bible Promises: H. God as Father, I. God as Master)

Day 2

Evaluating the Lesson

Comparison Activity, Maps and More 27

➤ Look at Maps and More 27.
➤ **What is the name of the bicycle that the three different stores are selling?** *(the Rolly 500)*
➤ **Read the price for this bicycle at each store.**
➤ **Which store offers the best buy on the Rolly 500?** *(A to Z Save-A-Center)*
➤ **What type of government is represented by these three stores?** *(capitalist)*
➤ **Which type of government allows for competition?** *(capitalist)*
➤ Give some reasons that competition between businesses would be good for the people who buy the bicycles. *(Answers will vary but should include the ideas that the people will be given more choices, the cost will come down, the quality will go up, and the businesses will thrive.)*
➤ *Give your child the three price tags.*
➤ Pretend that the three stores on the chart are part of a socialist country. Write a price on each price tag for the Rolly 500 bicycle that would show that the stores are part of a socialist economy. *(The price should be the same on all three cards.)*

◆ **LEARNING HOW** ◆

Capitalism Works

1. Get your Notebook, a pencil, and a pair of scissors.
2. Cut out the coupons from Notebook page 65.
3. Listen to your teacher for explanations about what you will sell and buy.
4. Answer the questions on Notebook page 66 to compare capitalism and socialism.

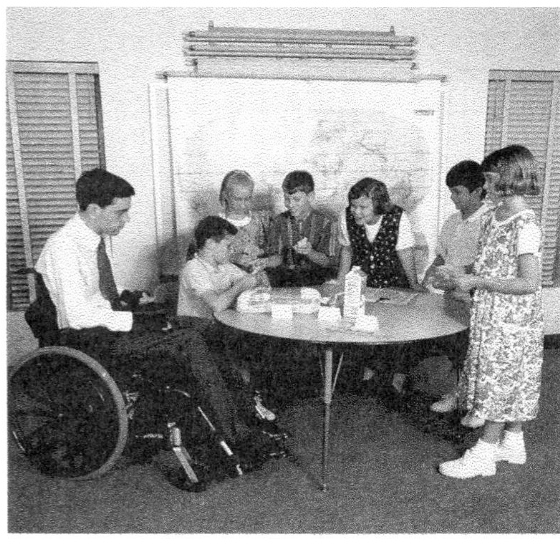

159

➤ **How would this pricing affect the choices of bicycles?** *(There would be little or no variety in choice; therefore, the competition would drop.)*

If you are teaching more than one child, the *Learning How* Activity will help to evaluate the lesson.

Learning How Activity, page 159 and Notebook pages 65-66 (optional)

➤ **Read and follow Step 1 on page 159.**
➤ **Read and follow Step 2.**
➤ **Read Step 3.**

Select two children to be shopkeepers. Give each shopkeeper a copy of the Socialist Prices cards that have prices already marked.

➤ Each shopkeeper should display the goods cards so that the other children can see the prices.
➤ You may use your coupons as money to make purchases at either store. Be sure to compare the stores to decide which store to buy from. *Allow a few minutes for them to make their purchases.*
➤ **What did you notice about the prices at these stores?** *(They were the same.)*
➤ *Choose two different shopkeepers and give each a copy of the Capitalist Prices cards without prices.*

Coupons—Same as Cash

Name ______________________

Cut out coupons to use in making your "purchases."

1 Credit | 10 Credits
5 Credits | 2 Credits
25 Credits | 20 Credits
3 Credits | 50 Credits
4 Credits | 7 Credits

© 1996 BJU Press. Reproduction prohibited.

Heritage Studies 4 Student Notebook — Lesson 41 Evaluating the Lesson 65

Capitalism or Socialism?

Name ______________________

Answer the following questions after you complete your shopping.

1. What type of economy was illustrated the first time you went shopping?
   socialist
2. What type of economy was illustrated the second time you went shopping?
   capitalist
3. At which shop were the prices the same for all the items? ***socialist***
   What do you think about this? ***Answers will vary.***
4. Which type of economy gave more choices? ***capitalist***
5. Which type of economy do you prefer? ***Answers will vary.***
   Why? ***Answers will vary.***

© 1996 BJU Press. Reproduction prohibited.

Heritage Studies 4 Student Notebook — Lesson 41 Evaluating the Lesson 66

Shopkeepers, please mark your own prices on your goods cards and display those prices. You are to try to sell as many items as you can. You may change the items or prices at any time during the sale.

Shoppers, use your coupons as money to make purchases at these stores. Be sure to compare the stores to decide which store to buy from.

➤ *Allow a few minutes for the children to make their purchases.*

➤ **Read and follow Step 4 on page 159.**

Going Beyond

Additional Teacher Information

The Secret Service is a law enforcement branch under the Treasury Department of the United States. One duty of the Secret Service is the identification of counterfeit money and the prosecution of counterfeiters or those involved with producing such money. Secret Service agents also investigate forged or missing checks issued by the United States government. Handwriting on such checks is compared with thousands of forgeries on file. Solving cases takes time and may involve an accumulation of many reports, many clues, and much information.

LESSON 42
Needs and Wants

Text, page 160

Preview

Main Ideas

- People have the same basic needs but different wants.
- Christians can trust God to meet their needs.

Objectives

- Distinguish between wants and needs
- Explain the lessons of Matthew 16:26

Materials

- Appendix, page A62: My List*
- A magazine with advertisements*

Lesson

Introducing the Lesson

Discriminating Activity

➤ *Give your child the My List page.*
➤ Circle all the items that can be eaten.
➤ Underline all items that can be worn.
➤ Put a star next to each underlined item or circled item that is necessary for life.

True needs are those things a person *must* have to live—water, food, shelter, and so on. Few things in life are true necessities.

Teaching the Lesson

Text Activity, page 160

➤ **Read the first two paragraphs on page 160 to find two things people should consider when making a purchase.** *(price and need)*
➤ Explain the difference between a need and a want.
➤ **Why do you think it is often hard to tell the difference between a need and a want?**

Discernment Activity

➤ *Give your child a magazine.*
➤ Choose an advertisement that causes you to consider buying something.
➤ **Read the third paragraph on page 160.**
➤ **Is the magazine advertisement that you chose for a service or a good?**

Needs and Wants

When you are thinking of buying something, what must you consider? Certainly the price is important. You should have enough money before you make a purchase.

But money may not be what you should think of first. You might ask yourself whether the item is something you *need* or you just *want*.

Businesses try to meet the needs and wants of people who buy. Businesses that sell things, or *goods*, and businesses that do work, or provide *services*, sometimes try to make people think they *need* what they really only *want*. For example, if a commercial tells about a new toy that "everyone is getting," you may think you have to get one. But the truth is that you only *want* one.

The Christian can trust in God to meet his needs. And he can know that his reward is eternal. He can believe that God, like a loving father, will give him "the desires of his heart." No Christian needs to fear the future or worry about the present. He need not entangle himself in the affairs of this world. His God will provide for him, no matter what governments and economies are doing.

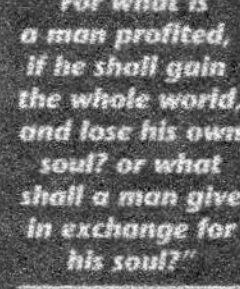

"For what is a man profited, if he shall gain the whole world, and lose his own soul? or what shall a man give in exchange for his soul?"
Matthew 16:26

God has promised to meet the needs of His children.

160

➤ **Does the service or good meet a need or a want?**

Wants can masquerade as needs. For example, although a boy needs shoes, he does not necessarily *need* a seventy-dollar pair of running shoes.

You may want to choose one or two advertisements to study and to identify ways the ads try to turn wants into needs.

➤ **Read the last paragraph on page 160 to see how a Christian should view his needs.** *(trusting God to take care of him)*

Some people think money can solve all their problems. People should rely on God, not money, to meet their needs. (BATs: 7d Contentment, 8a Faith in God's promises) Encourage your child to tell how God has met needs for him.

Evaluating the Lesson

Writing Activity, page 160

➤ **Read the verse Matthew 16:26 from page 160.**
➤ **What do you think it means to "gain the whole world"?**
➤ **What do think it means to "lose his own soul"?**

- **What would it profit someone who could "gain the world" but did not have salvation?**
- Write a paragraph, explaining how what appears to be gain is at last loss. Try to give examples of how people try to "gain the whole world."
- Be sure to include the most important need a person has *(salvation)* and how God has arranged for it to be met. (BAT: 1b Repentance and faith)

Going Beyond

Enrichment

Provide construction paper, felt-tip pens, glue, scissors, and magazines for your child to make "Gifts Money Cannot Buy." Instruct him to make coupons for family members, friends, or neighbors, offering his services for errands, and so on.

Additional Teacher Information

One million dollars would equal any of the following:

- one hundred million pennies towering approximately one hundred miles high.
- twenty million nickels filling an entire school bus.
- one million one-dollar bills weighing twenty-five hundred pounds and forming a stack approximately 360 feet tall.

When Oliver Winchester died, he left his wife, Sarah, with a fortune—money he had made from the invention of the Winchester rifle. But Sarah's great wealth did not make her happy. Soon after her husband's death, Sarah dreamed that she would die in order to atone for the deaths of all the people who had been killed by Winchester rifles. She dreamed that as soon as construction on her house was finished, she would die.

Without delay, Sarah hired carpenters to enlarge her house. She ordered them to tear out walls and add on rooms. She planned endless renovations: skylights, staircases, secret passageways, trap doors—anything at all to keep the workers busy. Over time, the eight-room farmhouse grew into a monstrosity as crews worked for decades enlarging the house. Sarah grew older, and her house took on a strange appearance. In all, Sarah's workmen built thirteen bathrooms, fifty-two skylights, and forty-seven fireplaces. When the workmen ran out of things to do, she ordered them to tear out walls and rebuild them in other places. Believing that she would live as long as she continued building, she asked her workmen to build staircases that led to dead ends and doors that opened onto solid walls. Some rooms were completely sealed off from the rest of the house. Ten thousand windows and fifty-two skylights could not let in enough light or fresh air to make Widow Winchester happy. Nothing she tried could alleviate her fear of death. At last, old and frightened, she died in her unusual house. Construction ceased that day. Today, the Winchester Mystery House is a tourist attraction in San Jose, California.

8 | LESSONS 43-48

Steam Engines and Smokestacks

This chapter traces the progression from hand machines to steam-powered machines and thus the establishment of America's early factories and mills. Your child will examine the changes in jobs, lifestyles, attitudes, and problems that came about as the Industrial Revolution grew and prospered. Lesson 43 presents a special dyeing project. Andrew Carnegie's success and generosity are highlighted in Lesson 48.

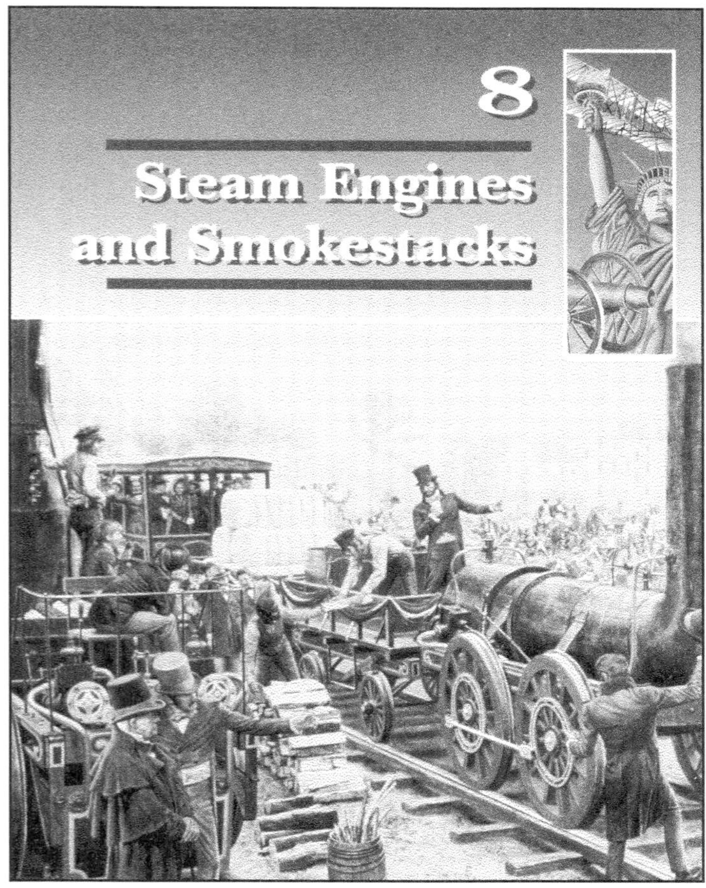

Materials

The following materials must be obtained or prepared before the presentation of the lesson. These items are labeled with an asterisk (*) in each lesson and in the Materials List in the Supplement. For further information see the individual lessons.

- Several homemade items (Lesson 43)
- Materials for dyeing cloth (Lesson 43)
- Appendix, pages A62-A63 (Lessons 43-48)
- A small paper sack (Lesson 44)
- Raw cotton or a cotton ball (Lesson 44)
- Appendix, page A64 (Lesson 45)
- Appendix, page A65 (Lesson 46)
- Appendix, page A66 (Lesson 48)

LESSON 43
By Hand

Text, pages 162-65
Notebook, page 67

Preview

Main Ideas

- People use the earth's resources to meet their needs.
- Early Americans made their own thread into cloth to make their clothing.
- People traded goods with others to meet their needs.

Objectives

- Dye cloth by hand
- Number in order the stages of early cloth making
- Draw a picture of a stage in cloth making in Colonial America

Materials

- Several homemade items (clothing, baskets, toys, small furniture)*
- Pieces of cotton cloth to dye (old socks, T-shirts, pillowcases)*
- 1 to 2 cups each of cut-up, stain-producing foods (red or yellow onion skins, spinach leaves, frozen blueberries, red cabbage, or beets)*
- 1 to 2 tablespoons coffee or saffron (optional)*
- Alum or white vinegar*
- Old nylon stockings*
- Several pots (glass, enamel, or stainless steel)
- Large, sturdy spoon
- A Bible
- *HERITAGE STUDIES Listening Cassette B*
- Appendix, pages A62-A63: The Wheel of Progress for the Industrial Revolution*

Day 1

Lesson

Introducing the Lesson

Guessing Activity

➤ *Display the homemade items.* All these things are alike in some way.

➤ **What do you think these items have in common?** These items were all made at home.

➤ I will read a riddle. Guess what adjective describes the item made at home. *(homemade)*

Not day after day in a factory line—
Not the long song of an engine's low whine—
I'm created at home with care from just one
Who patiently works 'til the task is all done.

Dyeing Activity

Prepare the materials needed for making homemade dye. Select one or more of the substances to create dyes. Collect or cut the pieces of cloth your child will be dyeing.

➤ You may assist me as we prepare a batch of homemade dye.

- Prepare individual dye bundles for each food variety by placing the measured amount of each vegetable, berry, or other substance in a separate nylon stocking.
- Tie each stocking using string or twist-ties.
- Place each bundle in a separate pot.
- Cover the bundle with two to three inches of water. You will need enough water to cover the cloth you will be dyeing.
- Add one teaspoon of alum or white vinegar to each pot. This will set the color so that it will not wash out.
- Boil for about an hour to extract the color. The color intensity is increased by adding more ingredients or boiling for a longer period of time. When the desired color is achieved, remove the nylon bundle. The dye is now ready.

➤ To begin the dyeing process, place one piece of cloth in each pan of dye.

➤ Soak and stir until the cloth reaches the desired shade.

➤ Remove the cloth from the pot, squeezing out any excess liquid.

➤ Hang the cloth to dry.

Today people can buy all kinds of clothes readymade.

Making Things

Before there were stores to buy clothes and food and tools and shoes in, before there were factories and big mills and plants for producing goods, people made their own goods—even toys and wagons and hats.

By Hand

If you had to make all of your clothes yourself, what would you do first? Go buy fabric? What if you had to make the cloth before you could sew the clothes? What would you do?

You could get a *loom*, a large frame used to make cloth from yarn or thread. You could weave cloth to make clothes. But where would you get the thread or yarn? Before there were yarn shops, people had to spin their own yarn and thread.

From what would you make your yarn or thread? You might choose wool or cotton. But first you would have to shear the sheep or pick the cotton. And before that, you would have had to raise the sheep or plant the cotton. Do you think you would have as many clothes as you do right now if you had to go through this process every time you needed a new piece of clothing?

Many people knit clothing, but few spin their own yarn first.

162

Shearing sheep

When the Separatists came to the New World on the *Mayflower*, they brought only a few extra clothes with them. But clothes wear out after a while. Where do you think they got new ones? Some ships from England brought more, including shoes. But the Separatists also made clothes.

Most women at that time knew how to make yarn, how to weave it into cloth, and how to make clothes from the cloth. It could take weeks or months to get a jacket or a skirt ready to wear. Why do you think it took so long?

Families often raised their own sheep. One of the children's jobs was to look after the flock. Why was this an important job? When the sheep's wool grew long, the farmer cut it off; he *sheared* the sheep.

Carding wool

Spinning yarn

After a sheep is sheared, the wool has to be combed, or *carded*, to smooth it out for spinning. *Spinning*, making a long yarn from the sheep's wool, requires a spinning wheel and someone to run the wheel. The person in this picture is making wool yarn. Then the wool is dyed. How much yarn do you think it takes to make a yard of cloth?

163

Day 2

Teaching the Lesson

Text Discussion, page 162

➤ **Read page 162 to find out about the process Colonial Americans went through to get new clothes.** *(They had to raise sheep for wool or plant cotton; spin the wool or cotton to make thread; weave the thread to make cloth; cut and sew the cloth.)*

The early colonists had to work hard in order to have clothes to wear, food to eat, and houses to live in. Most of the colonists' daily activities involved work for the adults and for the children. (BATs: 2c Faithfulness, 2d Goal setting, 2e Work)

➤ Look at the photograph of the child selecting clothes.

➤ **Did most children long ago have as many clothes as children do today?** *(no)*

Text Discussion, page 163

➤ **Read the first three paragraphs on page 163 to find out one important job that many Separatist children had.** *(looking after the flock of sheep)*

The Bible character David also had this job. Read aloud I Samuel 16:1, 11-13. Sing "The Lord Is My Shepherd" along with the recording from the listening cassette.

➤ **Read aloud the last sentence of the third paragraph on page 163.**

Shearing does not hurt the sheep; it is a little like giving a haircut. The shearer cuts the thick wool, or fleece, from the sheep. The sheep prances away with its new "hairstyle" and in a year needs another "haircut."

➤ **Read the last paragraph on page 163 to find out what is done with the wool after the sheep is sheared.** *(It is carded.)*

➤ **What happens when the wool is *carded?*** *(It is combed to make it smooth.)*

➤ **How does the carded wool become yarn?** *(It is spun on a **spinning wheel or machine**.)*

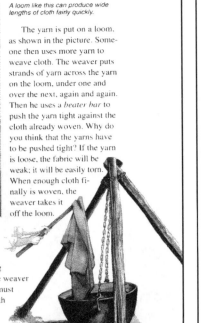

A loom like this can produce wide lengths of cloth fairly quickly.

The yarn is put on a loom, as shown in the picture. Someone then uses more yarn to weave cloth. The weaver puts strands of yarn across the yarn on the loom, under one and over the next, again and again. Then he uses a *beater bar* to push the yarn tight against the cloth already woven. Why do you think that the yarns have to be pushed tight? If the yarn is loose, the fabric will be weak; it will be easily torn. When enough cloth finally is woven, the weaver takes it off the loom.

Do you think the cloth is now ready to be used for clothing? Not yet. First it has to be washed and shrunk so that it will be sturdy. Making the cloth tighter by shrinking and pressing it is called *fulling*. If the weaver wants the cloth a different color, he must *dye* it by boiling it in water tinted with color. Then the cloth has to be dried and stretched before it can at last be used to make clothes.

Dyeing the cloth

164

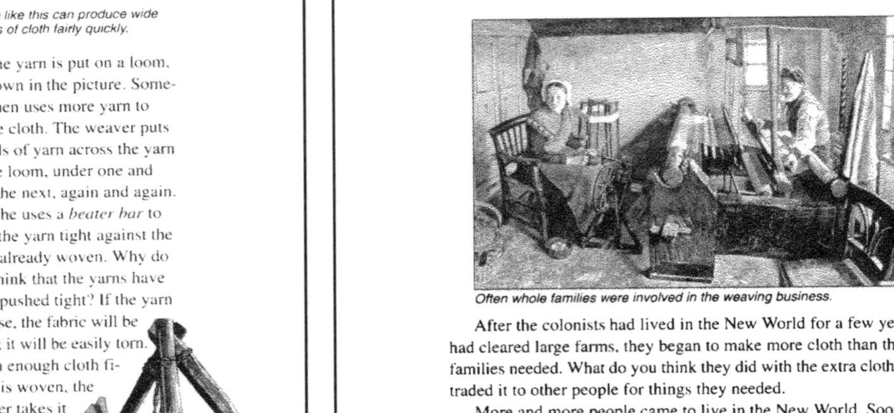

Often whole families were involved in the weaving business.

After the colonists had lived in the New World for a few years and had cleared large farms, they began to make more cloth than their own families needed. What do you think they did with the extra cloth? They traded it to other people for things they needed.

More and more people came to live in the New World. Soon some people who liked to weave began to make much cloth to sell. *Weavers* worked so many hours at their looms that they did not have time to make other things for themselves, such as shoes and tools. What do you think happened then?

The weavers traded their cloth for shoes, tools, and other items. They traded with people who mainly made shoes or tools. Soon, instead of families making all the things they needed for themselves, people were concentrating on making one product and trading for the rest. People began to *specialize*. What does that mean?

Suppose you were a weaver and you had more orders for cloth than you could fill. What could you do? You could hire people to help you; you would have to buy another loom and more yarn. But what if the spinners could not make enough yarn to keep your looms running?

165

Text Discussion, page 164

- ➤ **Read page 164 to find out how the yarn becomes a piece of cloth.** *(It is woven into cloth on a loom.)*
- ➤ **What happens when the cloth is *fulled*?** *(It becomes tighter by shrinking and pressing.)*
- ➤ **Why is some cloth dyed?** *(to add color)*

Although some cloth was dyed before making clothing, it was far more common to use the cloth in its natural state.

- ➤ Look at the page showing The Wheel of Progress for the Industrial Revolution.

We will be adding words to this spinning wheel as we study the change in production of goods which occurred in America.

- ➤ **Which words represent how goods were produced during these earliest days of our country?** *(handmade goods)* Glue these words to a spoke on the spinning wheel.

You may wish to have your child cut out the words before the lesson begins.

Text Discussion, page 165

- ➤ **Read page 165 to find out what people did when they made more cloth than they needed.** *(They traded it for other things that they needed, or they sold it.)*
- ➤ **Why did the weavers not have time to make tools or shoes for themselves?** *(They spent so much time at their looms making cloth that they did not have time to make other things.)*
- ➤ Listen as I read aloud the sentence that explains what they did: "People began to specialize."
- ➤ **What does *specialize* mean?** *(Answers will vary but should include that each person would make one specific product.)*

This system of making one specific product led to the need for more people. More people created a need for more machines. With more people and more machines, there was also a lot more of each product being produced.

Making Cloth Name ______________________

Read each statement. Number the statements in the order that they occurred.

1 Wool yarn was made on a spinning wheel.

4 The cloth was dyed.

3 The cloth was fulled.

5 Weavers sold their cloth or traded it for other things that they needed.

2 The yarn was made into cloth on a loom.

6 Other craftsmen began to specialize with the products that they made.

Draw a picture of one stage in cloth making.

© 1996 BJU Press. Reproduction prohibited.

Heritage Studies 4 Student Notebook

Lesson 43 Evaluating the Lesson 67

Evaluating the Lesson

Notebook Activity, page 67

➤ Read the instructions on Notebook page 67.
➤ Complete the page.

Going Beyond

Additional Teacher Information

Australia is the world's leading nation for sheep production. Most sheep live an average of seven years, and most ewes give birth to one or two lambs at a time. There are currently more than eight hundred breeds and varieties of domestic sheep throughout the world. Sheep yield wool, meat, and leather. They also furnish the raw materials for the production of glue, soap, fertilizer, cosmetics, and catgut used in stringing tennis rackets.

Most sheep shearers use power clippers. Expert sheep shearers clip two hundred or more animals in one day. The sheep shearers try to remove the fleece in one piece so that the parts can be sorted and graded more easily. The best wool comes from the shoulders and sides of the sheep. Sheep are usually sheared once a year, in the spring or in the summer.

All parts of the cotton plant are useful. Millers spin fibers (lint) into yarn and then weave the yarn into fabric. The very short fibers on the seeds (linters) are used in making paper, padding, and explosives. Refined oil from the seeds becomes an ingredient in food products such as margarine and salad dressing. Soap, cosmetics, and some medicines are made from unrefined cottonseed oil. Livestock eat the hulls of the seeds. Fertilizer is made from any remaining hulls and the stalks and the leaves of the cotton plant.

Lesson 44
By Machine

Text, pages 166-69
Notebook, page 68

Preview

Main Ideas

- Inventions and ideas spread from one part of the world to another.
- Individuals have unique attributes and skills.
- New machines improved the weaving industry.
- As technology changes, so do the ways people earn a living.

Objectives

- Read and interpret maps
- Read and interpret graphs
- Write a paragraph from the perspective of an unemployed hand weaver

Materials

- A small paper sack*
- Some raw cotton or a cotton ball*
- The Wheel of Progress from Lesson 43

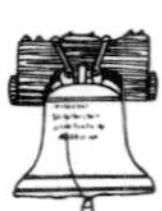

Place the cotton in the sack and close the sack before the lesson begins.

Day 1

Lesson

Introducing the Lesson

Mystery Item Identification

➤ *Place the paper sack on the table.*

➤ There is a mystery item in this sack. I will give you clues to help you guess what the item is. You may make a guess as soon as you think you know the answer.

Pause after giving each clue to allow your child time to guess what he thinks is in the sack. Allow him to look in the sack when he has guessed correctly or when all the clues have been given.

All of my parts are useful.
I am a kind of plant.
I begin as a seed.
My flower has five petals.

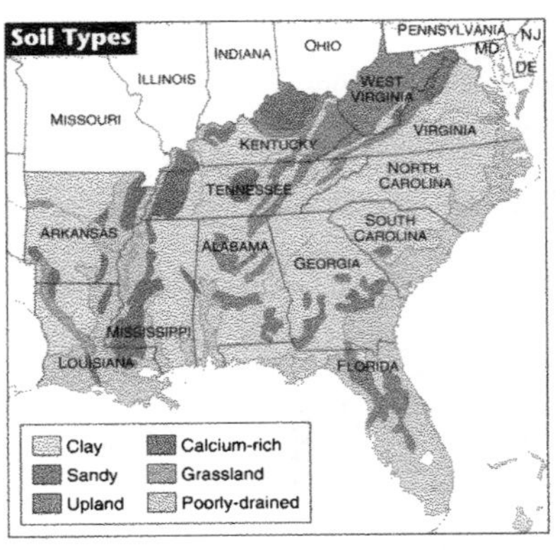

There are two kinds of cotton—long-strand and short-strand. The short-strand grows easily, but the seeds are hard to take out. The long-strand cotton needs a certain climate to grow well, but the seeds come out with less trouble. Mississippi, Alabama, and Louisiana grew the most short-strand cotton. The coasts of South Carolina and Georgia grew much long-strand.

Look at the soil and growing season maps. What kinds of soils and growing seasons do you think the two kinds needed?

169

My white flower turns pink and then purple before falling off.
My seedpod contains about thirty seeds.
My seedpod looks like a green walnut before it dries and cracks open.
I grow inside the pod.
I am white and fuzzy.
China and the United States lead in my production.
I am the most widely used plant fiber.
I am in many of your clothes.

Teaching the Lesson

Map-Reading Activity, page 169

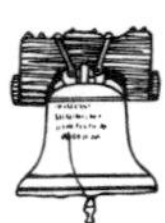

The pages in this section do not appear in order. Long-strand cotton is sometimes called New World cotton; short-strand cotton is sometimes called Old World cotton.

➤ **Read page 169 to find out the two kinds of cotton.** *(long-strand and short-strand)*

➤ Look at the map on this page showing the types of soil.

➤ **How many types of soil are shown in the key?** *(six)*

➤ **Read aloud the name of each soil type.**

➤ **Is there a state that has only one soil type?** *(no)* (*NOTE:* If your state is among those whose soil types are on the map, take time to locate your town and identify the soil type there.)

➤ **Which type of soil covers the largest area of the map?** *(clay)*

➤ Find the following states on the map, identifying the soil types: Louisiana, Mississippi, Alabama, South Carolina, and Georgia. *(Louisiana—clay, poorly drained, calcium-rich, grassland; Mississippi—clay, calcium-rich, poorly drained; Alabama—clay, sandy, upland, calcium-rich, poorly drained; South Carolina and Georgia—clay, sandy, poorly drained)*

➤ **Which two types of soil are in all of these states?** *(clay and poorly drained)*

➤ **In which type of soil do you think cotton grows?**

It grows best in clay soil. However, the type of soil is not the only important factor for the growth of cotton.

➤ Look at the map showing the growing seasons. **What color is used for the fewest number of days in the growing season?** *(purple)*

➤ Point to the places with the shortest growing season. *(northeastern West Virginia, some places in Virginia, eastern Tennessee, and western North Carolina)*

➤ **What color is used for the longest growing season?** *(green)*

➤ Name the state whose whole area has over 240 days that make up the warm and sunny growing season. *(Florida)*

➤ Locate once again Mississippi, Alabama, Louisiana, South Carolina, and Georgia, telling how long the growing season is in each state. *(Mississippi and Louisiana—210 to over 240 days; Alabama and South Carolina—180 to over 240 days; Georgia—150 to over 240 days)*

Each type of land is just the way God intends for it to be. God rules over the land, the things that it grows, and, of course, the people who tend the land. (Bible Promise: I. God as Master)

➤ **What kind of weather is necessary for growing cotton, based on the information gained from the map?** *(warm, sunny climate)*

In this lesson we will learn about the machines used in the early cotton industry.

By Machine

When the demands got bigger than people could meet, something had to change. A man named James Hargreaves had an idea. He made a machine called a *spinning jenny* that helped a spinner make twenty times as much yarn or thread in a day. Hargreaves lived in England, and he wanted to keep his idea just for the English. But the idea spread to other places. Why do you think he wanted to keep the idea in England? How do you think ideas get from one country to another?

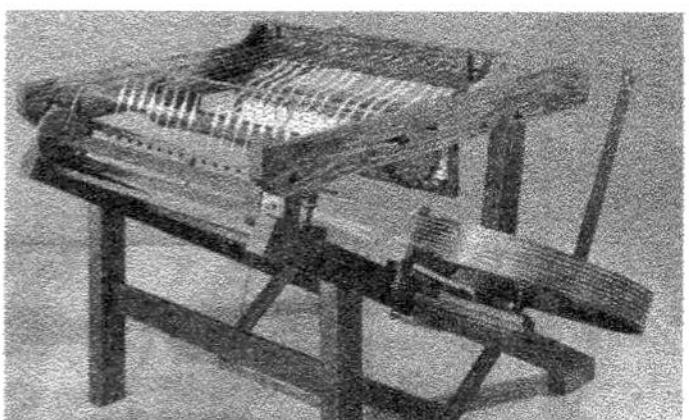

Hargreaves's spinning jenny

Then Samuel Crompton, another Englishman, made an even better machine. It ran on steam power; it made two or three hundred times more yarn in a day. Now spinners could supply all the yarn needed.

In fact, the spinners made far more yarn than the weavers could use up. For a while, the weavers worked faster and faster. But at last the weavers saw that they could not keep up. Then what do you think happened? The weaving business had to make some changes. A new weaving machine had to be invented.

Amount of Spinning in One Day by One Person

166

Text Discussion, pages 166-67

➤ **Read page 166 to find out which machines improved the making of thread.** *(spinning jenny and Samuel Crompton's steam-powered machine)*

➤ **What is shown on the graph on page 166?** *(the amount of spinning done in one day by one person)*

The spinning jenny made it possible for a person to make twenty times as much yarn as by hand.

➤ **What powered the machine which increased production by two or three hundred times?** *(steam)*

The steam-powered machine which Samuel Crompton invented was called the ***spinning mule***.

➤ **Look at the picture on page 167 and read the caption.**

➤ Choose the two sets of words which represent the improvements to the production of goods. Add these to The Wheel of Progress. *(steam power and spinning jenny)*

➤ **Read aloud the paragraph on page 166 which describes the problem created by Samuel Crompton's invention.** *(the last paragraph)*

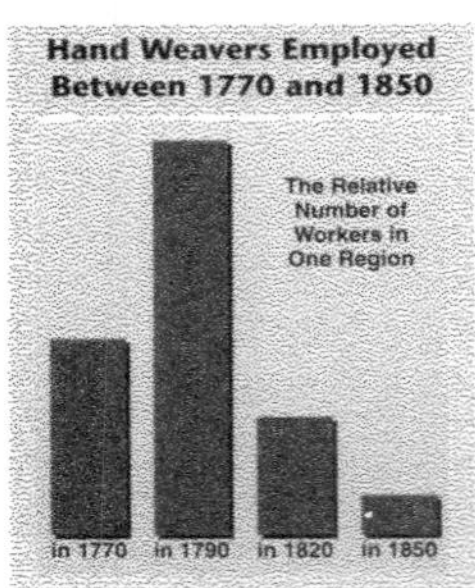

And soon it was. A large engine-driven loom changed forever how weaving was done. No longer did someone sit at a small loom and make a yard or two of fabric a day. Now one person could run a big machine that made that much or more in an hour. If such a machine could do the weaving of a dozen people, what do you think happened to the weavers who used the old looms? They soon had no work. How do you think those people felt about the new machines?

Some people who lost their work hated the new inventions. A few even broke into shops at night and smashed the machines. Others tried to get laws passed that would keep machines out of their towns. But the speed and power of the machines made them too useful to be ignored. Owners of businesses saw that with the faster methods they could make a lot of money. They did not want to worry about the craftsmen who were "going out of style."

Running a spinning mule, based on Crompton's design

167

When the weavers and spinners began to work much faster, what do you think happened to the cotton growers? They soon found that people wanted far more cotton from them than they could get ready. Although they could grow enough, they couldn't get the seeds out of it fast enough. Do you remember who invented a machine to take care of that problem?

Compare the graphs. By how much did the cotton gin increase the amount of cotton cleaned in a day? How did the gin affect cotton growing?

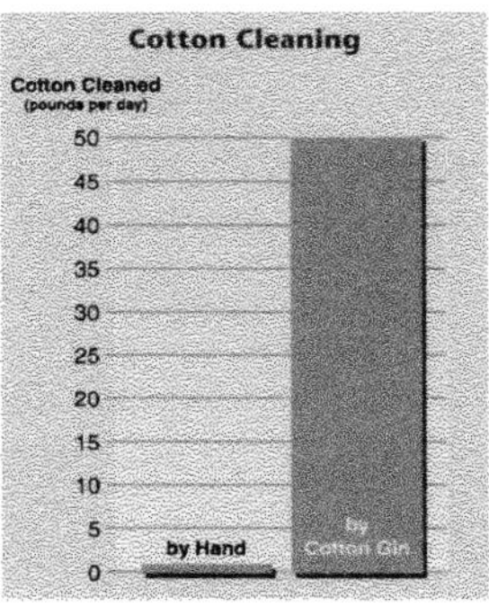

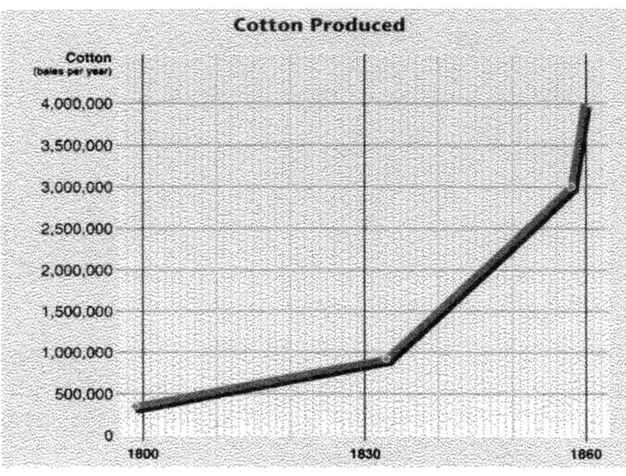

168

- ➤ **Read page 167 to learn about the next invention that changed the weaving industry.** *(a large engine-driven loom)*
- ➤ Look at the graph on page 167. **When were the most hand weavers employed?** *(1790)*
- ➤ **What was invented between 1790 and 1820 that made the work for hand weavers decrease?** *(An engine-driven loom was invented.)*
- ➤ **Read aloud the paragraph on page 167 that tells what some of the hand weavers did when no more work was available for them.** *(last paragraph)*

The weavers acted this way out of anger and desperation, but their actions were unkind and wrong. (BATs: 2d Goal setting, 2e Work, 3c Emotional control)

- ➤ **What are some other ways that the weavers could have dealt with this situation?** *(Possible answers are that they could have learned to operate the new machines and work for other people or that they could have gotten different kinds of jobs.)*

Chart-Reading Activity, page 168

- ➤ **Read page 168 to find out what other group of people had more work as a result of the success of the large steam-powered weaving machines.** *(the cotton growers)*
- ➤ Look at the graph entitled "Cotton Produced." **How many bales of cotton were grown in 1800?** *(fewer than five hundred thousand)*
- ➤ **How many bales were produced in 1830?** *(just under one million)*
- ➤ **How many bales were grown in 1860?** *(four million)*
- ➤ **Who invented the machine that took the seeds out of the cotton?** *(Eli Whitney)* (*NOTE:* If your child does not remember Whitney's name, refer to Chapter 6.)
- ➤ Look at the bar graph labeled "Cotton Cleaning." Compare the figures on the graph. *(approximately one pound cleaned by hand compared to fifty pounds cleaned by a cotton gin)*

With so much more cotton cleaned and ready for the large looms, the production of cloth became big business.

A Weaver's Story

Name ____________________

Read the following story starter.
Write your reactions to the situation that is described.

Pretend that you are a weaver, a good weaver who has worked steadily for several years in the colonies. Weaving on your hand loom is the way that you make your living to provide for your family. Sometimes you weave items to sell to others in order to buy food or other things that your family needs. Sometimes you trade your woven goods in exchange for items that someone else has made.

But now the orders have become fewer and fewer. Your house needs a new roof, and you do not have the money or materials to fix it. Your son needs new shoes, but you have nothing to trade with the cobbler. What has happened? Why do people not want your business anymore? A new steam-powered weaving machine has come to town. It does the weaving that it used to take a dozen people to do—and it does it faster. Nobody wants to wait around any more for the hand weaver to complete a job when the machine can do the job more quickly.

How does this situation make you feel? What will you do now to make money to support your family and to take care of their needs?

Heritage Studies 4 Student Notebook — Lesson 44 Evaluating the Lesson — 68

Evaluating the Lesson

Notebook Activity, page 68

- ➤ Read the instructions on Notebook page 68.
- ➤ Complete the page.

Going Beyond

Enrichment

Make arrangements to tour a textile mill, factory, or local weaver's shop.

Additional Teacher Information

In addition to the cotton and wool used to make cotton and wool yarn, the fibers of the flax plant were used to make linen yarn.

The following people and their inventions contributed greatly to the development and growth of the textile industry in early America.

> James Hargreaves invented the spinning jenny about 1767. *Jenny* was another word for *gin,* which was short for *engine.* Coarse yarn was produced with the spinning jenny as the weaver turned a crank that connected vertically mounted spindles.
>
> In 1769, William Arkwright patented a water-powered spinning frame that used the same motions that human hands had used when doing the work.
>
> In 1779, Samuel Crompton invented the spinning mule, which combined the actions of the spinning jenny, spinning frame, and the use of bobbins. It produced very fine yarn.
>
> Edmund Cartwright's invention of the large steam-powered loom was completed in 1789.
>
> Eli Whitney's cotton gin of 1793 greatly aided the process of cleaning raw cotton.

LESSON 45
More Machines

Text, pages 170-72
Notebook, page 69

Preview

Main Ideas

- As technology changes, so do the ways that people earn a living.
- Steam-powered machines affected almost every business in early America.
- People use technology to adapt to different environments.

Objective

- Match words with their definitions

Materials

- 6 small containers
- Appendix, page A64: terms and definitions*

Tape one of the six term labels to each container. Cut apart the definitions and place them in the labeled containers according to the following symbols: balderdash—•, sawyer—*, boom—+, spinster—#, vendor—$, teamster—? If the symbols at the end of each definition will confuse your child, you may cut off the symbol after organizing the definitions in the proper containers.

Day 1

Lesson

Introducing the Lesson

A Game

➤ Remove the definitions from the container labeled *balderdash.*

➤ **Read aloud the definitions one at a time, choosing the definition that you think is the correct one for *balderdash.***

Your child is not expected to know these terms yet. Guide him in the process of elimination to choose the most likely answer.

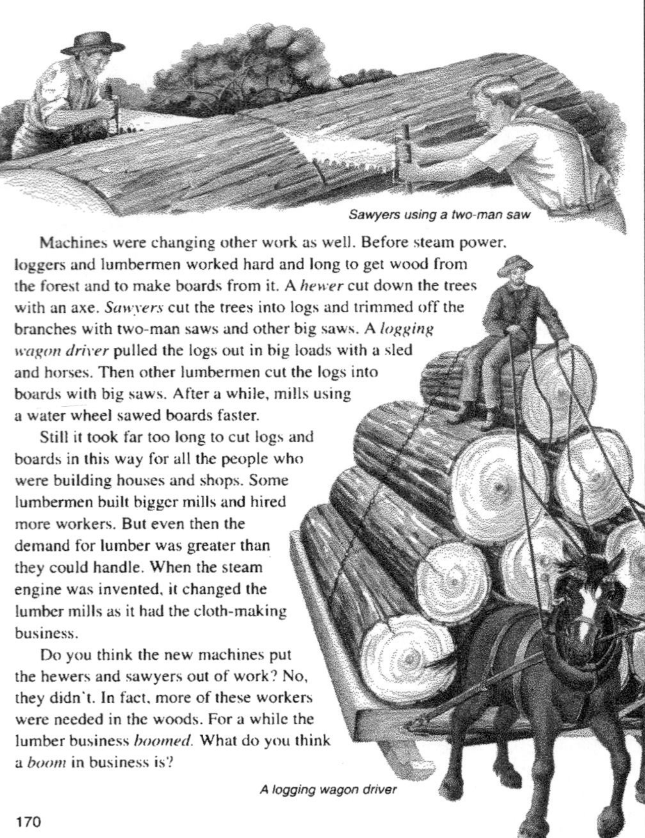

Sawyers using a two-man saw

Machines were changing other work as well. Before steam power, loggers and lumbermen worked hard and long to get wood from the forest and to make boards from it. A *hewer* cut down the trees with an axe. *Sawyers* cut the trees into logs and trimmed off the branches with two-man saws and other big saws. A *logging wagon driver* pulled the logs out in big loads with a sled and horses. Then other lumbermen cut the logs into boards with big saws. After a while, mills using a water wheel sawed boards faster.

Still it took far too long to cut logs and boards in this way for all the people who were building houses and shops. Some lumbermen built bigger mills and hired more workers. But even then the demand for lumber was greater than they could handle. When the steam engine was invented, it changed the lumber mills as it had the cloth-making business.

Do you think the new machines put the hewers and sawyers out of work? No, they didn't. In fact, more of these workers were needed in the woods. For a while the lumber business *boomed.* What do you think a *boom* in business is?

A logging wagon driver

170

The correct definition for balderdash is nonsense. The game Balderdash is a game that includes nonsense definitions as well as the correct definition of a word. The goal is to determine which definition is the real one. We will play a version of Balderdash with words from this lesson.

➤ Follow the same procedure to choose the correct definition for each of the terms: ***sawyer*** *(someone who cuts wood),* ***spinster*** *(an older single woman),* ***teamster*** *(a truck driver),* ***boom*** *(a time of great success),* ***vendor*** *(a salesman).*

If you are teaching more than one child, allow the children to take turns reading aloud the definitions. After all the definitions for one term have been read, allow each child to vote for the one he thinks is the correct definition. Give the correct definition before going to the next word.

➤ In this lesson we will learn more about these terms and how they came about.

This steam engine powered a grist mill.

Thomas Edison used this steam engine to power tools in his laboratory at Menlo Park.

Hardly a business was untouched by the new steam-powered machines. Sheep shearers now had steam-powered clippers that could quickly cut the wool from ewes. Farmers began to use reapers and threshers run by steam engines. Horses and carriages were replaced by trains running on steam. How do you think these changes made life different for everyone?

One change was in prices—they went down on many items. Now more people could afford to buy clothes and tools rather than make them for themselves. Another change was in the places people lived. Before the machines, most people lived on small farms. As mills and shops became bigger, more people began to move to the towns and cities to live and to work at jobs other than farming. Life was quite different in the city for people used to living in the country.

171

ECHOES IN HISTORY

Names

Although the new machines caused many jobs to disappear, some of the names still "echo" in our times. Just the meanings have changed. For example, someone who spun thread was called a *spinster.* Often this person was a woman who stayed with her parents to take care of the spinning, weaving, and other household work. The word has since come to mean any unmarried woman past the usual age for marrying.

Being a crossing guard is a big responsibility.

A *vendor* was once (and still is in some of the larger cities) a person who sold goods from a small street cart. Oystermen, muffin men, peanut girls, gingerbread ladies, and fish sellers were vendors on streets long ago. Today the word *vendor* usually means a person or a company that provides a service or goods.

Teamster used to refer to someone who drove a wagon and horses. Today the word *teamster* is used in a more general way. The Teamsters' Union includes truck drivers and warehousemen and others, but none of them work with horses.

Once a *crossing guard* stopped people from crossing tracks when a train was coming. What does the modern crossing guard do?

This vendor carts apples through the streets, calling, "Apples, fresh apples!"

172

Teaching the Lesson

Text Discussion, pages 170-71

➤ **Read page 170 to find out the difference between a *hewer* and a *sawyer.*** *(A **hewer** cuts down the trees with an axe. A **sawyer** uses saws to cut the trees into logs.)*

➤ **Why did the people want wood from the forest?** *(to make boards for building houses and shops)*

➤ **What powered the saws in the first sawmills?** *(water wheels)*

➤ **Did the invention of the steam machines put the hewers and sawyers out of business?** *(no)* Explain why. *(The lumber business was very successful and needed more and more wood from the hewers and sawyers.)*

➤ During this time, the lumber business boomed. **What do you think a boom is?** A ***boom*** is a time of success and prosperity.

➤ Look at the picture of a grist mill on page 171.

The ***grist mill*** ground grain for bread and cereals. Steam power was used to run this mill just as steam was used to power lumber mills and sawmills.

➤ **Read page 171 to find out some other businesses that were affected by the steam-powered machines.** *(Sheep were clipped quickly; farmers used steam engines to harvest their crops; trains replaced horses and carriages.)*

➤ **What changes did these machines bring about in America?** *(Prices went down on many items; therefore, more people could afford to buy more things. Many people moved to towns and cities.)*

Text Discussion, page 172

Although many jobs of long ago no longer exist today, some words and names associated with those jobs have become part of our modern vocabulary.

➤ **Read page 172 to find out what a *spinster* was originally and what the word means today.** *(Long ago a spinster was a woman who spun thread, often staying at home to take care of her parents. Today the term refers to an unmarried woman who is past the usual age of marriage.)*

➤ **Do you know what name is given to the machines from which you can buy crackers, candy bars, and sodas?** *(vending machines)*

The companies supplying these machines are called ***vendors***.

➤ If you have ever seen street vendors, tell where you saw the vendors and what they were selling.

➤ **What term is used for a pair of horses that work together to pull a wagon?** *(team)*

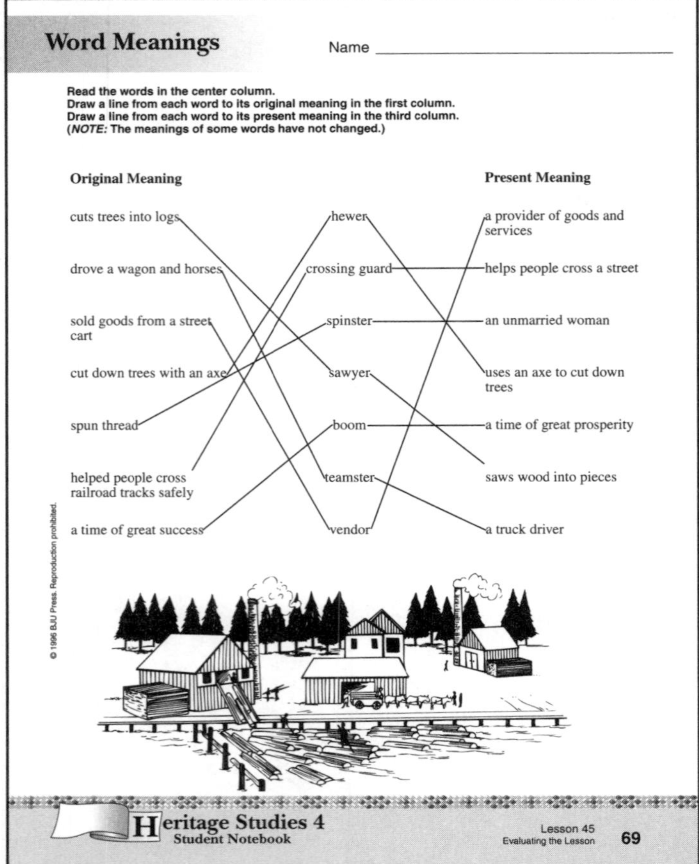

Word Meanings Name ____________

Read the words in the center column.
Draw a line from each word to its original meaning in the first column.
Draw a line from each word to its present meaning in the third column.
(*NOTE:* The meanings of some words have not changed.)

Original Meaning		Present Meaning
cuts trees into logs	hewer	a provider of goods and services
drove a wagon and horses	crossing guard	helps people cross a street
sold goods from a street cart	spinster	an unmarried woman
cut down trees with an axe	sawyer	uses an axe to cut down trees
spun thread	boom	a time of great prosperity
helped people cross railroad tracks safely	teamster	saws wood into pieces
a time of great success	vendor	a truck driver

Heritage Studies 4 Student Notebook — Lesson 45 Evaluating the Lesson 69

Teamwork, cooperation with others to achieve the same goal, is important for Christians who wish to accomplish the work of the Lord. (BATs: 2c Faithfulness, 2e Work)

➤ **What did *teamster* mean long ago and what does it mean now?** *(Long ago a teamster drove a wagon and horses. Today teamsters are truck drivers, warehousemen, and others, but none of them work with horses.)*

➤ **What did a *crossing guard* do long ago and what does he do now?** *(Long ago the crossing guard stopped people from crossing the tracks in front of a train; now he stops vehicles so that people can safely cross the road.)*

As times change and new things are invented, new words become part of our language, often changing the meaning of other words.

Evaluating the Lesson

Notebook Activity, page 69

➤ Read the instructions on Notebook page 69.

➤ Complete the page.

Although the meanings of some words have not changed, the definition is worded differently for each column.

Going Beyond

Enrichment

Encourage your child to make either a vendor's cart or a tractor-trailer truck with vendor advertising on the side. Provide several small boxes (small cereal boxes or boxes from tea bags would work well) for making vendor carts. Boxes from tubes of toothpaste may be used to construct the tractor-trailer trucks. Also have available several buttons or small caps like those from medicine bottles, milk jugs, and film canisters. Glue, tape, felt-tip pens, old magazines, and construction paper to cover the boxes are also necessary. Encourage your child to be creative.

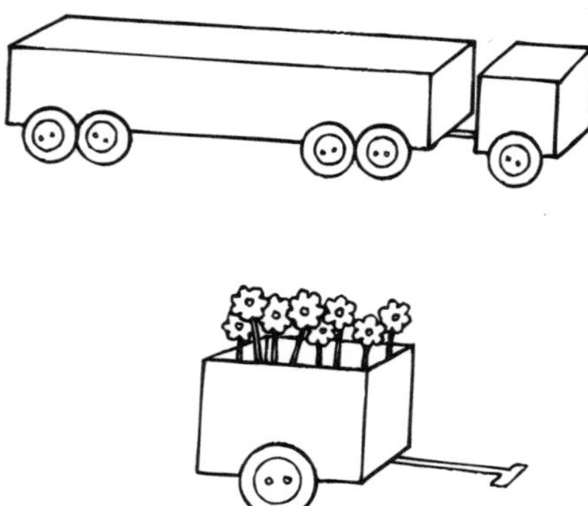

Additional Teacher Information

The first known vending machine dispensed holy water in a Greek temple in Alexandria, Egypt, in 215 B.C. In the United States, the first vending machines appeared in New York City in 1888 and dispensed chewing gum. Vending machines for candy and cigarettes first appeared in the 1920s.

The official name of the Teamsters Union is International Brotherhood of Teamsters, Chauffeurs, Warehousemen, and Helpers of America. Members of the Teamsters Union include truck drivers, chauffeurs, industrial workers, airline and public service employees, warehouse workers, workers in the automotive industry (including salesmen and garage and service station employees), and employees in dairy, brewery, soft-drink, and food-processing plants.

LESSON 46
The Industrial Revolution

Text, pages 173-76, 271, 313
Notebook, pages 70-71

Preview

Main Ideas

- Industry is important to a community.
- The Industrial Revolution changed the way people lived and worked.
- The physical environment makes a difference in the way people live and work.
- Using machines helped meet the needs of the American Civil War.

Objectives

- Complete a chart, listing changes caused by the Industrial Revolution
- Answer questions using a distribution map

Materials

- Appendix, page A65: Changes chart*
- The figure representing the Industrial Revolution (1830) from the TimeLine Snapshots
- The Wheel of Progress from Lesson 44

Notes

The Changes chart on the Appendix page will show the following changes when completed.

country ➡ city
farm ➡ factory
wilderness paths ➡ railroads
handwork ➡ machines
family work ➡ big business

Day 1

Lesson

Introducing the Lesson

Word-Completion Activity

➤ *Place the incomplete Changes chart on the table.*

➤ **Read the words or phrases shown on the left of this chart.**

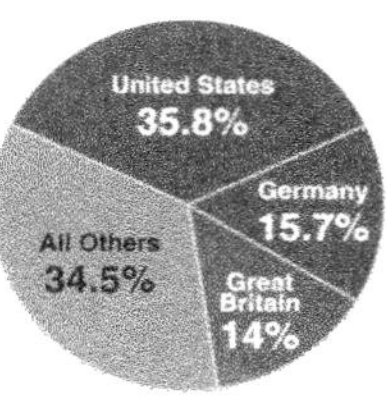

World Manufacturing in 1913

It Was Called a Revolution

Revolution usually means a big change which comes suddenly and often with violence. Do you think the change from handwork to machines should be called a revolution? In America, the change was not as dramatic as the word *revolution* might make it sound.

Money Spent on Running Factories in the U.S.

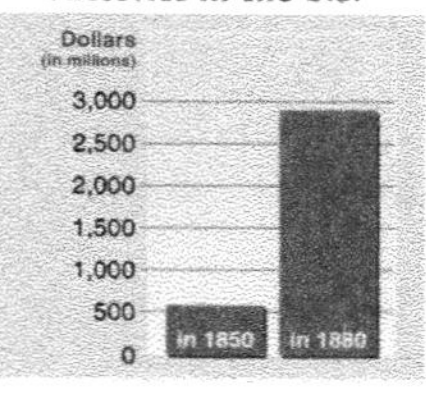

Number of People Working in Factories in the U.S.

Number of Workers: 3,000,000; 2,500,000; 2,000,000; 1,500,000; 1,000,000; 500,000; 0 — in 1850, in 1880

Although the change took many years, it made life in the United States completely different after the American Civil War. Many families now saw each other only when they were not working at a factory. Towns and cities grew fast; the nation became more "city" than "country."

In England, using more machines and factories was called the *Industrial Revolution*. *Industry* comes from an old word meaning "skill." *Factory*, a place where industry goes on, comes from an old word that means "a place for makers." The word *manufacture* comes from words meaning "to make by hand." How did the Industrial Revolution change the definition for that word?

Look at the graphs. What changes occurred in thirty years? How much money was being spent on factories by 1880? Where could you learn how much is being spent today? What country was first in manufacturing by 1913? Which country was second?

173

As more machines were invented in early America, many changes came. We will be completing this chart during our lesson today. For each term on the left, you will write a word or phrase that expresses the change brought about by new inventions. The chart will compare the old ways with the new ways.

Teaching the Lesson

Text Discussion, page 173

➤ **Read page 173 to find out the name of a special revolution in England and America.** *(the Industrial Revolution)*

➤ **What does the word *revolution* mean?** *("a big change which comes suddenly and often with violence")*

➤ **Did the Industrial Revolution bring a big change to America?** *(yes)*

➤ **Do you think the Industrial Revolution came suddenly?** No, the changes took many years.

➤ **Read the first term on the Changes chart.**

➤ **What word would describe the change in where people lived?** *(city)* Write the word beside the arrow.

➤ **What words did the word *manufacture* come from?** *(words meaning "to make by hand")*

After the Industrial Revolution the meaning of this word changed. The word now refers to products that are produced by large machinery in large quantities, usually in a factory.

TimeLine Snapshots Activity, page 271

➤ Add the figure representing the Industrial Revolution to the TimeLine at the year 1830.

The Industrial Revolution began in the late 1700s and continued through the mid 1800s. The greatest period of industrial growth in the United States occurred during the 1830s. The date 1830 is a representative date for the period known as the Industrial Revolution.

➤ **Who was president of the United States during the changes of the 1830s?** *(Andrew Jackson)*

➤ **In what year did Andrew Jackson enter office?** *(1829)*

➤ **Read the additional information about President Jackson found on page 271.**

Graph-Reading Activity, page 173

➤ Look at the graph showing how much money was spent on running factories in the United States. **What years are shown on the graph?** *(1850 and 1880)*

➤ **How many years were there between the two years shown on the graph?** *(thirty years)*

➤ **How much money was being spent on factories in 1850?** *(a little over five hundred million dollars) Write this number.*

➤ **Can you tell how much money was being spent in 1880?** *(almost three billion dollars) Write this number also for your child to read. Help him to compare the two numbers.*

➤ Look at the graph showing the number of factory workers. Calculate the increase of workers from 1850 to 1880. *(2,250,000−750,000=1,500,000 more factory workers) (NOTE:* Numbers are approximate. Accept any reasonable answer.)

➤ **What caused the increase in money spent and workers needed in the factories?** *(more machines, more factories, more business, and more products)*

In the early years of the Industrial Revolution, England had many more factories than America, but even with its slow start, America's Industrial Revolution continued to grow.

➤ Look at the circle graph. **Did England or the United States have more manufacturing in 1913?** *(the United States)*

The American Industrial Revolution

Americans had their reasons for not using machines and setting up factories as soon as other countries did. For one, the land in America was vast and unsettled. People who came from the crowded cities in other countries wanted to spend their money buying land. They did not want to stay in the towns. Even factory owners who paid good wages could not compete with the American desire to own land.

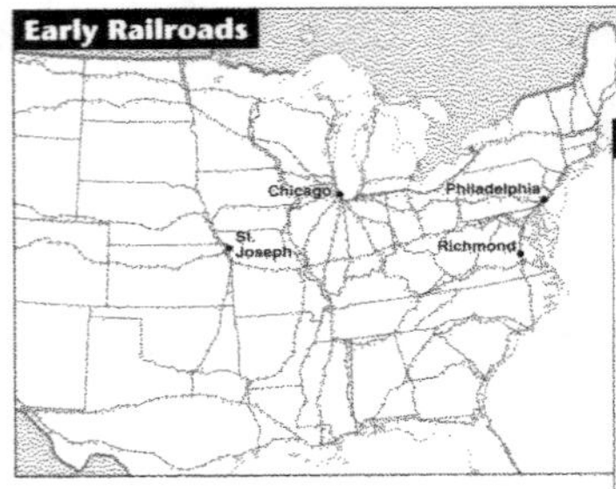

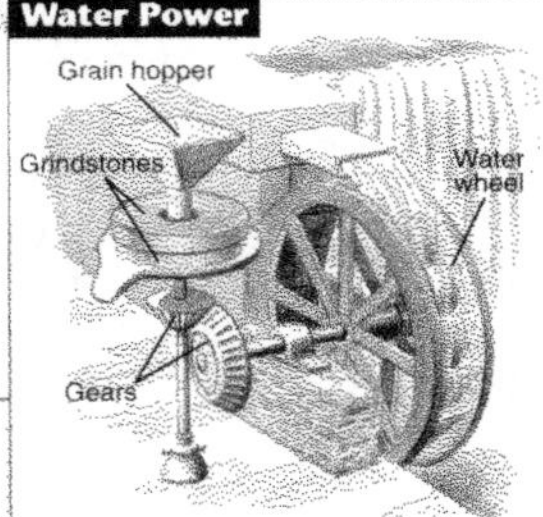

The "revolution" was slow in America also because it was a land with thousands of streams and rivers. Why, said the mill owners, should steam engines be used where the water power is easy to get and free? Although it was free, water did have its drawbacks: it sometimes froze in winter and dried up in summer. Then the mills and workshops had to close down and wait for better weather.

Perhaps the biggest problem for American business was the terrible condition of most of the roads. Many were still just paths through the wilderness. A factory owner could have steam-powered machines and good workers to run them but not have a way to get products to market. One thing that most helped solve this problem was the railroad.

174

➤ **What other country had "a slice of the pie," and what percentage did that country have?** *(Germany had 15.7%.)*

➤ **Read the second term on the Changes chart.** Write the word that tells where most people now worked. *(factory)*

➤ Add the word *factories* to the spinning wheel on The Wheel of Progress page.

➤ **Do you think manufacturing in the United States has increased from 1913 to the present?**

Text Discussion, page 174

➤ **Read page 174 to find out why the Industrial Revolution had a slow start in the United States.** *(People wanted to buy land and live in the country; mill owners wanted to use water power, not steam engines; roads were bad, so products could not be sent to market.)*

➤ **What solved the problem of getting the products to market?** *(the building of railroads)*

➤ Look at the railroad map on page 174. **Which city has the most railroads coming to and going from it?** *(Chicago)*

Chicago became a leader in meat processing in the 1880s. The development of the refrigerated railroad car by Gustavus F. Swift added much to Chicago's success as a center for manufacturing. The railroad system enabled ranchers from all over to send their livestock to Chicago's stockyards. Once there, the animals were prepared for sale as meat and other products; then with the use of the refrigerated railroad cars, the products could be sent to many distant markets.

➤ Name the towns on the map which would have been markets where products from Chicago's meat-packing industry could have been taken. *(Any town on the map is correct.)*

➤ **Read the third term on the Changes chart.** Write the new means of transportation. *(railroads)*

The text pages are discussed out of order in this lesson.

Text Discussion, page 176

➤ **Read page 176 to find out if the American Civil War interrupted the manufacturing success in the United States.** *(No, it made more businesses necessary to supply the demands of America's armies.)*

➤ Name some things that the armies needed. *(clothing, food, guns, tents, and other supplies)*

➤ Look at the Resources map on page 176. **Where did most of the farming occur in 1850?** *(in the eastern and central parts of the United States)*

➤ **Where did most of the grazing occur?** *(in Texas and California; in the Southwest)*

➤ **Read aloud each of the resources from the map key and locate areas where the resource is found.**

If your area is represented, locate it and use the map key to identify the land use and resources there.

➤ Look at the population map on page 176. **Why do you think the population was so much larger in some areas than in others?**

More manufacturing was located along the waterways. More people were needed to operate the businesses in the centers of manufacturing. Notice also that the centers of population and manufacturing were located in the areas with the most coal and iron or metal ore. These raw materials were necessary for the factories to produce goods.

Population Centers, 1845

When the Union and the Confederacy went to war, industries sprang up almost overnight. Suddenly armies needed clothes, food, guns, tents, and other supplies—more than handworkers toiling night and day could get made in time. Machines were the only answer.

Most factories burned coal to make steam to run the engines. Compare the two maps on this page. Where were the best deposits of coal and metal ore? Why do you think the population was so much larger in some areas than others? Compare these maps with the railroad map on page 174. Why did the railroad companies build the tracks where they did?

Resources, 1850

176

➤ **Why do you think the railroad companies built the railroads near the larger population areas?**

The railroads connected the manufacturing centers with numerous markets across the country. They also made it possible to ship raw materials, such as coal and iron, to other factories.

➤ **Read the rest of the terms on the Changes chart.** Add words or phrases to show what life was like after the Industrial Revolution. *(machines, big business)*

Labor Day

Labor Day is a holiday honoring working people. Matthew Maguire, a machinist from New Jersey, and Peter J. McGuire, a carpenter from New York City, are credited with suggesting this holiday. In September 1882, the two men took part in the nation's first Labor Day parade. The earliest parades were held in New York City and Philadelphia, but in 1887 Oregon became the first state to make Labor Day a legal holiday. Then in 1894, President Grover Cleveland signed a bill that made Labor Day a national holiday.

Many people celebrate Labor Day with a picnic.

In the United States, Puerto Rico, and Canada, Labor Day is celebrated on the first Monday in September. Though some organizations sponsor Labor Day festivities, most people enjoy time off from work for rest and relaxation.

313

◆ LEARNING HOW ◆

To Use Distribution Maps

1. Get some colored pencils or crayons and Notebook page 70.
2. Color the map and key as your teacher tells you.
3. Then read the map and answer the questions.

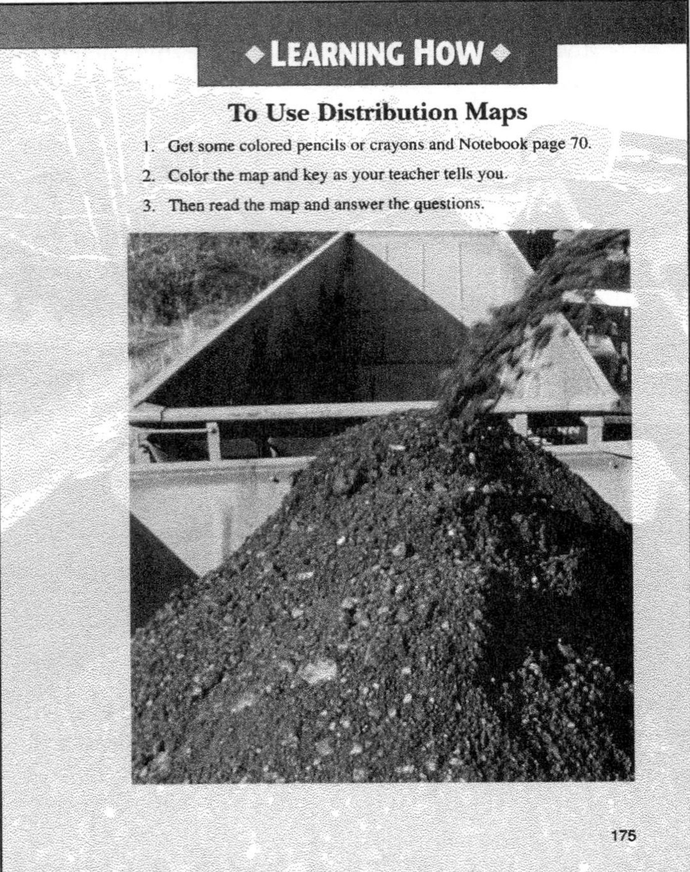

175

Day 2

Text Discussion, page 313

➤ **Read page 313 to find out what people are honored on Labor Day.** *(working people)*

The work of Christians should be done for the glory of the Lord. It is God who gives Christians the work and the strength to do it. We should be willing to work for others and for the Lord. (BATs: 2c Faithfulness, 2d Goal setting, 2e Work, 2f Enthusiasm)

➤ **Which president signed the bill to make Labor Day a legal holiday?** *(Grover Cleveland)*

➤ **When is Labor Day celebrated in the United States?** *(the first Monday in September)*

Learning How Activity, page 175 and Notebook page 70

➤ **Read the steps on page 175.**

➤ Select various colors of pencils or crayons to color over the shaded areas on the map and key.

➤ Use the map key to answer the questions on Notebook page 70.

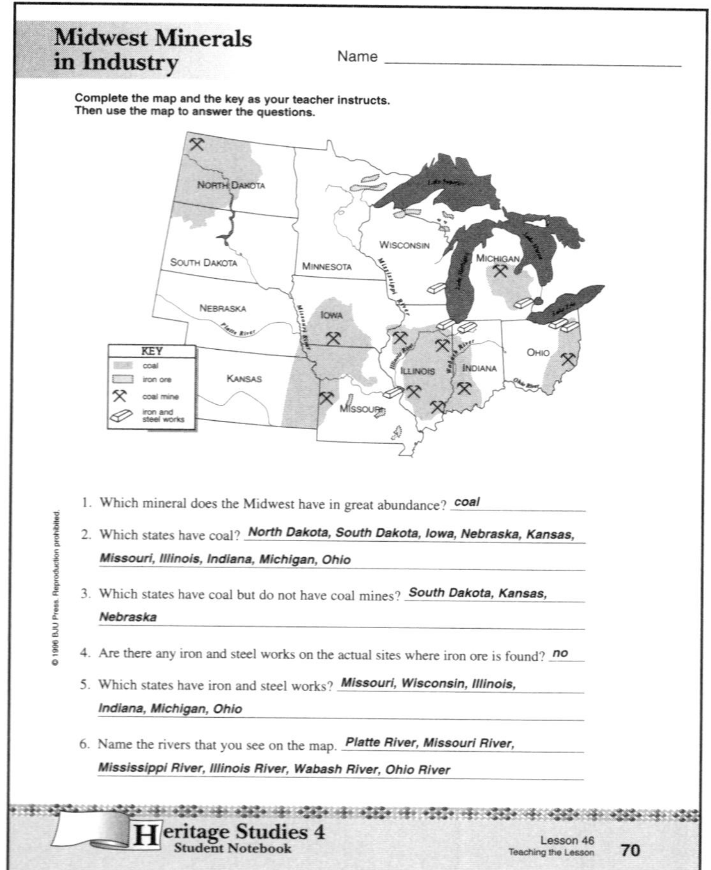

Midwest Minerals in Industry Name ____________

Complete the map and the key as your teacher instructs.
Then use the map to answer the questions.

KEY
coal
iron ore
coal mine
iron and steel works

1. Which mineral does the Midwest have in great abundance? *coal*
2. Which states have coal? *North Dakota, South Dakota, Iowa, Nebraska, Kansas, Missouri, Illinois, Indiana, Michigan, Ohio*
3. Which states have coal but do not have coal mines? *South Dakota, Kansas, Nebraska*
4. Are there any iron and steel works on the actual sites where iron ore is found? *no*
5. Which states have iron and steel works? *Missouri, Wisconsin, Illinois, Indiana, Michigan, Ohio*
6. Name the rivers that you see on the map. *Platte River, Missouri River, Mississippi River, Illinois River, Wabash River, Ohio River*

© 1996 BJU Press. Reproduction prohibited.

Heritage Studies 4 Student Notebook — Lesson 46 Teaching the Lesson — 70

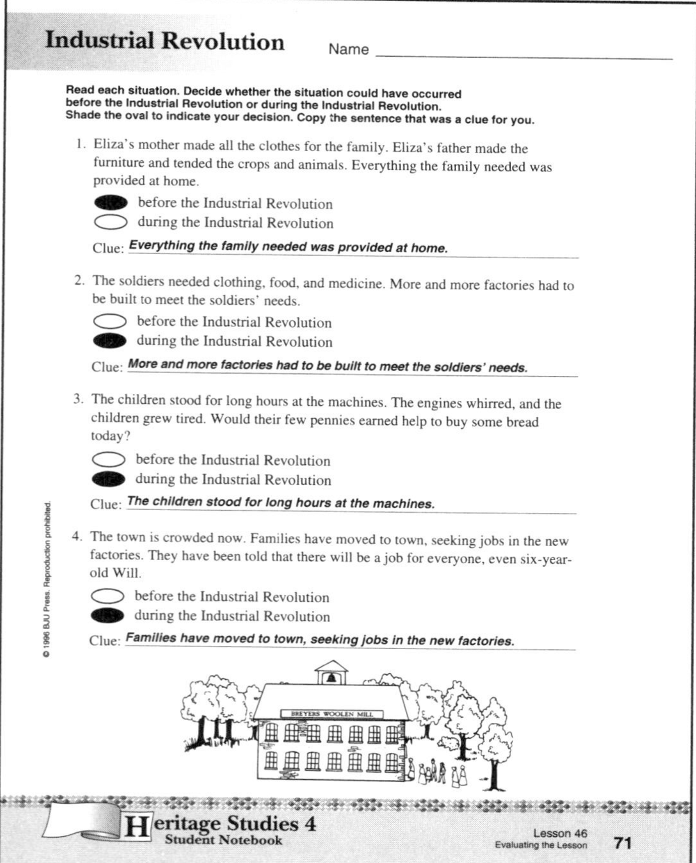

Industrial Revolution Name ____________

Read each situation. Decide whether the situation could have occurred before the Industrial Revolution or during the Industrial Revolution. Shade the oval to indicate your decision. Copy the sentence that was a clue for you.

1. Eliza's mother made all the clothes for the family. Eliza's father made the furniture and tended the crops and animals. Everything the family needed was provided at home.
   - ● before the Industrial Revolution
   - ○ during the Industrial Revolution

   Clue: *Everything the family needed was provided at home.*
2. The soldiers needed clothing, food, and medicine. More and more factories had to be built to meet the soldiers' needs.
   - ○ before the Industrial Revolution
   - ● during the Industrial Revolution

   Clue: *More and more factories had to be built to meet the soldiers' needs.*
3. The children stood for long hours at the machines. The engines whirred, and the children grew tired. Would their few pennies earned help to buy some bread today?
   - ○ before the Industrial Revolution
   - ● during the Industrial Revolution

   Clue: *The children stood for long hours at the machines.*
4. The town is crowded now. Families have moved to town, seeking jobs in the new factories. They have been told that there will be a job for everyone, even six-year-old Will.
   - ○ before the Industrial Revolution
   - ● during the Industrial Revolution

   Clue: *Families have moved to town, seeking jobs in the new factories.*

© 1996 BJU Press. Reproduction prohibited.

Heritage Studies 4 Student Notebook — Lesson 46 Evaluating the Lesson — 71

Evaluating the Lesson

Notebook Activity, page 71

- ➤ Read the instructions on Notebook page 71.
- ➤ Complete the page.

Going Beyond

Additional Teacher Information

Until the early 1900s, Western Europe was the center of the world's manufacturing. During World War I, the United States became the leading manufacturing nation in the world and today continues to rank as the world's greatest producer of manufactured goods. The top three manufactured products in the United States are chemicals, transportation equipment, and food products.

No matter what the product, the basic steps in manufacturing are the same. First, the manufacturer designs the product. Next, the raw material is purchased to make the product. Then the manufacturer produces the product and inspects it. Finally, the product is distributed to stores, where customers may purchase it.

LESSON 47
The Workers

Text, pages 177-81
Notebook, pages 72-73

Preview

Main Ideas

- As technology changes, so do the ways people earn a living.
- People work to provide money for goods and services.
- People use technology to adapt to different environments.

Objectives

- Pantomime jobs
- Complete a crossword puzzle
- Write a journal entry

Materials

- The Wheel of Progress from Lesson 46

Day 1

Lesson

Introducing the Lesson

Pantomime Activity

➤ I will pantomime a job. You are to guess what the job is. *Pantomime a job your child will recognize that is done only by adults.*

➤ **Is this a job for adults or a job for either children or adults?** *(for adults)*

➤ I will pantomime another job. Guess what this job is. *Pantomime a job that can be done by either children or adults.*

➤ **Is this a job for adults or a job for either children or adults?** *(a job for either)*

➤ Now you are to pantomime jobs, and I will guess what they are and who does them.

➤ **Have you ever done a job for which you were paid?** Tell what the job was, how long you worked, and how much you were paid.

There was a time in which children were required to do the work of adults. This lesson tells about some very difficult conditions of children working long ago in America.

The Workers

David was eight years old when his father decided to move the family to town. A cotton mill there had a job for him. He could make more money there than he could on the farm. And with five children, he needed to. David hated to leave his big garden and the woods where he played sometimes. But he knew his father wanted to do the best for them.

The house that David's family moved into was much smaller than the one they had had in the country. His mother made it look like home when she put the rocking chair by the window and set the cradle by the chair. David's little brother Joshua lay in the cradle and held up his hand to a beam of light.

Man working in a textile mill

David's father went to the mill right away. He worked until late at night. He left early every morning. David rarely saw him until Sundays. If David got up before the sun came up, he could talk to his father as he was eating or making a fire in the stove. But mostly, David had to wait until Sunday afternoon. It had never been that way on the farm. There his father had always been around somewhere.

One day, just before David turned nine, his father came home earlier than usual. He said he wanted to ask David a question.

177

Teaching the Lesson

Text Discussion, pages 177-78

➤ Tell what your father does at his workplace.

➤ **Read page 177 to learn about the jobs David's father had in the late 1800s.** *(farming and working in a cotton mill)*

➤ Compare David's life on the farm to his new life in town. *(Answers will vary but may include that on the farm he got to see his father more and he could enjoy the outdoors more.)*

A mill was a place where raw materials, such as cotton, grain, or lumber, were processed to produce useful products.

➤ **What useful products could be made from cotton?** *(yarn or thread to make clothing)*

➤ **Read page 178 to find out what important question David's father asked him.** *("What would you say to working at the mill with me?")*

➤ **Read aloud the sentences that tell what David thought of the job and what his father thought about David's working there.** *("To David the job seemed like an adventure. To his father, it was the end of a too-short childhood for David.")*

"What is it, Papa? Did I do something wrong?"

His father smiled and shook his head. "No, Son. Not at all. Down at the mill—" He paused. "Down at the mill, they have a job for a boy. Running errands for Mr. Shapp, the owner. What would you say to working at the mill with me?"

David felt his heart pounding. "Me? I could go to work?"

"I need you to, Son."

"Yes, Papa. Tell them yes!"

David's father nodded and looked away. He did not smile or say any more. David wondered why his father was not as happy as he was. He could hardly wait to be earning money. It would be like being all grown up. He was bursting to tell his younger brothers and sisters.

There were no rules then about how old someone had to be before he could go to work. Sometimes children as young as six or seven had to help support the family. To David, the job seemed like an adventure. To his father, it was the end of a too-short childhood for David.

Children sometimes worked in mills at machinery such as this.

178

Girls aged 6, 8, and 10 returning from a day of work shucking oysters

Child Labor

David worked for Mr. Shapp, a kind man, who asked him to run with messages to different parts of the mill. Sometimes he sent David with a letter to the post office. Other times David waited for the train and directed businessmen to the mill. Although David worked from seven in the morning until six at night, others his age had harder jobs.

Some children worked in coal mines, staying in the dampness and the dark for fourteen hours a day. They could come up into the sunshine for lunch—always for less than an hour. Sometimes miners would scare them with stories of monsters in the tunnels. Many children got sick, but they had to work anyway. How was this child labor different from the apprenticeships of Benjamin Franklin's time?

Other children had to help run the noisy, dangerous machines. And because they worked such long hours, they often fell asleep at the job. What do you think happened then? At best, they would be rapped with a stick and told to wake up and get back to work. At worst, they would fall into the machine and get badly hurt.

179

➤ **What do you think David's father wished his son could be doing instead of working at a job?**

His father wanted him to enjoy being a child, playing, relaxing, and working at home.

Day 2

Text Discussion, pages 179-80

➤ **Read aloud the heading on page 179.**

This phrase, ***child labor,*** is used to refer to the hiring of children to work in a business.

➤ **Read the first paragraph on page 179 to find out what hours David worked in the mill.** *(7:00 A.M. to 6:00 P.M.)*

➤ Calculate how many hours a day David worked at the mill. *(eleven hours)*

The average worker today works about eight hours daily.

➤ **Would David have had time to go to school?** *(no)*

➤ **Do you think David's enthusiasm for the job continued after working the long hours day after day?**

David probably lost his enthusiasm after a while. Children in nineteenth-century America worked hard at these jobs to help their families. The children did not earn very much—sometimes just seven or eight cents a day. They did not get to keep the money they earned; they gave it to their families to buy food, clothing, or other things that were needed. (BATs: 2e Work, 5a Love, 5b Giving)

➤ **Read the rest of page 179 and the first paragraph on page 180 to find out where besides the mill children worked.** *(coal mines and factories)*

➤ Describe the working conditions for many of these children. *(Answers will vary.)*

Although the conditions of child labor were frightening and terrible, they were something that the families and the children had to endure to make a little money to help them survive. There were no laws to regulate the age of the workers or to protect them or improve their working conditions. Children had always worked hard at home to help their families. But child labor in a factory was a totally new idea.

➤ **Do you think there are laws now regarding how old you have to be in order to work at a job?**

Now there are specific laws for hiring young workers. These laws tell how old a person must be in order to work at certain jobs as well as the number of hours and the time of day that he may work.

➤ Add the words *child labor* to The Wheel of Progress page.

A few factory owners took good care of the children who worked for them. They made sure they were schooled and had plenty to eat and did not work where it was dangerous. But far more owners cared more about their machines than they did for the boys and girls who worked them. Many factory children could not write their own names, and they often worked fourteen or fifteen hours a day. Their wages were only pennies a day.

Women worked as long and hard as men in factories.

The Men and Women Who Worked

Many women also began to work away from home. They became seamstresses in factories, ran machines that made thread and cloth, and did other jobs that women had never done before. How do you think that changed life at home?

Men had to learn new jobs too. Think of the weavers who lost their work when machines were invented to do weaving faster. What do you think those people did? Some of them learned to run the new machines. Others went into different work. And others moved to towns where hand-weavers could still make a living. What would you have done?

Many of the machines were open; that is, they had no covers over the chains and gears. There were many bad accidents before owners of factories put rails and shields around machinery that could hurt people. The faster way to work had many prices—many of which no one foresaw. It cost children their childhood, many people their jobs, some people their homes, and even a few people their lives.

180

Protest signs and riots sometimes accompanied strikes.

Some people tried to make the owners of factories help the workers more. These people, mostly the workers themselves, asked for shorter hours. They said ten hours a day would be better. How many hours a day do most people now work?

The workers wanted safer machines. When the owners ignored the workers' requests, the workers decided to band together and demand what they felt were their rights. They formed *unions*, groups of workers who join together, or unite, to help each other.

The unions asked the owners to listen to them. Many owners did. Although the workers did not get everything they wanted, they did get a ten-hour day and attention to the needs of the children.

Later, when unions were bigger, the members refused to work if their requests were not answered. They called the time when they would not work a *strike*. Have you heard of any strikes today? What do you think happened when workers went on strike? Sometimes the owners met the demands right away. Sometimes they fired the workers. Sometimes the workers and the owners went to court.

Most of the time, the judges decided that the workers were wrong to strike, and the workers had to return to their jobs—usually losing pay for when they did not work. Workers had been hired by agreement—so much work for so much pay. When they went on strike, they broke a contract. How else might they have made their needs known to the owners? They could have gone to court.

181

Text Discussion, pages 180-81

➤ **Read pages 180-81 to find out what changes workers wanted their bosses to make.** *(shorter workdays, safer conditions)*

Working conditions were difficult for all of the workers, including women and children. But the owners did not want to change things. They feared that they would not make as much money.

➤ **What was the first step workers took to get their bosses to listen?** *(They formed unions.)*

➤ **Read the definition of *union* given on page 181.** *("groups of workers who join together, or unite, to help each other")*

Workers formed unions because they would have more influence than one or two people.

➤ Add the word *unions* to The Wheel of Progress page.

➤ **When union requests were not met, what did the workers do?** *(refused to work, went on strike)*

➤ Explain what a ***strike*** is. *(It is the period of time when workers refuse to work until the conditions of their demands are met.)*

➤ **Read the caption under the picture on page 181.**

Often during a strike, the employees march in lines in front of the workplace, carrying signs, stating their demands. In this way they draw attention to themselves in order to persuade their employers to meet their demands more quickly. Open, fair communication between employers and employees often solves the problems and satisfies both groups. (BATs: 2a Authority, 2c Faithfulness, 2e Work, 3c Emotional control)

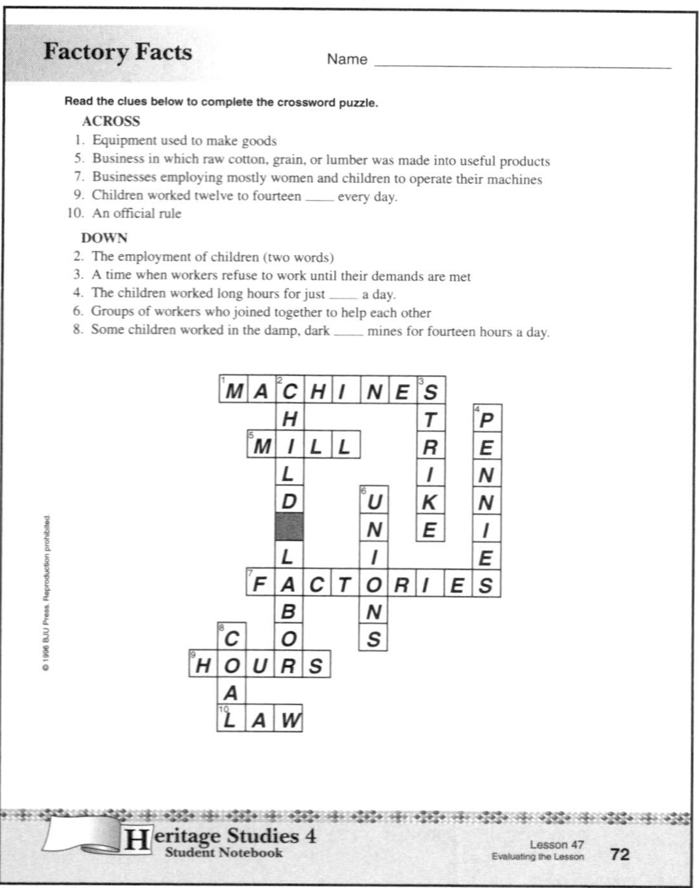

Factory Facts Name ____________

Read the clues below to complete the crossword puzzle.

ACROSS
1. Equipment used to make goods
5. Business in which raw cotton, grain, or lumber was made into useful products
7. Businesses employing mostly women and children to operate their machines
9. Children worked twelve to fourteen ____ every day.
10. An official rule

DOWN
2. The employment of children (two words)
3. A time when workers refuse to work until their demands are met
4. The children worked long hours for just ____ a day.
6. Groups of workers who joined together to help each other
8. Some children worked in the damp, dark ____ mines for fourteen hours a day.

All in a Day's Work Name ____________

Follow your teacher's instructions.

The date today is ____________.

I, ____________, *am writing to tell about* ____________

Evaluating the Lesson

Notebook Activity, pages 72-73

- ➤ Read the clues and complete the crossword puzzle on Notebook page 72.
- ➤ Make a journal entry in the space provided on Notebook page 73.

Write the account as though you are a nine year old working in a nineteenth-century mill or mine. Include observations on a strike or give details about how you feel about your work and wages.

Going Beyond

Additional Teacher Information

The late nineteenth century brought masses of European immigrants to America. The census of 1870 counted 750,000 workers under the age of fifteen employed in American industry. These child laborers were employed mostly in textile mills, mines, and factories. The reports of the children's working conditions sounded like horror stories. It was common for six and seven year olds to work as long as sixteen hours each day, often without uttering a single word. There were even a few reports of children being chained to their machines in the factories.

Some children were employed in home or neighborhood industries, often called *cottage industries* or the *sweating system.* Factories would commission these neighborhood industries to do some work for them in their apartments or basements. Because women and children worked long hours day and night in these dark, ventless basements, the term *sweatshop* was applied to their workplace.

Gradually, countries passed laws to protect the young laborers. In 1802, England passed the first law regulating child labor. This law prohibited the employment of pauper children under the age of nine in the cotton mills. It also forbade pauper children under fourteen from working at night and limited their workday to twelve hours. In 1819, the law was extended to include all children, but it was not until 1833 that any provision was made to try to enforce these laws. One of the most effective attacks on child labor came from Charles Dickens's novel *David Copperfield.*

In the United States, Massachusetts passed the first state child labor law in 1836. The law prohibited children under fifteen from working in any factory unless they had attended school for at least three months during the preceding year. Enforcement of the laws was extremely difficult. In 1904, the National Child Labor Committee was formed by people who wanted to establish and enforce child labor laws. It was not until 1916 that the first federal child labor law was passed; two years later the Supreme Court declared the law unconstitutional. Many amendments and laws were attempted but failed in trying to protect the nation's youth. The Fair Labor Standards Act of 1938 finally brought about child labor laws that regulate the employment of children. Today the federal government of the United States, as well as every state, has child labor laws. Federal and state laws vary widely, but when both state and federal laws apply, the higher standard must be observed.

LESSON 48
Big Business

Text, pages 182-84

Preview

Main Ideas

- As technology changes, so do the ways people earn a living.
- Inventions and ideas spread from one part of the world to another.
- In its first hundred years, the United States changed from an agricultural country to an industrial country.
- Andrew Carnegie was a good businessman who prospered immensely, sharing his wealth in numerous ways.

Objectives

- List ways of giving away $2,000,000
- Subtract large numbers
- Answer questions in a review activity

Materials

- Appendix, page A66: paper bills (cut apart)*
- The Wheel of Progress from Lesson 47
- An atlas
- The figure of Andrew Carnegie (1870) from the TimeLine Snapshots

Day 1

Lesson

Introducing the Lesson

Listing and Subtracting Activity

➤ *Give your child the paper bills.*
➤ Pretend that you have $2,000,000 to give away.
➤ Write *$2,000,000* at the top of a sheet of paper.

Think of the people or places or organizations to which you would like to give money. List the name of the recipient and the amount of money to be given next to each name. Subtract each amount. Use your paper bills to demonstrate the amounts you are giving away. *An example is shown on the next page.*

	$2,000,000
1. Faith Baptist Church	– 100,000
	$1,900,000
2. cars for missionaries	– 100,000
	$1,800,000
3. Cedars Hospital	– 100,000
	$1,700,000

Discuss what things must be considered as your child is making his choices. Help him to realize how difficult such decisions would be if he actually had that much money to give away.

No matter how much or how little money we have, it all truly belongs to the Lord. Christians should be content with what they have, knowing that God will supply their needs. They should be willing to give back to the Lord and to share with others. (BATs: 5b Giving, 7b Exaltation of Christ, 7d Contentment)

In this lesson, we will learn about a real man who tried to give away millions of dollars.

Teaching the Lesson

Text Discussion, page 182

- ➤ **Read page 182 to find out how America changed from a country of farms to a country of businesses.**
- ➤ Add the words *big business* to the spinning wheel on The Wheel of Progress.
- ➤ **Read aloud the first sentence on page 182**.
- ➤ **Do you remember the official date of America's birthday?** *(July 4, 1776)* Write the date 1776.
- ➤ **What was the one important business at that time?** *(farming)*
- ➤ Look at the time line on pages 182-83. Find the date of the first successful factory in America. *(1790)*
- ➤ Write 1790 above 1776. Calculate to find out how old America was then. *(fourteen years old)*
- ➤ **Read the events listed between 1790 and 1815 on the time line.**

Big Business

When America was a brand new country, its biggest business was farming. In 1925, President Calvin Coolidge said, "The business of America is business." What do you think he meant? And what had happened in one hundred ten years to change our country from a country of farms to a country of businesses? Look at the time line.

In 1815, England shipped many goods to the United States at low prices. The prices were so low, in fact, that the English were selling them at a loss. Why do you think the English were willing to do that? What else is happening on the time line right then? The United States is just beginning to build factories. England is already running big factories. How would selling English goods cheaply keep factories out of America?

How would a new patent law, making inventions easier to protect and easier to sell, help the Industrial Revolution? It encouraged people to come up with new ideas for faster and better machines. Americans have always been known for improving inventions and thinking up new ways of doing things.

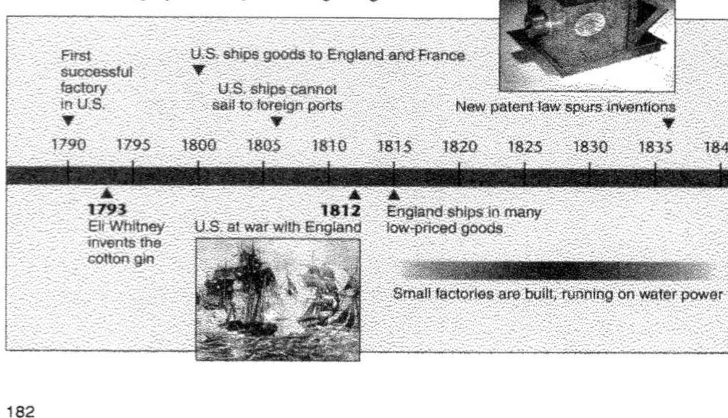

First successful factory in U.S.
U.S. ships goods to England and France
U.S. ships cannot sail to foreign ports
New patent law spurs inventions
1790 1795 1800 1805 1810 1815 1820 1825 1830 1835 1840
1793 Eli Whitney invents the cotton gin
1812 U.S. at war with England
England ships in many low-priced goods
Small factories are built, running on water power

182

- ➤ **What was happening between the United States and England in 1812?** *(They were at war.)*
- ➤ **What did England begin shipping to America in 1815?** *(many low-priced goods)*
- ➤ **Read the caption for the gray bar to find out what was happening in America from 1815 to 1840.** *(Small factories were being built.)*

England wanted to supply goods to America rather than to have America build its own factories to make its own goods. If Americans bought British goods, it would guarantee that money kept flowing back to England.

- ➤ Find the date on the time line telling when the new patent law was passed. *(1836)*

This new law protected inventors and their inventions and encouraged other Americans to try new ideas. God gives each person special abilities. Christians should do everything for His glory. (BATs: 3a Self-concept, 7b Exaltation of Christ)

In little more than ten years' time, the Industrial Revolution turned cities like Wichita, Kansas, from small cattle towns into prospering industrial centers.

Although there were problems that came with new industry, there were many advantages too. Lower- and middle-class people had more money; they lived longer; they had better houses and furniture; they had some time for leisure. Life improved for nearly everyone, not just the rich.

Can you name some reasons that people came to the United States after 1840? How would suddenly having many more people help the Industrial Revolution? There were now plenty of workers for the factories.

It was because of the thousands of people who were willing to work hard at unpleasant jobs that the United States got its railroads built, its roads paved, and its industries growing. The work they accomplished actually made more jobs; as the nation got richer and more powerful, it needed more and more work done. Although at first it seemed the many newcomers would destroy America's big business, they indeed ensured its success.

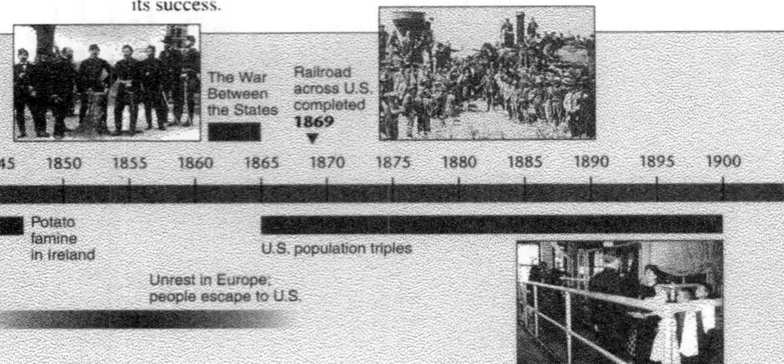

183

◆ FAMOUS PEOPLE ◆

Andrew Carnegie
(1835-1919)

A weaver who lost his job in Scotland moved to America in 1848. His thirteen-year-old son, Andrew, became a bobbin boy in a cotton mill; he worked twelve hours a day six days a week and made $1.20 a week. How much was that an hour?

Do you think Andrew Carnegie ever regretted the hard work he had done as a teenager?

Andrew later worked as a messenger boy for a telegraph office for $2.50 a week. He went early every day to learn how to send telegrams. When he was seventeen, he was so skillful that a superintendent of the Pennsylvania Railroad hired him to send his messages. Andrew learned about the train business and, seven years later, became vice president.

As he always had, Carnegie saved all his money. When he had enough, he invested it in oil, a grain elevator, and an iron business. From then on, the more money he made, the more businesses he bought. After the American Civil War, when other businesses failed, Carnegie's prospered. By age sixty, he was one of the wealthiest men in the world.

"Seest thou a man diligent in his business? he shall stand before kings; he shall not stand before mean men."
Proverbs 22:29

But his last ambition was to die poor. Andrew Carnegie gave money to build over three thousand libraries; he built schools and gave millions of dollars to universities (because he had been able to go to school so little himself). And he bought beautiful organs and furniture for churches. Despite his goal to become poor, he died still having $22,000,000!

184

Text Discussion, page 183

- ➤ **Read page 183 to find some advantages resulting from the Industrial Revolution.** *(Lower- and middle-class people had more money and nicer things; they lived longer and had more leisure.)*
- ➤ Look at the time line again, noting especially the time after 1845.
- ➤ **What caused many people to come to America after 1845?** *(the potato famine in Ireland)*
- ➤ **What do we call people who come to the United States from different countries?** *(immigrants)*
- ➤ **In what ways did the immigrants help in America's Industrial Revolution?** *(They worked hard at unpleasant jobs to build railroads and develop more industries, thereby making more jobs.)*

Map-Reading Activity

- ➤ Find the world map in your atlas.
- ➤ Locate the places I name for you. *Name places such as the following.*

Atlantic Ocean	Asia	Spain
Pacific Ocean	Africa	France
North America	Australia	England
South America	Antarctica	Scotland
United States	Europe	

Day 2

Text Discussion, page 184

Page 184 tells about an immigrant family, the Carnegies, who in 1848 left Scotland to find jobs in America.

- ➤ **Read page 184 to find out what made Andrew Carnegie famous.** *(his wealth and generosity)*
- ➤ **What was Andrew's first job?** *(He was a bobbin boy in a cotton mill.)*
- ➤ **How long did he work and how much money did he make?** *(He worked twelve hours a day, six days a week, and made $1.20 a week.)*
- ➤ Figure how many hours a week Andrew Carnegie worked. *(12×6=72 hours a week)*
- ➤ Figure how much money Andrew Carnegie made an hour. *($1.20÷72=$0.016 or less than two cents per hour)*

Remember that many children, some even younger than Andrew, worked long, hard hours day after day to earn whatever they could to help their families survive. The money earned by these children was not spent on candy or toys; the money was used to buy food and clothing, or was saved for a future need. Andrew Carnegie and other children in early America were willing to work hard to help those that they loved survive. (BAT: 2c Faithfulness, 2e Work)

- ➤ **What did Andrew Carnegie do with the money he earned?** *(He saved it.)*
- ➤ **Are you saving money for something? What?**
- ➤ **Read aloud the second sentence of the third paragraph that tells us what Carnegie did with his money after he had saved enough.** *(He invested it.)*

The term ***invested*** simply means that Andrew Carnegie loaned his money to successful businesses, enabling them to become even more prosperous. These businesses then were able to return to Carnegie even more money than he had loaned to them in the first place.

- ➤ Add the words *Andrew Carnegie* to The Wheel of Progress.

TimeLine Snapshots Activity

- ➤ Add the figure of Andrew Carnegie to the TimeLine at 1870.

It was in the year 1870 that Carnegie's annual income rose to $50,000 and he started giving money away.

Text Discussion, page 184 (cont.)

- ➤ Another word for ***ambition*** is *goal.* **What was Andrew Carnegie's last ambition or goal?** *(to die poor)*
- ➤ **What does this desire tell us about Andrew Carnegie?** *(He was generous, unselfish, and kind.)*
- ➤ Name some ways in which Carnegie gave away his money. *(He built many schools and libraries. He bought organs and furniture for churches.)*

Andrew Carnegie also set up numerous funds to help students get an education.

- ➤ *Read aloud Proverbs 22:29 from the text page.*
- ➤ **What do you think *diligent* means?** Look up ***diligent*** in the dictionary and read aloud the definition(s). (*NOTE: American Heritage Dictionary* defines *diligent* as "marked by persevering, painstaking effort," but it simply means "hard working.")
- ➤ **Was Andrew Carnegie diligent in business?** *(yes)*

> God wants us to be diligent in all that we do as a good testimony to others and for God's glory. (BATs: 2c Faithfulness, 2e Work, 3a Self-concept, 4a Sowing and reaping, 7b Exaltation of Christ)

Evaluating the Lesson

Review Activity

- ➤ *Give your child the $100,000 paper bills again.*
- ➤ Pretend that you are Andrew Carnegie giving away your money to worthy projects.

Your ambition is to give away all of your money. I will ask you questions from this lesson. For each correct answer $100,000 can be given away. I will be the banker to handle the money you give away.

> If you are teaching more than one child, divide them into two teams. Give each team ten of the bills. The first team to successfully give away $1,000,000 (or to come closest) wins the game.

- ➤ *Ask questions such as the following:*
  - **When America was a new nation, how did most people make their money?** *(in farming)*
  - **Which U.S. president said, "The business of America is business."** *(President Calvin Coolidge)*
  - **Which country had factories first—the United States or England?** *(England)*
  - **When was the first successful factory established in America?** *(in 1790)*
  - **Who invented the cotton gin?** *(Eli Whitney)*
  - **With whom was the United States at war in 1812?** *(England)*
  - **What was the source of power for the early machines in small factories?** *(water)*
  - **Why did many Irish immigrants come to the United States around 1845?** *(There was a famine in Ireland because of a potato blight.)*
  - **What country shipped many goods at low prices to the United States in 1815?** *(England)*
  - **What kind of law protects the inventor and his invention?** *(a patent law)*
  - **What was the name of the revolution involving factories, mills, and other businesses in early America?** *(the Industrial Revolution)*
  - **What were the people coming to America from other countries called?** *(immigrants)*
  - **What war occurred in the United States from 1860-65?** *(the American Civil War, or the War Between the States)*
  - **The Carnegie family came to America from what country?** *(Scotland)*
  - **What job did Andrew Carnegie's father have in Scotland?** *(weaver)*
  - **What was Andrew Carnegie's first job at age thirteen?** *(bobbin boy in a cotton mill)*
  - **Did Andrew Carnegie make more or less than three dollars a week at his first job?** *(less than three dollars a week)*
  - **For which railroad did Andrew Carnegie work and then become vice president of?** *(the Pennsylvania Railroad)*
  - **What did Andrew Carnegie do with the money that he earned?** *(He saved it.)*

- **When Mr. Carnegie had a lot of money, in which business did he invest his money?** *(in oil, a grain elevator, or an iron business)*
- **What was Mr. Carnegie's last ambition?** *(to die poor)*
- **What kinds of things did this rich man do with his money?** *(He helped build libraries and schools. He bought beautiful organs and furniture for churches. He helped students.)*
- **Was Andrew Carnegie diligent or lazy?** *(diligent)*

Going Beyond

Additional Teacher Information

Andrew Carnegie, a poor son of a weaver, knew how to work and save. Everything he bought or invested in prospered.

He cared for his mother all his life and remained a bachelor until her death. Shortly thereafter, he married Louise Whitefield, a longtime friend. Together they gave away money to worthy causes. When Andrew Carnegie died of bronchial pneumonia in 1919, he had achieved all of his ambitions except two—he had not achieved world peace, and he did not die a poor man.

9 LESSONS 49-54

Stoking the Fires

Change often brings conflict. This chapter discusses conflicts in the United States from the late 1860s to 1900. Your child will learn about the settlers' movement to the West and the numerous changes it brought in the land, the people, and the government. He will learn about the building of the transcontinental railroad with the conflict between the Irish and Chinese workers. The conflicts between the settlers, the government, and the Native Americans will also be addressed. As people settled and moved onward, new towns were born and other towns died, becoming "ghost towns." Your child will locate a ghost town on a map and write for more information. Finally, he will learn that amid all the moving and changing within the country, America became involved in the Spanish-American War. Highlighted during this period are Clara Barton, Theodore Roosevelt, William Randolph Hearst, and Joseph Pulitzer.

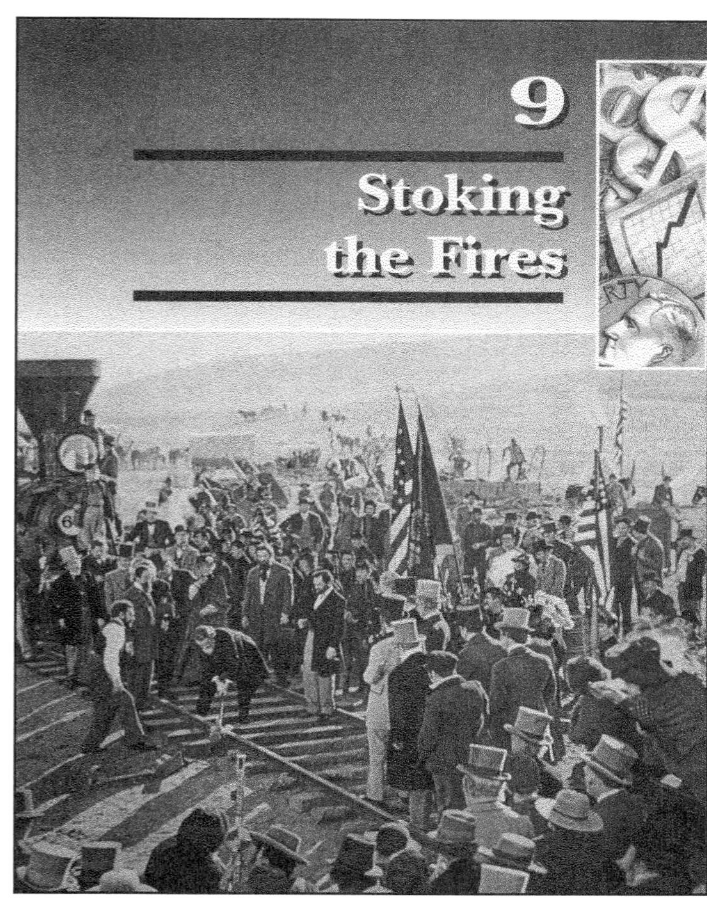

Materials

The following materials must be obtained or prepared before the presentation of the lesson. These items are labeled with an asterisk (*) in each lesson and in the Materials List in the Supplement. For further information see the individual lessons.

- Appendix, pages A67-A68 (Lesson 49)
- A feather (Lesson 51)
- An atlas that lists populations for cities (Lesson 52)
- Front-page newspaper headlines from old newspapers (Lesson 54)
- The front page of a newspaper (Lesson 54)

LESSON 49
The Railroad: Workmen and Weather

Text, pages 186-92, 320-321

Preview

Main Ideas

- Landforms, climate, and resources influenced individuals and societies.
- Many individuals and groups have shaped the nation's heritage.
- The Chinese and the Irish influenced American culture.

Objective

- Answer questions about the building of the transcontinental railroad

Materials

- Maps and More 28, 29, and 30, pages M13-M14
- Appendix, page A67: Lesson 49 Story
- The figure of the transcontinental railroad (1869) from the TimeLine Snapshots
- Supplement, page S12: Irish and Chinese
- Appendix, page A68: train tickets*
- A hole punch

Day 1

Lesson

Introducing the Lesson

Story and Discussion, Maps and More 28

➤ **Have you ever been in a situation where you were different from everyone else?**

➤ Describe the situation and tell me how you felt.

➤ Listen as I read a story of a young girl who was different. *Show Maps and More 28 as you read the story.*

➤ **What would you do if a young girl like Tomoko came to your Sunday school class?**

➤ **What besides her appearance might be different about Tomoko?** *(Answers should include language, food choices, and customs.)*

God made each person special. Even though many of us speak the same language and have similar likes, we are all different. God wants Christians to get along with others no matter how different they are. Christians should be friendly, showing God's love. (BATs: 3a Self-concept, 5a Love, 5d Communication, 5e Friendliness)

➤ This lesson tells about some people who contributed greatly to America's heritage but who were often mistreated because of their differences.

Teaching the Lesson

Review, pages 320-21 and Maps and More 30

To help your child better understand this lesson, take a few minutes to review some concepts that he learned in third grade about the transcontinental railroad.

➤ **Do you remember what the word *transcontinental* means?** *(across the continent)*

➤ **What type of transportation was being built across the United States in the 1860s?** *(the railroad)*

If the transcontinental railroad figure is displayed on the TimeLine, use the TimeLine to help your child answer this question. If it is not displayed, you will want to add it during the discussion.

➤ Look at the map on pages 320-21.

Remember that there were two railroad companies building the transcontinental railroad. Each of the companies was coming from a different direction to meet in the middle.

➤ **Where in California did the Central Pacific Railroad start building its part of the railroad?** *(Sacramento)*

Poster announcing coast-to-coast travel

America was getting richer and stronger all the time. Its machines and inventions, its immigrants and settlers, its resources and vast lands made it the envy of the world. But what seemed growth and light to some was destruction and darkness to others.

Railroad Ties

The railroads made travel easier and faster than many could ever have imagined just a few years before. The steam engines sped people and goods from one side of the country to the other. In many ways, the railroads united the people of America. But the builders of the rails found out how hard it is for different people to get along, to understand each other, and to work together.

When the transcontinental railroad was being built, many more workers were needed than was originally thought. Many men wanted to go west to look for gold rather than to labor on the endless rails. So the man in charge of the railroad builders, Charlie Crocker, decided to send to California for Chinese workers. Many of the men already working for the railroad were Irish; they did not like the idea of Chinese men working on the railroad. Why do you think that was?

186

Building a railroad was exhausting labor; these men looked forward to rest.

Other leaders in the railroad business thought Crocker had a bad idea. But Crocker said that the Chinese people had built the Great Wall of China and they certainly would be able to help with a railroad. They proved him right: the Chinese were efficient, diligent, and quick to learn the work. And they were often given the hardest and most dangerous jobs.

There were many reasons that people did not get along. For one thing, the Irish ate beef, bread, potatoes, and coffee; and they could not understand why the Chinese ate fish, seaweed, pork, and tea. They did not like the woven hats the Chinese wore, and they did not like it that the Chinese behaved differently from them.

The Irish workers talked and sang as they worked. The Chinese rarely made any noise, except for the thud of their picks and the chug and swish of their shovels. When the Irish shouted names at them, they expected the Chinese to return the insults. But the Chinese, who did not understand what was said or pretended not to understand, kept on working in silence.

187

➤ **What was the difficult kind of land that the Central Pacific Railroad crossed?** *(mountains)*

➤ Find the Sierra Nevada mountains on the map.

Remember that the Central Pacific Railroad had to cross and cut through this mountain range to build its part of the railroad.

The Union Pacific Railroad began building in Omaha, Nebraska.

➤ *Show Maps and More 30.* **Do you remember where the two railroad companies met?** *(Promontory Point, Utah)*

Text Discussion, pages 186-89 and Maps and More 29

➤ **Read pages 186-89 to find out about the two groups of workers who were different from each other and different from the Americans.** *(the Chinese and the Irish)*

➤ **What were the workers building?** *(the transcontinental railroad)*

➤ Find the sentence on page 186 that tells why the railroad needed more workers than they had originally thought. *("Many men wanted to go west to look for gold rather than to labor on the endless rails.")*

➤ Find the sentence that tells why Charlie Crocker hired Chinese workers. *("But Crocker said that the Chinese people had built the Great Wall of China and they certainly would be able to help with a railroad.")*

The silence was a far greater insult to the Irish than any reply could have been. Some of the Irish picked up clods of dirt and threw them at the Chinese. Still they worked on quietly. The Irish were furious by then. Some of them took the heads off their picks and attacked the Chinese with the wooden handles. Since the Irish were almost a foot taller than most of the Chinese workers, they thought it would be a quick and easy fight. They were wrong.

The Chinese at last fought back. They came at the Irishmen by twos, one throwing himself at an Irishman's legs, the other grabbing his shoulders and throwing him off balance. Pick handles were of little use to a man lying on his back with the opposition on top of him. In a short while, the Irish went back to their work. But the trouble was not over.

188

Some of the non-Chinese workers made hand bombs from the explosives meant for blasting rock. Most that they threw at the Chinese never went off. But a few of these bombs actually worked. Many Chinese workers were seriously hurt. Charlie Crocker tried to stop the fighting. Other leaders of the railroad work demanded that it stop. But it took more than their words to get results. It took a terrible accident.

An explosion, possibly meant to injure more Chinese, caused an instantaneous and huge avalanche. Rocks and earth crashed down into a hollow where many Irish workers were. Many, many men died suddenly, with no hope and no warning. All the men, Chinese and Irish and others, were stunned. After that, neither side made any moves against the other.

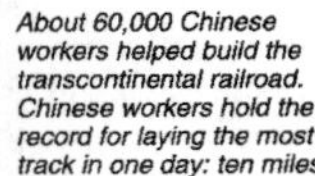

About 60,000 Chinese workers helped build the transcontinental railroad. Chinese workers hold the record for laying the most track in one day: ten miles.

189

➤ Look at Maps and More 29.

This is a picture of the Great Wall. This four-thousand-mile wall of stone and brick is the longest structure ever built. Chinese workers built the Great Wall completely by hand hundreds of years ago.

➤ **Did the Chinese workers with the transcontinental railroad work as well as Charlie Crocker had predicted?** *(yes)*

➤ Find the words on page 187 that describe the type of workers the Chinese were. *("efficient, diligent, and quick to learn the work")*

> These are fine qualities for any worker to have. Christians should work willingly and efficiently for God's glory. (BATs: 2c Faithfulness, 2d Goal setting, 2e Work, 4a Sowing and reaping)

➤ **What happened to stop the fighting between the Irish and the Chinese?** *(A big explosion caused an avalanche that killed many men.)*

➤ **Do you know what an avalanche is?** An ***avalanche*** is a fall or slide of a large amount of rocks or snow down a mountainside.

Contrasting Activity

➤ *Show your child the Irish and Chinese page. Cover the Chinese half of the page with a sheet of paper.*

➤ **Read a characteristic of the Irish.**

➤ Tell me a contrasting or similar characteristic about the Chinese. I will uncover the Chinese characteristic so that you may check your answer.

➤ *Follow the same procedure with each characteristic.*

These differences caused strong emotions, even hatred, to grow among the workers. The bad feelings soon led to bad actions. The Irish and the Chinese often had fights, some of which resulted in death.

> Remember that we are to show love and kindness toward others, even toward those who are different from us. (BATs: 3c Emotional control, 4b Purity, 5a Love, 5d Communication)

The Blizzards of 1866-67 and 1886-87

The weather could prove a worse enemy to railroad builders and ranchers and others than almost any other threat. The winter of 1866 blew in cold and sudden. Few people in the Sierra Nevada had any idea what lay ahead.

The railroad builders, most of them Chinese, worked through deep snow in November, December, and January. Thousands of men did nothing but shovel snow to keep the way clear for those who tried to lay the track. Others built snow sheds, shelters for the workers. Then in February, there came a blizzard like none had seen before. It raged for twelve days and nights. Drifts over sixty feet high made going on almost impossible. Shelters collapsed; people froze to death. If one man was more than a yard from the next, he could neither see nor hear his companion, so loud was the wind, so thick was the snow.

The golden spike is hammered in; it was a moment workers had dreamed of for years.

Some men died in avalanches; a few were found encased in ice, standing, still holding their pickaxes, nearly three months later. Little progress was made on the tracks over the mountains that month. The miracle is that any track was laid at all. But by the end of the summer, the worst part of the mountains was behind the workers. The driving of the golden spike was less than two years away.

190

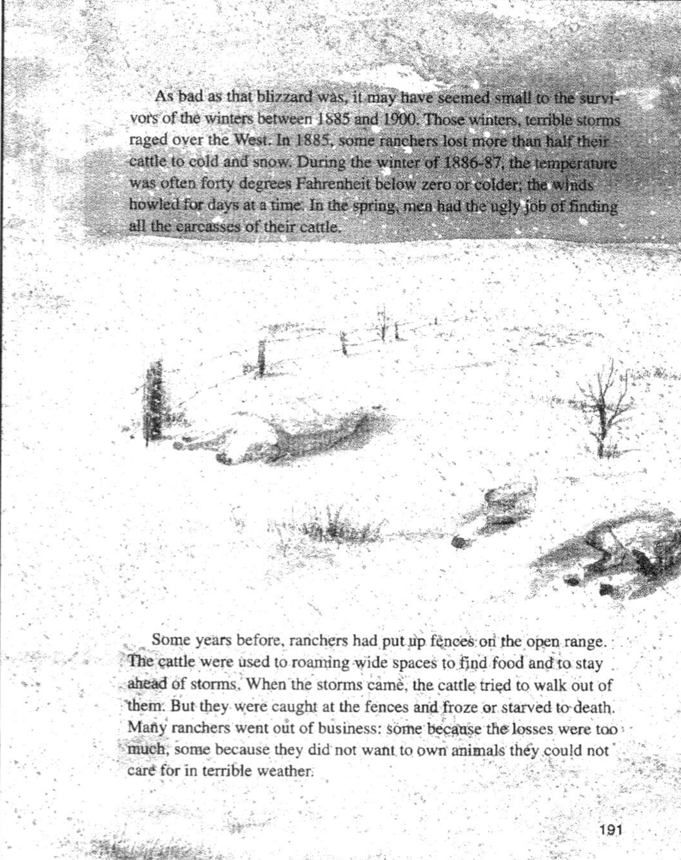

As bad as that blizzard was, it may have seemed small to the survivors of the winters between 1885 and 1900. Those winters, terrible storms raged over the West. In 1885, some ranchers lost more than half their cattle to cold and snow. During the winter of 1886-87, the temperature was often forty degrees Fahrenheit below zero or colder; the winds howled for days at a time. In the spring, men had the ugly job of finding all the carcasses of their cattle.

Some years before, ranchers had put up fences on the open range. The cattle were used to roaming wide spaces to find food and to stay ahead of storms. When the storms came, the cattle tried to walk out of them. But they were caught at the fences and froze or starved to death. Many ranchers went out of business: some because the losses were too much, some because they did not want to own animals they could not care for in terrible weather.

191

Day 2

Text Discussion, page 190

- ➤ On page 190 there is a term that may not be familiar to you. **Do you know what a blizzard is?** A ***blizzard*** is a fierce snowstorm.
- ➤ *With excitement in your voice, read page 190.*

Even in terrible weather conditions, the Chinese laborers continued their work of laying the railroad track. Remember that God controls all things. He has power to give life and to take it away. He has power to cause the storm or to calm it. Christians can pray for God's protection during times of danger or trouble. (BATs: 6b Prayer, 8d Courage; Bible Promises: H. God as Father, I. God as Master)

Text Discussion, pages 191-92

- ➤ **Read pages 191-92 to find out what happened to many ranchers in the severe winter storms that raged over the West in early America.** *(They went out of business.)*
- ➤ **When did the most famous blizzard along the eastern coast occur?** *(1888)*
- ➤ Tell what twelve-year-old Milton Daub did that was heroic. *(He made himself snowshoes and then got milk, food, and medicine for his family and neighbors on the worst day of the blizzard.)*
- ➤ **What does this sentence mean: "But the grateful people gave him many tips"?** *(The people were so thankful that they gave him extra money.)*
- ➤ Name some character qualities of Milton Daub. *(Answers will vary but may include unselfish, courageous, strong, uncomplaining, inventive.)* (BATs: 2b Servanthood, 2c Faithfulness, 2e Work, 2f Enthusiasm, 3a Self-concept, 4a Sowing and reaping, 5b Giving)

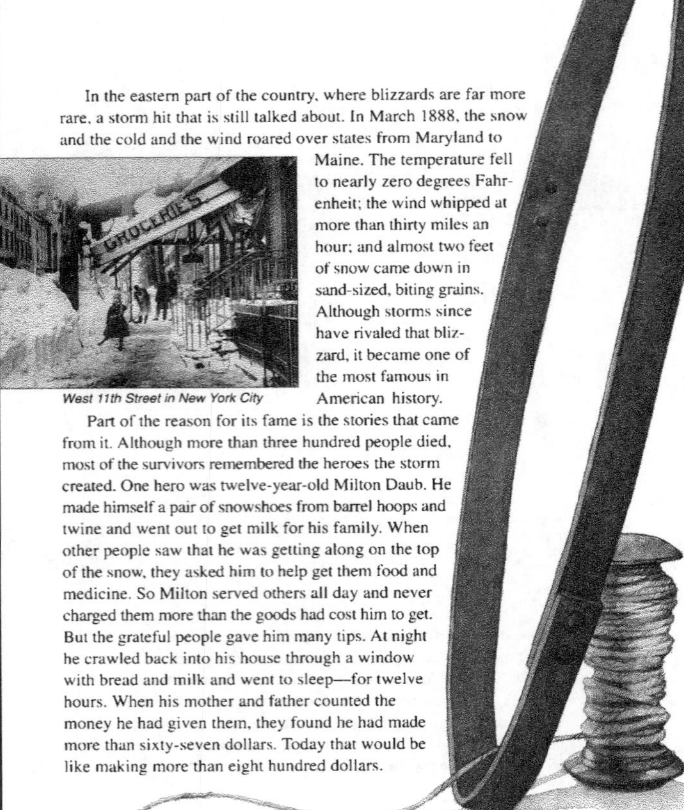

In the eastern part of the country, where blizzards are far more rare, a storm hit that is still talked about. In March 1888, the snow and the cold and the wind roared over states from Maryland to Maine. The temperature fell to nearly zero degrees Fahrenheit; the wind whipped at more than thirty miles an hour; and almost two feet of snow came down in sand-sized, biting grains. Although storms since have rivaled that blizzard, it became one of the most famous in American history.

West 11th Street in New York City

Part of the reason for its fame is the stories that came from it. Although more than three hundred people died, most of the survivors remembered the heroes the storm created. One hero was twelve-year-old Milton Daub. He made himself a pair of snowshoes from barrel hoops and twine and went out to get milk for his family. When other people saw that he was getting along on the top of the snow, they asked him to help get them food and medicine. So Milton served others all day and never charged them more than the goods had cost him to get. But the grateful people gave him many tips. At night he crawled back into his house through a window with bread and milk and went to sleep—for twelve hours. When his mother and father counted the money he had given them, they found he had made more than sixty-seven dollars. Today that would be like making more than eight hundred dollars.

192

Evaluating the Lesson

Train Ticket Punch

➤ *Give your child two railroad tickets.*

I will read some questions. Each time your answer is correct, I will punch your train ticket. The first punch will be at Sacramento, the beginning of the building of the railroad that stretched across the country.

➤ You will be trying to pass through each station to reach Promontory Point. See how many punches you can get with your correct answers.

- **What was the railroad called that stretched from one side of the continent to the other?** *(transcontinental railroad)*
- **Who hired many Chinese workers to build the railroad?** *(Charlie Crocker)*
- **What other group of foreign workers labored to build the transcontinental railroad?** *(the Irish)*
- **Who were usually taller—the Chinese or the Irish?** *(the Irish)*
- **What did the Chinese workers usually like to drink?** *(tea)*
- **What did Chinese workers build long ago in China that was made of stone and brick and was four thousand miles long?** *(the Great Wall of China)*
- **Who worked more efficiently—the Chinese or the Irish?** *(the Chinese)*
- **What is a fierce snowstorm called?** *(a blizzard)*
- **What was the name of the rugged mountains that the railroad workers had to cross during the severe winter of 1866-67?** *(the Sierra Nevada)*
- **What is the name given to the sliding of a large amount of snow down a mountainside?** *(an avalanche)*
- **Which people lost more than half their cattle to the cold and snow of 1885?** *(ranchers)*
- **When did the most famous blizzard occur in the eastern part of the United States?** *(in 1888)*
- **What did Milton Daub make from barrel hoops and twine?** *(snowshoes)*
- **What did the grateful people give to Milton?** *(tips)*

If you are teaching a group of children, you may want to divide the group into teams. Give each team a ticket.

Going Beyond

Additional Teacher Information

Thousands of Chinese men went to California in the 1850s in search of the much-talked-about "mountain of gold." After the long journey in overcrowded ships, the Chinese were willing to work at any job to pay back people in China who had provided their passage money. The Central Pacific Railroad employed about twelve thousand Chinese workers to build the transcontinental railroad; nine out of ten workers were Chinese. They worked in gangs of twelve to twenty men, from sunrise to sunset, doing the hardest, most dangerous jobs for $1 a day. (White workers were paid $3-$5 daily and were given food and housing.) Each gang had a Chinese cook to prepare meals—dried oysters, vegetables, pork, poultry, rice, and boiled tea. (The white workers lived on beans, beef, bread, potatoes, and cold water.) Without the diligent work of the Chinese, the transcontinental railroad would have taken much longer to complete. Unfortunately, even at the 100th anniversary celebration at Promontory Point, no one mentioned the Chinese railroad men.

After the ceremony in 1869, the golden spike was replaced with a regular railroad spike. The golden spike is now on display in the Stanford Museum in Palo Alto, California.

LESSON 50

Deliberations: The Chiefs and Government

Text, pages 193-97, 273, 322-23
Notebook, page 74

Preview

Main Ideas

- The West has a unique history of exploration, settlement, and growth.
- Places change over time.
- As white settlers moved farther west, the land of the Native Americans grew increasingly smaller.
- Native Americans were forced to live on reservations.

Objectives

- Participate in a role-playing activity
- Complete a word puzzle about Native Americans

Materials

- Maps and More 31, page M15

Day 1

Lesson

Introducing the Lesson

Role-Playing Activity

You will want to take your child to his bedroom so that he may better visualize the following scenario. Ask him to sit in the middle of the room where he will not feel crowded. It may be necessary to change some of the purchases in the story to fit your child's room.

➤ I will read a story that you will help to "act out." *Give your child directions as indicated.*

We have enough money to buy a new bookshelf and bean bag chair for your bedroom. To make room for these things, you will have to move some of your furniture so that it is touching. *(If this is easily done, you may want to move a few pieces of furniture closer together.)*

Oh, my! We've just received an exciting letter. Your grandparents would like to purchase a new computer and computer desk for your room. You may have to move things a little closer, but we must make room for this gift. *(Direct your child to move to one side of the room. Move some items in the room such as pillows, chairs, or toys so that he begins to feel a little crowded.)*

I know that you are crowded already, but we need to make some more changes to make room for three foster children who are coming to live with us for a while. They are coming from Germany. Please make these new children from a foreign land feel welcome in our home. To make these children even more comfortable, we will give them your bed. You can sleep on a quilt on the floor. *(Direct your child to a corner of the room. Tell him that he should stand while you continue the story.)*

We know that it will be a little difficult at first since most of these children have never been in America before and do not speak English. Adjustments will be made to help the German children get settled and feel more comfortable here. Most of our lessons will be taught in German so that the foster children will understand them. You can read the directions for yourself on your papers in English. For our meals, we will have favorite German foods, such as sauerkraut and sausages, cheeses, beets, onions, and turnips. We hope you will adapt to this new menu and will learn all you can about Germany—the country and its people.

Discussion

➤ **How would you feel if something like this *really* happened to you?** *Encourage your child to give some adjectives to describe what happened and how he would feel about it.*

In the story, we acquired some good things—new furniture, a new computer, and new foster children, but along with these good things, some problems resulted.

➤ Name some of the problems. *(overcrowded conditions, changes in food, changes in the way of teaching, different language being used)*

This activity is an illustration of what has occurred time and again in America's history. As new people settled an area, the people originally there were driven out or forced to make changes. Even today, as the rights of one group of people are protected, the rights of another group of people are affected.

Remember that the Lord encourages Christians to live together peaceably, accepting differences as just differences, not wrongdoings. (BATs: 5a Love, 7d Contentment)

Geronimo, an Apache warrior, led many raids on settlers and soldiers.

Words of the Chiefs

When the railroads and the telegraph lines were finished, there was almost no hope for the Sioux and other peoples who had lived in the lands that were now the United States to regain their old way of life. Some chiefs wanted to keep fighting, to try to hold back the tide of people they saw as invaders. Others began to realize that the fight was useless.

The Apaches had lived peaceably with white settlers for many years. After the War Between the States, though, the Apaches began to defend their homes and to raid white settlements. At last, the United States government demanded that the Apaches move to a reservation in New Mexico. An Apache chief, Cochise, made a speech then. The general who was sent to make the Apaches move was so impressed by the speech that he asked the government to let the people stay. Here is part of Chief Cochise's speech:

> When I was young I walked all over this country, east and west, and I saw no other people but Apaches. After many summers I walked again and found another race of people had come to take it. How is it? Why is it that the Apaches wait to die—that they carry their lives on their fingernails? They roam over the hills and plains and want the heavens to fall on them. The Apaches were once a great nation. They are now only a few.

193

Viewing a vanishing way of life

What do you think Chief Cochise meant when he said that his people carried their lives on their fingernails? Why do you think that the Apaches wanted the heavens to fall on them? What reasons can you give for the Apache nation's becoming small?

Chief Ten Bears, speaking for the Comanches, tried to hold on to the buffalo lands his people had always hunted on:

> Two years ago, I came upon this road, following the buffalo, that my wives and children might have their cheeks plump and their bodies warm. But the soldiers fired on us. And since that time there has been a noise like thunder, and we have not known which way to go. . . .
>
> I was born on the prairie, where the wind blew free and there was nothing to break the light of the sun. I was born where there were no fences and everything drew a free breath. . . . I know every stream and every woods between the Rio Grande and the Arkansas. I have hunted and lived over that country. I live like my fathers before me and, like them, I live happily.
>
> When I was at Washington the Great Father told me that all the Comanche land was ours, and that nobody should stop us from living on it. So why do you ask us to leave the rivers, and the sun, and the wind?

194

- ➤ **What could we have done to prevent so many problems from occurring with the addition of new things and new children from a different country?** *Discuss the concept of* compromise *as ideas are suggested.*
- ➤ This lesson is about a similar experience that happened during the settlement of the Wild West.

Teaching the Lesson

Text Discussion, pages 193 and 322-23

- ➤ *Point out the word* Cochise *to your child on page 193 and give the pronunciation (kō chēs´).*
- ➤ **Read page 193 to find the names of two groups of Native Americans whose lives changed with the coming of the white settlers.** *(Sioux and Apache)*
- ➤ Turn to the map on pages 322-23 to find out where the Sioux used to live in America long ago.

The Apache were nomadic, always on the move, especially in the plains of New Mexico and western Texas.

- ➤ **How did the coming of the railroads and telegraph lines influence the lives of the Native Americans?** *(More white people were moving west, claiming the land of the Native Americans for themselves.)*

There were no contracts or laws stating to whom the land belonged, but the Native Americans were living on the land first. No compromise or agreement was reached between the white settlers and the Native Americans. The whites just took what they wanted. They stole land from the Native Americans, often by lying or breaking promises. (BATs: 4c Honesty, 6c Spirit-filled, 6d Clear conscience, 7d Contentment) The whites did not treat the Native Americans as fellow Americans. The Native Americans were often treated as nonpeople.

> Remember that God made each of us exactly the way that He wanted. We are unique, with special features, characteristics, and abilities. We are not to think of ourselves more highly than of others. (BATs: 3a Self-concept, 4d Victory, 5a Love)

- ➤ **Read aloud from page 193 the speech made by Cochise, the Apache chief.**

Chief Joseph

Another chief, Chief Joseph, also made a speech about the plight of his people, the Nez Perce. President Grant had declared that the people would never have to leave their homes. They lived in the rich and beautiful valley of the Clearwater River, now in Washington State. But the land there was so good that soon the other settlers wanted it; they did not care what the president had promised. What do you think happened?

Soon the president's order was taken back and the Nez Perce were told to leave the valley. They were told to go to a reservation within thirty days. Chief Joseph asked for more time because he had many women, children, horses, and goods to move. But the general in charge, the same one who had helped Cochise, said no. Chief Joseph told his people to get ready to move. The Snake River was flooded; it would be hard to cross. But the Nez Perce had no choice.

They made the crossing, but it was dangerous and tiring. While they were crossing, some white people came and stole some of their cattle. A few of the young Nez Perce men wanted revenge; they killed some white people. Then the war was on.

195

Chief Joseph led his people toward Canada to escape the army that wanted to capture him and his people. He outwitted and outfought a force twice the size of his own many times. But at last he and his people, weary and despairing, gave up. Chief Joseph appealed to his captors:

> I know that my race must change. We cannot hold our own with the white men as we are. We ask only an even chance to live as other men live. We ask to be recognized as men. We ask that the same law work alike on all men. If the Indian breaks the law, punish him by the law. If the white man breaks the law, punish him also.
>
> Let me be a free man—free to travel, free to stop, free to work, free to trade where I choose, free to choose my own teachers, free to follow the religion of my fathers, free to think and act and talk for myself—and I will obey every law, or submit to the penalty.
>
> Whenever the white man treats the Indian as they treat each other, then we will have no more wars.

What do you think of Chief Joseph's requests? Check his requests against the first nine amendments of the Constitution of the United States. Which of his requests did the writers of that document consider important too?

Like many other Native Americans, Chief Joseph was heartsick at "all the broken promises."

196

Text Discussion, page 194

➤ **Read the first paragraph on page 194, and we will discuss the questions.**

➤ **What do you think Cochise meant by saying that "his people carried their lives on their fingernails"?**

The Apaches were forced to move so many times and never knew what to expect next. They felt unstable and very fragile, as temporary as fingernails.

➤ **What do you think Cochise meant by saying that the Apaches wanted "the heavens to fall on them"?**

The Apaches were sad about what was happening to their nation. They often wished for a great disaster to occur to end all the trouble or to make the current disaster not seem so bad.

➤ **Read the rest of page 194 to find out another chief who made a speech about freedom for Native Americans.** *(Chief Ten Bears)*

➤ **How did Chief Ten Bears feel about the prairie?** *(He felt that he was free there. He knew the land well.)*

➤ **How did Chief Ten Bears feel about leaving his land?** *(He felt that he and his people should not have to leave the land where they had lived for so long.)*

Day 2

Text Discussion, pages 195-97 and 273

➤ **Read page 195 through the first paragraph on page 197 to find out which president of the United States promised that the Nez Perce (*nĕz ´ pûrs ´*) would never have to leave their homes.** *(President Grant)*

➤ Find the figure of President Grant on the TimeLine Snapshots at the year 1869.

➤ Read the additional information about President Grant on page 273.

➤ **Why was President Grant's order reversed, and why were the Nez Perce told to move?** *(White settlers wanted the land for themselves.)*

➤ **Do you think this change of decision came from President Grant alone?** It did not.

➤ **What do you think could have influenced the president to cause him to reverse his orders?**

➤ **How long did the Nez Perce have to move?** *(thirty days)*

This undertaking was a difficult task, like moving a whole city with many women, children, animals, and goods across the flooded Snake River.

➤ **Where were the Nez Perce told to go?** *(to a reservation)*

Chief speaking at a council meeting

What do you think happened? Some of Chief Joseph's people were allowed to go back to their homes. But Chief Joseph and others were not. They had to go to a reservation far from their beloved river valley. Chief Joseph died there. The doctor at the reservation said in his official report that the chief had died of "a broken heart."

Why do you think that the leaders of the Nez Perce and the Apaches and other peoples were such good speakers? One reason is that the ability to speak well was considered a great art—greater than painting or carving. Since decisions in most of the nations were made by the whole group, not by just a few leaders, speakers needed to be able to persuade others to agree with them. Those who could speak most movingly became leaders.

Few words of the great chiefs and poets and singers exist today. The poems and speeches and songs were spoken or sung but not written down. How do you think we have any of the words? Some were written down by white translators. But these translators sometimes added their own ideas to the speeches; sometimes they did not translate correctly at all. At the ceremony in which the Union Pacific and Central Pacific Railroads were joined with the golden spike, for example, a Native American made a speech. He said that his people and many others had been cheated by the railroad. But the translator told the crowd that the man had said he was happy that the rails had crossed the land.

197

Native Americans Name ____________________

Read the clues to complete the word puzzles.

1. Fighting that results in a major conflict is called a (W) A R.
2. The leader of the Nez Perce was C H (I) E F J O S E P H.
3. A highly respected Apache chief was (C) O C H I S E.
4. The Nez Perce had to cross the flooded S N A (K) E River when they were ordered to leave their valley.
5. The Nez Perce were made to live on a R E S E R V A T (I) O N.
6. The railroads and telegraph lines took land away from the S I O (U) X nation also.
7. Cochise and the other A (P) A C H E S lived peaceably among the white settlers for many years.
8. T R A N S L A T O R (S) knew the language of both the Native Americans and the white settlers and could help them communicate.

Now write each circled letter in the corresponding box below.

What did Apaches call their small, dome-shaped huts made of poles and brush?

W I C K I U P S

Heritage Studies 4 Student Notebook — Lesson 50 Evaluating the Lesson 74

A ***reservation*** is land set aside by the government for Native Americans. In addition to providing the land, the government often promised to give the Native Americans livestock, manufactured goods, and medicines. Sometimes these promises were kept, but often they were ignored.

- ➤ **Where did Chief Joseph lead his people in order to escape the army and war?** *(toward Canada)*
- ➤ **Why did Chief Joseph and his people finally give up trying to escape?** *(Answers will vary.)*

Comparison Activity, page 196 and Maps and More 31

- ➤ *With great intensity and meaning, read Chief Joseph's speech.*
- ➤ **What do you think about Chief Joseph's requests?**
- ➤ Look at Maps and More 31.

This is a simplified version of the Bill of Rights. This is what the first ten amendments to the U.S. Constitution are called.

- ➤ *Read each amendment in turn, discussing what it means.*
- ➤ **Reread Chief Joseph's speech to find two requests that match the first amendment.** *("free to follow the religion of my fathers" [freedom of religion] and "free to think and act and talk for myself" [freedom of speech])*
- ➤ **Were Chief Joseph's requests unjust or reasonable?** *(reasonable)*

Text Discussion, page 197

- ➤ **Read the last two paragraphs on page 197 to find out whether the chiefs alone made the decisions for the Native Americans.** *(No, most decisions were made by the whole group, but often the chief spoke to help persuade the people in the way he thought was best.)*
- ➤ **How were the white people able to understand the words of the Native Americans?** *(through translators who knew the languages of the Native Americans)*
- ➤ **Do you know what a translator is?** A ***translator*** is a person who tells you what is being said in a different language from the one you speak.
- ➤ **What are some problems that were often associated with the use of translators?** *(They sometimes added their own ideas to the speeches. Sometimes they did not translate correctly at all.)*

This type of action was unfair and dishonest. God wants Christians to deal honestly and kindly with all men. (BATs: 4c Honesty, 5d Communication)

Evaluating the Lesson

Notebook Activity, page 74

- ➤ Read the instructions on Notebook page 74.
- ➤ Complete the page.

Be sure your child understands that the circled letters are to be written in the order in which they appear in the questions.

Going Beyond

Enrichment

If you live near a reservation or Native American museum, arrange a field trip.

Additional Teacher Information

In 1824 the U.S. government set up the Bureau of Indian Affairs and placed it under the War Department's control. In 1849 the Bureau became part of the Department of the Interior.

In 1830 Congress passed the Indian Removal Act, which allowed the government to move the remaining Native Americans west of the Mississippi River. The government moved more than seventy thousand Native Americans across the Mississippi within ten years. On this Trail of Tears many Native Americans died.

Today there are about two million Native Americans in the United States. They may live anywhere they want, but about half live on reservations. The United States has over 280 federal and state reservations, most of which are west of the Mississippi River. The Bureau of Indian Affairs, an agency of the Interior Department, manages the federal reservations.

In 1980 the Supreme Court of the United States ordered the federal government to pay approximately $105 million to eight Sioux tribes. The money was for Native American land in South Dakota that the U.S. government had seized illegally in 1877.

LESSON 51
Conflicts: The Laws and the Land

Text, pages 198-99

Preview

Main Ideas

- Many individuals and groups have shaped America's heritage.
- The history of the United States records diverse cultures forming a strong, free nation.

Objective

- Identify statements about Native Americans as either true or false

Materials

- A ruler
- A feather

Day 1

Lesson

Introducing the Lesson

Text Discussion, page 198

- ➤ **Read page 198 to find the name of the law that tried to make the Native Americans live and act like white people.** *(the Dawes Act)*
- ➤ **What were the Native Americans told to do for a living?** *(farm)*
- ➤ **Why was this order difficult for many Native Americans?** *(Most of them were hunters and traders, not farmers. Much of the land was hard and dry, not good farmland.)*
- ➤ **Why could the Native Americans no longer live in large groups, with grandparents, aunts, uncles, father, mother, and children all working together?** *(They were being forced to move and spread out, with each father farming the land that was given to him.)*
- ➤ **Did the Dawes Act improve life for Native Americans?** *(No, it made life worse.)*

Help That Did Not Help

Not all white people wanted to harm the Native Americans. But sometimes they did not know what to do to help. By 1887, people who thought that what was happening to the Apaches and others was wrong demanded that the government help. The Congress passed the Dawes Act to try to make the situation better.

George Catlin, Bull Dance, Mandan Okipa Ceremony, *National Collection of Fine Arts, Washington, D.C.*

The act said that because the Native Americans' ways of living would no longer work, the Native Americans would have to learn white ways. The people could no longer live in large groups as they always had, with grandparents, aunts, uncles, father, mother, and children all working together. Each father was given up to 160 acres of land and told to become a farmer.

Many of the western peoples were hunters and traders. How do you think they liked being told to become farmers? How do you think they liked being told that they could no longer live in large family groups? Some tried to do as they were told. But the land they were given was usually dry, poor land that the white men did not want. On 160 acres of such ground, few could grow enough for a family to eat.

> *"Providing for honest things, not only in the sight of the Lord, but also in the sight of men."*
>
> **II Corinthians 8:21**

Do you think the Dawes Act made life any better for those who had lost much already? It actually made things worse. The people who had always lived on the open plains were not used to owning land. When dishonest settlers or gold seekers offered to buy the land, they easily cheated the new owners.

198

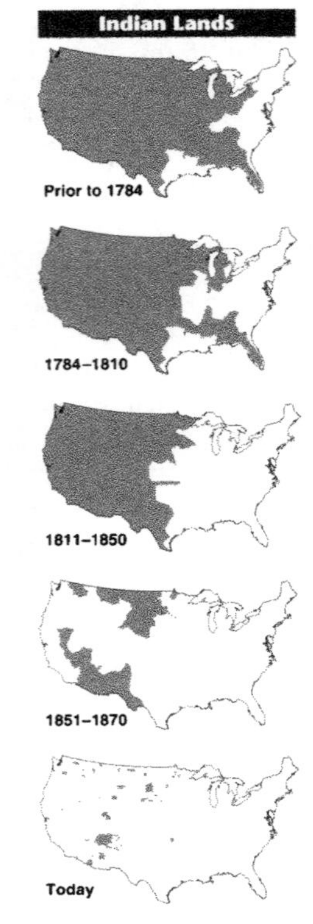

Why do you think the white people wanted the Native American people to be like them? Some thought that the white man's ways were the best ways. They thought the white man's houses were better, the white man's clothes were better, and the white man's rules were better. Some even thought that all Native Americans were like small children who needed to be taken care of.

Many believed that it was kindness to make the Native Americans live on *reservations,* special lands set apart for them, and to let the government provide their food and clothing. But was it? When the Cheyenne, for example, could no longer hunt their own food and make the beaded leather clothes they used to wear, they became unhappy; they had nothing to do, nothing to live for. White people who saw them said they were lazy and glum. The white people then tried harder to make the Cheyenne change.

The Native Americans had heroes and criminals among them, just as the white people did. They had good ways and bad ways, just as the white people did. But because they were fewer and because they did not have one leader, like a president, they did not have the power to keep their way of life. And as white hunters killed off the buffalo, more and more Native Americans had to live on reservations and look to the government for food, clothing, and shelter.

199

➤ **Read the sentence that tells how the Dawes Act made life worse for Native Americans.** *("When dishonest settlers or gold seekers offered to buy the land, they easily cheated the new owners.")*

> Read II Corinthians 8:21 from page 198. God admonishes Christians to be honest in all things. (BAT: 4c Honesty)

Teaching the Lesson

Text Discussion, page 199

➤ **Read page 199 to find out what many white people believed about Native Americans on reservations.** *(Many believed that it was kindness to make the Native Americans live on reservations and to let the government provide their food and clothing.)*

➤ **Why did the white people want the Native Americans to change?** *(Some thought that the white man's ways were the best ways.)*

➤ **How did the whites describe the Cheyenne when they just sat around and did nothing?** *(lazy)*

➤ **Why did the Cheyenne do nothing?** *(They could not do the things that they were used to doing.)*

> God made each of us exactly as He wanted. We all dress, talk, and eat differently. Cultural differences do not make us wrong or right; they just make us different. (BAT: 3a Self-concept)

Evaluating the Lesson

Coup Activity

The Native Americans had often fought battles in which no one was killed or injured. Each warrior had a long stick with a feather tied to the end. When a warrior touched an enemy with his stick, the warrior was said to be "counting coup" *(kū).* The term *coup* means "hit or strike." Counting coup was as brave as killing an enemy.

➤ Get your ruler.

➤ Tape the feather to the end of the ruler. The ruler will be your coup stick.

➤ I will read statements relating to this lesson. If the statement is true, tap the desk with your coup stick.

➤ If the statement is false, hold your stick over your head.

- All white settlers wanted to harm the Native Americans. *(False)*
- Congress passed the Dawes Act to try to improve the situation for the Native Americans. *(True)*

- The Dawes Act required the Native Americans to learn the ways of the white man. *(True)*
- The Native Americans could still live in large groups with their grandparents and aunts and uncles. *(False)*
- Each Native American father was given fifty acres of land. *(False)*
- Each Native American father was told to be a farmer. *(True)*
- Many Native Americans were used to being hunters and traders, not farmers. *(True)*
- All Native Americans refused to obey the Dawes Act. *(False)*
- Much of the land they were given was dry, bad land for growing crops. *(True)*
- Most Native Americans could not grow enough to feed their families. *(True)*
- The Dawes Act made life worse for Native Americans. *(True)*
- *Reservations* are special lands set aside for the Native Americans to live on. *(True)*
- When the Cheyenne could no longer hunt their own food or make their beaded leather clothes, they were unhappy. *(True)*
- When the white people saw the unhappy Native Americans with nothing to do, they thought the Native Americans were lazy. *(True)*
- The ways of the Native Americans were bad, and the ways of the white people were good. *(False)*
- The Native Americans and the white people each had heroes and criminals among their groups. *(True)*
- The Native Americans had a president to lead them. *(False)*

Going Beyond

Enrichment

Give your child an atlas, maps of your state, and writing paper. Direct him to look at a map to find the name of an Indian reservation in his state or in a neighboring state. (*NOTE:* Contact the Bureau of Indian Affairs, U.S. Department of the Interior, Washington, D.C., or your state tourism department for a list of Indian reservations and their addresses.) Encourage your child to write a letter to the Indian reservation, requesting information about the reservation and/or requesting the name and address of a fourth-grade pen pal from the reservation. Address the envelope with the name of the reservation and the state.

Additional Teacher Information

In 1871 Congress ruled that the tribes were no longer separate, independent governments; therefore, the government did not need to make treaties with the Native Americans. In 1887 Congress passed the Dawes Act (also called the General Allotment Act) to divide tribal lands into small property units.

In 1934 Congress passed the Indian Reorganization Act to restore tribal ownership of reservation lands. It also set up a credit fund for land purchase. But by this time, land owned by Native Americans had dropped from about 138 million acres in 1887 to 48 million acres.

LESSON 52
Towns: Changes Through Time

Text, pages 200-203
Notebook, pages 75-76

A bustling midwestern town

Ghost Towns and Boom Towns

Not everyone benefited from the railroad. Can you tell how the railroads helped take more land from the Native Americans? Can you think of others who might have lost their homes or wealth because of the rails? Some towns had bustled before because they were located on stagecoach roads. But if these towns were too far from the new tracks, people left them to go to towns where railroad stations brought in lots of money.

Some towns just got smaller; a few people stayed, keeping the towns alive. Other towns were deserted altogether. The buildings began to fall apart; the streets blew full of dust and tumbleweeds; the roads grew up with brambles. The towns became *ghost towns*. Why do you think people called them that?

A ghost town in Montana

200

Preview

Main Ideas

- Places change over time.
- Each town has a unique history of exploration, settlement, and growth.
- Many individuals and groups have shaped America's heritage.

Objectives

- Locate a ghost town on a map
- Write a letter requesting information about a ghost town

Materials

- An atlas*

The atlas for today's lesson needs to list populations for cities.

- An envelope
- A sheet of stationery

Day 1

Lesson

Introducing the Lesson

Story

➤ Listen as I read a story.

Every settler going west spoke of it. As wagon passed wagon, folks greeted each other, calling out the news. "Have you heard? Tom Ryan's found gold! Yes, gold in the new Wyoming territory! Gonna try my hand at it too!"

And so began the journey of settler after settler, hoping to strike it rich. Ryan's gold mine became the center of excitement. First, just a few hardy men, then a handful, came. They came and they stayed, eager to mine for gold. One by one, week after week, month after month, year after year, men with their families journeyed to this new land. Many brave souls, longing for more adventure and more "elbow room" traveled on the Oregon Trail through the town that came to be called South Pass City. In less than twenty years, South Pass City boasted over three thousand citizens. The town was thriving. Everyone was pleased with the progress of the town and content with life in the West.

But in just two years, life turned upside down for the people of South Pass City. The gold veins gave out. Days on end passed with few settlers or wagons passing through the town. The transcontinental railroad had come but was sixty miles beyond South Pass City. The townspeople didn't want to leave, but they had no other choice. In order to survive, miners and their families packed up all their belongings and moved away. The streets lay quiet—no footsteps or laughter any more. The wind groaned around the empty buildings, windows staring blankly on the sad death of a town. South Pass City, Wyoming—once an active, growing town—had become a ghost town.

➤ The story is an account about the beginning and end of a real town in the days of the Wild West. You will learn more about ghost towns in this lesson.

Teaching the Lesson

Text Discussion, page 200

➤ **Read page 200 to find out why people left towns in the old West.** *(because railroads were too far away from their homes)*

Some towns died out; others sprang into existence. People built many towns in a hurry. The gold rush created towns; the camps that men lived in sometimes turned into places like Red Dog and Rich Bar, California. Silver mining also generated towns: Aspen, Colorado, started as one man's small staked claim. Other towns built up around work like logging. Look at the chart that shows the stages of getting a tree from the forest to the sawmill to the carpenters. At which stages do you think a town might develop? Towns that grow quickly because a big business begins are called *boom towns*. What might the name suggest about these towns?

What businesses do you think came first to boom towns? Blacksmithing and storekeeping were needed right away. But no matter how many smithies and shops a place had, it could not be officially called a town until it had a United States post office. Aspen, for example, was just a claim on the Roaring Fork River. The man who owned the claim went to Washington, D.C., to ask for a post office; he planned to name the town Ute City. When he got back, someone had stolen his land and named the place Aspen.

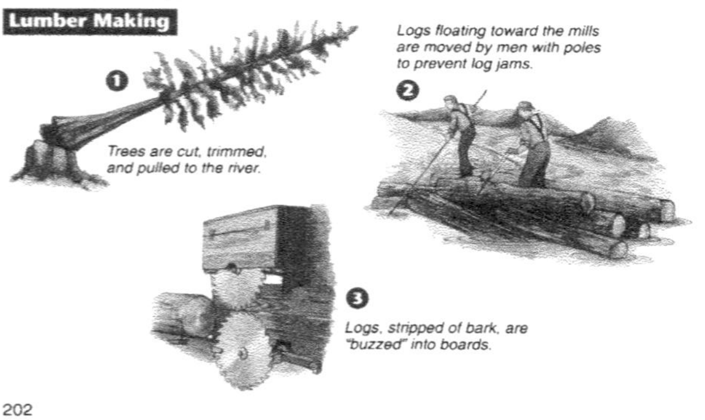

Lumber Making
1
Trees are cut, trimmed, and pulled to the river.
2
Logs floating toward the mills are moved by men with poles to prevent log jams.
3
Logs, stripped of bark, are "buzzed" into boards.

202

The Children Too

Sometimes it seems that only adults had adventures and important work to do. But in almost every job, except in building railroads, children were working right along with the adults. Even in the sawmills, children oiled the machinery and swept sawdust from under the saws. They helped look after the horses. If they did not keep to their work, all work slowed down. There was time to play, however. In the summer, the mill pond was good for fishing and swimming; in the winter it was good for skating.

A one-room school in Kansas

For many years, children did not have to go to school regularly. It was more important that they help get work done. Farmers' children, for example, could go to school only when there was not planting or harvesting to be done. When did they go to school? Some children in cities never went at all. Because children's wages were less, they were given jobs that adults usually did. By 1900, however, every state had laws that said all children had to go to school for at least a few years. Why do you think those laws were made? Partly it was to get some of the children's jobs back for the adults.

Schools today have grades, like the fourth grade. But in the 1800s, schools were not always separated into grades. In the big city schools, where there were more children than places for them, teachers began to put students of the same age together: eight grades in elementary, four in high school. In smaller schools and in country schools, many students were put together in one room, taller and older students in the back and younger and smaller ones in the front. Students in such schools were often grouped by ability rather than by age. Which school would you have liked better?

203

- **What does the term *deserted* mean?** *(left empty or alone; abandoned)*
- **Read aloud the sentence on page 200 that describes how these deserted towns might have looked.** *("The buildings began to fall apart; the streets blew full of dust and tumbleweeds; the roads grew up with brambles.")*
- Compare the pictures on the page.

The text pages are taught out of order in this lesson.

Text Discussion, page 202

- **Read page 202 to find out what *boom towns* are.** *(towns that grow quickly because a big business begins)*
- Give examples of businesses that started boom towns. *(silver mining, logging)*
- **Read aloud the stages of getting a tree from the forest to the sawmill to the carpenters.**
- **What did a town need to be officially called a town?** *(a United States post office)*
- **Why do you think a post office was important in the establishment of a town?**

Text Discussion, page 203

- **Read page 203 to find when every state had laws that required children to attend school.** *(by 1900)*
- Describe some of the tasks children did. *(The children worked in sawmills, sweeping floors and oiling machines. They also cared for the horses or worked on farms.)*
- **When were working children able to go to school?** *(only when their work was done)*
- **Why were laws made requiring children to attend school?** *(so that adults could have the children's jobs)*
- **What were schools like in the 1800s?** *(Students were often grouped according to age or ability, not by grades.)*

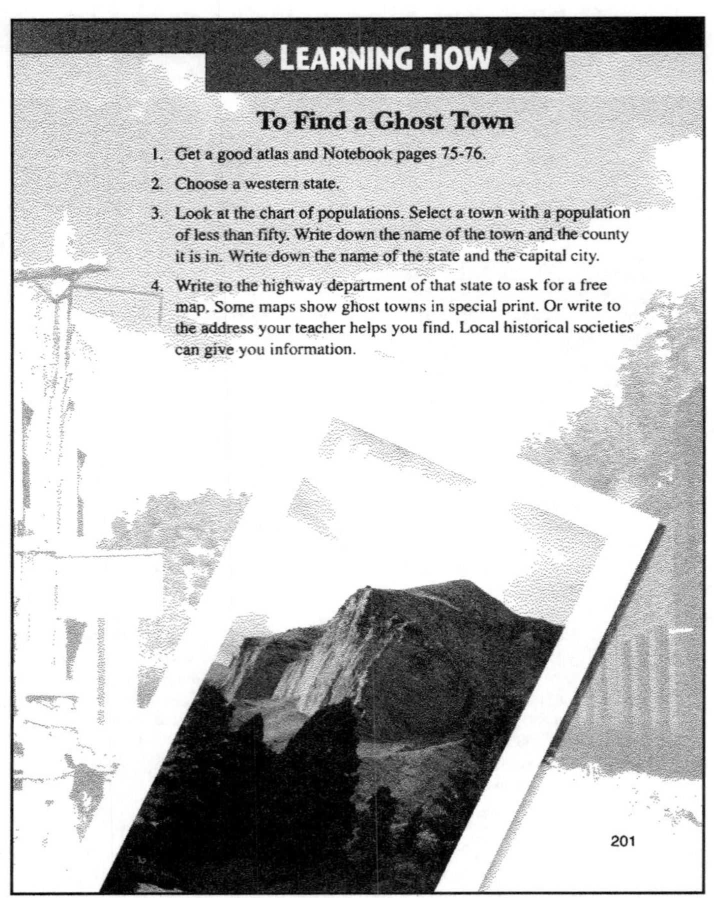
◆ LEARNING HOW ◆

To Find a Ghost Town

1. Get a good atlas and Notebook pages 75-76.
2. Choose a western state.
3. Look at the chart of populations. Select a town with a population of less than fifty. Write down the name of the town and the county it is in. Write down the name of the state and the capital city.
4. Write to the highway department of that state to ask for a free map. Some maps show ghost towns in special print. Or write to the address your teacher helps you find. Local historical societies can give you information.

201

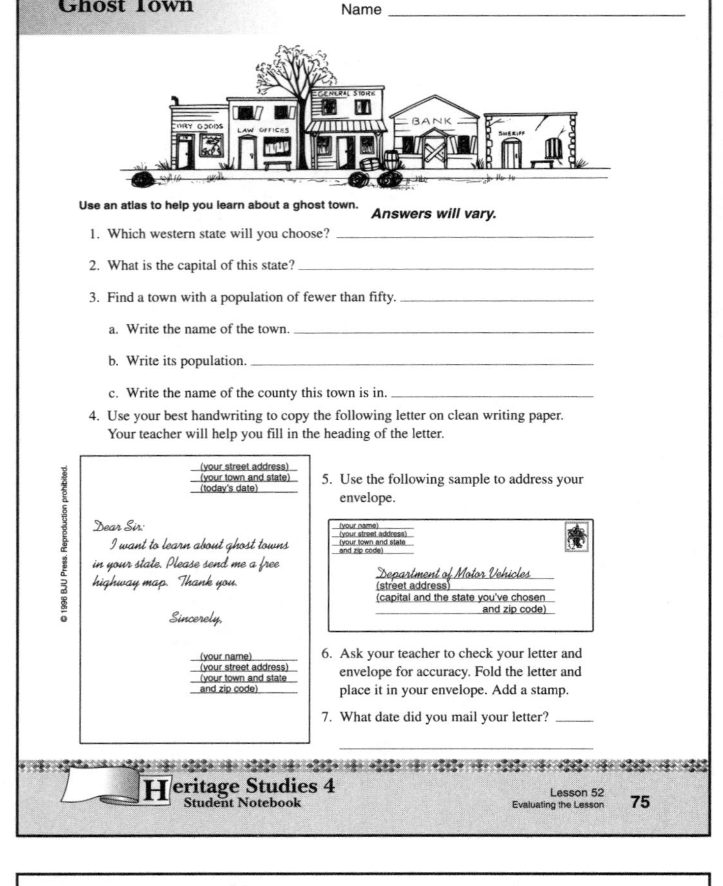

Ghost Town Name ____________________

Use an atlas to help you learn about a ghost town. ***Answers will vary.***

1. Which western state will you choose? ____________
2. What is the capital of this state? ____________
3. Find a town with a population of fewer than fifty. ____________
   a. Write the name of the town. ____________
   b. Write its population. ____________
   c. Write the name of the county this town is in. ____________
4. Use your best handwriting to copy the following letter on clean writing paper. Your teacher will help you fill in the heading of the letter.

(your street address)
(your town and state)
(today's date)

Dear Sir:
I want to learn about ghost towns in your state. Please send me a free highway map. Thank you.

Sincerely,

(your name)
(your street address)
(your town and state and zip code)

5. Use the following sample to address your envelope.

(your name)
(your street address)
(your town and state and zip code)

Department of Motor Vehicles
(street address)
(capital and the state you've chosen and zip code)

6. Ask your teacher to check your letter and envelope for accuracy. Fold the letter and place it in your envelope. Add a stamp.
7. What date did you mail your letter? ____________

Evaluating the Lesson

Learning How Activity, text page 201 and Notebook pages 75-76

➤ **Read the steps on text page 201.**

➤ Complete the information requested on Notebook page 75.

➤ After receiving your reply about the ghost town, complete Notebook page 76.

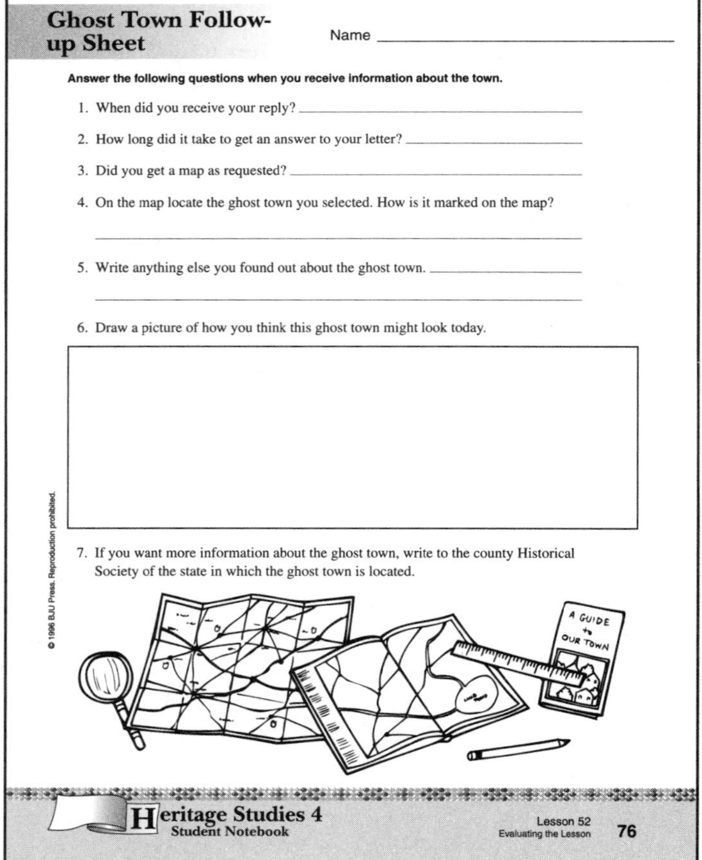

Ghost Town Follow-up Sheet Name ____________________

Answer the following questions when you receive information about the town.

1. When did you receive your reply? ____________
2. How long did it take to get an answer to your letter? ____________
3. Did you get a map as requested? ____________
4. On the map locate the ghost town you selected. How is it marked on the map? ____________
5. Write anything else you found out about the ghost town. ____________
6. Draw a picture of how you think this ghost town might look today.
7. If you want more information about the ghost town, write to the county Historical Society of the state in which the ghost town is located.

Going Beyond

Enrichment

Display the song "Tumbling Tumbleweeds" (Supplement, page S13). Play the recording of "Tumbling Tumbleweeds" from *HERITAGE STUDIES Listening Cassette B.* Invite your child to sing along.

Have available stationery and an envelope. Encourage your child to send a letter to a ghost town, maybe in care of the capital city of the state in which it is located. Tell him to request information about the ghost town's founding, history, and current status.

Additional Teacher Information

After the completion of the transcontinental railroad, thousands of Chinese workers needed jobs and places to live in the United States. Few people would hire these men with the almond-shaped eyes and strange speech and customs; therefore, many Chinese journeyed more than eight hundred miles back to the California coast, their original port of entry. Some settled, though, in Tuscarora, Nevada, where gold had been discovered in 1864 by brothers, Steve and John Beard. Here the Chinese could band together and freely practice their beliefs at the Chinese temple in the center of the town. Many Chinese in Tuscarora worked as cooks, cleaners, and gardeners. Tuscarora boomed from 1872 to 1876, boasting six mining mills. But by 1900, everyone had moved away, adding the name of Tuscarora to the list of ghost towns. Currently the population of Tuscarora, Nevada, is between twenty and fifty, depending on the season. A pottery school is the only active business in the town.

In early America, promoters of the frontier would often choose a site for a town, usually where trails crossed or where rivers joined. The promoters would lay out a plan for the town, sell lots, and try to *boom,* or promote, the town. A typical boom town grew out of the sudden influx of people seeking wealth from the discovery of gold or silver. In modern America, boom towns could arise from the discovery of a vital resource, the development of a new industry, or, in wartime, the building of a special defense project.

LESSON 53
War: The Beginning

Text, pages 204-6
Notebook, page 77

Preview

Main Ideas

- Many individuals and groups have shaped America's heritage.
- The Spanish-American War influenced America's history.

Objectives

- Locate Cuba on a map
- Locate Spain on a map
- Measure distances on a map

Materials

- A centimeter ruler
- A globe or atlas (optional)
- Appendix, page A69: map of Cuba*

Day 1

Lesson

Introducing the Lesson

Map Activity, Notebook page 77

- ➤ Find the east coast of the United States on the map on Notebook page 77.
- ➤ Color this portion of the United States green.
- ➤ Place your finger on the southernmost state on the east coast of the United States.
- ➤ **Do you know the name of this state?** *(Florida)*
- ➤ Move your finger farther south to the large island under Florida.
- ➤ Identify this island. *(Cuba)*
- ➤ Color Cuba red.
- ➤ Place your centimeter ruler on the dot at Key West, Florida, and measure the distance to Havana, Cuba. *($\frac{1}{2}$ centimeter)*
- ➤ Find the scale of miles on the map.
- ➤ **Read the scale of miles. What is the distance from Cuba to Florida?** *($\frac{1}{2}$ cm = 100 miles; Havana, Cuba, is one hundred miles from Key West, Florida.)*
- ➤ Fill in the information to the first question at the bottom of Notebook page 77.

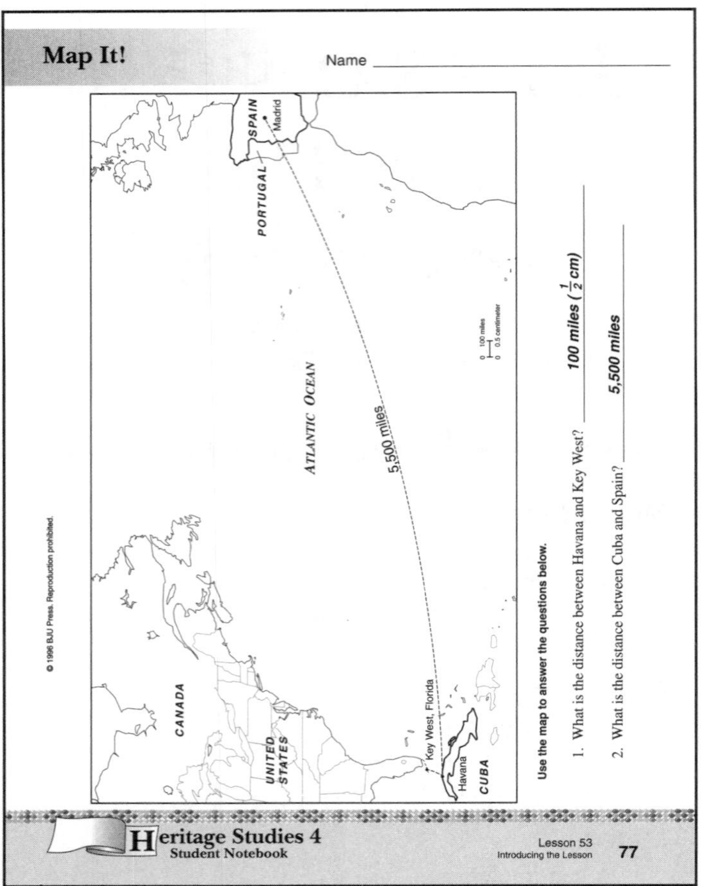
Map It!

Name ____________

Use the map to answer the questions below.

1. What is the distance between Havana and Key West? *100 miles ($\frac{1}{2}$ cm)*
2. What is the distance between Cuba and Spain? *5,500 miles*

Heritage Studies 4 Student Notebook — Lesson 53 Introducing the Lesson — 77

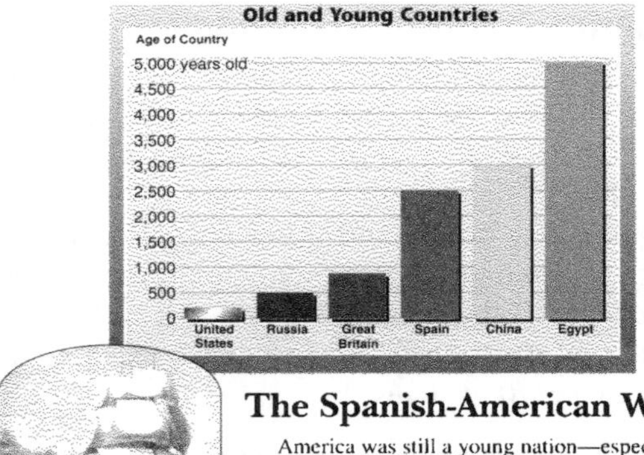

The Spanish-American War

America was still a young nation—especially in the eyes of the old countries in Europe. Many Americans wanted to prove that their nation was a world power. How do you think countries become important powers among other countries?

One way is to be wealthy. Having a lot of money to spend makes a country seem important. Another way is to have a strong army and navy that command respect. Although America had won independence from England in 1776 and had held its own in the War of 1812, the young nation was not yet considered a military power.

Spain was an old country with a long history of exploring, conquering, and settling. Other countries viewed Spain as powerful and important. Americans knew that their country was not feared as Spain was. Some Americans wanted to change that view; they wanted to gain more land and make a great army and navy. Others wanted America to mind her own business.

204

Give the name of a town or well-known place that is one hundred miles away from your home to help your child realize better what one hundred miles represents.

- ➤ **Do you think that the United States should be concerned about what goes on in Cuba? Why?**
- ➤ A long time ago Cuba was owned and controlled by Spain. Move your finger on the Notebook page map from Cuba across the Atlantic Ocean to the continent of Europe.
- ➤ Find Spain and color it orange.
- ➤ **How far away is Spain from Cuba?** *(about 5,500 miles)*
- ➤ Fill in this information on the bottom of Notebook page 77.

Spain was a long way from Cuba. The Spanish rulers needed to know what was happening in Cuba. This was a problem. The year being discussed in this lesson is 1898, before the invention of the airplane, helicopter, television, radar, tape recorder, or computer.

Below are the invention dates for the items mentioned in the previous paragraph:

airplane—1903	helicopter—1904
television—1920	radar—1935
tape recorder—1940	computer—1946

- ➤ **How do you think Spain could keep track of events in Cuba when it was so far away?**

Teaching the Lesson

Text Discussion, page 204

- ➤ Look at the graph on page 204. **Which country is the oldest and which country is the youngest?** *(oldest—Egypt; youngest—United States)*
- ➤ **Read page 204 to find out how countries become important powers.** *(having a lot of money and having a strong army and navy)*
- ➤ **Which country was older—Spain or the United States?** *(Spain)*
- ➤ **Which had a stronger army and navy—Spain or the United States?** *(Spain)*
- ➤ **Which was richer—Spain or the United States?** *(Spain)*
- ➤ **Which was more powerful—Spain or the United States?** *(Spain)*

ECHOES IN HISTORY

The Monroe Doctrine

In 1823, President James Monroe told the countries of Europe that the United States did not want them to make any more colonies in the New World. He said that the United States was establishing a democracy and that governments holding colonies were "dangerous to our peace and safety." What do you think he meant?

Do you think President Monroe could make his declaration work? What would he need if some country refused to go along with his statement? He needed a strong army and navy to enforce his new rule. But America's navy was small.

England had the strongest navy in the world then. England agreed to help America make other countries obey the Monroe Doctrine. But England did not help out just to be neighborly. English leaders wanted to trade with South American countries, and they did not want Spain to take back its South American colonies. America was happy to have English help, whatever the reason.

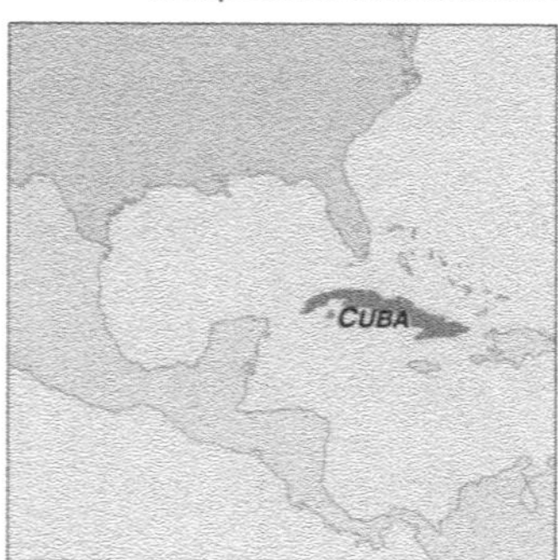

By the time Cuba, a Spanish colony, tried to get out of Spain's control in 1895, Americans had built a powerful navy. Some people tried to get the United States government to help Cuba, claiming that the Monroe Doctrine demanded such action. But did it? The doctrine said only that new colonies should not be made; it said nothing about removing existing ones. Nonetheless, the Monroe Doctrine "echoed" wherever there was a debate over Cuba.

205

➤ **What did Americans in 1898 want?** *(Some wanted other countries to view America as a powerful nation. Some wanted to get more land and to make a great army and navy. Others wanted America to mind her own business.)*

Day 2

Text Discussion, page 205

➤ The desire for a strong army and navy in America was not a new idea. **Read page 205 to find out which early president needed a strong army and navy in order to carry out his new rule.** *(James Monroe)*

➤ **What was the new rule called?** *(the Monroe Doctrine)*

The word ***doctrine*** means "rule or law."

➤ **What did the Monroe Doctrine say?** *(The countries of Europe would not be allowed to make any more colonies in the New World.)*

➤ **Which country offered to help the United States in case of any trouble with countries refusing to obey the Monroe Doctrine?** *(England)*

If your child does not remember where England is located, use a globe, an atlas, or Notebook page 77 to help him locate the country.

➤ **Was England just being kind or did the country's leaders have other reasons for helping America?** *(They had other reasons.)*

➤ **Read aloud the sentence from page 205 that tells what England's real reason was for helping.** *("English leaders wanted to trade with South American countries, and they did not want Spain to take back its South American colonies.")*

It did not matter to the United States *why* England was helping her; she was just thankful to have the assistance.

➤ **Do you think England's assistance made the United States appear still weak and in need of help?**

Because of England's help in making countries follow the Monroe Doctrine, America was well on her way to developing a strong army and navy.

➤ **When was the Monroe Doctrine once again brought up in disputes between nations?** *(when Cuba tried to get out of Spain's control)*

➤ **Was Cuba a new colony?** *(no)*

➤ **Did the Monroe Doctrine make any reference to removing existing colonies?** *(no)*

Rumblings of Trouble

How do you think a war gets started? Wars have started for many reasons—most of them seemingly small reasons. Some wars have started by accident—neither side meant to begin the fighting. The Spanish-American War had several causes.

Early in the war, American papers mocked the Spanish view that America was weak.

"Notice of funeral hereafter."

For one thing, two newspapermen were trying to outdo each other in sales. They each tried to get the biggest news first and put it in their newspapers. Sometimes, when the news was not exciting enough, these men would "spice it up" a little. Do you think that is right? William Randolph Hearst and Joseph Pulitzer said that they had a right to print what they wanted.

In 1898, Hearst and Pulitzer were looking for some really big news to print. But, for the moment, there were no big troubles in the world. There were only the usual stories—such as President McKinley's unpopularity because some people thought he was not using the Monroe Doctrine in the right way. What could Hearst and Pulitzer put in their newspapers to make people buy them? They decided to check into the trouble in Cuba.

206

Text Discussion, page 206

- **Read page 206 to find the names of two influential newspapermen who affected what happened in Cuba in 1898.** *(William Randolph Hearst and Joseph Pulitzer)*
- **What does it mean that they "were trying to outdo each other in sales"?** *(Each man was trying to get more people to buy his newspaper.)*
- **What did these men do to try to boost the sales of their newspapers?** *(They tried to get the biggest news first for their papers. When the news was not exciting enough, they would "spice it up.")*
- **What do you think the phrase "spice up the news" means?** It means to exaggerate the story.
- **Do you think this was honest, accurate reporting of the news?**
- **Do you think that this type of reporting still goes on?**
- **Do you think an exaggeration of the news could start a war?**

The Lord expects Christians to be honest in all things. (BATs: 4b Purity, 4c Honesty, 4d Victory)

Evaluating the Lesson

Map Activity

- *Give your child the map of Cuba from the Appendix.*
- **What do we call the declaration or rule made that said there were to be no more colonies in the New World?** *(the Monroe Doctrine)*
- **What country wrote the Monroe Doctrine?** *(the United States)*
- Locate the United States on your map and color it brown.
- **What country decided to help the United States enforce the Monroe Doctrine?** *(England)*
- Find England on your map and color it red.
- **About what country did William Randolph Hearst and Joseph Pulitzer decide to "spice up" the news?** *(Cuba)*
- Locate Cuba on your map and color it blue.
- **What country owned and controlled Cuba?** *(Spain)*
- Find Spain on your map and color it yellow.

Going Beyond

Enrichment

Have available a "C" encyclopedia and resource books about Cuba. Encourage your child to use the research materials to help him complete the questionnaire (Appendix, page A70).

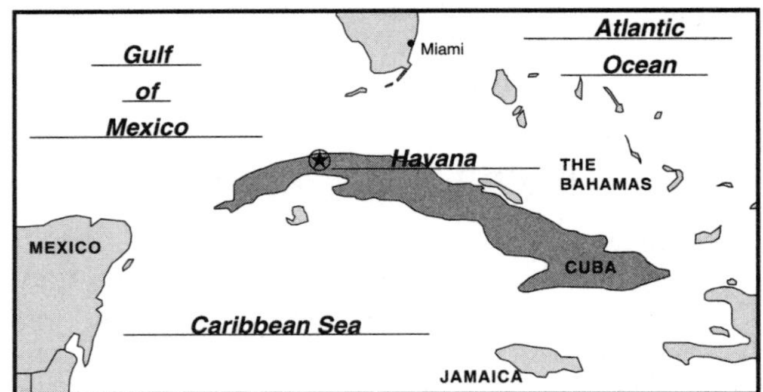

Answers to reproducible questions.

4. ***Havana***
5. ***Spanish***
6. a. ***Spain***
   b. ***1898***
   c. ***Batista***
   d. ***Castro***

Additional Teacher Information

William Randolph Hearst (1863-1951) came from a wealthy family. He was given the *San Francisco Examiner* by his father in 1885. Hearst made this newspaper a financial success, and in 1895 he bought the *New York Journal.* The *Journal* battled Joseph Pulitzer's *New York World* for top circulation sales, reaching its height in 1898 during the Spanish-American War. William Randolph Hearst bought other newspapers and magazines, and by 1937 he owned twenty-five large dailies. He founded the International News Service in 1909 to aid his newspapers. He was one of the first to produce color comics, Sunday supplements, banner headlines, and editorials. Some of his magazines included *Harper's Bazaar, House Beautiful,* and *Good Housekeeping.* Hearst was a U.S. Representative from New York from 1903 to 1907. His estate, San Simeon, with 240,000 acres of land, fifty miles of ocean frontage, and four castles filled with priceless art collections, was, by far, one of the grandest private dwellings in the United States. In 1958, the main castle and some land became a California state park.

Joseph Pulitzer (1847-1911), born in Hungary, left home at age seventeen in search of military adventure. Because of his poor health and bad eyesight, Joseph was rejected by the armed forces of England, France, and Austria. He traveled to Germany, where a United States recruiter enlisted him to fight with the Union forces in the American Civil War. After the war, Pulitzer settled in Missouri and became a United States citizen. In 1868, Joseph Pulitzer worked as a reporter for a German-language newspaper in St. Louis. In just four years, he had risen to managing editor and part-owner of the newspaper. In 1876, Pulitzer moved to Washington, D.C., serving as a correspondent for the *New York Sun.* In 1878, he bought two newspapers, the *St. Louis Dispatch* and the *St. Louis Evening Post.* He combined them into one newspaper, the *St. Louis Post-Dispatch,* and made a fortune. In 1883, Pulitzer bought the *New York World* and by 1887 had transformed it into an aggressive, crusading newspaper with the largest circulation in the nation at that time. At his death, Pulitzer gave five hundred thousand dollars each to the New York Philharmonic Society and to the Metropolitan Museum of Art. He also left two million dollars to Columbia University in New York City for the establishment of a graduate school of journalism. Pulitzer specified that after the school had operated for at least three years, prizes should be awarded for the advancement of education, journalism, literature, music, public morals, and public service. The Pulitzer Prizes were first awarded in 1917 and are now awarded every year for distinguished achievement in journalism, literature, drama, and music. There are numerous categories of prizes available, with awards in each category being either gold medals, citations, and/or three thousand dollars.

Lesson 54

The Fighting: Important People and Events

Text, pages 207-10, 275
Notebook, page 78

Preview

Main Ideas

- Many individuals and groups have shaped America's heritage.
- The Spanish-American War influenced America's history.

Objectives

- Identify headlines in a newspaper
- Select true "headlines" related to the Spanish-American War

Materials

- The front page of a newspaper*
- Front-page newspaper headlines from old newspapers*
- Maps and More 32, page M15
- The figure representing the Spanish-American War (1898) from the TimeLine Snapshots
- An atlas

Day 1

Lesson

Introducing the Lesson

Newspaper Headlines, Maps and More 32

➤ *Give your child the front page of a newspaper. Call attention to the name of the newspaper, the place in which it was published, and the date of publication.*

➤ **Read aloud the captions under the pictures on your front page.**

➤ Count the news articles that are on the front page.

➤ Look at the largest letters on the page or the top banner of words.

This is called the ***headline.*** Its purpose is to attract the attention of the passerby and to get him to buy the newspaper to read more about the headline and other articles.

- **Read the headline aloud.**
- *Show any headlines or front pages of old newspapers.*
- **Read aloud each headline.** *Mention briefly the event that the headline highlighted, giving the date if possible.*
- **How do you think these headlines may have affected the people who read them?**

The *Maine* was a United States warship that had been sent to Cuba to protect Americans and their property in case of fighting. It also reminded Spain of America's power.

- Look at Maps and More 32.
- **Read aloud the headline regarding the explosion of the *Maine.*** *(DESTRUCTION OF THE WAR SHIP MAINE WAS THE WORK OF AN ENEMY)*
- **How do you think Americans reacted to this headline?**
- **Do you think the Spanish destroyed the *Maine?***

After reading the headlines, many Americans thought that the Spanish destroyed the *Maine* purposely. An explosion on the *Maine* caused the ship to sink, killing over two hundred fifty crewmen and starting the Spanish-American War. (*NOTE:* A naval court of inquiry concluded that a submarine mine had caused the explosion. The United States blamed Spain, of course. But Spain claimed that an explosion inside the ship caused the disaster. In 1976, U.S. Navy researchers studied the incident again and concluded that a fire in a coal bin exploded a supply of ammunition stored nearby.)

- This lesson tells more about this incident as well as the people and events of the Spanish-American War.

The text pages are taught out of order in this lesson.

Teaching the Lesson

Text Discussion, page 208

- **Read page 208 to find out the name of the man who led the group known as the "Rough Riders."** *(Theodore Roosevelt)*
- **What do you think the name "Rough Riders" tells about the group?**
- **Who was president of the United States during this time?** *(President McKinley)*
- Find the figure of William McKinley on the TimeLine Snapshots at the year 1897.
- Read the additional information about President McKinley on page 275.

Theodore Roosevelt (in glasses beside flag) with the "Rough Riders"

Hearst and Pulitzer read about the trouble in Cuba. They decided to send writers there. Soon many reports were printed in the newspapers, telling the Americans that the Spanish were cruel and wicked, that the Cubans were dying only because the Spanish treated them so badly. Americans were angry. Those Spanish had to be stopped! The newspapers were not telling *all* the story. However, Americans did not seem to want to hear any more; they wanted action.

President McKinley said that America's army was not ready to go to war. He wanted to talk to the Spanish. And he did. The Spanish did not want a war either; they were too far from home to take on the United States in battle. To show that they did not want to fight, the Spanish sent one of their generals back to Spain. He was the general that the papers in the United States had been calling a "butcher." What do you think the Americans thought of this action?

Many Americans were somewhat calmed when the Spanish sent their general home. A few still wanted to make the Spanish do more. One of these was a man named Theodore Roosevelt. Roosevelt was in charge of a group of men called the "Rough Riders." What do you think the name tells about the group? Roosevelt wanted a war, and he wanted to be ready for it.

208

- **Which of these two men—William McKinley or Theodore Roosevelt—wanted war with Spain in Cuba?** *(Roosevelt)*
- **Why did President McKinley not want America to go to war?** *(America's army was not ready to go to war.)*
- **Why did McKinley want to talk with the Spanish?** *(He wanted to persuade Spain to change its dealings with Cuba. He wanted to discourage a war with Spain.)*
- **Read the sentences on page 208 that tell what Spain wanted and what the Spanish did to show their true feelings.** *("The Spanish did not want a war either; they were too far from home to take on the United States in battle. To show that they did not want to fight, the Spanish sent one of their generals back to Spain. He was the general that the newspapers in the United States had been calling a 'butcher.'")*
- **What do you think the newspapermen were trying to tell the public by using the term "butcher" with the Spanish general's name?** This general was mean and cruel. He was responsible for having many people killed.

The stories in newspapers are not always accurate or complete. We must read newspapers carefully and cautiously, asking for more information when we are not sure what the article is really trying

A Mysterious Explosion

The Americans sent a ship, the *Maine*, to Cuba to show that they could back up their demands. The Spanish did not like to see the ship come, but they were polite; they gave the Americans gifts and treated them with respect. Everyone began to believe that a war would not happen.

Then one night, as the sailors slept, a huge explosion lifted the great ship out of the water. She immediately began to take on water and to sink. The captain could not save his ship. By morning, with the help of a nearby Spanish ship, the captain had rescued 102 of his men. But more than 250 had died.

No one knew exactly what had caused the ship to explode. President McKinley sent men to find out, but they could not say for sure. Many experts thought it was an accident. But the newspapers in America printed headlines like these: "*Maine* Blown Up by Enemy," and "Split in Two by Enemy's Secret Infernal Machine." What do you think headlines like that did to the Americans' desire for war?

The Spanish did not want war. They quickly did everything that the United States wanted—and more. But it was not enough. America declared war on Spain.

An artist's version of the wreck of the Maine

209

A Short War

The American navy sent more ships to fire on Spanish forts in Cuba. Then the American army went on land to fight the Spanish soldiers. Teddy Roosevelt's Rough Riders were among the first to go in. They were indeed a rough group who did not always see the need to obey rules. But they were brave in a fight, and they liked Roosevelt enough to do as he said under fire.

The Americans thought that the Cubans they were rescuing would help with the fighting. But the Cubans were not prepared to fight; they had little training and few weapons. So the war that was supposed to be almost bloodless began to cost many American lives.

Soon the Americans had control of the whole island. The American generals, some of whom had fought in the American Civil War, demanded that the Spanish surrender. At first the Spanish said no. Then the United States offered to take all the Spanish soldiers home to Spain on American ships. The Spanish quickly surrendered. The Spanish flag that had flown over Cuba for almost four hundred years came down. The Stars and Stripes went up.

Back in the United States, everyone was celebrating. America had gone to war against an important country and had won. Now America had new lands—the island of Cuba and other islands.

210

to say. Writers often report only part of the story, maybe just the part that they agree with, or maybe just the part that is sensational or controversial.

Text Discussion, page 209

- ➤ **Read page 209 to find out what many experts thought about the explosion of the *Maine.*** *(It was an accident.)*
- ➤ **What were some of the headlines about the incident?** *("*Maine *Blown Up by Enemy" and "Split in Two by Enemy's Secret Infernal Machine")*

Remember that Hearst and Pulitzer used sensational headlines to try to sell more newspapers, though the information in the headlines had not been proved true.

- ➤ **What do you think those types of headlines did to the Americans' desire for war?**
- ➤ **Did the Spanish want war after the *Maine* incident?** *(no)*
- ➤ **Do you think the Spanish-American War could have been avoided?**

The strong public opinion, caused by the sensational reporting of the newspapers, persuaded Congress and President McKinley to declare war on Spain.

God's Word can be trusted, since it does not include man's opinion. We must read our Bibles daily, memorize Scripture, and use God's Word as a standard for judging man's words and actions. (BATs: 6a Bible study, 6b Prayer, 8b Faith in the power of the Word of God)

TimeLine Snapshots Activity

- ➤ Add the figure representing the Spanish-American War to the TimeLine at the year 1898.

Day 2

Text Discussion, page 210

- ➤ **Read page 210 to find out why the Cubans did not help the Americans fight for the Cuban land.** *(They had little training and few weapons.)*
- ➤ **What caused the Spanish finally to surrender to the Americans?** *(when the United States offered to take all the Spanish soldiers home to Spain on American ships)*

The Spanish-American War took place from April 21 through August 13—four months of battle. Although this was a short war, blood was shed and many soldiers died.

- ➤ **What country ruled Cuba after the Spanish-American War?** *(the United States)*

◆ FAMOUS PEOPLE ◆

Clara Barton
(1821-1912)

As a girl Clara Barton had traveled with her father when he fought with the Indians out West. Then, as a young woman, she served as a nurse in the Civil War. She spent her own money to find missing soldiers and to get help for the badly hurt. The group called the American Red Cross came to be because Clara Barton believed that such a group was needed. Perhaps you have seen a truck or a building with the red cross on it.

In 1898, Clara, then seventy-seven years old, heard that people in Cuba were suffering under the Spanish rulers. She could never hear of suffering without trying to help. She went to President McKinley and asked whether she could take some food and medicine to the Cuban people. He told her she could.

Clara Barton

When she got there, Miss Barton saw people starving and beaten. She saw little children with no food or clothes. She was horrified and grieved. She wrote a book, *The Red Cross*, to tell what life was like for some in Cuba.

Miss Barton had no idea how her book would be used. She had no idea how large and important the American Red Cross group would become. She only knew she had to live her life to help others.

207

Headlines Name ____________________

Read each pair of headlines. Draw a line through the false headline in each pair.

1. BARTON GOES TO CUBA
   ~~CUBANS CRY, "LEAVE US ALONE!"~~
2. RED CROSS SENDS AID
   ~~RED CROSS—FOR AMERICANS ONLY~~
3. HEARST AND PULITZER SWAP STORIES
   ~~HEARST HAS THE WHOLE TRUTH~~
4. SPANISH CRUELTY KILLS CUBANS
   ~~NO BLOODSHED IN CUBA~~
5. ~~SPANISH WANT WAR!~~
   ROUGH RIDERS READY TO FIGHT
6. ~~AMERICANS WITHDRAW IN RELIEF~~
   "BUTCHER" RETURNS TO SPAIN
7. ~~SPANISH WELCOME *MAINE*~~
   EXPLOSION SINKS *MAINE*
8. MCKINLEY DECLARES WAR!
   ~~NO WAR!~~
9. SPAIN SURRENDERS!
   ~~SPANISH SOLDIERS AS PRISONERS~~
10. ~~SPAIN RULES CUBA~~
    STARS AND STRIPES OVER CUBA

Heritage Studies 4 Student Notebook — Lesson 54 Evaluating the Lesson 78

➤ Look at the world map in your atlas.

Point out and name the lands that Spain ceded to the United States after the Spanish-American War: Cuba, Guam, Puerto Rico, and the Philippines. (*NOTE:* The United States paid Spain $20 million for the Philippine Islands.)

➤ **Read aloud the sentence on page 210 that explains how the Americans felt about the outcome of the Spanish-American War.** *("Back in the United States, everyone was celebrating.")*

Text Discussion, page 207

➤ **Read page 207 to find the name of the woman who helped the soldiers during the Spanish-American War.** *(Clara Barton)*

➤ **In what other war had Clara Barton helped?** *(the American Civil War)*

➤ **What was the name of the organization Miss Barton worked with?** *(the American Red Cross)*

➤ **How old was Miss Barton when she went to Cuba to help?** *(seventy-seven years old)*

➤ **What did Clara Barton take to the Cuban people?** *(food and medicine)*

The American Red Cross is still a vital, important organization today. The workers of the Red Cross help people in times of disaster, such as floods, hurricanes, and war. They provide shelter, medicine, food, and clothing to the victims or those in need.

You may want to talk to someone from your local Red Cross or visit the organization.

The help the Red Cross gives is valuable and kind. We need to be alert to the needs of others and to be willing to share what we have with those who are in need. (BATs: 4a Sowing and reaping, 5a Love, 5b Giving)

Evaluating the Lesson

Notebook Activity, page 78

➤ Read the instructions on Notebook page 78.

➤ Complete the page.

Going Beyond

Enrichment

Play Quest for Cuba with your child. Give him a game board (Appendix, page A71). Tell him that one of you will represent the United States and the other will represent Spain. Direct your child to cut out his flag, tape it to a toothpick, and stick it into a small ball of clay to serve as a base. Do the same with the other flag. To start the game, place the flags in any space in the outside rows on opposite sides of the game board. As you read the list of events given, one by one, direct your child to move his game marker only if his country received the greatest benefit as a result of that event. Explain that if each flag is moved correctly, the country that took Cuba in 1898 will be left standing on the board. The game may also be played with one player. The player must choose which flag to move for each event.

Additional Teacher Information

Clara Barton (1821-1912) began her career as a teacher. She later served as the first female clerk in the United States Patent Office. Soon after the outbreak of the American Civil War in 1861, Clara Barton carried clothing, food, and medicine to soldiers on the battlefield. Her courage and unselfish care for the wounded and needy soldiers earned her the nickname "Angel of the Battlefield." It was while she was resting in Switzerland in 1869 that Barton learned of the International Committee of the Red Cross. Back home in the United States, she led a campaign to start an American Red Cross chapter in 1881. Barton served as its first president and held the job from 1882 to 1904. It was Barton who was instrumental in having the clause added to the Red Cross constitution to provide aid for needy persons in times other than war. Clara Barton lived her life serving others with the Red Cross, writing books, and lecturing on various topics of health. In 1974, the thirty-eight-room house in Glen Echo, Maryland, headquarters for the American Red Cross for many years, became the Clara Barton National Historic Site.

Theodore Roosevelt was born into a prosperous, old New York family on October 27, 1858. As a child, "Teedie" (his childhood nickname) was interested in animals, writing his own Natural History of Insects at age nine and setting up his specimens in a display that he called the Roosevelt Museum of Natural History. As a young man, he studied law for a time in his attempt to improve the politics of New York City. He was active in the Republican Club and was elected to the New York state legislature as his first political office. He served as president of the police commission of New York, reducing corruption in the police force. Under William McKinley's presidency, Theodore Roosevelt was appointed secretary of the navy. When America declared war on Spain in 1898, Roosevelt resigned his position with the navy and accepted a commission as lieutenant colonel in the First Volunteer Cavalry Regiment, known as the "Rough Riders." In July 1898, Roosevelt and his Rough Riders raised the U.S. flag over San Juan Hill in Cuba as America won the Spanish-American War over Spain. Roosevelt became the hero of the Spanish-American War and one of the most famous men in America at that time. Later that year he was elected governor of New York, and in 1901 he became William McKinley's vice president. An assassin's bullet took the life of McKinley on September 14, 1901, making Theodore Roosevelt, at age forty-two, the youngest president in the history of the United States.

10 LESSONS 55-60

Getting the Message

This chapter follows the development of early communication in America. The transfer of news begins with the pony express, followed by America's first newspapers. Samuel F. B. Morse and his telegraph come on the scene, with Alexander Graham Bell and his telephone close behind. As each new mode of communication is met, your child will also examine people's reactions and the changes in lifestyle that resulted. He will learn how to write and interpret Morse Code and make and use a simple telegraph and telephone. A board game, Get the Message, is included as a chapter review in the Enrichment section of Lesson 60.

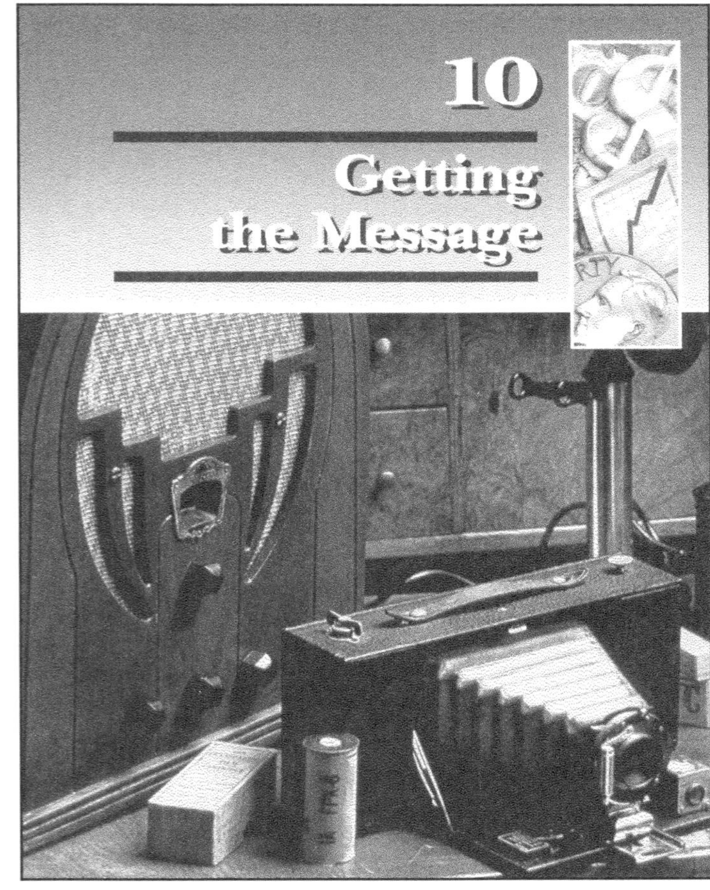

Materials

The following materials must be obtained or prepared before the presentation of the lesson. These items are labeled with an asterisk (*) in each lesson and in the Materials List in the Supplement. For further information see the individual lessons.

- A newspaper (Lesson 56)
- Newspapers that contain *Gazette* as part of their name (Lesson 56)
- 2 paper cups (Lesson 59)
- 25 feet of string (Lesson 59)
- A telegram (optional) (Lesson 60)
- Appendix, page A71 (Lesson 60)

LESSON 55
Hoofbeats A-Coming

Text, pages 212-13
Notebook, page 79

Preview

Main Ideas

- People in the United States are linked by transportation and communication.
- The pony express improved communication in early America.

Objective

- Complete sentences about the pony express

Materials

- An atlas

Day 1

Lesson

Introducing the Lesson

Listening Activity

➤ Listen as I read aloud a poem about communication in early America. (*NOTE:* You may want to read the poem a second time, allowing your child to strum his fingers on the desk in a rhythmic, galloping meter.)

They were Bob, Billy, Jay, Alexander, and Joe—
The "Pony Boys" who carried the mail.
Courageous though small, wiry, and strong,
Over miles they blazed the trail.

Determined and quick, their brave hearts astir,
The post riders raced 'cross the land.

They rode all the day, and through the night too,
These boys who too soon would be men.
To get the mail through, safe and on time
Was the goal that never had end.

Determined and quick, their brave hearts astir,
The post riders raced 'cross the land.

The dangers were great; the glories but few,
But the riders gave that no heed.
With news from afar leather pouches were full.
They pressed on—each man and his steed.

Determined and quick, their brave hearts astir,
The post riders raced 'cross the land.

➤ Today we will learn about the mail system known as the pony express which was used to carry important messages and very small packages across the western part of America during the early 1860s.

Teaching the Lesson

Text Discussion, page 212

➤ *Write and pronounce the word* mochila (mo chee lah).

A ***mochila*** was a lightweight leather saddlebag used to carry the mail on horseback. It lay across the saddle of the horse and was held in place by the weight of the pony express rider.

➤ **Read page 212 to find out why the pony express rider was always in a hurry.** *(His job was to get the mail through quickly.)*

➤ **What did the pony express rider do when he reached a new station?** *(He threw the leather pouch of letters onto a fresh horse and rode on his way—usually in less than a minute.)*

The stations at which the riders changed horses were about ten to twenty miles apart. Riders rode the horses as fast as they would go—about ten miles an hour—between stations. They learned ways to change riders in the least amount of time possible.

➤ **Do you think the pony express rider had to record his arrival and departure times at the stations?**

➤ **Do you think that the rider could have slowed down a bit and still have done a good job?**

Only lightweight young men could become express riders. Most were boys less than 18 years old. Their "uniforms" consisted of red shirts, blue trousers tucked into fancy boots with silver spurs, and a fringed buckskin jacket.

The accounts about the pony express riders claim that they pushed themselves to be as fast as they could be. They were determined, trustworthy, strong, and brave. Often they had to ride through terrible weather—driving snow, pouring rain, or even the hot, beating sun—but we do not read of any complaints or excuses being made.

Did You Hear?

A drumming of hooves and then a shout brought a man out from the pony express station. He ran to the barn to get the fresh horse—it had been saddled and waiting for two hours.

The rider galloped in, pulled up his horse, and leaped off. "Morning," he said to the man holding the fresh horse by the reins. He snatched the *mochila* from the back of the winded horse and threw it onto the new mount. The letters inside the leather pouch shifted.

"Coffee?" said the man still holding the horse.

"Can't," said the rider. "Late." He rolled his shoulders and stretched. Then he hauled himself into the saddle. He nodded to the station man and then pressed his heels into the horse's side. The horse sprang away. Not even a minute had passed since the rider had come in.

Why do you think the rider was in such a hurry? He had just come twenty-five miles, and he had another twenty-five miles to go. He was in a hurry because his job was important: to deliver the mail safely and quickly. But how quick is quick?

A mochila

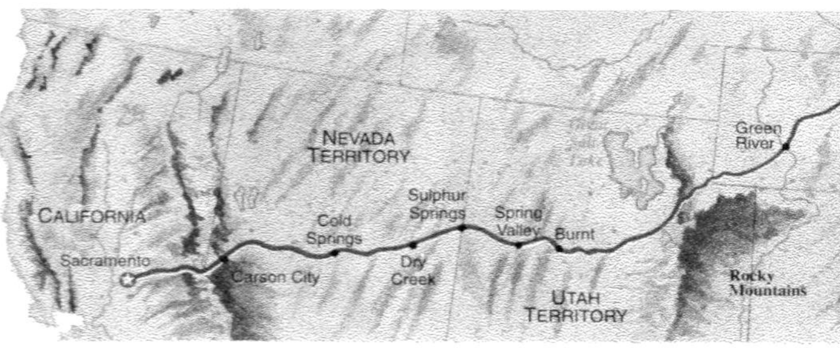

212

When the mail was carried on stagecoaches, it took at least three and a half weeks for a letter to get from St. Joseph to Sacramento. The pony express could get it there in as little as ten days.

How fast can you get a message to some distant place now? A few minutes? Even seconds? What inventions have made such communication possible?

Newspapers

Once, there were few ways to get news from one place to another. Long ago, most news traveled slowly; usually one person told another and he told another and so on. People who traveled from one town to another carried the news with them. Letters, too, spread information. The Separatists sent letters back to England, telling of their new life in the New World. Much of what we know about earlier times comes from these old letters.

After the printing press was developed, someone in England got another idea about getting the news out. The new idea was called the *London Gazette*. It was a printed paper that told the news. *Gazette* used to mean "official publication."

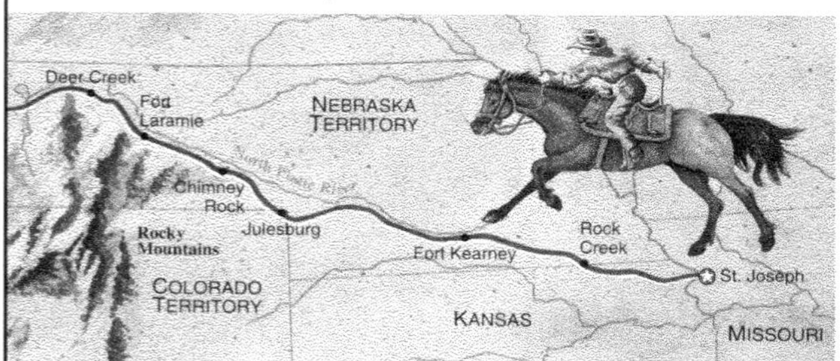

213

It is important to do your schoolwork and chores with the same attitudes that were evidenced by the pony express riders. God sees all we do, hears all we say, and knows everything that we think. All that Christians do should be for the glory of God. (BATs: 2c Faithfulness, 2d Goal setting, 2e Work, 2f Enthusiasm, 4a Sowing and reaping)

Map Reading Activity, pages 212-13

- ➤ Look at the map of pony express routes on pages 212-13.
- ➤ **Which town was the starting point for the pony express in the East?** *(St. Joseph)* **Where did this route end?** *(Sacramento)*
- ➤ **Which town was the starting point for the pony express in the West?** *(Sacramento)* **Where did this route end?** *(St. Joseph)*
- ➤ **Read aloud some of the names of towns in between these points.** This route covered almost two thousand miles.
- ➤ Look at the map of the United States in your atlas. Find St. Joseph and Sacramento on this map.
- ➤ **About how much of the distance from the East Coast to the West Coast was covered by the pony express routes?** *(a little more than half)*
- ➤ **How do you think the mail got from St. Joseph to New York?**

If a letter was leaving California and going to New York, it could travel quickly by pony express as far as St. Joseph. The remainder of the journey from there to New York had to be on the stagecoach.

Text Discussion, page 213

If your student text names the cities of New York and San Francisco in the first sentence on page 213, you will want to correct it to read St. Joseph and Sacramento.

- ➤ **Read the first two paragraphs on page 213 to find out how long it took to get a letter from St. Joseph to Sacramento when there was only the stagecoach.** *(at least three and one-half weeks)*
- ➤ Calculate how many days are in three and one-half weeks. *(twenty-four to twenty-five days)*

This would be like someone in St. Joseph sending a letter on May 1 to someone in Sacramento. The letter may contain news of a relative's illness or death, but the person in Sacramento would not read this news until about May 24.

- ➤ **How many days did it take when the pony express was used?** *(ten days)*

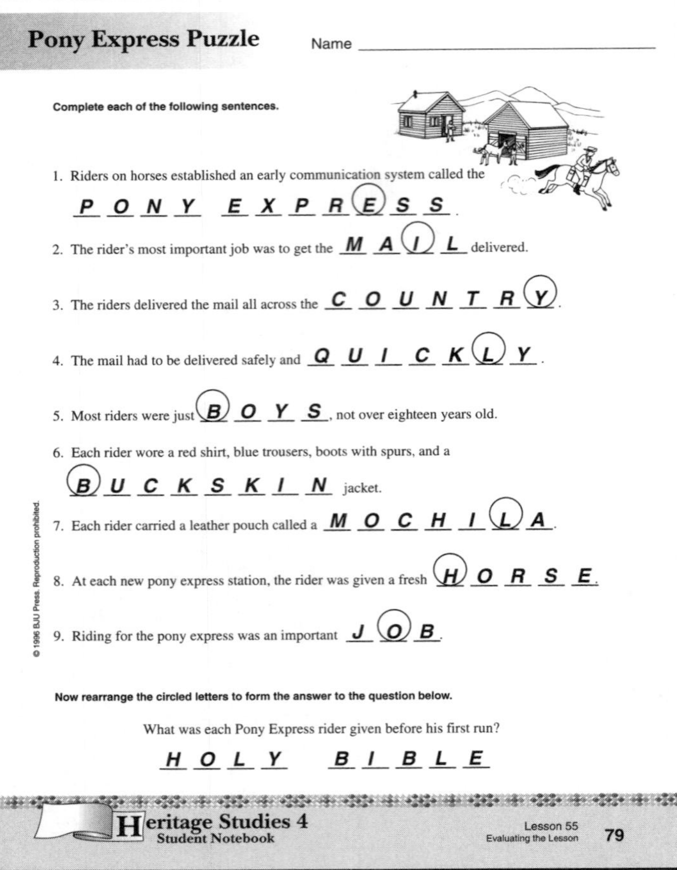
Pony Express Puzzle Name ____________

Complete each of the following sentences.

1. Riders on horses established an early communication system called the P O N Y E X P R E S S.
2. The rider's most important job was to get the M A I L delivered.
3. The riders delivered the mail all across the C O U N T R Y.
4. The mail had to be delivered safely and Q U I C K L Y.
5. Most riders were just B O Y S, not over eighteen years old.
6. Each rider wore a red shirt, blue trousers, boots with spurs, and a B U C K S K I N jacket.
7. Each rider carried a leather pouch called a M O C H I L A.
8. At each new pony express station, the rider was given a fresh H O R S E.
9. Riding for the pony express was an important J O B.

Now rearrange the circled letters to form the answer to the question below.

What was each Pony Express rider given before his first run?

H O L Y B I B L E

Heritage Studies 4 Student Notebook — Lesson 55 Evaluating the Lesson — 79

This would mean that the letter sent from St. Joseph on May 1 would arrive in Sacramento around May 10, thereby making the news in the letter a little more up-to-date.

Today a letter can go from Missouri to California in as little as three days.

➤ Name some other means of getting the news even faster today. *(by telephone, telegraph, e-mail, fax machine, etc.)*

Evaluating the Lesson

Notebook Activity, page 79

➤ Read the instructions on Notebook page 79.
➤ Complete the page. Find the answer to the final question.
➤ **What was each pony express rider given before his first run?** *(a Bible)*

Going Beyond

Enrichment

Provide your child with stationery on which he may write a letter. If possible, have available the name and address of a fourth-grade pen pal in a distant state or country. Encourage him to write a friendly letter, specifically asking the pen pal to make note of the date that the letter was received and to give that date in his response. Instruct him to record the date that he mails his letter. Tell him also to record the date that he receives a response to the letter. Encourage him to continue writing to his new pen pal.

Additional Teacher Information

The pony express began on April 3, 1860, covering a route that stretched over 1,840 miles. The service started at St. Joseph, Missouri, and ended in Sacramento, California. The line passed through Kansas, Nebraska, Colorado, Wyoming, Utah, and Nevada. Riders changed horses at relay stations every ten to twenty miles.

The riders' "uniforms" consisted of red shirts, blue trousers tucked into fancy boots with silver spurs, and a fringed buckskin jacket. Each rider rode as fast as his horse would go—about ten miles an hour—until he reached the next station. He blew a horn to signal his arrival at each new station. There the rider swung from his horse, switching the mochila filled with letters to the back of a fresh horse. Only one or two minutes passed before the rider was on his way again.

Mail delivery by pony express cost five dollars for each half-ounce letter. Later this charge was reduced to one dollar. At first the mail run was made once a week in both directions. Before too long, the management increased the pony express mail service to two times weekly. On the first run, the mail was carried across the nation in just ten days! Americans thought the age of speed had finally come!

LESSON 56
Read All About It!

Text, pages 213-14
Notebook, page 80

Preview

Main Ideas

- People in the United States are linked by transportation and communication.
- Inventions and ideas spread from one part of the world to another.
- Newspapers helped more people learn about more news more quickly.

Objectives

- Find items in a newspaper
- Write articles for a newspaper

Materials

- A newspaper*
- A dictionary
- Newspapers that contain *Gazette* as part of their names (optional)*

Day 1

Lesson

Introducing the Lesson

Notebook Activity, page 80

➤ Collect items for a Notebook activity. You will need a newspaper, scissors, glue, and Notebook page 80.

➤ **Read the labels in each section on Notebook page 80 to determine what kind of articles you will be looking for.**

➤ **Do you know what an *obituary* is?** You may look up the word in the dictionary. *(a notice of someone's death)*

➤ Search the newspaper to find and cut out one example of each item called for on the Notebook page.

➤ Glue the newspaper parts in the proper place on the Notebook page. If parts are too large to fit on the page, glue them on notebook paper, making sure to label the parts.

➤ **What other kinds of items does the newspaper contain?** *(Answers will vary.)*

➤ We will learn about early newspapers in this lesson.

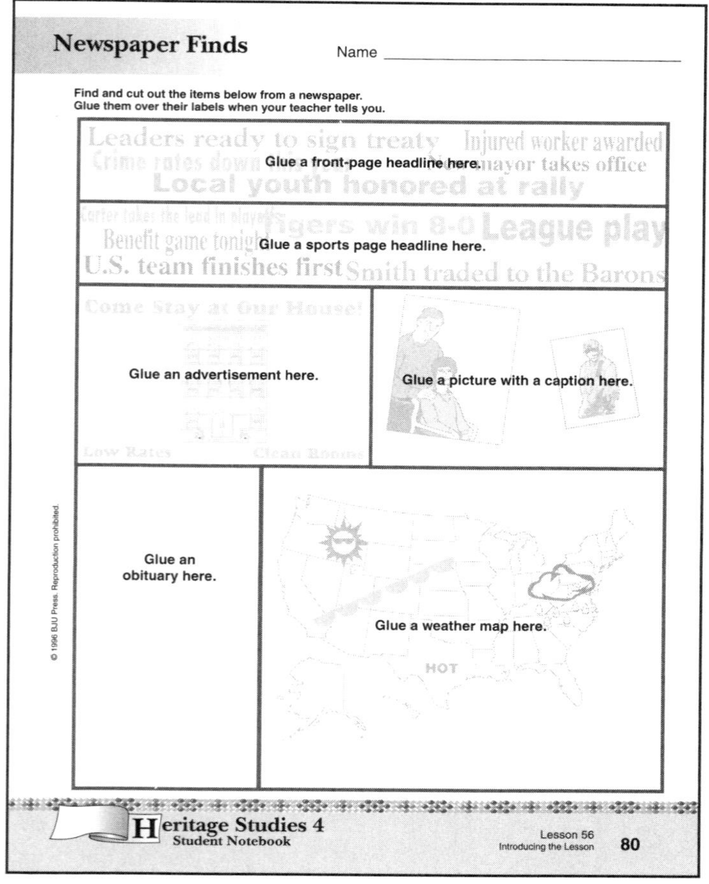

Newspaper Finds Name ______________________

Find and cut out the items below from a newspaper.
Glue them over their labels when your teacher tells you.

Glue a front-page headline here.

Glue a sports page headline here.

Glue an advertisement here.

Glue a picture with a caption here.

Glue an obituary here.

Glue a weather map here.

Heritage Studies 4 Student Notebook — Lesson 56 Introducing the Lesson — 80

Day 2

Teaching the Lesson

Text Discussion, page 213

➤ **Read the last two paragraphs on page 213 to find out some ways in which news was spread before the newspaper.** *(person to person and letters)*

Of course, news is still spread from person to person and by letter today.

> A Christian's words should be honest and bring glory to the Lord. (BAT: 5d Communication)

➤ **Where did the idea of a newspaper come from?** *(from someone in England)*

➤ **What was this first newspaper called?** *(the* London Gazette*)*

➤ **What does the word *gazette* mean?** *("official publication")*

➤ **Why was it an appropriate word to use for the newspaper?** *(The newspaper was an official publication with printed pages that told the news.) Show any examples of newspapers with the name* Gazette *that you have obtained.*

A few years later the word *newspaper* became the name for such publications as the *London Gazette*. In America, the first paper that stayed in business and made money was the *Boston News-Letter*. It did not look like a newspaper today; it was about as big as a sheet of notebook paper. How much news do you think could fit on both sides of one sheet of notebook paper?

Newspapers in those days might better have been called "oldspapers." The "news" in them was sometimes months old by the time the readers got them. They were not published every day either. Why do you think that was?

In 1833, the *New York Sun* changed the way papers were published. The *New York Sun* was bigger—nearly like today's papers. It cost only a penny, and it was published every day. It was the first paper to do other things too. It printed advertisements; it was the first to be delivered to houses; and it was the first to be sold on the street.

Newspapers changed the way people got their news. More people could know about events more quickly. How do you think newspapers changed the way people lived?

Even so, news traveled slowly by modern standards. When George Washington died in 1799, it was an event of world importance. But people in Massachusetts did not read about it until two weeks later. And people in Ohio saw the news in their papers almost three weeks after the funeral.

The 1704 Boston News-Letter

214

Text Discussion, page 214

- **Read page 214 to find out the names of some early American newspapers.** *(the* Boston News-Letter *and the* New York Sun*)*
- Describe what the *Boston News-Letter* looked like. *(It was about as big as a sheet of notebook paper. It had news printed on both sides.)*
- **Which newspaper became the first to be published every day in America?** *(the* New York Sun*)*
- Describe the *New York Sun* of early America. *(It cost one penny. It printed advertisements. It was the first to be delivered to houses. It was the first to be sold on the street.)*
- Discuss how much a daily newspaper costs in your town, whether it is delivered to houses, and how it is sold on the street.

Evaluating the Lesson

Writing Activity

Imagine yourself living in the time period of America's first newspapers. Brainstorm for ideas of what you might have written and submitted to a newspaper. (*NOTE*: Possible ideas for articles include a famous person, a fast pony express rider, a town celebration, a new sheriff or marshal, or a change in the newspaper office.)

- Write a rough draft of an article on notebook paper. I will read and edit your article when you are done.

If you are teaching more than one child, encourage them to create the front page of a newspaper using their articles. Direct them to include the name of the paper and the date. You may want to add handwriting lines and some column divisions to help guide them. Allow them to type or print neatly their articles into the columns. If you have a computer, guide the children in some simple desktop publishing.

Going Beyond

Enrichment

Arrange a field trip to your town's newspaper office to see how the local newspaper is produced. As a follow-up activity, encourage your child to write a thank-you letter to the newspaper's editor, telling what he learned or liked best about the visit.

Additional Teacher Information

During the mid-1440s, Johannes Gutenberg, a goldsmith in Germany, introduced printing using movable metal type. He cast letters of the alphabet from lead and put them in a frame, or galley, to make up words. Gutenberg could print different pages of a book by using the same pieces of type over and over again. Gutenberg's Bible is one of the most beautiful books ever printed.

LESSON 57

Morse and His Telegraph Machine

Text, pages 215-17
Notebook, pages 81-83

Preview

Main Ideas

- Individuals have unique attributes and skills.
- People in the United States are linked by communication.
- Samuel Morse experimented with electricity to develop a telegraph machine.

Objectives

- Use Morse Code to decode a message
- Solve a word puzzle about Samuel Morse and the telegraph

Materials

- The figure of Samuel Morse (1844) from the TimeLine Snapshots

Lesson

Introducing the Lesson

Notebook Activity, page 81 and text page 217

➤ **Have you ever used a secret code?** Tell how that code worked.

➤ Look at the code in the colored box on text page 217.

The International Morse Code is a special kind of code that telegraph and radio operators all over the world still use.

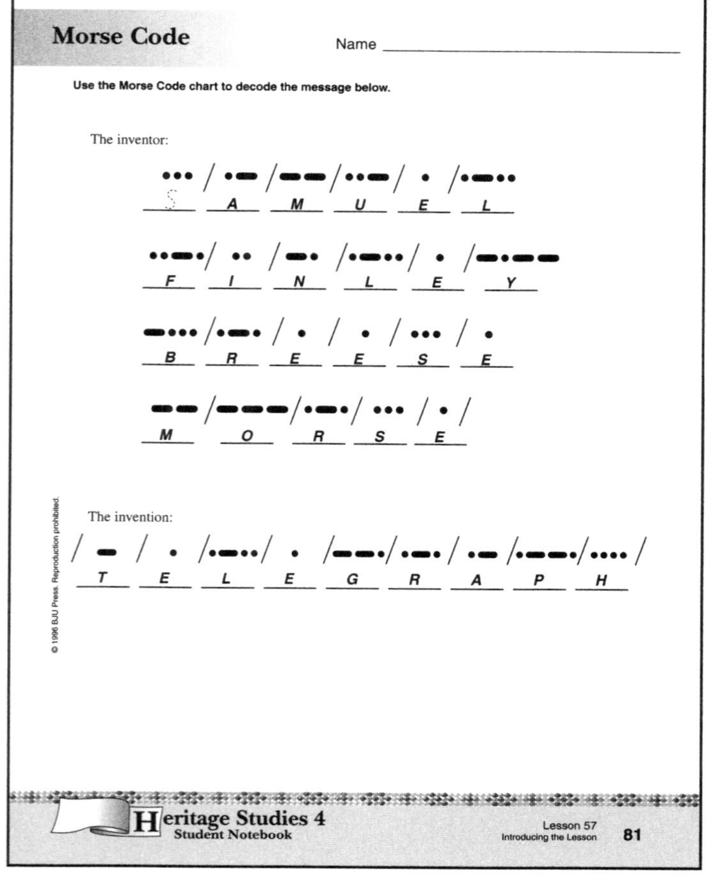

Morse Code Name ______________

Use the Morse Code chart to decode the message below.

The inventor:

··· / ·− / −− / ··− / · / ·−··
S A M U E L

··−· / ·· / −· / ·−·· / · / −·−−
F I N L E Y

−··· / ·−· / · / · / ··· / ·
B R E E S E

−− / −−− / ·−· / ··· / · /
M O R S E

The invention:

/ − / · / ·−·· / · / −−· / ·−· / ·− / ·−−· / ···· /
T E L E G R A P H

Heritage Studies 4 Student Notebook — Lesson 57 Introducing the Lesson — 81

➤ Read the instructions on Notebook page 81.

➤ Use the code on text page 217 to figure out the coded message on the Notebook.

It will reveal the inventor and invention that we will learn about in this lesson. *(Samuel Finley Breese Morse; telegraph)*

The Telegraph

Samuel F. B. Morse

America was becoming a big country. Newspapers and pony express mail kept the news traveling, but some people had been looking for faster ways to communicate. One of them was a famous painter named Samuel Morse.

Morse had been in France and was coming home by ship. During the long trip, he heard men talking about electricity. Since Benjamin Franklin's experiment with the kite and lightning, people had been fascinated by the possibilities of this energy.

"It's called an electromagnet," one man said. "Looks like a big horseshoe with wire wrapped around it. I saw it back in New York."

"What's the purpose of it?" said another.

"See," said the first man, "when electricity is passed through the wire, the horseshoe becomes magnetic. Works like a giant magnet, it does."

"Really!" said the other. "Does it matter how much wire is used? Does the current slow if the wire is long?"

"No, not at all. Electricity passes instantly from one end to the other no matter how long the wire is."

215

"Then," said Morse, speaking up for the first time, "I think that wire and electricity might be used to send messages over long distances."

The others talked on, hardly noticing that a painter of portraits had gotten an idea that would soon change the world.

Morse worked on his idea for years, but he had to keep painting and teaching to make a living. In 1837, Morse had his message machine ready to test. He hung seventeen hundred feet of wire around the walls of his classroom in New York University. At one end he attached a device connected by a wire to a battery. The device had a base and a metal arm that could be pressed down. At the end of the arm was a funnel-shaped *key*. When that key was pressed down to touch a similar key on the base, electricity from the battery passed through the device and all the way to the end of the wire strung about the room.

"It works!" said one of his students.

"Now to prove it to the rest of the world," said Morse.

"What will you call it?" said the students.

"A *telegraph machine*," Morse said, "because *tele-* means 'far off,' and *-graph* means 'writing.' "

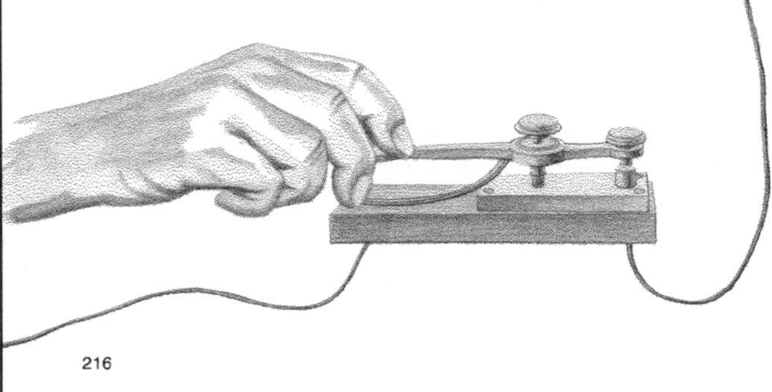

216

Teaching the Lesson

Text Discussion, pages 215-16

➤ **Read pages 215-16 to find out what machine Samuel Morse invented.** *(the telegraph, or a message machine)*

➤ **What jobs did Samuel Morse have before he became an inventor?** *(a painter and a teacher)*

Samuel Morse painted portraits of famous people, including President James Monroe. There was not enough work for an artist to make a living, so he did many other things besides. He had several strong abilities that he developed and used well.

> Each person has special abilities and talents that make him unique. Christians need to use their abilities for the Lord. (BAT: 3a Self-concept)

➤ **What were the men on ship discussing on Morse's return trip to America?** *(electricity)*

➤ **How did one man describe the electromagnet?** *(It looked like a big horseshoe with wire wrapped around it.)*

➤ **Read aloud the fifth paragraph on page 215, which tells the purpose of the electromagnet.**

➤ **What idea did Samuel Morse get as a result of this discussion about the electromagnet?** *(He thought that wire and electricity could be used to send messages over long distances.)*

➤ **Did the other men like this idea?** *(They did not even seem to be paying attention. They said nothing about the idea.)*

➤ **How long did Samuel Morse work on making a machine that would send messages over long distances?** *(years)*

Morse had set a goal, worked hard, and was determined not to give up until he had the telegraph just right. These are admirable traits for all of us. (BATs: 2d Goal setting, 2e Work)

➤ **Read aloud paragraph three on page 216, which describes how Samuel Morse tried out his new invention for the first time.**

➤ **Did Morse's invention work the way he wanted?** *(yes)*

➤ **What does the word *telegraph* mean?** *("far-off writing")*

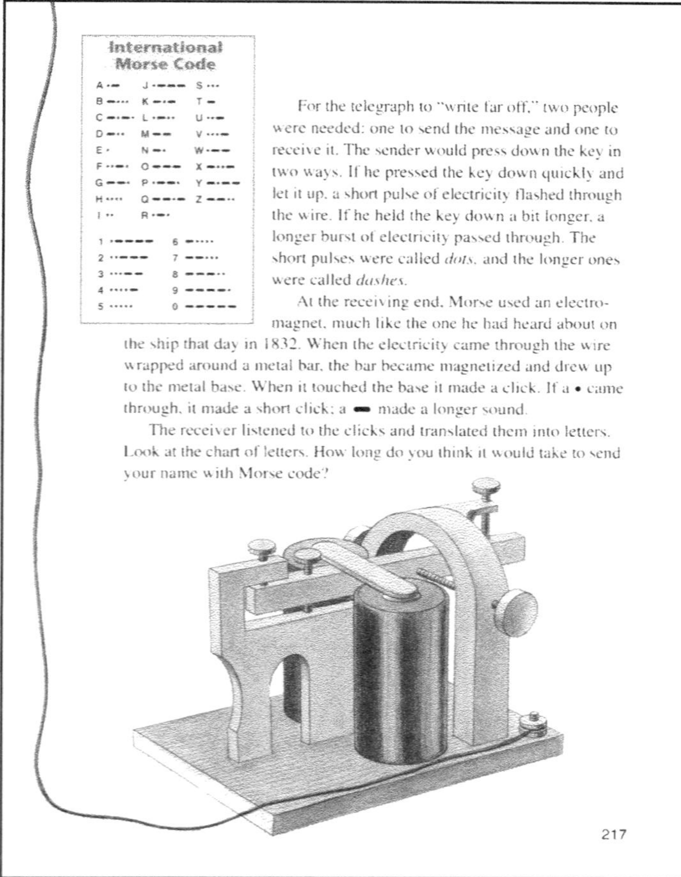

International Morse Code

A •—	J •———	S •••
B —•••	K —•—	T —
C —•—•	L •—••	U ••—
D —••	M ——	V •••—
E •	N —•	W •——
F ••—•	O ———	X —••—
G ——•	P •——•	Y —•——
H ••••	Q ——•—	Z ——••
I ••	R •—•	

1 •————	6 —••••
2 ••———	7 ——•••
3 •••——	8 ———••
4 ••••—	9 ————•
5 •••••	0 —————

For the telegraph to "write far off," two people were needed: one to send the message and one to receive it. The sender would press down the key in two ways. If he pressed the key down quickly and let it up, a short pulse of electricity flashed through the wire. If he held the key down a bit longer, a longer burst of electricity passed through. The short pulses were called *dots*, and the longer ones were called *dashes*.

At the receiving end, Morse used an electromagnet, much like the one he had heard about on the ship that day in 1832. When the electricity came through the wire wrapped around a metal bar, the bar became magnetized and drew up to the metal base. When it touched the base it made a click. If a • came through, it made a short click; a ▬ made a longer sound.

The receiver listened to the clicks and translated them into letters. Look at the chart of letters. How long do you think it would take to send your name with Morse code?

217

Telegraph Clues

Name ____________________

Use the clues below to complete the telegraph puzzle on page 83.

ACROSS

2. power made by electric current
3. initials of the inventor of the telegraph
4. another word for portrait painter
6. means *writing far off*
7. symbols used to send messages by way of the telegraph
8. short and long pulses that translate into letters

DOWN

1. Morse connected wire to a(n) ______.
2. This object looked like a big horseshoe with wire wrapped around it.
5. Electricity passes through a(n) ______.

Heritage Studies 4 Student Notebook — Lesson 57 Evaluating the Lesson — 82

Text Discussion, page 217

- **Read page 217 to find out how the telegraph machine was operated.**
- **How many people were needed to make the telegraph "write far off"?** *(two; one person to send and one to receive)*
- **What kinds of symbols did the short clicks and long clicks make?** *(Short clicks made dots; long clicks made dashes.)*

Samuel Morse used these patterns of dots and dashes to make his Morse Code. The invention of the code was just as important as the invention of the telegraph.

TimeLine Snapshots Activity

- Add the figure of Samuel Morse to the TimeLine at the year 1844.

We will learn more about this persistent inventor in the next two lessons. And we will find out what was significant for Samuel Morse in 1844.

- Look at the TimeLine to find out who was president in 1844. *(John Tyler)*
- Read the additional information about President Tyler on page 271.

Evaluating the Lesson

Notebook Activity, pages 82-83

- Read the instructions on Notebook page 82.
- Complete the crossword puzzle on Notebook page 83, using your text as needed.
- Look at the design of the puzzle. It shows how Samuel Morse's first telegraph receiver looked.

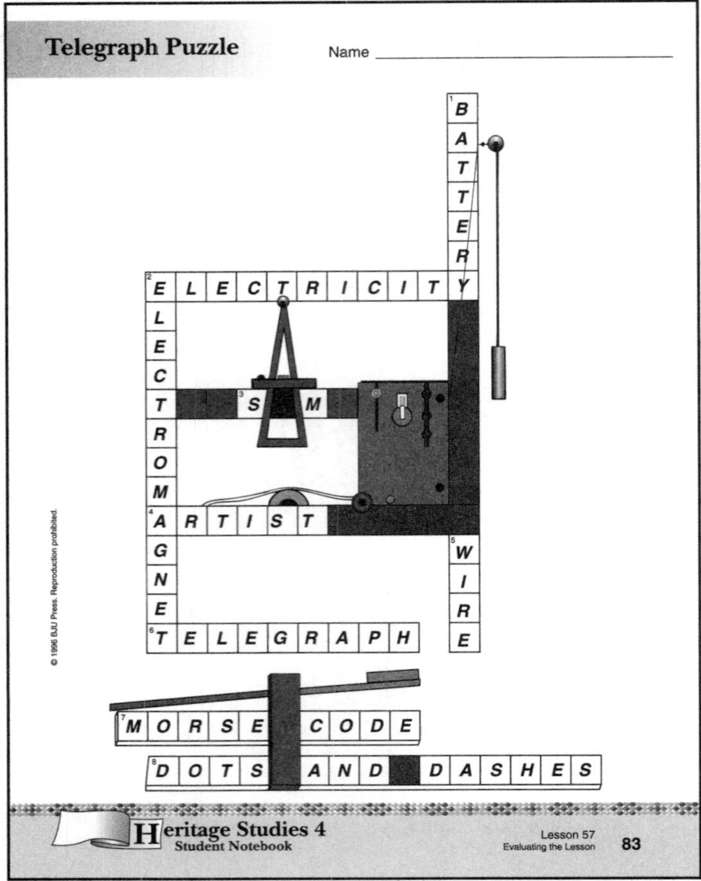

Going Beyond

Enrichment

Provide your child with colored 4"×6" index cards and felt-tip pens to make name tags. Direct him to use text page 217 as a reference. Encourage him to write his name in Morse Code on an index card, decorating the edges of the card if he wishes. To make sure that his name will fit, suggest that he write the code in pencil first, making a slash after each letter, before he traces over the marks with a felt-tip pen. Encourage your child to make cards for other family members if he is interested.

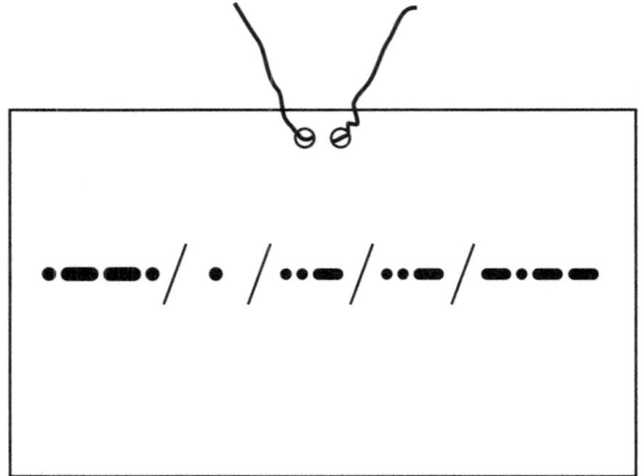

Additional Teacher Information

Samuel Finley Breese Morse was born in Charlestown, Massachusetts, on April 27, 1791. At age fourteen, Samuel entered Yale and studied in the field of science. In addition to his scientific knowledge, Samuel had a natural aptitude for drawing and eventually studied art in London. It was said that Samuel Morse was among America's finest painters, having among his credits exceptional portraits of President James Monroe and the Marquis de Lafayette. The orders for portraits were extremely infrequent, so the idle artist became a busy inventor.

While in Europe, Morse became fascinated with semaphores, tall platforms built for the purpose of passing along messages. To relay a message, a man climbed to the top of each semaphore and held up a huge pole with movable arms. By changing the positions of the arms, he could send a coded message for the man on the next semaphore to see and pass on. Morse wondered whether electricity could be passed on in a similar way. His first telegraph was built in his brother's living room. The simple talking machine was constructed from a picture frame, a table, wheels of an old clock, wooden drums, a pencil, metallic forks, mercury cups, and wire strung all over the room. The wire came in pieces that Morse had to join and insulate with cotton—a huge task in itself. The first demonstration of the telegraph was in 1837. Though the first telegraph message was sent in 1844, it was still several years before Morse's invention was recognized as a valuable communication tool.

In the midst of waiting, more experimenting, and demonstrating the telegraph, Samuel Morse began practicing daguerreotypy, one of the earliest forms of photography, thereby gaining the title Father of American Photography.

LESSON 58
Dots and Dashes

Text, pages 218-20, 271
Notebook, page 84

Preview

Main Ideas

- People in the United States are linked by communication.
- A code is made up of symbols used in communication.
- Lifestyles change as people use new inventions and improved technology.

Objectives

- Decode messages using Morse Code
- Make up a coded message using Morse Code
- Identify statements about Samuel Morse as either true or false

Materials

- A Bible
- An atlas

Lesson

Introducing the Lesson

Learning How **Activity, page 218 and Notebook page 84**

➤ **Read and follow the instructions in Step 1 on text page 218.**

➤ **Read Step 2.** Use the Morse Code chart on page 217 to decode the first message sent by Morse's telegraph. *(What hath God wrought)*

This message was taken from a verse in the Bible.

> Read aloud Numbers 23:22-23. In this passage the children of Israel are giving praise to the Lord for bringing them out of Egypt. All that we have and all that we do is because of the Lord. All praise belongs to Him. (BATs: 7b Exaltation of Christ, 7c Praise)

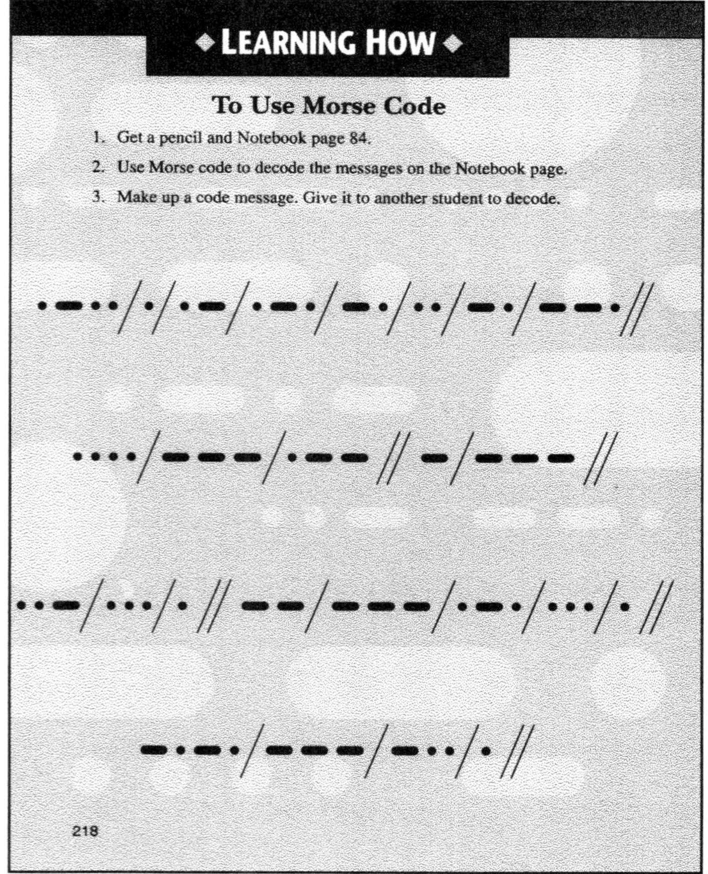

◆ LEARNING HOW ◆

To Use Morse Code

1. Get a pencil and Notebook page 84.
2. Use Morse code to decode the messages on the Notebook page.
3. Make up a code message. Give it to another student to decode.

218

➤ Place a piece of paper below the first line of the coded message on page 218. The double lines at the end indicate the end of a word. Decode the first word of this message. *(learning)*

➤ Fold your paper down and continue the decoding procedure for the rest of the page. *(Learning how to use Morse Code)*

➤ **Read Step 3.** Choose another family member to receive a special message from you. Complete your own message on Notebook page 84 by shading in either the dot or the dash in the space provided.

In this lesson we will learn more about Samuel Morse and his wonderful wires.

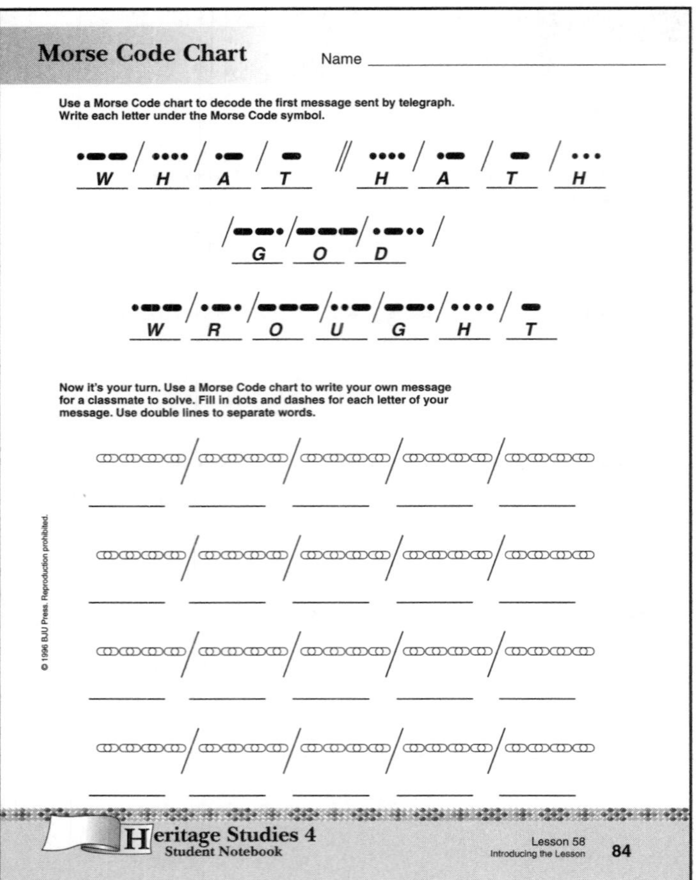

Morse Code Chart Name ______________________

Use a Morse Code chart to decode the first message sent by telegraph. Write each letter under the Morse Code symbol.

W H A T // H A T H

G O D

W R O U G H T

Now it's your turn. Use a Morse Code chart to write your own message for a classmate to solve. Fill in dots and dashes for each letter of your message. Use double lines to separate words.

Heritage Studies 4 Student Notebook — Lesson 58 Introducing the Lesson 84

Inventions such as the telegraph created opportunities for women to have jobs in offices.

Morse took his invention to President Martin Van Buren and his cabinet. He strung ten miles of wire around a room in the Capitol. He sent signals just as he had in his classroom in New York. He stepped back expecting everyone to be amazed and pleased. Do you think they were? Most of the people there said it was all nonsense and a waste of time. Morse was vastly disappointed.

But Morse did not give up. Six years later he went back to Congress with an improved telegraph. He put up wires between rooms in the Capitol and sent messages. Still the people laughed at Morse's "talking wires." When he asked the Congress for money to run a telegraph wire over the forty miles between Washington, D.C., and Baltimore, Maryland, the congressmen made jokes.

"According to this time it shall be said of Jacob and of Israel, What hath God wrought!"
Numbers 23:23b

But finally Morse was granted the money, and he built the telegraph. On May 24, 1844, a small group of people sat in a Capitol room waiting to receive the first formal telegraph message. Annie Ellsworth, the daughter of one of Morse's friends, leaned over and told Morse the message she had chosen to send. He sent it, clicking the key in a steady rhythm. In just a few seconds, the receiver at Baltimore sent the same words back: *What hath God wrought!*

219

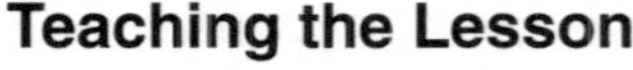

Teaching the Lesson

Text Activity, pages 219 and 271

➤ **Read page 219 to find out who watched the first demonstration of Morse's telegraph.** *(the president of the United States and his cabinet)*

➤ **Do you know what the president's cabinet is?**

It is a group of people chosen by the president to advise him in making decisions.

➤ Find the figure of Martin Van Buren on the TimeLine. **In what year did he begin his presidency?** *(1837)*

➤ **Read the additional information about President Van Buren on page 271.**

➤ **What did Samuel Morse do to demonstrate his telegraph?** *(He strung ten miles of wire around a room in the Capitol and sent signals through the wire.)*

➤ **What reaction did Morse expect from President Van Buren and his cabinet?** *(He expected everyone to be amazed and pleased.)*

➤ **Read aloud the sentence that tells what the reaction was.** *("Most of the people there said it was all nonsense and a waste of time.")*

Even though Samuel Morse was disappointed with their reactions, he did not give up. (BATs: 2d Goal setting, 2e Work)

➤ **How many years passed before Samuel Morse once again demonstrated his telegraph to important people in the government?** *(six years)*

➤ **Do you know what Congress is?** *(a group of people elected from all the states that makes the laws of the United States)*

➤ **Why did Samuel Morse want the people of Congress to like his invention?** *(He wanted them to give him money to run a telegraph wire over the forty miles between Washington, D.C., and Baltimore, Maryland.)*

➤ **Did Morse get his money from Congress at this time?** *(no)*

➤ **Read aloud two sentences from page 219 which describe the reactions of the people of Congress.** *("Still the people laughed at Morse's 'talking wires.' When he asked the Congress for money to run a telegraph wire over the forty miles between Washington, D.C., and Baltimore, Maryland, the congressmen made jokes.")*

➤ **Did Samuel Morse give up his idea of the telegraph after this kind of reaction?** *(no)*

➤ **When Morse was finally granted the money from Congress to build his telegraph, where did the first message originate?** *(in Washington, D.C.)*

➤ **Where was the first message received?** *(in Baltimore, Maryland)*

➤ Find the Northeastern United States page in your atlas. Point to the locations of Washington, D.C., and Baltimore, Maryland.

Remember that the distance between the two cities is about forty miles.

➤ **How long did it take for the telegraph message to travel this distance?** *(just a few seconds)*

➤ **How do you think the people reacted to this demonstration?** *(Answers will vary but will probably include amazed, pleased, and excited.)*

All of Samuel Morse's hard work and patience finally paid off, and the world was given a new, efficient communication tool.

It was appropriate that a Bible verse was used as the first telegraph message sent since it is God who should receive the praise and glory for everything that is accomplished. (BATs: 7b Exaltation of Christ, 7c Praise)

Day 2

Text Discussion, page 220

➤ **Read page 220 to find out what jobs were created with the acceptance of the telegraph.** *(telegraph receivers, linemen, and lumbermen)*

➤ **What happened to the pony express riders and their jobs?** *(They were no longer needed.)*

➤ **Why were people happy to have a telegraph station built in their town?** *(It made them feel closer to other cities since messages could be passed more quickly from place to place.)*

➤ **What do you think people meant when they said that the wires on the poles were shrinking the country?**

Communication was faster between cities and states, making those places seem closer together.

➤ **What caused the worst problems for the telegraph stations?** *(the bison)*

➤ Look at the bison on page 194 of your textbook.

Many people call this strong, large-headed, humped animal a ***buffalo***. A ***bison*** or buffalo can have a pair of horns that spread to thirty-five inches at their widest part. A full grown bull (male) measures from ten to twelve feet long and as much as five to six feet in height. Bulls usually weigh between two and three thousand pounds.

➤ **What were some ways that the telegraph was used?** *(Railroads monitored the train routes. Reporters and military leaders sent news messages.)*

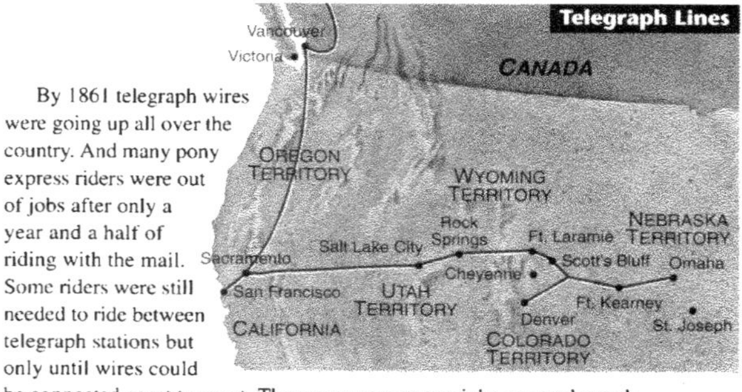

By 1861 telegraph wires were going up all over the country. And many pony express riders were out of jobs after only a year and a half of riding with the mail. Some riders were still needed to ride between telegraph stations but only until wires could be connected coast to coast. There were many new jobs now: telegraph receivers, who took and sent messages; linemen, who put up the lines and looked after them; lumbermen, who cut the poles.

Everywhere a new telegraph station was built, there was much celebration. Why do you think people were happy to have a station in their town? The speedy telegraph made them feel close to cities that only the day before had been days or weeks away. Some people said that the wires on the poles were shrinking the country. What do you think they meant?

The telegraph companies expected to have trouble from storms, the Civil War, and perhaps thieves. But some of the worst trouble came from an unexpected source—the bison. The great, shaggy beasts discovered that the telegraph poles made wonderful rubbing posts. Several would gather at a pole and scratch their backs on it. And soon the pole would wobble and tip over. Sometimes the poles would splinter in two. Then linemen had plenty of work to keep them busy.

Railroads began to use the telegraph to monitor train routes. Reporters during the Civil War used it to send news. Even military leaders used the telegraph to send messages. How do you think the telegraph changed the way people lived? How do you think having such fast communication changed the people themselves?

220

Evaluating the Lesson

Oral Evaluation Activity

➤ *Tell your child the following Morse Code "sound effects."*

T (for True)—"dah"

F (for False)—"di-di-dah-dit"

➤ I am going to read some statements about Samuel Morse and his telegraph.

➤ If the statement is true, say "dah" *(dä)*; if the statement is false, say "di-di-dah-dit" *(dĭ dĭ dä dĭt).*

Practice these two Morse Code "sound effects" with your child.

- President Van Buren was pleased with the telegraph and granted Morse money right away. *(F)*
- Samuel Morse's first demonstrations of the telegraph used wire strung between towns. *(F)*
- The clicks of the telegraph translated into dots or dashes. *(T)*
- Most people thought Morse's telegraph was an excellent invention. *(F)*
- Samuel Morse had to wait for years before his telegraph was accepted as a useful communication tool. *(T)*

- When Congress finally granted Morse money to build his telegraph, wire was strung forty miles between Washington, D.C., and Baltimore, Maryland. *(T)*
- The president of the United States sent the first telegraph message. *(F)*
- The first message was *What hath God wrought!* *(T)*
- This first message was received in just a few hours. *(F)*
- Many pony express riders lost their jobs when the telegraph was in full use. *(T)*
- Most townspeople were happy when a new telegraph station was built in their town. *(T)*
- Storms caused the most trouble for telegraph companies. *(F)*
- A bison is a buffalo. *(T)*
- A lineman put up the telegraph poles and took care of them. *(T)*
- Railroads used the telegraph to monitor train routes. *(T)*
- People felt that the telegraph was bringing the country closer together. *(T)*

Going Beyond

Additional Teacher Information

In Morse Code, the most frequently used letters have the shortest codes while letters that are not used often have longer codes. Even today, the International Distress call, or *SOS,* is used whenever there is trouble. The SOS code is "di-di-di-dah-dah-dah-di-di-dit."

The first telegraph message was sent on May 26, 1844, with Samuel Morse sending the message from Washington, D.C., to his partner Alfred Vail in Baltimore, Maryland. That same year, the telegraph was put to good use during the Democratic National Convention, held in Baltimore. Morse's telegraph worked, but it was extremely expensive. Samuel Morse offered to sell his invention to the U.S. government for $100,000 but was flatly refused. Through numerous obstacles and lawsuits against others who laid claim to the invention of the telegraph, Samuel Morse never gave up. Finally in 1854, the United States Supreme Court upheld the ruling that Samuel F. B. Morse was the sole inventor of the Electromagnetic Recording Telegraph.

LESSON 59
Words over a Wire

Text, pages 221-24
Notebook, page 85

Preview

Main Ideas

- Inventions spread from one part of the world to another.
- Alexander Graham Bell used what he knew about the telegraph, electricity, and sound to invent the telephone.

Objectives

- Make a simple telephone
- Answer questions about Alexander Graham Bell

Materials

- 2 paper cups*
- 2 paper clips
- 25 feet of string*
- The figure of Alexander Graham Bell (1876) from the TimeLine Snapshots

Day 1

Lesson

Introducing the Lesson

Simple Telephone Activity

- ➤ *Give your child the paper cups, paper clips, scissors, and string to make a simple telephone.*
- ➤ Carefully poke a small hole in the bottom of each cup.
- ➤ Pull the ends of the string through the holes in the cups.
- ➤ Attach a paper clip to the string inside each cup, tying a knot in each end to help secure the string.
- ➤ We will each hold one of the cups. Walk slowly away from me until the string is taut, or tight.
- ➤ To use the telephone, hold the open end of the cup to your ear while I talk into the open end of my cup. *Take turns listening and talking.*

The Telephone

Fast as the telegraph was, it was not fast enough. People were still looking for better ways to communicate over long distances. One of them was Alexander Bell, a teacher of deaf students.

Bell taught all day and then worked late into the nights trying to improve on the telegraph. He had a helper, Thomas Watson, who could build almost anything and build it quickly. Together they tried and tested many variations on the telegraph.

"You know," said Bell to a friend one day, "I have read somewhere that the tension in a wire changes the way electricity passes through it. If that is so, I wonder—" He stopped and looked thoughtfully away.

"What is it, Bell? What are you thinking?"

Bell brought his gaze back to his friend. "I was wondering whether there is a way to make electricity and wire transmit the sounds of the human voice."

The friend, Joseph Henry, an old man and himself a great inventor, turned a wondering look on Bell. "This," he said, "is the germ of a great invention. Stop all you are doing and work on this alone!"

Alexander Graham Bell later in his career

221

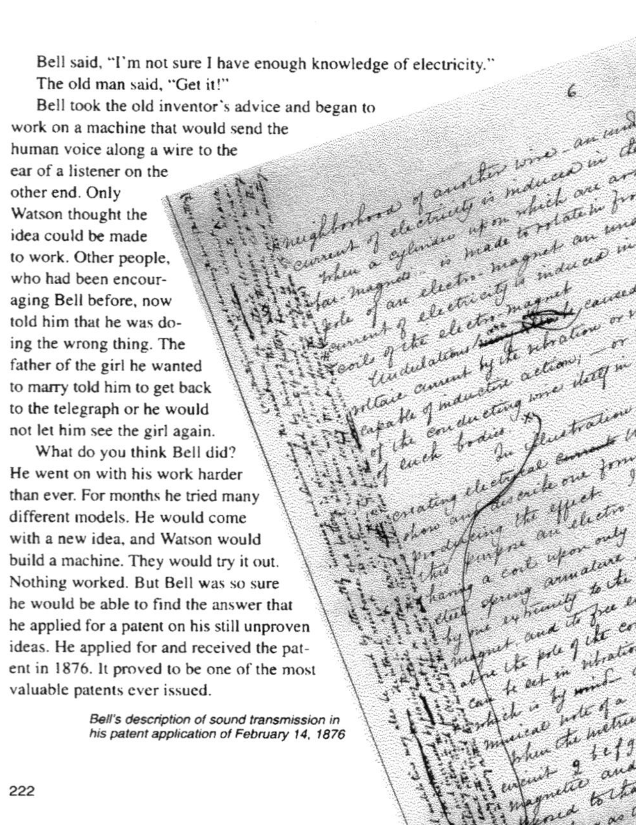

Bell said, "I'm not sure I have enough knowledge of electricity."

The old man said, "Get it!"

Bell took the old inventor's advice and began to work on a machine that would send the human voice along a wire to the ear of a listener on the other end. Only Watson thought the idea could be made to work. Other people, who had been encouraging Bell before, now told him that he was doing the wrong thing. The father of the girl he wanted to marry told him to get back to the telegraph or he would not let him see the girl again.

What do you think Bell did? He went on with his work harder than ever. For months he tried many different models. He would come with a new idea, and Watson would build a machine. They would try it out. Nothing worked. But Bell was so sure he would be able to find the answer that he applied for a patent on his still unproven ideas. He applied for and received the patent in 1876. It proved to be one of the most valuable patents ever issued.

Bell's description of sound transmission in his patent application of February 14, 1876

222

When someone speaks into the cup, the bottom of the cup vibrates. These vibrations travel along the string to the bottom of the other cup, where the sound is heard. Even though this explanation about sound travel seems very simple, it took a wise, hard-working inventor to make it work.

Teaching the Lesson

Text Discussion, page 221

➤ **Read page 221 to find out what Alexander Bell spent his nights doing.** *(trying to improve the telegraph)*

➤ **Read Bell's full name, found in the caption below the picture.**

At age eleven, Alexander Bell, with the consent of his parents, chose the name Graham as a middle name for himself.

➤ **What was the name of Alexander Bell's helper?** *(Thomas Watson)*

➤ **What was Alexander Bell's real job?** *(teaching deaf students)*

➤ **What did Bell begin to wonder about as he was working on the telegraph?** *(whether there was a way to make electricity and wire transmit the sounds of the human voice)*

➤ **What did Bell's friend Joseph Henry advise him to do?** *(Stop everything else and work just on this idea.)*

Text Discussion, page 222

➤ **Read page 222 to find out if Alexander Bell followed the old inventor's advice.** *(Yes, he did.)*

➤ **What did Bell need to learn more about in order to make electricity and wires carry the sounds of the human voice?** *(electricity)*

Alexander Bell and Thomas Watson worked long and hard to develop a machine to send the human voice along a wire. They failed over and over again. Many people criticized their efforts and told them to "stop this invention nonsense." The inventor and his helper kept to the task until they had a workable machine.

➤ **Do you think Bell and Watson ever grew discouraged and wanted to give up?**

Goal setting, dependability, and hard work are admirable qualities for all of us as we work. (BATs: 2c Faithfulness, 2d Goal setting, 2e Work)

◆ HOW IT WAS ◆

Boston, Massachusetts
Friday, March 10, 1876

Evening

Bell and Watson were setting up to test their newest model.

Bell accidentally spilled some acid on his clothes.

He called out, "Mr. Watson, come here. I want you."

In another room, Watson heard the words clearly over the new device.

Bell had proved that his wild idea was not so wild after all.

223

What do you think is important about that first message? It represents what Bell wanted his invention to do: help people. It is fitting that the first words over the wire, although not planned, should be a call for help.

Bell named his device the *telephone*, which means "far-off sound." He took his new machine to Philadelphia, where there was a huge celebration going on: the United States was one hundred years old. People came from all over the country to the Centennial Exposition, a display of inventions, machinery, and other exhibitions showing the greatness of the country.

Everyone who listened on one end of the wire was amazed to hear a voice, another human being, speaking to him. At last, Bell had support. People wanted to start using his invention.

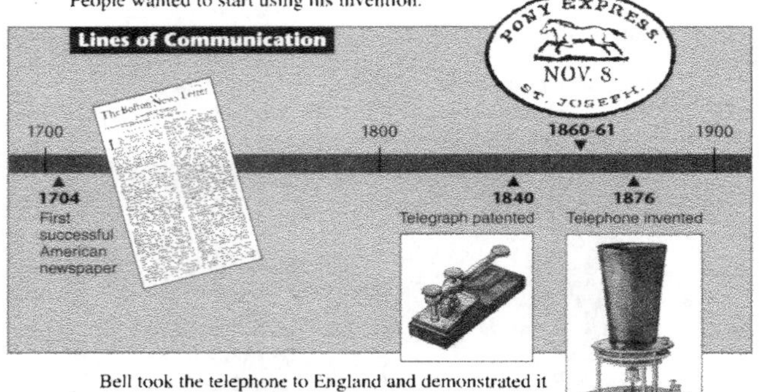

Bell took the telephone to England and demonstrated it for Queen Victoria. She listened quietly to words coming through the receiver. "Most extraordinary," she said. Bell could not have known how his telephone would extraordinarily change not only the United States but the whole world in just a few years.

224

Day 2

TimeLine Snapshots Activity

- ➤ **What did Alexander Bell receive in 1876?** *(a patent for his ideas about using electricity and wires to carry the voice)*
- ➤ Add the figure of Alexander Graham Bell to the TimeLine at the year 1876.
- ➤ Name several events shown on the TimeLine which occurred before or after this date.

How It Was Activity, page 223

- ➤ **Find the date and place of this historic moment by reading the titles on page 223.** *(the evening of Friday, March 10, 1876, in Boston, Massachusetts)*
- ➤ **Read page 223 to find out what important event occurred on this date.** *(Watson heard Bell over his new device.)*

> If you are teaching more than one child, allow one child to be Bell, one to be Watson, and one to be a narrator as they act out the scene on page 223.

- ➤ You may choose to be the narrator or Alexander Bell. We will act out the scene that is described on page 223.

- ➤ **How do you think Bell and Watson felt on the evening of March 10, 1876?** *(Answers will vary but may include excited, happy, surprised.)*

Text Discussion, page 224

- ➤ **Read page 224 to find out why Alexander Graham Bell named his new invention the *telephone*.** *(It means "far-off sound.")*
- ➤ **What did Bell do to let people know about the telephone?** *(He demonstrated the telephone at the Centennial Exposition.)*
- ➤ **What was the Centennial Exposition?** *(It was a celebration of the 100th birthday of the United States.)*
- ➤ **In what year did the United States become a country?** *(1776)*
- ➤ Calculate how old the United States is now.

The celebration of two hundred years, called the Bicentennial, was in 1976.

- ➤ Calculate when the celebration of three hundred years, the Tricentennial, will occur. *(in 2076)*
- ➤ Calculate how many more years there are until the United States Tricentennial.
- ➤ **What kinds of things do you think might be demonstrated or displayed at the Tricentennial?**
- ➤ **To whom did Alexander Bell take his invention next?** *(to Queen Victoria in England)*

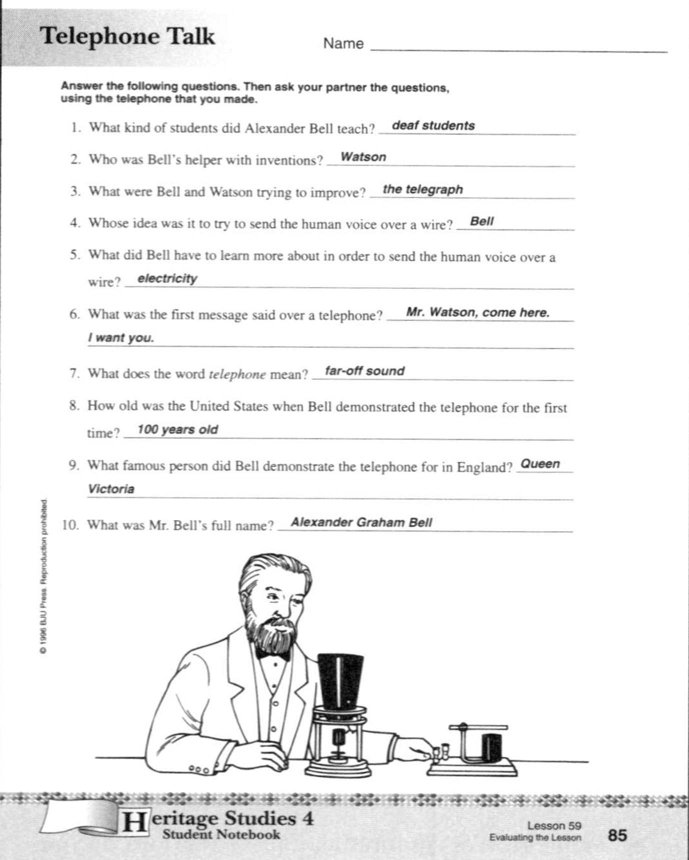
Telephone Talk Name ____________

Answer the following questions. Then ask your partner the questions, using the telephone that you made.

1. What kind of students did Alexander Bell teach? *deaf students*
2. Who was Bell's helper with inventions? *Watson*
3. What were Bell and Watson trying to improve? *the telegraph*
4. Whose idea was it to try to send the human voice over a wire? *Bell*
5. What did Bell have to learn more about in order to send the human voice over a wire? *electricity*
6. What was the first message said over a telephone? *Mr. Watson, come here. I want you.*
7. What does the word *telephone* mean? *far-off sound*
8. How old was the United States when Bell demonstrated the telephone for the first time? *100 years old*
9. What famous person did Bell demonstrate the telephone for in England? *Queen Victoria*
10. What was Mr. Bell's full name? *Alexander Graham Bell*

Heritage Studies 4 Student Notebook

Lesson 59 Evaluating the Lesson 85

Evaluating the Lesson

Evaluating Activity, Notebook page 85

- ➤ Read the instructions on Notebook page 85.
- ➤ Complete the page.

If you are teaching more than one child, allow the children to take turns asking each other the questions and answering them by using their telephones.

Going Beyond

Enrichment

Encourage your child to write a story entitled *A Special Telephone Call.* Have available the writing sheet with a picture of a modern telephone from Appendix page A71. Encourage him to write about a special telephone call that someone in his family received. Suggest that it might be a call from someone in another country, a call from a famous person, or a call giving exciting news.

Additional Teacher Information

Alexander Bell was born in Edinburgh, Scotland. His father and grandfather were well-known speech teachers and the developers of Visible Speech, an aid to teach the deaf to lip-read and to talk. Because of their influence and the fact that his mother was nearly deaf, Aleck had a remarkable understanding of sounds and tones. As young boys, Aleck and his brother Melville made a "talking machine" that made a sound, resembling the word "mama." After graduation, Aleck Bell became a teacher of deaf children. In any free time, he experimented with tuning forks and tones on the piano, trying to invent a telegraph that could send more than one message on the wire.

In 1870, after the death of two of Aleck's brothers from tuberculosis, the Bell family emigrated to Canada where the climate was drier and therefore more healthful. Bell's health improved, allowing him to move to Boston and gain a position as professor of Vocal Physiology and Elocution at Boston University. He continued his scientific experiments and enlisted the help of Thomas Watson.

In 1876, Alexander Graham Bell applied for a patent for his new invention, first called the "talking telegraph," then the "undulatory-current instrument," and now simply the telephone. One of Bell's early designs for the telephone had a connecting bar across two posts and was called a "gallows" telephone. The first voice sounds transmitted over Bell's telephone were on June 3, 1875, and the first words were transmitted in March 1876. Bell and Watson seemed tireless in their efforts to make this invention work and to continue to improve it.

LESSON 60
Better and Faster

Text, pages 225-28

Preview

Main Ideas

- People in the United States are linked by communication.
- People use technology to adapt to different environments.
- New inventions affect the attitudes and lifestyles of many people.

Objective

- Identify true and false statements about the telephone

Materials

- Appendix, page A73: What's the News?*
- A dictionary
- A telegram (optional)*

Notes

The board game Get the Message is introduced in the Enrichment section. If you choose to use the game, refer to Lesson 36 for instructions to assemble the game pieces.

Day 1

Lesson

Introducing the Lesson

Time Line Review

➤ **Read aloud each of the four dates shown on the What's the News? page.**

➤ Name the invention that corresponds to each date.

Remember that Samuel Morse's telegraph was patented in 1840.

➤ **What important event occurred on May 24, 1844?** *(The first telegraph message was sent between Baltimore, Maryland, and Washington, D.C.)*

Although telegraph wires and stations began springing up across the United States, it was not until 1861 that the connection was made that actually linked the east coast to the west coast. It was during that time that the pony express helped speed the messages coming from California to the nearest telegraph station in Missouri.

➤ **Have any improvements been made in communication since the invention of the telephone?** *(yes)*

➤ Name any new inventions that you know about. *(computers, fax machines, etc.)*

➤ **Look up and read the definition for *fax* in the dictionary.**

Your child may like to draw pictures of inventions to extend the What's the News? time line. Or he may choose to color and cut out the pictures and the date boxes. Direct him to glue the dates on the pictures and add the pictures to the TimeLine on the wall.

➤ **What kind of communications inventions do you think might occur in the future?**

In this lesson we will learn more about the effects of improvements in communications.

If you do not have some of the newest technology in your home, you may want to visit an office to see a computer, a fax machine, and any other modern communications equipment.

Bell married the girl whose father had so opposed his work, and her father put money into the first telephone company. After a few years, Bell lost interest in the telephone and began experimenting with other inventions—some of which are only today being used. One was a system to send sound over a beam of light. Today we call that sort of transmission fiber optics.

Bell's invention has helped save an untold number of lives.

Bell wanted the telephone to make life better and safer for everyone. The cost of owning a telephone was not high, about the same as the cost of heating a house with gas. Soon many businesses and homes had telephones. Today there are millions and millions of telephones in the United States. Can you count how many telephones you see in a week?

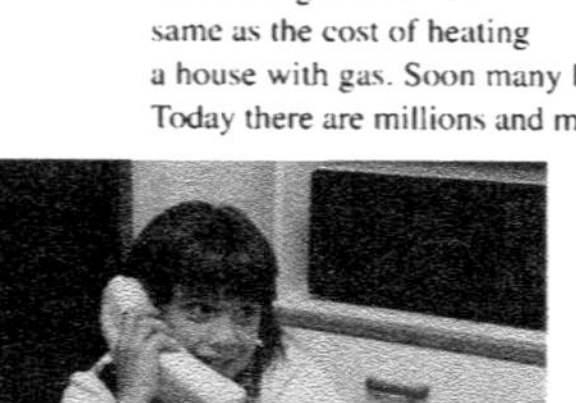

Using a telephone is no longer a remarkable event.

Do you think the telephone put the telegraph companies out of business? No, it did not. Telegraph companies still run today. People send telegrams on special occasions and to places that do not have telephones.

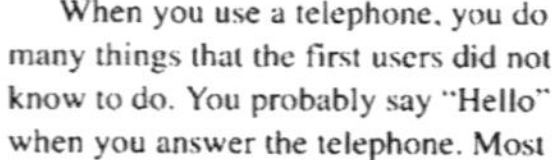

When you use a telephone, you do many things that the first users did not know to do. You probably say "Hello" when you answer the telephone. Most people did not know what to say at first. Bell wanted everyone to say "Hoy, hoy" when picking up the receiver. He was disappointed when the word *hello* became the most popular greeting.

225

Often people using the telephone would talk at the same time and then complain to the telephone company that the device did not work right! Part of the problem was that with the early telephones, the caller had to speak into and listen to the same part of the telephone. After speaking, he had to quickly move the piece to his ear. If the person on the other end started talking too soon, the caller missed some of the message.

The 1879 wall-mounted telephone used a microphone and receiver designed by Thomas Edison.

The brass desk set was invented in 1897.

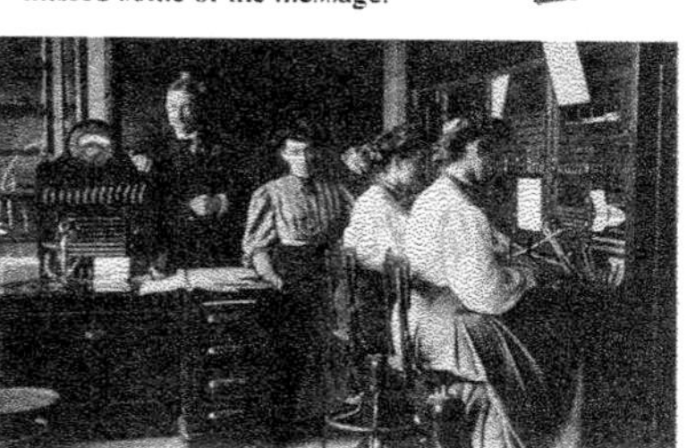

A Bell telephone office in 1900

Another thing happened to those first telephone owners that probably never happens to you. They picked up the receiver and suddenly got "stage fright." They could not think of anything to say. It took years before telephone manners developed to everyone's satisfaction.

Still, not all wanted to use the new invention. Some people thought it was just a toy that would go out of style. Others thought it was evil, a thing to be shunned. And others thought it was all a trick. Why do you think people had such notions?

226

Teaching the Lesson

Text Discussion, page 225

- **What do you say when you answer the telephone?**
- **Read page 225 to find out what Alexander Graham Bell wanted everyone to say when answering the telephone.** *("hoy, hoy")*
- **Did Bell ever marry the girl whose father did not believe in his efforts to invent the telephone?** *(yes)*
- **Was the cost of a telephone too expensive for people and businesses?** *(No, many bought them.)*
- **Do people today still use telegrams?** *(sometimes, on special occasions, or to send messages to remote places)* *If you have a telegram, show it to your child.*
- **What was Alexander Bell's invention known as *fiber optics*?** *(a system to send sound over a beam of light)*

Text Discussion, page 226

- **Read page 226 to discover some problems that early telephone users experienced.** *(talking at the same time, speaking and listening with the same part of the telephone, not knowing what to say, developing telephone manners)*
- *Talk about good telephone manners.*
- **Why did some people dislike the new invention called a telephone?** *(They thought it was just a toy, a trick, or an evil thing.)*

The Changes in Every Way

Letters and important papers can be transmitted through a fax machine.

Headsets allow people to keep their hands free while talking on the phone.

For good and for bad, the new inventions were here to stay. Inventors like Bell thought only that the new devices would make communication easier, which they did. But they also changed many other things.

Businesses

Before the telegraph and telephone, businesses in cities were built close together. Why do you think that was? People had to walk from one place to another or send messengers if they wanted to communicate with each other. The closer the buildings were, the faster people could communicate.

Today, businesses across the country from each other can do business over the telephone and with a newer invention, the *fax* machine. What do you think Alexander Bell would say about that?

The telephone also made business move faster; more work could be done more quickly. That swiftness caused more money to be made and spent by more people. And the more money that changed hands, the better businesses did. A country needs strong business to keep growing.

227

The Bell Telephone Company itself—started by Bell, his father-in-law, and Watson—changed American business. It eventually became the largest company in the world, employing thousands and thousands of people directly and making available thousands of other jobs, such as in plastics.

Lifestyles

Before telephones, people presented cards when they came to visit. If you did not want to see a person, you did not let him in. But when someone answered the telephone, he could not know who would be on the other end of the line. The rules separating upper and lower classes had to change because almost everyone could use a telephone.

Ideas about the world changed too. Everything seemed much closer together, much easier to keep up with. Towns no longer were places unto themselves; they were influenced immediately by changes and events in places far away. America was no longer the slowly growing country it had been. It was on its way to becoming the richest, most powerful country in the world.

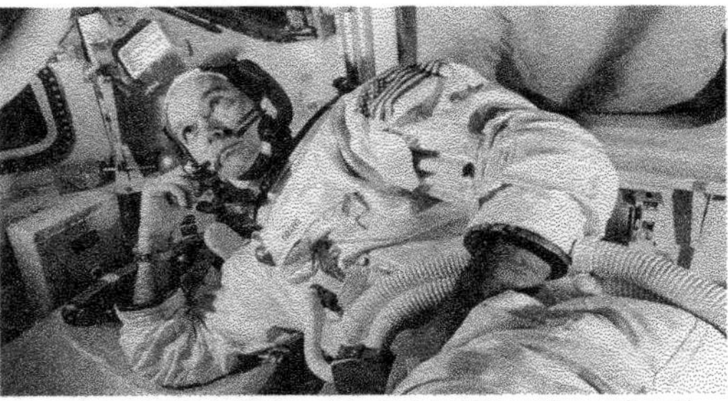
Communication reaches farther now than even Bell might have dreamed it would.

228

Text Discussion, pages 227-28

➤ **Read page 227 and the first paragraph on page 228 to find out how the telephone changed business in America.** *(Businesses did not need to be close together in order to succeed. Businesses moved faster, so people could make and spend more money.)*

➤ **Why is strong business so important to a country?** *(It helps the country to grow.)*

The telephone had a great influence on businesses in America. The businesses in America became more successful, and America became a stronger, more secure country.

➤ Name the company started by Alexander Bell that quickly became the largest company in the world. *(Bell Telephone Company)*

➤ **Why did jobs in plastics increase because of the invention of the telephone?** *(Many telephone parts were made of plastic.)*

➤ **What other jobs do you think were created as part of the production and use of the telephone?**

New jobs were available in the manufacturing of parts—metal, wire, electromagnets, cables, bells, and computers. There were jobs for telephone operators, telephone repairmen and installers, telephone company office personnel, etc.

➤ **Do you know someone who works in a job that is somehow connected to the telephone industry?**

God gives each of us unique abilities to use for Him. We should be willing to do our best at all times. (BATs: 2c Faithfulness, 2d Goal setting, 2e Work, 2f Enthusiasm, 3a Self-concept)

➤ **Read the rest of page 228 to find out how the telephone and other inventions in communications influenced people all over the world.** *(Places seemed closer together. News spread faster. People seemed more united as both the rich and the poor used these new inventions.)*

➤ **Read aloud the last sentence on page 228, which sums up the great influence that the telephone had on America.**

Evaluating the Lesson

Oral Evaluation

➤ I will read statements related to this lesson.
➤ If the statement is true, you should say "hoy, hoy."
➤ If the statement is false, you should say nothing.

1. Alexander Graham Bell invented more than the telephone. *(T)*
2. Bell was so busy with his inventions that he never married. *(F)*
3. Fiber optics sends sound over a beam of light. *(T)*
4. The telegraph is still used today. *(T)*
5. The early telephone cost so much that it was years before the average homeowner could afford to get one. *(F)*
6. "Hello" became a more popular greeting than "hoy, hoy" for telephone users. *(T)*
7. On early telephones, people spoke and listened with the same part of the telephone. *(T)*
8. Everyone liked using the new telephones because they made life so much easier. *(F)*
9. Before the use of telegraphs and telephones, businesses were built closer together. *(T)*
10. Alexander Graham Bell started the Bell Telephone Company on his own. *(F)*
11. The telephone seemed to bring people and places closer together. *(T)*
12. The telephone industry helped America become a strong, powerful country. *(T)*

Going Beyond

Enrichment

Introduce the Get the Message board game (Appendix, pages A73-A77). First, point out the *Start* and indicate the two paths players may choose in order to reach the *Finish.* Point out the spaces marked *Express Card.*

Show the Express Cards, explaining that before each round of play, the cards should be shuffled and placed facedown beside the game board. Show the colored buttons to be used as game markers.

Give directions for playing the game. All players begin with their game markers at the *Start.* Each player spins once, the one with the highest number going first. Then, in turn, each player spins again and moves his game marker the number of spaces indicated. A player may choose either path. If a player lands on a space marked *Express Card,* he should draw an Express Card from the pile, read it aloud, and move as the card indicates. Play continues as the players move their markers around the board. The first player to reach the *Finish* wins.

If you wish to use an alternative activity, arrange a field trip to a telephone company or a telegraph office.

Additional Teacher Information

Alexander Graham Bell continued improving his telephone and in 1877 patented the box telephone, the first commercial telephone. Later that year, Bell and his partners established the Bell Telephone Company, which has grown to be the American Telephone and Telegraph Company, or AT&T. The Bell Telephone Laboratories continue to conduct research on the telephone, radar, satellites, and lasers. It was in the "Bell Labs" that the transistor was invented.

It is reported that Alexander Graham Bell once said, "An inventor can no more help inventing than he can help thinking or breathing." The telephone was not Bell's only invention. He also invented the photophone (which transmits sound through beams of light), a vacuum jacket (which aided respiratory patients), a metal detector, an audiometer (which measures sound and tests hearing), and a machine for sorting punch-coded cards. Bell also improved the phonograph and the hydrofoil speedboat. He studied flying and organized a group called the Aerial Experiment Association. He was greatly involved in the National Geographic Society. He was also a personal friend of Helen Keller, encouraging her and guiding her education. Though Bell was a man of great accomplishment, his grave in Scotland is marked by a simple stone which bears his name and words that Bell himself chose: Citizen of the United States and Teacher of the Deaf.

11 Lessons 61-65

Struggles Far Away

This chapter discusses the Boer War in South Africa and the Boxer Uprising in China in the years immediately surrounding 1900. Your child will see that both conflicts show the desire of settled people to be free of foreign control. He will learn how South Africa was settled by Europeans and how the discovery of gold and diamonds influenced people's actions. The lesson on the Boxer Uprising emphasizes the Christian response of missionaries and Chinese believers through this difficult time. The final lesson of the chapter focuses on imperialism, the desire of powerful countries to gain control, and the Industrial Revolution. Your child will learn about family and societal changes that resulted from the new inventions of the eighteenth and nineteenth centuries.

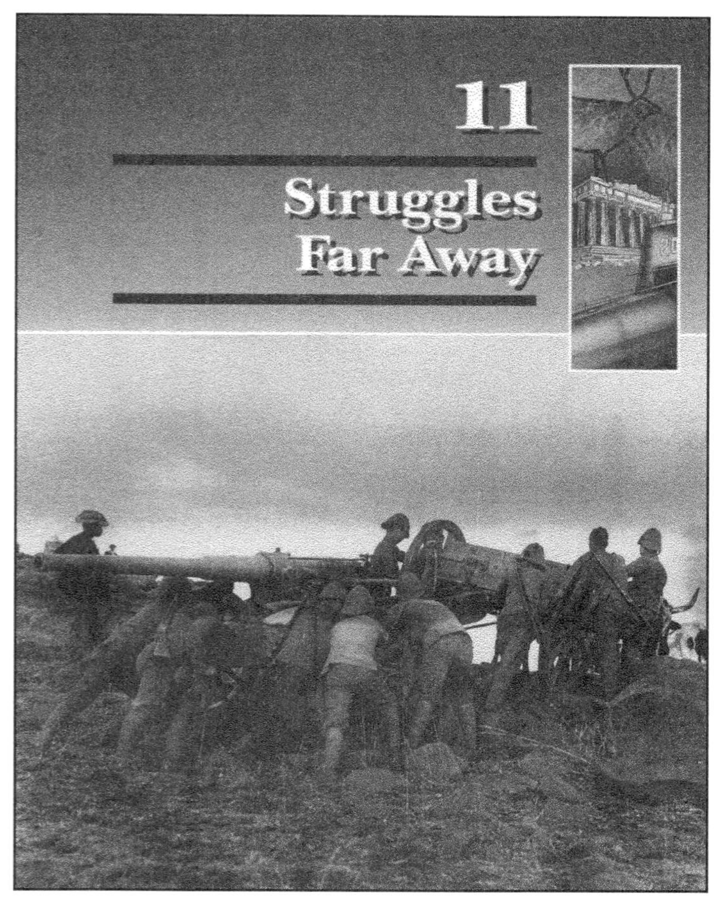

Materials

The following materials must be obtained or prepared before the presentation of the lesson. These items are labeled with an asterisk (*) in each lesson and in the Materials List in the Supplement. For further information see the individual lessons.

- A large rock outside (Lesson 61)
- A small piece of leather (or similar material) (Lesson 61)
- Appendix, page A79 or a wall map of the world (Lessons 61-64)
- Appendix, page A80 (Lessons 61-64)
- A picture of Buckingham Palace (Lesson 62)
- Appendix, page A81 (Lesson 62)

Lesson 61
Diamonds and Gold

Text, pages 230-33, 316-17
Notebook, page 86

Preview

Main Ideas

- All societies have some kind of government.
- The Boers were farmers who did not want to be ruled by England.
- Gold was found in the Boer territory of Transvaal.
- England decided to take over the Boer territory of Transvaal.

Objective

- Match terms with their correct descriptions

Materials

- A letter
- A large rock outside*
- A small piece of leather (or similar material)*
- An atlas
- Maps and More 35, page M16
- Appendix, page A79 or a wall map of the world*
- Appendix, page A80: figure of gold miner*

Notes

Write a short letter to your child. Fold the letter and wrap it in the leather. Place the wrapped letter under the rock before beginning the lesson. Do all this without your child's knowledge.

Give your child the figure of the gold miner to color and cut out before or during the lesson.

Lesson

Introducing the Lesson

Post Office Activity

➤ **Do you like to receive letters in the mail?**

➤ **How do you think mail travels from one country to another today?**

Hundreds of years ago, English sailors and merchants traveled from England to India to trade and settle. But there were no airplanes, no postal trucks, and no post offices.

➤ Turn to a world map in your atlas. Find England and India on the map.

➤ **How do you think the merchants who settled in India were able to send letters to their loved ones in England hundreds of years ago?**

The travelers from England and India used a system of ***post office rocks*** on the coast of South Africa.

➤ *Take your child out to the rock.* See what you can find under the rock.

➤ Unwrap the bundle to see what is hidden inside.

➤ Read the letter.

Long ago sailors would place their letters, wrapped in leather pouches, under the rocks. The letters would lie there for many months until sailors from another ship passed by and retrieved "the mail."

Sailors on the next ship heading home from India to England would stop and look under the post office rocks to see whether there were any letters to be taken home. Those sailors would leave any letters they wanted sent on to India for an India-bound ship to pick up and deliver.

➤ Later today you will write a letter to another family member and place it under the rock. You may tell that person to check the post office rock for mail.

> If you are teaching several children, you may choose to select one child to retrieve the letters at a certain time and to deliver them.

Teaching the Lesson

Map Activity, Maps and More 35

➤ Find the world map in your atlas again and point to England and India once more.

➤ Now point to the continent of Africa.

Hundreds of years ago, African kingdoms began to develop. European powers established colonies along the coast of Africa beginning in the 1400s. During the late 1800s Cecil Rhodes, an English businessman and statesman, was the greatest influence in helping England gain control over southern Africa. He spent his money freely to achieve his goals. Through his influence and that of others, almost all of Africa was under European control by the 1920s.

You and your child will be writing several names and terms during this lesson. He will then have the page to use as a study guide. This is good preparatory work for learning to take notes.

- *Write the name* Cecil Rhodes.
- Write a short description of who Cecil Rhodes was. *(an English businessman and statesman)*
- Locate South Africa on the map.
- **In what portion of the continent is South Africa located?** *(southern portion)*
- **Why do you think this area was important to trading ships?**

The journey from Europe around Africa to India took many months. Ships needed places to stop along the way for rest and to resupply with food and water.

- Trace this route with your finger on the map. Begin at France and then go around South Africa to the southern tip of India.

In 1652, Jan van Riebeeck was sent from the Dutch East India Company in the Netherlands to Cape Town to set up a "refreshment station" to resupply trading vessels going around the Cape of Good Hope to India.

- *Write the name* Jan van Riebeeck. **What company sent this man to Cape Town?** *(Dutch East India Company)*
- Find the Netherlands on your map in the atlas. It is north of France. *You may ask your child to look at the insert on student text page 316 to get a clearer picture of the Netherlands.*
- **What was Jan van Riebeeck's assignment?** *(to build a station for supplies for trading vessels)*
- Write this information next to Jan van Riebeeck's name.
- Find Cape Town on Maps and More 35 and in your atlas.

Notice the small piece of land projecting into the ocean just south of Cape Town. A piece of land that projects out into the water is called a ***cape***. The name of this cape is the Cape of Good Hope. It is around this cape that sailing vessels must pass to reach India.

- Find the area on Maps and More 35 labeled as Cape Province.

This southern part of Africa was known as the Cape Colony during the late 1800s. The name was later changed to Cape Province. Cecil Rhodes was the wealthy prime minister of Cape Colony from 1890-1895.

- Write *prime minister of Cape Colony* after Cecil Rhodes's name on your list.

As time passed, other Europeans settled in the Cape Colony. The early Dutch settlers in Cape Colony became farmers and were known as the ***Boers.*** Many of these Boers owned slaves to help them on their farms. The British took control of Cape Colony in 1806 and outlawed slavery in 1807. Consequently, the Boers—many of whom owned slaves—moved north.

- *Write the term* Boers.
- Write an explanation for who the Boers are. *(Dutch settlers in Cape Colony who became farmers)*
- **Why do you think the British and European nations came to Africa?**

European countries wanted to control cities along Africa's coasts so that their ships could stop to rest or resupply.

Remember that when the British tried to control America, the Americans fought for their freedoms. This war was called the Revolutionary War. Although nearly all of Africa was now under the control of other countries, there had been no wars.

- **Why do you think the black Africans did not fight a war against the white settlers?**

The Africans were not united into one nation; they were divided into many small groups of people. These groups could not individually face the strong European armies. And the black Africans had no guns to use in battle.

At Gettysburg, one of the bloodiest battles of the American Civil War was fought.

What do you think is worth fighting a war for? Some wars have been fought over land, some over money or gold, some over ideas. Do you remember why the American Civil War happened?

Both sides in that war, the North and the South, believed in different ways of living. Many in the North lived in cities and worked in factories; their Southern neighbors preferred a more rural life and farming. More importantly, the two sides disagreed about what laws the states should be allowed to make for themselves. The South said that slavery should be left up to the states; the North said it should not.

In another country, about thirty years later, slavery helped to cause another war. But that war was also about gold and land and the right of people to govern themselves. It was called the *Boer War*.

230

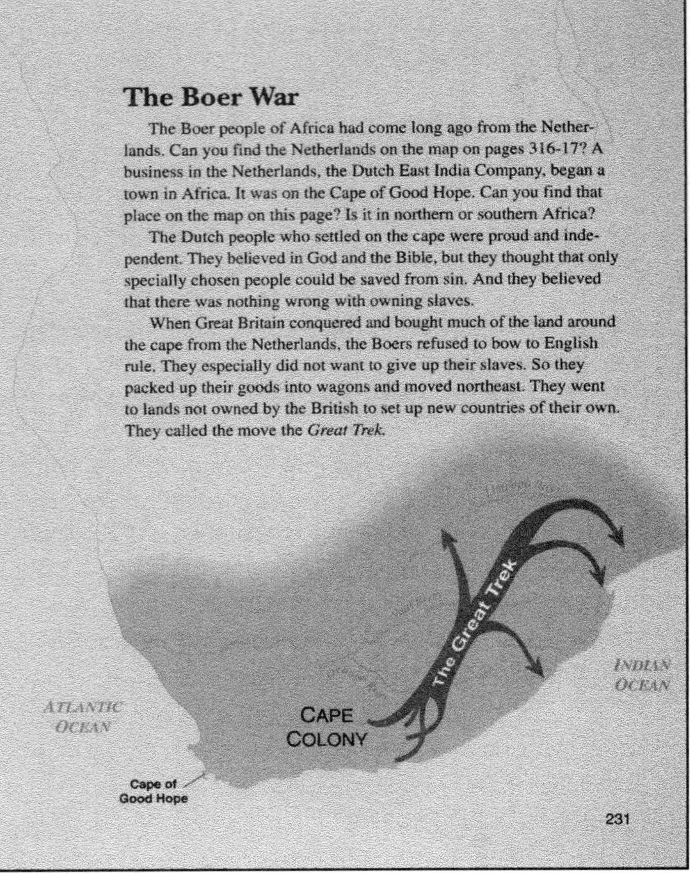

The Boer War

The Boer people of Africa had come long ago from the Netherlands. Can you find the Netherlands on the map on pages 316-17? A business in the Netherlands, the Dutch East India Company, began a town in Africa. It was on the Cape of Good Hope. Can you find that place on the map on this page? Is it in northern or southern Africa?

The Dutch people who settled on the cape were proud and independent. They believed in God and the Bible, but they thought that only specially chosen people could be saved from sin. And they believed that there was nothing wrong with owning slaves.

When Great Britain conquered and bought much of the land around the cape from the Netherlands, the Boers refused to bow to English rule. They especially did not want to give up their slaves. So they packed up their goods into wagons and moved northeast. They went to lands not owned by the British to set up new countries of their own. They called the move the *Great Trek*.

231

Day 2

Text Discussion, page 230

➤ Wars are fought for a variety of reasons. **Read page 230 to find out why the American Civil War was fought.** *(over what laws each state should be allowed to make, over whether states should be allowed to choose slavery)*

➤ **What are some other reasons wars are fought?** *(over land, money, or ideas)*

➤ **What war erupted in South Africa, where slavery was an issue?** *(the Boer War)*

➤ **What were the other reasons the Boer War was fought?** *(over gold, land, and the right of people to govern themselves)*

The Boer War was fought in South Africa during the years 1899-1902.

➤ Calculate how many years ago this war was fought.

Text Discussion, page 231

➤ **Read page 231 to find out what the *Great Trek* was.** *(a migration north by Boers to land not owned by the British)*

The word ***trek*** means journey or great movement. The Great Trek was made in 1836. The Boers who made the journey were called ***voortrekkers***. *Write the term.*

The word *voortrekker* means "front trekker." The voortrekkers traveled in wagon trains from Cape Colony to new lands in northern South Africa. They wanted to set up an independent area to farm.

➤ **What were the two main reasons that the Boers moved northeast?** *(They wanted to keep their slaves, and they did not want to live under British rule.)*

➤ **Do you think the voortrekkers met any people on their journey?**

The Boers met some black Africans. Some of the African people attacked the Boers who settled on their lands. The Boers had guns, however, and killed thousands of black Africans who fought against them.

Some Boers stopped in a grassy flatland. Others went on farther north. From these two groups, two states grew. For a while, the Boers were free to wander on the open land, farming and keeping their traditional ways. What does the picture tell you about the Boer life?

These Boer travelers have stopped for the night. After supper, some will sleep in the wagon and some under it, guns always ready.

But the Boers in the two states could not get along with each other. Their governments could not control the people. When money became hard to get, the two groups began to fight each other. The British decided to take over the states.

Do you think the Boers liked British rule? They did not. After four years, they attacked British soldiers in several cities. Taken by surprise, the British lost the skirmishes. Great Britain decided to let the Boer states be independent again.

232

Then an unexpected thing happened: someone found gold, much gold, on Boer land. How do you think that changed history? Men from all over began to go there looking for gold. The whole Boer area got rich; in fact, it became the richest place in Africa.

Since gold had not been discovered while the British had been in charge, the Boers claimed that God meant the gold only for the Boers. They were not about to share it.

The Boer leaders began to think that they could run the British out of more places in Africa. They thought that the Boers should rule the whole southern tip of Africa. Why do you think they thought they could beat the British?

General Piet Cronje sent a message to the British: "I shall not surrender alive."

President Paul Kruger, a puzzle to his enemies

233

Text Discussion, page 232 and Maps and More 35

- ➤ **Read page 232 to find out how many states were established by the Boers.** *(two)*
- ➤ Look at Maps and More 35 to find the Transvaal and the Orange Free State. These were the two states established by the Boers.
- ➤ **Did the Boers like to settle down and build homes on their land?** *(No, they wandered on the open land.)*
- ➤ **How did the Boers in the Transvaal get along with the Boers in the Orange Free State?** *(They fought each other.)*
- ➤ **What happened when the two groups began to fight?** *(The British decided to take over the Transvaal and the Orange Free State.)*
- ➤ **Did the Boers like being under British rule?** *(no)*
- ➤ **How long were the Boers ruled by the British before the Boers tried to drive them out?** *(four years)*
- ➤ **What was the outcome of those battles?** *(The British lost, so they decided to let the Boers govern themselves again.)*

Text Discussion, page 233 and Maps and More 35

- ➤ **Read page 233 to find out what was discovered on the Boers' land.** *(gold)*
- ➤ Point to the Transvaal on Maps and More 35. This is the area where the gold was found.
- ➤ **What would you do if gold were discovered on a vacant lot near our home?**

Thousands of people moved to the Boer land to look for gold for themselves.

- ➤ **Did the area become wealthy?** *(yes, wealthier than any other place in Africa)*

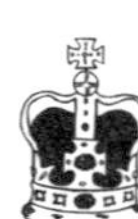

To help your child associate events and locations, he will be placing the pictures related to specific events on a map. You may use your own wall map, or you may have him color and post the map from the Appendix. Your child may attach the pictures to the map itself or place them on the wall around the map and connect them, using string or yarn.

- ➤ Attach the gold miner figure to South Africa on the map.

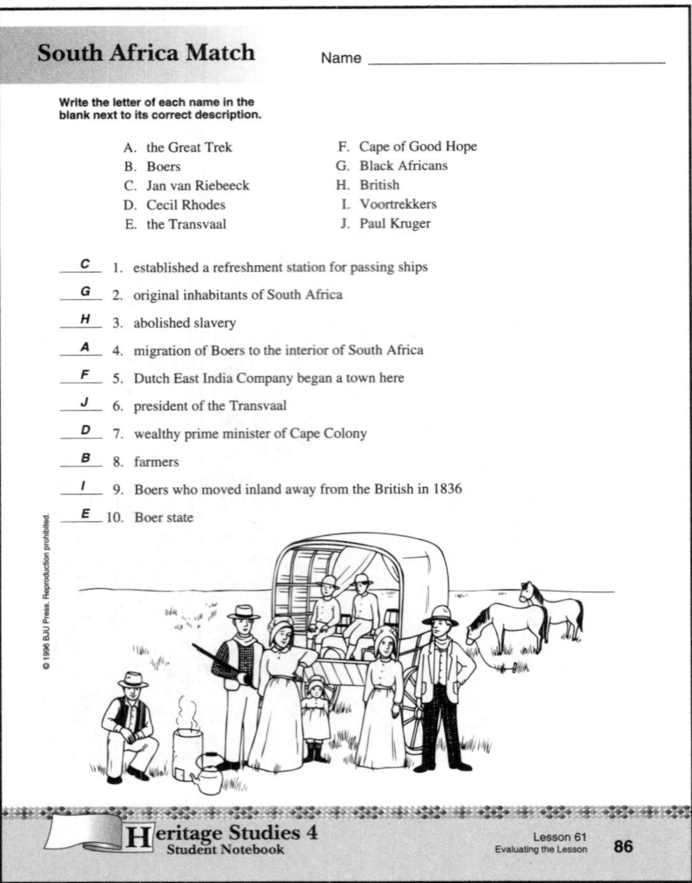
South Africa Match Name ______

Write the letter of each name in the blank next to its correct description.

A. the Great Trek
B. Boers
C. Jan van Riebeeck
D. Cecil Rhodes
E. the Transvaal
F. Cape of Good Hope
G. Black Africans
H. British
I. Voortrekkers
J. Paul Kruger

C 1. established a refreshment station for passing ships
G 2. original inhabitants of South Africa
H 3. abolished slavery
A 4. migration of Boers to the interior of South Africa
F 5. Dutch East India Company began a town here
J 6. president of the Transvaal
D 7. wealthy prime minister of Cape Colony
B 8. farmers
I 9. Boers who moved inland away from the British in 1836
E 10. Boer state

© 1996 BJU Press. Reproduction prohibited.

Heritage Studies 4 Student Notebook Lesson 61 Evaluating the Lesson 86

➤ **Did the Boers want to share the gold with non-Boers?** *(no)* **Why not?** *(They thought that God wanted them to have all the gold for themselves.)*

➤ Look at the picture of Paul Kruger on text page 233.

Paul Kruger was the president of the Transvaal. President Kruger thought that God had chosen only the Boers to rule South Africa. When many non-Boers moved into the Transvaal in search of gold, President Kruger refused to give them political rights; these non-Boers were not allowed to vote. Some British people tried to overthrow President Kruger, but Kruger's men were able to defeat them.

Evaluating the Lesson

Notebook Activity, page 86

➤ Read the instructions on Notebook page 86.

➤ Complete the page.

Statement 5 and choice F. may be different on your child's notebook page. You may change them to match what is in your teacher's edition or delete that item.

Going Beyond

Enrichment

Provide paper and crayons for your child. Encourage him to draw a picture of something that is made with diamonds or gold.

Additional Teacher Information

Cecil Rhodes came to South Africa as a young man because it was thought that the climate there would be more healthful for him than England's climate. He dreamed of expanding the British Empire and worked for that end. His hope was to have all of Africa in the empire. By the age of twenty, Rhodes had become very rich through the diamond mines of South Africa. He had plenty of money with which to mine gold when the gold fields of Witwatersrand were opened up in 1886. The country of Rhodesia (now Zimbabwe) was named after Cecil Rhodes. He defended the city of Kimberley during the Boer War but died at age forty-nine before the end of the war. A bequest in his will provides scholarships to Oxford University in England for scholars from around the world. Those who are awarded this opportunity for study at Oxford are called Rhodes Scholars.

LESSON 62
The Boer War

Text, pages 234-37

Preview

Main Ideas

- When people are dissatisfied with their government, they respond in different ways.
- The British greatly outnumbered the Boers.
- The Boers fought fiercely for their land.
- The British defeated the Boers after three years.

Objectives

- List reasons the British and the Boers were fighting the Boer War
- List the advantages the British had
- List the advantages the Boers had
- Tell which side won the Boer War

Materials

- Supplement, page S14: "The British Grenadiers"
- A picture of Buckingham Palace*
- *HERITAGE STUDIES Listening Cassette B*
- Maps and More 35, page M16
- Appendix, page A80: figure of soldier with cannon*
- Appendix, page A81: question cards*

Notes

Give your child the figure of the soldier firing a cannon either before or during the lesson to color and cut out.

Day 1

Lesson

Introducing the Lesson

Singing Activity

➤ **Can you name some patriotic songs?** *("America the Beautiful," "The Star-Spangled Banner," and so on)*

➤ *Turn to "The British Grenadiers" in the Supplement.*

All countries have patriotic songs. The name of a British patriotic song is "The British Grenadiers." The ***grenadiers*** were soldiers specially trained in the use of hand grenades. This regiment, known as the British Grenadier Guards, fought during the colonial wars. Today it guards England's royal palace. *Show the picture of Buckingham Palace.*

One reason was that the Boers had beaten the British before. They did not stop to think, though, that the British had not been ready or serious. Also, with all their new wealth, the Boers had been buying weapons from other countries—the biggest, most modern guns they could get. And finally, the Boers believed that God was on their side.

A Boer scout with his cartridge belt, rifle, water bottle, and bedroll

Boer soldiers were excellent horsemen. They were used to sleeping on the ground and getting along on little food. And they were not just paid to fight, as their enemies were; they fought for their families and their farms. They wanted to win, and they wanted to live to go home. Why do you think this attitude made them soldiers to be feared?

Great Britain has never liked to look as though she started a war. So the government has always tried to talk over a problem with the enemy, to see whether terms could be worked out. Why do you think Great Britain wanted to talk first and to appear as though she were pushed into war?

234

➤ Listen as I play the recording of "The British Grenadiers." This song was sung by British soldiers during the Boer War.

➤ Sing along with the tape as I play again "The British Grenadiers."

Teaching the Lesson

Text Discussion, page 234 and Maps and More 35

Remember that the Boers were trying to run the British out of the southern part of Africa.

➤ **Read page 234 to find out why the Boers thought they could beat the British.** *(They had beaten them before; they had bought new weapons; they believed God was on their side.)*

➤ **What were the Boer soldiers fighting the British for?** *(control of South Africa; their families and their farms)*

➤ Point to the Transvaal on Maps and More 35.

Remember that this is the area in which gold was found. The British wanted to control this area.

➤ **What advantages did the Boers have on their side?** *(guns bought from other countries, belief that God was on their side, excellent horsemen, used to hard life, fighting for families and land, wanted to win)*

British soldiers retreating to Ladysmith

The Boer leaders agreed to talk. They may have wanted to get their way without war. But they were also waiting for good weather on the plains. The rains had to come so that there would be grass for their war-horses. What do you think happened?

The peace talk went nowhere. The British were not going to meet the Boer terms, and the Boers were not going to meet the British terms. Soon the summer rains began to fall. Now there would be plenty of grass for the horses. The Boers were ready for war.

The British soldiers were not prepared for fighting in the south of Africa. Nor did they understand the enemy. They believed what leaders in the area said: "It will all be over in two weeks."

In the first battle of the war, the British made the Boer soldiers retreat. But at the next battle—and the next and the one after that—the Boers outsmarted and beat the British. The defeats were a terrible embarrassment to the British, with their history of being great in war.

235

The British used observation balloons to try to find the Boer trenches.

The war went on for three years. The Boers' skill in riding and shooting made them tough enemies. But the British had more men and more money, and in 1902 they finally won. The Boer soldiers had fought long and hard and bravely. They had to give in, but they still carried their heads high and sang their songs. They were a proud people who had fought an enemy that outnumbered them ten times.

The British let the Boers take part in the new government. And England spent much money and gave many goods and animals to help the Boer country rebuild. Many Boer soldiers refused to believe that England ruled them at all. They held on to their old ways and their own language. Some Boers thought it best to get along with the British, but they kept a love for their old country in their hearts. Do you think the British really won? Most British did not think so.

236

➤ **How would the ability to sleep on the ground and get by on little food be an advantage to the Boers?** *(They would be able to endure the hard conditions of war.)*

➤ **What did Great Britain want to do instead of fighting?** *(talk about terms to settle the problem)*

Text Discussion, page 235

➤ **Read page 235 to find out why the Boers agreed to peace talks and drew them out for so long.** *(so that the rains would fall to provide enough grass for their horses to eat)*

➤ **Were either the Boers or the British willing to give in?** *(No, neither side was willing to give in.)*

Let's think about an example of this type of situation. Suppose two children both wanted to play with the same toy at the same time and neither one was willing to share.

➤ **What might happen with the toy?** *(There might be pulling and tugging on the toy. The toy might get broken.)*

When two countries or two sections within a country disagree strongly about who will control the government or land, war can result. However, in most cases, disagreements can be resolved in other ways.

➤ **How long did the British think the war would last?** *(two weeks)*

They thought the Boers were untrained and had few weapons. The British did not expect any real fighting.

➤ Think about two men fighting to defend a home. **Who would fight harder, the man who owns the home or the one who is just visiting?** *(the man who owns the home)*

➤ **Who won most of the opening battles of the Boer War in 1899?** *(the Boers)*

The Boers were fiercely independent and were fighting to protect their families and their way of life. They won the first battles because they were so determined.

➤ Attach the figure of the soldier firing a cannon to South Africa on the world map used in our last lesson.

Day 2

Text Discussion, page 236

➤ **Read page 236 to find out what made the Boers hard to beat.** *(their skill in riding and shooting)*

➤ **How long did the war last?** *(three years)*

➤ **Who won the war?** *(the British)*

The Boers still wanted the British to leave them alone. They rebelled again twelve years later, but the British soldiers held them back. Then they began to think: most of the leaders were Boer, and few British lived in their lands. They decided to wait, to use their heads instead of their guns. In 1960, only fifty-eight years after the war, the children and grandchildren of the Boer soldiers were allowed to vote themselves free of Britain. The Republic of South Africa became its own country.

South Africa today is rich and powerful. But it has many problems. The people who settled the area—Dutch, Bantu, British—often had conflicts. Although the Dutch and British made up only one-fifth of the population, they built the big cities and farms. They controlled the government. To protect their control, they lived by *apartheid*, a rule that kept blacks from voting and from living and working wherever they wanted.

Why do you think the blacks wanted change? Why do you think the whites did not? Other nations began to condemn South Africa's racist policies, isolating the country by refusing to buy or sell certain goods to it. The South African government began to change. Under President F. W. de Klerk, the government abolished many apartheid laws. In 1990 the president released a prisoner named Nelson Mandela, a black man who had served twenty-six years for violence against the government. In 1994, Mandela ran for president—and won. How do you think South Africa has changed?

Modern Johannesburg, the largest city in South Africa, resulted from the discovery of gold in 1886.

237

- ➤ **Why did the British win the war even though the Boers had won the first several battles?** *(The British had more men and more money.)*
- ➤ **How many more British soldiers were there than Boer soldiers?** *(ten times more)*

The British Empire stretched around the world and, therefore, had almost unlimited resources of men and weapons for fighting a war. The Boers were unable to keep up the fight, so they surrendered to the British in 1902.

- ➤ **Were the Boers allowed a part in the new government of South Africa after the war?** *(yes)*

There have been many times in history in which Christians have been outnumbered by people who hated them. Christians should depend on the Lord to help them through any difficulty and should stand up for their beliefs regardless of circumstances. (BATs: 8a Faith in God's promises, 8d Courage)

Text Discussion, page 237

- ➤ **Read page 237 to find out whether Britain rules South Africa today.** *(no)*

Many changes have occurred in South Africa over the years. In 1910 the Union of South Africa was formed as a British commonwealth country.

- ➤ **In what year did the Republic of South Africa come into being as an independent country, free of British rule?** *(1960)*

The Dutch, Bantu, and British who had settled in the southern part of Africa were happy with the new government. But the many black people who originally lived in the land were not happy.

- ➤ **Why did the blacks in South Africa want a change?** *(They were not allowed to vote or to live and work where they wanted.)*
- ➤ Find the term that describes the rules which kept the black people from having these freedoms. ***(apartheid)***
- ➤ **What did other nations do that put pressure on South Africa to end apartheid?** *(They refused to buy or sell with South Africa.)*

After a while, many of the racist laws of South Africa were changed.

- ➤ **Who was elected president of South Africa in 1994?** *(Nelson Mandela)*
- ➤ **How was Nelson Mandela different from previous presidents?** *(He had served time in prison for violence against the government; he was the first black man elected president of South Africa.)*

Evaluating the Lesson

Discussion Question Activity

- ➤ *Give your child the question cards and writing paper.*

These cards contain thinking questions from the material we have just read. You may read through the cards to see what the questions are about. Then you will answer several of the questions on your writing paper.

- ➤ Choose four of the cards.
- ➤ Read one of the cards you chose. Think through the situation and write the answer you think is correct.
- ➤ Follow the same procedure for the other three cards.

Encourage your child to mention a Scripture reference or principle if possible that applies to the situation. Writing exercises encourage him to think through issues critically. Avoid giving him the right answers.

Going Beyond

Additional Teacher Information

Winston Churchill, future prime minister of England, was a twenty-five-year-old war correspondent in 1899, reporting the Boer War for the *Morning Post.* When the armored train he was riding was attacked by the Boers, Churchill was taken as a prisoner of war. He escaped from the prison camp by sneaking over the wall, traveled hundreds of miles through hostile territory, and finally reached British-controlled territory. In England, he was lauded as a hero. Shortly thereafter, Churchill won his first seat in Parliament.

South Africa is a very rich country. More than half of the world's gold is mined there. South Africa is also the world leader in diamond mining, and 85 percent of the world's platinum is mined there.

LESSON 63
China in Conflict

Text, pages 238-41, 316-17
Notebook, pages 87-88

Preview

Main Ideas

- Nations try to gain territory in different ways.
- Foreigners went to China as missionaries and merchants.
- The empress dowager of China imprisoned the emperor and ruled China alone.
- The Boxers were Chinese patriots who wanted to drive all foreigners out of China.

Objective

- Complete a crossword puzzle about the Boxer Uprising

Materials

- An atlas
- Appendix, page A80: missionary family*
- A dictionary

Notes

Give your child the figure of the missionary family either before or during the lesson to color and cut out.

Day 1

Lesson

Introducing the Lesson

Missionary Discussion

➤ Share experiences you have had with missionaries.
➤ **What is a missionary's main goal?** *(to give the gospel to people who have not heard about Jesus)*
➤ Find China on the world map in your atlas.

During the 1800s and early 1900s, hundreds of missionaries gave the gospel throughout China. Thousands of Chinese people were led to Christ.

➤ **Do you remember the name of the English doctor who started the China Inland Mission?** *(Hudson Taylor)*
➤ Point to the figure of Hudson Taylor on the TimeLine Snapshots.

After the missionaries left China, the Chinese Christians continued to spread the gospel in China. More than one billion people live in China now. This is about one-fourth of the people in the world. The Chinese government does not permit missionaries to come to China, but millions of Chinese Christians hold secret church services in homes.

➤ **How would you feel if we had to meet secretly for church?** It is important for us to pray for the people of China. (BAT: 5c Evangelism and missions)

Teaching the Lesson

Text Discussion, page 238

➤ **Read page 238 to find out who the *Boxers* were.** *(Chinese people who hated missionaries and Chinese Christians; those who blamed China's troubles on Christians and other foreigners)*

➤ **Why were these people called Boxers?** *(They did exercises like boxers did.)*

➤ **Why did the Boxers hate foreigners?** *(They said that foreigners did not show respect and were ruining the Chinese way of living.)*

The Boxers were angry with Europeans who had forced China to trade with other nations and brought foreign religion and inventions into China. The Boxers wanted China to be *only* Chinese.

➤ **How did the Boxers plan to make China happy again?** *(by killing all Christians and making all foreigners leave)*

➤ **How do you feel about people from other countries bringing foreign ideas into our country?**

➤ **Why do you think the Boxers hated Christians so much?**

The Boxers believed in Buddhism, Taoism, or Confucianism. These are false religions that cannot provide forgiveness of sin or a way to heaven. We know that the only way to heaven is through the righteousness of Christ. (BAT: 1a Understanding Jesus Christ)

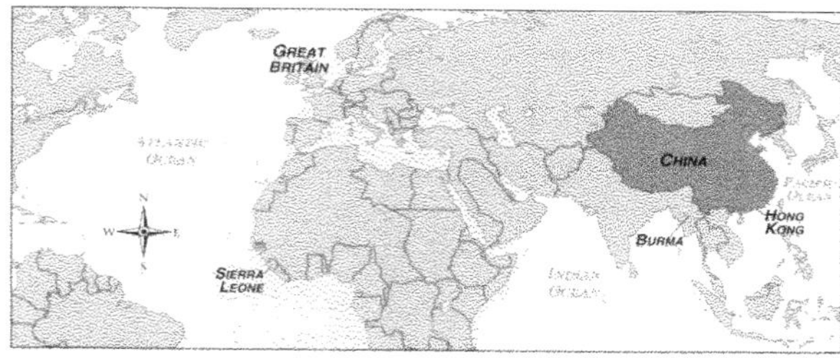

The Boxer Uprising

Do you remember reading about the missionaries to China? Find China on the map. What continent is it on? What direction is it from England? Many Christian workers went to China, and many Chinese people became Christians and left their old religion. The old religion required the people to worship their ancestors. Some missionaries made enemies by trying to change the customs and to interfere with the government in cities. Others stirred up bad feelings by treating the Chinese people as servants or inferiors.

Many Chinese said that Christians did not show respect to the ancestors; they said that Christianity was ruining the Chinese way. Soon groups of people who wanted to keep the old ways began to burn the Christians' property and sometimes attack the Christians themselves. The groups hated the missionaries, but they hated the Chinese Christians more.

One group was bigger and more powerful than any other. They did exercises to make their bodies strong for fighting. Since the exercises looked like the exercises boxers did, the group became known as the *Boxers*. The Boxers wore red to show who they were. Although the Boxers hated all foreigners, they blamed the troubles of China on the Christians. If the Christians were killed, they said, all foreigners would leave and China would again be happy.

238

The Boxers did not understand the love of Christ. They felt that Christianity was a *foreign* religion. They did not understand that Jesus came into the world to save people of every nation.

Read aloud Revelation 5:9b, "For thou wast slain, and hast redeemed us to God by thy blood out of every kindred, and tongue, and people, and nation." (BAT: 1a Understanding Jesus Christ)

The Boxers thought the Chinese Christians were traitors because they believed a foreign religion. The Boxers were very cruel. They killed not only adults but also children.

But China's troubles were not caused by Christians. Many of the problems began in the court of the old empress, Cixi. She wanted power more than anything else. She made sure her son would be the emperor by having the three highest officials killed. When her son died young, she made everyone agree to let her nephew become the next emperor. She schemed her whole life to get things the way she wanted them. And she thought everything was working out just right.

The Empress Dowager, Cixi

Her nephew, although he said he was grateful to the empress, really disliked her running his life. Even when he was a grown man and the emperor of all China, he had to ask the old empress about everything he did—what trips he took, which people could work for him. The empress declared that she loved him dearly, but secretly she was afraid he would take her power and so had him watched all the time. With all the scheming going on, no one was taking care of China.

The emperor wanted to let China learn from the English and others who came to his land. He thought some of their new ideas were good. But the empress hated all new thinking; she thought it was disloyal to the ancestors—and a threat to her control. What do you think she did? She had the emperor taken to an island and held prisoner. Then she ruled China by herself.

239

The palace in the Forbidden City can now be visited by anyone.

The empress wanted the Boxers to hurt the foreigners and to destroy their property. She thought such treatment would make the foreigners go home. So no matter what the Boxers did or how many laws they broke, she did nothing to stop them. When the foreigners saw that the empress was not going to help them, they asked their own governments to send soldiers. Soon soldiers from England, Russia, Japan, Austria, Germany, Italy, and the United States were in China. Do you think the trouble stopped?

The Boxers believed that no foreigner's gun and no foreigner's sword could hurt them. They believed their chants would protect them. They were completely unafraid of fighting anyone of another race. Soon the missionaries and the Chinese Christians in Beijing (spelled Peking on older maps) decided to leave their houses and stay together in a mission. It was easier to defend. They began to put barbed wire around the outside of the mission.

Beijing, the capital, was where the empress lived. Her part of Beijing was walled off from the rest of the city; she lived in the Forbidden City. What does the name tell you about the place?

240

Text Discussion, page 239

- ➤ **Read page 239 to find out who was ruling China during the time of the Boxer Uprising.** *(Cixi)*

Cixi was called the ***empress dowager.*** She was the widow of a former emperor and had been empress while her husband lived. Cixi had done everything she could to maintain her power.

- ➤ **What ideas did the young emperor have that the old empress did not like?** *(He would have allowed his people to learn English, and he welcomed some of the foreigners' ideas.)*
- ➤ **What did Cixi do to make sure the new emperor followed her wishes?** *(made all his decisions, had him watched all the time)*
- ➤ **What did Cixi do to the emperor when her control was threatened?** *(She had the emperor imprisoned.)*
- ➤ **Is it right to resort to bad behavior in order to get your own way?** *(no)* (BATs: 4c Honesty, 6d Clear conscience)

Day 2

Text Discussion, page 240

- ➤ **Read page 240 to find out how the Boxers treated foreign people.** *(They hurt them and destroyed their property.)*
- ➤ **What did the empress do to protect the foreigners from the Boxers?** *(nothing)*

The missionaries and merchants who were being hurt and killed were from many different countries. When they received no help from the empress, they sent word back to their own lands.

- ➤ **How did the home countries of the foreigners in China get involved?** *(They sent troops.)*
- ➤ Name countries that sent troops to China. *(England, Russia, Japan, Austria, Germany, Italy, and United States)*
- ➤ **Were the Boxers afraid of the troops?** *(No, they thought they could not be hurt.)*

The Boxers recruited soldiers by telling them that bullets fired from a foreigner's gun could not hurt them.

➤ **Was this true?** *(no)*

The Christian missionaries did not keep weapons with them and did not defend themselves from the Boxers. Instead, the missionaries stayed as long as they could in their homes. Then they traveled to mission stations to live together and fortified themselves against the enemy. Some of them even fled from the country to save their lives.

➤ Attach the picture of the missionary family to China on the world map that we are using in this chapter.

➤ **Did the empress live in a part of Beijing where everyone was allowed to visit?** *(no)*

➤ **Why do you think she have wanted to isolate herself from her people?**

Text Discussion, page 241

➤ **Read page 241 to find out what happened as the foreign soldiers marched toward Beijing.** *(There was fighting all along the way. Many people on both sides were killed.)*

Many missionaries were living in mission compounds during this time, waiting for the European, Japanese, and American soldiers to free them. Some missionaries reached safety in Beijing, Hangzhou, or Shanghai. Others, however, were killed in their homes or while they were trying to escape to safety.

The Chinese name for the Boxers means ***Righteous and Harmonious Fists.***

➤ Look up *righteous* and *harmonious* in the dictionary and read the definitions.

➤ **Did the Boxers behave in a righteous or harmonious way?** *(no)*

➤ **Did the Boxers respect the government officials of Beijing?** *(No, they robbed them.)*

Do you think the foreigners were safe now? No, the Boxers burned down the mission and several other churches. The foreigners moved to another place. The soldiers from the other countries were trying to get to Beijing. Can you follow their route on the map? The soldiers had to fight the Boxers all along the way. They took the city of Tientsin from the Boxers first. About eight hundred foreign soldiers had died and almost five thousand Chinese soldiers and Boxers.

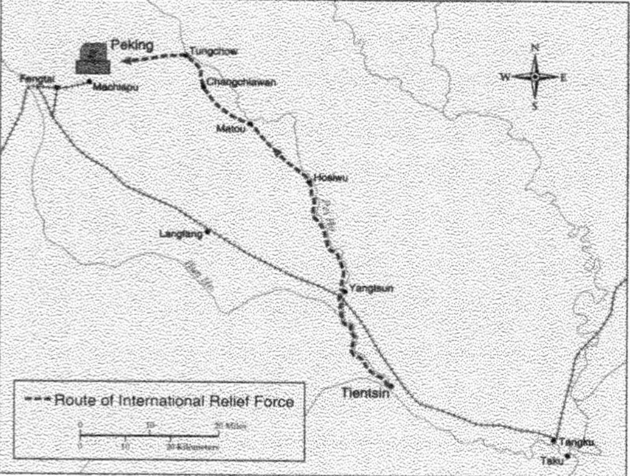

In Beijing the fighting got worse. And more than two thousand Chinese students and Christians went to the foreigners for help. The Boxers (more than 150,000 were in Beijing) had begun to rob anyone, even a Chinese governor. The empress was becoming disgusted; the Boxers were turning into thieves. They were not the brave patriots she had thought.

241

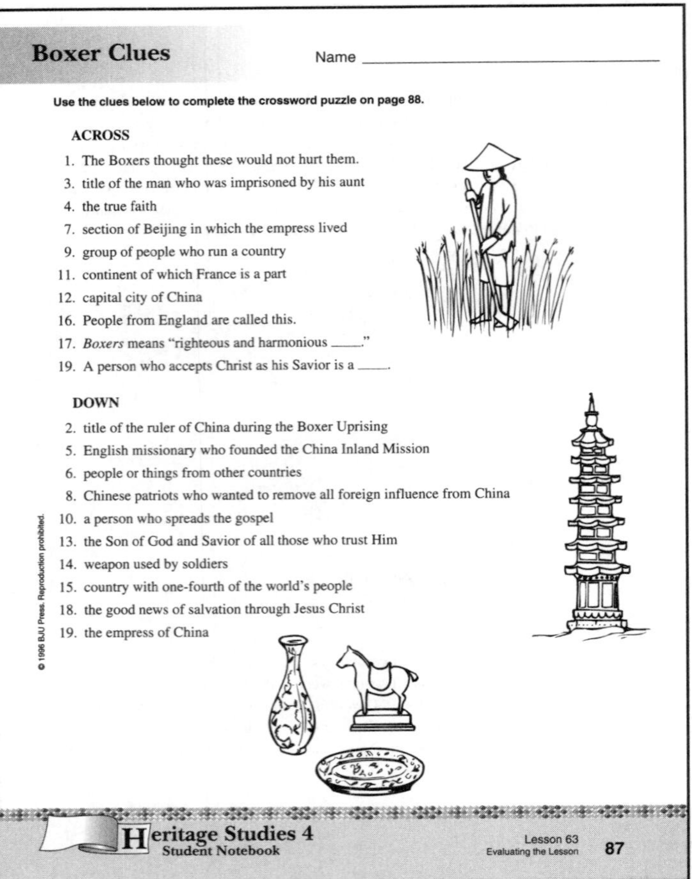

Boxer Clues Name ______________________

Use the clues below to complete the crossword puzzle on page 88.

ACROSS

1. The Boxers thought these would not hurt them.
3. title of the man who was imprisoned by his aunt
4. the true faith
7. section of Beijing in which the empress lived
9. group of people who run a country
11. continent of which France is a part
12. capital city of China
16. People from England are called this.
17. *Boxers* means "righteous and harmonious ____."
19. A person who accepts Christ as his Savior is a ____.

DOWN

2. title of the ruler of China during the Boxer Uprising
5. English missionary who founded the China Inland Mission
6. people or things from other countries
8. Chinese patriots who wanted to remove all foreign influence from China
10. a person who spreads the gospel
13. the Son of God and Savior of all those who trust Him
14. weapon used by soldiers
15. country with one-fourth of the world's people
18. the good news of salvation through Jesus Christ
19. the empress of China

Boxer Puzzle Name ______________________

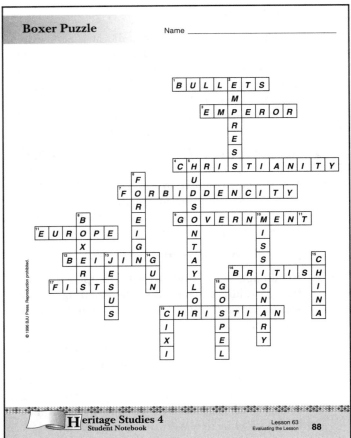

Evaluating the Lesson

Puzzle Activity, Notebook pages 87-88

- ➤ Read the instructions on Notebook page 87.
- ➤ Complete the puzzle, using the textbook if necessary to find the answers to the clues.

Going Beyond

Enrichment

Encourage your child to make a Chinese fan. Tell him that Chinese fan paintings were considered a serious art during the sixteenth and seventeenth centuries. Many of the fans were painted on silk. Provide parchment-type stationery with an outline of a fan as shown in the figure below. Direct him to decorate the fan by coloring pictures of flowers or birds. Instruct him to cut out the fan. Explain that the fan may be folded in an accordion-type fashion.

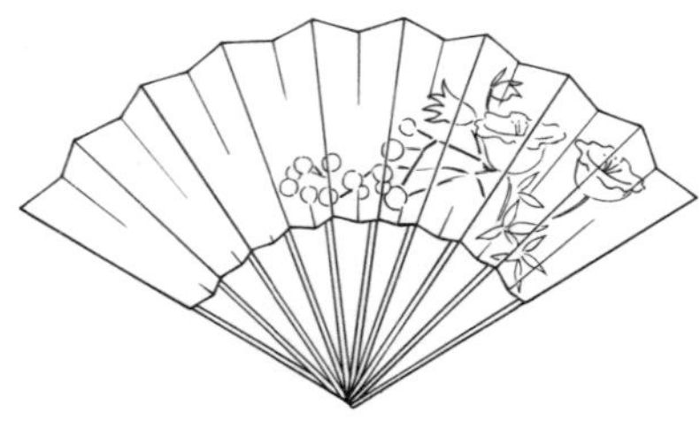

Additional Teacher Information

The word *Beijing* means "northern capital." For many years the word *Beijing* was spelled *Peking* when written in English. However, *Beijing* is closer to the Chinese pronunciation and is the correct word to use when referring to the capital of China.

One factor leading to the Boxer Uprising was the Opium War. In the early 1800s, British merchants sold opium to the Chinese people. Chinese authorities outlawed the importation and possession of opium. When the British continued to import opium into China, the Chinese government seized all the opium that was in the port warehouses and held the British merchants hostage. The Chinese then burned the two thousand tons of opium. To keep the market open for opium, the British attacked the city of Canton and demanded payment for the opium that had been destroyed. The battles that followed are called the Opium War. The British won the war and opened several other ports for the importation of opium and other goods.

After the Opium War, there was talk among European countries of partitioning China in the same way Africa had been partitioned, with the entire country under foreign rule.

LESSON 64
Christians in the Boxer Uprising

Text, pages 242-44
Notebook, pages 89-90

Preview

Main Ideas

- Missionaries and Chinese Christians were persecuted and killed by the Boxers.
- Foreign soldiers defeated the Boxers to end the uprising.
- The empress dowager instituted reforms in China after the uprising.

Objectives

- Choose the correct term to answer questions about the terms and events of the Boxer Uprising
- Sequence a list of events surrounding the Boxer Uprising

Materials

- A Bible
- Appendix, page A80: empress as peasant*

Notes

Give your child the figure of the empress as a peasant either before or during the lesson to color and cut out.

The board game Escape in China is introduced in the Enrichment section. If you choose to use the game, refer to Lesson 36 for instructions to assemble the game pieces.

The missionary figures will be used as game markers. Make a copy of the figures. (*NOTE:* See the Appendix, page A86.) Cut out the missionary figures and the bases and affix them to a stiff backing. After laminating the figures, cut a slit along the dark cutting line and slide each missionary figure onto a base.

Lesson

Introducing the Lesson

Listening Activity

➤ Listen as I read a story.

A wicked artist lived near his village temple in China. Even though his family was religious, this man was very evil. Ever since he was a boy, he had done whatever he wanted. Some things he did, like drawing and painting and sculpting, were good things. But this man also broke the village laws, and he worshiped false gods.

The artist became a leader in his village. He was famous for the paintings he did in the temple. All the villagers came to buy the idols that he sculpted out of gold and silver. All the village children and most of the adults were afraid of the wicked artist. He was a proud fighter, and he led many other evil men in fierce battles against other villages. He was often arrested, beaten, and thrown into prison.

The artist's brother was a wicked man too. Together the brothers raided neighboring villages. One day, the artist heard something that infuriated him. A villager had told him that his brother had become a Christian and would not raid villages anymore. He grabbed his weapons and ran to his brother's house. He was determined to murder the missionary who had led his brother to Christ.

➤ **Could a man like the artist in the story ever be saved?** *(yes)*

> God saves His people out of every people, tongue, and nation. The wickedness of a man's life cannot hinder the work of the Holy Spirit of God in saving a man. (BAT: 1b Repentance and faith)

➤ We will learn more about this wicked idol maker in this lesson.

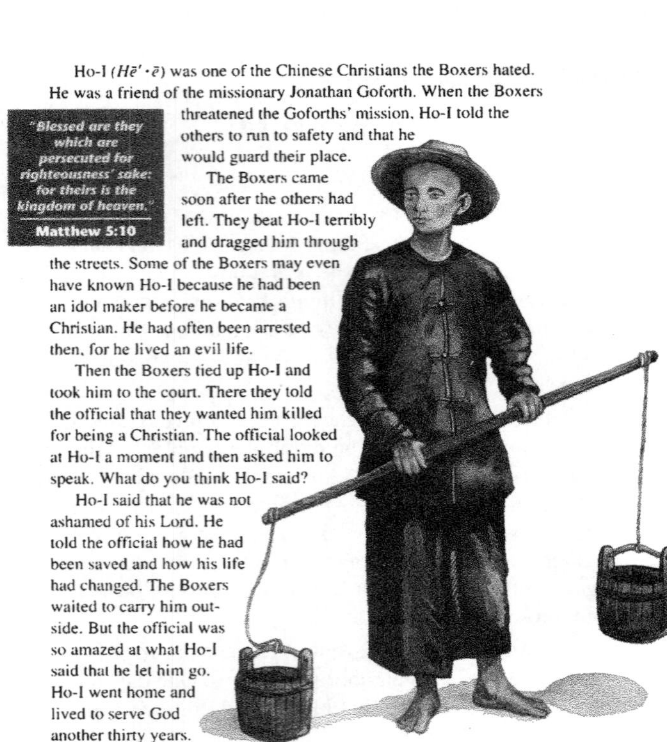

Ho-I (*Hē′·ē*) was one of the Chinese Christians the Boxers hated. He was a friend of the missionary Jonathan Goforth. When the Boxers threatened the Goforths' mission, Ho-I told the others to run to safety and that he would guard their place.

> *"Blessed are they which are persecuted for righteousness' sake: for theirs is the kingdom of heaven."*
> **Matthew 5:10**

The Boxers came soon after the others had left. They beat Ho-I terribly and dragged him through the streets. Some of the Boxers may even have known Ho-I because he had been an idol maker before he became a Christian. He had often been arrested then, for he lived an evil life.

Then the Boxers tied up Ho-I and took him to the court. There they told the official that they wanted him killed for being a Christian. The official looked at Ho-I a moment and then asked him to speak. What do you think Ho-I said?

Ho-I said that he was not ashamed of his Lord. He told the official how he had been saved and how his life had changed. The Boxers waited to carry him outside. But the official was so amazed at what Ho-I said that he let him go. Ho-I went home and lived to serve God another thirty years.

242

American, Japanese, and British troops storm the palace at Beijing.

The foreigners held off the Boxers for many weeks until the armies from their countries got to Beijing. Then the fighting was bitter and swift. Foreign soldiers pushed into the city. At last, the empress and her court had to flee. They traveled miles from Beijing and hid. After some time, the foreign soldiers broke down the last defenses and walked into the Forbidden City, a place no foreigner had ever been.

The Boxers also fled. They began to realize that foreign bullets and swords could indeed kill them. The foreign soldiers looted the city, taking anything they wanted—furs, silver, dishes, silk. With almost a third of the city burning and the rest being smashed, the empress finally agreed to talk peace.

For more than a year, the peace talks went on. At last, the empress signed a paper that changed many things in China. Many of the old leaders were put to death. It became a law that no one was allowed to join an antiforeign group. And China had to pay the winning countries millions of dollars.

How do you think events might have been different if the empress and other leaders had accepted new ideas earlier?

243

Teaching the Lesson

Text Discussion, page 242

- ➤ **Read page 242 to find out how one Chinese Christian answered when asked to give up his faith or be killed.** *(He said he was not ashamed of the Lord.)*
- ➤ **What is the name of this man?** *(Ho-I [Hē′·ē])*
- ➤ **Was Ho-I a brave man?** *(yes)*
- ➤ **Was Ho-I killed by the Boxers?** *(No, the government official let him go free.)*

Ho-I was the wicked artist from our story. Although he had been very angry that his brother became a Christian, he too came to know the Lord. Although he was faced with men who said they would kill him, Ho-I knew the Lord would not forsake him. (BAT: 8a Faith in God's promises)

- ➤ **Do you remember the biblical account of Shadrach, Meshach, and Abednego?**

These men also were asked to give up their faith or be killed. Because they would not bow to the king, they were thrown in the fiery furnace. But God saved them.

- ➤ **Is God more powerful than wicked men?** *(yes)*

God is greater and more powerful than any trouble we will ever encounter. Christians should trust the Lord to help them through times of trouble. (BAT: 8a Faith in God's promises) Read Mark 13:11. The Holy Spirit will help us just as He helped Ho-I say the right things in his time of trial. (BAT: 5d Communication)

Text Discussion, page 243

- ➤ **Read page 243 to find out what the empress did as the foreign soldiers advanced.** *(fled and hid)*
- ➤ **Why would the empress want to leave Beijing?** *(She might have been afraid of being hurt or killed by the foreign soldiers.)*

The empress disguised herself as a peasant, hid in a cart, and escaped the city.

- ➤ Attach the figure of the disguised empress to the world map that we are using for this chapter.
- ➤ **What did the foreign soldiers see that no foreigner had ever seen?** *(the Forbidden City)*
- ➤ **Why did the Boxers begin to flee also?** *(They realized they could be hurt or killed by the foreign soldiers' bullets and swords.)*
- ➤ **What did the foreign soldiers do once inside the Forbidden City?** *(They took anything they wanted and burned or smashed the rest.)*

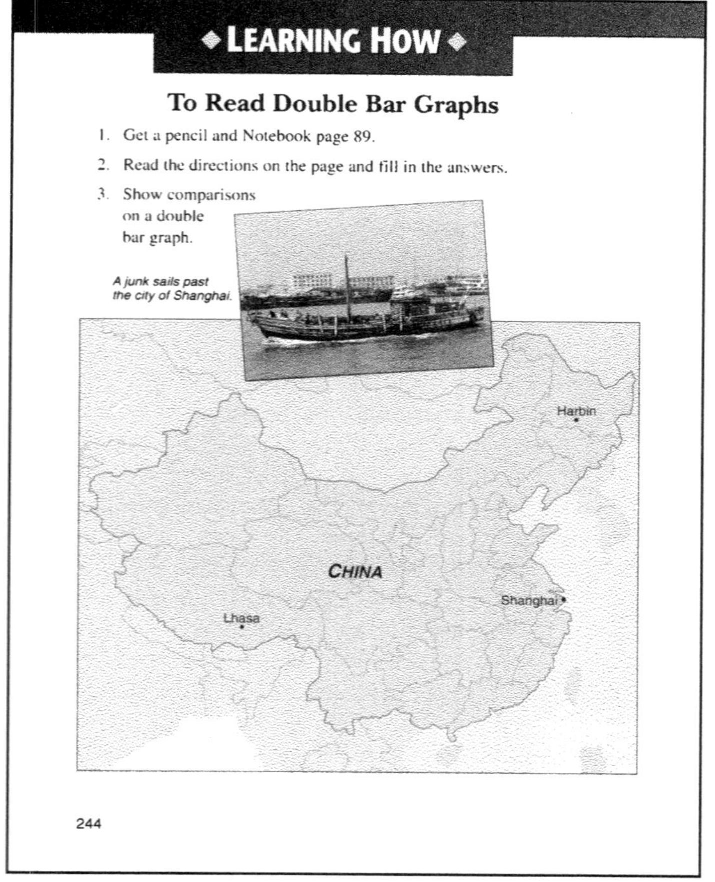

◆ LEARNING HOW ◆

To Read Double Bar Graphs

1. Get a pencil and Notebook page 89.
2. Read the directions on the page and fill in the answers.
3. Show comparisons on a double bar graph.

A junk sails past the city of Shanghai.

244

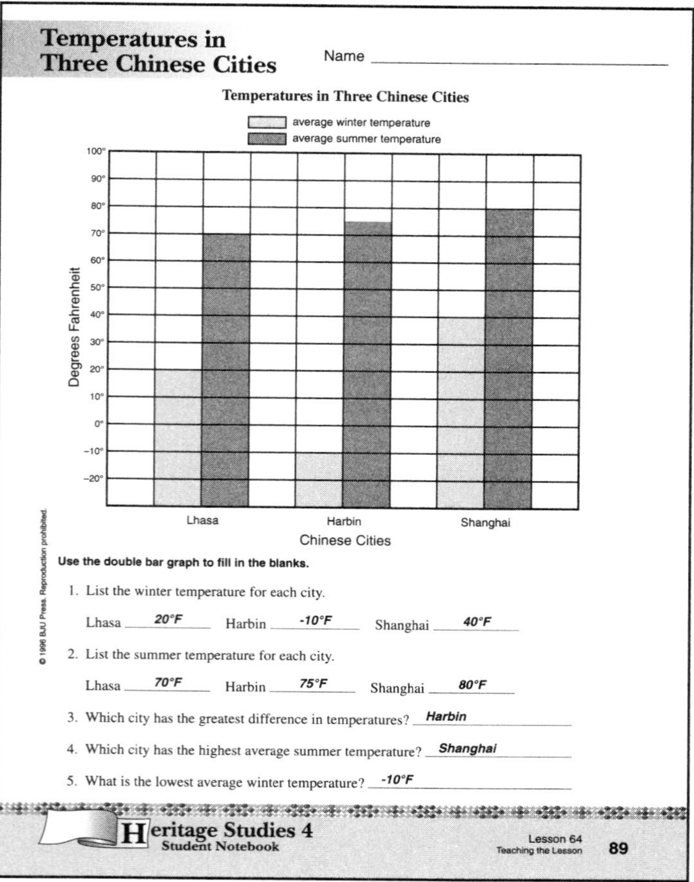

Temperatures in Three Chinese Cities

Name ______________________

Use the double bar graph to fill in the blanks.

1. List the winter temperature for each city.
   Lhasa ___*20°F*___ Harbin ___*-10°F*___ Shanghai ___*40°F*___
2. List the summer temperature for each city.
   Lhasa ___*70°F*___ Harbin ___*75°F*___ Shanghai ___*80°F*___
3. Which city has the greatest difference in temperatures? ___*Harbin*___
4. Which city has the highest average summer temperature? ___*Shanghai*___
5. What is the lowest average winter temperature? ___*-10°F*___

Heritage Studies 4 Student Notebook

Lesson 64 Teaching the Lesson 89

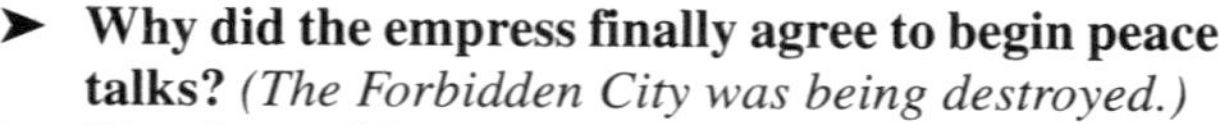

➤ **Why did the empress finally agree to begin peace talks?** *(The Forbidden City was being destroyed.)*

➤ **How long did the peace talks last?** *(over a year)*

➤ **What changes came to China as they met the conditions of the peace treaty?** *(Many old leaders were put to death, antiforeign societies were outlawed, and the winning countries were paid millions of dollars.)*

Day 2

Learning How Activity, page 244 and Notebook page 89

➤ **Read the title on page 244.** Today we will be reading a double bar graph.

➤ **Read all the steps on page 244 and then follow Step 1.**

➤ **Read aloud the title of the graph on Notebook page 89.** *(Temperatures in Three Chinese Cities)*

➤ **What do the numbers along the left side of the graph indicate?** *(the temperature in degrees Fahrenheit)*

➤ **What do the words across the bottom of the graph represent?** *(the names of three cities in China)*

➤ **What do the darker columns indicate?** *(the average summer temperature for each city)*

➤ **What do the lighter shaded columns show?** *(the average winter temperature for each city)*

➤ Complete the Notebook page.

The Boxer Uprising Name ____________________

Choose the correct word to fill in the blank. Words may be used once or not at all.

empress	emperor	India	Ho-I
Boxers	Forbidden City	million	Beijing
China	foreign soldiers	new ideas	Jonathan Goforth
bullets	government official		

1. Many Chinese patriots wanted things to stay the same in China. They did not want to accept ___*new*___ ___*ideas*___.
2. The ___*emperor*___ was kept a prisoner by his powerful aunt.
3. The soldiers who persecuted the Chinese Christians were called ___*Boxers*___.
4. ___*Beijing*___ is the capital city of China. The Forbidden City was within its walls.
5. Hudson Taylor was a missionary to the country of ___*China*___.
6. After the war, the Chinese had to pay 330 ___*million*___ dollars to the victors.
7. ___*Ho-I*___ stood firmly for the gospel in the face of persecution.
8. ___*Jonathan*___ ___*Goforth*___ was the missionary who led Ho-I to Christ.
9. The empress lived in the part of Beijing called the ___*Forbidden*___ ___*City*___.
10. The ___*foreign*___ ___*soldiers*___ defeated the Boxers in the Boxer Uprising.
11. The ___*empress*___ escaped from Beijing dressed as a peasant woman.
12. A ___*government*___ ___*official*___ let Ho-I go free.

Number the statements in the order they occurred.

___*3*___ Foreign troops burned the Forbidden City.

___*1*___ Christians were persecuted by the Boxers.

___*2*___ Missionaries left their stations and went to Beijing.

___*4*___ The Empress agreed to hold peace talks.

Heritage Studies 4 Student Notebook — Lesson 64 Evaluating the Lesson — 90

Evaluating the Lesson

Notebook Activity, page 90

➤ Read the instructions on Notebook page 90.
➤ Complete the page independently.

If you are teaching several children, you may make the checking of this page into a game. Divide the group into two teams: the French army and the British army. Read aloud each question in turn from Notebook page 90, calling on a child to give the correct answer. Each team member raises his hand if he has the correct answer written on Notebook page 90. Count and record the number of children from each army who answered correctly. Each correct answer will recruit a soldier for the representative army. When all the questions on the Notebook page have been answered, the army with more recruits wins.

Going Beyond

Enrichment

Introduce the Escape in China game (Appendix, pages A81-A85). First, show the game board. Point out the map of China in the background and the spaces to be traveled around the outside of the game board. Trace the direction of "traffic" with your finger, showing the possible added loop (detour). Point out Mr. Wu's house, the river crossing, the cave, the wheat field, and the mission compound.

Call attention to a space that has a star. Explain that whenever a player lands on a starred space, he should draw one card, follow the directions on the card, and then replace the card on the bottom of the pile.

Give directions for playing the game. Explain that the object of the game is to move a missionary to the *Mission Compound.* All players begin with the game markers at the *Start.* Each player spins once, the highest number going first. Then, in turn, each player spins again. Each player moves his marker ahead as many spaces as the spinner indicates, drawing a card if he lands on a starred space. Play continues until a player reaches the mission compound. A player must reach the mission compound by the exact number on the spinner.

Additional Teacher Information

Of the Protestant missionaries in China at the time of the Boxer Uprising, 133 adults and 48 children were killed by the Boxers. No one knows how many Chinese Christians were killed. However, after the uprising, missionaries returned to their stations in China. Thousands of Chinese people were saved in the years between the Boxer Uprising and 1949, the year of the Communist takeover of China. At that time, missionaries were forced out of the country.

LESSON 65
The Industrial Revolution and Imperialism

Text, pages 245-48
Notebook, pages 91-92

Preview

Main Ideas

- The Industrial Revolution changed the way of life for people in Europe and the United States.
- The conquering of other lands by a country is called *imperialism.*
- Great Britain amassed a huge empire during the reign of Queen Victoria.
- The United States has territories and possessions.

Objectives

- Identify inventions of the Industrial Revolution
- Identify changes in home life brought about by the Industrial Revolution
- Identify possessions and colonies of Great Britain and the United States

Materials

- Maps and More 25, page M12

Day 1

Lesson

Introducing the Lesson

Listening Activity

➤ Listen as I read a journal entry.

It is nine o'clock at night, and this is the first moment I have had to write. After getting up at six o'clock this morning, I made my bed and helped Mother get the other children ready. That is one of the jobs I have because I'm the oldest. I'm ten years old. At six-thirty I started for work. My little brother Benny went with me. We worked at the factory from seven in the morning until seven at night. I wish I could stay home and play or go to school, but Mother and Father need the money that Benny and I earn.

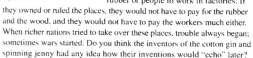

ECHOES IN HISTORY

The Industrial Revolution

Inventions like the cotton gin made a need for more inventions. Can you think of any of them? The spinning jenny was one. Because more cotton could be seeded by the gin, bigger machines were needed to make thread. As thread production increased, weavers needed machines to make cloth faster. And on it went.

Why do you think nations want bigger and better machines to make more things faster? It is because they make money by selling the things. The more they make, the more they can sell. The more they sell, the richer they become. The richer they become, the more powerful they are.

After a while, nations with bigger and better machines could not grow enough cotton or find enough iron or cut enough wood to keep all the machines busy. So they began to look for such things in other places. When a country buys goods from another country, it *imports* the goods, or brings them in. Imported goods have to be paid for, however. Can you think of a reason not to import goods to make things from?

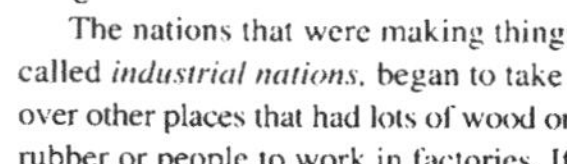

A table leg made from imported mahogany wood

The nations that were making things, called *industrial nations,* began to take over other places that had lots of wood or rubber or people to work in factories. If they owned or ruled the places, they would not have to pay for the rubber and the wood, and they would not have to pay the workers much either. When richer nations tried to take over these places, trouble always began; sometimes wars started. Do you think the inventors of the cotton gin and spinning jenny had any idea how their inventions would "echo" later?

245

Benny and I ate our brown bread together at noon time. Mother's bread is very good, and it was a fresh loaf. After work, we walked home in the dark. I had a penny, so I bought a sweet roll from the baker and shared it with Benny. Mother had bean soup on the stove for us when we got home. It was hot, and it warmed me up. Better get to sleep now—six o'clock comes early.

During the time of the Industrial Revolution, many children worked ten or twelve hours a day in factories or mines.

Teaching the Lesson

Text Discussion, page 245

➤ **Do you remember what a spinning jenny was?** *(a machine that made thread)*

➤ **Read page 245 to find out why the spinning jenny was invented.** *(Because the cotton gin could seed so much cotton, a machine was needed that could spin the cotton quickly into thread.)*

➤ **How would a business profit from being able to spin a lot of thread quickly?** *(It would have more thread to sell.)*

Imperialism

Look at the map. What are some of the countries in Europe? Why do you think countries like England and France sent some of their people to other countries, such as South Africa and China? What were some of the reasons that people wanted to go live in China and Africa? One reason was money; the Boers found gold, and soon many others wanted it. China had silks and tea, goods which brought much money.

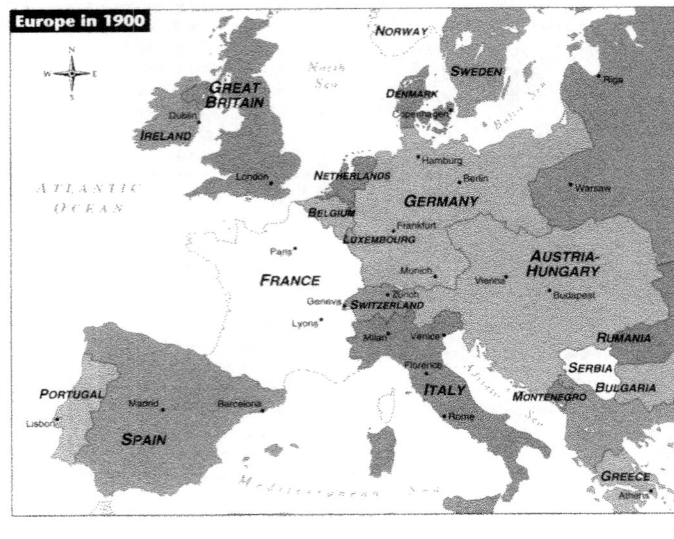

246

> *"For we preach not ourselves, but Christ Jesus the Lord; and ourselves your servants for Jesus' sake."*
> **II Corinthians 4:5**

Another reason was that the people in Europe felt they were better than other people. They thought they should teach their ways to the Chinese, the Indians, the Boers, and others. Do you think missionaries felt this way? Some of them did. Some, though, wanted only to serve God.

Yet another reason Europeans went to other countries is nationalism. If a country like England did not own lands somewhere else, it looked weak and small to the other countries. So most nations tried to get *colonies*, or territories. England had colonies all over the world. What happened to her colonies in the New World in 1776?

Why do you think most colonies try to get free of the country that established them or that took them over? Sometimes, as in the case of the Boers, they have their own government and customs. In other cases, such as in America, colonists grow away from the old country. They begin to think of themselves as a separate people. Why do you think the Chinese did not want others to rule them? Perhaps it was partly because they did not want their ways to change. Another reason was that most Chinese thought of themselves as better than all foreigners.

What do you think happens when many countries try to get the same land? Suppose three people want a bike that you own. How might they try to get it? One may offer to buy it. One may try to take it. Another may try to prove that it should be his by law. What would you do with your bike?

247

➤ **How was thread spun before spinning machines were invented?** *(Each housewife spun her own thread on a hand-operated spinning wheel.)*

Because women no longer had to spin their own thread, some of them went to work in the textile or fabric factories. The factories were built to make clothes more quickly. Then shops were opened to sell the clothes.

Many people were hired to work in the factories and shops, including children. Entire families worked six days a week for many long hours to produce thread, cloth, shoes, or furniture.

➤ **Would a home shoe factory or a large machine-driven shoe factory produce more shoes per day?** *(the large factory)*

Although working in the factories was difficult work for the laborers, many modern advances were made. Goods became more plentiful, and many people were able to afford the new conveniences. Railroads were built to carry large amounts of goods to market.

In order to keep the factories running, huge amounts of natural resources were needed.

➤ **How did the *industrial nations* get the additional resources they needed?** *(They **imported** them from other countries.)*

➤ **To make importing goods easier, what did the large nations do to the smaller countries?** *(They took over their lands.)*

The larger industrial nations, such as England and France, began to acquire other territories which they then controlled.

Text Discussion, pages 246-47

➤ Find Great Britain on the map on pages 246-47.

In 1900 Great Britain was actually made up of four countries: England, Scotland, Wales, and Northern Ireland. All of Great Britain was ruled from the capital city of London.

➤ **Read pages 246-47 to find out why Europeans started settlements in Africa and China.** *(to earn money, to teach their ways to these people, to share the gospel, to gain territories)*

➤ **What had the Boers found that interested the British?** *(gold)*

➤ **What goods did China have that other countries wanted?** *(silk and tea)*

➤ **Read aloud the paragraph on page 247 that tells why England wanted territories.** *(the second paragraph)*

A country that has colonies is called an *empire*. Getting or keeping colonies is *imperialism*. Both terms come from an old word that means "command." What does that definition tell you about the way empires were usually made?

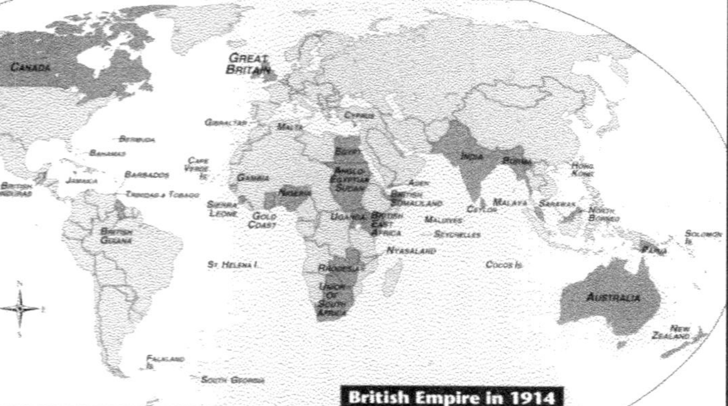

Look at the map. How many colonies did England have by 1914? What do you think people meant when they said that the "sun never sets on the British flag"? They meant that the colonies were so spread out over the world that in at least one of them, it would be daytime at any hour during the twenty-four hours in a day.

Today, few countries still own colonies. Most colonies have become their own nations. How many years ago did the American colonies become the United States of America? What do you know about the American colonies' struggle to become a nation?

248

- ➤ **How would England have looked if it had had no colonies?** *(small and weak)*
- ➤ **Did most colonies like being controlled by another country?** *(no)*
- ➤ **Why did colonies try to become independent?** *(They had their own customs and government. They did not want to be told how to live. They grew away from the old country.)*

Text Discussion, page 248

- ➤ **Read page 248 to find the meaning of the term *imperialism*.** *(getting or keeping colonies)*
- ➤ **What are a country and its colonies called?** *(an empire)*
- ➤ **What does the phrase "the sun never sets on the British flag" mean?** *(Britain had colonies spread out around the world so that at least one of them was in daylight at any given time.)*

Queen Victoria ruled Great Britain during the time most of the colonies were conquered. In the 1920s some large lands controlled by Britain included Australia, Canada, India, and South Africa. These colonies are now independent nations.

- ➤ Find Australia, Canada, India, and South Africa on the map on page 248.
- ➤ Do most countries today have colonies? *(no)*

Map Activity, Maps and More 25

- ➤ Look at Maps and More 25.

This map shows the worldwide possessions of the United States. The dark shaded sections are places that are under the control of the United States.

- ➤ Find Guam in the Pacific Ocean near the mainland of Asia.
- ➤ Find Puerto Rico in the Caribbean Sea off the southern coast of the United States.

These regions are two of the largest United States territories. There is discussion about the possibility of Puerto Rico's becoming a state, and even Guam has discussed this possibility over the years.

- ➤ **How many states would there be if either Puerto Rico or Guam were to become a state?** *(fifty-one)*
- ➤ **How many would there be if both Puerto Rico and Guam became states?** *(fifty-two)*

Review Puzzle

Name ______________________

Use the clues below to fill in the acrostic on page 92.

1. This invention spun thread quickly.
2. During the 1800s many people worked for very little ____.
3. Mothers, fathers, and even ____ worked in factories.
4. ____ is a territory of the United States.
5. Colonies supplied natural ____.
6. A spinning jenny made ____.
7. ____ is a continent in the Pacific Ocean once ruled by Great Britain.
8. During the Industrial Revolution, people worked ____ days a week.
9. ____ is an island in the Pacific Ocean belonging to the United States.
10. The British Empire was ruled from London, the capital of ____.
11. The policy of taking over other countries is called ____.
12. Many people worked ____ hours a day during the Industrial Revolution.
13. ____ was queen of England during the growth of the British Empire.
14. During the Industrial Revolution, a typical workplace was a ____.
15. The thirteen American ____ were once part of the British Empire.
16. Guam is a possession of the ____.
17. Weaving machines make ____ from thread.
18. Tea and ____ were products of China.
19. The spinning jenny was a direct result of the invention of the ____ gin.
20. Many new machines were ____ during the Industrial Revolution.

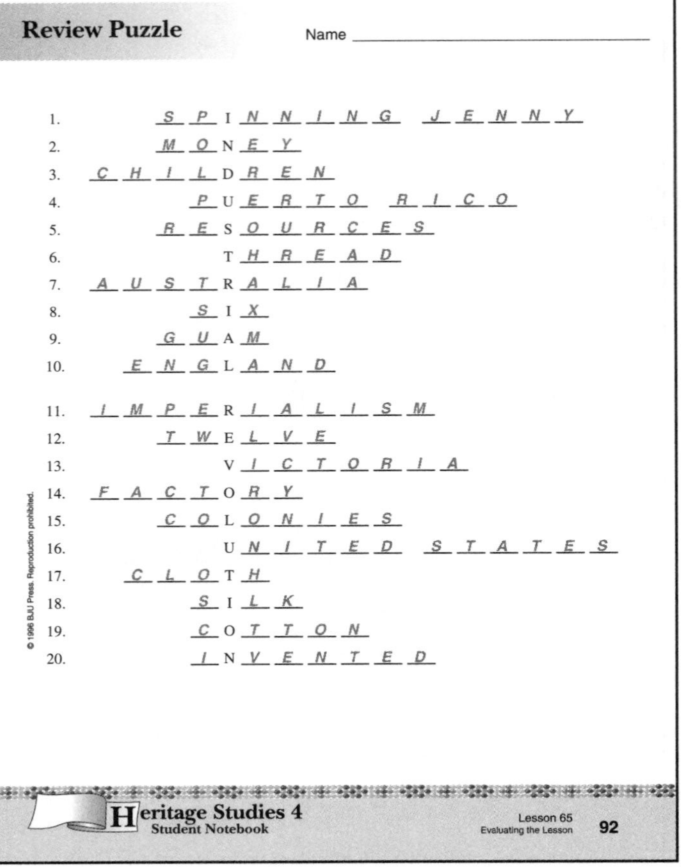

Review Puzzle

Name ______________________

1. SPINNING JENNY
2. MONEY
3. CHILDREN
4. PUERTO RICO
5. RESOURCES
6. THREAD
7. AUSTRALIA
8. SIX
9. GUAM
10. ENGLAND
11. IMPERIALISM
12. TWELVE
13. VICTORIA
14. FACTORY
15. COLONIES
16. UNITED STATES
17. CLOTH
18. SILK
19. COTTON
20. INVENTED

Evaluating the Lesson

Notebook Activity pages 91-92

- Read the instructions on Notebook page 91.
- Write the words to complete the acrostic puzzle on Notebook page 92.

You may find it beneficial to work this page with your child. Some of the answers are found only in the Teaching information. We do not recommend using this page for a grade.

Going Beyond

Enrichment

Provide your child with drawing paper and crayons. Copy and cut apart the "Invention/Modification" cards from Appendix, page A87. Place the cards in a box. Encourage your child to choose one of the cards and to draw a picture and write a description of an invention or modification to an existing product that would solve the problem mentioned on the card. Allow him to construct a model of the invention if possible.

Additional Teacher Information

At its height in the 1920s, the British Empire encompassed one-fourth of the world's people and about one-fourth of the world's land.

12 LESSONS 66-70

By the People

This chapter highlights the workings of the American democracy. Your child will learn that the heartbeat of the United States government is the people—the citizens who contribute to their nation by obeying laws, voting, and paying taxes. The chapter focuses on the Constitution, which was carefully constructed to protect the citizens by creating a system of checks and balances among the executive, legislative, and judicial branches. Your child will also review the Bill of Rights, which guarantees additional freedoms to the people. Through this study of the United States democracy, he will gain a greater appreciation for the freedoms he exercises on a daily basis as well as a determination to become a worthy citizen, preserving the American way.

Materials

The following materials must be obtained or prepared before the presentation of the lesson. These items are labeled with an asterisk (*) in the lesson and in the Materials List in the Supplement. For further information see the individual lesson.

- Two shoe boxes or ballot boxes (optional) (Lesson 66)
- Appendix, page A88 (optional) (Lesson 66)
- Appendix, page A90 (Lesson 67)
- Several items from the store that still have the price tags (Lesson 69)
- Appendix, pages A92-A93 (Lesson 69)

Since this chapter introduces the concepts of voting and making laws, a number of the activities will work better with more than one child. Perhaps other siblings of similar age can join you in the discussions, or other home schooled children can participate in this chapter. These group activities will enhance your child's understanding of the concepts being taught. If he is unable to participate in group activities, he will still be able to learn many of the concepts.

LESSON 66
By the People

Text, pages 250-53, 269-70
Notebook, page 93

Preview

Main Ideas

- All societies have some kind of government.
- Governments make laws, enforce laws, and provide a system of justice.

Objectives

- Use terms from the lesson to complete statements
- Demonstrate the principle of majority rule in a voting activity

Materials

- Two shoe boxes or ballot boxes (optional)*
- Appendix, page A88: figures of the donkey and the elephant (optional)*

Notes

If you are teaching this chapter in a group situation, assign the children to two teams, the Republicans and the Democrats. Prepare two ballot boxes or shoe boxes. You may use the figures of the donkey and the elephant found on Appendix page A88 to place on each box. Assign each child a number that he will use in all the lessons. After each child has completed each Notebook page, he will write his number on the ballot (Notebook page), fold his completed page lengthwise like a ballot, and then drop the ballot into his team's box as indicated in each lesson. At the end of this chapter, grade the Notebook pages, giving points for correct answers. The team, or party, with more points wins the "election."

Day 1

Lesson

Introducing the Lesson

Voting Activity

> The following activity is more appropriate as a group activity.

- ➤ *Give two options to vote on, such as going out to play or playing a special game inside.*
- ➤ Vote for the activity you prefer by writing your choice on a piece of paper.

A modern farm, in a long American tradition

The United States of America has been a country for more than two hundred years. During that time it grew from a few tiny colonies huddled beside the Atlantic Ocean to fifty states spanning the continent of North America. Farms and factories filled the land. Millions of immigrants came to find work and a new home. But the United States was not the only country where land and work and homes could be found. What made the United States seem better than other countries? Of all the new homes people could have chosen, why choose America?

One important thing that made this country the best choice for so many was the kind of government it had. Our *Founding Fathers*, the early leaders of the United States, did not like the old governments in England and other European countries. So they made a different kind of government, unlike any other, for the new country. But what is a government?

A policeman helps enforce the laws.

A *government* is a system of rules and authority. Every group of people has some kind of government. Of course, countries have governments. So do states, cities, towns, and even businesses and schools. Each group has rules it must follow. Each group has leaders with the *authority*, or power, to help it follow the rules.

250

- ➤ Count the number of votes for each activity. The activity that receives the most votes wins.

Voting is an important part of the political processes in a democracy. We will be learning more about democracy in this chapter.

Teaching the Lesson

Text Discussion, page 250

- ➤ **Read page 250 to find what the word *government* means.** *(a system of rules and authority)*
- ➤ **Why do you think America has grown so much since Colonial days?**
- ➤ **What was one important factor, other than land and resources, that drew people to America in the early days?** *(the government)*
- ➤ **Read aloud the explanation of who the *Founding Fathers* were.** *(the early leaders of the United States)*
- ➤ **Why did the Founding Fathers create a new type of government?** *(They did not like the old governments in their homelands.)*
- ➤ Look at the presidential figures on the TimeLine Snapshots.
- ➤ Find the figures of Washington, Adams, Jefferson, and Madison. These men were influential Founding Fathers.

Think about your school. Can you name some of the rules of your school? Who helped to make those rules? Probably the principal and teachers made many of them. What would happen in your school if your principal did not make rules? It is a good thing he does. You obey the rules at school because you accept his authority.

Your town has rules too. There are rules about how you should cross the street, where you can ride your bike, and what you should do when you see something you want in a store. Who made those rules? The leaders of your town's government did. Can you guess who made the rules for the United States?

"Submit yourselves to every ordinance of man for the Lord's sake: whether it be to the king, as supreme; Or unto governors, as unto them that are sent by him for the punishment of evildoers, and for the praise of them that do well."
I Peter 2:13-14

Students obeying the rules at school

Rules help to make our schools, towns, and country a safe and orderly place if everyone obeys them. What makes a person obey all the rules? Perhaps you obey rules because you know you will be punished if you do not. That is enough reason for some. But Christians have another reason for obeying rules. God's Word tells us that we must obey the rules made by people in authority.

251

It might seem that all governments are the same. All governments have rules, or *laws*. And they all have people with authority to make and carry out the rules, but not all governments make and enforce laws the same way. Do you know how the government of the United States is different from other governments?

A Democratic Government

The government of the United States is a type of democracy. *Democracy* comes from two Greek words. The first, *demos*, means "the people." *Kratos* means "authority or government." What can you say about a democracy, then? It is a government by the people.

In a democracy, the people work together to make important decisions. Together they choose their leaders. Together they make the laws for their government. Not everyone needs to agree on a law or a leader. But more than half the people must. When more than half the people make a decision, all the people accept it. We call this process the principle of *majority rule*.

252

For additional information about these presidents, refer your child to pages 269-70.

- ➤ **What are the two main characteristics of government that states, cities, businesses, and even schools have?** *(rules and leaders)*
- ➤ **Do you think these places could exist without some form of government?**
- ➤ Explain what the word ***authority*** means. *(power to help others follow the rules)*
- ➤ Name some people who have authority over you. *(parents, teachers, pastors)*
- ➤ **Why should you respect and obey these people?**

The Bible says Christians are to obey those who have authority over them. (BAT: 2a Authority)

Text Discussion, page 251

- ➤ **Read page 251 to find out why people obey rules.** *(They obey to avoid punishment, to protect themselves, to do what is right, or to obey God's commandment to submit to authority.)*
- ➤ Tell some rules that we have made for you.
- ➤ **Why do you obey these rules?**

Remind your child that love should also be a motivation for us to obey. If we love our parents, we will want to obey them to show that love. That is the same way with God—if we love Him, we will want to obey Him. (BAT: 5a Love)

- ➤ **Read aloud I Peter 2:13-14 from page 251.**
- ➤ **What does "every ordinance of man" mean?** *(laws or rules)*
- ➤ **How does this verse tell Christians to respond to these ordinances?** *(They are to submit to them.)*
- ➤ **Read aloud the phrase in the verse that tells Christians why they should obey these ordinances.** *("for the Lord's sake")* (BAT: 2a Authority)

Text Discussion, page 252

- ➤ **Read page 252 to find out what type of government the United States has.** *(a democracy)*
- ➤ **What does the word *democracy* mean?** *(government by the people)*
- ➤ Name some types of government leaders in the United States. *(mayors, governors, senators, representatives, or the president)*
- ➤ Name some types of government leaders in other countries. *(kings or queens, prime ministers, or dictators)*
- ➤ **How do you think a government by the people is different from a government with these other types of leaders?**

In a democracy, the people make decisions and choose their leaders to govern. In other types of governments, the leaders are appointed or rule because they are born into a royal family. Some leaders, such as dictators, govern because they have more power and military strength than other leaders.

Although kings and queens are considered rulers, many of the modern monarchs are mere figureheads. Instead, the real governing is done by parliaments, cabinets, or even prime ministers.

Word Study

➤ A democracy involves people working together as one unified group. **How do you think all the citizens of the United States come to agreement in selecting leaders and in making laws?**

It would be impossible for all citizens to agree on the same laws and leaders.

➤ *Write the word* major.
➤ **What does *major* mean?** *(most, main, chief)*
➤ *Write the word* majority *next to the word* major.
➤ **What does the word *majority* mean?** *(the most)*
➤ **How does your textbook explain majority rule?** *(when more than half the people make a decision and all the people accept it)*

Even on the playground, decisions are often made based on the principle of majority rule. The majority-rule principle usually applies when there are only two candidates or choices.

➤ *Write the word* plural. **What does this word mean?** *(more than one)*
➤ *Write the word* plurality *next to its root word.*
➤ **What do you think *plurality* means?**

When there are three or more candidates, the principle of plurality applies. Plurality occurs when one candidate receives more votes than the others yet not always the majority of the votes.

➤ **What things are important when working together as one group?** *(Possible answers include discussing, not arguing, and allowing each person to ask questions and offer opinions.)*

Working together involves communicating clearly and also being united. (BATs: 3a Self-concept, 5d Communication)

Exercising the freedom of speech

In America, all people have the same rights.

The *minority,* or smaller group, must follow the laws and leaders chosen by the majority. What would happen if they did not? But the people need to be careful about the laws they make. Because everyone will have to obey the laws, the people cannot make laws that might be unfair to a few.

Equality is another important principle of democracy. All people are equal in a democracy. That does not mean that they have equal wealth, or education, or physical strength. We know that God created each person special and different. Instead it means that the government thinks of everyone as the same. It does not give special protection or power to a person because he is rich and famous, or poor and unknown, or somewhere in between.

One last principle makes a democracy special: freedom. A democratic government gives the people freedom to do many things other kinds of government do not. They have the freedom to worship and serve God as they believe they should. They are free to make their own decisions. And they are free to choose their own laws and leaders.

253

Text Discussion, page 253

➤ *Write the word* minor.
➤ **What does this word mean?** *(smaller or lesser)*
➤ *Write the word* minority *next to its root.*
➤ **Read page 253 to find the text definition of *minority.*** *(smaller group)*
➤ **Why do you think it is important that the minority obeys the laws and the leaders that are chosen by the majority?**

Everyone must obey the laws if society is to function properly. Even if we do not agree with some rules or laws, we still need to obey them. (BAT: 2a Authority)

➤ *Write the word* equal.
➤ **What does *equal* mean?** *(having the same rights)*
➤ *Write the word* equality *next to its root word.*
➤ **What does the word *equality* mean?** *(It means being equal or the same.)*
➤ **How can people in a democracy be equal when each person is unique?** *(The government thinks of everyone as the same and treats everyone equally.)*

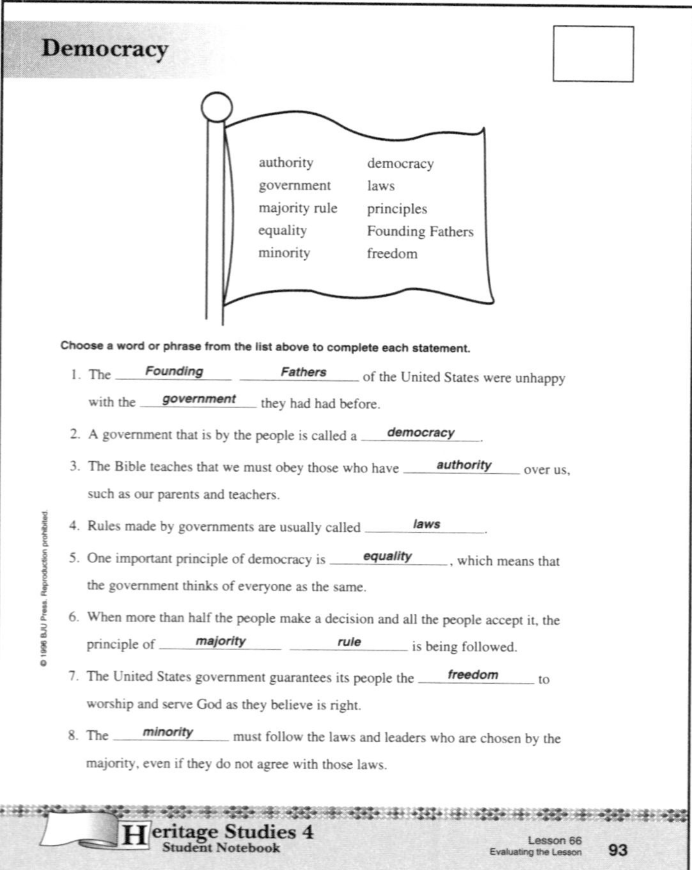

Democracy

authority	democracy
government	laws
majority rule	principles
equality	Founding Fathers
minority	freedom

Choose a word or phrase from the list above to complete each statement.

1. The *Founding* *Fathers* of the United States were unhappy with the *government* they had had before.
2. A government that is by the people is called a *democracy*.
3. The Bible teaches that we must obey those who have *authority* over us, such as our parents and teachers.
4. Rules made by governments are usually called *laws*.
5. One important principle of democracy is *equality*, which means that the government thinks of everyone as the same.
6. When more than half the people make a decision and all the people accept it, the principle of *majority* *rule* is being followed.
7. The United States government guarantees its people the *freedom* to worship and serve God as they believe is right.
8. The *minority* must follow the laws and leaders who are chosen by the majority, even if they do not agree with those laws.

Heritage Studies 4 Student Notebook   Lesson 66 Evaluating the Lesson   93

America is a nation made up of many different people, each person contributing different things to its culture. Although Americans are each different, they all have equal opportunities and rights offered to them by the government and its laws. (BAT: 3a Self-concept)

➤ Name another principle besides equality that makes a democracy special. *(freedom)*

➤ **What types of freedoms do Americans have?** *(Possible answers include freedom of speech, freedom of religion, and the freedom to live as they want.)*

Americans should be thankful for the freedoms they have and should be willing to do whatever possible to preserve these freedoms. (BAT: 7c Praise)

Evaluating the Lesson

Notebook Activity, page 93

➤ Read the instructions for Notebook page 93.

➤ Complete the page.

If you are following the group procedure for this chapter, instruct each child to put his number in the box at the top of the Notebook page, fold it as a ballot, and put it into his party's ballot box. See the Notes section in this lesson.

Going Beyond

Enrichment

Give your child a copy of the "We the People" page (Appendix, page A89). Instruct him to write a paragraph, telling what freedom means to him or allows him to do.

Additional Teacher Information

There are two basic systems of government—unitary and federal. In the unitary system, the central government retains most of the power, creating the state and local governments. Countries with the unitary system of government include France, Italy, and the United Kingdom.

In the federal system of government, several states join to make a union or nation. Power is in the hands of not only a central government but also state and local governments. The final authority rests in the hands of the people. Countries with the federal system of government include Argentina, Australia, Austria, Brazil, Burma, Canada, India, Mexico, Switzerland, and the United States.

LESSON 67
Democracy Comes to America

Text, pages 254-57, 316-17
Notebook, page 94

Preview

Main Ideas

- Democracy has been in existence for centuries.
- There are two types of democracy: direct democracy and indirect democracy.
- The beliefs for which the American colonists fought are the basis for the freedoms protected by the Constitution.

Objectives

- Distinguish between a direct democracy and an indirect democracy
- Create some of the main points of a new constitution

Materials

- Appendix, page A90: Our Constitution activity page*
- The figure of the signing of the Constitution (1787) from the TimeLine Snapshots

Day 1

Lesson

Introducing the Lesson

Constitution Activity

If you are teaching this chapter to several children, divide the children into groups. Let each group represent a committee of leaders deciding on a constitution for their new nation. Give each group a copy of the Our Constitution page. Each group will need to choose a secretary to complete the form. Each group will vote on the information.

➤ *If you are teaching one child, give him the Our Constitution page.*

➤ Let's work together to fill out the form, pretending we are creating a new nation.

ECHOES IN HISTORY

The First Democracy

Democracy is not a new idea. Do you remember where the word *democracy* comes from? It comes from two Greek words; the Greeks were the first people to have a democratic government.

The people of Greece were artists, writers, and thinkers. People who lived in the city of Athens were especially talented in these ways. Athenians studied history, math, science, and medicine. They built some of the most beautiful buildings in the world. Others wrote stories and poems that are still read today. Athenians set up a great culture about five hundred years before Christ was born.

The Greeks voted by dropping bronze disks into a ballot box.

Greek democracy began in the city of Athens. Every free man of that city helped to make laws and choose leaders. The men met every ten days or so to vote on new laws. Do you think slaves could take part in this democracy? They could not, and neither could women. But more people had a voice in Athens's democracy than in any other government of the time.

The democracy in Athens did not last. Other countries took over the Greek cities. They made the Greek people obey their laws and follow their kings. But the words and ideas of the Greek people "echoed" around the world and across more than two thousand years. They were an example of a government in which the power was in the hands of the people.

254

As you work with your child, you may want to have an opinion on some questions different from your child's. You can then work on compromises. If another sibling is able to help, you can even vote on some decisions.

Day 2

Teaching the Lesson

Text Discussion, pages 254 and 316-17

➤ **Read page 254 to find out where Greek democracy began.** *(Athens)*

➤ Find Greece on the map on pages 316-17. You will be able to see it better in the inset of the map.

➤ **What does the Greek word *demos* mean?** *("the people") If your child has difficulty with the meaning, let him look back at page 252.*

➤ **What does the Greek work *kratos* mean?** *("authority or government")*

➤ Name some of the things that the Athenians studied and accomplished. *(They studied history, math, science, and medicine; wrote poems and stories; and built great buildings.)*

➤ **In what way was the Greek form of government a democracy?** *(Men voted on laws and leaders.)*

➤ **Do you think that the Greek democracy was fair?**

Two Kinds of Democracy

Democracy—government by the people—can take one of two forms. It can be a *pure*, or *direct*, *democracy*. In a pure democracy, all the citizens, or members, meet together to decide on their laws. The government in the Greek city of Athens was a pure democracy. The town meetings held in some places in New England even today could be called pure democracy. Pure democracy works best when the people are few and they live close together. What problems would a large number of people have in a pure democracy?

Every citizen should vote.

Campaign rally for George Bush

Large groups of people can also have a democratic government. It is a democracy by the people's *representatives*. The citizens in this kind of democracy choose people to make the laws for them. The representatives listen to the citizens who have chosen them, and they make laws the citizens agree with. This kind of democracy is called a *representative*, or *indirect*, *democracy*. Can you guess what kind of democracy the United States has?

255

The American Democracy

On May 25, 1787, men from thirteen states met in the State House in Philadelphia. Four years before, the states had won a war against England. With that victory, they won the right to make their own laws. But now the states were fighting among themselves; they could not agree on what laws to follow. The states sent their best leaders to Philadelphia to work on the problem.

The problem was not easy to solve. The new country had not made one good government. Instead, each state had its own government. Each state acted like a separate country. The states needed a government that would help them to work together, but the men did not want a government like the one in England.

Who made the laws in England and in most other countries in Europe? A king made the laws. The people could not choose their king. All kings were born into a king's family. Once a man became king, he was king until he died. Then his son became the king. Why do you think the men from the states did not want this kind of leader?

The men wanted the chance to choose their own leaders. They wanted the people to have a say about their laws. And they wanted to be able to pick new leaders if they did not agree with the laws their leaders made.

256

In that time, neither slaves nor women could vote. For many years in the United States, only certain people were allowed to vote. Some people were not allowed to vote because of their race or gender.

> Although people have been treated unfairly, God sees all people as equal, and He loves all people equally. (BAT: 5a Love; Bible Promises: H. God as Father, I. God as Master)

- ➤ **What eventually happened to the democracy that was in many Greek cities?** *(Other countries eventually took over and made the Greeks obey their laws and follow their kings.)*
- ➤ **What do you think the statement "the ideas of the Greek people 'echoed' around the world and across more than two thousand years" means?**

The Greek idea of democracy has influenced many countries and people over the years.

Text Discussion, page 255

- ➤ **Read page 255 to find out what type of democratic government large groups of people can have.** *(a **representative democracy**)*
- ➤ Explain the difference between a ***direct democracy*** and an ***indirect democracy.*** *(Each person votes on every law in a direct democracy. In an indirect democracy, representatives are chosen to vote for a large group of people.)*
- ➤ **Which type of democracy did Athens have?** *(direct democracy)*
- ➤ **Could the United States have a direct democracy?** *(no)*
- ➤ Explain why a direct democracy would not work in America. *(because the nation is too large and there are too many people for everyone to meet in one place to vote)*
- ➤ **Why must an indirect democracy choose representatives?** *(There are too many people to gather together in one location.)*
- ➤ Give another name for an indirect democracy. *(a representative democracy)*
- ➤ Explain what a ***representative*** is. *(a person who acts for another)*

In a representative democracy, representatives are chosen by the people to make laws and decisions for them. Representatives are needed in countries that are large like the United States.

Day 3

Text Discussion, page 256

- ➤ **Read page 256 to find out what type of government England and other countries had that made the Founding Fathers want a different government.** *(government by king or queen, with the*

It took many months, but the men finally solved the states' problem. Together they made a plan for a strong national government. The plan allowed the national government to make laws that all the states must follow. But the plan also let each state's government make some of its own laws. Do you think this was a good idea? Now the democratic thing to do was to ask the citizens what they thought.

The men took their plan back to the people. The citizens in each state read and talked about the plan. Some thought that the national government needed more authority. Others thought the states gave too much authority away. Finally the time came to vote on the plan.

The citizens of each state decided how they felt about the plan. If the majority of the states liked the plan, it would become the law. What do you think happened? Every state accepted the plan. It was now the most important law of the new country, the United States.

Signing the Constitution
by Howard Chandler Christy

The Constitution

The plan the men wrote in Philadelphia is known as *the Constitution.* The Constitution does more than set the rules for the government of America. It protects the rights of all the citizens. Its laws help to guard freedom.

257

Pure or Representative?

Complete the statements.

1. A pure democracy may also be called a(n) ___*direct*___ democracy.
2. Another name for a representative democracy is a(n) ___*indirect*___ democracy.

Write a *P* in the blank if the statement describes a pure democracy, *R* if it describes a representative democracy, or *N* if neither applies.

___*P*___ 3. The type of government the Greek city of Athens had.
___*N*___ 4. A king rules in this type of government.
___*P*___ 5. Some town meetings are an example of this type of democracy.
___*R*___ 6. The citizens of this type of government choose people to make laws for them.
___*N*___ 7. The citizens of this type of government combine both a direct and an indirect democracy.
___*P*___ 8. This type of democracy works best when people are few and live close together.
___*R*___ 9. The United States has this kind of government.
___*R*___ 10. When there is a large number of people, this kind of democracy works the best.

Heritage Studies 4
Student Notebook
Lesson 67
Evaluating the Lesson
94

people not having much involvement with important decisions)

- **Who made the laws long ago in England and in most other European countries?** *(the king)*
- **How do kings usually become leaders?** *(They are born into royal families.)*
- **What possible problems do you think may arise from a leader's being chosen because of his family?** He may not be qualified or ready to lead a country.
- **Why did the Founding Fathers not want this type of leader?** *(They wanted people to participate more in the governing of their country.)*

Text Discussion, page 257

- **Read page 257 to find out what plan the Founding Fathers decided upon.** *(the Constitution)*
- **How did the Constitution divide power between the states and the central government?** *(The Constitution created a strong national government, yet it allowed each state to make some of its own laws.)*
- **What do you think the United States would be like today without the Constitution?**

Americans probably would not have the freedom to do as they choose to do. We should be thankful for the freedoms we enjoy.

Christians enjoy an even greater freedom—the freedom from the penalty of sin. (Bible Promises: A. Liberty from Sin, B. Guiltless by the Blood)

TimeLine Snapshots Activity

- Add the figure of the signing of the Constitution to the TimeLine at the year 1787.

Remember that the meeting in Philadelphia to write the constitution was called the Constitutional Convention.

- **Why did the people feel that the convention in Philadelphia was needed?** *(The states were fighting among themselves and could not agree on what laws to follow.)*
- **Why did the states need one government?** *(Each state was acting on its own. The states were not unified because there was not one government to settle disputes.)*

Evaluating the Lesson

Notebook Activity, page 94

➤ Read the directions on Notebook page 94.
➤ Complete the page.

Follow the procedure given in Lesson 66 for forming a ballot with the Notebook page if you are teaching a group of children.

Going Beyond

Enrichment

Give your child a piece of colored construction paper, scissors, glue, and a copy of the Preamble page (Appendix, page A91). Tell him to cut out his copy of the Preamble, glue it on colored paper, and decorate it. Tell him to roll his paper from both ends as a scroll.

Additional Teacher Information

The Constitutional Convention was held in Independence Hall in Philadelphia, Pennsylvania, in 1787. For sixteen weeks, the Founding Fathers deliberated over the document that was to have a monumental impact on the new nation called the United States of America. This group of fifty-five men included such greats as George Washington, Benjamin Franklin, Thomas Jefferson, and Alexander Hamilton. The average age of the founders was forty-three. Most of them were fairly wealthy, with occupations ranging from lawyer to planter and merchant. The workings of politics were not a new concept to the fifty-five, for many of them had fought in the American Revolution, and six were signers of the Declaration of Independence. John Adams described the Constitutional Convention as "the greatest single effort of national deliberation that the world has ever seen."

Lesson 68
Checks and Balances

Text, pages 257-61
Notebook, pages 95-96

Preview

Main Ideas

- In the United States the interests of individuals, cities, states, and the nation are protected by the government.
- The United States government rests on the Constitution.
- The United States government is divided into legislative, executive, and judicial branches.

Objectives

- Read a flow chart
- Identify basic functions of the legislative, executive, and judicial branches of the government

Materials

- Maps and More 36, page M16

Notes

You will need an area with chairs set up in a semicircle like a courtroom or a Congressional decision chamber.

Day 1

Lesson

Introducing the Lesson

The purpose of the following activity is to see the three branches of the government at work. It is best used with a group. If several children are not available, you may omit this activity.

Rule-Making Activity

➤ *Place the children into three groups: a Rule-Writing group, a Rule-Checking group, and a Rule-Interpreting group.*
➤ The Writing group may come to the decision chamber.
➤ Make a rule about something in the home, such as chores or free time. (*NOTE:* If the children in your group have another common connection, such as the

same Sunday school class or same home school association, adjust the rule to fit your situation.)

- *When the rule is written, call the Checking group to the decision chamber to discuss and approve it.*
- *Call the Interpreting group to the decision chamber to determine whether the new rule is compatible with the rest of the rules already established for the group.*
- *Allow the other two groups to ask the Interpreting group questions such as "Can the rule apply every day or just on certain days?" or "Who must obey the rule?" Tell the Interpreting group to make decisions about the rule based on these questions.*

Passing laws involves a similar process, moving through three branches of government before becoming the law of the land.

Day 2

Teaching the Lesson

Text Discussion, pages 257-58

- **Reread the last paragraph on page 257 to find the purpose of the Constitution.** *(to protect the rights of all citizens and to guard their freedoms)*
- **How can this one document protect people?** *(It is the law and must be obeyed.)* (BAT: 2a Authority)
- **Read page 258 to find out what the two parts of Congress are.** *(the Senate and the House of Representatives)*
- **Why were three branches of government created?** *(so that no one person or group of people could get power over the whole country)*
- **Is this system of checks and balances good or bad?** *(good)*
- Explain what the legislative branch does. *(writes the laws)*
- **What are the two parts of the legislative branch?** *(the House of Representatives and the Senate)*
- **How long does a senator serve in office?** *(six years)*
- **How many senators are there in all?** *(one hundred)*
- **How often are members of the House of Representatives elected?** *(every two years)*

The number varies for each state because the representatives are chosen according to the population of the state.

- **How many members are there in the House of Representatives?** *(435)*

Flow Chart Activity, Maps and More 36

- Look at Maps and More 36.

This is a diagram of the Great Compromise of 1787, which established two houses in the legislative branch of the government. The compromise satisfied both the large states and the small states.

The Constitution says that the government should be divided into three parts, or *branches*. Each branch has its own job to do. And each branch checks up on the other branches to be sure they are doing their jobs right. With the authority of the government divided in this way, no one person or group of people can get power over the whole country.

The *legislative* branch writes the laws. The United States Congress makes up this branch. The legislative branch is the only one divided again into two smaller parts. Do you know the names of the two parts?

The first part is made up of 435 people. The citizens of the United States choose these people every two years. They are the citizens' representatives, and the whole group is called the *House of Representatives*. The map below shows how many representatives each state sends to Congress.

The second part of Congress is the *Senate*. The men and women of the Senate are also the citizens' representatives, but we call them senators. Senators serve their states for six years. The citizens of each state choose two senators. How many senators are there all together?

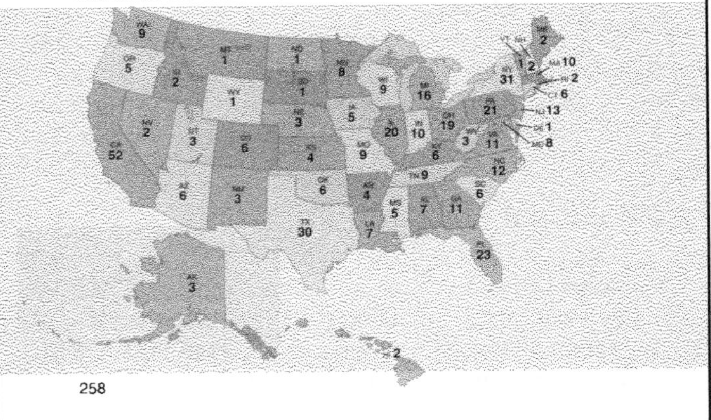

- Look at the figures on the Senate side of the diagram. **Would New Jersey or Virginia have more votes in that part of Congress?** *(Both states would have two votes.)*
- Look at the figures on the House of Representatives side of the diagram. **How many more votes would Virginia have than New Jersey in that part of Congress?** *(five more)*
- The states did not think they were getting the same number of representatives. **Which part of the Great Compromise made the small states happy?** *(the number of votes in the Senate)*
- **Which part made the large states happy?** *(the number of votes in the House of Representatives)*
- **What job do the Senate and the House have in government?** *(They make the laws.)*

Map Activity, page 258

- Look at the map on page 258.
- Find out how many representatives are in our state.
- Name the states that have thirty or more representatives. *(California, Texas, and New York)*
- Name the states that have only one representative. *(Alaska, Montana, Wyoming, North and South Dakota, Delaware, and Vermont)*

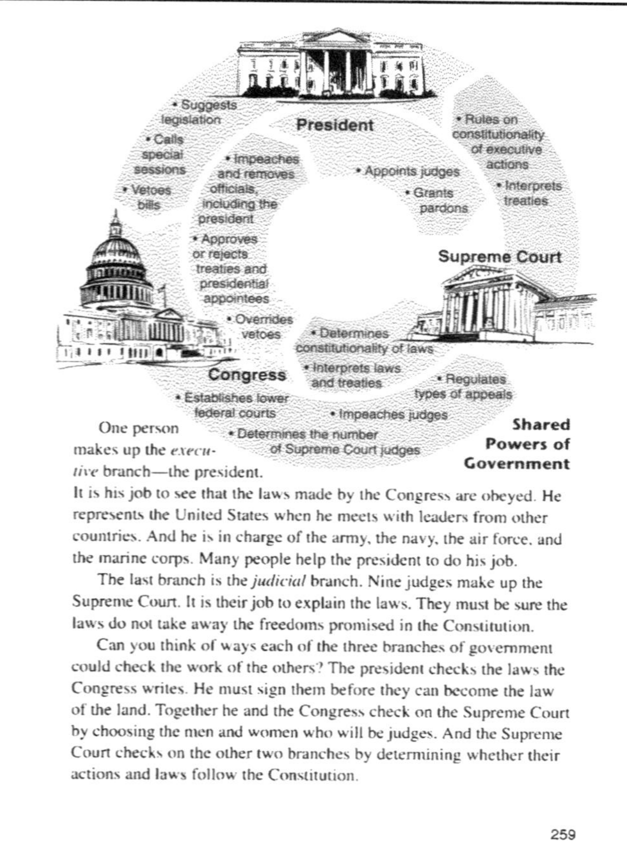

One person makes up the *executive* branch—the president. It is his job to see that the laws made by the Congress are obeyed. He represents the United States when he meets with leaders from other countries. And he is in charge of the army, the navy, the air force, and the marine corps. Many people help the president to do his job.

The last branch is the *judicial* branch. Nine judges make up the Supreme Court. It is their job to explain the laws. They must be sure the laws do not take away the freedoms promised in the Constitution.

Can you think of ways each of the three branches of government could check the work of the others? The president checks the laws the Congress writes. He must sign them before they can become the law of the land. Together he and the Congress check on the Supreme Court by choosing the men and women who will be judges. And the Supreme Court checks on the other two branches by determining whether their actions and laws follow the Constitution.

259

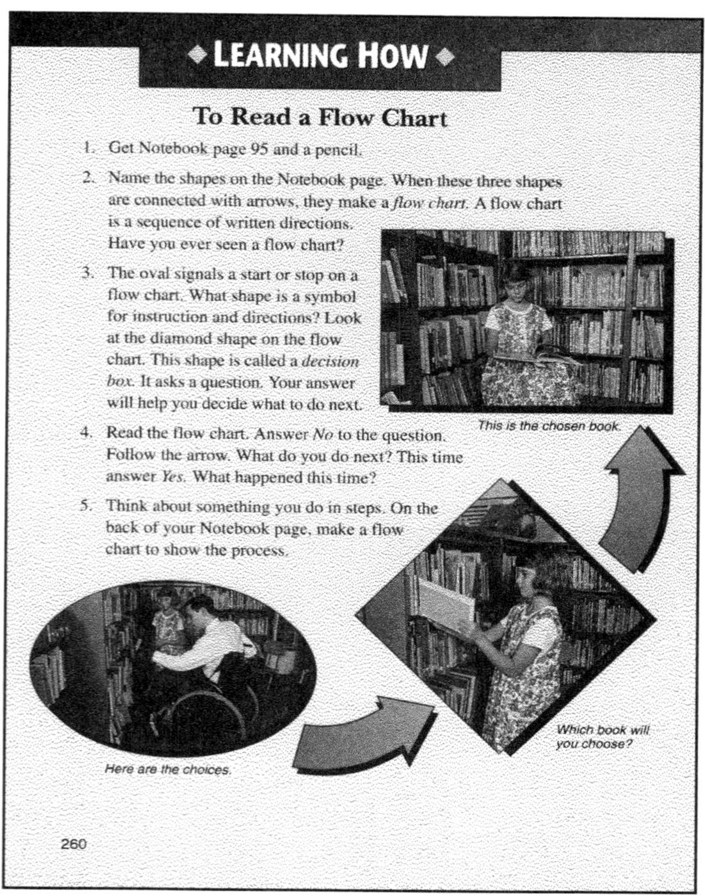

◆ LEARNING HOW ◆

To Read a Flow Chart

1. Get Notebook page 95 and a pencil.
2. Name the shapes on the Notebook page. When these three shapes are connected with arrows, they make a *flow chart*. A flow chart is a sequence of written directions. Have you ever seen a flow chart?
3. The oval signals a start or stop on a flow chart. What shape is a symbol for instruction and directions? Look at the diamond shape on the flow chart. This shape is called a *decision box*. It asks a question. Your answer will help you decide what to do next.
4. Read the flow chart. Answer *No* to the question. Follow the arrow. What do you do next? This time answer *Yes*. What happened this time?
5. Think about something you do in steps. On the back of your Notebook page, make a flow chart to show the process.

This is the chosen book.

Which book will you choose?

Here are the choices.

260

Text Discussion, page 259

➤ **Read page 259 to find out who the head of the executive branch is.** *(the president)*

➤ **What are some of the duties the president has as the leader of the executive branch?** *(He enforces laws made by Congress, meets with leaders from other countries, and leads the armed forces.)*

➤ **Who is in the judicial branch of the government?** *(nine justices of the Supreme Court)*

➤ Describe the function of the judicial branch. *(explain the laws, ensure that the laws do not take away any of the freedoms promised in the Constitution)*

Chart-Reading Activity, page 259

➤ **Read the last paragraph on page 259 again.**

➤ Look at the chart on page 259.

➤ **How does the president keep a check on Congress?** *(He must sign a law before it becomes the law of the land.)*

➤ **How do the president and Congress check the Supreme Court?** *(They choose the judges who will serve in the Supreme Court.)*

➤ Explain how the Supreme Court can check on the other two branches. *(by determining whether their actions and laws follow the Constitution)*

Learning How Activity, text page 260 and Notebook page 95

➤ **Read and follow Steps 1 and 2 on page 260.**

➤ **What is a *flow chart*?** *(a sequence of written directions)*

➤ **Read Step 3 on page 260.**

➤ Look at the flow chart on Notebook page 95.

➤ Explain the significance of each shape. *(The oval represents a start or stop. The rectangle represents instructions. The diamond represents a question that forces a decision.)*

➤ **Read Step 4.**

➤ Let's read the flow chart and answer the questions at the bottom of the Notebook page.

➤ **Read and follow Step 5.**

Follow the procedure for forming a ballot if you are teaching a group of children.

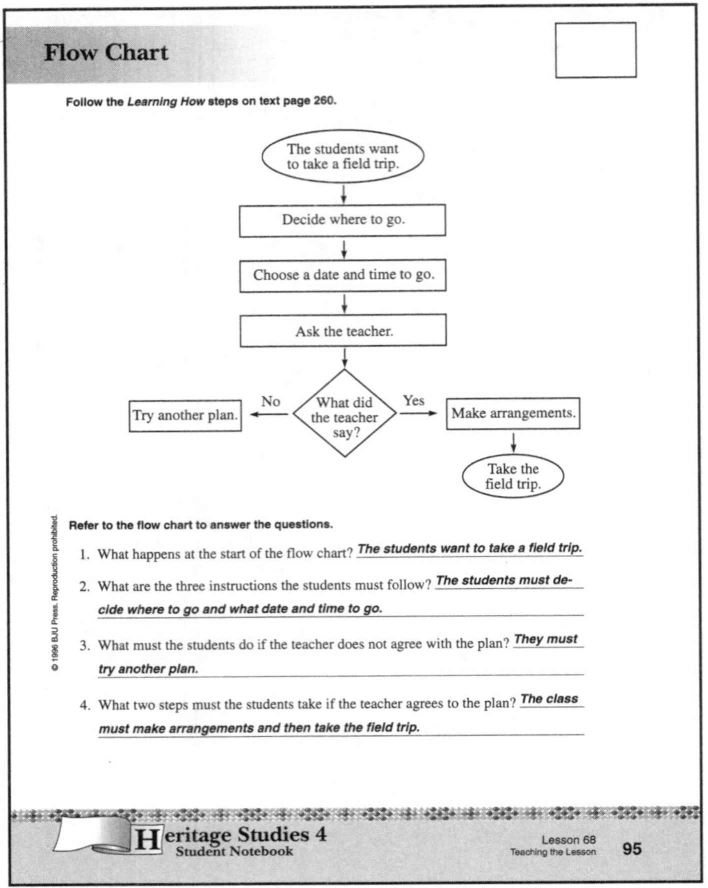
Flow Chart

Follow the *Learning How* steps on text page 260.

The students want to take a field trip. → Decide where to go. → Choose a date and time to go. → Ask the teacher. → What did the teacher say?

No → Try another plan.

Yes → Make arrangements. → Take the field trip.

Refer to the flow chart to answer the questions.

1. What happens at the start of the flow chart? ***The students want to take a field trip.***
2. What are the three instructions the students must follow? ***The students must decide where to go and what date and time to go.***
3. What must the students do if the teacher does not agree with the plan? ***They must try another plan.***
4. What two steps must the students take if the teacher agrees to the plan? ***The class must make arrangements and then take the field trip.***

Heritage Studies 4 Student Notebook — Lesson 68 Teaching the Lesson — 95

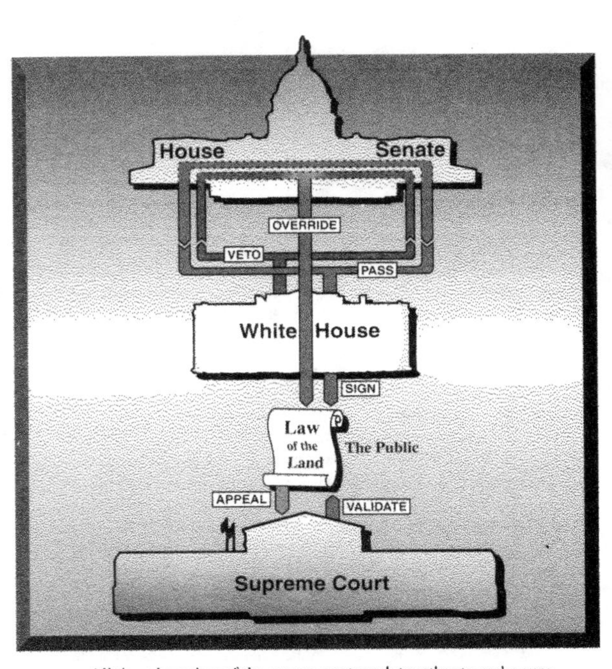

All three branches of the government work together to make sure the country's laws protect the citizens' freedom. A bill, an idea for a new law, must take several steps to become a law. Each branch has a part. Which branch do you think has the most important job?

261

Text Discussion, page 261

➤ **Read page 261 to find out what the word *bill* means in the government.** *(an idea for a new law)*

➤ **Do you think it is good or bad that a bill must go through so many branches and steps before it can be passed?**

It is sometimes considered a good system because bills must be carefully considered, and no one branch has all the power. It is sometimes considered a bad system because it can be a very long and difficult process to pass some bills.

➤ **Which branch do you think is the most important?**

Each branch of government has a part in deciding the laws of the land.

Evaluating the Lesson

Notebook Activity, page 96

➤ Read the instructions on Notebook page 96.

➤ Look at the three pictures on the right.

The top picture represents the legislative branch. The middle picture represents the executive branch, and the last picture, the judicial branch of the government.

➤ Complete the page. You may refer to the circle graph on page 259 of your textbook.

Follow the procedure for forming a ballot if you are teaching a group of children.

Going Beyond

Enrichment

Help your child write a letter to any one of the following leaders: a U.S. senator or representative, the governor of the state, or the president of the United States. His letter could ask a leader to pass into law a holiday that he has invented. Encourage him to tell what the holiday is about, why it should be celebrated, when it will take place, and who will be able to celebrate it.

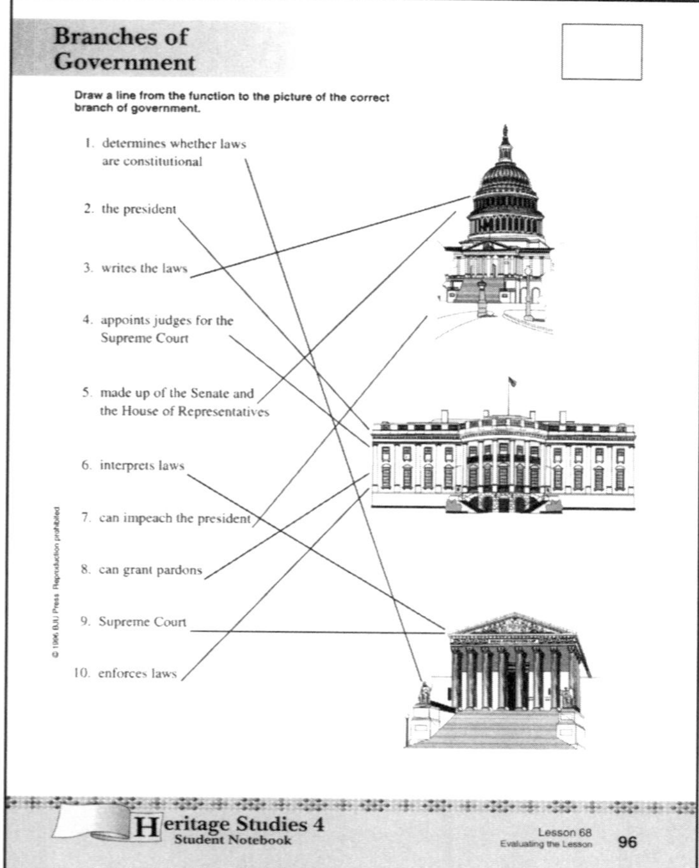

Branches of Government

Draw a line from the function to the picture of the correct branch of government.

1. determines whether laws are constitutional
2. the president
3. writes the laws
4. appoints judges for the Supreme Court
5. made up of the Senate and the House of Representatives
6. interprets laws
7. can impeach the president
8. can grant pardons
9. Supreme Court
10. enforces laws

© 1996 BJU Press. Reproduction prohibited.

Heritage Studies 4 Student Notebook — Lesson 68 Evaluating the Lesson — 96

LESSON 69
Citizenship

Text, pages 262-63
Notebook, page 97

Preview

Main Ideas

- Citizens have rights and responsibilities.
- People pay taxes to provide for parks, schools, libraries, and other services.

Objective

- Demonstrate an act of good citizenship

Materials

- Several items from the store that still have the price tags (e.g., a cake mix or a bag of rice)*

If you do not have any items with price tags, make price tags for the items you choose.

- The figure of the Bill of Rights (1791) from the TimeLine Snapshots
- Appendix, pages A91-A92: the Bill of Rights pages*
- A dictionary

Additional Teacher Information

The bicameral, or two-chamber, United States Congress makes up the legislative branch. This branch of government derives most of its power from its ability to control the government's finances.

To qualify for office as a U.S. representative, a person must be at least twenty-five years old, a United States citizen for at least seven years, and a resident of the state he wishes to represent. One running for a position in the Senate must be at least thirty years old, a United States citizen for at least nine years, and a resident of the state he wishes to represent.

The focal point of the executive branch is the president of the United States. A candidate running for the presidency must be at least thirty-five years old and have lived in the United States for at least fourteen years. The Constitution stipulates that the president must be a "natural-born" United States citizen. However, there has been some debate as to whether the qualification of being natural-born means only those born in the United States and its territories or whether it applies to those who are born to United States citizens, regardless of location.

The Supreme Court is the protector and interpreter of the Constitution. The Court's nine members include a chief justice and eight associate justices. The justices may remain in office for life—with a set salary. These stipulations were made to protect the justices from political and financial influences.

Day 1

Lesson

Introducing the Lesson

Pricing Activity

➤ *Show your child the items with the price tags.*

➤ **Does a person paying for these items in the store pay the exact amount on the tag or a little more?** *(a little more)*

➤ The government charges extra money on items that are bought. **Do you know what this extra money is called?** *(sales tax)*

Sales tax must be paid on certain items. There is a different rate for different states. Some states charge five cents or six cents or more per dollar. Sales tax is just one type of tax that citizens must pay.

The Bill of Rights

The Constitution solved the problem of making the new country. But more than that, it has kept the country working for more than two hundred years. The men who wrote the Constitution made sure that it could change as the country changed. The changes that have been made since the Constitution was first written are called *amendments.*

The first ten amendments are special. They were added to the Constitution soon after it was accepted by all the states. The first Congress wrote these amendments because the citizens asked for them. They wanted the Constitution to name the rights the government could not take away. These ten amendments are called the *Bill of Rights.*

The Bill of Rights was added to the Constitution in 1791. Since then, seventeen more amendments have been added to the Constitution. The Thirteenth Amendment ended slavery in all the states. What war was fought before this amendment was added? The Fifteenth Amendment gave all men the right to vote, no matter what their race or skin color. Where can you find a list of all the amendments?

262

A Citizen's Part

What law is this man obeying?

Writing good laws and protecting the freedoms of its citizens are the *responsibilities,* or duties, of a good government. Citizens expect their government to fulfill its duties. In return, good citizens should fulfill certain responsibilities. Can you think of some responsibilities of a good citizen?

The first responsibility of a citizen should not be difficult to guess. Citizens must obey the laws their government makes. No one can force a citizen to obey the laws. It is his choice. A good citizen obeys the law because it is the right thing to do. The laws of our states and country are written to protect us and all other citizens.

Most citizens do not enjoy their second responsibility. But a good citizen pays taxes, even when he wishes he did not have to. *Taxes* are money given to keep the government working. The money helps to pay for things the government does for its citizens. Taxes pay representatives for their work in the government. Tax money also pays for libraries, parks, and roads. Do you know other things the government uses taxes for?

Taxes help pay road builders.

263

You may want to show your child how to figure the final price, including sales tax, according to the rate charged in your state.

Teaching the Lesson

Text Discussion, page 262

- ➤ **Read page 262 to find out what was added to the Constitution in 1791.** *(the Bill of Rights)*
- ➤ Explain what an ***amendment*** is. *(a change in a law)*
- ➤ **What was the *Bill of Rights?*** *(a list of amendments)*
- ➤ *Give your child a copy of the Bill of Rights pages.*
- ➤ **Read aloud each amendment.**
- ➤ *Discuss with your child the meaning of each law.*
- ➤ **Why did the citizens want to add the first ten amendments to the Constitution?** *(They wanted to have rights that the government could not take away.)*
- ➤ **Why has the Constitution worked well for so many years?** *(The Founding Fathers made the Constitution a plan that could change with the country.)*

TimeLine Snapshots Activity

- ➤ Add the figure of the Bill of Rights to the TimeLine at the year 1791.
- ➤ **How much time passed between the writing of the Constitution and the adding of the Bill of Rights?** *(four years)*
- ➤ **How many amendments are there all together?** *(twenty-seven)*
- ➤ The Thirteenth Amendment ended slavery. **What war did it follow?** *(the American Civil War)*
- ➤ Explain what the Fifteenth Amendment did. *(It gave all men the right to vote regardless of their race or skin color.)*
- ➤ **Why do you think these amendments were created?**

Issues such as freedom and slavery were addressed during and after the American Civil War. The Thirteenth, Fourteenth, and Fifteenth Amendments were a result of these issues, creating new freedoms for those who had never had them before.

- ➤ **Where can you find a list of these three amendments and all the other amendments?** *(in the Constitution)*

Day 2

Text Discussion, page 263

- ➤ Explain what the word ***responsibility*** means. *(a duty or something that must be done)*
- ➤ **Read page 263 to find out what some of the government's responsibilities are.** *(to write good laws and protect the freedoms of its citizens)*
- ➤ **What is the first responsibility of a citizen?** *(to obey the laws made by the government)*

Citizenship

Follow your teacher's instructions.

My project was ______________________

____

______________________.

I did my project on ______________________.
(date)

I spent ____________ doing my project.
(amount of time)

Doing my project made me feel ______________________

____

______________________.

____
(my signature)

____
(parent's signature)

Every person has responsibilities to fulfill. Part of a Christian's testimony is meeting those obligations and duties. God rewards those who are faithful. (BATs: 2a Authority, 4a Sowing and reaping)

- ➤ **What is the second responsibility of citizens?** *(to pay taxes)*
- ➤ **Read aloud the definition of *taxes* from a dictionary.** *("money given to keep the government working")*
- ➤ **Have you been in a public library or park?**

These places are available because of tax money. Roads, highways, and police and fire protection are also made possible by taxes.

God wants Christians to obey the laws and to pay taxes. He also wants them to give back to Him cheerfully a portion of what they have. (BAT: 5b)

Evaluating the Lesson

Notebook Activity, page 97

Citizenship is more than merely living in a country. Citizenship involves helping other people as well as one's community or country.

- ➤ Choose a project which you could do that involves performing a helpful deed for another person or for the community.
- ➤ Look at Notebook page 97. After you have completed your citizenship project, you will fill out this form and draw a picture to illustrate what you did.

Some suggestions are cleaning for an elderly person or picking up trash along the road. You may choose to give your child or group as much as a week to complete the project. You will want to decide whether to include this in the ballot box.

Going Beyond

Enrichment

Give your child five 15"×2" strips of red crepe paper, five 15"×2" strips of white crepe paper, one 18"×8" piece of blue construction paper, one twelve-inch piece of yarn, and his copy of the Bill of Rights pages that were used in the Teaching the Lesson section.

Your child will need to cut out the rights listed on the reproducible page, gluing one strip on each piece of crepe paper so that the words face out. Then he should glue each strip of crepe paper to the blue construction paper, folding the blue paper into a cylinder as shown. Your child will write on a piece of white construction paper the word *RIGHTS*, gluing the white paper to the blue paper. After he has completed these steps, he can punch holes at the top of the cylinder and loop the yarn through them so that the windsock can be hung.

Additional Teacher Information

Taxes, though often viewed as an unpleasant responsibility of citizenship, are also a necessary duty. The three major kinds of taxes are those on property, income, and transactions. Property taxes are collected on property such as farms, houses, land, and factories. They are also called *direct taxes* because they are levied directly on the people. Income taxes must be paid on the salary an individual earns. This income can be money made from businesses and even from estates and trusts. The third type of tax is one that applies to transactions that include the sale of goods or privileges such as the right to participate in an activity. Taxes that must be paid for privileges, such as getting married or going hunting or fishing, are called *excise* taxes. Only Congress has the right to levy taxes.

LESSON 70
We the People

Text, pages 264-66
Notebook, page 98

Preview

Main Ideas

- Voting is a method of group decision making.
- Elizabeth Cady Stanton and Susan B. Anthony paved the way for the passage of the Nineteenth Amendment.
- The people have made democracy work in the United States.

Objective

- Identify true and false statements about democracy

Materials

- The figure of Elizabeth Cady Stanton and Susan B. Anthony (1869) from the TimeLine Snapshots
- The figure representing the Nineteenth Amendment (1919) from the TimeLine Snapshots

Lesson

Introducing the Lesson

Campaign Activity

Personalize the following activity by choosing a group that your child is a member of, such as a sports team, a gymnastics group, or a church group.

- ➤ Plan a commercial that promotes a candidate for the president of your group.
- ➤ Think about issues that are important to you, such as more planned get-togethers, less homework, or new sports equipment.
- ➤ Think of things the candidate could do for the group and his fellow members.
- ➤ Write a slogan about the candidate. The slogan can be a short statement such as "Vote for this candidate because he cares."
- ➤ Think of things that would please the rest of the group so that the members will choose their candidate.

Voters might use a ballot like this.

105 0408
This Ballot Stub shall be removed by Mgr. before Ballot is placed in the Ballot
Initials of Box Mgr.
To cast a write-in ballot, the name of candidate and the office must be filled in stub.
Candidate   Office
PLACE HOLES OVER POSTS
INSERT CARD   THIS SIDE UP

A good citizen does one more thing: he gets involved. The government will have problems that need to be solved. Spending more money on schools is one problem the government might face. How to help people without jobs is another. Can you think of more problems for the government? Citizens do what they can to help solve these problems.

How can a citizen know whether an action will solve a problem? He must do his best to learn all he can. In school, he can find out how a democracy works. He should listen to the news reports and read the newspaper. Then he must decide what he believes about the things he has heard. He can vote for the man or woman who offers the best solution.

Voting is the easiest and most important way for a citizen to get involved. Today, citizens eighteen or over have the right to vote. But voting is more than a right; it is a responsibility too. Voting allows all to help in making decisions for the country. What would happen if people did not vote? The decisions would be made by a few people. How would that be bad for the country?

Voting is a right—and a privilege.

264

Being able to choose their own leader, the members would be having a part in the leadership of the group. This involvement is why voting is so important to citizens.

Teaching the Lesson

Text Discussion, page 264

- ➤ **Read page 264 to find another important way for a citizen to get involved in his country.** *(by voting)*
- ➤ Name some of the problems the government must deal with. *(money for schools, jobs for the people, poverty, and crime)*
- ➤ **What can a citizen do to help solve these problems that the government must deal with?** *(learn all he can about society and the government; acquire skills that will improve society)*

Learning a lot and doing well in your schoolwork will help you to become a better citizen. The more you know, the more you will be able to contribute to society.

- ➤ **How can listening to the news and reading the newspaper help a person to be a better citizen?** *(He will know what is happening in the world around him and will be able to make better decisions.)*

◆ FAMOUS PEOPLE ◆

Elizabeth Cady Stanton/Susan B. Anthony
(1815-1902) (1820-1906)

As a young girl, Elizabeth Cady studied law books in her father's office. Because she was a woman, she could not become a lawyer. But her studies helped her to understand that the laws did not treat women the same as men. In 1848 Stanton planned a women's meeting in her hometown of Seneca Falls, New York, to discuss the laws and to make a list of rights they believed they should have, including the right to vote.

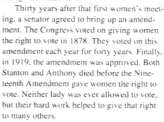

Stanton met Susan B. Anthony about three years later. In Anthony's family, men and women were treated equally. It was hard for her to understand why all women were not. Both women worked for women's *suffrage*, or the right to vote. They believed that if women could vote, they could change the unfair laws.

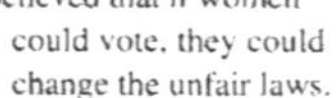

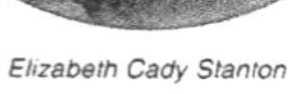

Elizabeth Cady Stanton

Thirty years after that first women's meeting, a senator agreed to bring up an amendment. The Congress voted on giving women the right to vote in 1878. They voted on this amendment each year for forty years. Finally, in 1919, the amendment was approved. Both Stanton and Anthony died before the Nineteenth Amendment gave women the right to vote. Neither lady was ever allowed to vote, but their hard work helped to give that right to many others.

Susan B. Anthony

265

A statue of Jefferson at the University of Virginia

The Founding Fathers—men like George Washington, James Madison, and Thomas Jefferson—wanted a country where all the people could have a say. At first it was an experiment. No one was sure such a government could last.

What made our democratic government work? The people did: people who were born in the United States and spent their whole lives here; people who came here from other countries looking for freedom and equality for themselves and their children; people who, after years of slavery, were finally free too. All these people believed in the principles of the Constitution. Together they made it work.

Each American must do his part to make sure that the government keeps working. It is every citizen's responsibility to protect the freedoms promised in the Constitution. All citizens must remember what that freedom meant in America's past and what it means to the future.

A welcoming parade for soldiers returning from war

A military salute at the Tomb of the Unknown Soldier

266

➤ **Who in the United States is allowed to vote?** *(all citizens who are eighteen years old or older)*

➤ Explain how voting is both a right and a responsibility. *(It is a right because America has a government by the people. It is a responsibility because those elected can greatly affect the lives of the citizens.)*

➤ **How do you think the United States would be different if the citizens were not allowed to vote?**

Americans would not have many of the freedoms that they have today. Voting is a freedom that every American should be thankful for. (BAT: 7c Praise)

Text Discussion, page 265

➤ **Read page 265 to find out what the Nineteenth Amendment did.** *(gave women the right to vote)*

➤ **How did Elizabeth Stanton become interested in women's rights?** *(She studied law and realized that it treated men and women differently.)*

➤ **How did Susan B. Anthony's family life help to shape her thinking?** *(Men and women were treated equally.)*

➤ Explain what the word ***suffrage*** means. *(the right to vote)*

➤ **Why did Elizabeth Stanton and Susan B. Anthony work so hard for women's suffrage?** *(They felt that if women could gain the right to vote, they could also change some of the unfair laws.)*

➤ **Do you think these women were right about the power of voting?**

➤ **How long did it take the Nineteenth Amendment to pass?** *(forty years)*

Although Stanton and Anthony caused laws to change, both used means that were either unlawful or questionable. Their accomplishments are noted here because of their historical significance.

TimeLine Snapshots Activity

➤ Add the figure of Elizabeth Cady Stanton and Susan B. Anthony to the TimeLine at the year 1869.

During the year 1869 Elizabeth Stanton and Susan B. Anthony were successful in forming a National Woman Suffrage amendment which was added to the Constitution. Through the years not every United States citizen has been able to vote. These two women did a lot to make it possible for women to vote.

➤ Add the figure representing the Nineteenth Amendment to the TimeLine at the year 1919.

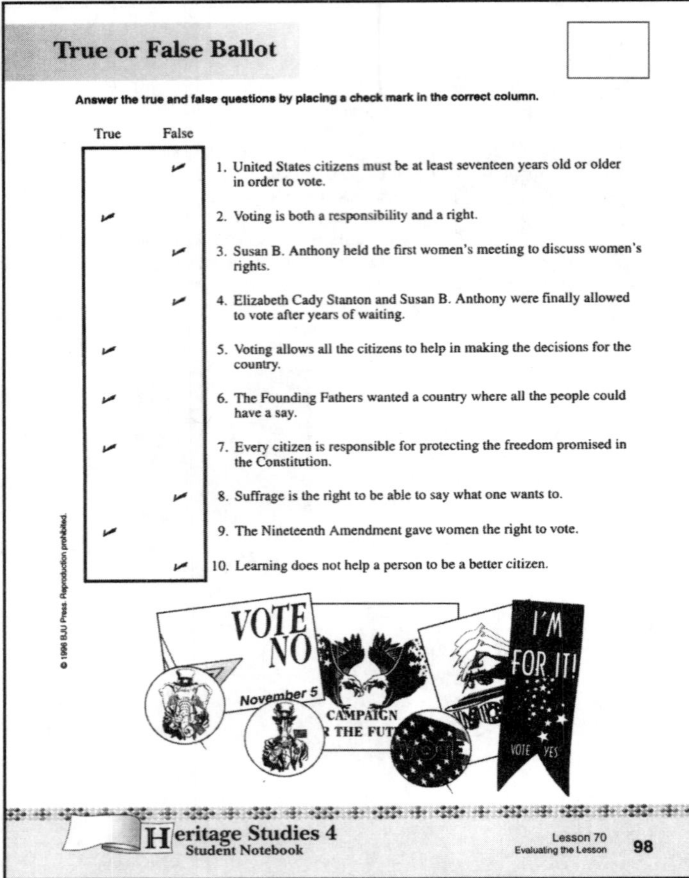
True or False Ballot

Answer the true and false questions by placing a check mark in the correct column.

True	False	
	✓	1. United States citizens must be at least seventeen years old or older in order to vote.
✓		2. Voting is both a responsibility and a right.
	✓	3. Susan B. Anthony held the first women's meeting to discuss women's rights.
	✓	4. Elizabeth Cady Stanton and Susan B. Anthony were finally allowed to vote after years of waiting.
✓		5. Voting allows all the citizens to help in making the decisions for the country.
✓		6. The Founding Fathers wanted a country where all the people could have a say.
✓		7. Every citizen is responsible for protecting the freedom promised in the Constitution.
	✓	8. Suffrage is the right to be able to say what one wants to.
✓		9. The Nineteenth Amendment gave women the right to vote.
	✓	10. Learning does not help a person to be a better citizen.

Heritage Studies 4 Student Notebook — Lesson 70 Evaluating the Lesson — 98

Text Discussion, page 266

➤ **Read page 266 to find out what has made America's democratic government work.** *(the people)*

➤ **What kind of country did the Founding Fathers want?** *(a country in which all the people could have a say)*

➤ **What is every citizen's responsibility?** *(to protect the freedoms promised in the Constitution)*

Freedom is important to every citizen, and each one must do his part to preserve the freedoms that America offers. In the same way, a Christian must be faithful in every task he does. (BATs: 2c Faithfulness, 2e Work, 2f Enthusiasm)

Evaluating the Lesson

Notebook Activity, page 98

➤ Read the instructions on Notebook page 98.

➤ Complete the page.

Follow the procedure for adding this page to the ballot box if you are teaching a group of children. Collect the ballots from each box and tally the points for all correct answers to see whether the Democrats or the Republicans won.

Going Beyond

Enrichment

Give your child colored paper, crayons or felt-tip pens, glue, and scissors. Instruct him to create campaign posters, buttons, or bumper stickers, using the slogan he made up in the Introducing the Lesson section or others he has written.

Additional Teacher Information

Elizabeth Cady was born in Johnstown, New York, in 1815. She gained an interest in law through her father, Judge Daniel Cady. She studied law on her own and later went on to study at Troy Female Seminary. She experienced disappointment and frustration with the mundane, basic courses offered at the seminary. Situations like this and the general attitude of the day toward women spurred Elizabeth Cady on to action.

Elizabeth Cady became the leader of the early women's rights movement, organizing some of the first suffrage meetings in the United States. In 1840, she married Henry B. Stanton, an abolitionist and reformer. Elizabeth Stanton became friends with Susan B. Anthony in 1851. Together these two women worked for women's rights, forming a National Woman Suffrage amendment to the Constitution in 1869.

Susan Brownwell Anthony was born in Adams, Massachusetts, in 1820. Her father, the owner of a cotton mill, was a Quaker who had married outside his religion. Susan grew up influenced by Quaker tradition and practice. Her father emphasized learning and working. Susan attended Deborah Moulson's Seminary for Females in Philadelphia and then taught from 1838-49. She entered the temperance movement and later joined forces with Elizabeth Stanton. Unmarried, Susan soon devoted her life to feminist work, becoming what the newspaper termed "the Napoleon of the Women's Rights Movement."

Elizabeth Cady Stanton and Susan Brownwell Anthony worked together for over fifty years, enduring criticism, frustration, and even, in Anthony's case, arrest. Despite a lifetime of work, the two women did not live to see the fulfillment of their accomplishments—the Nineteenth Amendment passed after both women had died. Henry Stanton reportedly said to his wife, "You stir up Susan, and she stirs up the world." Indeed, these two ladies helped to change the role of women in society, not only in America, but also around the world.

Immigration to the United States Between 1620 and 1920

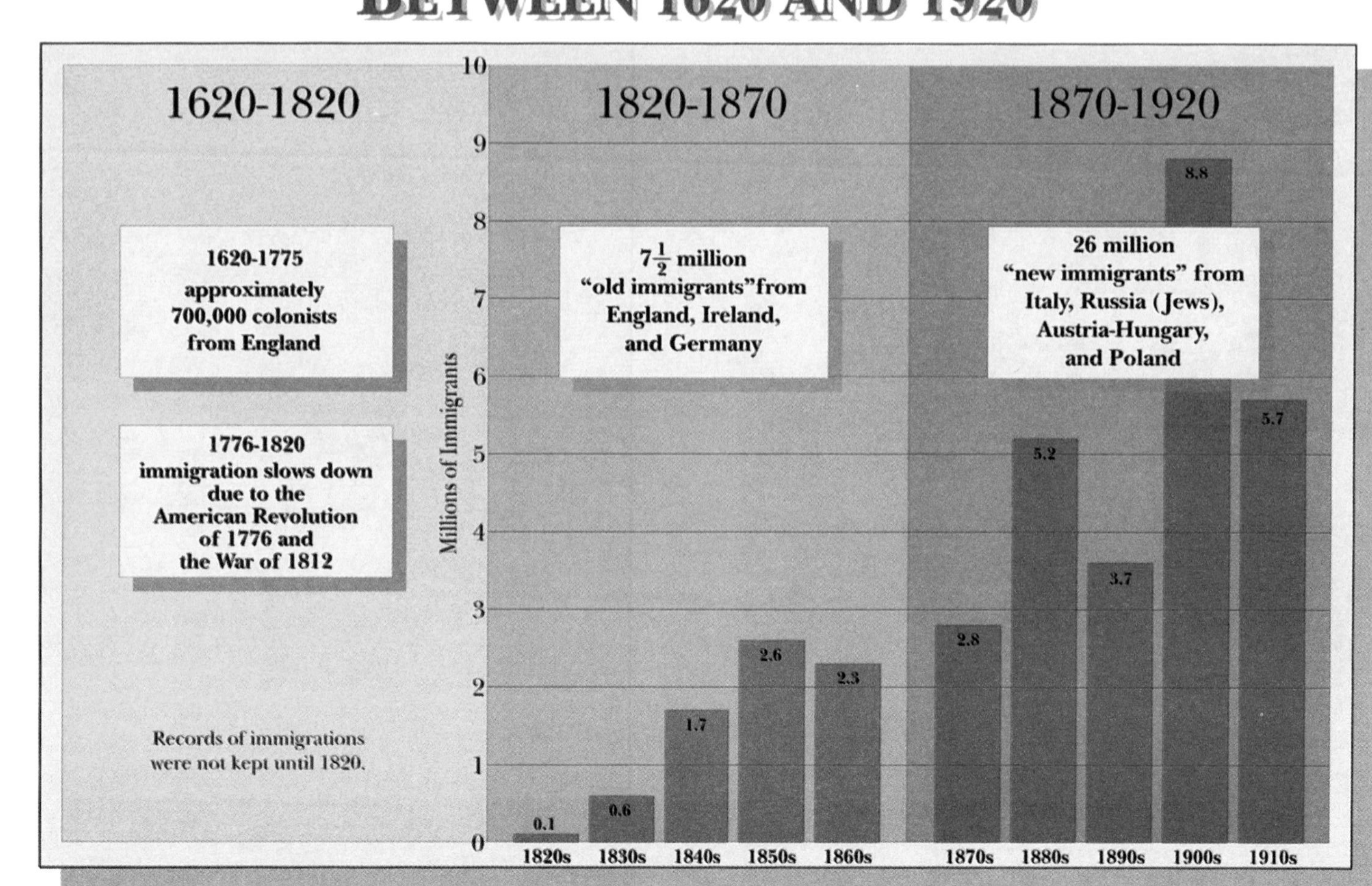

Maps and More 2

Maps and More 5

Maps and More 6

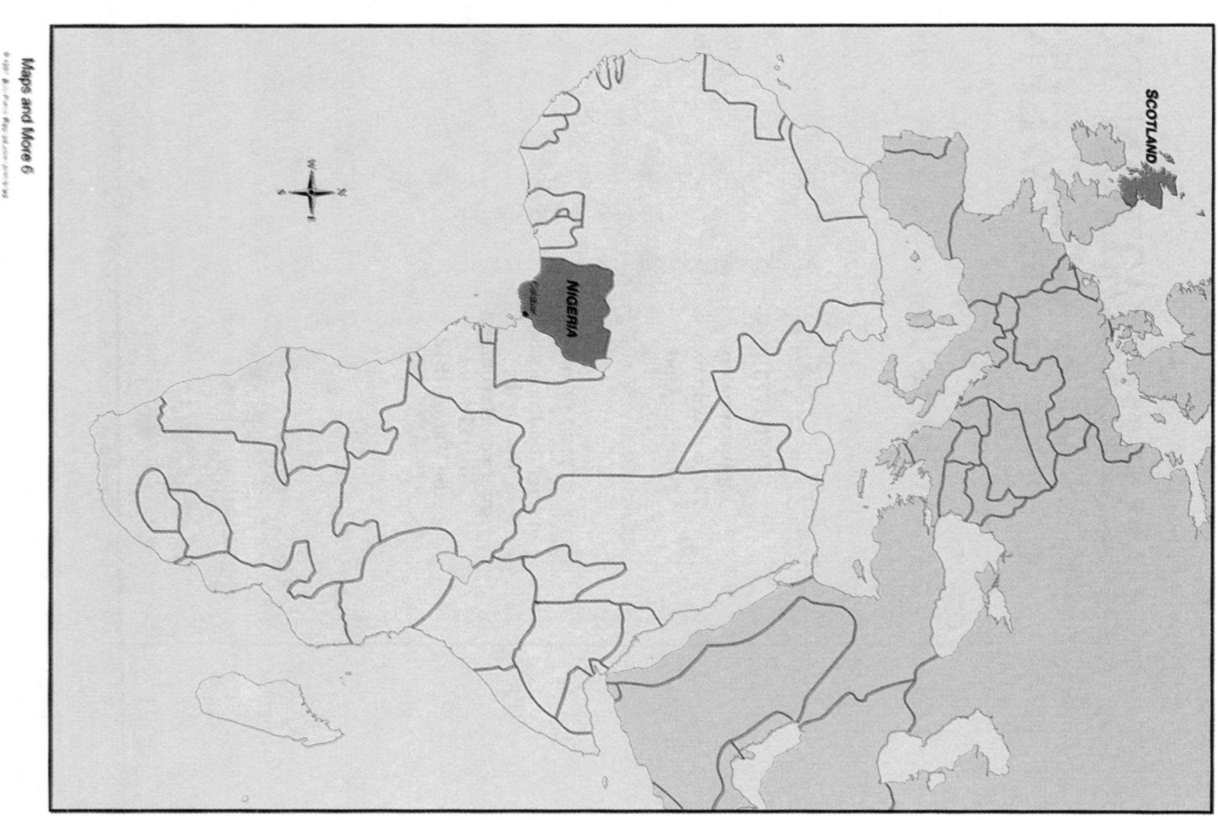

Maps and More 7

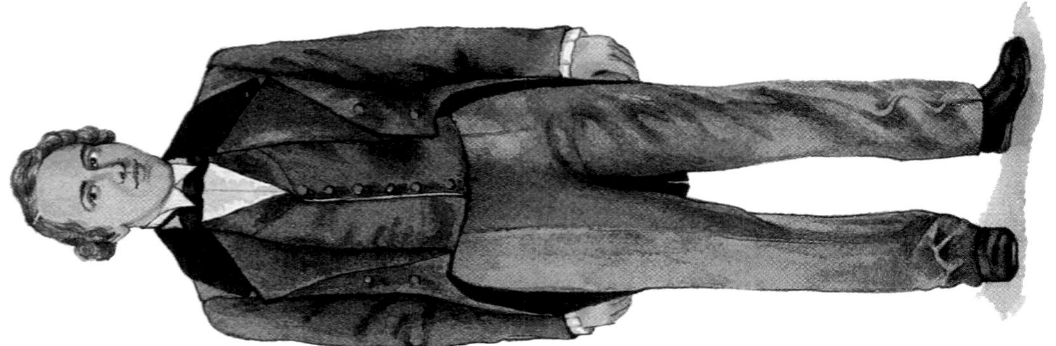

Maps and More 8

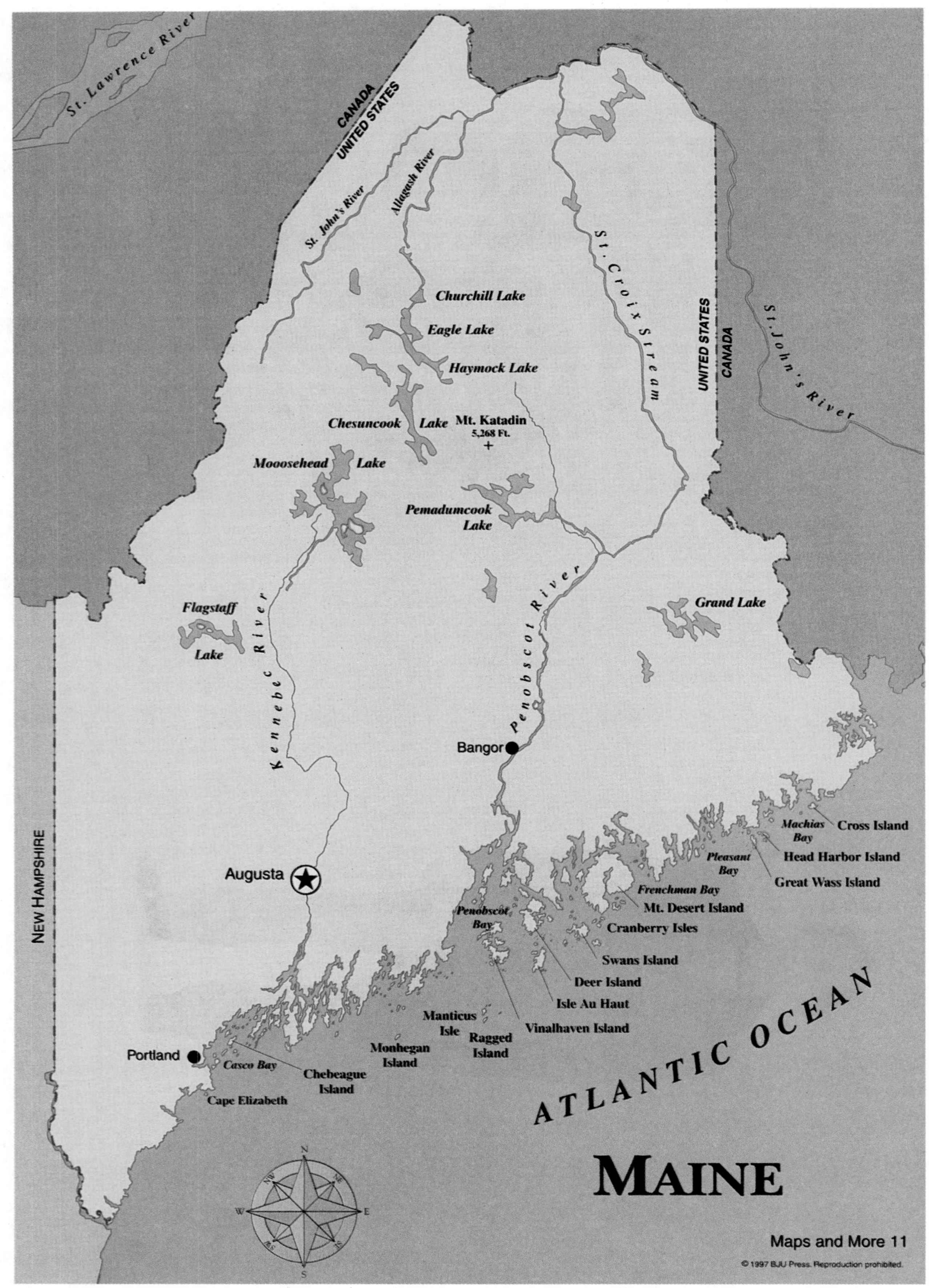
St. Lawrence River
CANADA
UNITED STATES
St. John's River
Allagash River
Churchill Lake
Eagle Lake
Haymock Lake
Chesuncook Lake
Mt. Katadin
5,268 Ft.
Mooosehead Lake
Pemadumcook Lake
St. Croix Stream
UNITED STATES
CANADA
St. John's River
Grand Lake
Flagstaff Lake
Kennebec River
Penobscot River
Bangor
Augusta
NEW HAMPSHIRE
Machias Bay
Cross Island
Pleasant Bay
Head Harbor Island
Great Wass Island
Frenchman Bay
Mt. Desert Island
Penobscot Bay
Cranberry Isles
Swans Island
Deer Island
Isle Au Haut
Vinalhaven Island
Manticus Isle
Ragged Island
Monhegan Island
Portland
Casco Bay
Chebeague Island
Cape Elizabeth
ATLANTIC OCEAN
MAINE
N
NE
E
SE
S
SW
W
NW
Maps and More 11
© 1997 BJU Press. Reproduction prohibited.

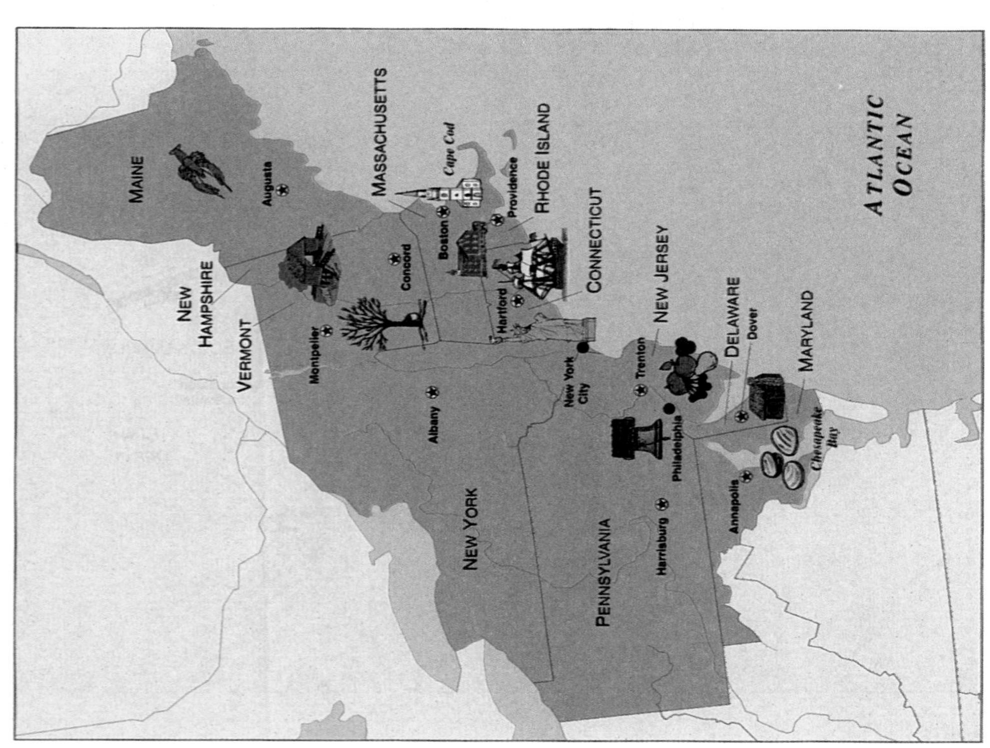
NORTHEAST REGION
MAINE
Augusta
NEW HAMPSHIRE
VERMONT
Montpelier
Concord
MASSACHUSETTS
Cape Cod
Boston
Providence
RHODE ISLAND
CONNECTICUT
Hartford
NEW YORK
Albany
New York City
NEW JERSEY
Trenton
DELAWARE
Dover
MARYLAND
Chesapeake Bay
Annapolis
Philadelphia
PENNSYLVANIA
Harrisburg
ATLANTIC OCEAN
Maps and More 10

Maps and More 12
© 1997 BJU Press. Reproduction prohibited.

Southeast Region

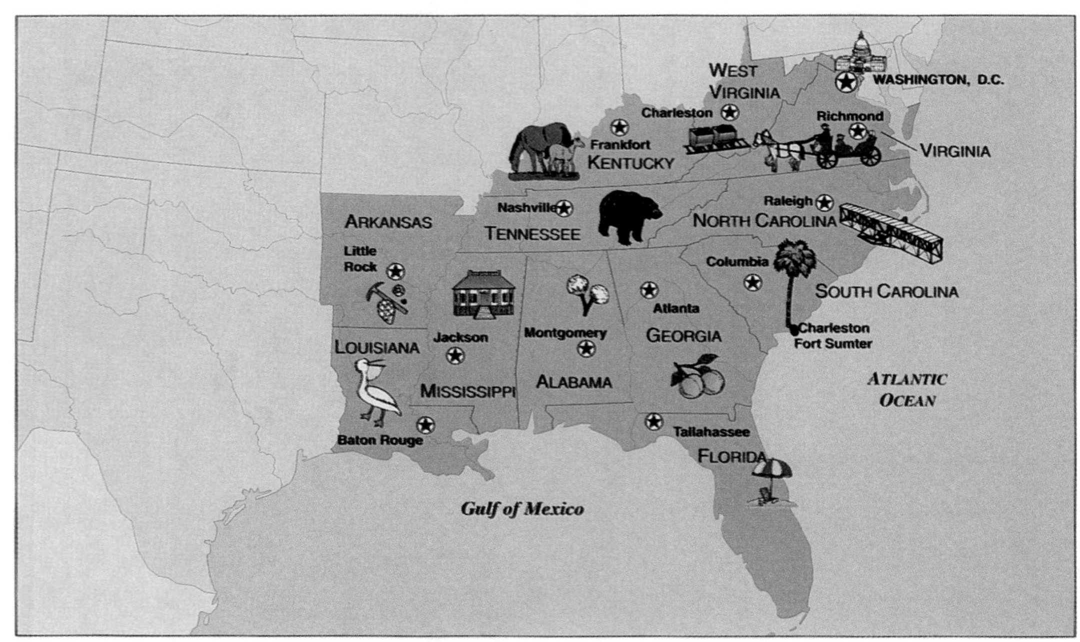

Maps and More 13

Middle West Region

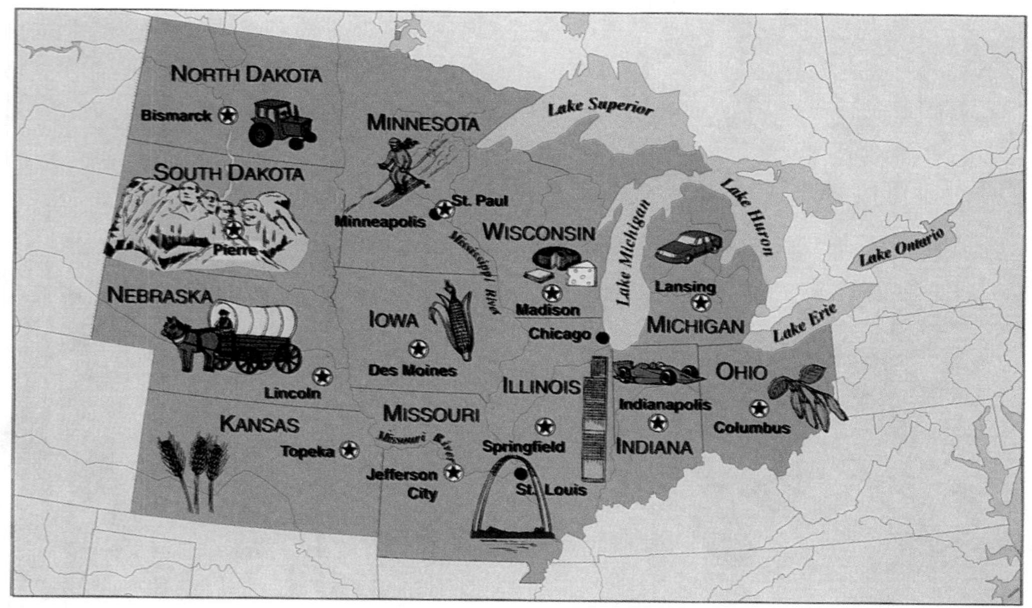

Maps and More 15

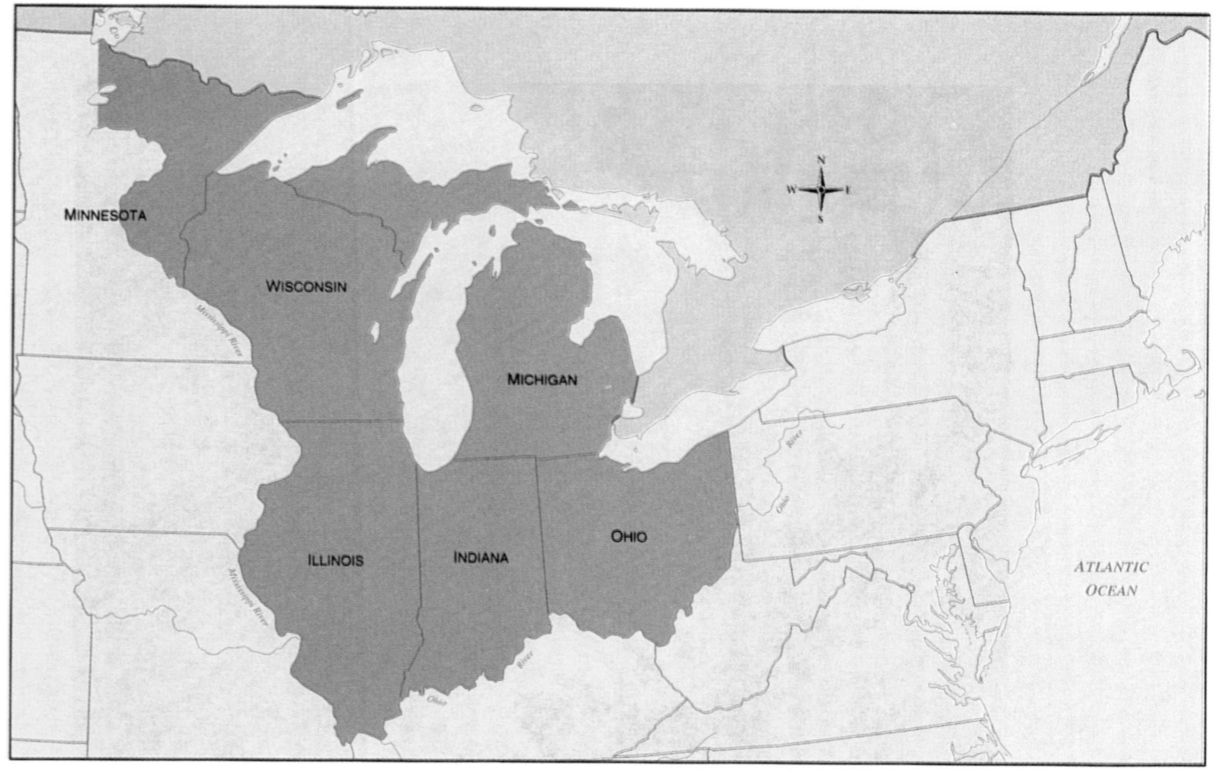
MINNESOTA
WISCONSIN
MICHIGAN
ILLINOIS
INDIANA
OHIO
ATLANTIC OCEAN
Mississippi River
Ohio River
N
S
E
W

Maps and More 16

WASHINGTON
OREGON
IDAHO
CALIFORNIA
WYOMING
COLORADO
NORTH DAKOTA
SOUTH DAKOTA
NEBRASKA
KANSAS
TEXAS
MINNESOTA
IOWA
MISSOURI
WISCONSIN
ILLINOIS
MICHIGAN
INDIANA
OHIO
KENTUCKY
TENNESSEE
ALABAMA
GEORGIA
SOUTH CAROLINA
NORTH CAROLINA
VIRGINIA
MARYLAND
PENNSYLVANIA
NEW YORK
N
S
E
W
Major corn-producing areas (Corn Belt)
Other corn-producing areas

Maps and More 17

Maps and More 18

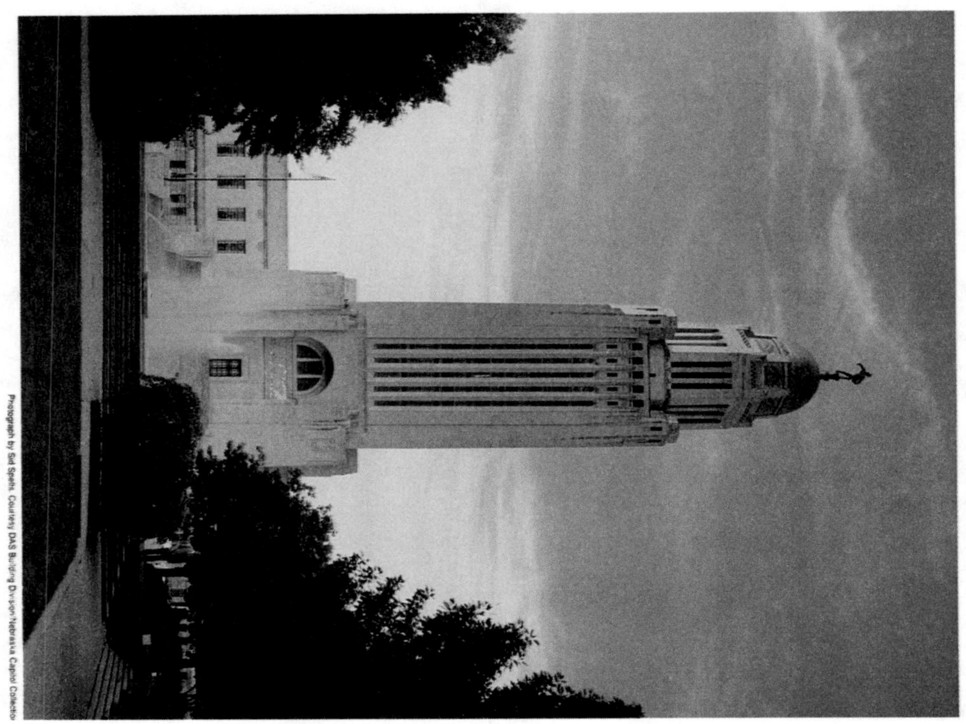

SOUTHWEST REGION

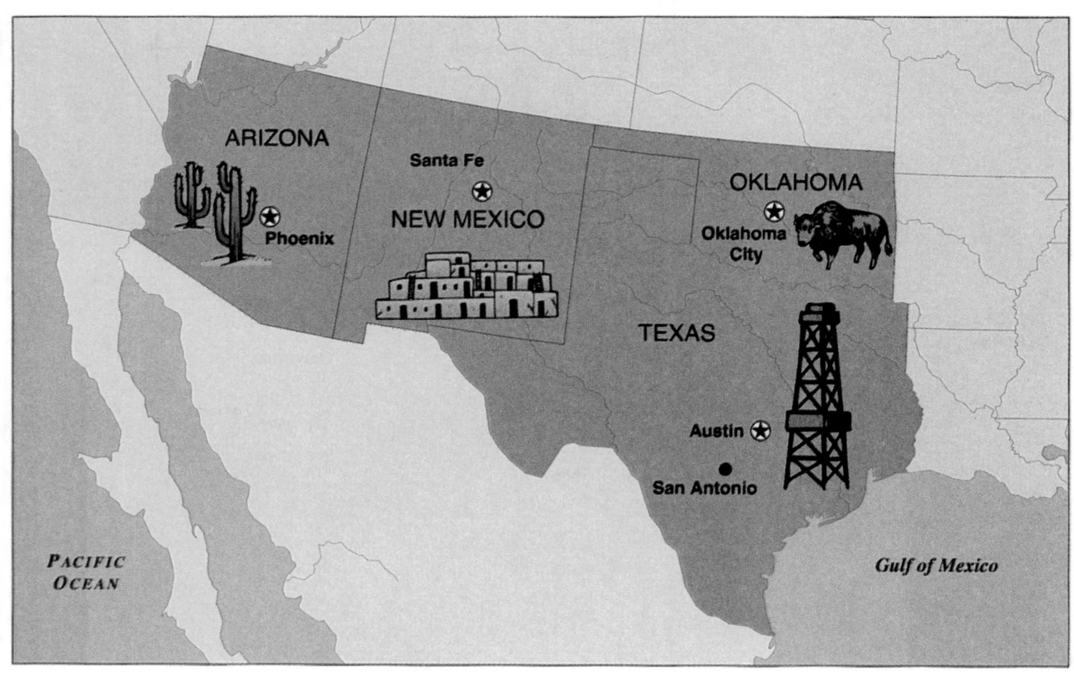

Maps and More 19

Petrified Forest

NPS photograph by Fred E. Mang Jr.

Painted Desert

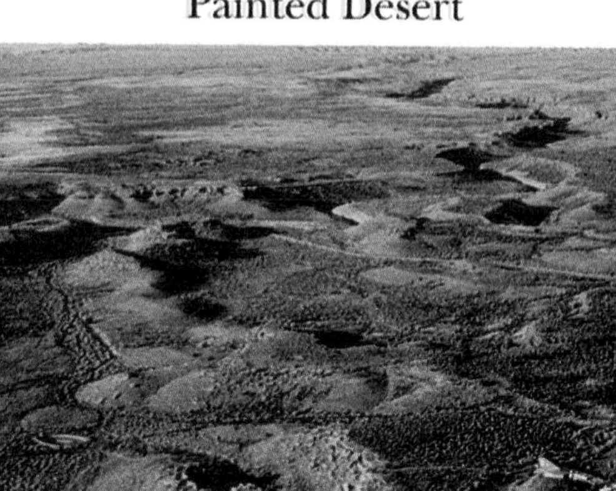

NPS photograph by Fred E. Mang Jr.

Maps and More 21

Rocky Mountain Region

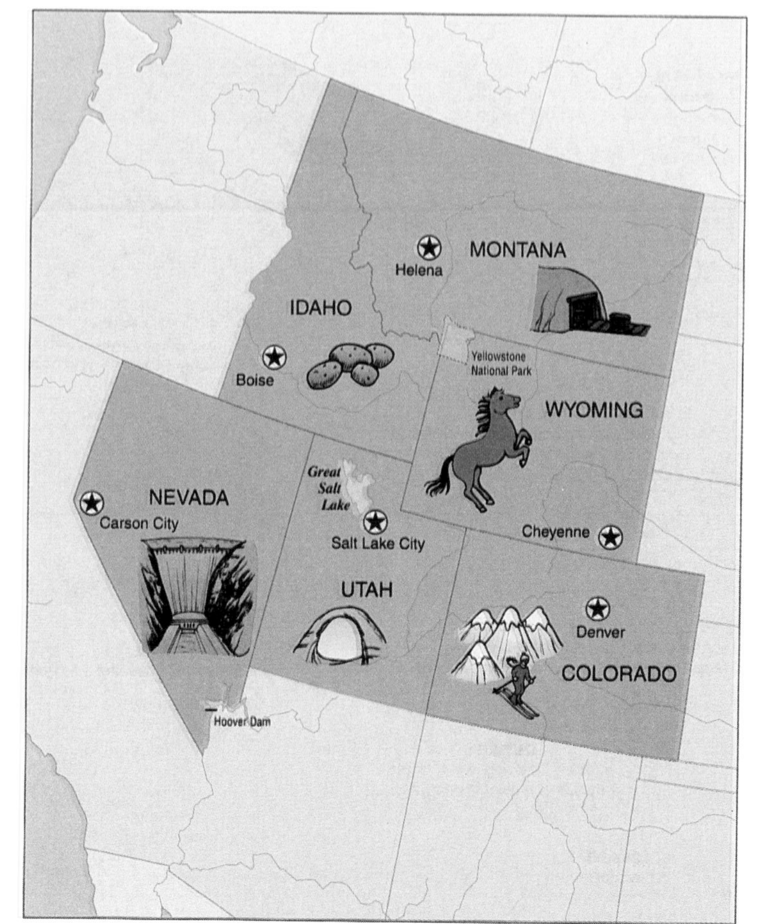

Maps and More 22

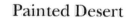

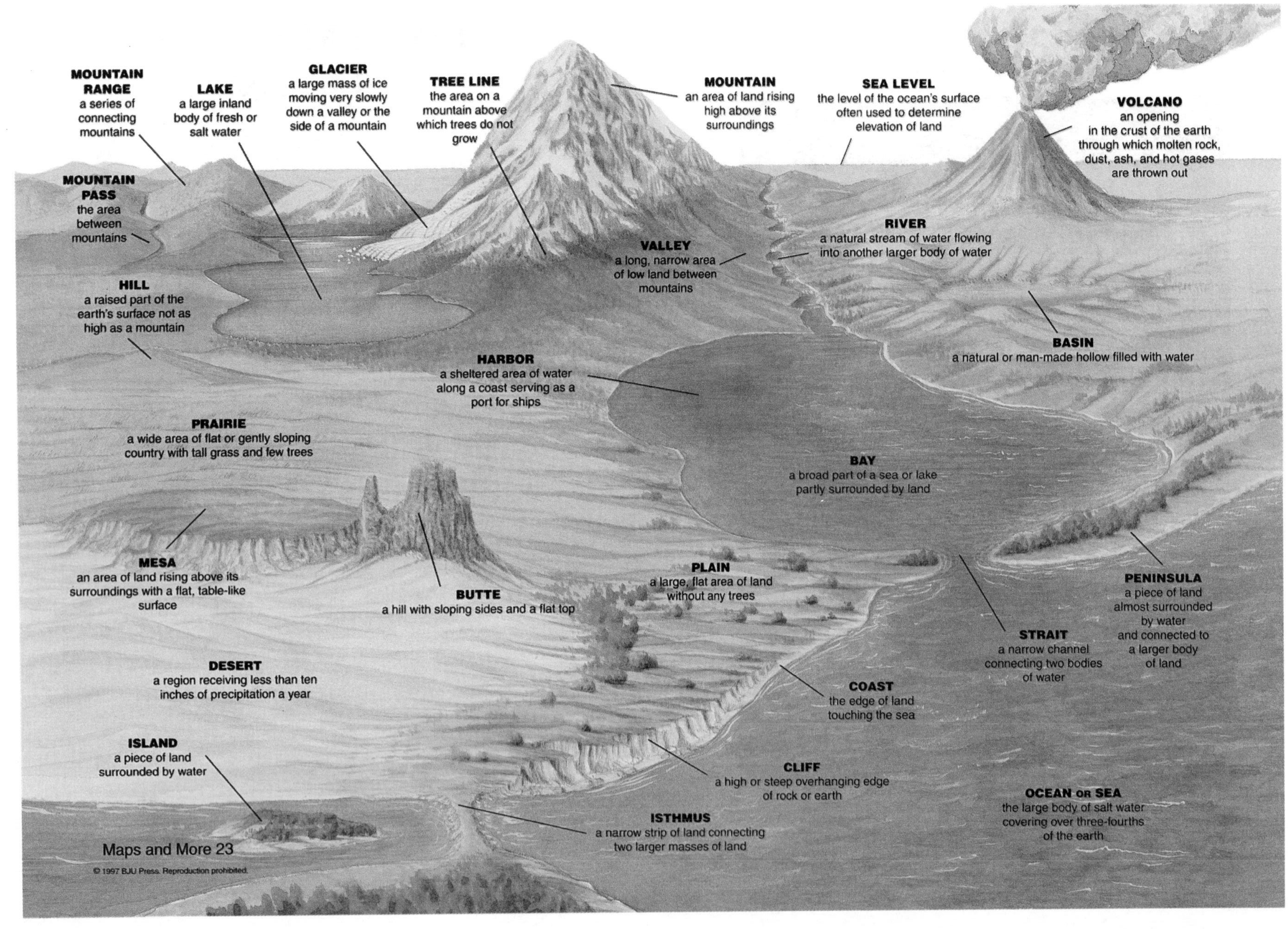

MOUNTAIN RANGE
a series of connecting mountains
LAKE
a large inland body of fresh or salt water
GLACIER
a large mass of ice moving very slowly down a valley or the side of a mountain
TREE LINE
the area on a mountain above which trees do not grow
MOUNTAIN
an area of land rising high above its surroundings
SEA LEVEL
the level of the ocean's surface often used to determine elevation of land
VOLCANO
an opening in the crust of the earth through which molten rock, dust, ash, and hot gases are thrown out
MOUNTAIN PASS
the area between mountains
VALLEY
a long, narrow area of low land between mountains
RIVER
a natural stream of water flowing into another larger body of water
HILL
a raised part of the earth's surface not as high as a mountain
BASIN
a natural or man-made hollow filled with water
HARBOR
a sheltered area of water along a coast serving as a port for ships
PRAIRIE
a wide area of flat or gently sloping country with tall grass and few trees
BAY
a broad part of a sea or lake partly surrounded by land
MESA
an area of land rising above its surroundings with a flat, table-like surface
PLAIN
a large, flat area of land without any trees
BUTTE
a hill with sloping sides and a flat top
PENINSULA
a piece of land almost surrounded by water and connected to a larger body of land
STRAIT
a narrow channel connecting two bodies of water
DESERT
a region receiving less than ten inches of precipitation a year
COAST
the edge of land touching the sea
ISLAND
a piece of land surrounded by water
CLIFF
a high or steep overhanging edge of rock or earth
OCEAN OR SEA
the large body of salt water covering over three-fourths of the earth
ISTHMUS
a narrow strip of land connecting two larger masses of land
Maps and More 23
© 1997 BJU Press. Reproduction prohibited.

Pacific Region

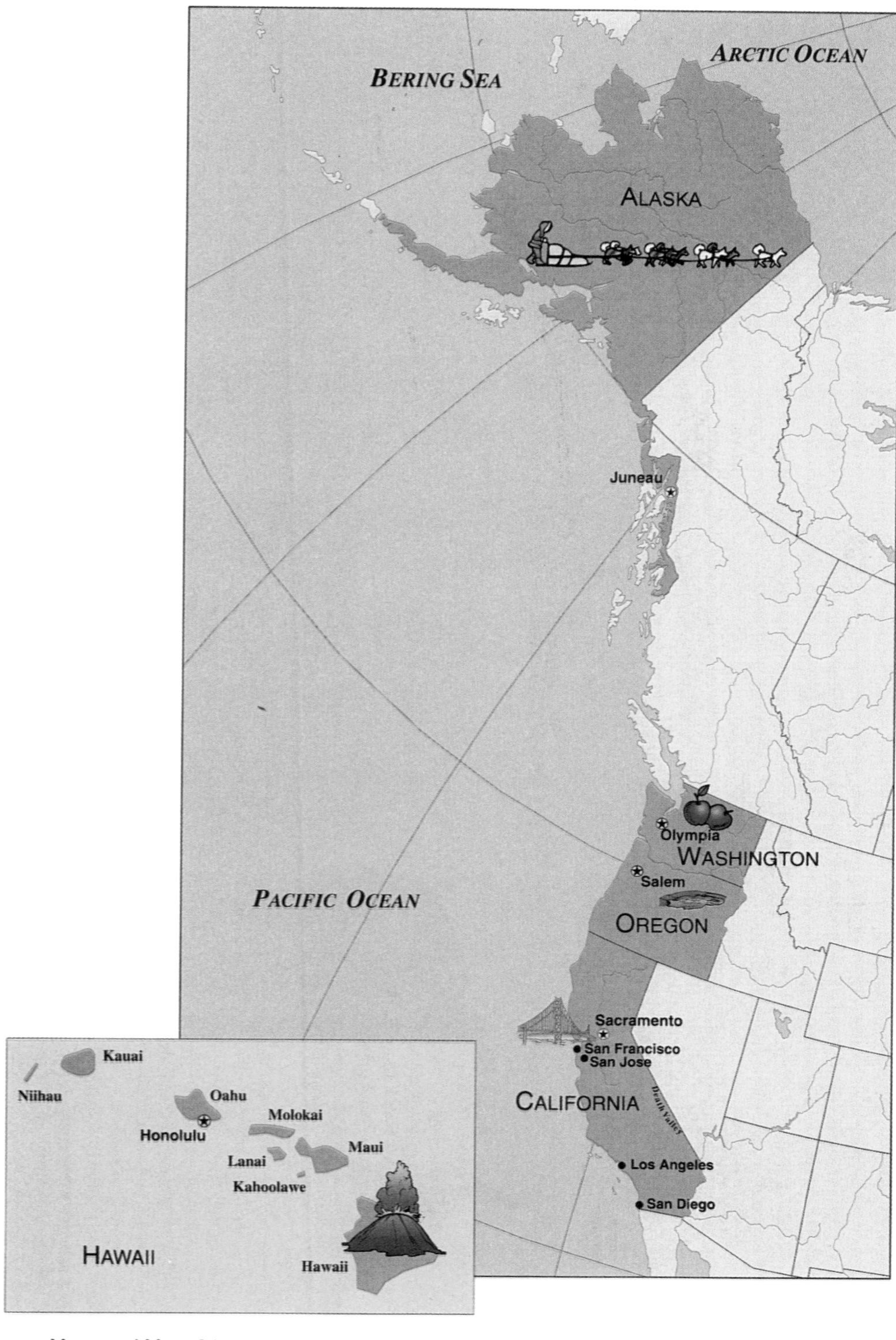

Maps and More 24

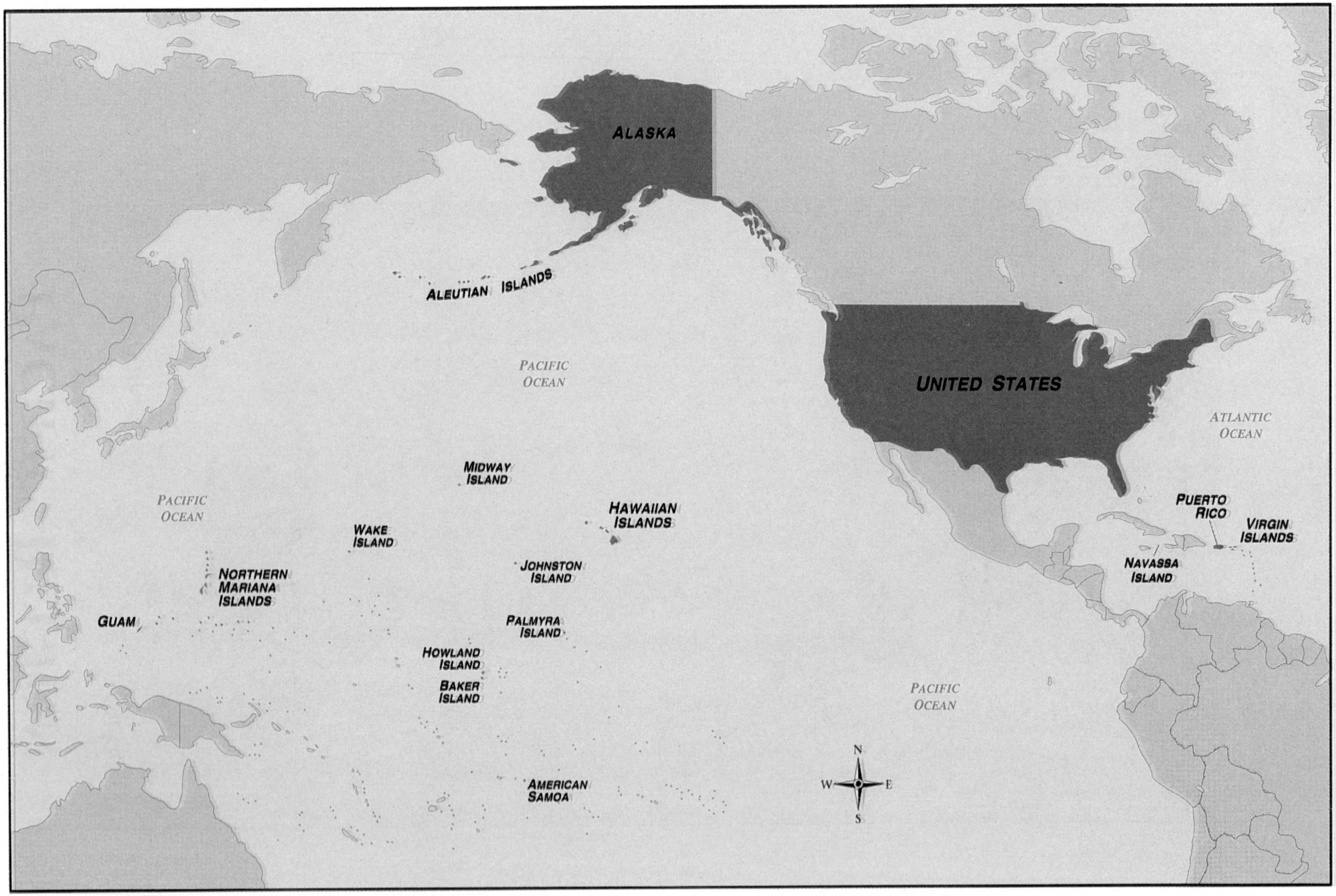

Maps and More 25

GUAM

PACIFIC OCEAN

NORTHERN MARIANA ISLANDS

WAKE ISLAND

HOWLAND ISLAND

BAKER ISLAND

MIDWAY ISLAND

ALEUTIAN ISLANDS

PACIFIC OCEAN

PALMYRA ISLAND

JOHNSTON ISLAND

AMERICAN SAMOA

HAWAIIAN ISLANDS

ALASKA

W N S E

PACIFIC OCEAN

UNITED STATES

NAVASSA ISLAND

PUERTO RICO

VIRGIN ISLANDS

ATLANTIC OCEAN

A to Z SAVE • A • CENTER
BIKE CLEARANCE
EAST SIDE BIKE SHOP
ROLLY 500
26" 21-speed
rapid shift
Mountain Bike
$229.97
free assembly
ROLLY 500
$179.95
Rolly 500
26" 21-speed
mountain bike
Reg. $199.95
DIRTMASTER
$99.95
Dirtmaster
24" 18-speed
All Terrain Bike
Reg. $120.00
TRUE SPEED
$149.95
True Speed
20" 18-speed
all-terrain bikes
TRUE SPEED
$299.99
fully automatic
5 speed shifting
26" bike
men's and women's
ROLLY 500
$199.99
Rolly 500
26" 21-Speed
Rapid Shift
Mountain Bike
$99.99
Cross country bikes
men's & women's
$149.99
All-Terrain bikes
KIDS
$89.99
"Buster" 16" Bikes
only at Southern VALUE STORES
Maps and More 27

Maps and More 28

Photograph by Carson Fremont

Maps and More 29

Photograph by Union Pacific Railroad

Maps and More 30

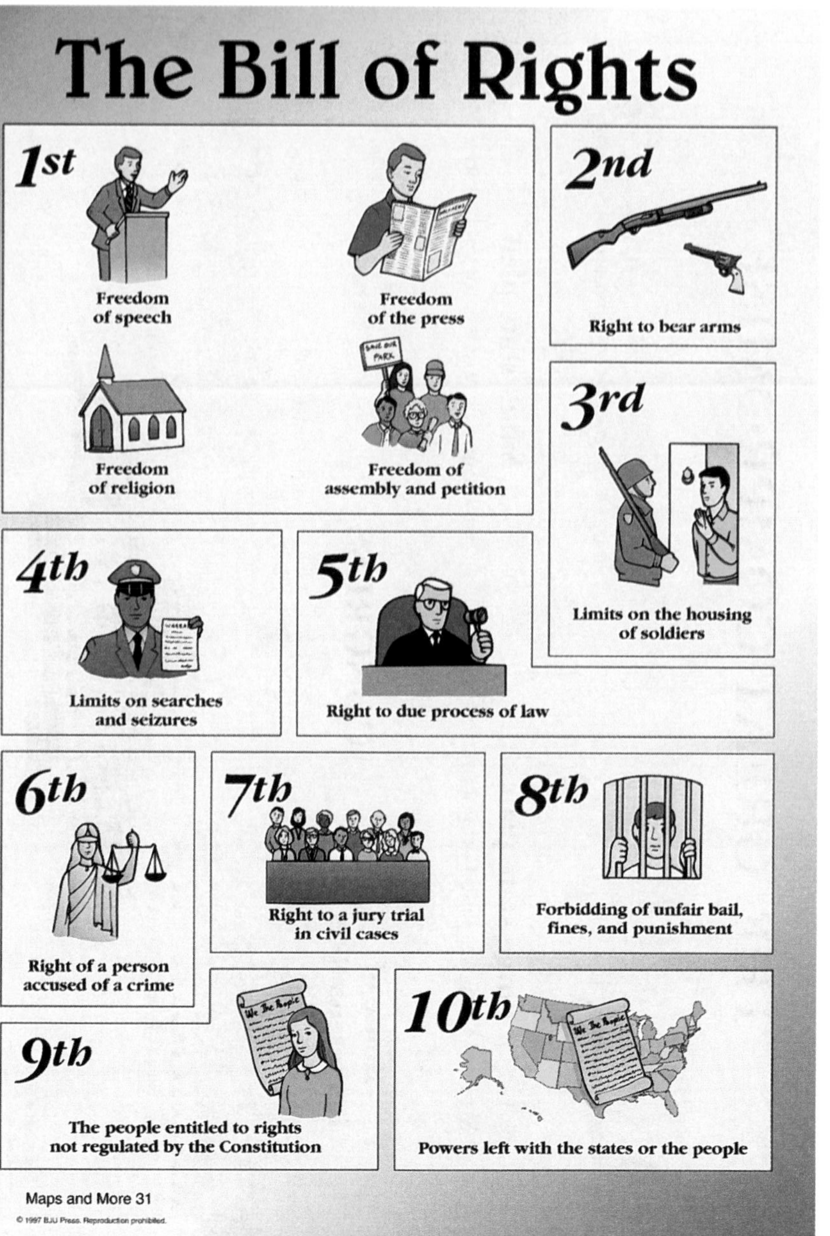
The Bill of Rights
1st
Freedom of speech
Freedom of the press
Freedom of religion
Freedom of assembly and petition
2nd
Right to bear arms
3rd
Limits on the housing of soldiers
4th
Limits on searches and seizures
5th
Right to due process of law
6th
Right of a person accused of a crime
7th
Right to a jury trial in civil cases
8th
Forbidding of unfair bail, fines, and punishment
9th
The people entitled to rights not regulated by the Constitution
10th
Powers left with the states or the people
Maps and More 31
© 1997 BJU Press. Reproduction prohibited.

$50,000 REWARD.—WHO DESTROYED THE MAINE?—$50,000 REWARD.

EDITION FOR GREATER NEW YORK

NEW YORK JOURNAL

AND ADVERTISER.

NEW YORK, THURSDAY, FEBRUARY 17, 1898.—16 PAGES.

DESTRUCTION OF THE WAR SHIP MAINE WAS THE WORK OF AN ENEMY.

$50,000!

$50,000 REWARD!
For the Detection of the Perpetrator of the Maine Outrage!

Assistant Secretary Roosevelt Convinced the Explosion of the War Ship Was Not an Accident.

The Journal Offers $50,000 Reward for the Conviction of the Criminals Who Sent 258 American Sailors to Their Death. Naval Officers Unanimous That the Ship Was Destroyed on Purpose.

$50,000!

$50,000 REWARD!
For the Detection of the Perpetrator of the Maine Outrage!

NAVAL OFFICERS THINK THE MAINE WAS DESTROYED BY A SPANISH MINE.

Hidden Mine or a Sunken Torpedo Believed to Have Been the Weapon Used Against the American Man-of-War—Officers and Men Tell Thrilling Stories of Being Blown Into the Air Amid a Mass of Shattered Steel and Exploding Shells—Survivors Brought to Key West Scout the Idea of Accident—Spanish Officials Protest Too Much—Our Cabinet Orders a Searching Inquiry—Journal Sends Divers to Havana to Report Upon the Condition of the Wreck. Was the Vessel Anchored Over a Mine?

BY CAPTAIN E. L. ZALINSKI, U. S. A.

Assistant Secretary of the Navy Theodore Roosevelt says he is convinced that the destruction of the Maine in Havana Harbor was not an accident.

The Journal offers a reward of $50,000 for exclusive evidence that will convict the person, persons or Government criminally responsible for the destruction of the American battle ship and the death of 258 of its crew.

The suspicion that the Maine was deliberately blown up grows stronger every hour. Not a single fact to the contrary has been produced.

Captain Sigsbee, of the Maine, and Consul-General Lee both urge that public opinion be suspended until they have completed their investigation. They are taking the course of tactful men who are convinced that there has been treachery.

Washington reports very late that Captain Sigsbee had feared some such event as a hidden mine. The English cipher code was used all day yesterday by the naval officers in cabling instead of the usual American code.

Maps and More 32

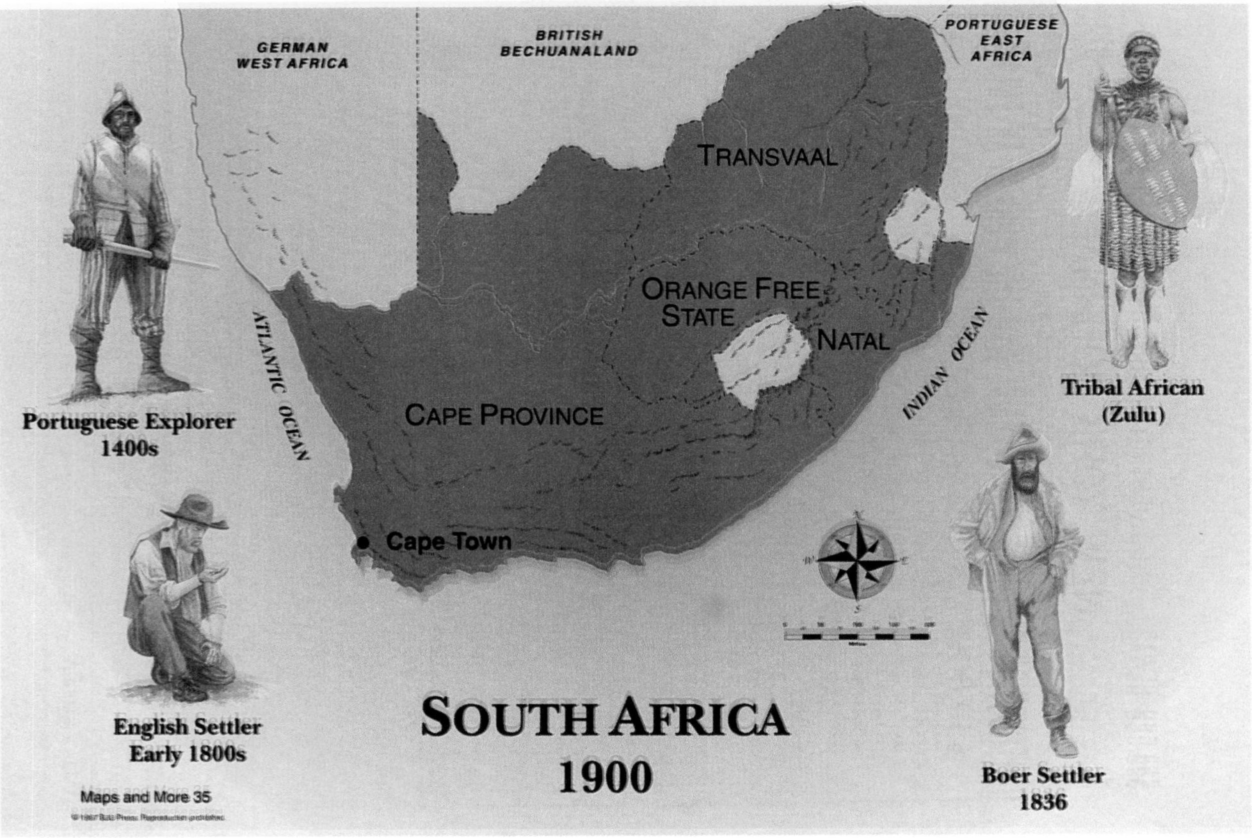

GERMAN WEST AFRICA

BRITISH BECHUANALAND

PORTUGUESE EAST AFRICA

TRANSVAAL

ORANGE FREE STATE

NATAL

CAPE PROVINCE

Cape Town

ATLANTIC OCEAN

INDIAN OCEAN

Portuguese Explorer
1400s

Tribal African
(Zulu)

English Settler
Early 1800s

Boer Settler
1836

SOUTH AFRICA
1900

Maps and More 35

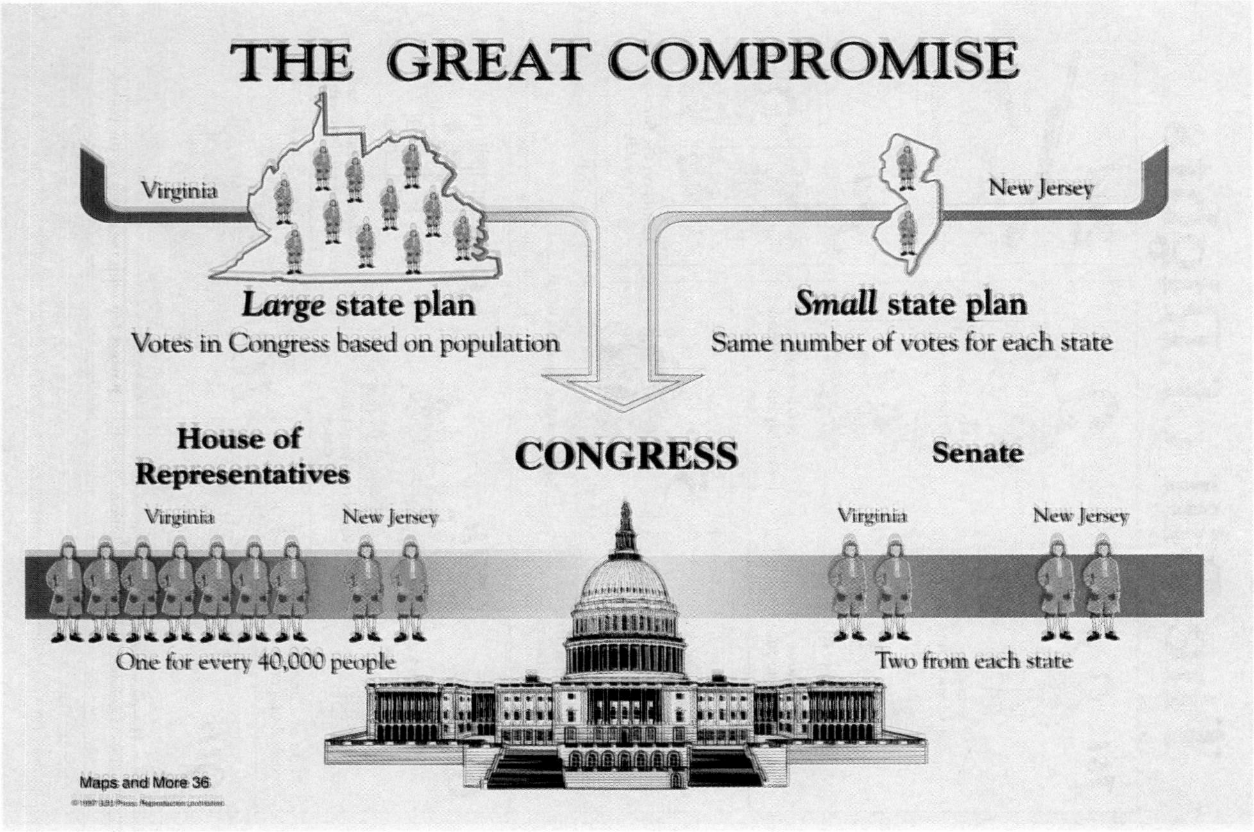

THE GREAT COMPROMISE

Virginia

New Jersey

Large **state plan**
Votes in Congress based on population

Small **state plan**
Same number of votes for each state

House of Representatives

CONGRESS

Senate

Virginia

New Jersey

One for every 40,000 people

Virginia

New Jersey

Two from each state

Maps and More 36

Supplement

©CHospPgh®

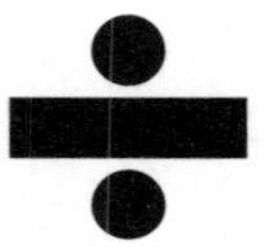

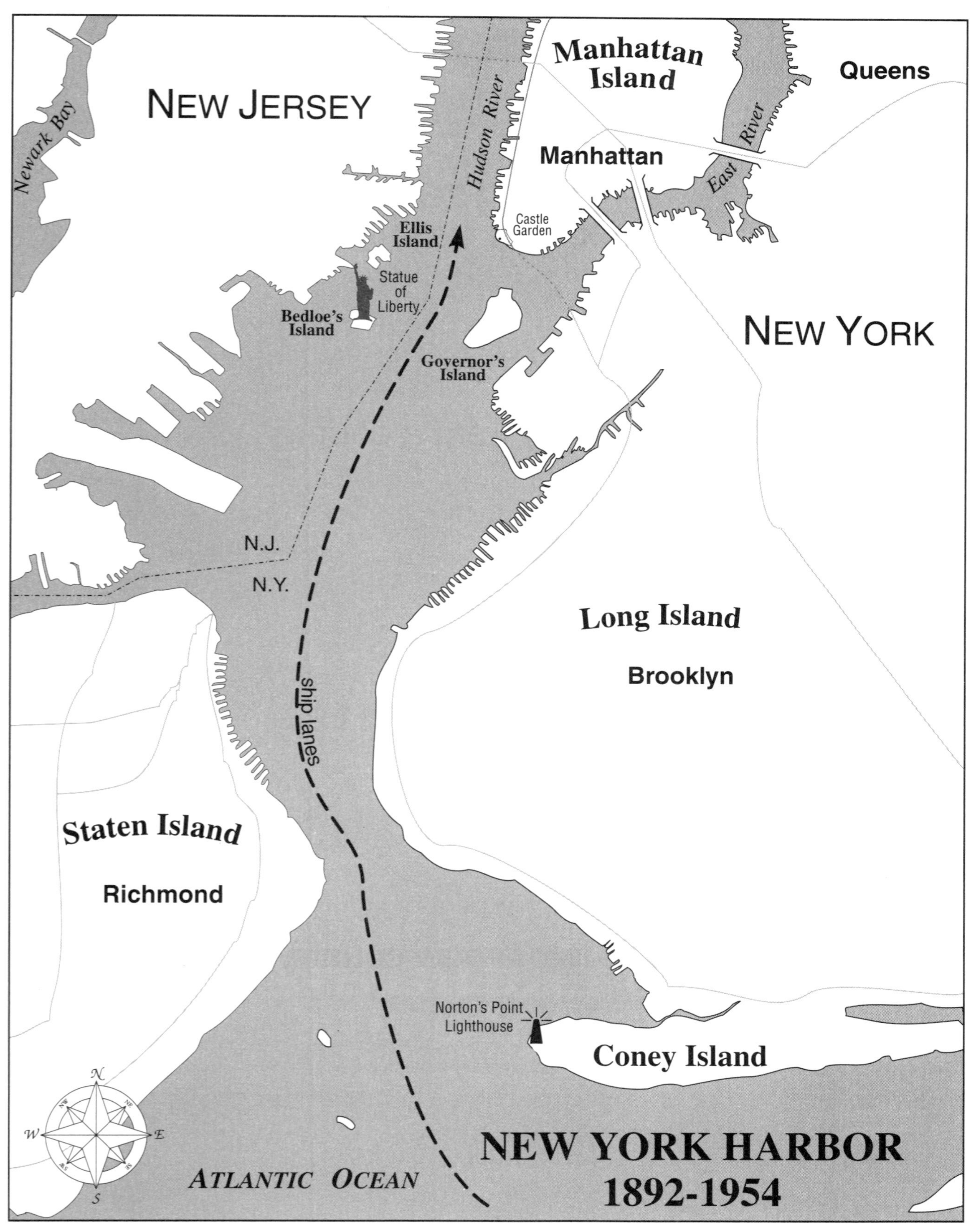
Manhattan Island
Queens
NEW JERSEY
Newark Bay
Hudson River
Manhattan
East River
Castle Garden
Ellis Island
Statue of Liberty
Bedloe's Island
NEW YORK
Governor's Island
N.J.
N.Y.
Long Island
Brooklyn
ship lanes
Staten Island
Richmond
Norton's Point Lighthouse
Coney Island
N
W
E
S
ATLANTIC OCEAN
NEW YORK HARBOR
1892-1954

Introduced in Lesson 6.

Terms

emigrants
x
i
t

move away from a country

immigrants
n
t
o

move into a new country

Total Population of the United States 1790

English and Welsh	1,939,396
African	856,770
Scots	261,138
Scots-Irish	190,662
Other Irish	116,248
German	279,220
Dutch	100,000
French	73,750
Spanish	25,625
Swedish	21,100
Unassigned	219,805
Total	4,083,714

CONSTITUTION OF THE UNITED STATES

Article II, Section 1, Paragraph 5

No person except a natural-born citizen, or a citizen of the United States at the time of the adoption of this Constitution, shall be eligible to the office of President; neither shall any person be eligible to that office who shall not have attained to the age of thirty-five years, and been fourteen years a resident within the United States.

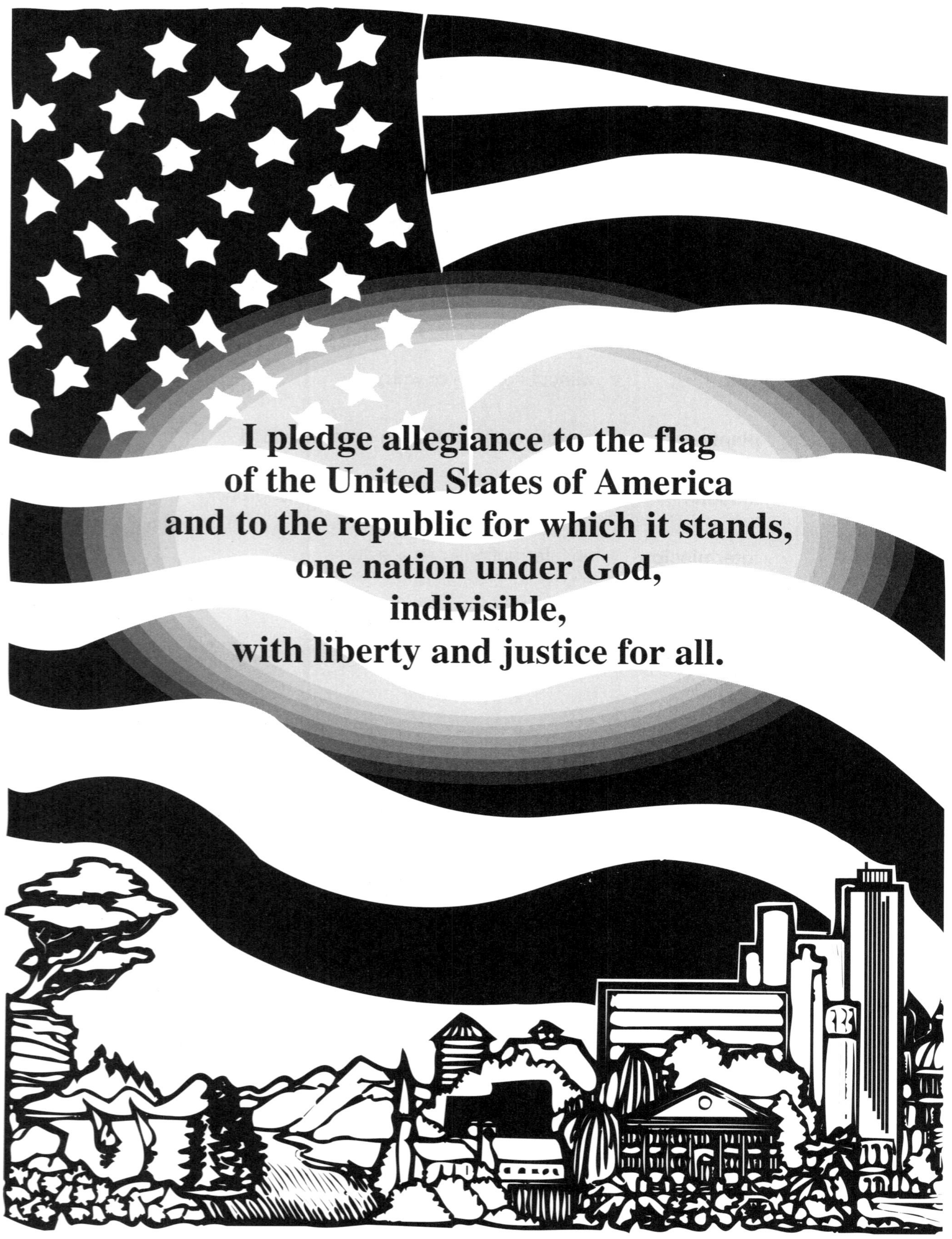
I pledge allegiance to the flag
of the United States of America
and to the republic for which it stands,
one nation under God,
indivisible,
with liberty and justice for all.

Definitions for Notebook Page 19

varied	of many kinds or forms
blithe	without concern or worry
plank	a thick, wide, long piece of sawed wood
mason	a person who builds things of stone or brick
intermission	an interruption in an activity
robust	full of health and strength

Major Points of Entry, 1985
(number of immigrants shown)

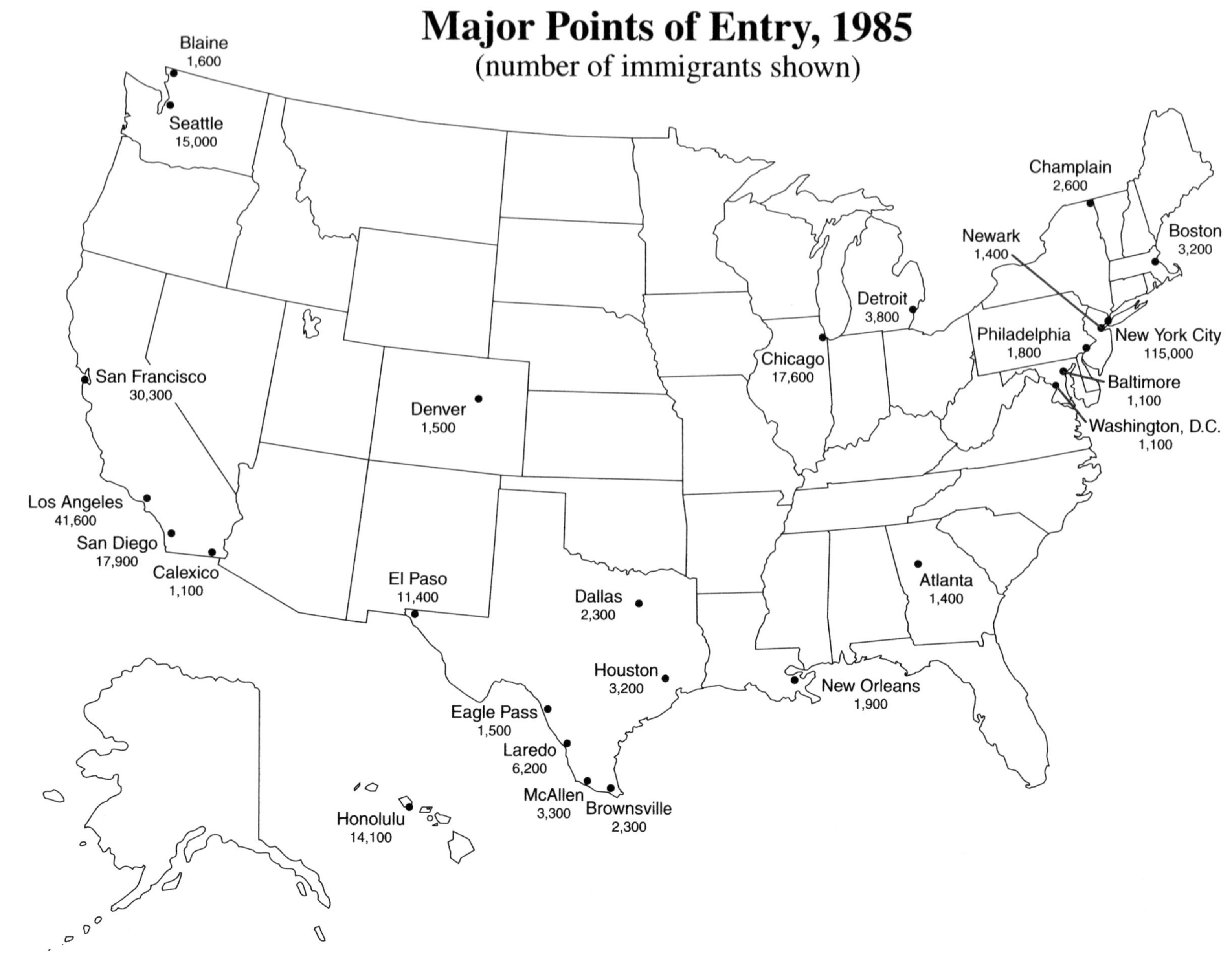

Brethren, We Have Met to Worship
George Atkins
William Moore
Breth-ren, we have met to wor - ship And a - dore the Lord our God;
Let us love our God su - preme - ly, Let us love each oth - er too;
Will you pray with all your pow - er, While we try to preach the Word?
Let us love and pray for sin - ners, Till our God makes all things new.
All is vain un - less the Spir - it Of the Ho - ly One comes down;
Then He'll call us home to heav - en, At His ta - ble we'll sit down;
Breth-ren, pray, and ho - ly man - na Will be show-ered all a - round.
Christ will gird Him - self, and serve us With sweet man - na all a - round.

Irish	Chinese
ate beef, bread, potatoes	ate fish, seaweed, pork
drank coffee	drank tea
wore no hats	wore woven hats
talked and sang	quiet workers
usually tall	usually short
spoke English	spoke Chinese

Tumbling Tumbleweeds
by Bob Nolan

I'm a roaming cowboy, riding all day long,
Tumbleweeds around me, sing their lonely song. Mm—
Nights underneath a prairie moon, Mm—
I ride alone and sing a tune. Mm—

Chorus:
See them tumbling down,
Pledging their love to the ground,
Lonely but free I'll be found,
Drifting along with the tumbling tumbleweeds. Mm—

Cares of the past are behind,
Nowhere to go, but I'll find
Just where the trail will wind,
Drifting along with the tumbling tumbleweeds.

I know when night has gone
That a new world's born at dawn,
I'll keep rolling along,

Deep in my heart is a song,
Here on the range I belong,
Drifting along with the tumbling tumbleweeds.

The British Grenadiers

English Folksong

Some talk of Al - ex - an - der, and some of Her - cu - les,
When e'er we are com - mand - ed to storm the pal - is - ades,
Of Hec - tor and Ly - san - der, and such great names as these;
Our lead - ers march with fus - es, and we with hand gren - ades;
But of all the world's brave he - roes there's none that can com - pare,
We throw them from the gla - cis, a - bout the en - e - mies' ears,
With a tow, row, row, row, row, row, To the Brit - ish Gren - a - diers.
With a tow, row, row, row, row, row, The Brit - ish Gren - a - diers.

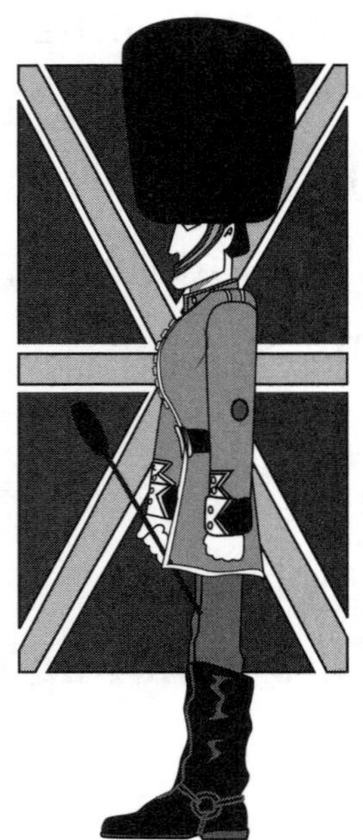

Materials List

Chapter 1

Lesson 1
- A globe
- A *Heritage Studies 4 Student Textbook*
- A *Heritage Studies 4 Student Notebook*
- Appendix, page A2: World Map 1
- Appendix, page A3: World Map 2
- Appendix, page A4: information cards

Lesson 2
- Appendix, page A5: World Map 3
- 2 oranges
- A knife
- A permanent marker
- An atlas
- A globe

Lesson 3
- World Map 3 used in Lesson 2
- A globe (optional)
- 2 small toy boats
- The TimeLine Snapshots
- The figure of Matthew Maury (1850) from the TimeLine Snapshots
- Appendix, page A6: temperature cards

Lesson 4
- An atlas with a map of the world
- A pair of sunglasses
- A heavy coat
- A knit cap
- A straw hat
- A packet of instant cocoa or a tea bag
- A glass of ice water
- A Bible
- Appendix, page A7: weather and rainfall cards
- Appendix, page A8: thermometer

Lesson 5
- The figure of Roald Amundsen (1911) from the TimeLine Snapshots
- An atlas with a map of the world
- Appendix, page A9: exploration questions
- An index card labeled with a "treasure," such as *an extra treat* or *stay up fifteen extra minutes*

Chapter 2

Lesson 6
- A cassette player
- *Heritage Studies Listening Cassette B*
- Family pictures (optional)
- Newspaper clippings (optional)
- 9" square of colored construction paper
- 8 pieces of yellow construction paper
- A Bible
- Felt-tip pens and colored pencils of various colors
- A patchwork quilt or a piece of patchwork
- Supplement, page S2: symbols
- Supplement, page S3: New York Harbor
- Supplement, page S4: Terms
- Supplement, page S5: population chart
- Appendix, page A14: Native American map
- Appendix, page A15: flashcards

Supplemental Lesson
- Presidential figures 1-25 from the TimeLine Snapshots
- Supplement, page S6: excerpt from the Constitution
- Appendix, page A17: research sheet
- Appendix, page A18: presidential profile sheet

Lesson 7
- A bowl with several unpeeled, boiled potatoes
- Some salt
- A small paring knife
- A table knife (optional)
- A scarf
- A shawl
- A globe

Lesson 8
- A dictionary (optional)
- Appendix, page A19: Brainstorming
- A Bible
- Maps and More 2, page M1

Lesson 9
- A Bible
- A cassette player/recorder
- A blank cassette
- A family Bible (optional)
- 15-20 play dollar bills or coins

Lesson 10
- 3 pieces of colored paper or index cards
- Appendix, page A22: Immigrant Questionnaire (optional)
- New York Harbor map from Lesson 6
- The figure of the Statue of Liberty (1886) from the TimeLine Snapshots
- Scarves to be used as head coverings and shawls (optional)
- Suitcases (optional)
- Paper bags (optional)

Lesson 11
- Appendix, pages A23-A24: I Am an American
- A calculator (optional)

Lesson 12
- An American flag
- A dictionary
- Supplement, page S7: pledge
- *Heritage Studies Listening Cassette B*

Chapter 3

Lesson 13

- *HERITAGE STUDIES Listening Cassette B*
- An atlas with a world map
- 2 pieces of construction paper
- A hole punch

Lesson 14

- 2 crib-sized bed sheets, towels, pieces of cloth, or women's long rectangular scarves
- Some safety pins and some hairpins
- Appendix, page A27: a man in ethnic costume
- Appendix, page A28: a woman in ethnic costume
- The figure of Jane Addams (1889) from the TimeLine Snapshots

Lesson 15

- A cookbook
- A world map in an atlas (optional)
- A set of encyclopedias

Lesson 16

- A dictionary

Lesson 17

- Appendix, page A29: signs in Spanish and German to be cut out
- Supplement, page S8: Definitions for Notebook Page 19

Lesson 18

- Three 4" lengths of yarn or ribbon
- The figure of the immigrants (1820) from the TimeLine Snapshots
- Supplement, page S9: Major Points of Entry, 1985
- A dictionary (optional)

Chapter 4

Lesson 19

- *HERITAGE STUDIES Listening Cassette B*
- Maps and More 5, page M2

Lesson 20

- Appendix, page A30: shoes
- A felt-tip pen (optional)
- A shoebox containing a pair of men's shoes
- The figure of D. L. Moody (1861) from the TimeLine Snapshots

Lesson 21

- Maps and More 6 and 7, pages M2-M3

Lesson 22

- Ingredients and utensils for baking fortune cookies *OR* construction-paper circles (about 3" diameter)
- Maps and More 8, page M3
- A globe or atlas with a world map
- 2 rice bowls or baskets
- A metal saucepan
- A rubber hammer or a large metal cooking spoon
- 24 fortune cookies, either baked or made of paper, with a strip containing one of the sentence parts inside each
- Appendix, page A31: sentence beginnings and endings

Lesson 23

- Two missionary prayer cards or letters (*NOTE:* Letters should represent different missionaries and different countries of the world.)
- A globe or atlas with a world map
- Two sheets of construction paper or tagboard
- 3 metal brads or 3 four-inch lengths of yarn
- A hole punch

Lesson 24

- A globe or world map
- A Bible

Chapter 5

Lesson 25

- A Bible
- Maps and More 10 and 11, pages M4-M5
- A pine cone
- A piece of granite
- *HERITAGE STUDIES Listening Cassette B*
- Supplement, page S11: fishermen with lobster pots
- A maple cookie (optional)
- Appendix, page A32: Regions map
- The figure of the signing of the Constitution (1787) from the TimeLine Snapshots
- The figure of the Declaration of Independence (1776) from the TimeLine Snapshots
- The figure of Francis Scott Key (1812) from the TimeLine Snapshots
- An atlas (optional)

Lesson 26

- A Bible
- Maps and More 12 and 13, pages M5-M6
- Several of the following items derived from peanuts: shoe polish, ink, soap, face powder, shaving cream, shampoo, paint, cooking oil, milk, flour, and coffee
- Several roasted peanuts in the shell
- A piece of coal
- A model of a horse
- A picture of the Smoky Mountains
- The figure of Wilbur and Orville Wright (1903) from the TimeLine Snapshots
- Appendix, page A35: Carver Story
- An atlas (optional)

Lesson 27

- A Bible
- Maps and More 15, 16, 17, and 18, pages M6-M8
- Several kernels of corn or a can of corn

- A cereal box (*NOTE:* You may wish to display a cereal brand based in Michigan, such as Kellogg's, Post, or General Foods.)
- A model of or picture of a cow
- A loaf of bread
- Appendix, pages A36-A37: product cards (cut apart and shuffled)
- Appendix, page A38: Products Chart
- An atlas (optional)

Lesson 28
- Maps and More 19 and 21, pages M8-M9
- A picture of the Grand Canyon
- A Bible
- The figure of the Alamo (1836) from the TimeLine Snapshots
- A road atlas
- Several road maps for adjoining states
- Appendix, page A39: United States map
- Appendix, page A40: the four Southwest state cards
- An atlas (optional)

Lesson 29
- Maps and More 22 and 23, pages M9-M10
- A large cardboard box with "Rocky Mountain treasures" (optional)
- *HERITAGE STUDIES Listening Cassette B*
- Appendix, page A41: "America the Beautiful"
- An atlas (optional)

Lesson 30
- A Bible
- Maps and More 23, 24, and 25, pages M10-M12
- A globe
- Approximately 25 buttons or dried beans
- An atlas (optional)

Supplemental Lesson
- Encyclopedias, travel brochures, and/or library books about the state that your child has chosen
- Appendix, pages A42-A47: the state booklet pages
- Materials to build a float: small box and art supplies

Chapter 6

Lesson 31
- A large plate or tray
- 10 items to go on the tray
- A large towel
- A blank sheet of paper
- A clock with a second hand or a stopwatch
- A zip-up jacket
- A button-up sweater with many buttons

Lesson 32
- The figure of James Watt (1769) from the TimeLine Snapshots

Lesson 33
- A bowl of wheat flour
- Packaged items containing wheat (bread, crackers, cereal, pasta, cookies)
- A stalk of wheat or a picture of a stalk of wheat

Lesson 34
- A sewing machine
- Two 4"×4" pieces of fabric for your child and four pieces for you
- A watch or clock with a second hand
- A needle and thread for each of you

Lesson 35

No additional materials needed

Lesson 36
- A ruler
- A large piece of paper
- Scrap paper
- Some books about inventions (from the library or your personal collection)

Chapter 7

Lesson 37
- 5 stones, beans, or buttons
- 2 pieces of candy
- Several quarters
- Several stickers
- A Monopoly game
- Appendix, page A53: Bookmarks
- A Bible

Lesson 38
- A Monopoly game
- The Community Chest and Chance cards from a Monopoly game
- A Bible
- An atlas

Lesson 39
- A Bible
- An expensive-looking necklace
- A book
- A wooden pencil
- A piece of paper
- A large rock

Lesson 40
- A candy bar
- Appendix, page A56: Demand Curve

Lesson 41
- Appendix, page A58: occupation cards (Choose one.)
- Maps and More 27, page M13
- Appendix, page A59: 3 price tags
- Appendix, page A60: Socialist Prices cards (optional)
- Appendix, page A61: Capitalist Prices cards (optional)

Lesson 42
- Appendix, page A62: My List
- A magazine with advertisements

Chapter 8

Lesson 43
- Several homemade items (clothing, baskets, toys, small furniture)
- Pieces of cotton cloth to dye (old socks, T-shirts, pillowcases)
- 1 to 2 cups each of cut-up, stain-producing foods (red or yellow onion skins, spinach leaves, frozen blueberries, red cabbage, or beets)
- 1 to 2 tablespoons coffee or saffron (optional)
- Alum or white vinegar
- Old nylon stockings
- Several pots (glass, enamel, or stainless steel)
- Large, sturdy spoon
- A Bible
- *HERITAGE STUDIES Listening Cassette B*
- Appendix, pages A62-A63: The Wheel of Progress for the Industrial Revolution

Lesson 44
- A small paper bag
- Some raw cotton or a cotton ball
- The Wheel of Progress from Lesson 43

Lesson 45
- 6 small containers
- Appendix, page A64: terms and definitions

Lesson 46
- Appendix, page A65: Changes chart
- The figure representing the Industrial Revolution (1830) from the TimeLine Snapshots
- The Wheel of Progress from Lesson 44

Lesson 47
- The Wheel of Progress from Lesson 46

Lesson 48
- An atlas
- Appendix, page A66: paper bills (cut apart)
- The Wheel of Progress from Lesson 47
- The figure of Andrew Carnegie (1870) from the TimeLine Snapshots

Chapter 9

Lesson 49
- Appendix, page A67: Lesson 49 Story
- Supplement, page S12: Irish and Chinese
- Appendix, page A68: train tickets
- The figure of the transcontinental railroad (1869) from the TimeLine Snapshots
- A hole punch
- Maps and More 28, 29, and 30, pages M13-M14

Lesson 50
- Maps and More 31, page M15

Lesson 51
- A ruler
- A feather

Lesson 52
- An atlas with populations listed
- An envelope
- A sheet of stationery

Lesson 53
- A centimeter ruler
- A globe or an atlas (optional)
- Appendix, page A69: map of Cuba

Lesson 54
- Front-page newspaper headlines from old newspapers
- The front page of a newspaper
- Maps and More 32, page M15
- The figure representing the Spanish-American War (1898) from the TimeLine Snapshots
- An atlas

Chapter 10

Lesson 55
- An atlas

Lesson 56
- A dictionary
- A newspaper
- Newspapers that contain *Gazette* as part of their names (optional)

Lesson 57
- The figure of Samuel Morse (1844) from the TimeLine Snapshots

Lesson 58
- A Bible
- An atlas

Lesson 59
- 2 paper cups
- 2 paper clips
- 25 feet of string
- The figure of Alexander Graham Bell (1876) from the TimeLine Snapshots

Lesson 60
- Appendix, page A73: What's the News?
- A dictionary
- A telegram (optional)

Chapter 11

Lesson 61
- A letter
- A large rock outside
- A small piece of leather (or similar material)
- An atlas
- Maps and More 35, page M16
- Appendix, page A79 or a wall map of the world
- Appendix, page A80: figure of gold miner

Lesson 62
- Supplement, page S14: "The British Grenadiers"
- A picture of Buckingham Palace
- *Heritage Studies Listening Cassette B*
- Maps and More 35, page M16
- Appendix, page A80: figure of soldier with cannon
- Appendix, page A81: question cards

Lesson 63
- An atlas
- Appendix, page A80: missionary family
- A dictionary

Lesson 64
- A Bible
- Appendix, page A80: empress as peasant

Lesson 65
- Maps and More 25, page M12

Chapter 12

Lesson 66
- Two shoe boxes or ballot boxes (optional)
- Appendix, page A88: figures of the donkey and the elephant (optional)

Lesson 67
- Appendix, page A90: Our Constitution activity page
- The figure of the signing of the Constitution (1787) from the TimeLine Snapshots

Lesson 68
- Maps and More 36, page M16

Lesson 69
- Several items from the store that still have the price tags (e.g., a cake mix or a bag of rice)
- The figure of the Bill of Rights (1791) from the TimeLine Snapshots
- Appendix, pages A91-A92: the Bill of Rights pages
- A dictionary

Lesson 70
- The figure of Elizabeth Cady Stanton and Susan B. Anthony (1869) from the TimeLine Snapshots
- The figure representing the Nineteenth Amendment (1919) from the TimeLine Snapshots

Appendix

All the pages that need to be copied for use in the lessons can be found in the Appendix. At the bottom of each page, you will find the corresponding lesson number. Some pages include the word *Enrichment* or *optional* beside the lesson number. You do not need to copy these pages if you will not be doing the Enrichment or optional sections of the lesson. If more than one copy of a page is necessary, it will be indicated at the top of the page. Some pages have gray shaded areas. If these areas do not copy, you may shade them an appropriate color. When teaching more than one child, you will need to refer to the individual lesson to determine whether the page needs to be copied additional times.

World Map 1

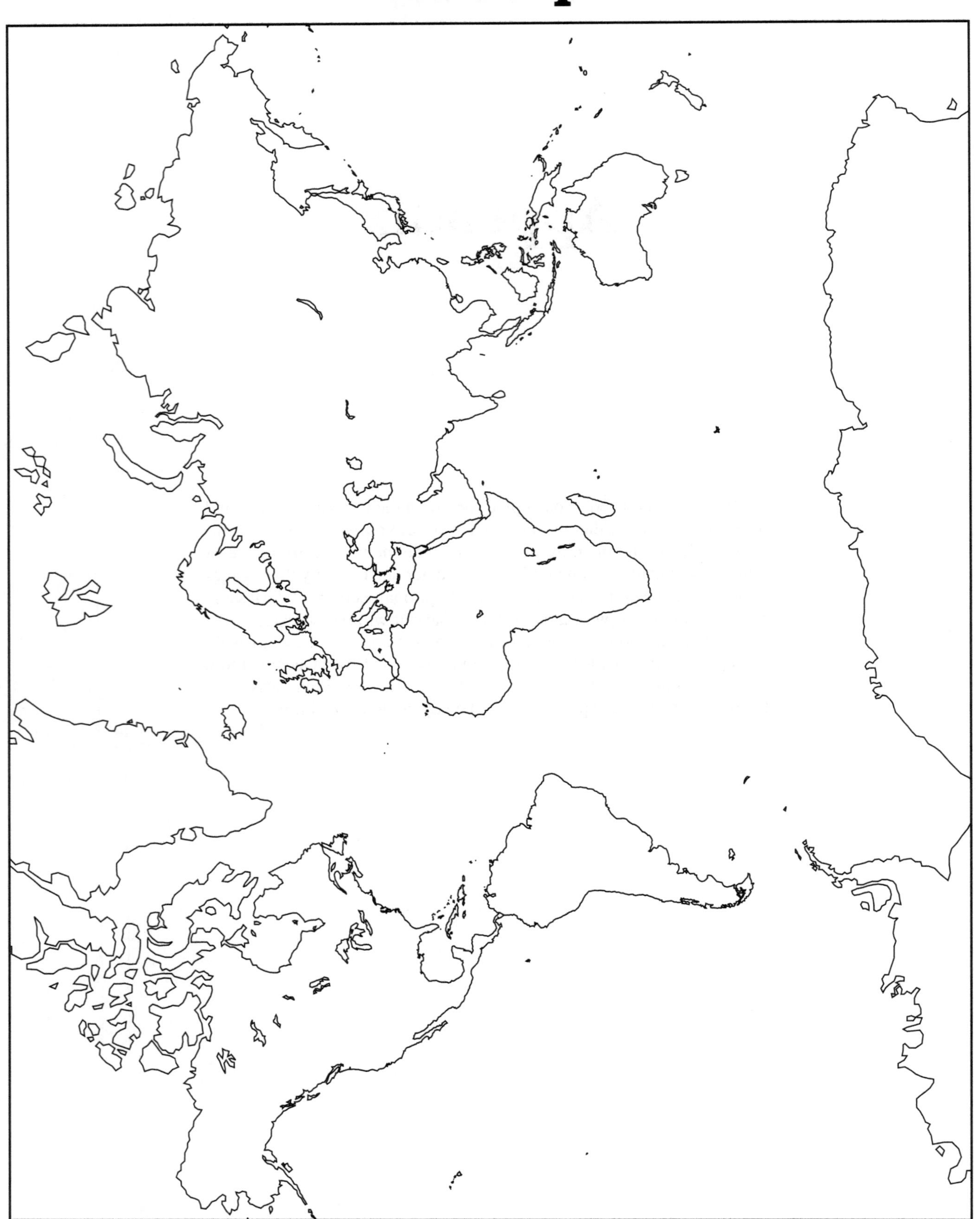

World Map 2

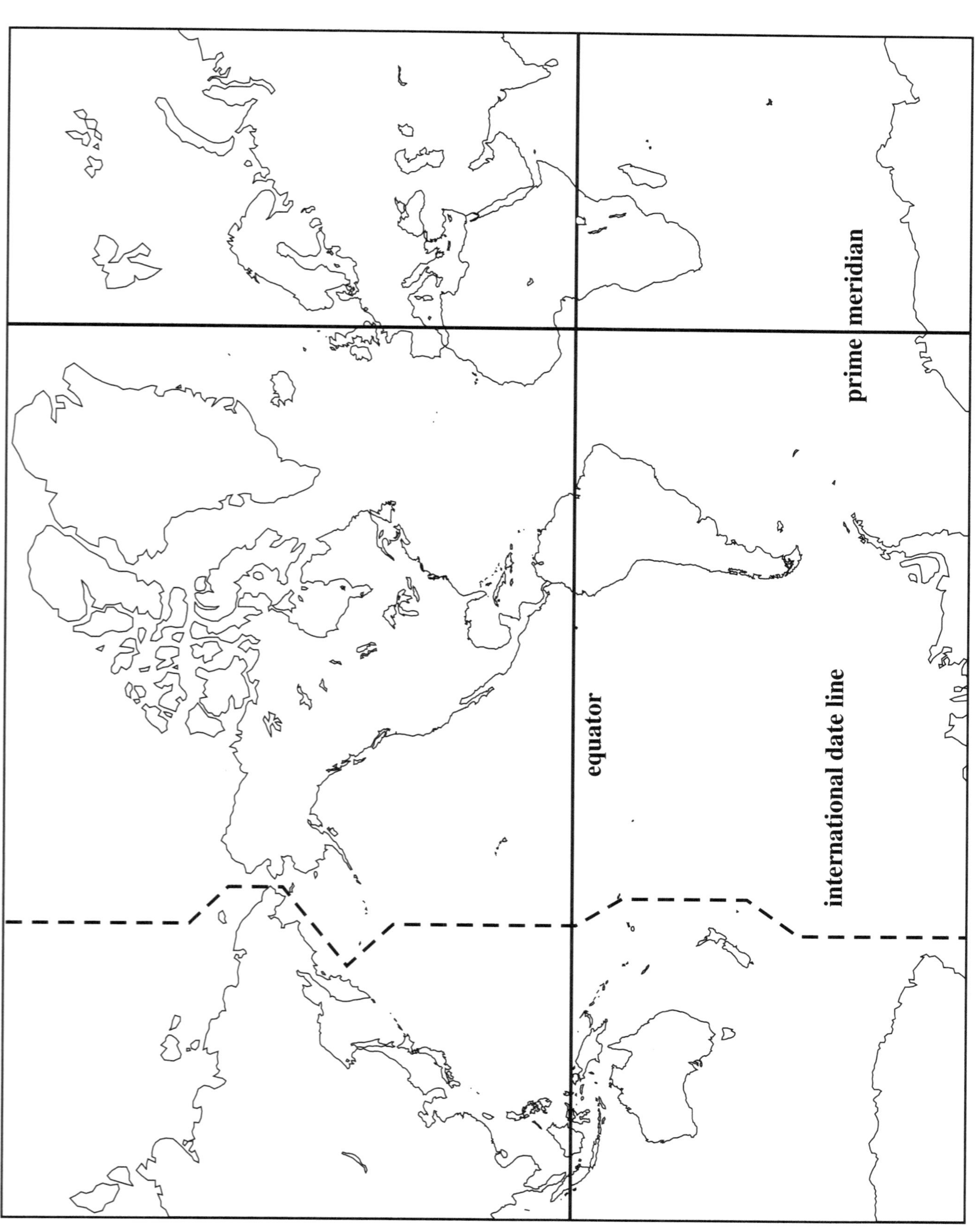

Use with Lesson 1.

Our continent is ______________________.	Our country is ______________________.
Our state is ______________________.	Our hemispheres are ______________________ and ______________________.
Our state borders the ______________________ Ocean.	

World Map 3

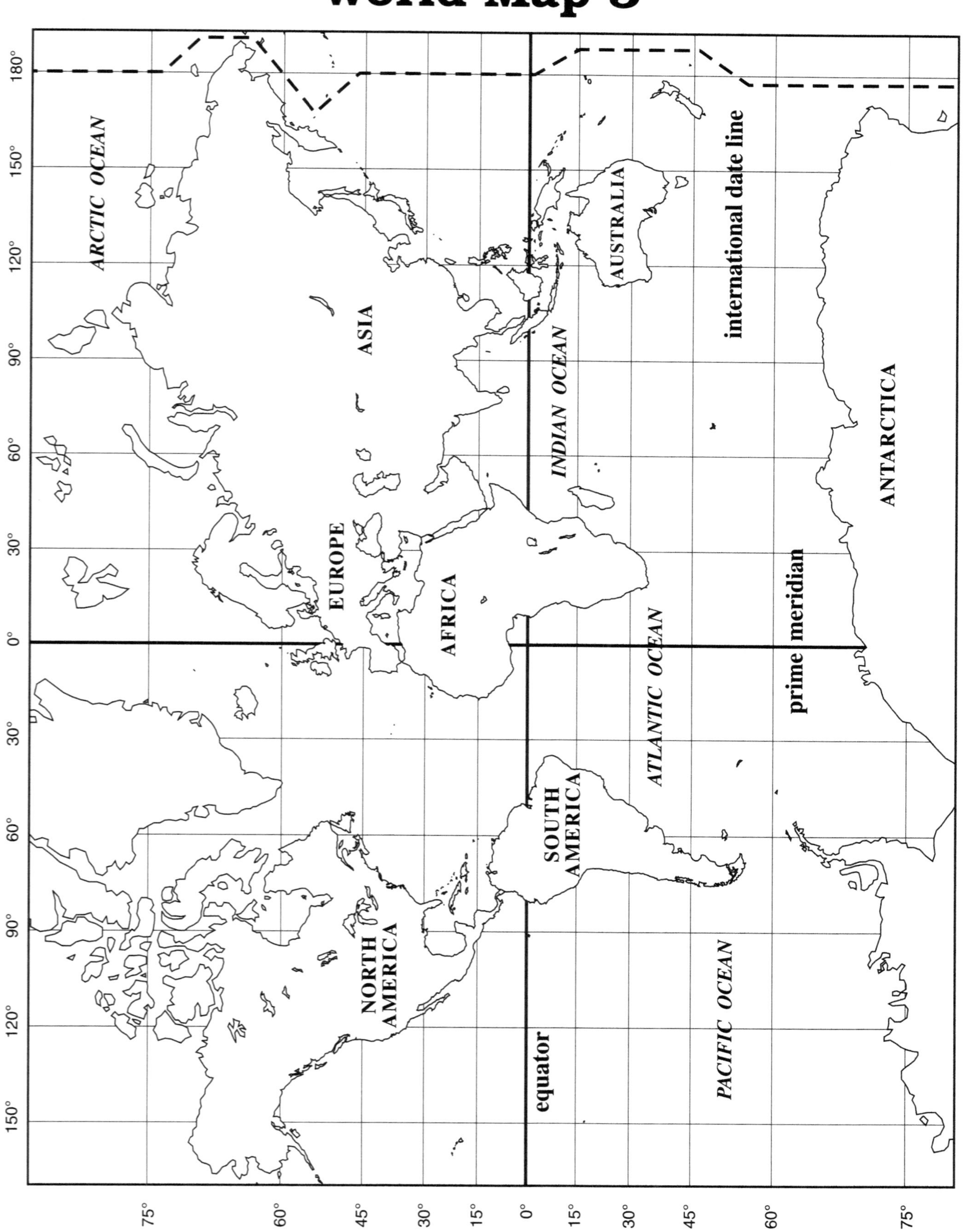

ARCTIC OCEAN
ASIA
EUROPE
AFRICA
INDIAN OCEAN
AUSTRALIA
international date line
ANTARCTICA
prime meridian
ATLANTIC OCEAN
SOUTH AMERICA
NORTH AMERICA
PACIFIC OCEAN
equator
180°
150°
120°
90°
60°
30°
0°
30°
60°
90°
120°
150°
75°
60°
45°
30°
15°
0°
15°
30°
45°
60°
75°

Average January Temperatures

High ________ Low ________

Average July Temperatures

High ________ Low ________

Average Yearly Rainfall

______________ inches

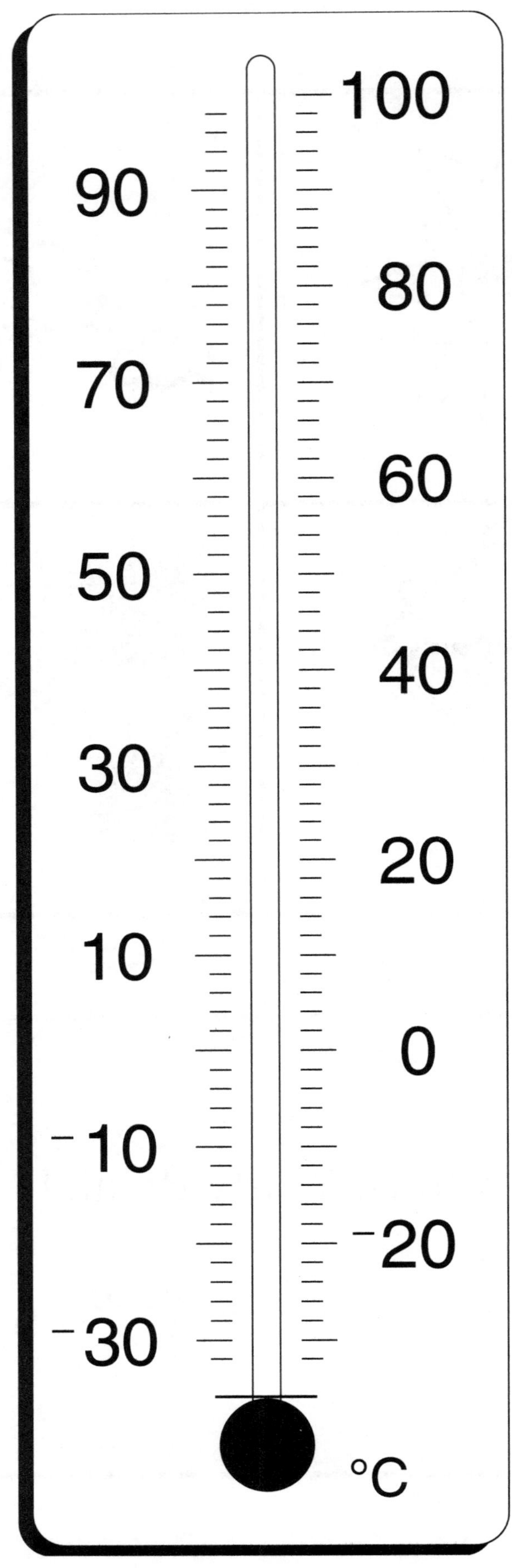
100
90
80
70
60
50
40
30
20
10
0
-10
-20
-30
°C

Exploration 1 Name the highest mountain in the world.	**Exploration 2** List three land formations found on the ocean floor.
Exploration 3 True or False: Amundsen discovered the North Pole.	**Exploration 4** List two characteristics that describe Amundsen's life.
Exploration 5 Name the longest river in the world.	**Exploration 6** Name the first European to see Victoria Falls.
Exploration 7 List one reason people explore the earth.	**Exploration 8** True or False: Antarctica was discovered in 1509.

front of clue cards

back of clue cards

highest mountain in the world	longest river in the world	height above sea level
He discovered the South Pole.	imaginary line that circles the globe at its "fattest" part	He charted ocean currents.
He was the first Englishman to see Victoria Falls.	imaginary north-to-south line that passes through Greenwich, England	what God put on the earth for our use and enjoyment
largest island in the world	the 180th meridian	largest ocean in the world
He led the second team to reach the South Pole.	the area between the tropic of Cancer and the tropic of Capricorn	the year Antarctica was discovered
deepest place in the ocean	the area north of 66°N latitude	the smallest of the seven continents
last continent to be discovered	the area south of 66°S latitude	combined name for the largest landmass in the world
imaginary lines that run north and south around the earth	imaginary lines that run east and west around the earth	the half of the earth that is north of the equator
the half of the earth that is south of the equator	the half of the earth that is east of the prime meridian	the half of the earth that is west of the prime meridian
the normal condition of the atmosphere at the earth's surface	mountain range with the highest altitude	English missionary who served God in China

Antarctica	Western Hemisphere	1820
Nile River	Matthew Maury	Southern Hemisphere
Climate	Antarctic Circle	Hudson Taylor

Robert Scott	Arctic Circle	Western Hemisphere
1820	Tropics	Southern Hemisphere
Nile River	David Livingstone	Prime Meridian

Mount Everest	Mariana Trench	Hudson Taylor
Greenland	Eastern Hemisphere	Meridians of Longitude
International Date Line	Altitude	Robert Scott

Arctic Circle	Climate	David Livingstone
Australia	Mariana Trench	Parallels of Latitude
Himalaya Mountains	Mount Everest	Natural Resources

Meridians of Longitude	Tropics	Northern Hemisphere
Antarctic Circle	Pacific Ocean	Antarctica
Prime Meridian	Equator	Himalaya Mountains

Greenland	Roald Amundsen	Matthew Maury
Eurasia	International Date Line	Equator
Eastern Hemisphere	Parallels of Latitude	Altitude

Mount Everest	Prime Meridian	Australia
Eurasia	Climate	Roald Amundsen
Natural Resources	Pacific Ocean	International Date Line

Equator	Eurasia	Altitude
Hudson Taylor	Northern Hemisphere	Climate
Arctic Circle	Meridians of Longitude	Roald Amundsen

Robert Scott	Altitude	David Livingstone
Parallels of Latitude	Antarctic Circle	Natural Resources
Pacific Ocean	Mount Everest	Arctic Circle

Robert Scott	Meridians of Longitude	Tropics
Natural Resources	Eurasia	Western Hemisphere
Australia	Nile River	Matthew Maury

Antarctica	Roald Amundsen	Parallels of Latitude
Eastern Hemisphere	Pacific Ocean	Hudson Taylor
Greenland	Matthew Maury	Southern Hemisphere

Greenland	1820	Matthew Maury
Equator	Prime Meridian	David Livingstone
Mariana Trench	Northern Hemisphere	Tropics

Indian Nations of Long Ago

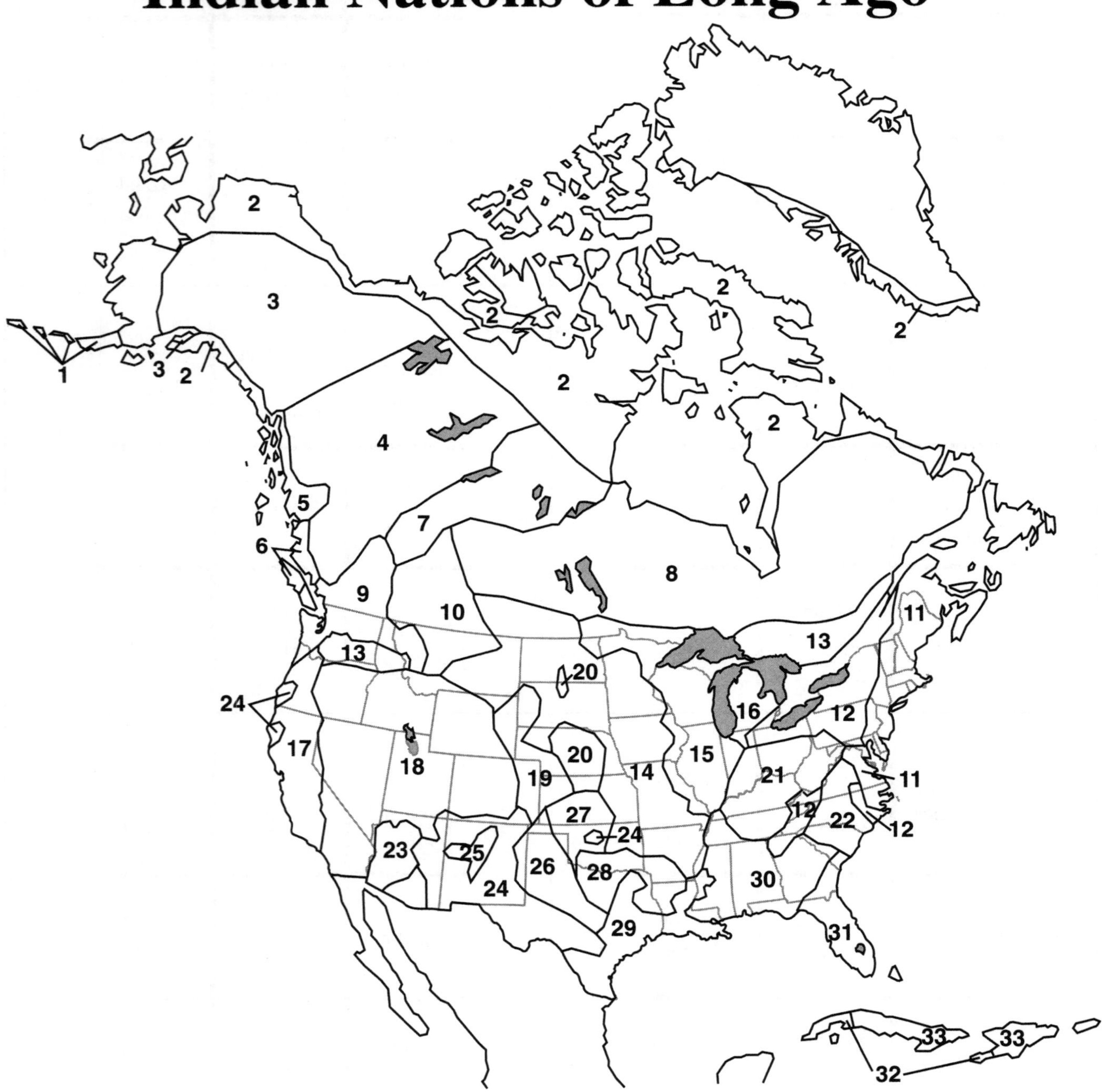

Colossus	a huge statue of a man that stood near a Greek harbor
brazen	made of brass
exiles	persons forced to leave their country
pomp	a magnificent display

Read the clues to complete the crossword puzzle.

ACROSS

4. The country that gave the Statue of Liberty to the United States
6. People whose first image of America is the Statue of Liberty
8. What the statue holds in her arm
10. The material from which the statue is made
11. The number of spikes on her headpiece
12. What Lady Liberty is wearing

DOWN

1. What the Statue of Liberty wears on her head
2. Another name for the base of the statue
3. What lies broken at Miss Liberty's feet
5. The last name of the author of "The New Colossus"
7. The color of the "door to America"
9. What the statue holds in her uplifted hand

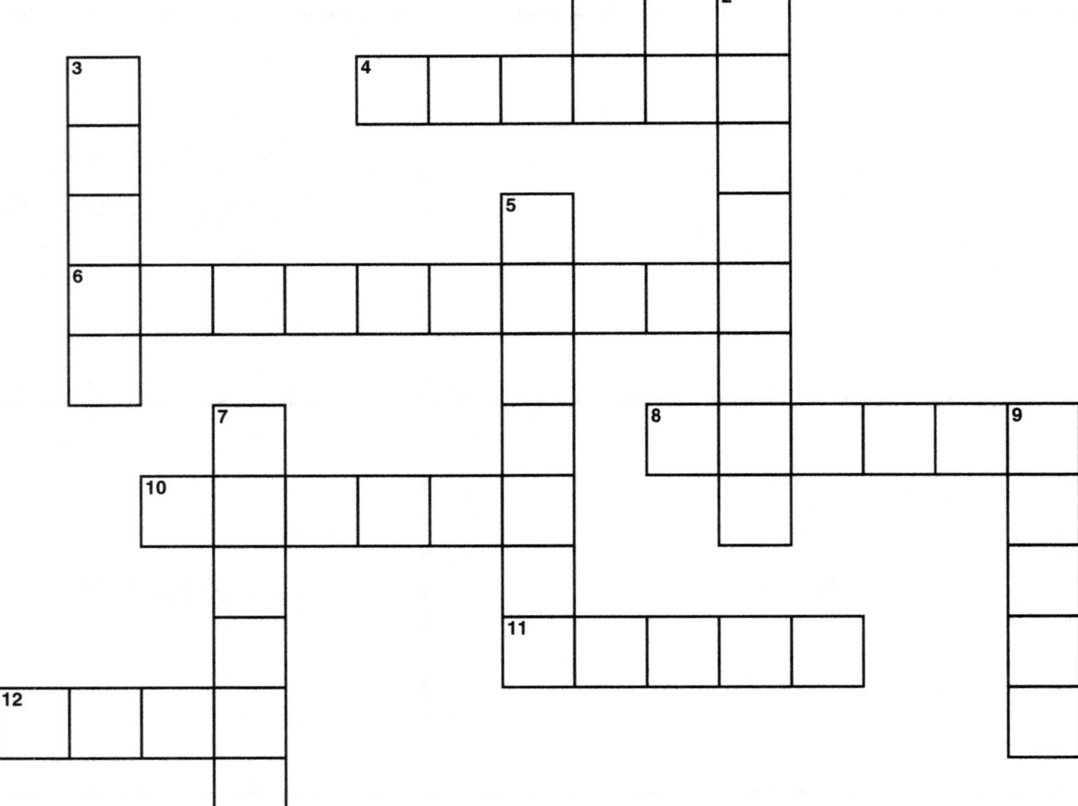

Research

Look for the information about these U.S. presidents using pages 268-79.

1. If you were Ulysses S. Grant, what would you have eaten for breakfast during the Civil War? ______________________________

____

2. On what day did presidents John Adams, Thomas Jefferson, and James Monroe die? ______________________________

____

What is significant about this day? ______________________________

____

3. Which president has two middle names? ______________________________

____

4. What was unique about James Knox Polk's inaugural address? ________

____

5. What did Franklin D. Roosevelt add to the White House? ____________

____

6. Which two presidents were born in 1767? ______________________________

____

7. President Kennedy is often referred to as "JFK." What do these initials stand for? ______________________________

8. Which president introduced ice cream, waffles, and macaroni to the United States? ______________________________

9. Which president gave the Gettysburg Address while suffering from smallpox? ______________________________

10. What was unique about the first president's teeth? ______________

____

Presidential Profile

Determine whether the person described is qualified to be president of the United States. If the person is qualified, circle the number. If he or she is not qualified, draw an *X* over the number.

1. Bill Smith was born in California and graduated with a degree in physics from Stanford. He is thirty-four years old.

2. Mark Franklin teaches sixth grade at an elementary school in Massachusetts where he was born. For his fortieth birthday, his students gave him a special book about the United States Constitution.

3. Miriam Anderson was born in Texas. She has taught economics at a college there for almost thirty years.

4. Walter Frederick, an English citizen, participated in the British Parliament for many years. Now he is in his late sixties and follows American politics with great interest.

5. Maria Valdez was born in California. She works for the United States Embassy in Puerto Rico as a translator. She has met many important government officials there and has learned a lot about politics. On her thirty-fifth birthday, she was appointed to be an ambassador.

6. Dr. Sarah Rennick has just set up a medical practice near Washington, D.C. At thirty-three years old, she follows politics very closely. She wants the government to represent and serve the people as much as possible.

7. Senator Johnson is in his early seventies. He is popular in his home state of Kansas.

8. Paul Craft was born in New York but has lived in France for most of his life. Out of his fifty years, he has spent only about ten years in New York.

Brainstorming

Pedro Amado and his family live in Brazil. Pedro will be coming to the United States and spending six months with our family. Brainstorm as a group and write your answers below.

1. What are some potential problems Pedro might have?____________________

2. How could our family prepare for his coming?____________________

3. How could our family make him feel welcome when he comes?____________________

Four-Generation Pedigree Chart

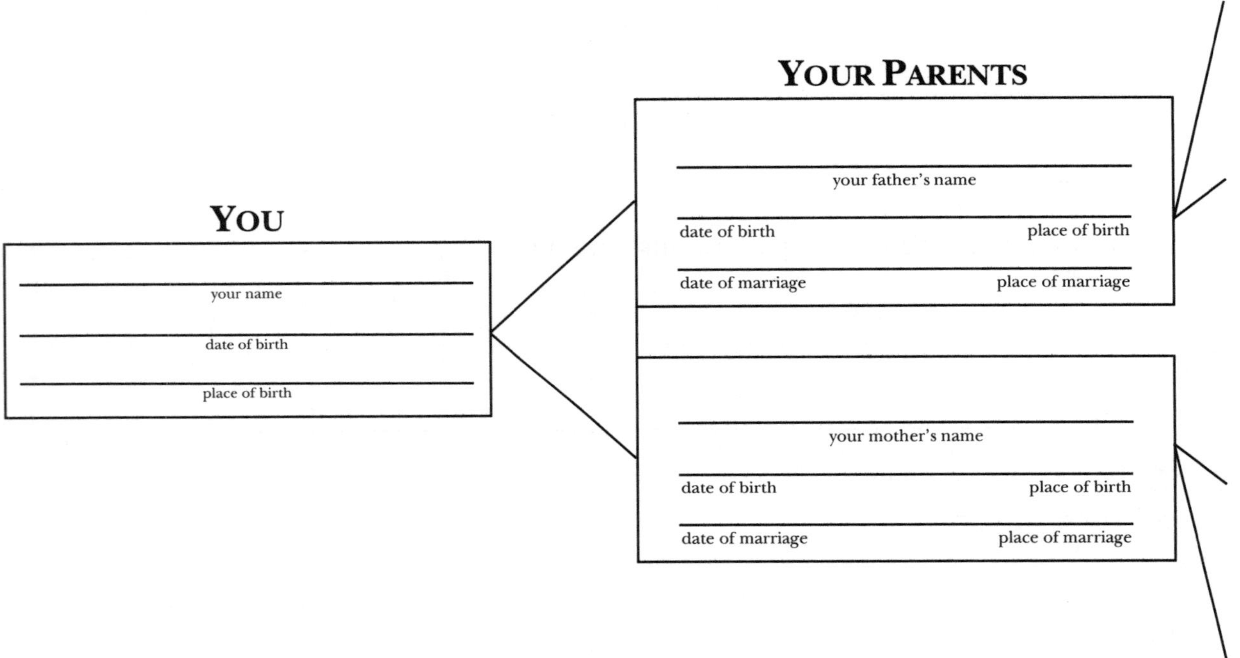

YOUR PATERNAL GRANDPARENTS

your father's father's name

date of birth — place of birth

date of marriage — place of marriage

date of death — place of death

your father's mother's name

date of birth — place of birth

date of marriage — place of marriage

date of death — place of death

YOUR PATERNAL GREAT-GRANDPARENTS

your father's father's father's name

date of birth — date of death

your father's father's mother's name

date of birth — date of death

your father's mother's father's name

date of birth — date of death

your father's mother's mother's name

date of birth — date of death

YOUR MATERNAL GRANDPARENTS

your mother's father's name

date of birth — place of birth

date of marriage — place of marriage

date of death — place of death

your mother's mother's name

date of birth — place of birth

date of marriage — place of marriage

date of death — place of death

YOUR MATERNAL GREAT-GRANDPARENTS

your mother's father's father's name

date of birth — date of death

Your mother's father's mother's name

date of birth — date of death

your mother's mother's father's name

date of birth — date of death

your mother's mother's mother's name

date of birth — date of death

OFFICIAL DOCUMENT

UNITED STATES OF AMERICA

1. What is your name? ______________________________

2. How old are you? ____________ Are you married or single? ______________

3. What is your occupation? ______________________________

4. Are you able to read and write? _____ What is your nationality? ______________

5. Where was your last residence? ______________________________

6. At which United States seaport did you land? ______________________________

7. What is your final destination in the United States? ______________________

8. Do you have a ticket to your destination? ______________________________

9. Did you pay for your passage to the United States? If not, who did? __________

____

10. Do you have money with you? How much? ______________________________

11. Are you going to join a relative? What relative? Name and address? __________

______________ ____

12. Have you ever been to the United States before? Where and when? __________

____

13. Have you ever been in prison, in a poorhouse, or supported by charity? ________

14. Are you under contract to perform labor in the United States? ______________

15. What is the condition of your health, mental and physical? ______________

____

I Am an American

Stanza 1

I am an American.
My father belongs to the Sons of the Revolution;
My mother, to the Colonial Dames.
One of my ancestors pitched tea overboard in Boston Harbor;
Another stood his ground with Warren;
Another hungered with Washington at Valley Forge.
My forefathers were America in the making:
They spoke in her council halls;
They died on her battlefields;
They commanded her ships;
They cleared her forests.
Dawns reddened and paled.
Staunch hearts of mine beat fast at each new star
In the nation's flag.
Keen eyes of mine foresaw her greater glory:
The sweep of her seas,
The plenty of her plains,
The man-hives in her billion-wired cities.
Every drop of blood in me holds a heritage of patriotism.
I am proud of my past.
I am an AMERICAN.

Elias Lieberman

I Am an American

Stanza 2

I am an American.
My father was an atom of dust,
My mother a straw in the wind,
To His Serene Majesty.
One of my ancestors died in the mines of Siberia;
Another was crippled for life by twenty blows of the knout.
Another was killed defending his home during the massacres.
The history of my ancestors is a trail of blood
To the palace-gate of the Great White Czar.
But then the dream came—
The dream of America.
In the light of the Liberty torch
The atom of dust became a man
And the straw in the wind became a woman
For the first time.
"See," said my father, pointing to the flag that fluttered near,
"That flag of stars and stripes is yours;
It is the emblem of the promised land.
It means, my son, the hope of humanity.
Live for it—die for it!"
Under the open sky of my new country I swore to do so;
And every drop of blood in me will keep that vow.
I am proud of my future.
I am an AMERICAN.

Elias Lieberman

Color the picture. Fill in the blanks.

Middle-Eastern Man
Late 1800s

Hats come in all shapes and sizes. People in different areas of the world wear different types of hats. Muslim and Hindu men wear a special hat called a ________________.

Turbans are worn to keep the head cool and to shield the face from sand.

Do people in your family wear turbans? ________________

Color the picture. Fill in the blanks.

Egyptian woman
Late 1800s

Women around the world wear different types of hats. Their hats vary in size, shape, and color. Some women wear hats because their religion demands it. Others wear hats because they want to look stylish. Women also wear hats to protect them from the hot sun.

Many Muslim women wear special hats called ____________. They wear veils to keep their faces hidden from the view of strangers. For them, veils symbolize the modesty required by their religion. Do any women in America wear veils? ___________

recién pintado

nasse Farbe

At age five, Hudson Taylor . . .	. . . decided to go to China..
Hudson Taylor was a missionary writer . . .	. . . and a doctor.
Hudson Taylor believed that the best way to reach the Chinese . . .	. . . was to become as nearly Chinese as possible.
Hudson Taylor had his head shaved except for a section in the back . . .	. . . which he had woven into a pigtail.
When Taylor dressed in Chinese clothing, the Chinese . . .	. . . received him eagerly and listened to the gospel.
When Taylor dressed in Chinese clothing, his English friends . . .	. . . scorned him, thinking he was crazy.
In 1860, Taylor returned to England because . . .	. . . he was sick.
While Taylor was in England, he revised . . .	. . . the Chinese New Testament.
When Taylor was burdened about the Chinese, he prayed for . . .	. . . twenty-four skilled and willing workers to go to inland China.
The China Inland Mission . . .	. . . was an organization dedicated to getting missionaries and funds to China.
Some Chinese hated foreigners and called them . . .	. . . "foreign devils" or "Western dogs."
By the time Hudson Taylor died, . . .	. . . the Chinese Inland Mission had mission stations in every province in China.

Regions

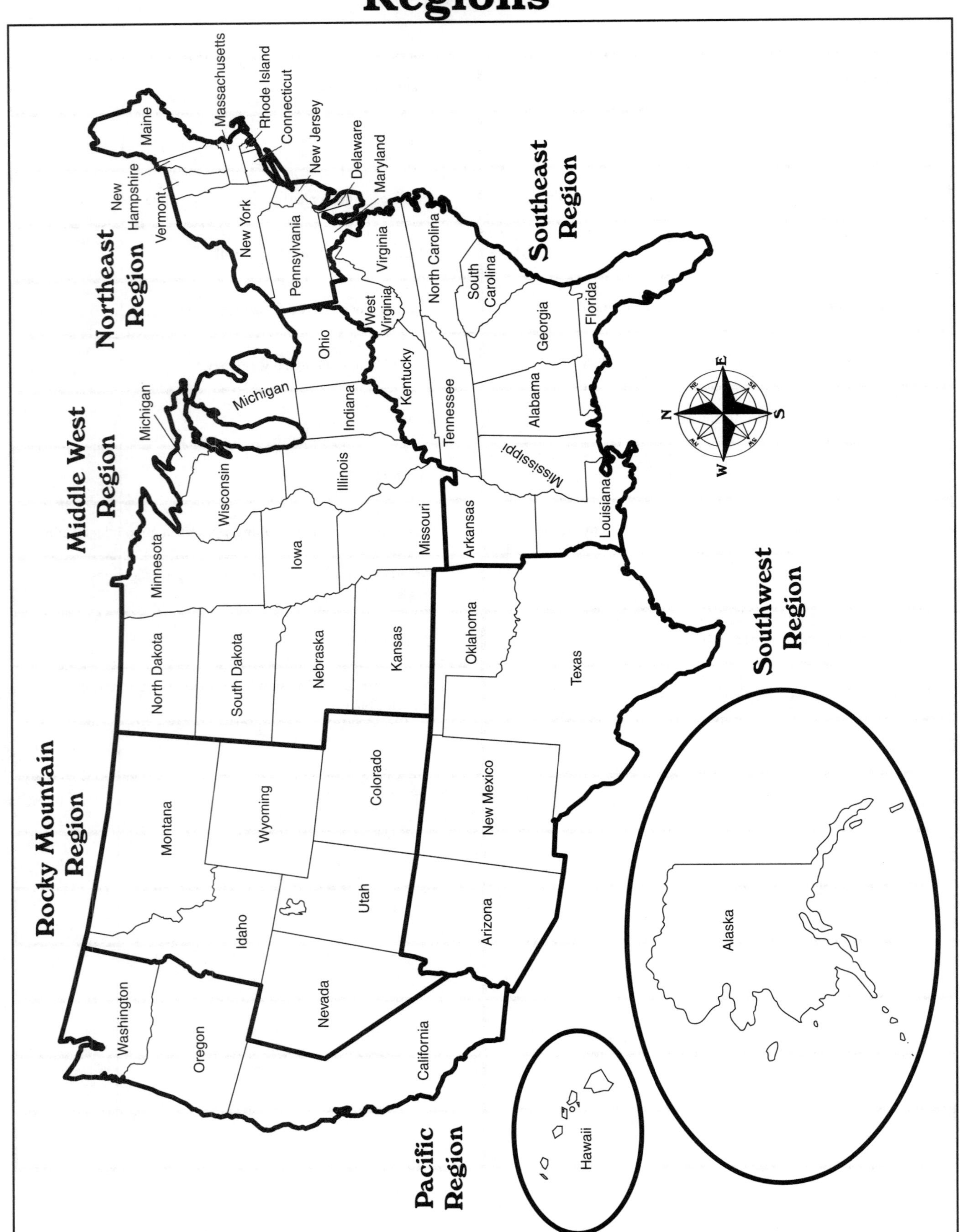

Northeast Region
Southeast Region
Middle West Region
Southwest Region
Rocky Mountain Region
Pacific Region
Maine
Massachusetts
Rhode Island
Connecticut
New Jersey
Delaware
Maryland
New Hampshire
Vermont
New York
Pennsylvania
Virginia
West Virginia
North Carolina
South Carolina
Georgia
Florida
Ohio
Michigan
Indiana
Kentucky
Tennessee
Alabama
Mississippi
Louisiana
Wisconsin
Illinois
Iowa
Missouri
Arkansas
Minnesota
North Dakota
South Dakota
Nebraska
Kansas
Oklahoma
Texas
Montana
Wyoming
Colorado
New Mexico
Idaho
Utah
Arizona
Nevada
Washington
Oregon
California
Alaska
Hawaii
N
S
E
W

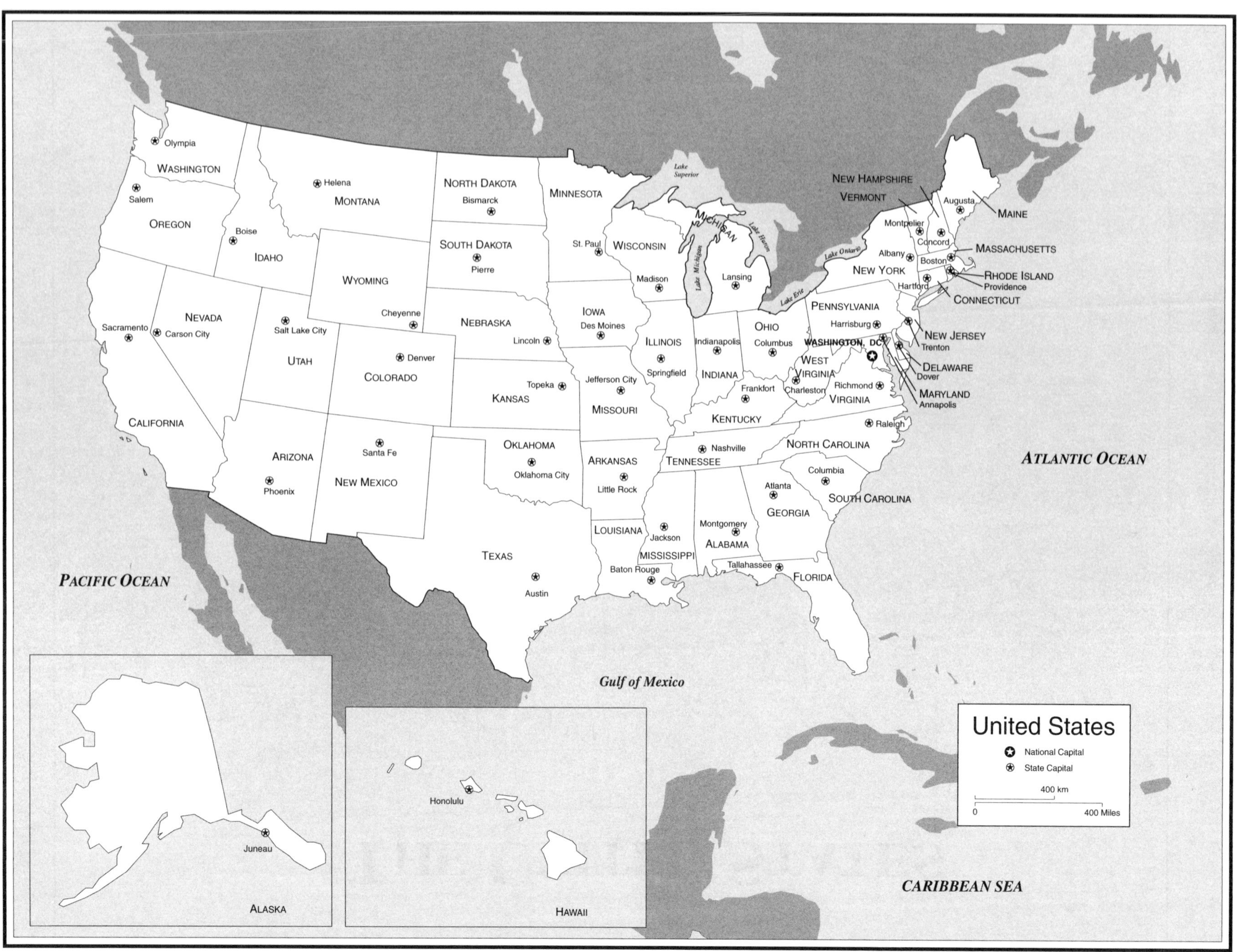
United States
National Capital
State Capital
400 km
0
400 Miles
ATLANTIC OCEAN
PACIFIC OCEAN
Gulf of Mexico
CARIBBEAN SEA
Lake Superior
Lake Michigan
Lake Huron
Lake Erie
Lake Ontario
WASHINGTON
Olympia
OREGON
Salem
IDAHO
Boise
MONTANA
Helena
WYOMING
Cheyenne
NEVADA
Carson City
CALIFORNIA
Sacramento
UTAH
Salt Lake City
COLORADO
Denver
ARIZONA
Phoenix
NEW MEXICO
Santa Fe
NORTH DAKOTA
Bismarck
SOUTH DAKOTA
Pierre
NEBRASKA
Lincoln
KANSAS
Topeka
OKLAHOMA
Oklahoma City
TEXAS
Austin
MINNESOTA
St. Paul
IOWA
Des Moines
MISSOURI
Jefferson City
ARKANSAS
Little Rock
LOUISIANA
Baton Rouge
WISCONSIN
Madison
ILLINOIS
Springfield
MICHIGAN
Lansing
INDIANA
Indianapolis
OHIO
Columbus
KENTUCKY
Frankfort
TENNESSEE
Nashville
MISSISSIPPI
Jackson
ALABAMA
Montgomery
GEORGIA
Atlanta
FLORIDA
Tallahassee
SOUTH CAROLINA
Columbia
NORTH CAROLINA
Raleigh
VIRGINIA
Richmond
WEST VIRGINIA
Charleston
WASHINGTON, DC
PENNSYLVANIA
Harrisburg
NEW YORK
Albany
NEW JERSEY
Trenton
DELAWARE
Dover
MARYLAND
Annapolis
CONNECTICUT
Hartford
RHODE ISLAND
Providence
MASSACHUSETTS
Boston
VERMONT
Montpelier
NEW HAMPSHIRE
Concord
MAINE
Augusta
ALASKA
Juneau
HAWAII
Honolulu

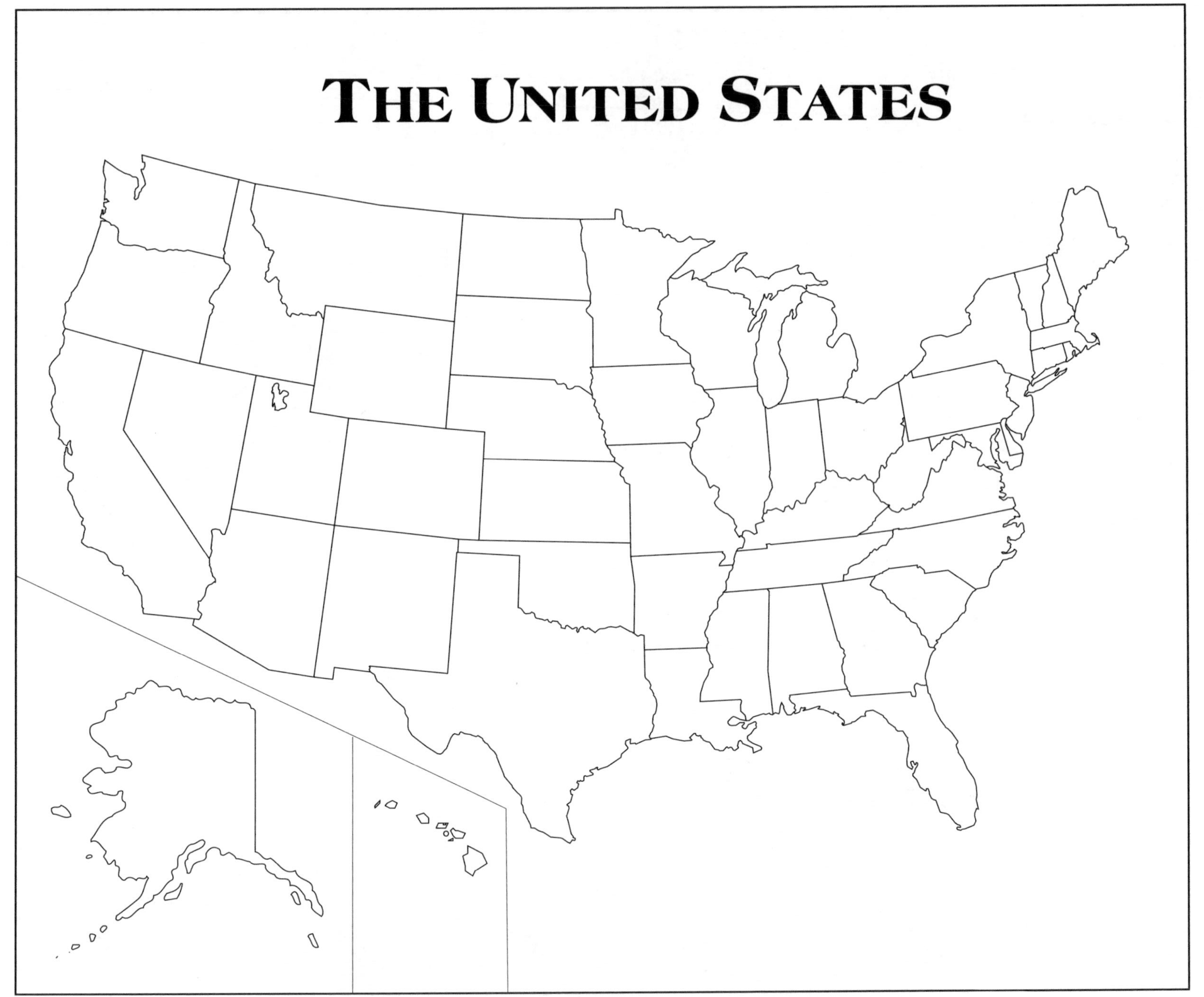
THE UNITED STATES

Carver Story

(Show your child Maps and More 12, pointing to young George Washington Carver as you read the story.)

Who is this small boy bending over a rosebush?

"Poor rosebush! You must be moved into the sun in order to grow in beauty!" he says.

Who is this frail lad, sickly most of his life?

"What a pity!" he thinks to himself. "Look at these wilting leaves! I must find a way to cure this poor plant."

Who is this curious youngster desiring to learn more?

"There is a flower that I've never seen," he says. "I'll take it with me and find out its name."

(Point to the picture of an older George Washington Carver as you continue reading the story.)

Who is this grown man graduating from college?

"What an opportunity—I'm going to teach in Alabama at Tuskegee Institute, a college for blacks," he says.

Who is this caring professor inspiring his students?

"Let me challenge you," he says. "Don't just learn the facts. Discover things for yourself."

Who is this remarkable scientist helping southern farmers?

"I have been experimenting with the peanut, and it is certain that this crop can help the soil and be profitable," he says.

Who is this small boy, frail lad, curious youngster, grown man, caring professor, and remarkable scientist?

"My name is George Washington Carver, otherwise known as 'The Plant Doctor.' After numerous experiments and much hard work, I developed more than three hundred uses for the peanut, including shoe polish, ink, soap, face powder, shaving cream, shampoo, paint, milk, cooking oil, flour, and coffee."

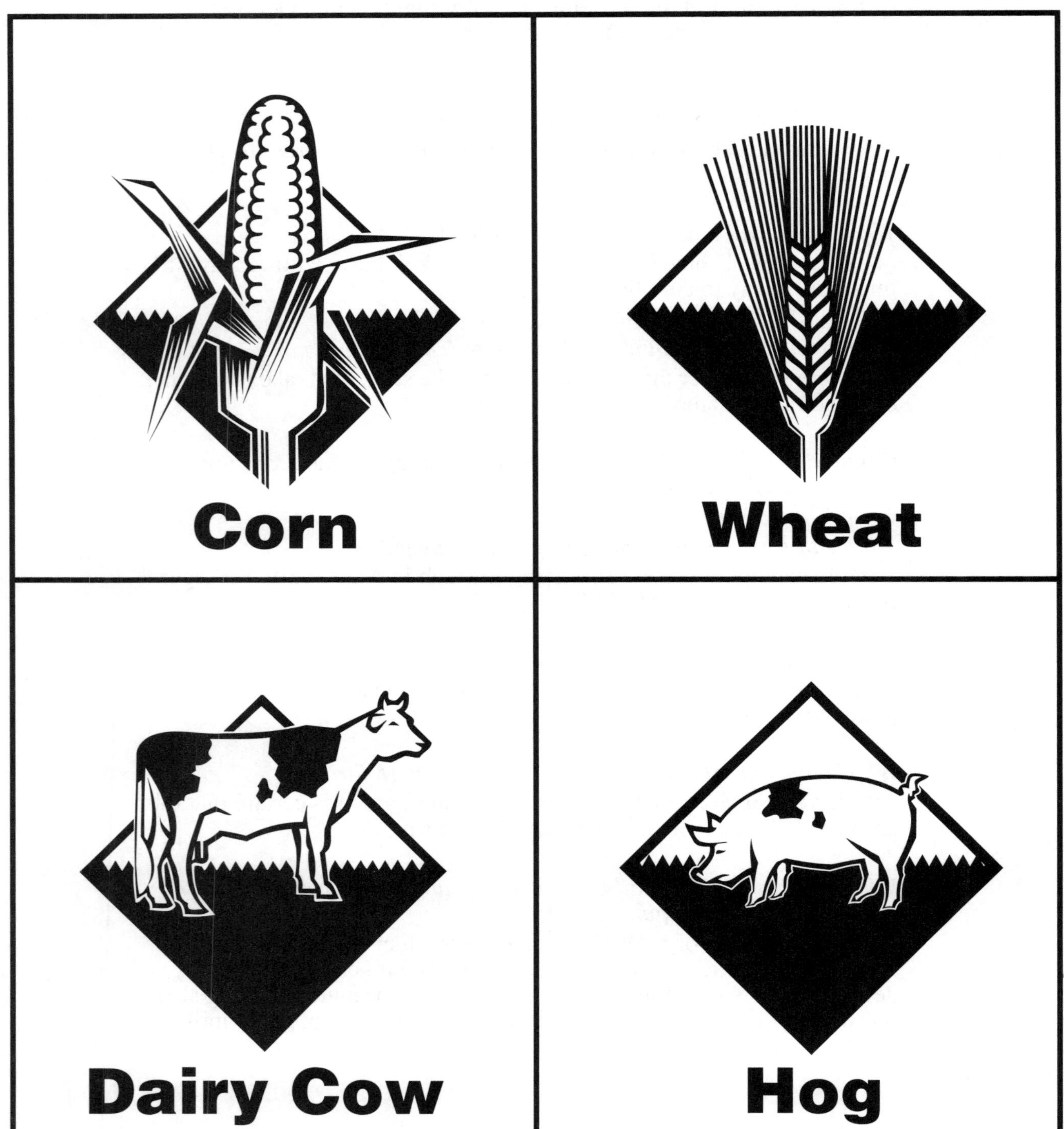
Corn
Wheat
Dairy Cow
Hog

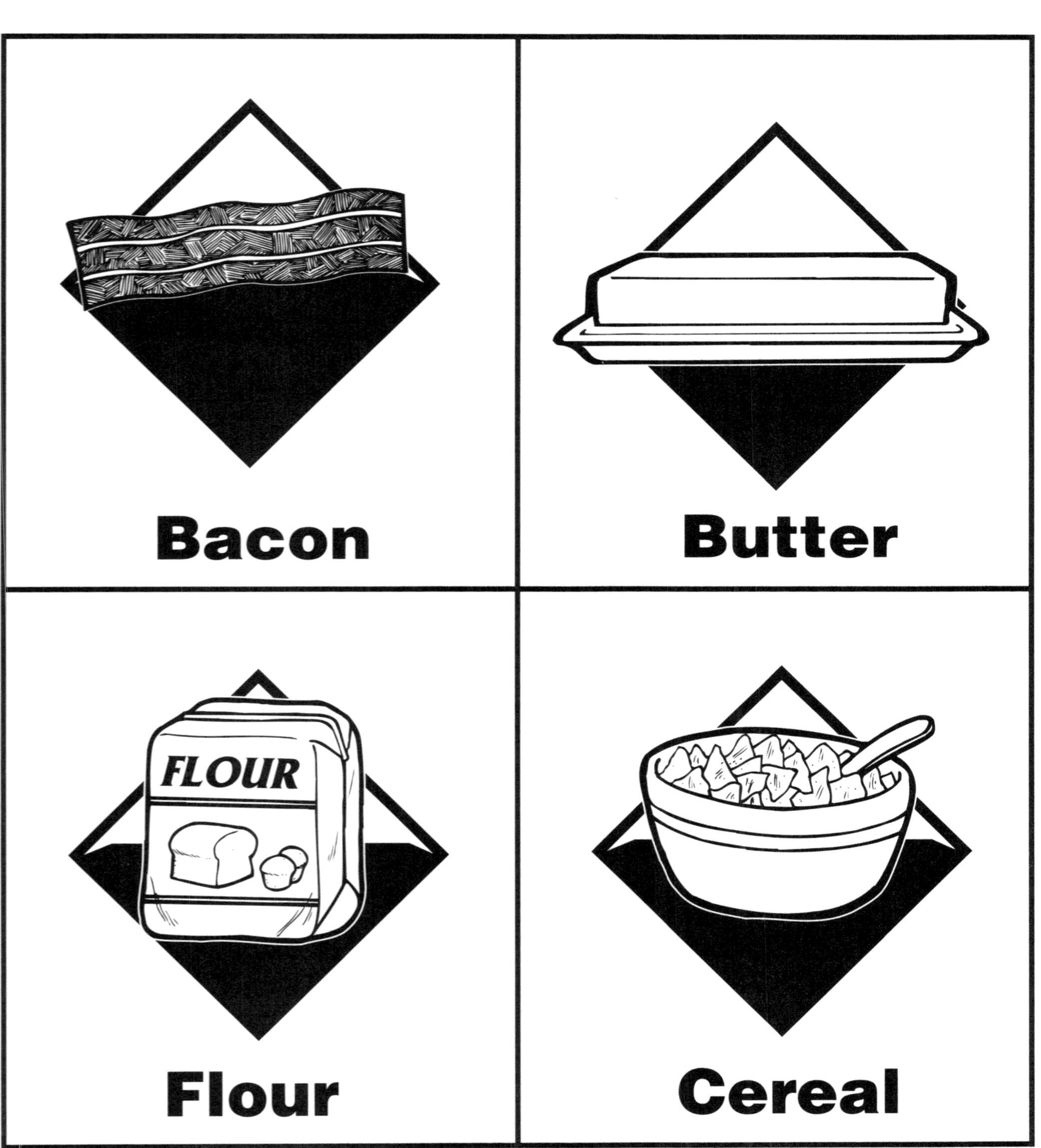
Bacon
Butter
FLOUR
Flour
Cereal

Products Chart

Agricultural (Farm)	Manufactured (Factory)

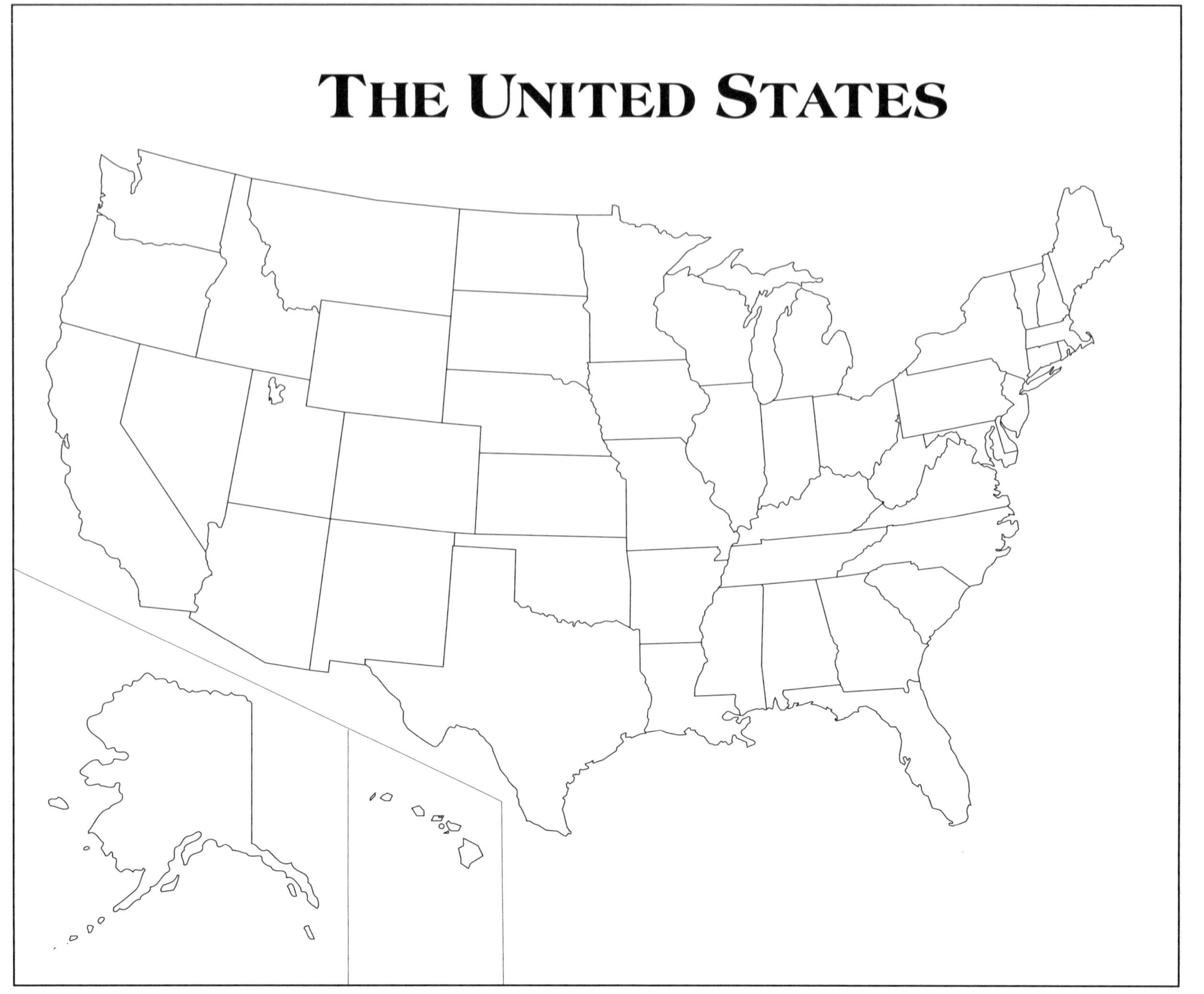
THE UNITED STATES

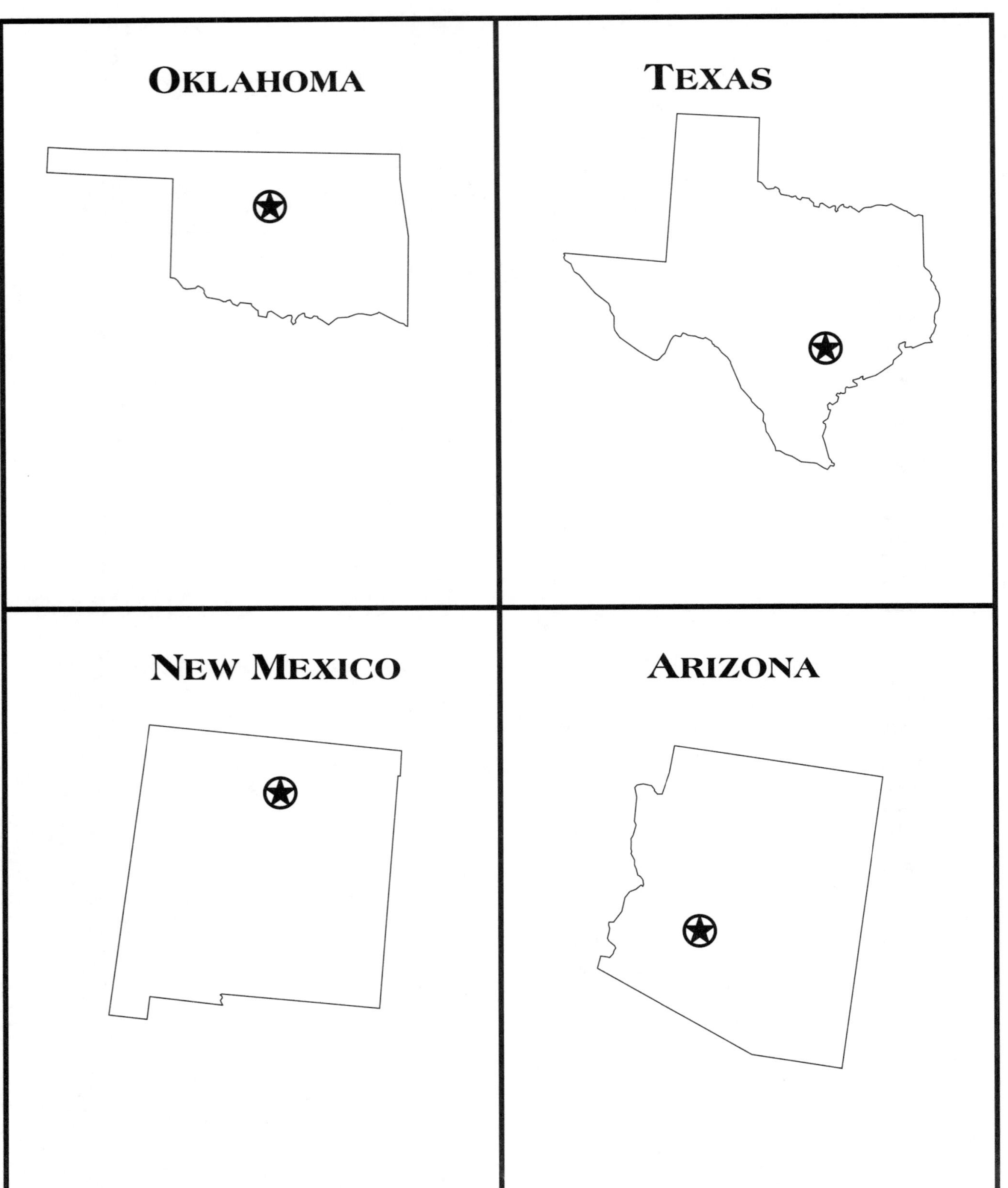
OKLAHOMA
TEXAS
NEW MEXICO
ARIZONA

America the Beautiful
Katherine Lee Bates
Samuel A. Ward
O beau - ti - ful for spa - cious skies, For am - ber waves of grain, For
O beau - ti - ful for pa - triot dream That sees, be - yond the years, Thine
pur - ple moun - tain maj - es - ties A - bove the fruit - ed plain! A -
al - a - bas - ter cit - ies gleam Un - dimmed by hu - man tears! A -
mer - i - ca! A - mer - i - ca! God shed His grace on thee, And
mer - i - ca! A - mer - i - ca! God shed His grace on thee, And
crown thy good with broth - er - hood From sea to shin - ing sea.
crown thy good with broth - er - hood From sea to shin - ing sea.

CONCLUSION

Write one interesting fact about your state.

Write about what you like best in your state.

Draw or glue a picture of a favorite place to visit in your state.

12

MY STATE

name of state

name

date

State report pages must be photocopied back-to-back in the order they appear.

LOCATION

Color your state on the map of the United States.

My state is bordered by

Check the box of the region where your state is located.

- ☐ Northeast
- ☐ Southeast
- ☐ Middle West
- ☐ Southwest
- ☐ Rocky Mountain
- ☐ Pacific

PLACES TO VISIT

Choose one vacation spot in your state. Use the lines below to describe this special place.

Create a post card of your vacation spot in the space below.

STATE HISTORY

Fill in the blanks.

date of statehood

number of statehood

Choose three more important dates in the history of your state to place on the time line below.

date

date

date

event

event

event

Write the name of a famous person from your state. Tell why this person is famous.

STATE MAP

Draw an outline of your state in the space provided. Label the capital and place a star (★) beside it. Label a major river or lake and a major city in your state.

GENERAL INFORMATION

Fill in the following information about your state.

Name of state: ____________________

Nickname: ____________________

Population: ____________________

Capital: ____________________

Flower: ____________________

Bird: ____________________

Tree: ____________________

Song: ____________________

Motto: ____________________

STATE RESOURCES

List three major resources in your state.

1. ____________________
2. ____________________
3. ____________________

Create an advertisement for one of your state's resources in the space provided below.

STATE GEOGRAPHY

Fill in the blanks below.

Two major rivers in my state are ______________________

____.

The highest point in my state is ______________________ (name)

____________________. It is ____________________ (height) high.

The lowest point in my state is ______________________ (name)

___________. It is ______________ (height) above/below sea level.

A famous geographical feature in my state is ___________

____

____.

STATE FLAG

Draw and color your state flag.

STATE FLOWER

Draw or glue a picture of your state flower in the space provided.

name

Describe your state flower.

STATE BIRD

Draw or glue a picture of your state bird in the space provided.

name

Write some interesting facts about your state bird.

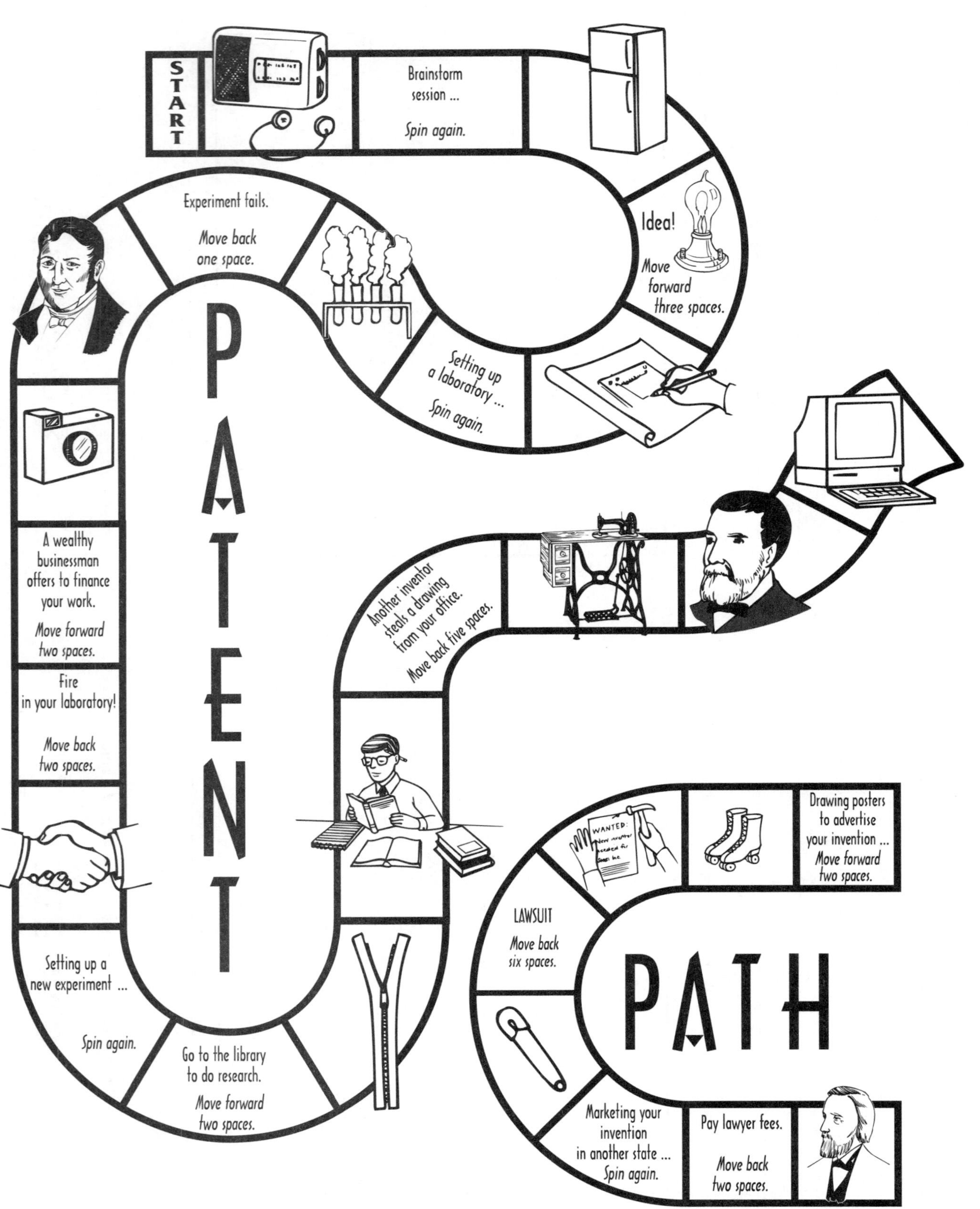
START
Brainstorm session ... Spin again.
Idea! Move forward three spaces.
Setting up a laboratory ... Spin again.
Experiment fails. Move back one space.
PATENT
A wealthy businessman offers to finance your work. Move forward two spaces.
Fire in your laboratory! Move back two spaces.
Setting up a new experiment ... Spin again.
Go to the library to do research. Move forward two spaces.
Another inventor steals a drawing from your office. Move back five spaces.
Drawing posters to advertise your invention ... Move forward two spaces.
WANTED:
LAWSUIT Move back six spaces.
PATH
Marketing your invention in another state ... Spin again.
Pay lawyer fees. Move back two spaces.

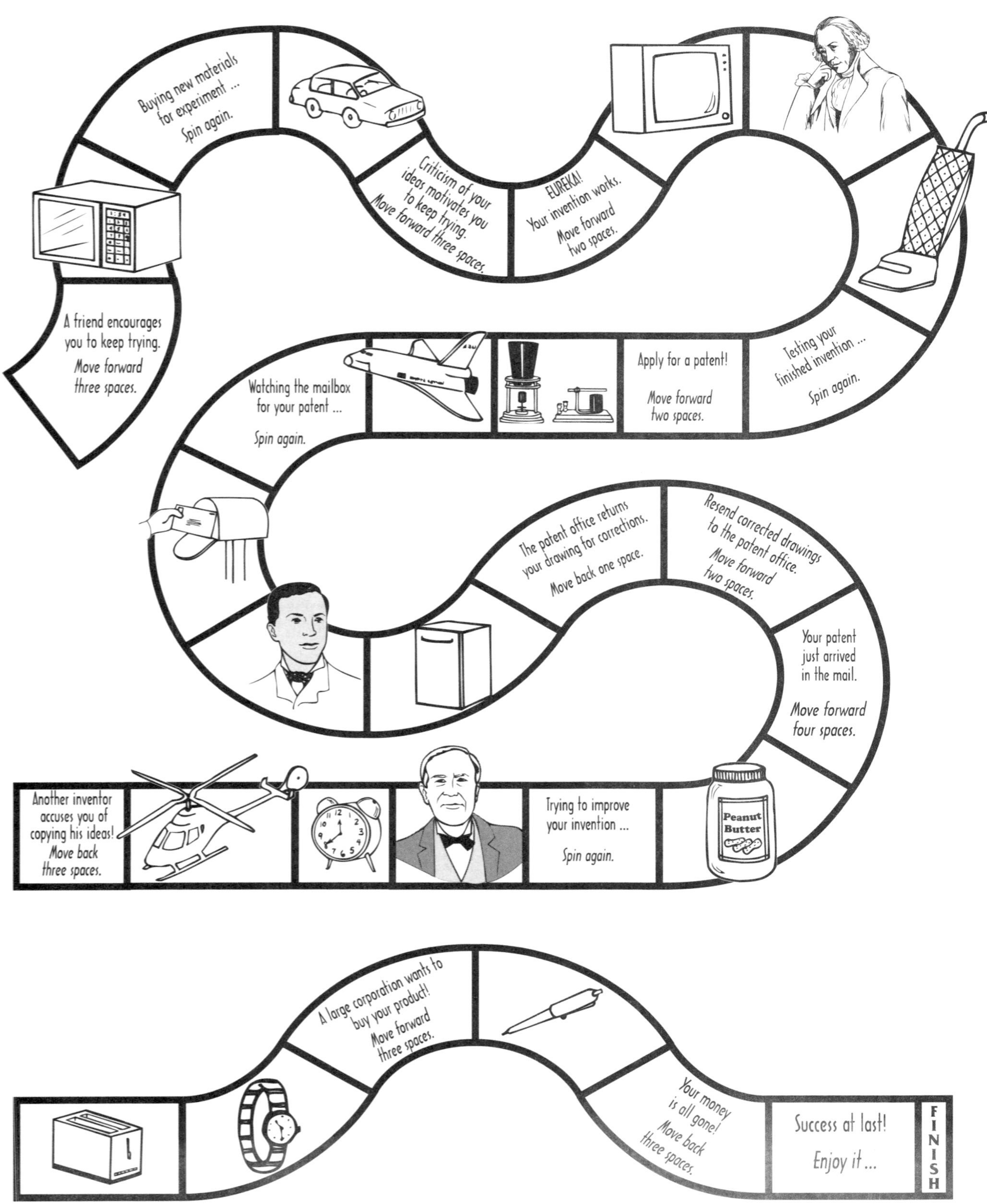
A friend encourages you to keep trying. Move forward three spaces.
Buying new materials for experiment ... Spin again.
Criticism of your ideas motivates you to keep trying. Move forward three spaces.
EUREKA! Your invention works. Move forward two spaces.
Testing your finished invention ... Spin again.
Apply for a patent! Move forward two spaces.
Watching the mailbox for your patent ... Spin again.
The patent office returns your drawing for corrections. Move back one space.
Resend corrected drawings to the patent office. Move forward two spaces.
Your patent just arrived in the mail. Move forward four spaces.
Peanut Butter
Trying to improve your invention ... Spin again.
Another inventor accuses you of copying his ideas! Move back three spaces.
A large corporation wants to buy your product! Move forward three spaces.
Your money is all gone! Move back three spaces.
Success at last! Enjoy it ...
FINISH

Famous Inventor

Famous Inventor

Famous Inventor

Famous Inventor

Famous Inventor

Famous Inventor

Famous Inventor

Famous Inventor

Famous Inventor

Famous Inventor

Famous Inventor

Famous Inventor

Famous Inventor

Famous Inventor

Famous Inventor

Famous Inventor

Q: What famous inventor traveled to England to sell his invention? **A**: Elias Howe	**Q**: What famous inventor worked in a shoe factory? **A**: Jan Matzeliger	**Q**: What famous inventor gave money to D. L. Moody? **A**: Cyrus McCormick	**Q**: What famous inventor said, “Genius is 99 percent perspiration and 1 percent inspiration”? **A**: Thomas Edison
Q: What famous inventor made guns from interchangeable parts? **A**: Eli Whitney	**Q**: What famous inventor taught botany classes at Tuskegee Institute? **A**: George Washington Carver	**Q**: What famous inventor led a church youth group? **A**: Jan Matzeliger	**Q**: What famous inventor thought of an important machine for cotton farmers? **A**: Eli Whitney
Q: What famous inventor established easy credit and guarantees for his customers? **A**: Cyrus McCormick	**Q**: What famous inventor supervised a print shop? **A**: Christopher Sholes	**Q**: What famous inventor developed new ways to use sweet potatoes? **A**: George Washington Carver	**Q**: What famous inventor joined in business with Matthew Boulton? **A**: James Watt
Q: What famous inventor patented more inventions than anyone else? **A**: Thomas Edison	**Q**: What famous inventor grew up in Scotland? **A**: James Watt	**Q**: What famous inventor made a machine that enabled more women to work in offices? **A**: Christopher Sholes	**Q**: What famous inventor received five dollars every time one of his machines was sold? **A**: Elias Howe

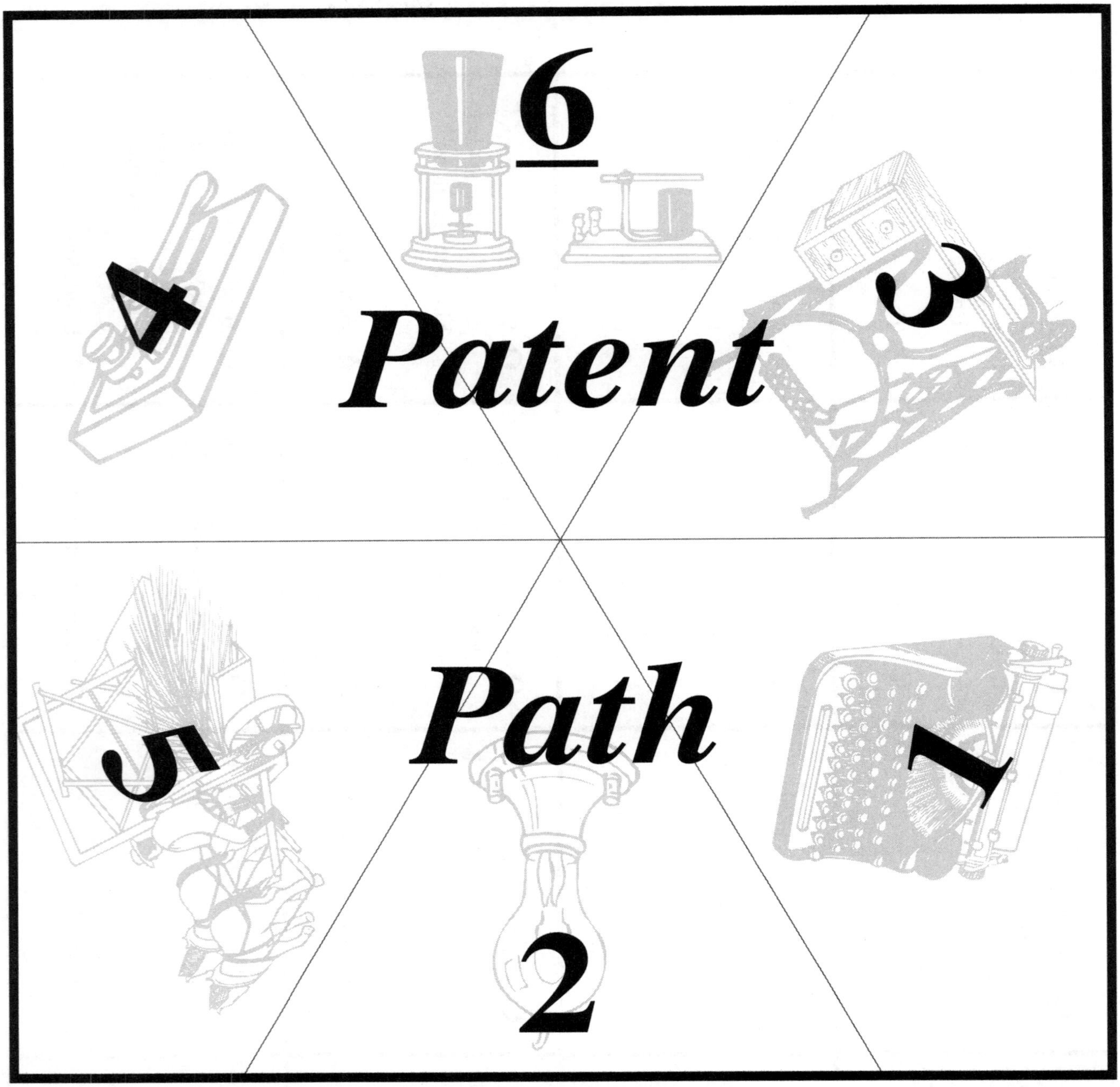

6

4

3

Patent

Path

5

1

2

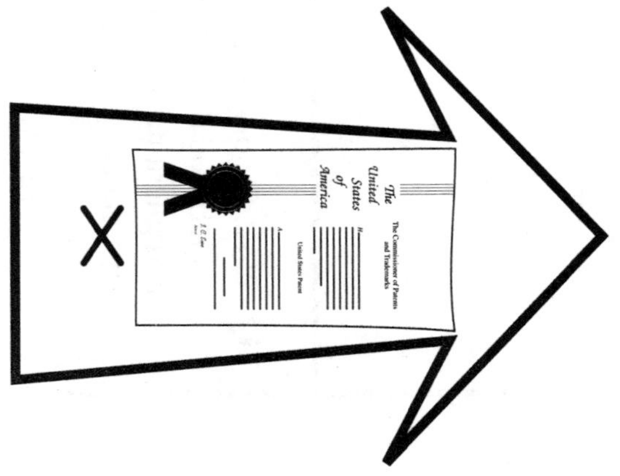

Bookmarks

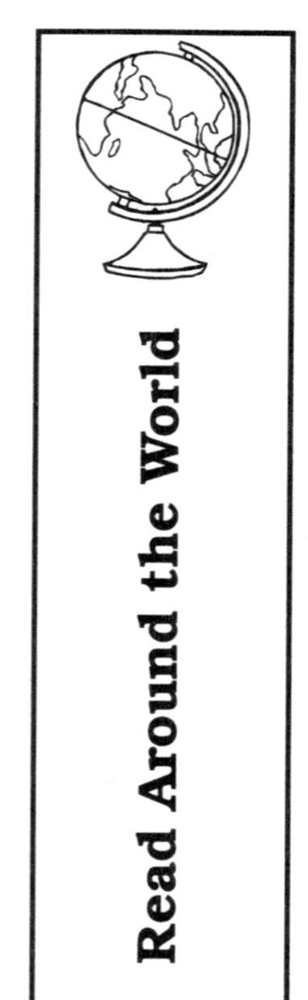

$0.40 ◯ $1.00

$$\begin{array}{r} \$1.00 \\ -0.40 \\ \hline \end{array}$$

Goods	Services

Examine the portion of the map of Atlantic City. Circle all the street names that correspond to property names on the Monopoly game board.

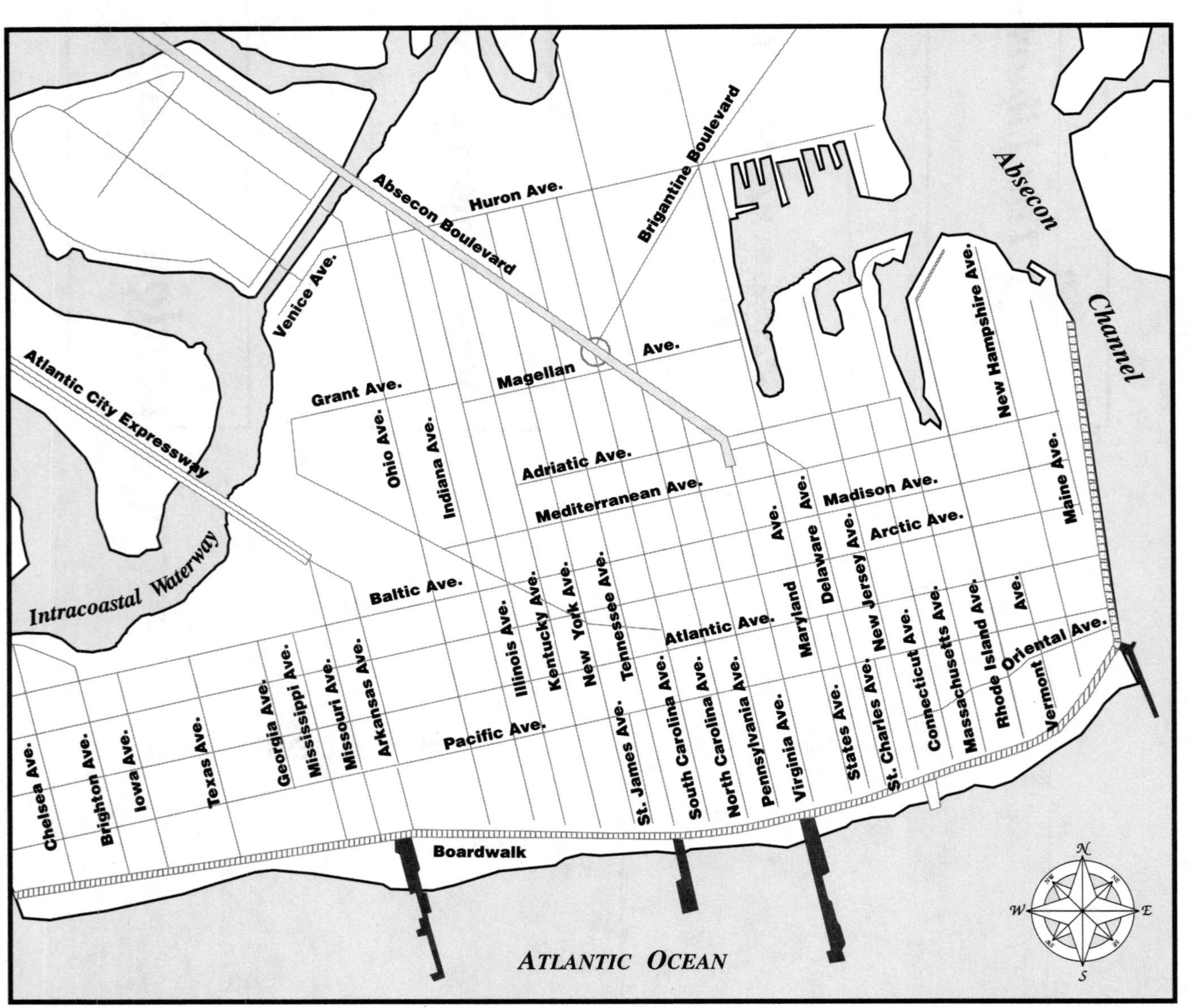

My Treasure

One item that is valuable to me is ______________________________

____

I value this item because______________________________

____

____

Other people may not see the value of this item because______________

____

Do you think your value of this item will ever change?______________

Why or why not?______________________________

____

Use with Lesson 39 (Enrichment).

DEMAND CURVE

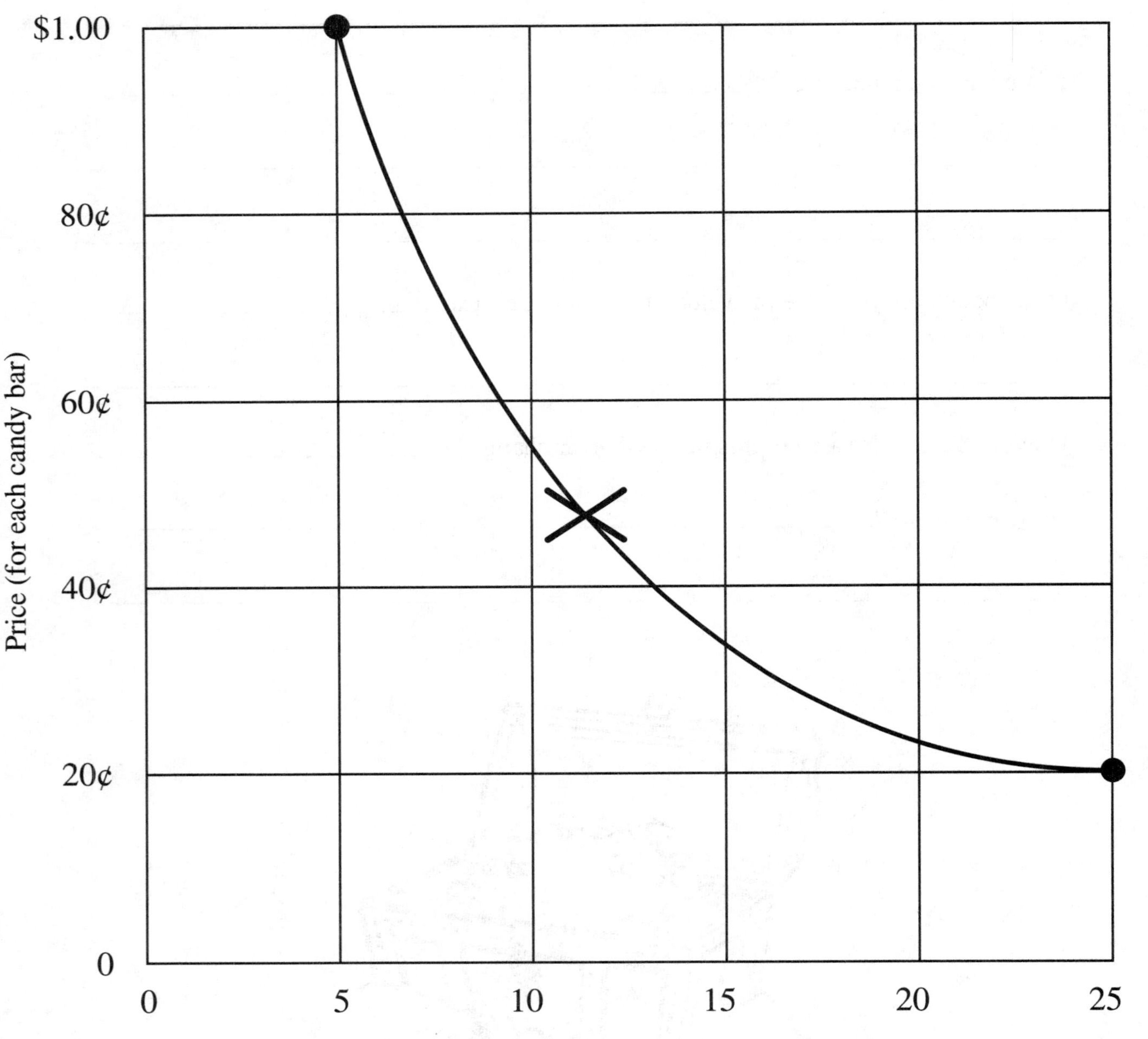

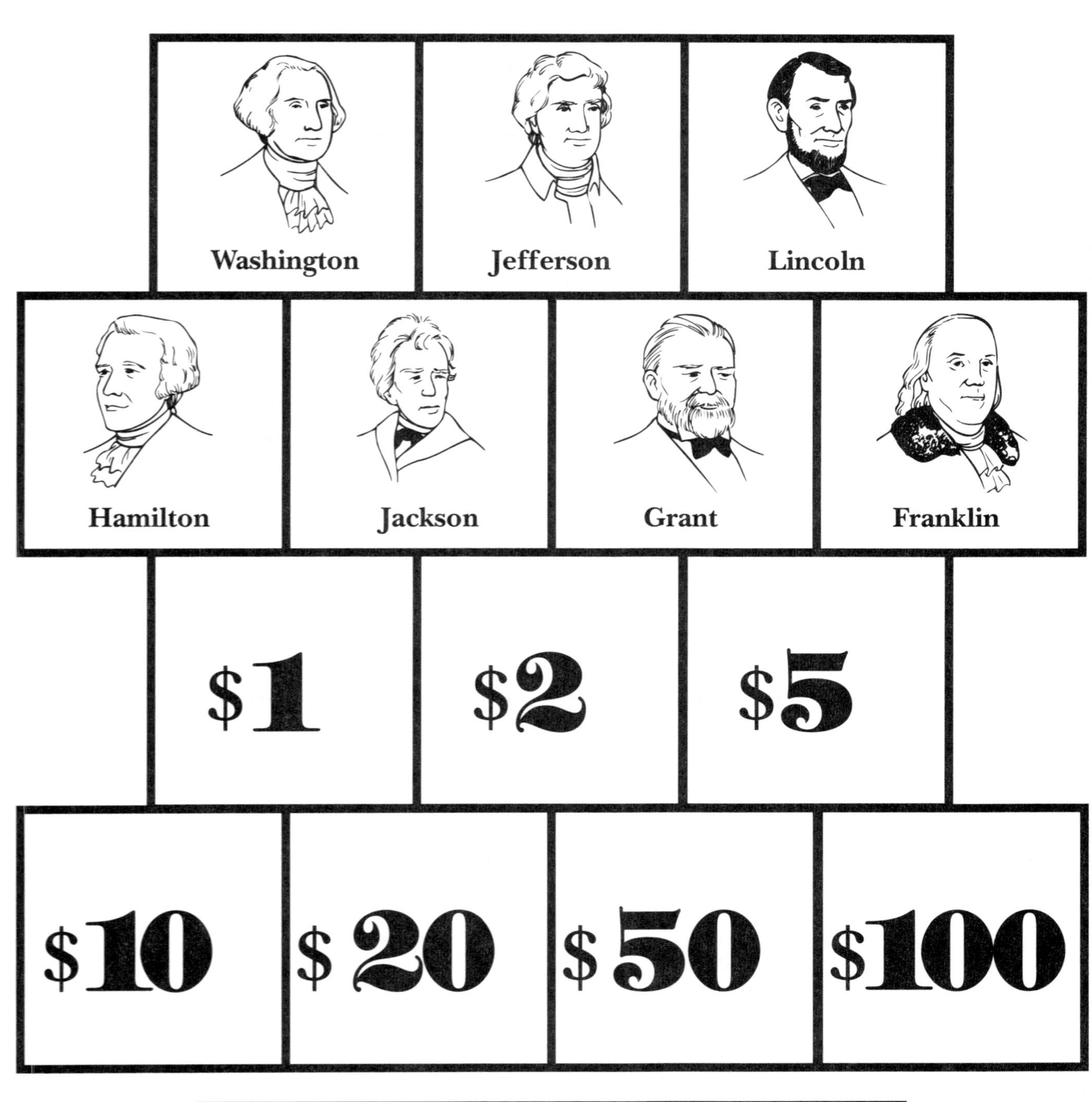

Answer Key

Washington *($1)*
Jefferson *($2)*
Lincoln *($5)*
Hamilton *($10)*
Jackson *($20)*
Grant *($50)*
Franklin *($100)*

Occupation Cards

I am a ______________________________

______________________________________.

My product or service is __________

______________________________________.

I charge ___________________________

______________________________________.

You are a ***doctor***

______________________________________.

Your product or service is ***to tend the sick***

______________________________________.

You may charge ***$50 per office visit***

______________________________________.

I am a ______________________________

______________________________________.

My product or service is __________

______________________________________.

I charge ___________________________

______________________________________.

You are a ***barber***

______________________________________.

Your product or service is ***to cut hair***

______________________________________.

You may charge ***$10 per haircut***

______________________________________.

fold here

cut apart

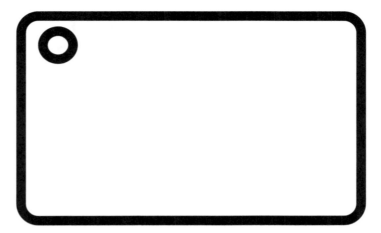

SOCIALIST PRICES

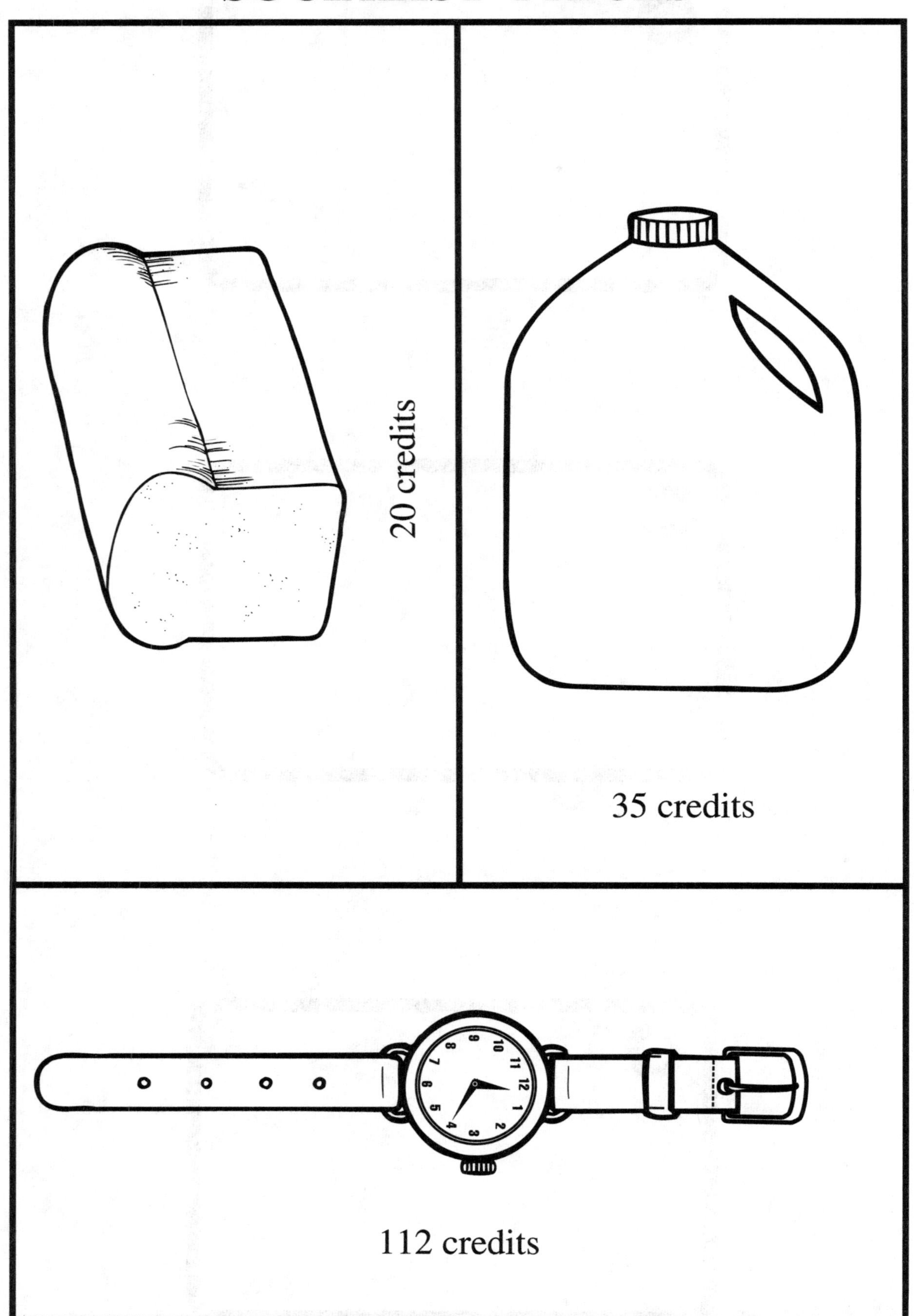

CAPITALIST PRICES

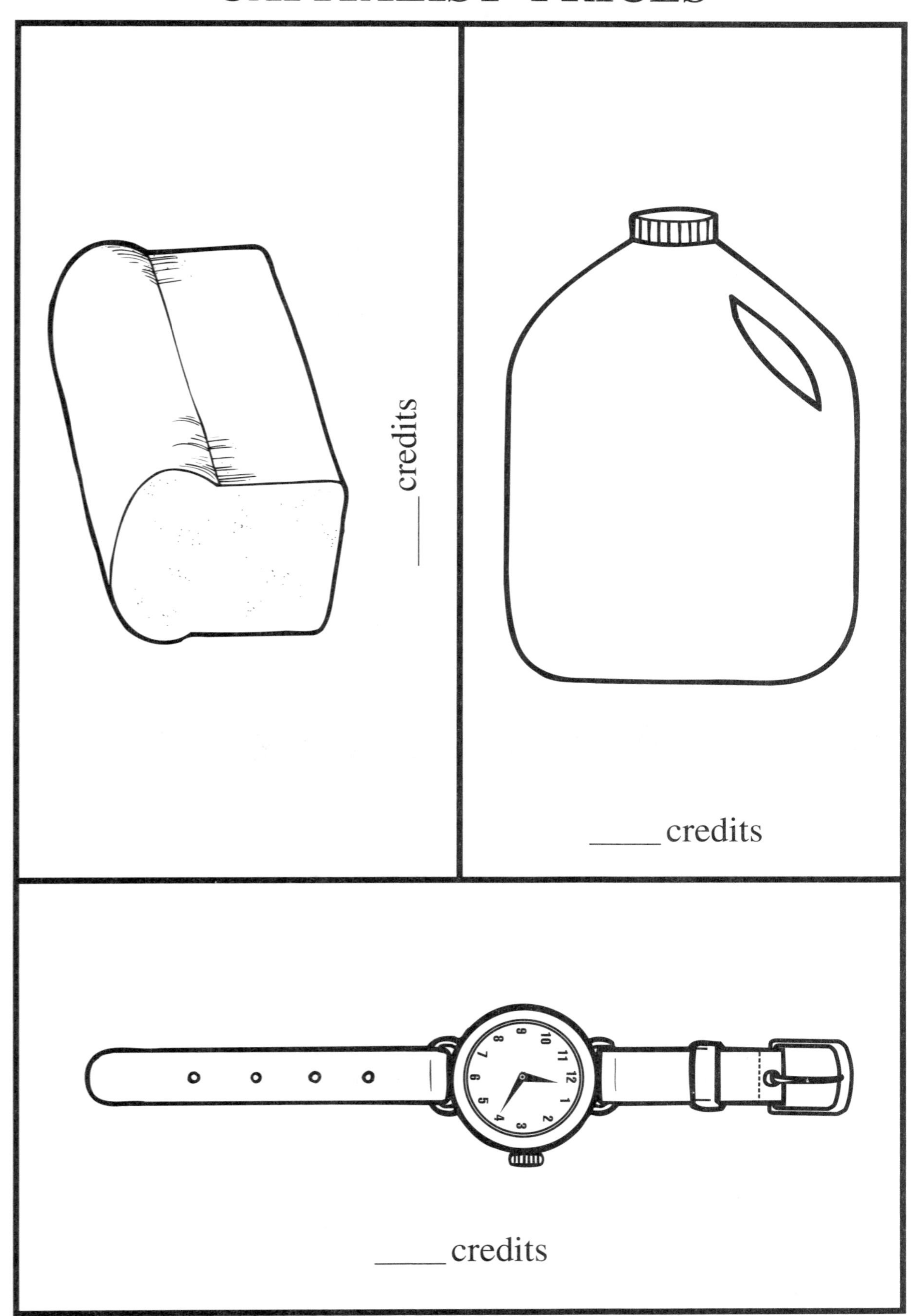

 Use with Lesson 41 (optional).

My List

shoes
house
water
apples
blouse
chewing gum
bread
socks
coat
candy
yo-yo

Use with Lesson 42.

Words for Wheel of Progress Spokes

handmade goods
spinning jenny
steam power
factories
child labor
unions
big business
Andrew Carnegie

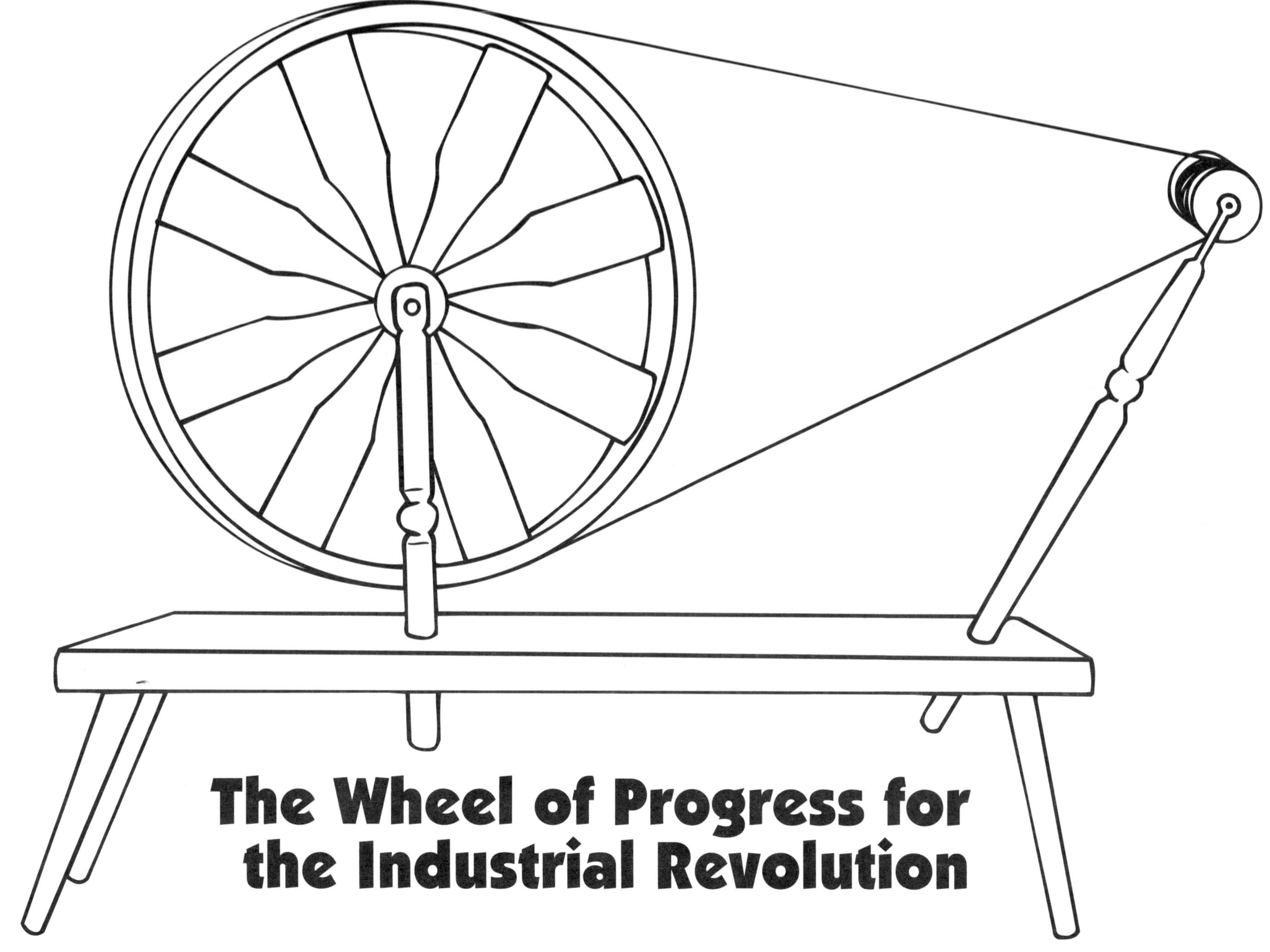
The Wheel of Progress for
the Industrial Revolution

teamster	boom	spinster
balderdash	vendor	sawyer

a treatment to grow hair	•	nonsense	•
spicy food from India	•	a seasoning for chicken	•
a punctuation mark	•	someone who writes children's books	*
an axe	*	a witness	*
a painter	*	someone who cuts wood	*
a device used for sweeping	+	a large gun	+
a very boring person	+	a good-luck charm	+
a time of great success	+	a type of washing machine	#
a machine for mixing batter	#	part of the backbone	#
an older single woman	#	an air vent	$
a race car	#	something that bends easily	$
a salesman	$	someone that loans things to others	$
chrome over a wheel of a car	$	a member of an organized group	?
the leader of a committee	?	a criminal	?
a tiny silver spoon	?	a truck driver	?

Changes

country →

farm →

wilderness paths →

handwork →

family work →

Make 2 copies.

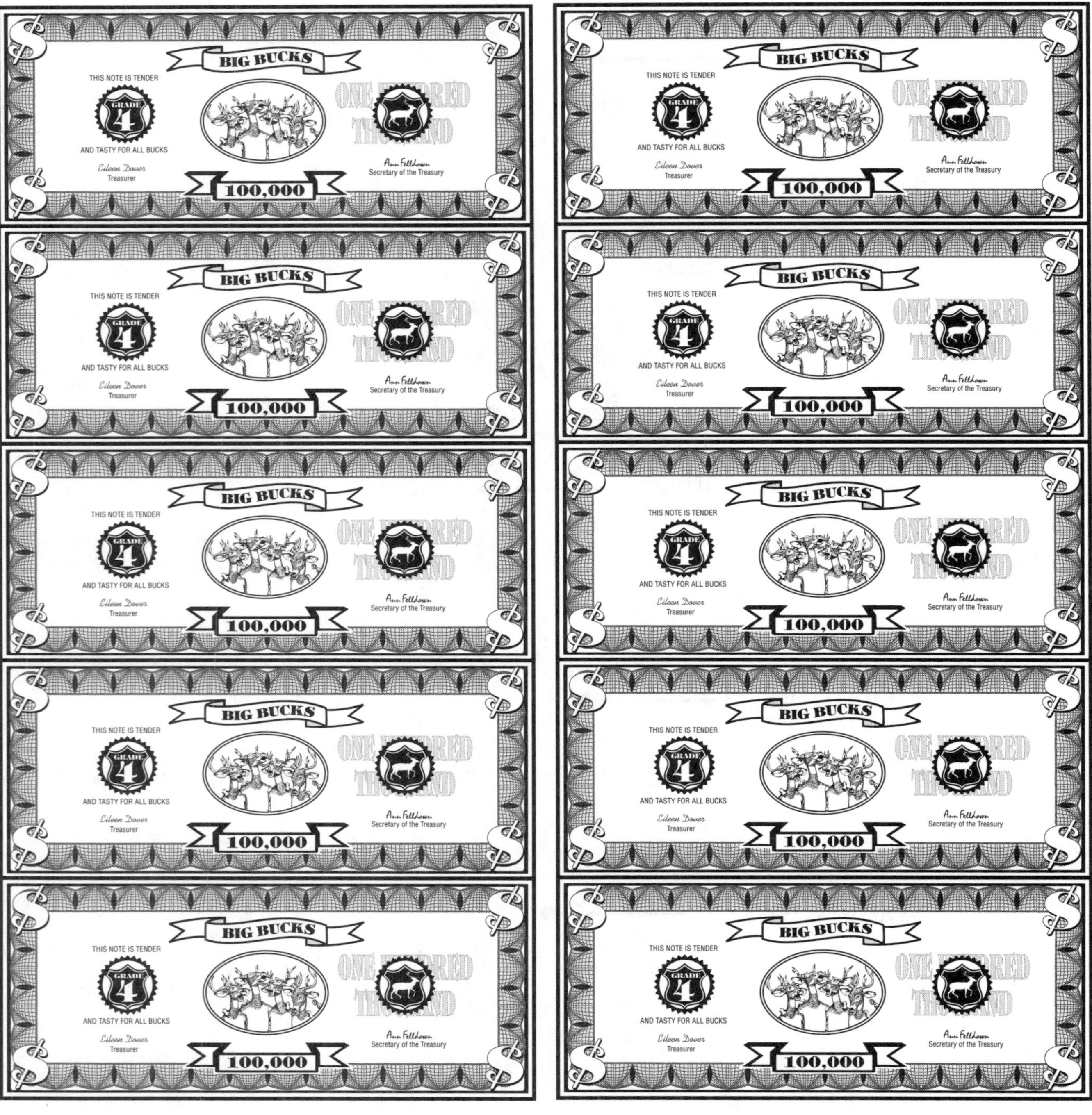

Lesson 49 Story

Behind my Sunday school teacher stood Tomoko Nagata, her black, almond-shaped eyes looking at the floor. As Miss Harris moved aside to introduce Tomoko, a ripple of snickers filled the room.

I didn't snicker or point. I stared, wide-eyed, at the tiny, costumed child. Her black hair glistened. Her almond eyes, full of fear, were still cast downward. Her robe (called a kimono, I later learned) was of shimmering lavender silk, hanging from her shoulders all the way to her ankles. It was straight with a lovely, wide sash at the middle and wide, wide sleeves. On the cuffs and down the middle of the robe were clusters of red, yellow, and blue flowers, sewn of shiny threads, close together. No buttons or zippers interrupted the scene; little coils of gold cording formed knots and loops that met to join the panels of graceful fabric. This Tomoko was the most beautiful person I had ever seen. She was so still, so perfect, so lovely, so different that somehow she didn't seem real. Part of me wanted to include her in my porcelain doll collection; part of me wanted to take her tiny hand and be her friend.

Sierra Nevada
Sacramento
Donner Pass
Central Pacific Railroad
PROMONTORY POINT
Shantytown
Great Salt Lake

Sierra Nevada
Sacramento
Donner Pass
Central Pacific Railroad
PROMONTORY POINT
Shantytown
Great Salt Lake

Sierra Nevada
Sacramento
Donner Pass
Central Pacific Railroad
PROMONTORY POINT
Shantytown
Great Salt Lake

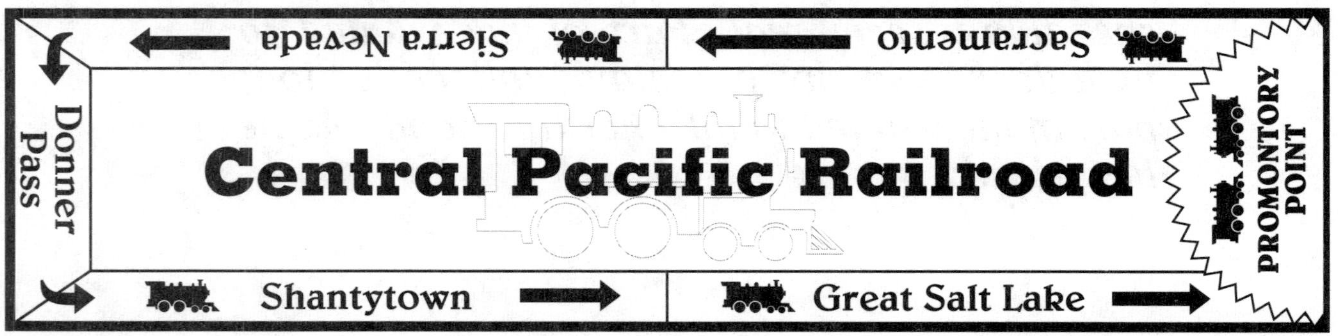
Sierra Nevada
Sacramento
Donner Pass
Central Pacific Railroad
PROMONTORY POINT
Shantytown
Great Salt Lake

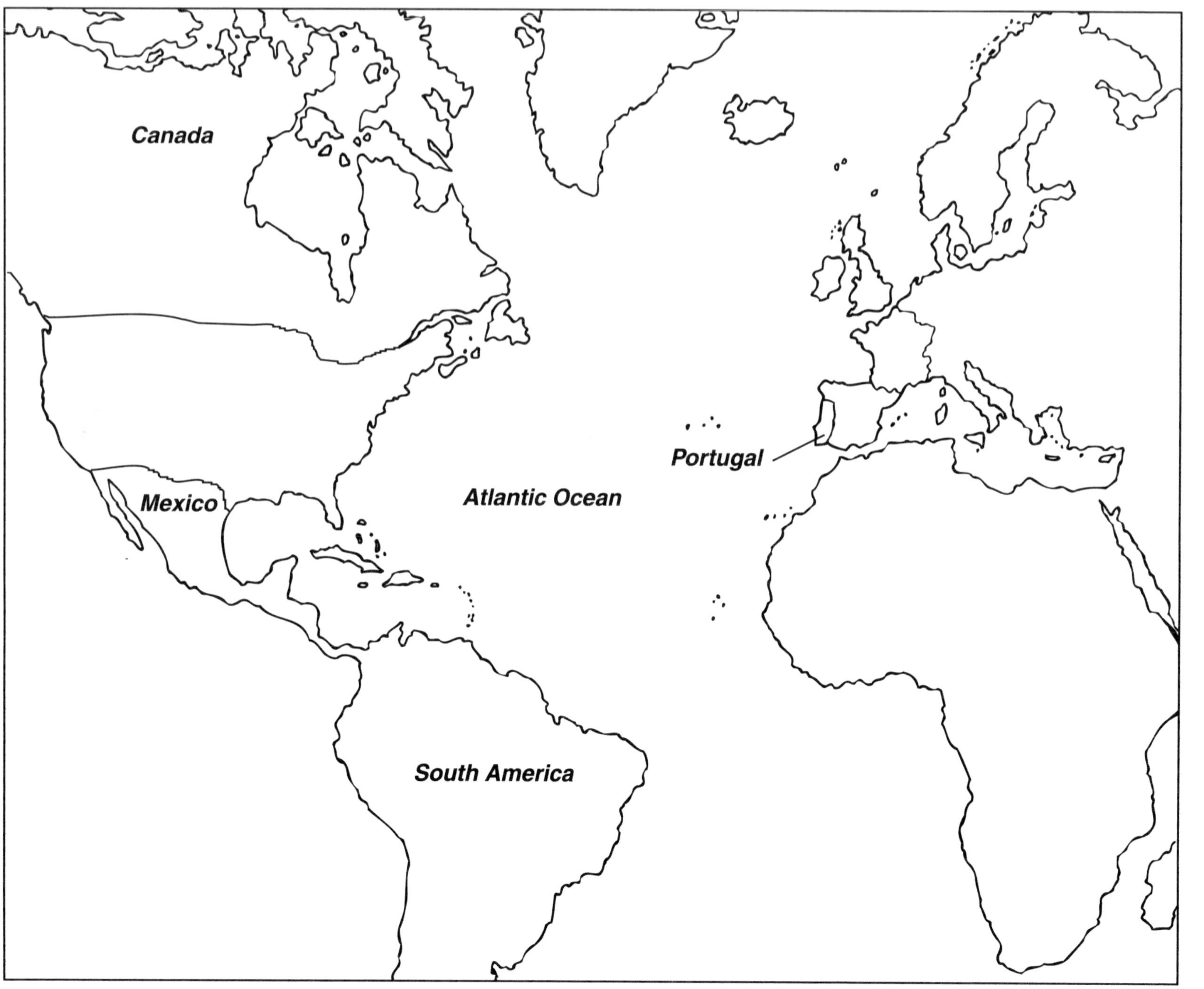
Canada
Portugal
Mexico
Atlantic Ocean
South America

Cuba Questionnaire

1. Label the bodies of water that surround Cuba.

Miami
THE BAHAMAS
CUBA
JAMAICA

2. Color Cuba's flag correctly.

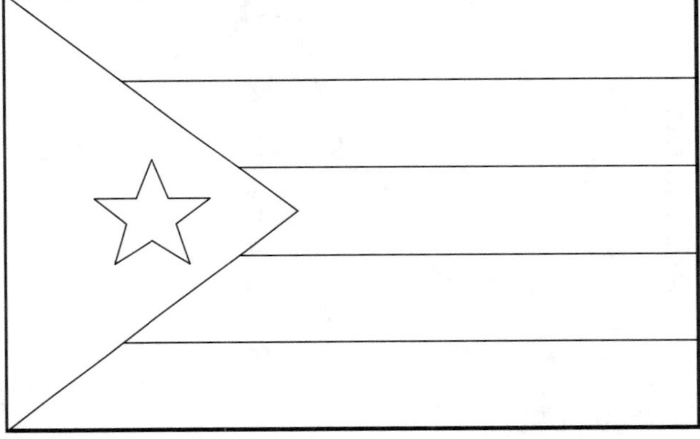

3. Connect the dots to reveal an important crop grown in Cuba.

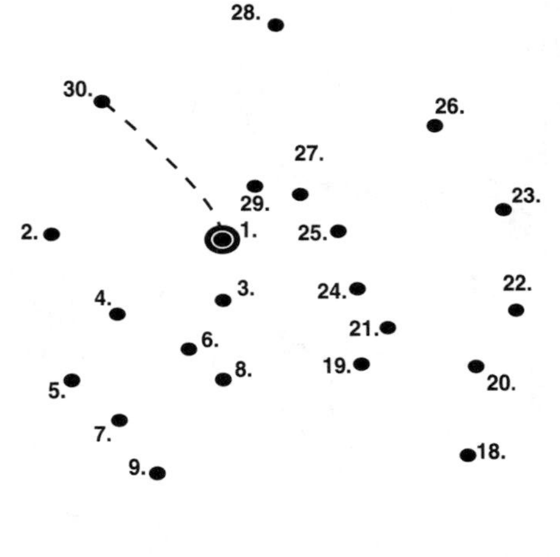

4. What is the capital of Cuba? ________________.
   Write the name on the map by the ⊛.
5. What is the official language of Cuba? ______________________
6. Complete the statements about the government of Cuba.
   a. For about 400 years, ____________________ ruled Cuba.
   b. A U.S. military government ruled Cuba from _________ to 1902.
   c. In the 1930s Cuba was controlled by a dictator, Fulgencio ________________.
   d. In 1959 Fidel _________________ took over and set up a socialist government.

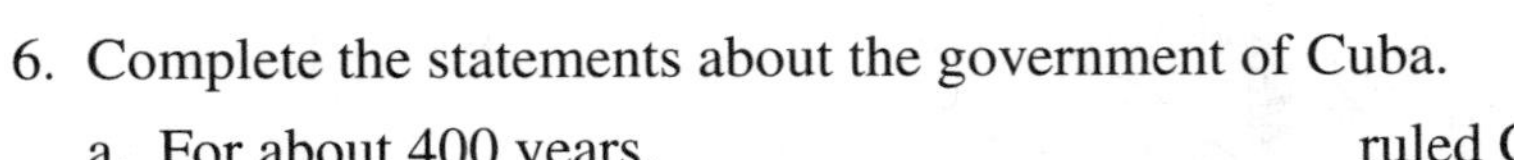

Quest for Cuba

1. Prepare your flag as your teacher directs.

2. Place a flag on any space in an outside row opposite your opponent.

3. Read the list of events.

4. Move your flag forward to the next row if the event was a benefit for your country.

5. Only one flag may move for an event.

6. On the last event, the flag that moves overtakes the other flag.

7. The flag remaining on the game board wins Cuba.

Events of the Spanish-American War

1. Spain acquires Cuba.
2. Cuba is not affected by the Monroe Doctrine.
3. The *Maine* goes to Cuba.
4. Hearst and Pulitzer publish sensational reports.
5. Roosevelt and the "Rough Riders" fight in the Spanish-American War.
6. The United States takes Cuba from Spain.

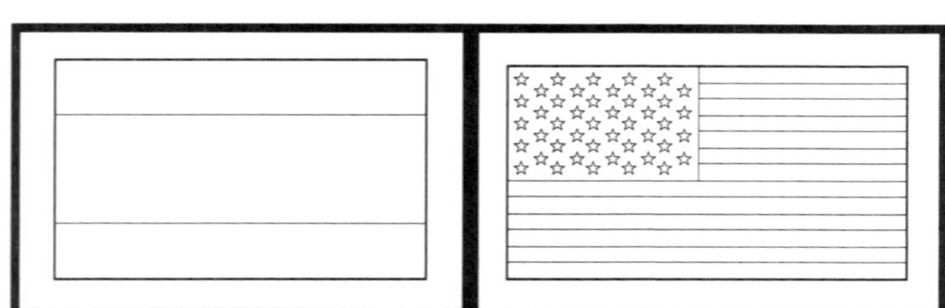

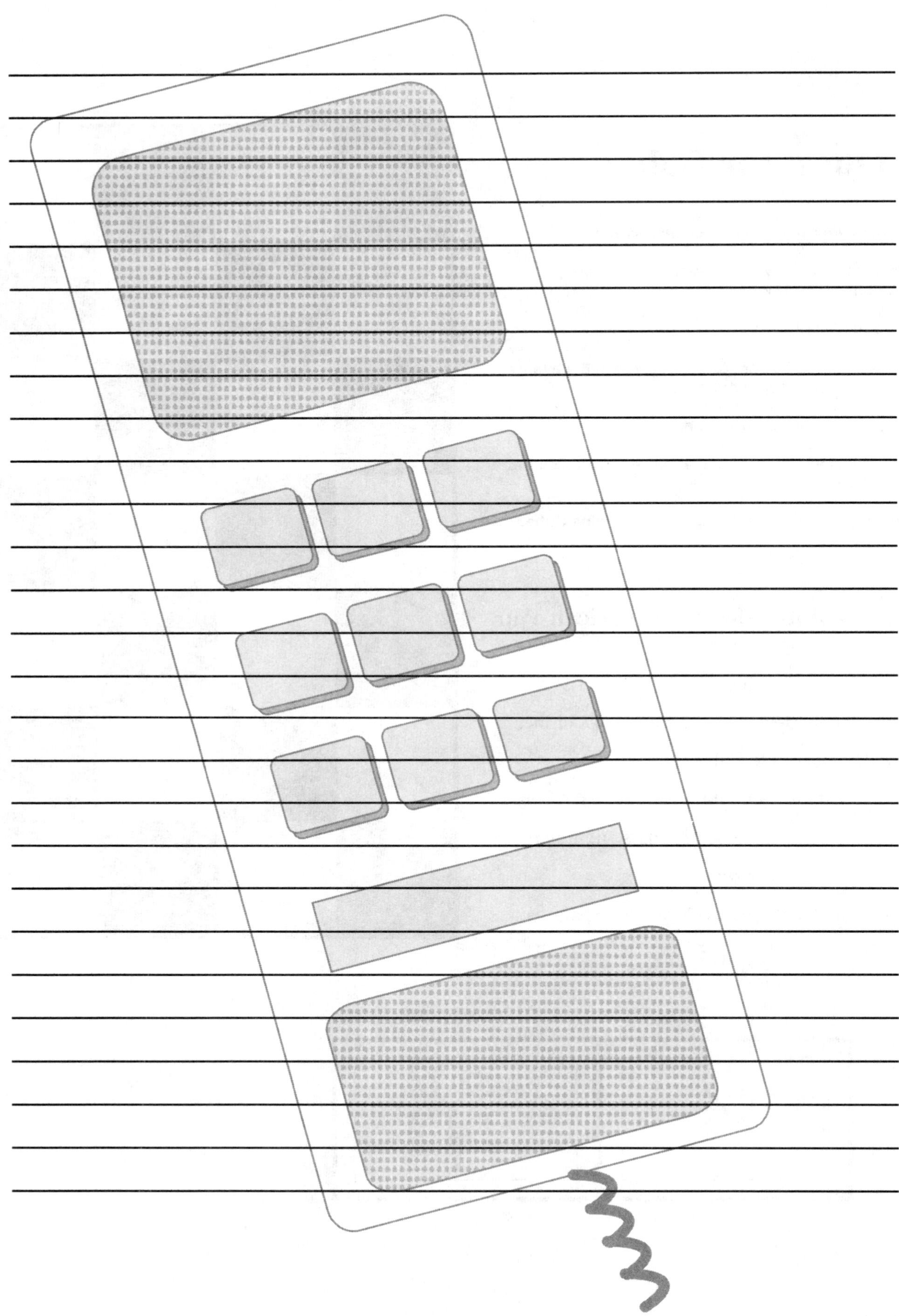

WHAT'S THE NEWS?
THE TIMES
OUR COUNTRY GOES TO WAR!
Newspaper
Telegraph
Pony Express
Telephone
1704
1844
1860
1876

Express Card	Express Card	Express Card
Express Card	Express Card	Express Card
Express Card	Express Card	Express Card
Express Card	Express Card	Express Card
Express Card	Express Card	Express Card
Express Card	Express Card	Express Card
Express Card	Express Card	Express Card
Express Card	Express Card	Express Card
Express Card	Express Card	Express Card
Express Card	Express Card	Express Card

In 1854, the U.S. Supreme Court upheld Samuel F. B. Morse as the inventor of the telegraph. **Move 3 spaces.**	A holiday was declared when the mail first reached Sacramento by pony express. **Move 1 space.**	The first *New York Sun* cost only 1¢. **Move 3 spaces.**
The fax is a facsimile machine that sends and receives images. **Move 5 spaces.**	Alexander Bell got tuberculosis while in Scotland. **Move *back* 4 spaces.**	The unit for measuring sound, the decibel, is named for Alexander Graham Bell. **Move 4 spaces.**
The world ignored Morse's telegraph for 12 years. **Move *back* 3 spaces.**	Gutenberg introduced movable type printing. **Move 2 spaces.**	Buffalo Bill Cody was a famous pony express rider. **Move 1 space.**
It took 10 days to carry letters from East to West by pony express. **Move 1 space.**	The telegraph was used during the Democratic National Convention in 1844. **Move 3 spaces.**	The pony express ended after the telegraph came into use. **Move *back* 1 space.**
Thomas Watson assisted Bell with the invention of the telephone. **Move 4 spaces.**	The fax machine transmits images over telephone lines. **Move 5 spaces.**	"Pony Bob" rode a record 380 miles in one mail run. **Move 1 space.**
Gazette means "official publication." **Move 2 spaces.**	The pony express routes went from St. Joseph, Missouri, to Sacramento, California. **Move 1 space.**	Alfred Vail helped Morse with the telegraph. **Move 3 spaces.**
Alexander Bell helped direct the education of Helen Keller. **Move 4 spaces.**	Alexander Bell demonstrated the telephone at the U.S. Centennial. **Move 4 spaces.**	The first newspaper was the *London Gazette*. **Move 2 spaces.**
The news in early newspapers was sometimes months old to the readers. **Move *back* 2 spaces.**	Alexander Bell and his partners started the Bell Telephone Company. **Move 4 spaces.**	Congress gave $30,000 to test Morse's telegraph. **Move 3 spaces.**
"What hath God wrought" was the first telegraph message. **Move 3 spaces.**	The *Boston News-Letter* was one sheet of paper printed on both sides. **Move 2 spaces.**	Alexander Bell taught Visible Speech to deaf students. **Move 4 spaces.**
Pony express riders were young, wiry, and brave. **Move 1 space.**	Samuel Morse painted a portrait of Lafayette. **Move 3 spaces.**	The *New York Sun* was delivered to homes. **Move 2 spaces.**

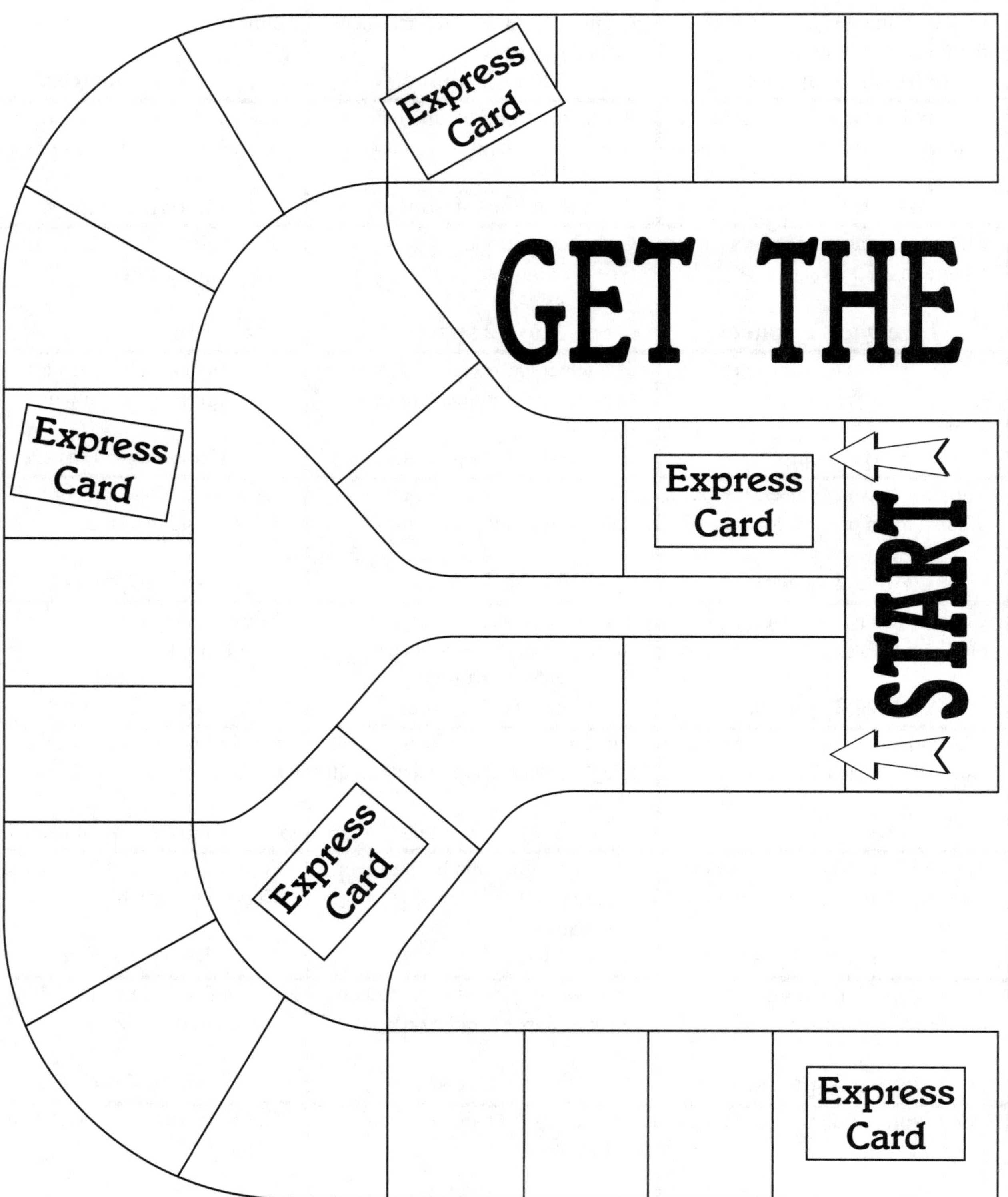
Express
Card
GET THE
Express
Card
Express
Card
START
Express
Card
Express
Card

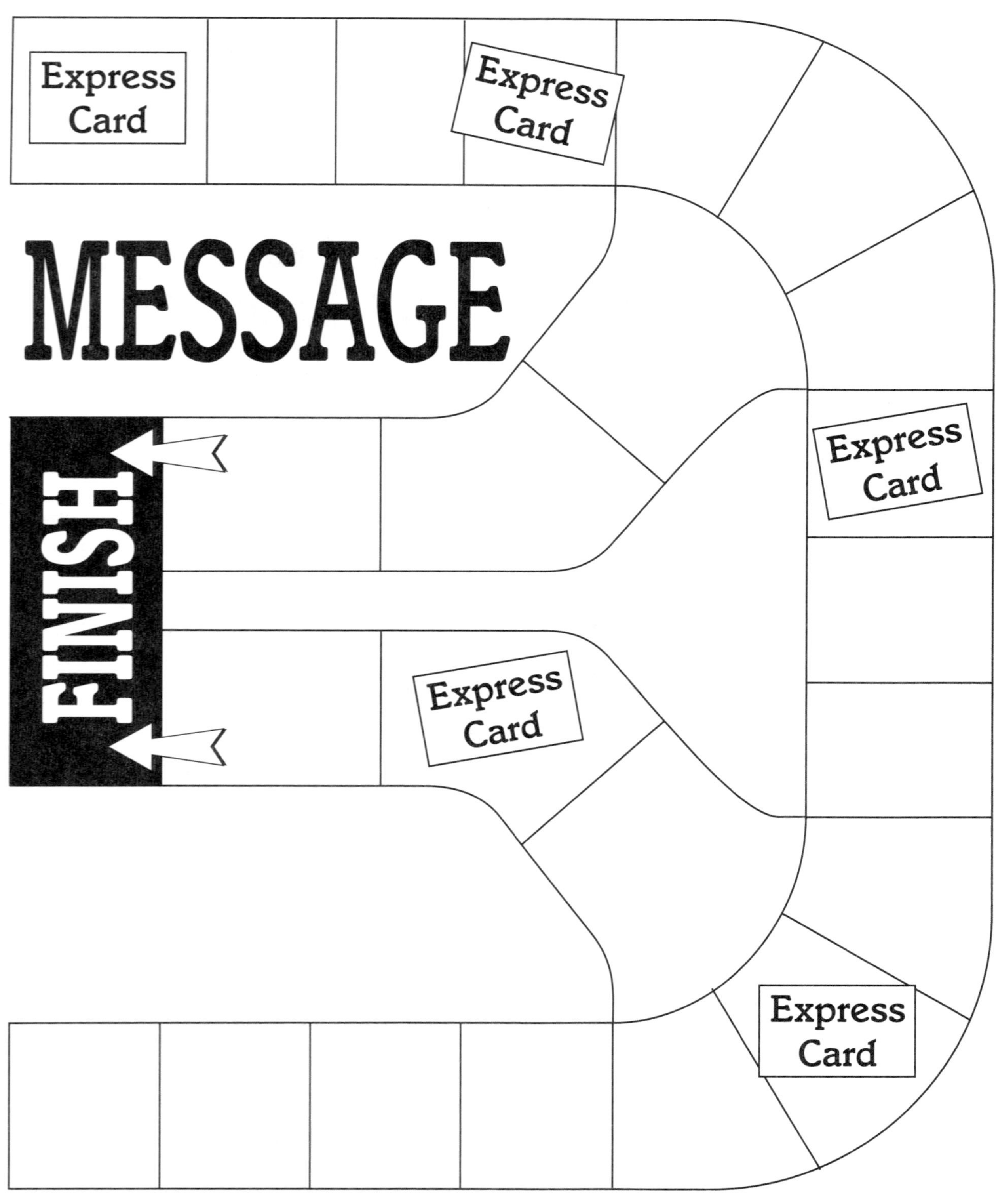
Express Card
Express Card
MESSAGE
FINISH
Express Card
Express Card
Express Card

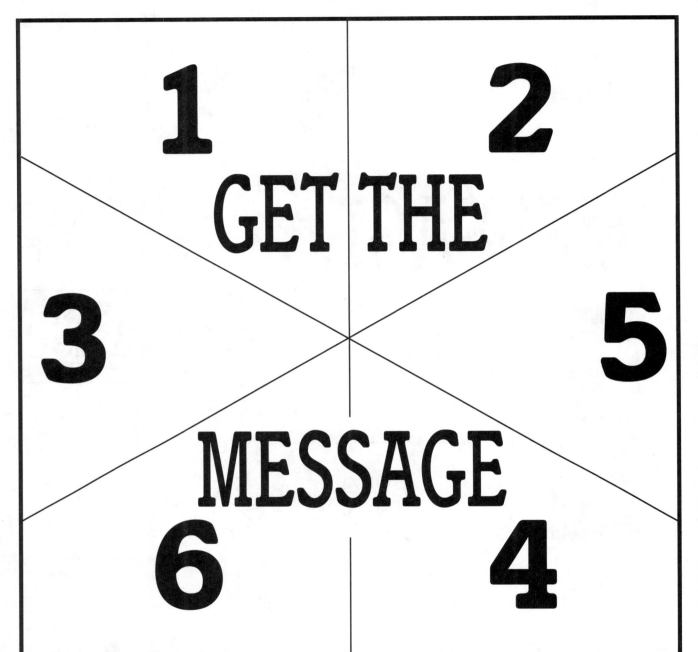

1	2
GET	THE

3 5

MESSAGE

6	4

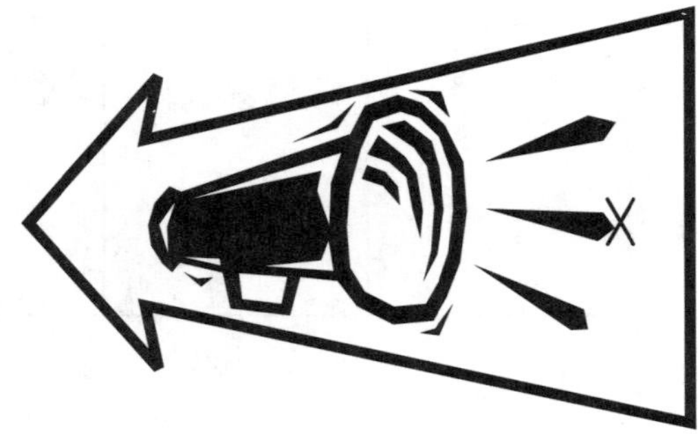

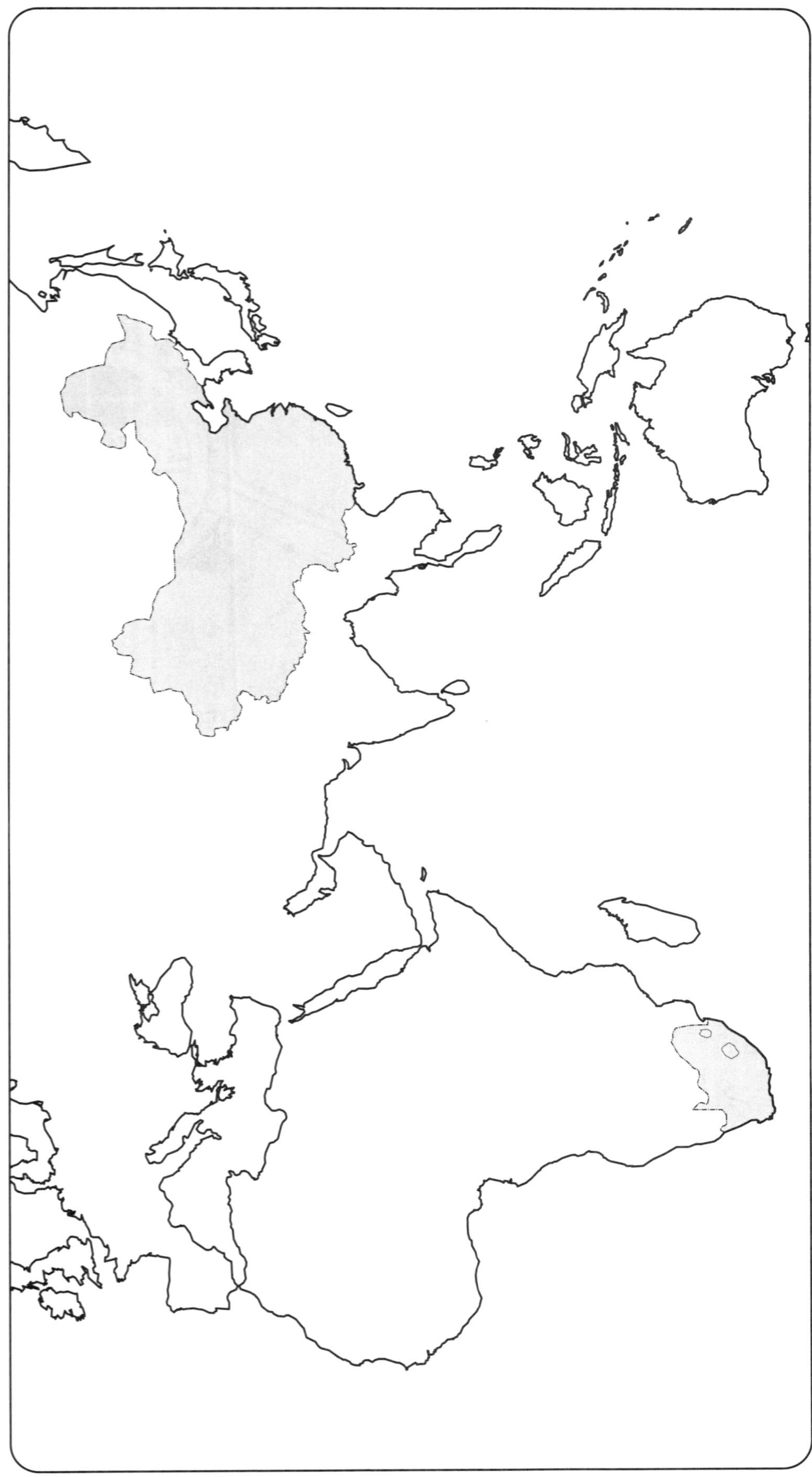

Introduced in Lesson 61 (optional).

The British soldiers sang "The British Grenadiers" during the Boer War. How could the singing help them?	The British wanted part of the gold in the Transvaal. Was this a good reason to go to war?	The Boers did not want to allow the British to vote in Boer elections. Do you agree or disagree with them? Explain.	The black Africans had very few rights in South Africa until 1994. What could have been done about this situation earlier?
You are a Boer soldier fighting in the Boer War. What will you do?	If you were a black African, who would you have wanted to win the Boer War? Why?	Should the British have fought against the Boers, or should they have let the Boers have all the gold?	Were the Boers right to fight back against the British, or should the Boers have given up since they knew they would lose in the end anyway?
Gold was found on your land, and hundreds of people came to dig it up for themselves. What will you do?	As an adult, you are not allowed to vote in your country's elections. What will you do?	You are a British soldier fighting in the Boer War. What will you do?	How could compromise have helped the British and the Boers?

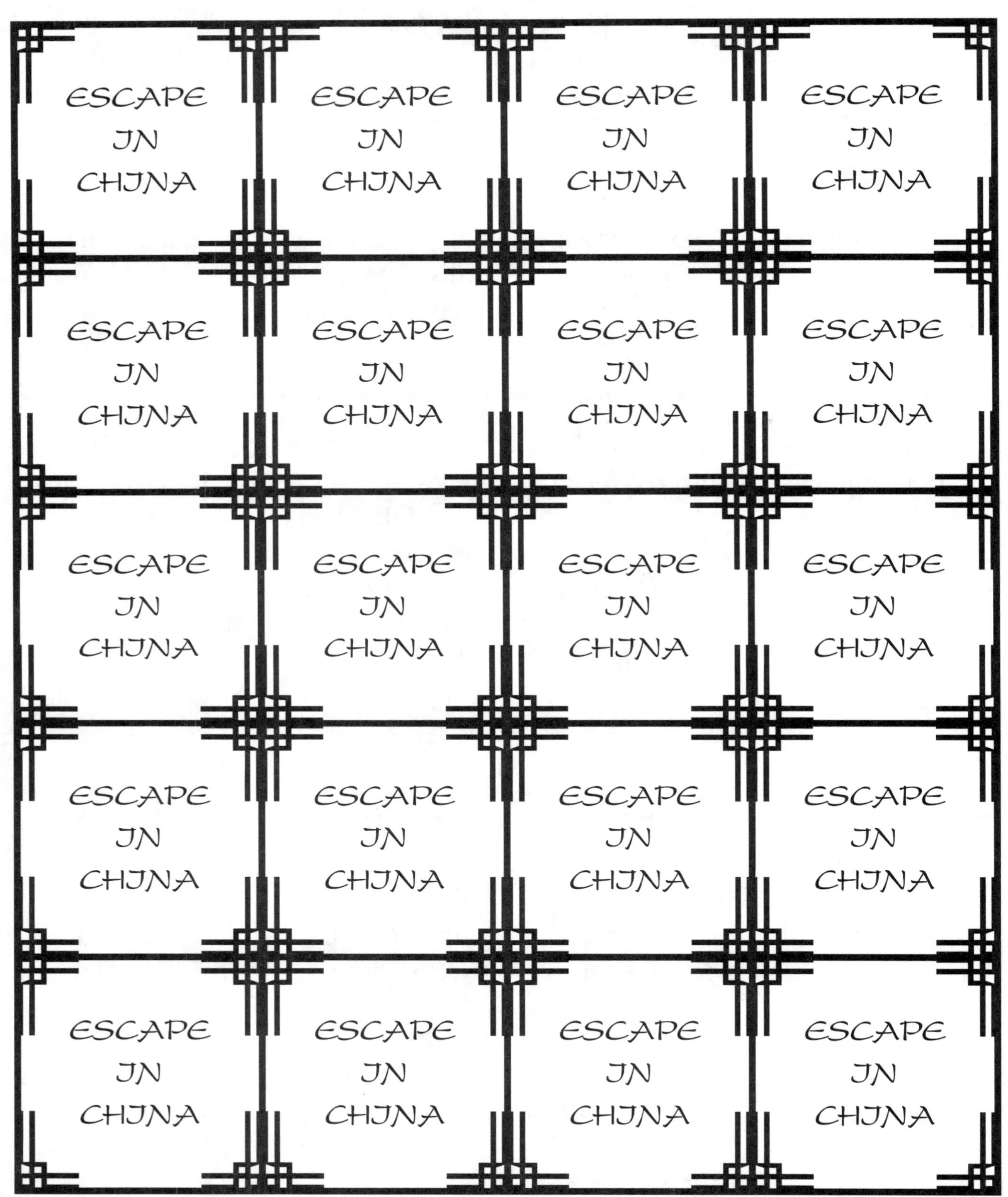
ESCAPE IN CHINA
ESCAPE IN CHINA
ESCAPE IN CHINA
ESCAPE IN CHINA
ESCAPE IN CHINA
ESCAPE IN CHINA
ESCAPE IN CHINA
ESCAPE IN CHINA
ESCAPE IN CHINA
ESCAPE IN CHINA
ESCAPE IN CHINA
ESCAPE IN CHINA
ESCAPE IN CHINA
ESCAPE IN CHINA
ESCAPE IN CHINA
ESCAPE IN CHINA
ESCAPE IN CHINA
ESCAPE IN CHINA
ESCAPE IN CHINA
ESCAPE IN CHINA

Your wife gets sick. Go back 1 space to care for her.	The Boxers are at the city you just left. Run ahead 2 spaces.	You are captured and brought before the city Yamen. Lose a turn.	You give a good testimony before the court. Go ahead 3 spaces.
Chinese Christians bring you food. Go ahead 2 spaces.	You receive a letter containing money. Go ahead 1 space.	You are unable to find food for two days. Go back 1 space.	Bandits attack your group and steal all your food and supplies. Go back to the beginning.
A Chinese man sees your bravery and asks to hear about the God you serve. Go ahead 3 spaces.	You are relieved to hear that your children are safe at the mission school in Che-foo. Go ahead 1 space.	You are attacked. One man is beaten by the Boxers. Lose a turn while you bandage his wounds.	The baby becomes ill. Run quickly ahead to the next space to get help.
Go to Mr. Wu's house to hide.	Go to the wheat field to hide.	Go to the cave to hide.	Go to the river crossing.
You see Chinese soldiers approaching. Hide until they pass. Lose a turn.	Your house at the mission station is burned. Run ahead 2 spaces to get away.	You are robbed by bandits. Go back 1 space.	You see a stream ahead. Run ahead 2 spaces to get a fresh water supply.

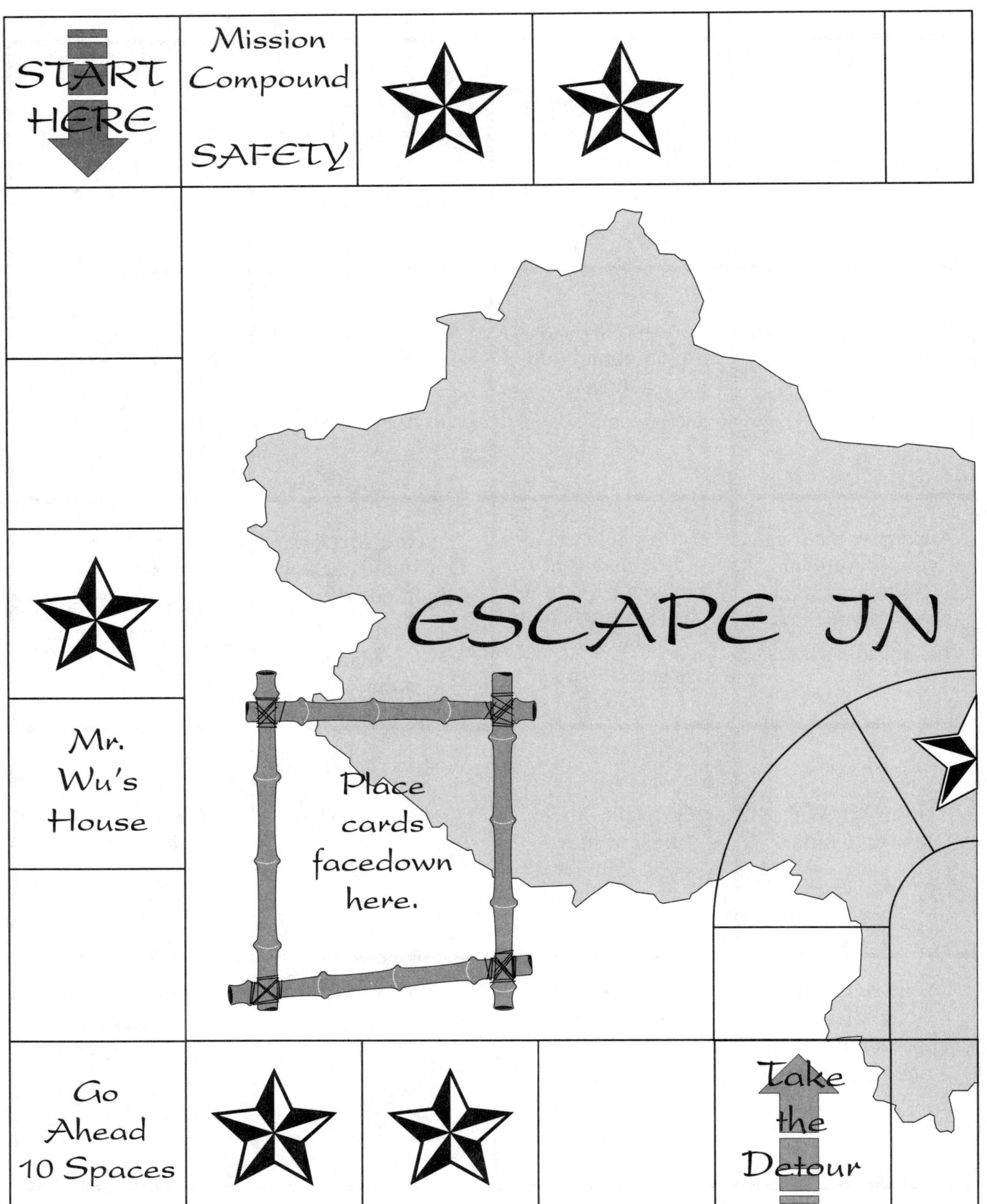
START HERE
Mission Compound SAFETY
ESCAPE IN
Place cards facedown here.
Mr. Wu's House
Go Ahead 10 Spaces
Take the Detour

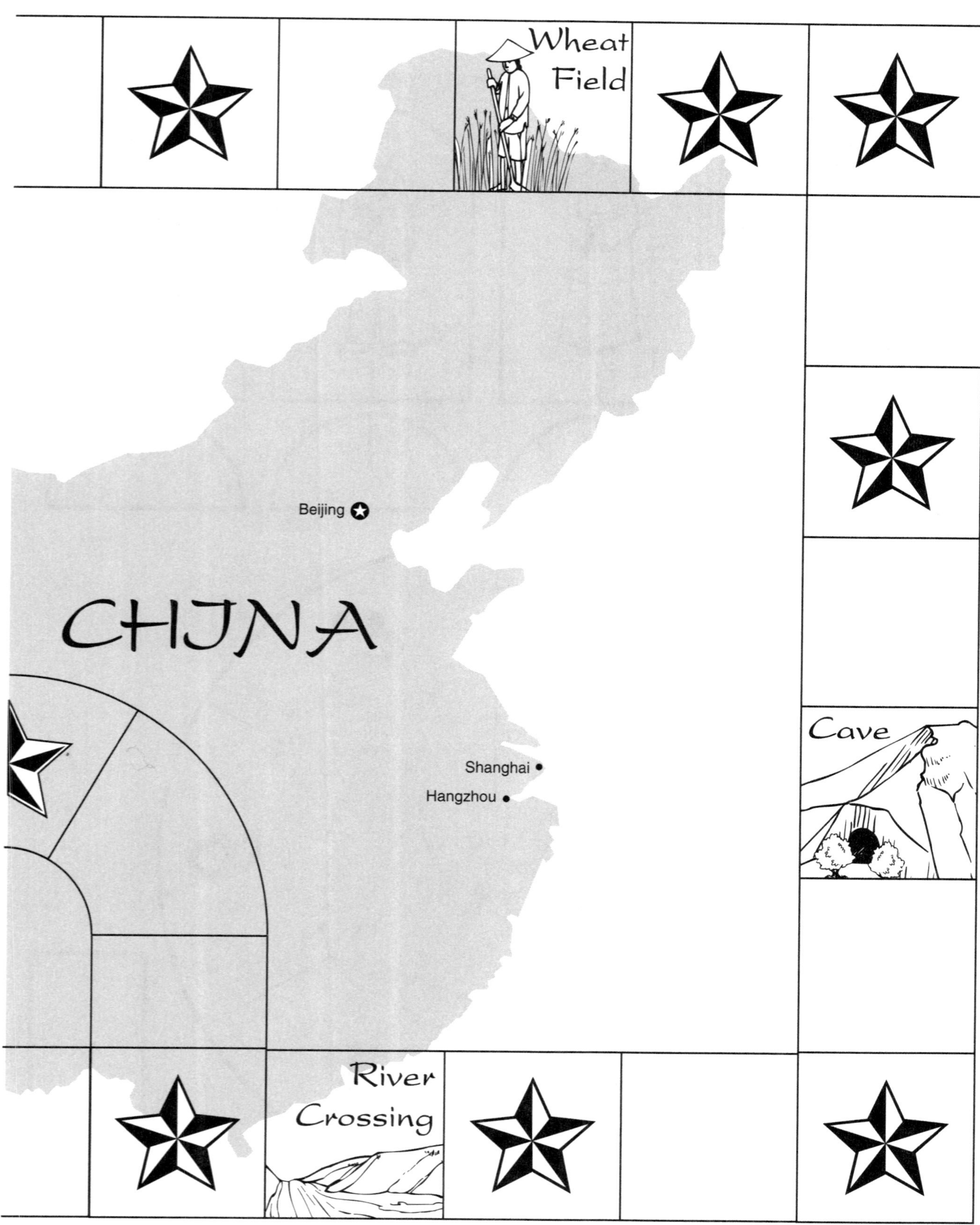
Wheat Field
Beijing
CHINA
Shanghai
Hangzhou
Cave
River Crossing

Cut out the missionary game pieces. Slide the parts together so they will stand.

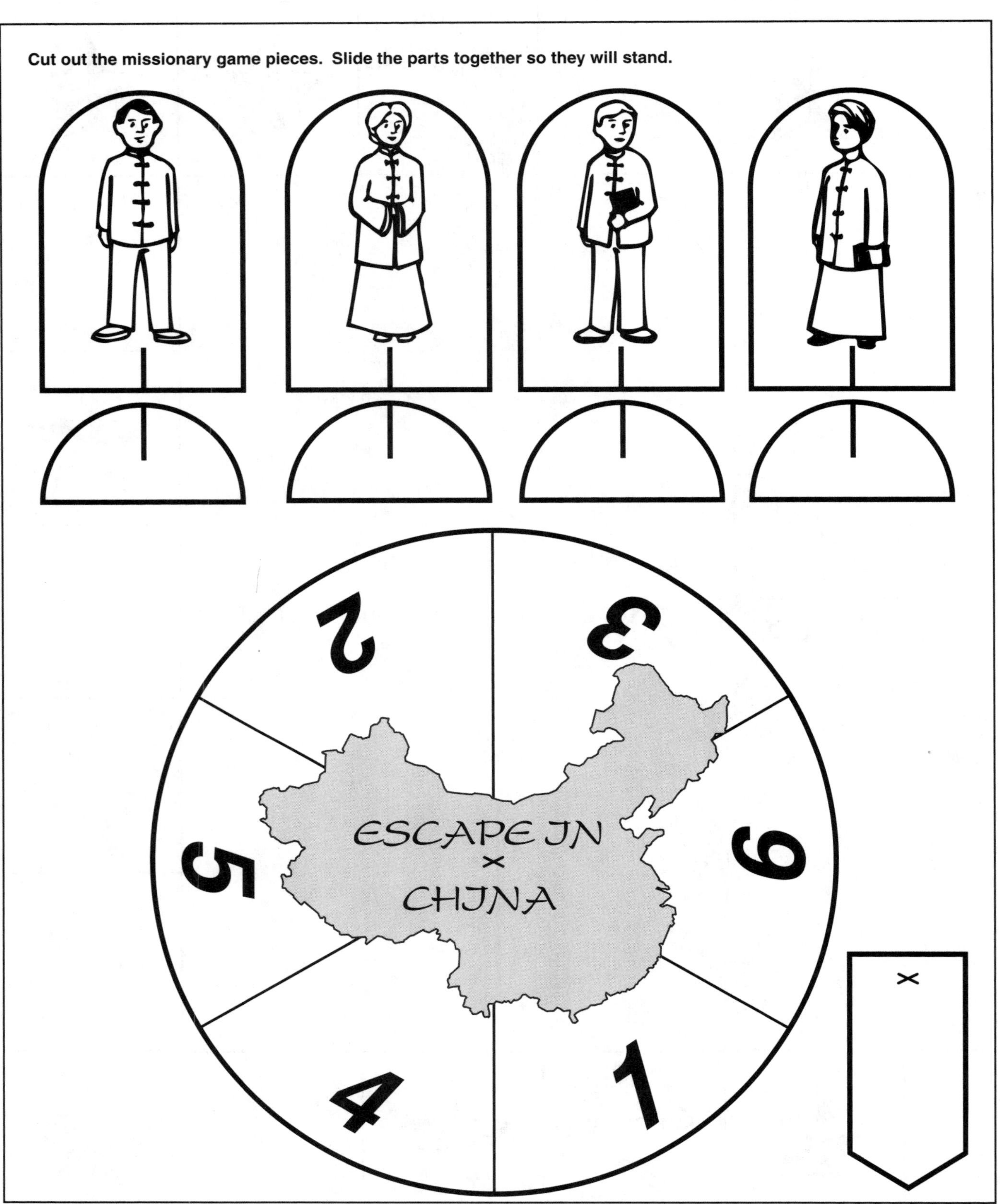

Invention/Modification Cards

Grandma is unable to open envelopes without tearing the letter inside. Invent a machine to help Grandma open her letters.	Tim cannot remember to brush his teeth. Invent a machine that will help Tim remember.	Sally loves to bake, but she finds it difficult to measure the correct amounts of ingredients. Invent a machine to help Sally measure.
The mailbox faces the street, and Mother does not want John to have to step out into the street to open the mailbox and get the mail. Make a modification to the mailbox so that John can get the mail without going into the street.	Dad always spills coffee out of his cup when he drives. Modify Dad's coffee mug so that coffee will not spill.	Invent a machine to roll Mother's skeins of yarn into balls.
Mary loses her glasses and then cannot see well enough to find them. Invent something that will help Mary find her glasses.	Jack loses his keys. Invent something that will allow Jack to find his keys.	Mr. Smith dislikes cleaning his barbecue grill. Invent a machine that will do this task for him.
Dad has asked Jenny to weed the garden. Jenny would like to go to her friend's house to play. Invent a machine to weed the garden for Jenny.	Your dad jogs in marathons and gets extremely thirsty, but he doesn't want to stop. Invent a lightweight water container for Dad that will not interfere with his running.	Your mother raises hybrid orchids. Everyone will be gone for three days. Invent a system to keep the flowers watered when nobody is at home.

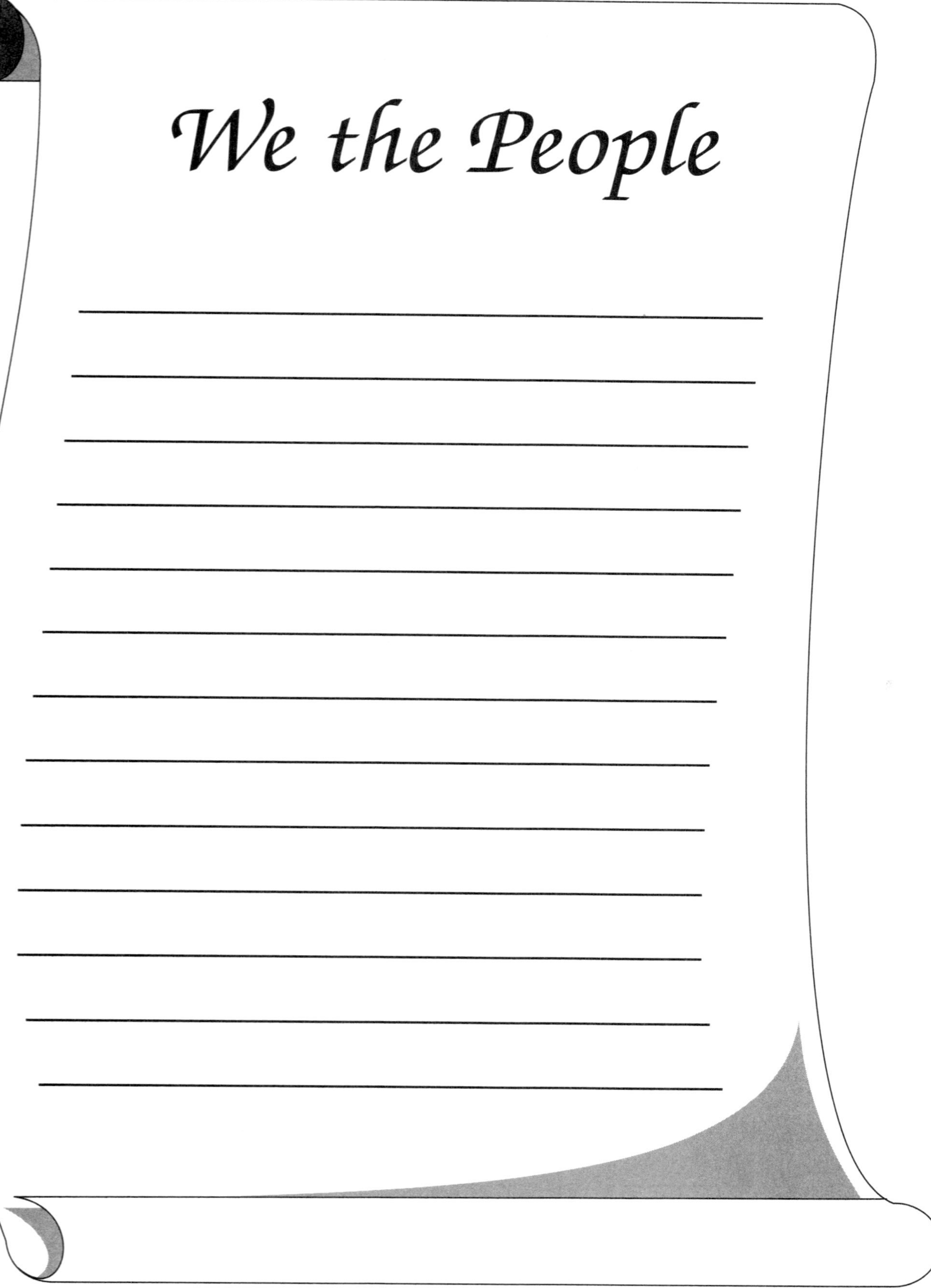

Use with Lesson 66 (Enrichment).

Our Constitution

Complete the form based on the decisions of your group.

1. Our new nation shall be called ______________________________________.

2. Our flag will look like this.

   It represents ______________________________
   ____
   ____
   ____
   ____

3. The leader of our government will be called the ______________________________.

   The ______________________________ will make the laws.

4. We wish for the citizens to have certain rights that will include the following:

   ____
   ____
   ____
   ____

5. The citizens will not be allowed to do the following: ______________________________

   ____
   ____
   ____

Signatures of the Delegates:

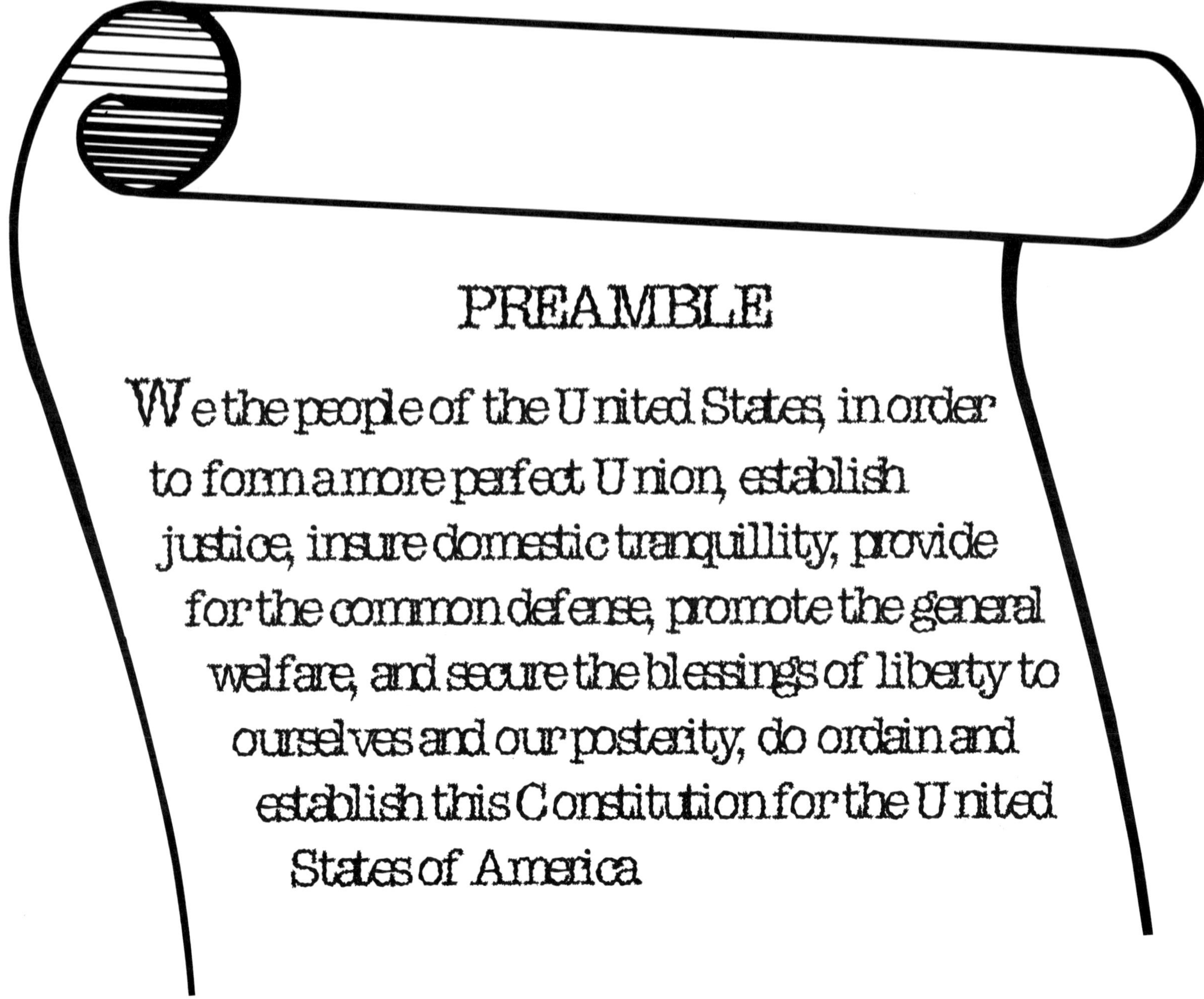
PREAMBLE
We the people of the United States, in order
to form a more perfect Union, establish
justice, insure domestic tranquillity, provide
for the common defense, promote the general
welfare, and secure the blessings of liberty to
ourselves and our posterity, do ordain and
establish this Constitution for the United
States of America

1. Freedom of religion, speech, and the press; rights of assembly and petition

2. Right to bear arms

3. Protection against having to house soldiers in times of peace

4. Right to be secure against unreasonable search and seizure

5. Rights in criminal cases

6. Right to a fair trial

7. Right to civil cases

8. Protection against excessive bails and cruel punishment

9. Rights retained by the people

10. Powers retained by the states and the people

Index

U

V

W

Y